PSYCHOLOGY of the CHILD

NEW YORK · JOHN WILEY & SONS, INC.

LONDON

ROBERT I. WATSON

Northwestern University

O F   T H E

Personal,

Social,

and

Disturbed

Child

Development

FOURTH PRINTING, JULY, 1962

Copyright © 1959 by John Wiley & Sons, Inc.

Library of Congress Catalog Card Number: 59–5875

Printed in the United States of America

Preface

IF THIS BOOK HAS ANY CLAIM TO UNIQUENESS AS A text in child psychology, it rests upon several interrelated purposes which guided me in writing. I wanted to find out the extent to which learning theory and psychoanalysis could be integrated with one another in the setting of child psychology. I considered that findings from clinical psychology had been relatively neglected in other publications. Believing that the developmental framework had been unduly neglected in most texts, I wished to combine the dramatic sweep of child development with the rigor and exactitude of the research studies contributing to it. I hold the opinion that it is heuristically desirable to go into more detail about selected studies than to cite a greater number of studies briefly; so I have tried to present enough material about the research being considered to allow the reader to see the study in the setting of the operations by which the conclusions were reached. As for my major reason in writing the book at all, I wanted to learn more about child psychology.

In any book such as this, the author's debt is manifold. There is my debt to those whose conceptions and researches have been learned from printed pages. There is my debt to publishers who have graciously permitted quotations, to whom specific acknowl-

v

edgments are made at the appropriate places throughout the book. There is my debt to an erstwhile colleague, Dr. Bettye M. Caldwell. Originally, we planned to write this book in collaboration, but press of other duties prevented her from writing more than most of Chapter 3. However, my debt to her in joint planning of the book and for reading critically several of the chapters goes beyond this particular chapter. There is my debt to Donald T. Campbell, John W. Cotton, Janet A. Taylor, and Brendan A. Maher, colleagues who took time away from their own scholarly work to offer criticisms of certain sections of chapters falling within their special areas of competence. There is my debt to my undergraduate assistants, Miss Barbara Bennett, Mr. Marvin Martin, Miss Nissah Mesch, and Mr. Daniel Murphy for many, many hours of editorial and library assistance. There is my debt to those efficient secretaries, Mrs. Irene Nolte, Mrs. Diana Theobald, Mrs. Kathryn Dieterich, and Mrs. Janice Bonge in helping me to carry through from scrawl to completed manuscript pages. There is my debt to my wife, Hazel, for reading the manuscript. To all of them go my thanks.

ROBERT I. WATSON

Evanston, Illinois
October, 1958

Contents

Part IV   Later Childhood

Part V   Psychological Disturbances in Childhood

PSYCHOLOGY of the CHILD

part I

*History
and
Principles*

chapter 1

History of the Study
of the Child

MANY PERSONS AND PROFESSIONAL GROUPS ARE IN-
terested in the behavior and experience of the child. Although having the common theme of psychological development, they have approached the problem differently according to their own interests
and training. Certainly at the top of the list of such interested
parties would be parents, who love their child and watch with interest and affection, if not awe, the developing personality with which
they are so intimately bound.

It is the child psychologist who is most directly concerned with all
aspects of behavior and experience of the child. As described in
Chapter 2, he attempts to study the child using his own approaches.
But he also looks to the work of others who are interested in the
study of the child and uses their findings to supplement his own.

Neither parents nor psychologists have a monopoly of interest in
children. Diverse aspects of development attract and hold the attention of representatives of other fields. The pediatrician, for example,
is concerned with the prevention and treatment of childhood diseases.
Since matters of child health are intimately related to other aspects
of development, psychological factors of behavior and experience fall
within his field of interest. The educator sees the child as a growing
plastic creature to be guided in learning those things the particular

society considers worthwhile. Therefore, psychological factors of interest and motivation and learning and growth loom large upon his horizon. The anthropologist and sociologist are interested in the child as influenced by society and as in turn influencing it. Psychiatrists and clinical psychologists concerned with behavior disorders of the early part of the life span see the child when unusual psychological difficulties appear.

It is not easy to draw a clear distinction between normal and disturbed infants and children. As a rule of thumb, the disturbed child needs special professional help in getting along with himself and society over and beyond that which the normal child requires. Consequently, disturbed infants and children become available for study as well as for help. While it is primarily with the disturbed child that they deal, they cannot afford to be unconcerned about broader aspects of normal child development. The philosopher, the artist, the obstetrician, the embryologist, indeed all whose fields touch the human being as a source of information, must have some degree of interest in the behavior and experience of the child.

We shall begin our study of the psychology of the child by examining the men and events charting its course. In this first chapter, we are concerned with presenting the study of the child in historical perspective in order to increase our understanding of the amazing series of changes taking place in the psychological development of each child. Specifically, we are going to examine the attitudes taken toward the child before child psychology emerged as a separate field, the men whose work founded the field, the subsequent history of the field, the influence other fields have had upon child psychology, and the current status of the field as expressed in the modern period in child psychology.

Early attitudes toward the child

Before the advent of child psychology as a branch of science there was one characteristic common to early attitudes held toward the child. This was the fact that interest in the child *as such* was virtually nonexistent. Almost always the interest was not in what he was but in what he had been or was to become. When viewed as a product of original sin, epitome of innocence, reflector of evolution, or future citizen—the child *as a child* was not of immediate concern.

When he was the subject for either scientific enterprise or philosophical speculation, he was regarded as in transition.   This does not imply that such views are entirely false, for indeed childhood is a period of transition.   But, strictly speaking, childhood is no more exclusively a period of preparation for adulthood than the adult years are preparatory for old age or old age preparatory for death.   Obviously, there is a serial sequence to these age periods, but each is worthy of observation in its own right, not merely as the culmination of the preceding period or the preface to the succeeding one.

It is now appropriate to examine more closely some of the earlier attitudes and theories which helped to structure the field of child development.

The Child as a Miniature Adult

Some historical evidence is available to suggest that one of the earliest views of the child was that he was but a miniature adult. Originally this was perhaps an expression of prehistoric man's anthropocentric view of nature; the child was regarded as merely a smaller, weaker, and more stupid version of himself.   As a child grew larger, stronger, and brighter, he revealed the adult characteristics which had been there all the time.   The primacy of this attitude toward the child is supported by the generality and relative simplicity of the concept.   Of course, this attitude did not stop with prehistoric man, for traces of it have been present in many more recent points of view that will be discussed shortly.   The child as a future citizen, as a carrier of inborn perversity or of moral goodness, or as a stage of evolution focuses in varying degrees upon a specific aspect of which the attitude toward the child as a miniature adult is a more general statement.

Over the centuries many specific instances of the way a child was regarded and treated originated from this general point of view. Smaller versions of adult clothes were worn by children and adult manners and customs were forced upon the child even while he was still a toddler.   Early biologists held that in mating the male transmitted to the female a completely formed but very minute adult human being.   The baby-man or homunculus, as it was called, grew in strength, size, intelligence, and so on; but when he became a man he was different only quantitatively from the way he had been as a baby.

The obvious differences in physical proportions of children as compared with adults were largely ignored by advocates of this point of view. We know today that the process of growing up involves a readjustment of the relation of the many structures of the mature organism. If the child grew into an adult only by increasing in height and weight, the results would be an enormous head, long thick trunk, and very short arms and legs. Physically, a child is definitely not a miniature adult.

With respect to intellectual qualities this attitude was also pervasive. Even well into modern times educational practice rested upon this attitude, as reflected by attempts to teach children in terms of adult interests and aspirations. Textbooks were written in a way to interest adults, not the children for whom they were intended. Education was regarded as an indoctrination into the ways of adult life and getting the child to behave like an adult as quickly as possible was one of its chief functions. Today education for the child, not the child for education, is the prevailing point of view (and one carried to extremes, according to some authorities). School buildings, schedules, curricula, and other facets of the educational process are designed with reference to the developing child. Qualitative, as well as quantitative, differences between the child and the adult are recognized.

The Child as a Future Citizen

In antiquity, one purpose of instruction was to mold the child into the adult he was to become, an aim not unrelated to that followed by both formal and informal educational systems today. Thus, a view of the child which has held firm with continuity to modern times is that of the child as a future citizen. In ancient civilizations, notably Greece and Rome, emphasis was placed upon assuring that the child grow up to be a good citizen. Plato, some 400 years before the Christian era, gave specific expression to this attitude by teaching that children are born with certain abilities and that it is the task of the state to guide the child into those activities in which his aptitudes would best serve the state. Laudable though this goal may be, when balanced by other intrinsic and extrinsic goals for childhood, it is relatively easily perverted when it is allowed to be the major goal. Hitler, too, saw childhood as a period of preparation for service to the state. Functioning alone this attitude paves the way for disregard of the child as an individual and is not conducive to the study of the child's nature apart from a preconceived optimal social order. Such an approach can be valuable when other ways of regarding childhood are also taken into account and the child *qua child* is seen as of intrinsic value and not merely as the adult he is to become.

The Child as Innately Depraved

Another view widely held for many centuries stressed the inborn sinfulness of man. If man was conceived and born in sin, childhood should be a crucial period for curbing and to some extent eradicating the evil in his nature. Without rigid discipline, presumably the child's nature would become progressively more sinful. Hence, harsh corrective measures were necessary, as exemplified in the dictum, "Spare the rod and spoil the child." Man and child would be prepared for the world to come by suffering in this one. Comprehension of the implications of such a doctrine, especially in combination with the conception of the child as a miniature adult, makes understandable the severity with which children were sometimes treated. The child who forgot to carry out some activity could be only expressing his evil nature and therefore entitled to punishment. Little distinction by those in authority was made between behavior which in an adult might be reprehensible and the groping of a child toward solution of a problem produced by sheer immaturity and lack of experience.

A correlate of the concept of innate depravity is the belief that children are born with an innate moral sense. Thus regarded, undesirable behavior was the result not of ignorance on the part of the child but of a moral violation. Though there was a general admission that it took some time to develop a sense of right and wrong, the period was quite short by modern standards. This fact helps to explain what appears today as the shockingly early age at which crimes of children were severely punished. Knowledge of right and wrong was presumed to be intuitive and needed only a relatively short time to develop. Such views would preclude interest in the *process* of learning as such, even though there was much concern with precisely *what* the child learned. It is possible that this and related points of view retarded investigation or even speculation about the learning process, closing out, as they do, any alternative explanations of the origin of various behavior patterns.

The Child as Inherently Good

Opposed to the view of the child as inherently sinful went the diametrically opposite belief. "For of such is the kingdom of heaven" implies a belief in the innate goodness of children. The teachings of the French philosopher, Rousseau, helped to promulgate the belief that the infant is unspoiled and pure but becomes corrupted through his contact with adults. If permitted to express his natural impulses and to develop without restriction the abilities given by nature, the developing child will show none of the depravity that is characteristic of adults. Expressed during the intellectual ferment of the eighteenth century, Rousseau's views found an enthusiastic audience. With political and religious practices in a state of flux, these ideas reflected the climate of the times and thus had a greater chance of being accepted. Soon educational practices, first in Germany and later in the United States, began to show the stamp of his thinking. The relation between this view of childhood and present-day emphasis upon freedom from repressive influences is more than accidental.

The Child as a Stage of Evolution

In the nineteenth century, the work of Charles Darwin and others on the study of evolution did much to stimulate interest in the study of the child. In testing the hypothesis of man's descent from animals, evidence derived from the study of children was utilized. The baby was regarded as a link between animal and man. Closely allied to this source of interest was the theory that the child relived or successively passed through the different stages of animal life (described by a phrase which a modern advertiser might well be proud to have coined—"ontogeny recapitulates phylogeny"). The crawling of the infant replicated the swimming movements of the fish, creeping, the locomotion of mammals, and running, the stage of man's movement. Survival of specific behaviors from prehuman days was sought, as in the grasp or "Darwinian" reflex, which, according to this theory, came about because the primate infant clung to the mother or tall branch for protection.

Today, the child is not regarded as a stage of evolution in the sense these early biological workers used this phrase. And yet childhood *is* a transitional period. Insofar as growth itself is a manifestation of the evolutionary process, then the child is one performer in the evolutionary tableau.

The theory of recapitulation, erroneous though it may be, was rooted in the biology of the day. Hence, in it a *scientific* interest in the child was apparent. This helped to pave the way for the advance of modern child psychology, suggesting concepts which lent themselves to experimental test instead of providing merely a loose philosophical scaffolding. Indeed, the influence of this idea was keenly felt by the early pioneers in the field of scientific child study.

The beginnings of child psychology

Child psychology came into being from the scientific study of the child. The work of investigators from other fields had a profound effect. Even psychologists who contributed to this beginning were drawn from various specialties other than child psychology. They all had the characteristic in common that they were not primarily identified with child psychology when they did their important work. When it was done, they were the first child psychologists.

Preyer and the Baby Biography

Systematic observation is basic to all scientific investigation as the account in Chapter 2 will attest. Although occasionally attempted before the nineteenth century (for example, Rousseau's *Émile*), relatively systematic observations of children reached a position of importance and significance in the last three decades of the past and the first decade of the present century. The first observational procedure used was the so-called baby biography. The observer, often both parent and scientist, made day-to-day observations of a single "normal" child, starting at or near birth. The work of Preyer, a physiologist, is one of the earliest examples (6). In his account of his son's mental development during the first four years, he recorded careful and detailed observations and added information contributed by others as well as comparative data from the behavior of animals. He observed the development of reflexes from birth and the influence of experience and learning. *The Mind of the Child* (20), the book resulting from his labors, although justly criticized for not sharply separating fact from inference, is one of the great classics of child psychology. Another pioneer biography was Charles Darwin's diary

(5) of his infant son which was begun in 1840, but did not appear in print until 1870. In it he revealed another facet of his interest in evolutionary processes as well as a broader concern with general development than is generally associated with him.

These biographies served the useful purpose of indicating clearly the necessity of careful observation and detailed study for the guidance of subsequent psychological workers. At the same time such intrafamily biographies have certain serious weaknesses. One of these is the fact that a naive observer is likely to see merely what he is looking for; especially desirable characteristics are apt to be noted, while such behavior as would blight the family escutcheon might be overlooked. Such biographies differ from observational studies carried out today, which define in advance what is to be included and excluded and make provision for a check on the reliability of observations. (Reliability in this case can be achieved through independent and simultaneous observation by more than one person.) In the baby biography many of the observations were fortuitous, were perhaps recorded long after the event had occurred, and were thus subject to memory distortion; furthermore, the children selected for study were not typical of children in general. In spite of these weaknesses the baby biographies helped to lay the groundwork for a scientific child psychology by raising problems which could later be answered more adequately by improved methods.

Hall and the Questionnaire

The next major development in the history of child psychology occurred in the United States under the leadership of G. Stanley Hall. In his thinking Hall was stimulated by the theories of biological evolution and recapitulation. He theorized that the normal growth of the mind is to be seen as a series of stages more or less corresponding to those which early man and his ancestors went through in the history of the race. He thus was influenced by the point of view sketched earlier of the child as a stage of evolution. Following up an idea he had acquired in Germany, he had teachers question children in the primary grades. By this rather simple technique of asking questions, a great assortment of facts about childhood experiences and problems was assembled. The findings are exemplified by Hall's paper on children's lies published in 1882 and his study of the contents of children's minds published in 1883. Shortly after the initial studies by Hall an abundance of efforts along similar lines by teachers, parents, and others appeared in the literature.   Societies and associations dedicated to the study of the child by this technique were formed both here and abroad.   The period of most intense activity of this way of studying children was from about 1890 to 1915.

It should be noted that Hall's own original work in this field was methodologically an improvement over both earlier and later studies using the questionnaire.   For example, in his first study (9) he used specially selected teachers, trained them to uniform methods of questioning, and met with them frequently for discussion and critique during data collection.   However, he and his students later began the practice of circulating to teachers and parents throughout the country questionnaires on various topics with blank spaces for the recording of answers.   In this way, much more information could be collected in a relatively short time over wide geographical areas.   If the questions were too difficult for the children, their teachers and parents were requested to interpret them to the children.   Still later the scope of the technique was broadened by circulation of questionnaires suitable for adults to record their childhood experiences as they remembered them.   Some of the topics (3) he studied from the questionnaire were appetites, fears, punishments, dreams, memories, toys, early sense of self, prayers, crying and laughing, perceptions of rhythm, and motor abilities.

Only the simplest of statistical devices were used in analyzing the data and no clearly defined or typical samples were gathered.   Often the questions were worded so as to suggest the desired answer.   The questionnaire as Hall used it also had certain inherent weaknesses. Direct questioning of children, as he attempted it, may produce careless, evasive, imitative answers of a sort the child thinks the adult wishes to hear.   Untrained recorders undoubtedly committed many sins both of omission and commission.

In large measure, the child study movement fell of its own weight. Parents and teachers uncritically, enthusiastically, and dogmatically stated the results of their superficial excursions into child development.   Hall himself began to lose enthusiasm and turned his energies toward some of his other manifold interests, especially religion and the psychology of senescence.

Despite its weaknesses, the child study movement of this period made definite contributions to the psychological study of the child. As Bradbury (3) summarizes, it led to increased recognition of the importance of empirical study of the child, brought forth a realization of the necessity of a critical evaluation of the methods used, and led to a recognition of the importance of childhood *per se*. It might also be added that the questionnaire approach fostered by Hall was in many respects the forerunner of modern psychological tests.

Binet and the Intelligence Test

In 1904, the French Minister of Education named a commission to study the measures to be taken to insure that defective Paris school-children receive the best possible educational training. This commission decided that no child suspected of mental retardation should be eliminated from ordinary school classes without first taking a special examination. The task of developing and applying such an examination was assigned to Alfred Binet. The patriarch of all later psychological tests—the Binet-Simon tests—was thus the direct result of an administrative decision in educational practice (2).

The first great advance that Binet made in intelligence testing was to abandon dependence upon the artificially simplified laboratory tasks used in the mental testing that had been attempted prior to his efforts. Short, discrete, simple tasks, such as tonal memory, estimation of distance, speed of reaction, and rate of tapping are examples of previously used items. Early tests such as these had been found to have little prognostic value in work with children. Whatever they were measuring, it was not intelligence as the term is used today.

Binet, after many years of preliminary work, chose to use the more complex and realistic tasks of everyday life. In his first, or 1905 scale, done in collaboration with Theophile Simon, there were thirty tests (1). Illustrative of the content were the tests requiring verbal knowledge of objects such as parts of the body, naming of common objects, repetition of digits, drawing of a design from memory, finding the right word to complete a sentence, and definitions of abstract terms. These tests were arranged in increasing order of difficulty. It was not until the 1908 and 1911 revisions of the scales that Binet made his second great contribution to mental testing—the grouping of tests as representative of the age at which they are usually passed. Mental age is the degree of intellectual development of an individual found by comparing his performance with that of other individuals of the same chronological age. Thus, a ten-year mental age is the degree of intellectual development attained by the average child of ten years. Through this procedure, a frame of reference for interpretation of the results of intelligence tests, the mental age, was established. Of course, crude comparisons using this concept had been known before, as exemplified in remarks such as, "He has no more sense than a child." It was Binet's work, however, which firmly established this means of assessing intelligence test results in quantitative form.

In 1916 in the United States, Lewis M. Terman restandardized and extended the original Binet-Simon Scale for American use and published it as the Stanford-Binet Intelligence Scale. This version soon became *the* standard testing instrument for measuring children's intelligence. In fact, it is no exaggeration to say that the principal task of many psychologists working with children was to administer the Stanford-Binet.

The Scale had the great merit and appeal of being carefully and objectively standardized. It was constructed with attention to the standards of scientific rigor of its day. As a tool it proved its value in predicting educational status of schoolchildren, in aiding in the diagnosis of mental deficiency in children, and in serving as a means whereby many problems of child psychology became open to investigation. In 1937 the presently used revision appeared. As Goodenough (8) indicates, the rapidity with which Binet testing was adopted in the United States can be traced to a number of conditions which made the times right for its appearance. Compulsory school attendance was beginning to be vigorously enforced and the length of the period of schooling was increased. Backward students in the schools thus became an increasingly important problem. Juvenile delinquency as a social problem was coming into active prominence, and emphasis upon social welfare and prevention of emotional and mental defects was becoming part of the American scene. Such problems called for large-scale assessment by means of a standardized instrument, a commission which was admirably fulfilled by the several revisions of the Binet scales.

Watson and the Conditioning Technique

The modern era in child psychology was ushered in by the work of John B. Watson on emotional responses in infants. Working with animals, particularly the white rat, and human infants, he found it impossible to use the then current major method of psychological investigation of introspection. The earlier investigators who had relied upon the method of introspection had ruled out children as suitable subjects for psychological investigations because they could not be trusted to report accurately their conscious experiences. In dismissing introspection, Watson made infants and children legitimate subjects for psychological experiments. He therefore militantly championed an approach to psychology, behaviorism, which stressed the behavioral aspects; hence, the name given by him to it.

The technique he used was that of conditioning. As Pavlov had established, when a dog is making a definite response to a particular stimulus, any frequently accompanying stimulus is likely to be responded to in the same way. Thus, a dog presented with food (to which he responds by a flow of saliva) and the sound of the bell at the same time will eventually respond by salivating to the sound of the bell alone. No introspection is either possible or necessary; the dog is presented with stimuli to which he responds.

This conditioning technique was applied by Watson (25) to newborn infants during the twenties. He was interested in the emotional responses of infants and used conditioning to demonstrate how emotional responses are acquired.

His most famous subject, Albert, aged eleven months, was reared in a hospital and showed no fear reaction to such stimuli as a white rat or rabbit, masks, or cotton wool. He reached for practically everything brought near him. Fear, however, was shown by Albert at the sound of a steel bar struck sharply. In one of his experiments, Watson presented the rat to Albert. Just as he was reaching for the rat, the bar was struck producing a loud sound. The infant jumped violently, burying his face in the mattress. When the rat was presented a second time and he again reached for it, the bar was struck once more. This time, in addition to jumping violently, Albert began to whimper. A week later, the rat was presented without the sound from the bar. Although he eyed the rat, there was no tendency to reach for it, and when the rat was placed near him, he withdrew his hand. Evidently, the two joint stimulations of sight of rat and sound of bar were not without effect. Thereafter, joint stimulations of rat and bar were made several times. After five simultaneous presentations, the rat was presented alone. The instant Albert saw the rat he began to cry and crawled rapidly away from it. Subsequent checks showed that several other objects that formerly brought no fear responses now did. The rabbit, the mask, and the white cotton wool all were reacted to violently.

This and other studies showed that fears are acquired by conditioning. Watson also demonstrated that there is a lack of specificity (stimulus generalization) of the S-R relation in that conditioned response formed to a certain specific stimulus was also excitable by other stimuli having certain visual similarities in common with it. These conditioned responses were found to persist over periods of time. In general, he demonstrated that many fears of infants are acquired. For present purposes, the most important implication of his work is his supplying the psychologist with a way of studying the infant objectively.

It was through the work of such men as Preyer, Hall, Binet, Terman, and Watson that a scientific child psychology came into being. Although working with different problems in different countries, these men all had something in common—a desire for objectivity and the conviction that through quantitative measurement this could be assured. Although interpreting objectivity in research with varying standards of exactitude, each turned his back on philosophical and theological explanations of child behavior and worked toward the goal of new explanatory systems based upon scientific research. Each is identified with a technique of study of the child, emphasizing to a greater or lesser degree exactitude and replicability of observations— the true beginnings of the scientific study of the behavior of the child.

Child psychology in the twenties and thirties

During the decades of the twenties and thirties, certain trends which had emerged a little earlier now came into sharp focus, whereas other areas of interest were abandoned or temporarily suppressed. One outstanding event of the period was the considerable influx of psychologically trained personnel into what was now recognized as the field of child psychology. No longer were there only a few isolated giants as in the past, but rather many capable workers collectively making a considerable contribution to knowledge of the child.

The type of research shifted during this period, with the new direction largely determined by advances in methodology made during the previous period. That is, devices for measuring diversified forms of behavior had been developed, and projects were now launched to measure these behaviors. These decades thus were characterized by specialized studies of the different capacities and traits of the child.

Research was vigorously carried out on hundreds of problems with little concern for their interrelationships. Piecemeal measurement became the order of the day. The soil was so rich that it encouraged snatching deposits of behavior here and there and then hurrying on to the next vein. Which shining nugget attracted attention was almost fortuitous. To be sure, one worked a claim registered under the name of "intelligence," "learning," or some one of the other conventional titles, but aside from this there was apt to be little of a theoretical map to guide these explorations.

To place it in perspective, these were the years in which specific traits and capacities were being investigated by the then current procedures. Emphasis was placed upon the quantitative and objective. Large samples of children were used, and to a large extent a single variable was investigated at a time. In other words, what would be known about the children would be the particular measure for each child under consideration and some conventional subsidiary information such as sex and chronological age; otherwise, little or nothing else was reported about the children.

Highly specialized studies dealing with learning, intelligence, sensory capacity, motor performance, emotion, language, thinking, and the like were carried on. Promising leads in method or theory drawn from anywhere in the general field of psychology were followed up avidly. Many workers would turn to a given field when a promising method or challenging theory was advanced, leaving other areas relatively inactive. Consequently, the growth of child psychology was not uniform. Among the areas mentioned previously the studies of intelligence and learning loomed the largest. These areas occupied the attention of the majority of child psychologists.

With the advent of World War I the opportunity for large-scale testing of army recruits arose. As a result, tests were developed that could be applied to groups of individuals simultaneously. In the face of their pragmatic demonstration of their usefulness during wartime, tests for peacetime uses in the school systems were extensively developed. The Stanford-Binet of Terman was often the original source of much of the work, as well as the criterion in terms of which a new instrument would be validated. This was done by correlating scores obtained on the new test with the scores made by the same individuals on independently administered Stanford-Binets. If the agreement were close, the test was judged to be a good measure of intelligence.

Many of the studies of this period were normative in the sense that they charted measurements of some segment of behavior by age, sex, socio-economic status, and the like. The measurement of intelligence with increasing age, with hundreds of new tests appearing during this period, was a characteristic type of endeavor. It was also characteristic to some degree that, in their preoccupation with *tests,* these psychological research workers lost sight of the *child* who was being measured.

This was the period of the investigation of "individual differences." At first this assertion may appear to contradict the comment just made that the individual child was lost to view. This concern with individual differences was, in one sense, curiously misleading. What was studied was group variation in respect to one variable at a time and not how one individual differs from another. By individual differences, then, workers made a study of group variation in respect to one trait or capacity at a time. For example, one might administer the Stanford-Binet to 100 children and calculate the average IQ, the spread of scores from low to high, and so on. Thus, a given child was close to the average, another only at the fifth percentile, another at the ninety-fifth percentile, and so on. But this, so far as research was concerned, was generally about all that was known about a particular child. At best, some investigators administered a group of tests, and scores on a series of tests might be available for each child. Although then they could make a series of separate statements about the child, nothing was done about how these trait scores were related to one another. So far as these workers were concerned, the child was merely a series of isolated scores.

But on this issue some voices of doubt could be heard now and then. "Where in this mass of facts," they asked, "is the child?" The segmentalized, compartmentalized approach was noted with some misgivings by parents, educators, and others who dealt with children in everyday situations. Johnny throwing a temper tantrum on the main floor of the town's largest department store was somehow different from the reactions described in the current textbook in child psychology's chapters on emotion, motor development, and learning. They asked for general principles that would make Johnny understandable, that would make the facts cohere. In short, they asked for general principles of personality organization or a theoretical framework into which the isolated facts could fit. This request, although justified, was, at this time, somewhat premature. What such critics neglected to see was that normative data are essential before a more integrated picture could be assembled. Before developing this theme, however, it is necessary to consider the influence upon child psychology of the work in other fields.

The influence of other fields upon child psychology

The beginnings of child psychology have been found in the work of certain pioneers, few of whom limited their interests exclusively to psychology. Perhaps a measure of the eminence of the individuals is the fact that their work extended beyond the confines of child psychology. Preyer was primarily an embryologist; Hall, although trained as a psychologist, could not really be pigeon-holed; Binet helped to found the first French psychological clinic and the first French psychological journal; Watson was an animal psychologist and the founder of the school of behaviorism which in many ways revolutionized the field of psychology as a whole. Men with interests even more distinctly in other areas also have contributed much to child psychology. Other fields of endeavor have influenced child psychology profoundly, some of which will now be examined.

Psychoanalysis

Undoubtedly, one of the greatest influences upon modern child psychology has come from the work of Sigmund Freud, the founder of psychoanalysis. His influence is to be found not only in the direct utilization of psychoanalytic concepts and findings in child psychology today, but also in the subtle, indirect, and sometimes unnoticed effect upon child training practices. Bearing the impact of his thinking, whether acknowledged or not, are present-day practices concerning the child's experiences in its motivated striving aspects, parent-child relationships, the effect of unconscious influences, and our understanding of deviant children. Even his most vehement opponents spread his doctrines by their very rebuttals.

Sigmund Freud was trained as a neurologist in Vienna and elsewhere. Toward the end of the last century, while still practicing as a neurologist, he became interested in the more psychological aspects of the problems of his patients who were emotionally disturbed. He began to search for a method of treatment to meet their problems. Ultimately he arrived at what is known as the method of free-association. In free-association the patient is expected to say anything that comes to his mind, to relate all his thoughts no matter how trivial, irrelevant, or distasteful they may be. His early patients spontaneously reported their dreams in the course of their sessions with him, and dream interpretation was subsequently incorporated into the psychoanalytic method.

According to Freud, this "verbal mind wandering" with little or no direction on the part of the psychoanalyst produced one invariable result. His patients reported many childhood experiences, and gradually Freud was led to the conclusion that adult personality maladjustments were directly traceable to unfortunate experiences in childhood. During the course of the psychoanalysis, as the therapeutic procedure came to be called, the patient not only recalled his childhood but he also relived some of his early experiences in the analytic hours, with the analyst serving as a sort of parent surrogate.

The principles and techniques of psychoanalysis were largely developed from work with adult patients. However, the crucial role of the patients' childhood experiences is stressed. Freud thus forcibly called attention to childhood as a most critical period of development. Indeed, it was not until Freud emphasized that adult neurotic symptoms were the outcome of childhood experiences that past histories were studied in order to explain present behavior.

Freud was a strict determinist. All human activities, no matter how trivial, were postulated as having been rooted in a meaningful cause-effect sequence. Indeed, slips of the tongue, dreams, and "minor" unnoticed gestures on the part of his patients were found to have profound significance. He was also struck by his patients' inability to see the sigificance of these activities in their proper light. Only after many psychoanalytic sessions did the patient gradually begin to have insight into their meanings. Thus, the extreme importance of unconscious determinants came to the fore. Freud was not the first to point out the significance of unconscious determinants, but he was the first to advance a method, free-association, whereby they could be thoroughly studied. It was to Freud, then, that child psychology owes interest in and appreciation of the significance of dynamic or motivational processes and unconscious influences upon the development of the child.

Freud found that his approach was also applicable to the problem of children. In collaboration with the father of a five-year-old boy, in 1909 he reported an analysis of the child's phobias. The method of free-association is obviously impossible to use with young children, requiring as it does a more advanced verbal level than they possess. He therefore emphasized the play activities of the child in securing data for analysis and interpreting their significance. He drew upon the symbolic significance he had found to be appropriate with his adult patients. His use of play was casual and his interest in child patients was far overshadowed by his time and attention to neurotic adult patients.

For many years Freud worked in Vienna in relative isolation from both psychiatry and from academic psychology. In 1909, G. Stanley Hall invited Freud to the United States, where at Clark University he gave a series of lectures on psychoanalysis which were later published in the *American Journal of Psychology*. His visit and his writings stimulated considerable interest, both positive and negative. It may be remarked here that his doctrines, centering as they did upon sexual functions, broadly interpreted, aroused considerable feeling. Once in the public spotlight his statements were seldom lightly received. For many years there was hardly any middle ground; either one was an enthusiastic adherent or a violent opponent. Only gradually were his views assimilated and placed in proper perspective, and even today his views are sometimes only gingerly touched by specialists in child behavior.

It was from the generation subsequent to Freud that the next major developments in child psychoanalysis were to come. One of his students, Melanie Klein (13), took the step of systematically applying play technique as a substitute for free-association. The essence of her approach is direct, immediate, verbal interpretations to the child of the symbolic nature of his play activity. They are not only direct and immediate but also uncompromisingly blunt. Thus, the bumping of toys together signifies sexual intercourse of the parents; questions about a sequence of alternating long and short words in a poem indicate thoughts of sex differences; a girl playing an "office" game reveals a desire to be a man; overturning a toy suggests an aggressive impulse; and so on. For several reasons, especially the conviction that her interpretations tend to be blunt and overreaching, her position has not had as much influence upon child psychoanalysis in the United States as has that of Anna Freud.

Anna Freud (7), the daughter of Sigmund Freud, also works with children in the psychoanalytic tradition. She feels that psychoanalytic therapy with children follows a clearly delineated sequence, and, that preceding psychoanalysis proper, there is a preanalytic phase of treatment. In the United States, where her point of view has had considerable influence, the induction phase of child guidance clinic procedures (to be described subsequently) often provides the means whereby this preanalytic phase is conducted. The need for this period comes about because the immature patient—the child—is not psychologically prepared for treatment and seldom sees any need for it. The intent is to enlist the cooperation of the child. Interpretations are neither as immediately nor as forcibly given the child as in the case with Klein and more use of indirection is employed. Her approach involves not only the use of play, especially drawings, but also the use of daydreams and dreams in the psychoanalytic sessions. After analysis, a postanalytic phase with the parents and teachers through the child guidance clinic helps to reinforce the gains made in the psychoanalysis itself.

The psychoanalyst spends his professional and scientific life examining in minute and exacting detail the behavior and experience of a very small number of individuals. Regularities are noted and any deviation, no matter how trivial, does not escape scrutiny. His training makes him sensitive to the nuances of behavior, the evasions and deceptions so common in our adjustive behavior. The analyst is thus in a favorable position to describe human behavior and to derive principles concerning it. Psychoanalysis is essentially a method of reconstruction of the individual's past, whether he be adult or child. These hindsights and clinical reconstructions accomplish a great deal. They are, however, more useful as a stimulation for research than as instances of verified research findings. From the point of view of the psychologist, their results are not sufficient, and the traditional further step of scientific verification of clinical findings is necessary.

Child Guidance

The original impetus for the formation of child guidance clinics arose from a desire to combat juvenile delinquency. Before the advent of such clinics, the child or adolescent might have had a physical examination by juvenile authorities, but no investigation into why he had performed the delinquent activities was conducted.

As a method of treating juvenile delinquency, the first child guidance clinic was founded in 1909 by William Healy in Chicago under the name, "The Juvenile Psychopathic Institute." One of the major forces operative at the beginning of this movement was the emphasis upon the psychopathology exhibited by the child delinquent. As the child guidance movement has spread, the link to delinquency has weakened, but not the other major force which led to the clinic's founding—the conviction that delinquency represented aberrant psychological behavior and that it was amenable to modification. However, there has been a gradual broadening of scope, as it was recognized that substantially the same means of treatment applicable to the delinquent could be applied to the emotionally disturbed nondelinquent child. This, however, waited upon the understanding that the delinquent himself was often an emotionally disturbed or otherwise maladjusted child; or, in other words, that delinquency and emotional maladjustments are different surface manifestations of what may be highly similar etiological pictures.

During the twenties, other child guidance clinics were organized in various cities. It was during this period that a shift from emphasis on the delinquent to work with children manifesting other types of disturbance took place. Although organized to combat juvenile delinquency, the clinics helped many children with problems not directly related to delinquency. Maladjustment in school and home, especially that centering upon parent-child relationships, came to the foreground. In many clinics today the influence of psychoanalysis is very evident. Adaptation of psychoanalytic principles and techniques to the setting and personnel of the clinic and to the nature and age of the patients came rapidly. The child, regarded during an earlier period as a passive victim of whatever circumstances were impinged upon him, came now to be viewed in the dynamic tradition of psychoanalysis as a very active participant who could be helped by psychotherapy.

The unique characteristic of the child guidance clinic is the use of the so-called team approach, or the coordinated services of the specialists on the staff. Instead of one clinician serving in all phases of work, a customary but flexible division of labor has evolved. In a typical child guidance clinic procedure, the social worker, as intake supervisor, talks to the person requesting clinical services and describes what might be done, provided the facilities of the clinic are appropriate for the child's needs. During the initial contact, a visit of both the parent (generally the mother) and the child is arranged. The child is seen by the psychologist for psychological testing; the child is observed, often in a playroom, by the psychiatrist; and the mother is seen by the social worker who secures a comprehensive family history and an account of the difficulties that the child is exhibiting. Often the psychiatrist also sees the mother. After sufficient information is collected to make possible some tentative diagnostic appraisal, a case conference is arranged. The psychiatrist, social worker, and psychologist review the information which has been gathered and each discusses his interpretation of the difficulties the child is facing. A general plan of treatment is worked out and a psychotherapist selected for both mother and child. In many clinics, the psychotherapist for a specific child is chosen more for his particular fitness or availability rather than because he is a representative of one or another of the disciplines. Thus, either a psychiatrist, a psychologist, or a social worker may be the psychotherapist for a specific child. From time to time, there may be conferences in which the talents of the staff are again pooled in efforts to further the progress of the child and mother.

Although sometimes working as a diagnostic agency only with referral elsewhere for disposition and treatment, the child guidance clinic in its more typical form also carries on psychotherapeutic functions. Many hours may be spent with the child and with his parents in exploring the reasons for his difficulty and many more in attempting to help him. Such a process provides the clinician an excellent opportunity for learning about children. What happens in the therapeutic process furnishes valuable information which is helpful in developing a coherent, clear, and complete understanding of child behavior.

Concern in such clinics is with the discrete, individual child. Each patient is unique, presenting a unique problem, personality, and array of environmental circumstances. To be sure, there are always threads of commonality, but the pattern is different in each instance and each child must be understood in terms of himself.

Clinical Psychology

Some of the same influences brought to bear upon child psychology were operative in helping to shape the history of clinical psychology. The psychological test tradition, the influence of psychiatry and psychoanalysis, and the child guidance movement had their effects upon its development. Clinical psychology, in turn, affected their development. Some of its roots have been traced elsewhere (27).

The opening in 1896 of the Psychological Clinic at the University of Pennsylvania is said to mark the advent of clinical psychology (4). Lightner Witmer, the founder and director of the clinic, became interested in helping the educationally retarded and handicapped child. As a consequence, the great majority of the cases seen in the clinic came from the school systems. Cooperation with special teachers of the blind, deaf, and mentally defective was stressed. This clinic, the first of many organized at universities and teachers colleges, found its particular area of competence in the everyday problems of the child, particularly those relating to academic success, such as reading. This is not to say that emotional or nonschool problems were ignored; rather, less stress was placed upon them (perhaps because at that time there was less understanding of them).

This tradition of close cooperation with the schools still has a respected place in the activities of the clinical psychologist. Nevertheless, for good or for ill, clinical psychology as a specialty has outgrown its beginning in a quasi-educational setting and found its place in mental hospitals, child guidance clinics, homes for the mentally defective, and many other settings (26).

Today, the clinical psychologist often carries on full diagnostic and therapeutic responsibility not only with the educationally or intellectually handicapped, but also with the emotionally disturbed child or adult. In the next chapter, these two facets of the clinical method of the psychologist, diagnosis and therapy, will be explored, not primarily because of their aim of alleviating distress, but rather as tools of research in furthering our understanding of the child.

An interest in clinical problems gave the psychologist an opportunity to study the child from a different point of view and under different circumstances, and provided a different approach for doing so.

Pediatrics

The pediatrician is likewise interested in the behavior and experience of the child, in health as well as illness (22). Pediatrics first emerged as a medical specialty in the middle of the nineteenth century as a field of teaching rather than of practice. Its origin provided another avenue of proof that the theory of the child as a miniature adult was inadequate, even with respect to diagnosis and treatment of physical disease. Even in this area the child presented his own unique problems.

Interest in the psychological aspects of child medical practice was slow to develop, not reaching any proportions until the end of the first quarter of the present century. Concerning these influences, Senn (22), a pediatrician, has stated that pediatric attention first focused on neurological conditions. This was followed by an interest in the testing of intelligence, which later broadened to an appreciation of the developmental sequence. In the meantime, knowledge of phenomena of conditioning and learning, particularly as stimulated by John B. Watson, led to suggestions on how to rear children.

Concerning subsequent developments, this same authority refers to the rise of psychiatric-pediatric collaboration and the appearance of child guidance clinics in which there was a provision for pediatric service. One way in which the importance of taking into consideration psychological aspects of development expressed itself was in attempts on the part of some pediatricians to combat the prevalent rigid, impersonal method of infant feeding by the clock and by the ounce. Now many medical schools arrange that some pediatrics be taught collaboratively with psychiatry, with at least some attention given to the personality of the child (22).

Pediatrics as a branch of medicine is concerned with physiology and anatomy. It is, however, also concerned with the child as an individual person and as a psychological being. The interrelation of the two areas, the physical and the psychological, leads to their integration in psychosomatic conditions, which will be discussed later.

Education and Educational Psychology

In many ways, child psychology and childhood as education and educational psychology view it owe their development to the same forces. The early attitudes toward the child previously sketched are as much the heritage of education and educational psychology as they are of child psychology. Preyer, Hall, and Binet are part of the history of educational as well as child psychology. Naturally, the educator and educational psychologist have emphasized the processes of learning and teaching.

In the more modern period, two individuals stand out as influencing studies of children's learning and of methods of teaching them—John Dewey and Edward L. Thorndike. John Dewey—philosopher, psychologist, and educator—probably had a more profound influence upon education than any other man of this century. His educational philosophy is widely known, though not always put into practice. Through his followers, his work led to the progressive education movement which in essence consists of the application of mental hygiene to education (15).

The studies of Edward L. Thorndike on learning and related topics are part of this common heritage. Sharing through his own research in learning the discovery of the child as an individual, he did much to document the newly appreciated fact of individual differences. The existence of individual differences was now established by research instead of being part of the intuitive grasp of the gifted few "born" teachers. Thorndike's first book on educational psychology was published in 1903. His emphasis upon drill as a means of learning, although influential for many years, is now seen in a broader perspective and is of less influence than formerly. The work of the educational psychologists and that of their colleagues in other disciplines has led to a concern with the growth and development of each child, in spite of the educator's responsibility for large groups of children. Differentiated curricula, the activity program, the advent of elective subjects, concern with each individual student's interest and motivation, and the appearance of learning readiness programs all attest to education's concern with the individual child and his emotional as well as intellectual needs.

Cultural Anthropology

Findings in cultural anthropology also have influenced child psychology. Workers in this field attempt to understand man as a social being. In the main they study the so-called primitive cultures throughout the world, although some anthropologists have begun to interest themselves in contemporary cultures such as our own.

Prior to 1920, cultural anthropology used a descriptive and historical approach relatively uninfluenced by events in other fields (14). E. B. Tylor in his volume, *Primitive Culture* (23), published in 1871, laid the foundation of what came to be called "cultural anthropology." His most celebrated doctrine was that of animism, the view that primitive man tends to look upon all things as if they had consciousness or "soul." This doctrine influenced the thinking of his contemporaries among evolutionists, especially those who viewed primitive man as essentially childlike. This doctrine came under well deserved suspicion as being too sweeping and in need of qualification. To be sure, there have been varied attempts by different individuals, including Freud, Wundt, and Hall, to use the primitive as an analogue of the child. For example, there are primitive cultures which foster the development of animistic thinking. Since children in our society think "animistically," an analogy is drawn. But the fact is (18) that there are primitive (that is, nonliterate) societies which discourage animistic thinking in an even more rigorous fashion than our own. Eventually, we have come to the position that there is no such thing as *the primitive;* rather there are *individuals* in many different societies. The pattern of living imposes individuality upon members of primitive societies no less stringently than in ours.

The anthropologist in the early years of this century spent much of his time in the field collecting discrete "facts." This search for facts came about because of the necessity of describing the primitive cultures before they were altered or destroyed by European influences. In a way, this collection of facts was somewhat similar both in form and spirit to the collecting of the artifacts—the baskets and spears for the museums—that accompanied it. Each bit of behavior was carefully noted and, to some extent, catalogued, but an understanding of the over-all pattern was lacking because theory was lacking. Gradually, a new point of view emerged. It is not the behavior in itself as an independent unit that is important, but its meaning, the assumptions underlying it, the way it is patterned, the motivation for it, and the satisfactions it brings that give it vitality and relevance. Working within such theoretical frameworks, whether psychoanalytically or nonpsychoanalytically oriented, and recognizing the implications of the units of behavior for an understanding of broader social processes are characteristic of modern cultural anthropology.

Many of the recent contributions of such distinguished anthropologists as Margaret Mead have been directed by a desire to test psychiatric-psychological hypotheses in other cultures (14). Often such studies focus attention on younger subjects and are avowedly developmental in character (19). For example, Mead's *Coming of Age in Samoa* (16) and *Growing Up in New Guinea* (17) reveal in their very titles a concern with the developmental sequence.

In her Samoan study, Mead (16) was interested in testing the hypothesis that the so-called storminess of adolescence was a result of particular cultural conditions instead of being an inevitable manifestation of maturational factors as it was generally assumed to be. Lacking power to construct experimental conditions, she turned to Samoa, a culture far different from our own. Careful and intensive study of 50 adolescent Samoan girls allowed her to supply evidence which demonstrated convincingly that adolescence is not a period of strain in Samoan society. Anthropology, then, contributes to child psychology through demonstrating the influence of society on child development.

One well-known contribution of anthropology to psychological knowledge has been the needed corrective of "cultural relativity." This term refers to the unjustifiability of generalizing a research finding to individuals of a culture different from those upon whom the finding was originally based. That is, any given behavior pattern is "relative" to the cultural experiences of the individual who exhibits it. Thus, knowledge of primitive cultures can be used to raise questions concerning psychological assumptions involving universal applicability of Western European or American behavior (for example, assuming that because adolescence is a period of stress and strain in American society, this must represent an innate physiological predisposition rather than a reaction to conditions within the culture). The concept of cultural relativity offers a corrective to overgeneralization when a child, reacting in a particular time, place, and set of circumstances, is interpreted by an investigator as exhibiting a pattern of behavior holding in all cultures and at all times. The task of the anthropologist then becomes the thankless one of gently but firmly indicating that in such and such a cultural setting this generalization does not hold and hence the behavior in question is culturally relative. To express the same issue more positively, anthropologists may test psychological formulations found to hold in our culture by examining children in other cultures to see if they also apply, which they must if they are to have general validity.

Findings of the anthropologists have forced a recognition that we can never observe human beings who have not been subject to cultural influences. Their findings further indicate that cultural factors are important during the formative phase of personality development; hence, the emergence of the problem of the interrelations between personality and culture, an issue to which we will turn later.

This brief review could not do justice to the manifold influences brought to bear upon our knowledge of the behavior and experience of the child. All of general psychology, but most particularly the field of learning theory, has contributed to child psychology in the modern period. The contribution of sociology, through its study of the family, has not been mentioned; nor have the insights and findings of the linguist, philosopher, artist, or religious leader. They, too, have made their contributions to the modern period in child psychology.

The modern period in child psychology

Certain characteristics of the modern period in child psychology will help set the stage for the account contained in the rest of this book. Themes running throughout much current activity in the field will now be summarized. They might be briefly identified by the catch words with which they are associated, namely, "development," "personality," "total situation," "multidiscipline research," "interplay of science and practice," and "behavior theory."/ Each will be considered in turn.

Workers in child psychology and related disciplines share with others the American tradition of emphasis on the worth and value of the developing individual. Development is the common interest of workers in all of these varied fields.   It is this theme of development which can be made central in discussions of child psychology, both as a concept and as a means of presenting the facts and theories concerning the psychological study of the child./ The concept can perhaps be made more specific and meaningful by referring to *personality* development.   Although variously defined, personality is concerned with the molar behavior and experience of the person.

/The present era is one in which *personality* investigation is paramount in child psychology./ We have on one hand certain views of personality long in theory but short on facts; on the other hand, we have various scientific findings short on theory but long on facts. Sometimes an individual child psychologist or a member of another field interested in the child reacts by slavishly accepting a certain theoretical position, say psychoanalysis, and then planning investigations which, provided one accepts the major tenets, can be cited as furthering our knowledge of personality theory.   Others refuse to see any problem and ignore theory while normatively mapping personality as a separate entity much as has been done in other areas such as learning or intelligence.   However, there is, as always, a middle ground.   Without allowing any one rigid theoretical position to pervade all of one's thinking, one can use theoretical constructs as a guide to hypothesis-making.   With continuing research, a picture gradually will emerge based upon scientifically verified facts. As these particular facts emerge into larger structures, a more unified picture combining theory and empirical data can be constructed. In the meantime, unverified but plausible hypotheses can be used to fill in the missing gaps *provided that they are recognized for what they are—as yet unverified assumptions.*   In this task of balancing fact and theory, the child psychologist, it is to be hoped, plays an important part.

/It is characteristic of the modern period in child psychology that the child is seen as having his psychological significance as an individual in a total situation.// The child functions as he does not only because of individually determined forces but also because of the environmental circumstances pressing upon him.// /The beginnings of this point of view were apparent in the earlier periods, as in the psychoanalytic point of view where Freud stressed the effect of adverse circumstances upon personality development. Even more clearly there was recognition of external influences in the child guidance movement. William Healy's first major work, significantly entitled the *Individual Delinquent*, showed that delinquency was a situational phenomenon, not a characteristic of the child himself and subject to change if circumstances were changed. Within child psychology itself, this stress upon total social situation gave us the flourishing field of the social psychology of childhood.

This emphasis upon the whole child in a total situation has added impetus to another trend of the modern period—the development of multidiscipline child research institutes. Although often psychologists predominate, the personnel of such institutes may also include individuals of different areas of specialty and interest, such as psychiatrists, pediatricians, nutrition experts, and physiologists.

The Institute of Child Welfare at the University of California is typical. In operation for many years, its research is directed along several lines (*12*). It is concerned with the investigation of the physical, physiological, and psychological development of children and adolescents. The Institute is dedicated to research, the development of theory, the training of students, the preparation of reports concerning the implications of their findings for schools, and practical problems in child training.

It is characteristic of the modern period in child psychology that there is an interplay between science and practice. The healthy integrating exchange thus coming about is borne out by many of the facets of history previously outlined. Clinical-child psychologists or, if you prefer, child-clinical psychologists are one manifestation. Still other child psychologists are to be found within education, home economics, pediatrics, parent education, marriage counseling, correctional work, and the gamut of children's agencies. Research stations such as those outlined before are very sensitive to questions of practice. It is recognized today that you cannot artificially separate science and practice. Nevertheless, there can be a division of labor.

The clinical psychologist working with children may on this basis be distinguished from the child psychologist. The former works primarily with disturbed children. The child psychologist, although cognizant of what his brother is doing and sometimes assuming the uneasy role of his brother's keeper, is more concerned with scientific advance and sees the problems of the child in a broader perspective.

He sometimes pays for this breadth by less appreciation of individual dynamics.

It is pertinent to report the opinion of others concerning these trends. One authoritative source is in the *Annual Review of Psychology*, in which current research is critically examined by experts in each of the specialties. In the 1955 volume, the Yarrows, who wrote the review of child psychology, have this to say: "Rather slowly, but very perceptibly, a new point of view is emerging in child psychology. It is not a point of view which is an irresponsible, radical departure from the conservative empiricism which has epitomized this discipline, but it is a reformulation of the problems in terms of a more dynamic conception of behavior and development" (28, 1).[1]

After examining briefly earlier developments in child psychology in a fashion not too different in spirit from this presentation, they go on to summarize the modern era as follows: "Childhood re-emerged as a crucial field of study (the fourth phase) when testable hypotheses based on clinical (mainly psychoanalytic) theories began to be formulated by systematically oriented researchers, when psychological theory and cultural anthropology converged, and when the genius of Kurt Lewin trained the experimental method upon meaningful social psychological questions within a framework of dynamic field theory" (28, 2).[1]

That we are not alone in taking this stand concerning the importance of the current dynamic-theoretical phase of child development is also borne out by their analysis of the United States Children's Bureau bulletin on current research in progress (24). Into the problem areas of personality dynamics, personality deviations, and parent-child relationships fall 41 per cent of all studies in progress reported in this presumably nearly exhaustive review. This is all the more significant when it is noted that clinical case studies are omitted. On the other hand, studies of physical growth, motor development, perception, hereditary and constitutional factors, and learning make up slightly more than ten per cent combined. Evidently, the current research scene reflects at least some aspects of the present contentions.

There are many indications, some of which have been sketched, that psychology as a science is becoming more closely united today than it has been in the past. There is an increasing recognition on the part of psychologists and others of the essential unity of the field.

[1] From Yarrow and Yarrow (28). Published 1955 by *Annual Reviews, Inc.*, and used with permission.

"Schools of psychology" which used to plague the field are almost nonexistent. This does not mean that there are no differences of opinion, but rather that these differences rest upon this or that specific point, not upon some fundamental principle which would tear the fabric of the field into bits. There is, to be sure, a "latitudinarian" left and a "rigorous" right, but such a distinction is a quantitative, not a qualitative, one. As Hebb puts it, "There appears to be a left wing and a right wing in psychology . . . the Right favors parsimony of explanatory ideas, a simple or mechanical account of behavior, and definiteness even at the cost of being narrow. The Left is prepared to postulate more fully and can better tolerate vagueness and lack of system in its account of behavior" (10, 47–48).[2]

There have been a number of attempts at integration of the areas of psychology—learning, motivation, perception, thinking, and the like—into one unified view. One of the signs of integration in psychology is what is known as behavior theory. Actually, there is a variety of behavior theories, having in common an interest to embrace and unify the various psychological phenomena into one system with emphasis upon learning. Each in its own way accounts for the acquisition and retention of new forms of behavior.

One major stream in behavior theory stems from the work of Clark L. Hull, whose volume, *Principles of Behavior* (11), epitomizes the approach. His efforts at integration are related to the earlier work of John B. Watson in behavioristic study of animals and man and to the work of Edward L. Thorndike on reward and punishment in learning. Hull represents the rigorous right in psychological theory. He was primarily concerned with an analysis of the learning process with particular attention to carefully controlled experimental situations. It was part of his strategy to begin the study of human behavior with animal subjects, hoping that their very simplicity would give him access to the fundamentals of learning.

His colleagues and students have extended his theoretical conceptions in an attempt to build a theory of personality development. They thus represent to some degree the latitudinarian left. These efforts have taken them beyond what Sears calls "the closely charted regions of rigorous stimulus response theory" (21, 61).[3] In no sense are matters in this extension of learning theory a settled issue. Many

---

[2] From Hebb (10). Copyright 1951 by Duke University Press, and published with permission.

[3] From Sears (21). Copyright 1947 by the University of Pittsburgh Press, and published with permission.

areas relevant to their efforts are simply not yet explored; others are only dimly understood and even in the most thoroughly explored areas there is only the most sketchy understanding. Different workers in this tradition have proceeded in different directions. This necessitates in a presentation such as the present one a choice from among them. At this point it is enough to say that the works of Dollard and Miller on social learning, Sears on frustration-aggression and patterns of child rearing, and Whiting and Child on socialization are emphasized. Each of these men were or are associated with the Institute of Human Relations at Yale University where Hull did his work. Each in his own way has been influenced by his account of learning theory. For present purposes their appeal lies in the fact that each in his own way emphasizes the social aspects of personality.

These related points of view have no commonly agreed-upon name. Following Hull, they might be called behavior theory, but this designation is perhaps best reserved for the more rigorous Hullian exposition. For convenience and for shortness of statement only, and with the warning that there is no general agreement about the choice of the term, behavior-social learning theory (learning theory, for short) will be used in referring to this point of view in the presentation to follow.

In furthering these themes of modern child psychology in later chapters, the usual format for a text in child psychology will not be followed. Typically in a treatise on child psychology, the topics of psychological growth are divided into areas, such as intelligence, learning, emotion, motor development, social development, and personality. Such a division, although conventional and therefore convenient, would be false to the aim of striving to see the whole child. Any child's behavior at a given moment overlaps these categories. To follow the usual chapter arrangement would also minimize the contribution of the other fields just discussed. Since the disciplines contributing to our knowledge of the behavior and experience of the child are all interested, broadly speaking, in personality development in a total situation, the natural sequence would be to follow the child from germination to end of childhood within a framework of these themes.

As a concession to the impossibility of considering all things at once, the following chapter will be devoted to a discussion of the methods of child study. Thereafter, chapters on basic principles and concepts of development are introduced. This is followed by an artificial, but necessary, separation of development into three periods—infancy, early childhood, and late childhood.

Two major considerations dictate the choice of infancy and early and late childhood as the periods of development into which childhood is divided for study. First, there is popular general acceptance and consequent understanding of this division. Infant, preschool child, and school child, for example, are used as synonyms for these ages in educational settings. Often research studies are designed expressly to cover the age span of one of these periods. In fact, if a given period is neglected with some promising technique or hypothesis, the very fact that the age period has not been investigated is stimulus for research efforts to fill this gap. Second, the tripartite age division corresponds to age stages used by the psychoanalyst, namely, the oral-anal stages, phallic stage, and latency period, respectively.

Within each age period a further subdivision is necessary. In one chapter, the infant is considered as relatively independent of the social situation. In the next chapter, he is viewed as a social being. Disturbances in infancy round out the discussion of that period. In subsequent chapters, early childhood is considered in terms of individual and social factors. Late childhood is similarly treated. Disturbances as shown in early and late childhood, instead of being discussed separately, are the common theme of the next chapter which closes the book.

Summary

Before the emergence of child psychology as a scientific discipline, there were a variety of points of view or attitudes toward the child. These views may be identified as seeing the child as a miniature adult, as a future citizen, as innately depraved, as inherently good, and as a stage of evolution. They had in common that they were expressions of points of view about what the child had been or was to become. Only with the advent of scientific study was there much interest in what the child *is*—a study of the child for his own sake.

The beginnings of the science of child psychology are to be found in the work of certain pioneers during the period from about 1880 to 1920. These early workers each contributed to the founding of the field through the first major application of some technique of scientific study. Thus Preyer used the baby biography, Hall the questionnaire, Binet the intelligence test, and Watson the conditioning technique. The techniques themselves are less important than what they represented—an attempt on the part of each of these workers to develop objective means of studying the child.

In the twenties and thirties of the present century, the greatly increased number of workers in child psychology proceeded to place child psychology upon a solid footing. Their research efforts may be characterized as *normative* in that they were concerned with carefully establishing what children at given ages were capable of doing, psychologically speaking. General personality organization and the dynamics whereby a given child might be understood were relatively neglected during this period.

It was from other fields that new influences came which helped to shape child psychology as it is today. Psychoanalysis was the most potent of these influences. Its influence was greatest upon the area of motivation, helping us to understand the dynamics of behavior— why a child did what he did. But child guidance, clinical psychology, pediatrics, education and educational psychology, cultural anthropology, and other fields also contributed to the modern period in child psychology.

In the modern period in child psychology, development emerges as the common element in the interest of these workers from the various disciplines, including the child psychologists. Even more specifically interest centers upon personality development. In order to hold this interest in focus, the child is customarily seen as functioning in a particular environmental situation. Following from these developments are other effects—the development of multidiscipline research institutes, the interplay of science and practice, and attempts at integration through more comprehensive theories. They also characterize the modern period in child psychology.

For Further Reading

For this and subsequent chapters, suggestions will be made about further readings. Wayne Dennis has written a brief account of the beginnings of child psychology on which the writer has leaned heavily. His presentation, "Historical Beginnings of Child Psychology," is to be found in the *Psychological Bulletin,* 1949, 46, 224–235. The influence of other fields upon orthopsychiatry and thus upon many aspects of child psychology is sketched by various authorities under the editorship of Lawson Lowrey in the book, *Orthopsychiatry 1923–1948:*

Retrospect and Prospect (New York: American Orthopsychiatric Association, 1948). This writer prepared "A Brief History of Clinical Psychology," appearing in the *Psychological Bulletin*, 1953, 50, 322–346. Some conception of the general status of child psychology, year by year, may be gained from the chapter devoted to the subject in the *Annual Review of Psychology* (Stanford, Calif.: Annual Reviews).

References

1. Binet, A., and Simon, T.   Methodes nouvelles pour le diagnostic du niveau intellectual des anormaux. *Annee psychol.,* 1905, 11, 191–244.
2. Binet, A., and Simon, T.   Upon the necessity of establishing a scientific diagnosis of inferior status of intelligence.   In W. Dennis (Ed.), *Readings in the history of psychology.*   New York: Appleton-Century-Crofts, 1948, 407–411.
3. Bradbury, D. E.   The contribution of the child study movement to child psychology. *Psychol. Bull.,* 1937, 34, 21–38.
4. Brotemarkle, R. A.   Clinical psychology 1896–1946. *J. consult. Psychol.,* 1947, 11, 1–4.
5. Darwin, C.   A biographical sketch of an infant. *Mind,* 1877, 2, 285–294.
6. Dennis, W.   Historical beginnings of child psychology. *Psychol. Bull.,* 1949, 46, 224–235.
7. Freud, Anna.   *The psychoanalytical treatment of children.*   London: Imago, 1946.
8. Goodenough, Florence L.   *Mental testing, its history, principles and applications.*   New York: Rinehart, 1949.
9. Hall, G. S.   The contents of children's minds on entering school. *Ped. Sem.,* 1891, 1, 139–173.
10. Hebb, D. O.   The role of neurological ideas in personality. *J. Pers.,* 1951, 20, 39–55.
11. Hull, C.   *Principles of behavior.*   New York: Appleton-Century-Crofts, 1943.
12. Jones, H. E.   Studies in child development. *Inst. Child Welf. Univ. Calif. Res. Bull.,* No. 16 Undated.
13. Klein, Melanie.   *Contributions to psychoanalysis, 1921–1945.*   London: Hogarth Press, 1948.
14. Kluckhohn, C.   The influence of psychiatry on anthropology in America during the past one hundred years.   In J. K. Hall (Ed.), *One hundred years of American psychiatry.*   New York: Columbia University Press, 1944, 589–617.
15. Krugman, M.   Orthopsychiatry and education.   In L. G. Lowrey (Ed.), *Orthopsychiatry 1923–1948: retrospect and prospect.*   New York: American Orthopsychiatric Association, 1948, 248–262.
16. Mead, Margaret.   *Coming of age in Samoa.*   New York: Morrow, 1928.
17. Mead, Margaret.   *Growing up in New Guinea.*   New York: Morrow, 1930.
18. Mead, Margaret.   Investigation of thought of primitive children with special reference to animism. *J. Roy. Anthrop. Inst.,* 1932, 62, 173–190.
19. Mead, Margaret.   Research on primitime children.   In L. Carmichael (Ed.), *Manual of child psychology* (2nd ed.).   New York: Wiley, 1954, 735–780.

20. Preyer, W. *Die Seele des Kindes*. Leipzig: T. Grieben, 1882.
21. Sears, R. R. Child psychology. In W. Dennis (Ed.), *Current trends in psychology*. Pittsburgh: University of Pittsburgh Press, 1947, 50–74.
22. Senn, M. J. E. Pediatrics in orthopsychiatry. In L. G. Lowrey (Ed.), *Orthopsychiatry 1923–1948: retrospect and prospect*. New York: American Orthopsychiatric Association, 1948, 300–309.
23. Tylor, E. B. *Primitive culture*. London: J. Murray, 1871.
24. United States Children's Bureau. Research relating to children. *U. S. Dept. Health, Educ. and Welf. Bull.*, 1953, No. 2.
25. Watson, J. B., and Raynor, Rosalie. Conditioned emotional reactions. *J. exp. Psychol.*, 1920, 3, 1–14.
26. Watson, R. I. (Ed.), *Readings in the clinical method in psychology*. New York: Harper, 1949.
27. Watson, R. I. A brief history of clinical psychology. *Psychol. Bull.*, 1953, 50, 321–346.
28. Yarrow, Marion R., and Yarrow, L. J. Child psychology. *Annu. Rev. Psychol.*, 1955, 6, 1–28.

The Scientific Study
of the Child

THE AIM OF PSYCHOLOGICAL SCIENCE IS THE SAME AS
that of any other science—the development of predictive accuracy in
antecedent-consequent relationships. In child psychology the aim
is to develop predictive accuracy about child behavior and experience—that is, to establish the lawful relationships among the phenomena which can be observed. To chronicle the facts of child development is not enough; laws or principles must be discovered which
will explain and give order to the facts.

It is obvious that this goal cannot be achieved by a mere accumulation of information. A thousand isolated facts about childhood
contribute little to our understanding of child behavior. Only the
placing of facts in larger perspective enables us to perceive the law-
fulness of behavior and thus to understand it. By interrelating established facts, *principles* or *laws* of behavior are derived, and it is
these laws or principles which identify a mature (or maturing) science. Our scientific task is to account for the multitude of particulars
that make up the behavior and experience of the child with as few
general laws as possible.

The chief test of the validity of a scientific law is whether it enables one to predict future events with reasonable accuracy. Such
prediction makes possible the elimination of those influences which

38

interfere with development—that is, which make for unhealthy and unhappy children—and to arrange for conditions which facilitate optimum growth. Lest it appear that "optimum growth" is regarded as some mystical, omnipresent factor which is the same for all children and all cultures, a reminder is in order here that it is difficult, if not impossible, to divorce science from the world of values. That is, behavior which is considered "healthy" by one group at a given time in history (for example, an authoritarian attitude among the children of Nazi Germany) might be regarded as grossly abnormal by another group or by the same group at a different time. Yet "control of behavior" implies that it might be possible in one or two short generations to manipulate conditions so that virtually everybody in a given social group behaved or thought in a certain way and that this pattern of behavior or thinking in turn precluded the development of different patterns. Conceivably, such arbitrary manipulation of conditions (environmental and perhaps genetic) might eventually make such scientific puppetry possible. A system, however, of checks and balances operates in this as in most aspects of social life, so that it is not likely in a diversified, democratic society.

The above description may seem to imply that scientific prediction (and thus control) is an all-or-none affair. This, however, is not the case; predictions are not statements of certainty but of probability. The degree of accuracy of prediction will depend upon, first, how many relevant variables (that is, conditions which can vary and thus influence results) affecting the behavior in question are known, and second, how much control can be exerted over the relevant variables.

Occasionally, a formulation of a scientific law will be made before all the relevant variables are known and prediction made only in terms of those which are recognized. The unidentified variables will always contribute a certain amount of error to the predictions made. For example, Boyle's calculations on the predicted relationship between pressure and volume of gases held only for experiments performed at a constant temperature. One source of predictive error remained until Charles, some hundred years later, worked out the precise relations of temperature to pressure and volume. With the recognition of this newly discovered variable, prediction became significantly more precise.

To choose an illustration from the field of child psychology, we might cite work in mental testing. Although never formulated as a law in the sense of Boyle's law, a principle which several workers in psychology have proposed is that the relationship between mental age and chronological age of a child is a constant. However, prediction for an individual child in terms of this presumably constant relationship (the intelligence quotient or IQ) can often be in error ten or more units. This error in prediction might be due to some weakness in the measuring instrument itself (just as predictions about the behavior of gases erred in part because of inadequate techniques for measuring pressure), but it might also indicate that other variables remained uncontrolled and lowered accuracy of prediction. Such variables have indeed been discovered and include such things as socio-economic status, health of the child at the time of examination, the amount of stress evoked by examination procedures, and so on.

Accuracy of prediction does not have to be perfect for predictions to be of value; actually, predictions may be valuable if they are barely better than chance. The closer predictions approach (but never reach) certainty, the more valuable they are. To defend this position concerning probability as differentiated from certainty, it is necessary only to remind the reader that in testing a certain hypothesis, not *all* humans can be studied. Generalizations are, of necessity, made on the basis of partial evidence even if there are no other limitations. All that can be done is to make inferences having a certain degree of probability. All branches of science share in this limitation. It may be that more established sciences, such as astronomy, have attained a higher degree of probability in their laws. Nevertheless, although it is highly probable that the sun will rise tomorrow, it is not absolutely certain!

Scientific advance may be interpreted, with some justice, as an increase in the ability to predict correctly. If there is a respectable degree of accuracy of prediction, the ability to control behavior comes into being. Thus, to take an oversimplified example, assume that it is known that environmental conditions A, B, and C produce in children effect Z. This knowledge makes it possible to take the further step of arranging for a given child to be exposed to an environment conducive to development of these conditions, which in turn leads to the desired effect. This would occur, of course, only if there were not too many unknown variables, such as D, E, and F, also related to effect Z.

There is also what might be called negative prediction and control. As a matter of fact, at the present limited level of knowledge, many of the more valuable contributions of child psychology arise from such negative or avoidance control. In such instances, we are not concerned with arranging a given effect to come about, but in preventing certain adverse effects from appearing. Thus, if L, M, and N produce effect Y, where Y represents a warped or some socially undesirable personality trait, conditions L, M, and N can be changed or eliminated so that this effect will *not* take place. Many selection procedures, such as those used in determining suitability of a child for entrance into public school or for readiness to read, are illustrative. Thus, if we know a child is not ready to read because certain predictive devices point to this lack of readiness, the frustrating experience of failure in this activity may be avoided by delaying reading.

In arriving at these laws, instead of dealing with the behavioral items or facts as they stand, sometimes constructs are used. Constructs, in the sense used here, are inferred attributes of the child's behavior. They are not immediate observables, but rather are ways of furthering understanding of certain observables. Behavior tendencies, such as aggression or dependence, are of this nature. No one has ever seen "aggressive tendencies." However real they may be to the experiencing person, they are abstractions, the existence of which the observer infers from behavior. The child behaves in such and such a fashion; the observer infers aggression and relates it to other experiences that may be subsumed under the same construct.

With this introduction we are now in a position to further refine the meaning of science. Although "science" has become a common household term, it is not an easy word to define. In a recent attempt to formulate a definition, Conant has written: "As a first approximation, we may say that science emerges from the other progressive activities of man to the extent that new concepts arise from experiments and observations, and the new concepts in turn lead to further experiment and observations" (6, 37).[1] It will be noted that this definition highlights the methods—experiment and observation—by means of which new concepts emerge. Of course, the terms "experiment" and "observation" connote various things to different people, for, to be sure, not all activities described as experiments warrant being termed "scientific." Also much observation is subjective and biased and not worthy of being designated as scientific activity. Only observations made and experiments conducted under carefully controlled conditions will permit reliable conclusions to be drawn from the data. Naive acceptance of presumed "facts" without concern for how the facts were obtained is inimical to science.

[1] From Conant (6). Copyright 1947 by the Yale University Press, and published with permission.

In recognizing the necessity for having some understanding of the process whereby worthwhile scientific investigations are conducted, the next section of this chapter is devoted to a review of methods of studying the child in ways that fulfill the criteria of the above definition of scientific activity.

The methods of study

Many different classifications of the scientific method may be found in the literature, but all of these can be recognized as offering to the investigator the opportunity to select one of two major procedures. Briefly, he may intervene with nature, and thus perform an experiment, or he may observe differences in nature as they are found, and thus use the differential method. Each of these will be considered in turn.

The Experimental Method

An experiment is a particular way of making observations. It differs from the differential method in that it affords the experimenter a greater degree of control over the variables involved in the situation. Those variables over which he has control are called *independent* variables. These he manipulates or changes as he sees fit, within the limits of his problem as he has defined it. As he varies the independent variable (or variables), he observes the changes occurring in some other variable (or variables) to see whether they are related to the changes introduced. These other variables in which the effects of the changes are observed are called *dependent* variables (that is, they are dependent upon certain other conditions). The investigator is seeking information on the concomitant variation between the independent and dependent variable. It is clear that this discussion of "identification" and "control" introduces the factor of prearrangement, and hence a laboratory situation is usually (but not always) the setting in which an experiment is performed. In summary, the task of the experimenter is to study the relationship or concomitant variation between independent and dependent variables.

As Woodworth (*13*) indicates, an experimenter makes an event happen at a certain time and place and thus is alerted to make accurate observations by knowing when and where to make them.

Also, he can systematically vary the independent variable through predetermined stages while noting the concomitant variations in the dependent variable. The factor of control, in the sense that the independent variable is varied in a specific and known manner, also makes possible the repetition of the experiment either by the original or by another investigator.

Not too many years ago it was considered essential that the experimenter hold constant all variables that might be independent variables (that is, "affect" the results) except one. Certain factors that might have affected the dependent variable are not allowed to vary during the course of the experiment, that is, are held constant. Here another meaning of control is introduced (4). If they had not been controlled *in the sense that they were kept constant,* they might have affected the measures under consideration, thus obscuring the effect of the independent variable under study. Of course, in another study they might themselves have been systematically studied or even, with a different experimental design, been included in the study under consideration. One independent variable studied at a time was at one time considered an essential rule. Now that certain advances in statistics, particularly analysis of variance, have been made, it is possible to handle several independent variables in a particular study at the same time. It is, moreover, also possible to observe more than one dependent variable in the same experiment.

When "control" of factors as a restraint of other variables is spoken of, it is important to emphasize that the control is not complete. Indeed, if complete control were possible, only one observation for each degree of change in the independent variable would be necessary. Since we do not always have exact control of variation of the independent variable, various degrees of stimulation are possible. We may vary the intensity, pitch, and timbre of an auditory stimulus through predetermined steps exactly controlled by the experimenter. This is likewise true in other sensory fields and for some other areas of child study. However, for many important problems, we simply do not know enough about the independent variable to vary it through finely graded steps. Thus, we study whether the presence or absence of a certain factor has any effect at all and leave for later research the study of gradation of effect.

There are certain different experimental procedures which might be identified briefly. Thus, one common research design calls for using the same subjects once under normal conditions and then again with one condition (the independent variable) changed. In this, the *method of difference,* a subject is his own control since he is studied under both conditions.

If practice effects are involved, as in studies of children's learning, it is not possible to use the same children under both conditions. If doing the task itself makes the child different because he has now learned something new or how to do something better because he went through the first session, he is no longer the same person as he was at the beginning of the session. In order to circumvent this blurring of results, the *control group* technique is used. In its simplest form, two groups are used. Children of the total sample are assigned to the two groups in such a manner as to make them as alike as possible. For example, suppose that in a study of reading ability one wishes to control (equalize) for the effect on the results of individual differences in intelligence. With scores on an intelligence test available, the top child may be placed in the experimental group, the next highest in the control group, the third highest in the experimental group, and so on, alternating between the groups. Thus, both the average intellectual level and the variability of the two groups are equalized.

The problem of placement becomes more complicated when other matching variables, such as sex, age, socio-economic status, and so on, must also be considered, but basically the way of equating is the same. In general, the intent is to make the experimental and control groups as similar as possible in the independent variables *not* under consideration; it may nonetheless cause concomitant variation in the dependent variable being studied. The choice of matching the groups on certain variables depends upon whether it is known or suspected that there is a concomitant variation with the dependent variable. For instance, as Anderson (2) observes, in studying motor skills with all except very young children, it is not necessary to control intelligence or socio-economic factors, because concomitant variation with motor ability is known to be very low. On the other hand, in studying language, which is positively related to (concomitantly varies with) these factors, both must be controlled.

Now that this necessity of equation of the groups has been indicated, it is possible to elaborate on the nature of the control group study. Two equated groups of subjects are used, differing only in that one group, the experimental, has the independent variable introduced (or has a greater or lesser magnitude, and so forth), while the second or control group does not. In the simplest form of this technique, both groups receive a prior test to establish equality; following this one undergoes the experimental procedure, while the other does not. Both then take a final test. The difference in this final test-results between the experimental group and the control group is considered the result of the experience undergone by the experimental group which the control group did not receive and is the measure of the effect of the experimental (that is, independent) variable.

An experiment is "manmade" in the sense that the investigator arranges the conditions. Thus, rigid control of conditions is possible. Since another person can do likewise, replication of the conditions under which a given experiment was performed is possible. Since science depends upon *verified* knowledge, and verification is relatively more exact with the experimental method, it is, in most instances, the method of choice. There are certain circumstances, however, in which arrangement of conditions by the experimenter is not feasible and he must seek a different method of verifying a hypothesis.

The Differential Method

In the experimental method, the distinguishing operation was the introduction or the manipulation by the investigator of some specific stimulating condition, the independent variable. But there are some problems in which this intervention on the part of the investigator is impossible or impractical. Indeed, there are sciences in which experiment is impossible, so far as major problems are concerned. This is the case with astronomy and geology. The space and time dimensions of these sciences do not permit manipulation. An astronomer cannot vary the orbit of a star to see its effect; nor can the geologist introduce an ice age to observe the resultant changes. These sciences, as well as certain problem areas in other sciences, depend in the main upon the differential method. This consists of the scientist studying differences found in certain conditions without purposive manipulation (other than selection of phenomena to be studied). A star already varying in its orbit is studied; evidence of the effect of ice ages is examined in relation to other events occurring at the same time.

Many psychological problems likewise do not permit experimental manipulation. Sometimes to do so would be too costly in time, money, or effort. Sometimes an attempt to study a problem experimentally would mean ethical or moral violation of the personal rights of others. An illustration would be the attempt to make the independent variable of an experiment the development of an experimental psychosis in a child; so, too, would be the placement of heretofore emotionally stable children in a family environment designed to produce emotional trauma. Moreover, respect for living things prevents workers in all sciences from inflicting unnecessary pain in the course of their experiments. Child psychologists are further limited in their use of the experimental method because of their desire to avoid interfering in any way with the best development of the child's personality. This precaution is followed even when harmful effects are but remotely suspected. For instance, a question, which is of considerable relevance for the field of child development and regarding which contradictory data have appeared in the literature, is whether insufficient oxygen (anoxia) at birth causes lasting damage to the child. The surest, most efficient technique of answering this question would be to subject large numbers of new-born infants to varying degrees of anoxia and to follow their subsequent development. However, so long as there is even the faintest suspicion that such a procedure might cause lasting damage to the children, such a method is not likely to be employed. Instead, the differential method, capitalizing upon cases of anoxia that occur despite the best obstetrical care, must be relied upon to answer the question.

For some problems, life as it is lived, and thus the differential method, offers greater promise than does an experiment. Studies of normal development, for example, are central to child psychology. Since we are interested in the *normal* changes concomitant with age, we do not attempt to alter the course of development precisely because it is the normal child we are trying to study. Sometimes the differential method is employed by necessity, but for certain problems it is the method of choice.

In using the differential method, the investigator finds a situation rather than arranges for it. The children are behaving in ways that are natural to them. The children are already "intelligent," "mentally retarded," or "disturbed" when the differential method is applied. Instead of setting up a situation and inducing the subjects to do something, they are already being, or doing, or experiencing what is to be investigated.

In psychology, the differential method employs individual differences among persons as the independent variable. Subjects are chosen according to a criterion, and the measurements themselves form the variable. Thus, the researcher does not manipulate the independent variable and, consequently, he has less control of it. However, concomitant variation, the use of control groups, and other characteristics of the experimental method are still possible.

Many studies using a correlation technique fall in the class of differential methods. Indeed, somewhat loosely, the term "correlational studies" (or "statistical studies") is used to describe what are called here instances of the differential method. Studies of intelligence, aptitude, and personality mostly take people as they are and are studied against some predetermined criterion.

Let us consider for a moment the use of the control group in research by the differential method. Suppose the problem is the relation of aggression in children to parental attitudes. By a means irrelevant to the issue at hand, 50 aggressive children are isolated. (Note they are already "aggressive," not made so by the research worker.) Let us further suppose that in 42 of the homes from which these aggressive children come, parental rejection of these children takes place. It would be tempting to conclude that parental rejection brings about aggressiveness. Actually, the study is inconclusive without a control group. We must isolate a control group of nonaggressive children to find out what proportion of parental rejection is present in this group as well. Then, and only then, can we speak with any degree of assurance about the meaning of the results.

The differential method is the basis for both the longitudinal and cross-sectional approaches to development.

The longitudinal and cross-sectional approaches. In investigating many problems in child psychology, interest focuses upon the course of development. It is enough to say at this point that for both practical and theoretical purposes knowing the rate and manner of change of psychological processes is central to an understanding of child behavior. Since knowledge is wanted about the normal course of development, the attempts to alter its course, which an experiment would do, make the differential method the more appropriate. There are two ways in which development may be studied differentially— the longitudinal and cross-sectional approaches.

In the longitudinal approach, the *same* children are studied at *different* ages. The same children may be studied when they are seven, when they are eight, and again when they are nine years old. In the cross-sectional approach, *different* children are studied at *different* ages. Thus, seven-, eight-, and nine-year-old children may be studied all at the same time. This latter approach is obviously both more economical of time and easier to arrange for, since a given child may be seen only once, with no necessity to wait to retest while time passes. Moreover, drawing new samples for various age levels introduces a check on the data found at other levels. Thus, if there is some bias in a given age sample, it might be more readily detected by the cross-sectional approach than if one sample were studied at several ages.

Despite this possible weakness, the longitudinal approach is generally to be preferred in developmental research. Cross sections give only approximations instead of the more accurate representations of the developmental process which the longitudinal approach affords. A study by the cross-sectional approach of 13-year-old girls would place together many girls past puberty with others who would not reach that developmental stage for some time. The longitudinal approach allows the study of individual as well as group development and an appraisal of the interrelations among developmental processes.

Use of the longitudinal approach, however, does require more care in selecting the sample and introduces the additional problem of keeping track of the original group for later study. Since only one sample is used, an "all eggs in one basket" approach, as it were, is unavoidable. Moreover, the corrective influence of other samples inherent in the cross-sectional approach is not present. Likewise, one may by choice bias the sample, for the sake of keeping track of the subjects for later study, by selecting a group which for some reason is judged to be geographically more stable and thus easier to locate at a later date. Thus, a community with known low mobility for its members may be used. But this introduces in itself a bias which will influence the findings. Moreover, individuals may be lost through death, or illness may make cooperation impossible, or individuals may show a changed attitude about cooperating. These very situations which make cases unavailable may actually have a bearing upon development which, of course, cannot be reflected in the results at the later ages. In fact, these difficulties have caused some investigators (for example 3), to advocate discarding data on incomplete cases. This, however, reduces the size of the sample, and in order to be so cavalier about discarding data, one has to start with a group considerably larger than that reported in the final results. Another complication of longitudinal research is that, during the course of the study, improvements in technique are made, but in order to make comparisons from one age level to another, continuity of measurement is desirable.

The longitudinal method is the only way of accurately measuring *individual* growth curves. At first glance it might appear that we could use a series of averages obtained from cross-sectional samples for this purpose. Actual comparison between norms developed in this way with individual curves shows that individual variability is blotted out, thus giving a distorted picture. For example, in a study of physical growth patterns, late maturing girls and early maturing girls showed different growth curves which were not apparent when age cross-sectional samples were used (11).

Variations of the longitudinal approach, each with its specific values and weaknesses, include the baby biography previously examined in historical perspective and certain aspects of the case history to be discussed later. Both baby biography and case study have in common certain limitations—a paucity of cases, a probably nonrepresentative selection, and the possibility of bias on the part of the observer. Furthermore, lack of control of other variables operating, although not necessarily inherent in either technique, operates to reduce their scientific usefulness.

The most systematic and thoroughgoing use of the longitudinal approach requires extensive facilities and continuity of personnel. Hence, it is not surprising that the child welfare stations, described earlier in connection with modern trends in the history of child psychology, take the lead in such studies. Investigators working in isolation from their colleagues seldom have the time, money, or patience to use this approach profitably. Cross-sectional studies do have value and are open to them. Not only do both the longitudinal and cross-sectional approaches give us information on the developmental process of childhood, but they also supply material to be used as norms with which the performance of other children can later be compared. A scale thus becomes available for the evaluation of other children. Height and weight charts, intelligence tests, motor development scales, reading tests, and vocabulary tests are simple illustrations. The child's present performance may be compared with children at his own, higher, and lower levels, thus accurately placing him—provided the groups on which the norms were based are representative of the population from which they have been drawn.

The techniques of study

Basic to all scientific research, psychological or otherwise, is observation—the noting of events as they occur. Both the experimental and differential method rely ultimately upon observation. Something is done to the child by the experimenter (experimental method) or by nature (differential method), and observations of the results are made. But our senses are faulty and limited, and our wishes as to the outcome can possibly distort our observations. We cannot see everything that is going on. A magician, for example, capitalizes on our limitations in this respect. Moreover, we are set to see certain things, so we see to a certain extent what we expect to see. Thus, one purpose of research techniques and devices is to increase the accuracy of our observations. A handmaiden of accurate observation is immediate and accurate recording. If what is observed is not recorded properly, then a source of error just as serious as inaccurate observation has been introduced. The necessity of immediate recording comes about from the well-known phenomenon of faulty and distorted memory to which all of us are subject.

Observation is an experience of the observer. In a sense, then, all observation remains subjective because it depends upon the organism of the observer. We attempt to make it as objective as possible by arranging conditions of observation so that the human element can be minimized (although never eliminated). Devices and procedures increasing objectivity are attempts to reach the goal of minimal dependence upon subjective impression. It follows that all such devices have varying degrees of objectivity-subjectivity. It is impossible, therefore, to speak as though differences among techniques are qualitative; rather they represent quantitative differences along the objectivity-subjectivity continuum.

In many research situations, but especially in clinical settings, the investigator is not merely passively recording observations but actively interacts with his subject. Thus, he becomes, in Sullivan's apt phrase, a "participant observer." This may lend subtlety to the situation, but it also makes it more complex. In effect, the investigator, because he is part of the research situation, becomes a variable in the research which may affect the results. Thus, it is necessary to study the investigator to see to it that his very participation does not cause him to make errors in his evaluation of the situation. Feelings of like or dislike may color his evaluations. Sometimes we must have observers watching the observers!

Many of the techniques discussed in this and later chapters—chronoscopes, tests, motion pictures, and so on—are means of making observations more correct and their recording less subject to error. Just as lenses are ground to enhance vision, the devices and procedures employed in psychological research are means of making more exact and more acute the observational processes of the investigator. And just as a voice recorder is used to capture historic events, the techniques to be discussed include those which help to make sure that what is observed is recorded accurately.

Once the method of study has been chosen, a problem facing the research investigator is the selection of the appropriate technique. That is to say, he must now decide within the limits set by his method of study what he is going to use to study the child. Will he observe through a one-way screen the child as he plays and rate his behavior on certain preselected characteristics? Will he record the child's response to intelligence test items and then score the test? Or will he have him learn to thread a maze and record time and errors? These and many other techniques may be used depending, of course, upon the problem to be solved. In fact, in many studies, several techniques are likely to be used.

The investigator's choice of study techniques will be dictated by certain considerations. Most important of all, he attempts to use a technique that is directly related to his problem. There must be as high a degree of congruence as he can arrange between his hypothesis and how he goes about studying it. If his hypothesis calls for an investigation of the differences between girls and boys in reading ability, he uses a test of reading, not a test of intelligence, to establish these differences. But the crucial point is more subtle. He wants to use a test of reading that, on the basis of earlier studies or his own experience with the test, he is confident actually measures reading. Hence, he wants a *valid* test, or one which measures what it is supposed to measure. Although validity is customarily treated as a topic to be discussed when tests are concerned, it enters into consideration in the selection of all techniques. It is merely that in a test its validity is not as self-evident or overt as it is with many other techniques. In learning studies, for example, one arranges for the child to be faced with a new problem, and if after practice trials the child commits fewer errors and takes less time, one can then say that learning has taken place; or he asks a child to tell which of two lights is the brighter, and he can then say that he has studied visual brightness discrimination. But in both these instances there must be some direct, unequivocal connection between that which he says he is studying and that which he actually is studying. The investigator describes the operations by which his results are obtained. Similarly, marks on a weight scale may be used directly to measure weight. But if weight is used indirectly as a measure of nutrition, then it is up to the investigator to demonstrate that there is a necessary connection. The relation between the indicator and that which it indicates must be determined. If it measures what it purports to measure, it is valid. If it is a valid measure of what he wants to investigate, the instrument is suitable for his purposes.

Emphasis so far has been on the selection of techniques by the investigator, but some mention should be made of the kinds of techniques open to his use. In this book we follow Rosenzweig (10) in dividing techniques into objective, subjective, and projective. A characterization of each of these classes is appropriate. It is probable that previous acquaintance is greatest with objective techniques, somewhat less with subjective techniques, and least of all with projective techniques. Hence, only a short account will be given of objective techniques, a somewhat longer statement about subjective techniques, and a much more detailed statement about projective techniques.

Objective Techniques

Objective techniques depend upon the subject's behavior as noted by the observer-investigator. The child does something either spontaneously in a free situation, such as a playroom, or on request, as when he reads from a book, pushes a button when he sees a light, learns a problem, or lifts a weight. Characteristics of his physiological processes such as blood pressure may also be investigated. In objective techniques, then, the observer looks at the subject and reports on his observations.

Subjective Techniques

Subjective techniques make use of what the subject has to say about himself to an observer. They consist of an account of his experiences, points of view, traits, aims, needs, or interests. These statements are taken by the investigator for what they are—disclosures by the subject about himself. Thus, the subject looks at himself and reports to the observer.

Subjective techniques are based upon what the individual can reveal and what he chooses to reveal about himself. Some things he does not know and other things he does not choose to tell. In other words, in varying degree, subjective techniques are weakened by selection on the part of the person concerned. Often subjective techniques depend upon the subject's interpretation of the meaning of the material at hand without his being given much of a guide or source of reference as to how to interpret the material. The autobiography, for example, has the disadvantages associated with its adult use— selection, conscious and unconscious, of what the informant should tell—plus the additional disadvantage of language and other developmental limitations of the child. Subjective techniques nevertheless possess value. It is undoubtedly important to know what a person thinks about himself. An unfounded belief, even if masquerading as a fact, is still a valuable datum for psychology. In addition, there are certain problems for which subjective techniques are particularly appropriate. With children the questionnaire and the interview are the most widely used of subjective techniques.

Projective Techniques

Projective techniques are not concerned with consciously held opinions of the subject nor with his overt behavior but with imaginative responses which aim to uncover indirectly whatever personality variables are under investigation. The subject reveals something about himself to the observer by the way he organizes the material presented to him—the way he projects meaning into neutral or ambiguous material. According to Rosenzweig (10), this is tantamount to having both the subject and the observer "look the other way" at some neutral object that is capable of permitting the subject's personality dynamics to be "projected" out where they can be observed.

Projective procedures use techniques which permit the individual to reveal aspects of his personality by the organization of stimulus material into which he projects the meaning it has for him. Since idiomatic responses are sought, no external criterion of what is right or what is wrong is used. Since the testing situation is arranged in such a fashion that the child does not know what is expected of him, he reveals by his spontaneous way of handling the stimulus materials some of the ways he organizes his view of the world. In the source of structuring the relatively unstructured material, the child reveals his structuring principles which are, it is hypothesized, the principles of his personality.

It is evident that the projective approaches put a heavy burden upon the interpreter. The clinician or researcher, since he is dealing with relatively unstructured material, must be alert lest he read his own projections into the material. The observer must ever be aware that his own anticipations are not those to be found à la Tom Thumb

This subjective element in interpretation of projective material has justifiably been a source of criticism. Only through the awareness of this danger, the use of norms, the investigation of validity and reliability, and careful cross-checking can this criticism partially be met.

Projective instruments such as the Rorschach Ink Blots, play techniques, drawings, and the spontaneous telling of stories to pictures all have in common the fact that they all are relatively unstructured and yet provide a standardized stimulus situation. They are stimuli which readily allow the child to impose upon them his own meaning and organization, private and idiosyncratic though they may be. The stimuli are to some degree unclear or equivocal, allowing the child to interpret or structure them himself. The same principle applies to the instructions given to the child. For all of these techniques in essence the instructions reduce to, "Do with or interpret the material as you want to."

The Rorschach Ink Blot examination. Looked at without any background of expectation and knowledge, the Rorschach Ink Blots are really meaningless blobs of ink on paper on which somehow we can see something. How can anything meaningful and worth while come from such unlikely material? Their "meaninglessness" is the crux of the matter. If the same splotch of ink looks like convicts, lizards and tigers, clowns, or rockets hurtling through space to different individuals, the diversity of response to the same physical stimulus must indeed appear provocative. In view of the identity of the stimulus for all seeing the blot, the differences must stem from the way the individuals perceive it, which in turn must be related to differences in their experience.

This lack of structure and idiomatic reactions to blots are shown in Table 1 which contains some hypothetical reactions of two children to a short series of ink blots.

TABLE 1

REACTIONS TO A SERIES OF INK BLOTS

	Child 1	Child 2
Blot A	Pretty flowers	Meat, all bloody
Blot B	Butterfly	A hobgoblin mask
Blot C	Ladies	Icicles
Blot D	Picture puzzle	A gorilla

The two children are seeing the blots, but "seeing" them differently. One does not have to know the nature of blots to see that there is a difference between the two children. Neither does it require clinical skill to recognize that if one had to choose which child was emotionally disturbed, the modicum of evidence we have would point to it being the second child. Of course, we do not have in this illustration enough evidence to make any such decision. Even a battery of test results would not be enough since the entire case history needs to be collected.

Ten symmetrical ink blots are used in the Rorschach examination. Five of the blots are grayish black, two are black and red, and the remaining three are multicolored. A blot resembling those developed by Rorschach, but not drawn from his series, is given in Figure 1. In actual presentation, the blot is in shades of gray for the side figures and in red for the right and left upper blobs and for the central detail. The blots are presented to the subject in numbered order one at a time. The instructions vary, but essentially they amount to, "Tell me everything you see in the blots." In keeping with the projective hypothesis, nothing is said about the basis on which the investigator's interpretation is to be made. Questions of what to see, how many things should be seen, whether turning the cards is permitted, and so on, are met with a noncommittal, "It's up to you." As soon as the subject is finished telling what he sees in one blot, the next is given to him without comment.

It is customary, although not mandatory, to wait until he is finished with all blots before securing the information which will round out the picture. The examiner will want to know *where* on the particular blot his response occurred, *how* he saw what he did see, and *what* it was he saw. This period is known as the inquiry. It allows the psychologist to fill in the gaps created by the fact that there were no instructions given the child to give his response in terms of these three aspects of what, where, and how.

In scoring, the "where" has to do with the area of the blot used, whether it was the whole blot, a regularly used detail less than the whole, or an unusual, not commonly used area. "How" is a more complex question to phrase to the young child, but it is necessary for uncovering the determinants of the responses. Form (shape, outline, contour) is the basis on which interpretation is most frequently made, but color, movement, and shading determinants also appear. They may be combined with form, dominating it or secondary to it. However, pure responses sometimes occur in which color or texture is the only determinant used. For example, in a response like "blood," redness is the only determinant admitted. This might be the case

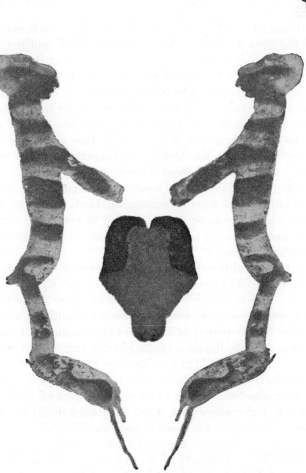

Figure 1. A blot in a series parallel to those used in the Rorschach Ink Blot Examination. (Copyright 1945 by M. R. Harrower, and published with permission.)

with the upper right or left blobs in the illustrative figure. "Clotted blood" as a response to the same area shows in the qualifying term that something else other than color is operative. Generally speaking, the first mentioned determinant, if more than one is given, is stronger and dominant. The last major aspect revealed through the Rorschach is "what" is seen or the "content." The ways of classifying content are legion, but there is general agreement that the majority of associations are human, human detail (part of person such as leg), animal, animal detail, and anatomy (differentiated from human detail by being similar to anatomical illustrations).

Some responses occur with such frequency that they have been classified as popular responses. Despite the fact that the blots do not represent any one thing, they do invite or predispose certain associations. For example, in the blot used for illustrative purposes on page 56, the popular response in order of frequency as established by Harrower and Steiner (7) are two animals (two side figures), face or head of a person (upper protuberance of long narrow figure), human beings (two side figures), a valentine heart (central detail), and tigers (two side figures).

The factors scored on the Rorschach are interpreted in a variety of ways but cannot be discussed here. The number of times each of these factors is used is determined. In addition, a variety of ratios and other mathematical indices comparing these factors is derived.

Until recently, the use of the Rorschach was hampered by lack of adequate norms for use with children. Fortunately, this in part has been remedied by Ames and her associates (1). Their findings also support the clinical impression that the Rorschach yields meaningful material for children even as young as two-and-one-half-years of age.

The various other facets which make the Rorschach both a delicate and hazardous instrument to use cannot be explored here. The severe limitation imposed in this present discussion is indicated when it is mentioned that many books have been written dealing with the Rorschach.

Thematic apperception technique. The Thematic Apperception Technique (TAT) is another widely used projective device. It consists of pictures somewhat similar to illustrations for magazine stories. Some pictures are suitable for children, some for adults, and some for both. The boy or girl is told that he is to be shown some pictures and that a story is to be made up for each one. In telling his story he is to imagine what led up to the event shown in the picture, to relate what is happening in the picture, and what the outcome will be. Any questions asked by him are answered noncommittally, with the nature of the situation and kind of story left entirely to the child.

The fundamental assumption concerning projection with the TAT is that the child identifies himself with a central figure in the story. The way the figure is described, the problem faced, and how it is handled are considered to be reflections of the child's own feelings and attitudes.

But how are these stories interpreted? There are various methods of anlaysis and norms toward which to turn (12). All methods of interpretation have in common the process of careful reading and inspection and assimilation of the stories by the interpreter. The first task is often considered to be the identification of the character in the story with whom the child has identified. Then an analysis is made of what happens to this central character. Is he seen as happy, defeated, rejected, or how? What are his needs? Victory at all costs, to be protected, to escape from the situation untouched by it, and the like? What are the environmental forces with which he must contend? Is it the family hampering him at every turn, is it an impersonal obstacle which blocks him in his efforts to reach his goal? What is the outcome? Is he successful in reaching his goal or does he suffer frustration and defeat? Special emphasis is placed upon recurrence of themes from one story to another—father-son conflict, feelings of guilt, hostility, etc. These recurrent trends are interpreted as revealing characteristic ways of responding to situations. Comparison with norms showing the recurrence of a given theme in comparable subjects is important, with more significance being attached to appearance of themes where normatively they are infrequent. This is in keeping with the assumption that if something is "pressing" at the child, he will use even unlikely materials on which to project this conflict. Telling gloomy stories about pictures generally interpreted in a more pleasant way would be a case in point. There are many nuances to the scoring and interpretation of TAT protocols which need not be discussed, but are presented in the extensive literature which has appeared, for example (12).

After this somewhat lengthy discussion of the techniques, it is appropriate to remind the reader that the discussion was placed in a setting where the ones that are available to the research investigator could be suitably chosen for his particular study. Once he has made his choice he then proceeds to apply the technique or techniques to his already selected subjects.

The clinical approach

The clinical approach [2] is an application of the scientific findings within a clearly recognized value system, namely, helping individuals. The clinical approach may be used for scientific research, but not all instances of its application have this aim. Rather, it is used most extensively to help individuals with their difficulties. It is in this sense that the approach will first be examined, leaving aside for the moment the scientific application which arises during the course of working with patients or clients.

In the previous chapter, a concrete illustration was given of the clinical approach in action in the setting of the child guidance clinic. The disciplines of psychiatry, clinical psychology, and social work have developed information that is useful in understanding and helping children. Some of the other settings in which a clinical approach is applied in work with children will be referred to in later chapters. It is enough to say at this point that they include special school agencies and classes, courts, hospitals, and homes for the delinquent, feeble-minded, and physically handicapped. Clinical workers include not only those from the major specialty groups already mentioned, but also a host of other workers, such as pediatricians, nurses, remedial teachers, speech and reading specialists, dentists, parole officers, social workers, and psychiatric aides.

The clinical approach refers to the evaluation of children in the course of their diagnosis and treatment. Originally confined to medical practice, the meaning of the clinical approach has been extended to include practice by nonmedical personnel. The essential spirit, however, is preserved. Whether it be a speech specialist, a clinical psychologist, or a school guidance expert, the task involved is to understand the difficulties of the patient or student in terms of the causes of his problem, how he reacted to them, and what can be done about them in order to correct the condition. A person comes to the clinician because he is troubled. As Klein says of the clinician, "How well he understands and ministers to his patient is the yardstick of his

---

[2] "Approach" is used to designate the matter under consideration to avoid using the word "method" in a second and confusing sense. The writer, as well as others, has in the past used the expression "clinical method" to refer to the questions discussed here. No fundamental change in position is implied by this change in terminology.

success" (8, 43). Those from whom the patient seeks help have in common an aim, the alleviation of his difficulties, and an approach, the clinical. This aim and this approach hold whether psychiatrists, pediatricians, clinical psychologists, or educational remedial specialists are called upon for this help. The clinician views the person as a *patient*, not as a *subject*. In this sentence is the essence of the clinical approach in differentiating it from use as a scientific method in studying children.

The clinician, in the course of diagnosis and treatment, uses knowledge obtained from the experimental and differential methods. In his approach he draws upon all that he knows based upon scientific research and applies it in connection with the needs of the specific patient. He also draws upon his personal-social heritage of insight into human nature and upon his personal clinical experience. Since the patient is a patient, he needs help *now*. The clinician cannot pause, as does the scientist, and depend only upon scientifically verified knowledge. Therefore, imperfectly validated diagnostic and therapeutic procedures may be used when there are no thoroughly established scientific guideposts to follow. The clinician does not necessarily hold that what he does could not benefit from scientific verification; it is merely that he cannot always wait before proceeding.

All clinicians share an interest or focus on the individual child. The nature of the professional activity calls for attention to the child as a person in his own right. Work is centered around individual sick children, and diagnostic decisions and plans for treatment are made on an individual basis. The clinician is also interested in the general. This interest in the general is as a guide to the particular. Hence, interest in diagnosis and classification, a reflection of this general interest, is a device to use other clinical experiences with the single case (8). There is no contradiction between placing primacy upon the unique, because in order to know the unique, one needs to know the common background—that is, that from which the individual case stands out as unique.

The clinician is interested in the individual child, whereas other specialists in child study are more concerned with development of generalizations about children as a group. This, however, is a matter of degree and some exceptions to these trends should be noted. The child psychologist studies individual differences, the educator, the causes and nature of school difficulties in individual deviant children. Conversely, medical men and clinical psychologists sometimes use larger groups of patients as research subjects. Nevertheless, such instances as these are exceptions to the general definition.

The clinical approach may be used for this service function and it may be used for research. In fact, in the clinical setting, research and practice are hard to distinguish, in that the noting of similarities and differences leads to both individual diagnostic and therapeutic skill and to the adroit formulation of fruitful hypotheses. In the course of ministering to his patients, the clinician may originate many promising ideas for research from what the patients reveal about themselves, from the professional contacts through colleagues as in seminar, and from his readings in the literature. Though vague and ill-formed at first, his idea will serve to sensitize him to other instances he finds in these same sources pointing in the same direction as his "hunch." The primary source is his contact with individual patients. A specific illustration is to be found in David Levy's account (9) of how his work in maternal overprotection came about. He reports that in listening to case reports being given at a staff meeting of the Institute of Child Guidance, someone discussed a woman having a child after ten years of sterility. The record also showed that she was very solicitous and indulgent toward this child. These two events were not in any way considered interrelated at this point. They were merely aspects of a voluminous case record. Levy raised the question to himself: Assuming she wanted the child, would not this ten years' wait cause her to be very solicitous toward him? The idea intrigued him and he began to search the case records of the clinic for cases showing maternal overprotectiveness and then to study the case records to see what other attitudes were shown by the same mother. His studies of maternal overprotection discussed in detail in Chapter 11 resulted from this experience. The similarity of this process of hypothesis forming and that sketched as taking place in scientific investigation in general can be readily noted.

The clinical approach, as well as other ways of studying the child, is used to obtain information about children. In the course of his daily work, the clinician develops hypotheses ("hunches") which may be tested against other patients seen subsequently. Thus, there is always a ragged advance guard of knowledge in that no man's land between pure speculation and scientific verification of knowledge. As a clinician, he finds that certain ways of viewing the patient strike him as true, and this apparent truth is accepted until verification of its truth or falsity can be brought about. Some clinicians, to be sure, hold that no verification by scientific procedures, in the sense we have described them, is necessary. They would argue that purely clinical procedures are all that are necessary. For example, the clinical procedure that Freud followed to formulate hypotheses was to draw upon his experience with patients, and then to test these hypotheses against later cases. If, in these later cases, consistency with the hypothesis was observed, he considered the hypothesis verified. As Boring puts it:

> Freud's technic lay somewhere between that of the experimental psychologist, who alters an independent variable and observes the result, and the philosopher-psychologist, who induces generalization about human nature from the reservoir of his experience. Freud made his generalization from a wealth of specialized experience and then tested his hypotheses out against particular cases, increasing his assurance about the validity of each induction as the number of consistent cases grew. He had, however, no control, either in the sense of the rigorous constraint of contributing factors or in the sense of adding the method of difference to the method of agreement. Indeed, he seems to have been restricted to Mill's method of agreement, pure and simple, a method which by itself is clearly unsafe (5, 436).[3]

Boring emphasizes the necessity of *controlled* research. In examining the studies of children to be reported later, appeal to controlled research will be made whenever it is available.

It is now possible to present a classification of the research studies considered in this book. It was demonstrated earlier that the scientific method embraced both experimental and differential methods. This was done in a setting primarily of the *laboratory approach* to child psychology. Now it is seen that there is also a second, the *clinical approach*. Studies using the experimental method and the differential method may be done either through a laboratory approach or through a clinical approach.

The clinical approach often does not offer as much opportunity for use of the experimental method as does the laboratory approach. Often, although not always, the differential method is used clinically. Frequently, clinical research is concerned with tracing back into the past for that which has made the child (or adult) patient what he is today, and thus depends upon the differential method. The effects of psychotherapy is a distinguished, although barely explored, area in which experimentation may be used.

Clinical research is by no means as fully developed as is laboratory

---

[3] From Boring (5). Copyright 1954 by The American Psychological Association, and published with permission.

research, because the clinician is usually confronted by a complex situation in which variables are more numerous and more uncontrollable than in a laboratory setting. He strenuously objects to attempts to simplify prematurely the task by experimental control of these variables. His objection may be stated in the form of an aphorism, "Research contamination is clinical enrichment." The clinician wants as much information about his patient as possible in reaching a decision. Since he is dealing with a patient in a complex, everyday setting, all sources are used. But allowing all these factors to vary without the control called for by scientific research, in effect, contaminates the situation so he cannot trace down the precise effect of each variable.

Greater rapprochement between traditional laboratory and clinical research has been made possible by the development of research methodology which permits concomitant variation in several variables being investigated simultaneously. The classic methods of experimental and differential research called for varying systematically a single factor and restraining all other factors which might affect the dependent variable. This way of studying children ran counter to the deeply held conviction of clinicians that the *interaction* among the various factors of the personality of his patient was important. As Klein puts it:

> In clinical practice it is a commonplace that similar symptoms may arise from quite different origins; or even that the same cause can give rise to very different symptoms. This observation is crucial for the clinician. Expressed conceptually, it tells us that the most basic attribute of an interacting set of variables is not the component variables themselves but the *interaction* (8, 43).[4]

Now that statistical techniques are available to permit simultaneous study of several variables used by both laboratory and clinical workers, this source of difference is disappearing. Thus, laboratory and clinical work share a common aim. Using different means to secure this information occasionally created a situation wherein those individuals or experimenters in one or the other tradition denied the value or even the respectability of the other. Arguments from the traditionalists center upon what they believe to be the lack of exactitude of the clinician, while those of the clinician seize upon what they consider to be the sterile rigor focused upon trivial problems of the

[4] From Klein (8). Copyright 1949 by The American Psychological Association, and published with permission.

more traditional researcher. It is neither profitable nor relevant to continue this line of discussion, except to state that the position taken in this book attempts to draw upon both methods for information. In so doing, the validity of both the charges of lack of exactitude of one and the incompleteness of knowledge of the other are tentatively accepted with this important reservation—that instead of rejecting one or the other, both are accepted with, it is hoped, some recognition of both the merits and deficiencies of each.

It is recognized that the psychology of the child is not a finished body of knowledge, but a very vital and rapidly changing field. All approaches have something cogent to say about the child. It is mandatory to use both the most accurate and the most meaningful contributions to a given problem. It does not follow, however, that accuracy and meaningfulness always reside to an equal degree in the same finding. Experimental-differential evidence found in the traditional fashion will be chosen when such is available and when it appears to be the appropriate method for a particular problem. There will be no hesitation, however, in using clinical findings when they are more meaningful and relevant than data obtained from laboratory investigations.

The frontiers of scientific knowledge of childhood behavior and experience are irregular. Sometimes our thinking about problems in this area can be based upon firm scientific foundations. But for other problems, our knowledge is as yet very incomplete and must be based, if we are to say anything at all, upon incompletely verified findings. Unfortunately, this is true concerning many important problems of the child personality. Dependence upon only that which has firm experimental foundation would result in a small but by no means compact structure. If a continuation of the analogy be permitted, many vital rooms and hallways (not to mention the plumbing) would be completely missing. Here, the structure we are building will be filled out by dependence upon clinical findings when they are appropriate and of value.

This intention to use clinical findings is reinforced by the conviction that many of the more vital problems of child behavior and experience have not as yet been investigated in the laboratory. What, for example, can we say about the infant's first experiences in this shining bauble of a world into which he has just been born? How does he "see" it? What are the effects of these first impressions? These and related problems are interesting and important, but there is a lack of information based upon experimental verification of hypotheses.

What little is known or speculated about them will be presented. It is important, however, to recognize that the charge of inexactitude of such findings has merit. The reader with an awareness of the importance of method can to some extent decide for himself, as the source of information will be identified.

Summary

Increasing the accuracy of predictions concerning child behavior is the aim of the scientific study of the child. Pursuing this aim, principles or laws are derived under which are subsumed a variety of facts. The crucial test of these laws is their predictive accuracy. However, these tests are not those of certainty of occurrence but of probability. Despite this uncertainty, they are still of value in advancing our knowledge of child behavior.

The methods of study used by the child psychologist are those he shares with other scientists—experiments in which he controls to some degree the independent variables; and observations in which he has no control over these independent variables, but, instead, depends upon their prior differential effect upon children. Both the experimental and the differential methods have their place and their particular advantages and disadvantages.

Specific techniques—instruments and procedures by which to secure the relevant data—are applied to the children. These techniques may be used with either the experimental or differential methods. They may be classified into three major categories: objective techniques involve the noting of the child's behavior by the psychologist; subjective techniques depend upon the child reporting his observations about himself to the psychologist; projective techniques depend upon the child giving his own meaning and organization to the material to which he is exposed, which is noted and then interpreted by the psychologist. Each of the three categories of techniques and the particular instruments included in these categories have their particular advantages according to the problem being investigated.

The clinical approach is used for helping disturbed individuals, including children. In the clinical approach diagnostic evaluation of the individual is carried out and a course of treatment followed. In addition to its service function, the clinical approach is also used in

connection with scientific research.   When used for research functions, the clinical approach most often involves applying the differential method, although the use of experimental method is not
impossible.   From clinical setting the psychologist often arrives at
fruitful hypotheses which he then proceeds to investigate in this
setting.   For a variety of reasons, but particularly because of lack
of appropriate controls for all relevant independent variables, sometimes (but not always), research done in clinical settings lacks precision and exactitude in contrast to research done in a laboratory
setting.   Choice among research efforts for presentation in the chapters to follow will depend not only upon their exactitude but also their
relevance to the problem at hand.   On this basis of this last criterion
there will be no hesitation in using clinical findings when clinical
research is judged important and relevant.

For Further Reading

Suggestions for further reading may be conveniently grouped as discussions of
methodology in general and statistics in particular.   Specific to methodology with
children, the long chapter by John E. Anderson in the *Manual of Child Psychology: Second Edition*, edited by Leonard Carmichael (New York: Wiley, 1954) is
unexcelled.   A more general account may be found in the book edited by T. G.
Andrews, *Methods of Psychology* (New York: Wiley, 1948).

Three excellent statistical texts are the books by Quinn W. McNemar, *Psychological Statistics: Second Edition* (New York: Wiley, 1955); Benton J. Underwood, Carl P. Duncan, Janet A. Taylor, John W. Cotton, *Elementary Statistics*
(New York: Appleton-Century-Crofts, 1954); and Palmer O. Johnson, *Statistical
Methods in Research* (New York: Prentice-Hall, 1949).   All three contain discussions of central tendency, variability, correlation, and tests of significance of differences, and Underwood *et al.*, in addition, are oriented about the use of statistics
in an experimental setting as such.

References

1. Ames, Louise B., Learned, Janet, Metraux, Ruth W., and Walker, R. N.
   Development trends in child Rorschach responses.   New York: Hoeber, 1952.
2. Anderson, J. E.   Methods of child psychology.   In L. Carmichael (Ed.),
   Manual of child psychology (2nd ed.).   New York: Wiley, 1954, 1–59.
3. Anderson, J. E., and Cohen, J. T.   The effect of including incomplete series
   in the statistical analysis of longitudinal measurements of children's dental
   arches.   *Child Develpm.*, 1939, 10, 145–149.
4. Boring, E. G.   The nature and history of experimental control.   *Amer. J.
   Psychol.*, 1954, 67, 573–589.

5. Boring, E. G. Review of Jones, E. The life and work of Sigmund Freud: Vol. 1. *Psychol. Bull.*, 1954, 51, 433–437.
6. Conant, J. B. *On understanding science.* New York: Mentor, 1951.
7. Harrower, Molly R., and Steiner, M. E. *Manual for psychodiagnostic inkblots (a series parallel to the Rorschach blots).* New York: Grune and Stratton, 1945.
8. Klein, G. S. A clinical perspective for personality research. *J. abnorm. soc. Psychol.*, 1949, 44, 42–49.
9. Levy, D. M. In J. Kasanin (Chm.), Research in orthopsychiatry. *Amer. J. Orthopsychiat.*, 1943, 13, 230–232.
10. Rosenzweig, S. Available methods for studying personality. *J. Psychol.*, 1949, 28, 345–368.
11. Shuttleworth, F. K. The physical and mental growth of girls and boys aged six to nineteen in relation to age at maximum growth. *Monogr. Soc. Res. Child Developm.*, 1939, 4, No. 3.
12. Watson, R. I. *The clinical method in psychology.* New York: Harper, 1951.
13. Woodworth, R. S. *Experimental psychology.* New York: Holt, 1938.

chapter 3

Development

THE TRANSFORMATION FROM A FERTILIZED EGG CELL to an adult organism closely resembling the parents is called the process of development. This process has two phases: embryonic or prenatal development and postnatal development from birth onward. Prenatal development will be considered first. A more general discussion follows in which development is examined for trends and manifestations. Since there is an essential continuity from prenatal to postnatal development, this section of the account draws upon both phases.

From cell to organism

The shuffling and chance recombinations which occur during germ cell maturation are completed, and a new zygote is formed. From the moment of conception its genetic history and, to a certain extent, its heritable future, are fixed. The genetic pool from which succeeding generations can draw is now organized. In the absence of extremes of environmental conditions (such as excessive dosages of X-rays) or of spontaneous modifications (mutations) which can alter the germ plasm, the genetic components available to future generations are fixed. Reproduction during maturity will provide the opportunity for interaction with new elements from a different genetic population, and the consequent assembling of a new genetic pool.

Although the genetic past and potential future of the new organism are now restricted and delimited, its present is far from stabilized. During the ten lunar months between conception and birth the genes are given an environment in which to produce their chemical reactions. This environment will be crucial for determining whether or not a given complex of genes will be permitted to express themselves in observable structure or function, or whether their influence will be suppressed or aborted. This generalization is true for any type of organism. For example, experiments have shown that vestigial wings which result from a hereditary mutation in Drosophila may fail to appear unless the larvae are kept at low temperatures. Animals with the same genetic history will, if incubated at higher temperatures, fail to develop the abnormal wing structure. This is no different from the practical situation faced by the farmer who knows that he will not get a good crop from the best of seeds unless optimal soil and weather conditions prevail.

The developing organism lives in a sequestered environment—the uterus of the mother—to which, except in cases of multiple birth, he has exclusive property right. During this period, the mother plays the truly unique role for which nature has so admirably equipped her. Although perhaps always of value, at no other time in life will she be completely indispensable to her child. In his *Brave New World,* Aldous Huxley fantasies a process by means of which children will develop in demijohns rather than uteri, will have a blood surrogate pumped mechanically through a synthetic lung, and, after having been exposed to a precisely regulated set of conditions, will eventually be decanted with a minimum of trauma. At our present state of knowledge, however, there appears to be no satisfactory surrogate for the mother during the vital phase of development from cell to organism.

Conditions for Development

In discussing external influences upon embryological development, Hamburger (10) has distinguished conditions for and modifiers of development. Certain essential agents found in the prenatal environment are conditions for development so long as they remain within the normal range. However, should they exceed this range, they become modifiers of development. An example is the amount of available oxygen. Should this deviate too drastically from an optimal level, then the course of development will be drastically modified by death or various kinds and degrees of fetal damage.

Sequence of prenatal development. Almost immediately following fertilization, the zygote begins the process of cell division which will transform it into a highly differentiated multicelled organism. This transformation occurs both by increase in the number of cells and by increase in size and weight of many individual cells. As direct observation of this process *in vitro* is impossible, precise charting of the embryological timetable, especially the first two weeks of intrauterine life, is difficult. During this period, the conceptus retains its egglike state and derives its nourishment from parts of the zygote which will not be used in the subsequent development of the organism. Appropriately, this period is generally called the ovular or germinal stage.

The period from about the second through the fifth weeks is called the embryonic stage. During this time, the important cellular layers are differentiated and the various body parts begin to appear. After the sixth week, the new organism is known as the fetus, and the period is designated as the fetal period.

In early divisions, the cells become differentiated into formative and auxiliary components of the ovum. One function of the auxiliaries is to form a covering for the cells from which the embryo proper will develop. Very soon fluid appears, giving the early ovum the appearance of a fluid-filled sphere. At this stage, it is known as a blastula. As this fluid collects, the formative cells are pushed into one side of the blastula and, with other cells of the region, form the embryonic disc, from which the embryo develops. In this clump of cells, a smaller cavity forms, later to be recognized as the amnion. The outer layer of cells, called the trophoblast, forms the means of attaching the embryo to the uterine wall and also prepares for the subsequent interchange of nutritive and waste products.

As the trophoblast cells produce a greater accumulation of fluid, the embryo becomes what is known as a blastocyst and is now ready for implantation. The inner mass of cells in this rapidly proliferating system quickly produces a new layer of cells, the endoderm, which will line the blastocyst and produce another closed space called the yolk sac. This is an extremely important structure in other species than man, as it is the chief source of nutritive materials during early developmental periods. In man, however, its value is transitory and by the end of the fourth week of gestation, it has largely disappeared.

Also arising from the endoderm is the allantois, a sausage-shaped tube which extends outward toward the periphery of the embryo. That part which remains in contact with the embryonic disc will ultimately comprise the bladder.

Soon a third layer of cells, the mesoderm, spreads out into the original blast-cyst cavity. These cells become thickened at one end and form the *body stalk*, which will fuse with the allantois to form the *umbilical cord*—the chief avenue over which maternal-fetal interchange will occur. The outer layer of the entire embryo is called the chorion. On the outside of the chorion, little spidery filaments, called villi (singular villus), appear and secure themselves in the endometrium or lining of the uterus. As soon as blood vessels appear, as they do from the allantois and body stalk, they find their way into the openings of the villi and thence into the uterine walls.

The nutritional demands of the rapidly growing embryo cannot for long be satisfied by materials contained within the ovum, and more permanent arrangements must be made. As soon as the zygote is implanted in the uterine wall, the *placenta* begins to develop. This new and temporary organ will handle the interchange of nutrients and waste products until such time as the new organism can sustain independent existence. The placenta is a truly amazing structure which shows great interspecies variability. Corner (4) has emphasized this fact with the reminder that placentas of such organisms as mouse, elephant, and man differ from one another more than do the brains or noses of these animals. In fact, a good case could be made for classifying mammals according to the type of their placentation.

Nature of the Mother-Child Relationship

An adequate discussion of the placenta requires clarification of the relationship between mother and child during the prenatal period. Essentially the relationship is that of host and parasite. The mother takes care of all the vital functions, including provision of nutrients and oxygen and the expulsion of carbon dioxide and other waste products. The nutrients provided the fetus are already carefully "screened"; that is, they are those that have already found their way into the mother's blood stream. Thus, the circulatory systems of the two organisms are of crucial importance for future development. Corner has provided an effective metaphorical description of the placenta-uterus association as follows:

If the reader has difficulty visualizing the relation of the placenta to the uterus, let him imagine a piece of ground (representing the uterine wall) beneath which is a network of terra cotta pipes (the blood vessels). Dig a hole in the ground, breaking off the pipes as you dig, and make it just large enough to receive the dense roots of a tree (the placenta). Pave the ground over the hole and all about it, the paving representing the chorio-amniotic surface of the placenta. . . . The trunk of your tree is the umbilical cord. The roots will be bathed in fluid from the cut ends of the underground pipes; in like manner the root system of the placental villi dips into a sort of pool filled with maternal blood from the opened ends of small arteries and drained by opened veins. This blood is the source of oxygen and nourishment for the infant and the means of disposal of carbon dioxide and organic wastes which filter back into it from the villi-roots of the embryo (4, 46).[1]

Should the placenta fail to develop properly, or should its function be seriously impaired at any time during the pregnancy, then damage to the fetus is virtually inevitable. The placenta is truly the lifeline of the new organism, and, no matter how excellent the seed which was fertilized and which formed the basis for the new life, normal development cannot occur without advantageous placental attachment.

Although the placental villi dip into "pools" or sinuses of maternal blood, there is no direct connection between the blood stream of mother and child. Indeed, during the early weeks of gestation, the infant does not have anything that could technically be called a blood stream. Rather he has cells that are developing into blood cells and the beginnings of a circulatory system capable of effecting transfer across the placental barrier. Very early in embryonic life the fetal heart begins to pulse and to force its own blood through its own closed vascular system. However, very quickly the outer layer of the embryo begins to form capillaries which terminate close to terminals on the maternal side. Actual exchange of chemical materials is accomplished by diffusion through these capillary walls. Thus, while there is no direct connection between the circulatory systems of the two organisms, there is certainly interaction between them.

We might want to inquire also about the other major circulating and communicating network—the nervous system. Again, there is no direct connection between mother and child in the sense that the nerve fibers of one organism comprise an open system and become affiliated with fibers from the other system. In order to help demolish certain persistent stereotypes about the influence of the mother on

---

[1] From Corner (4). Copyright 1944 by the Yale University Press, and published with permission.

the fetus, it has become customary in recent years to emphasize the lack of direct connection between the nervous system of the mother and that of the fetus. Montagu, however, insists that such assertions are based on an inadequate conception of the nervous system. He writes:

> A still widely prevalent belief has it that there is no connection between the nervous systems of mother and fetus. This notion is based on a very narrow conception of the nervous system. It is through the neurohumoral system, the system comprising the interrelated nervous and endocrine systems acting through the fluid medium of the blood (and its oxygen and carbon-dioxide contents), that nervous changes in the mother may affect the fetus. The common endocrine pool of the mother and fetus forms a neurohumoral bond between them. The endocrine systems of mother and fetus complement each other.
>
> All this is not to say that there is anything in the old wives' tale of "maternal impressions." The mother's "impressions," her "psychological states" as such, cannot possibly be transmitted to the fetus. What are transmitted are the gross chemical changes which occur in the mother and, so far as we know at the present time, nothing more (*18*, 152).[2]

Perhaps an accurate way of summarizing the relationship is that the two systems, although separate and distinct, nonetheless interact.

It is manifestly impossible to describe every significant event which occurs during the prenatal period and to expand on all the conditions for development which are crucial for later functioning. In Table 2 a brief summary of some of the more significant events in the prenatal calendar has been assembled. Study of this table will acquaint the reader with a rough sequence of prenatal growth and will give some idea of the patterning and interlocking of growth during this developmental phase.

TABLE 2

APPROXIMATE TIMETABLE OF PRENATAL DEVELOPMENT [*]

First Month

Fertilization, descent of ovum from tube to uterus. Early cell division and formation of embryonic disc from which new organism will develop. Early formation of three layers of cells—the *ectoderm*, from which sense organs and nervous system will develop; the *mesoderm*, from which circulatory, skeletal, and muscular systems will develop; and *endoderm*, from which digestive and some glandular systems will develop. The ovum becomes implanted in the walls of the uterus. Special layer of cells formed

[2] From Montagu (*18*). Copyright 1950 by the Josiah Macy, Jr. Foundation, and published with permission.

TABLE 2   (*Continued*)

in the uterus which will become the *placenta* and through which nutritive substances will be carried to the new organism and waste products carried away.   Special layer of cells forms the *amnion* or water-sac, which will surround the developing embryo except at umbilical cord.   Heart tube forms and begins to pulsate and force blood to circulate through blood vessels in embryonic disc.   Nervous system begins to arise, first in form of neural groove appearing at about 19 days.   Development of intestinal tract, lungs, liver, and kidneys begins.   By end of one month, the embryo is about one-fourth inch long, curled into a crescent, with small nubbins on sides of body indicating incipient arms and legs.   Eyes arise as two pouches thrust out from brain tube, and tissue which will produce inner ear forms.

Second Month

Embryo increases in size to about 1½ inches.   Bones and muscle begin to round out contours of body.   Face and neck develop and begin to give features a human appearance.   Mouth becomes reduced in size, and eyes move to front of face.   Forehead very prominent, reflecting precocious development of brain in comparison to rest of body.   Limb buds elongate.   Muscles and cartilage develop.   Sex organs begin to form, though still essentially identical in both sexes.

Third Month

Beginning of fetal period.   Sexual differentiation continues, with male sexual organs showing more rapid development and the female remaining more neutral.   Buds for all 20 temporary teeth laid down.   Vocal cords appear; digestive system shows activity.   Stomach cells begin to secrete fluid; liver pours bile into intestine.   Kidneys begin functioning, with urine gradually seeping into amniotic fluid.   Other waste products passed through placenta into mother's blood.   Bones and muscles continue development, and by end of third month spontaneous movements of arms, legs, shoulders, and fingers are possible.

Fourth Month

Lower parts of body show relatively accelerated rate, so that head size decreases from one-half to one-fourth of body size.   Back straightens; hands and feet are well-formed.   Whorl patterns appear on fingers and toes; skin appears dark red, due to coursing of blood showing through thin skin, and wrinkled, due to absence of underlying fat.   Finger closure is possible.   Reflexes become more active as muscular maturation continues.   Fetus begins to stir and to thrust out arms and legs in movements readily perceived by the mother.

TABLE 2 (*Continued*)

Fifth Month

Skin structures begin to attain final form. Sweat and sebaceous glands are formed and function. Their secretions, plus dead cells sloughed off from the skin, form a paste called the *vernix caseosa* covering the entire body. Skin derivatives also appear—hair, nails on fingers and toes. Bony axis becomes quite straight, and much spontaneous activity occurs. Fetus is lean and wrinkled, will be about one foot long and weigh about one pound. If aborted, it may respire briefly, but will soon die as it seems unable to maintain movements necessary for continued breathing.

Sixth Month

Eyelids, which have been fused shut since third month, reopen; eyes are completely formed. Eyelashes and brows begin to develop. Taste buds appear on tongue and in mouth and are, in fact, more abundant than in the infant or adult. If born, the six-month fetus will perhaps live a few hours or longer if protected in an incubator. During brief extrauterine life, may exhibit "Moro" or startle responses.

Seventh Month

Organism capable of independent life from this time one. Cerebral hemispheres cover almost the entire brain. Seven-month fetus can emit a variety of specialized responses. Generally is about 16 inches long and weighs about three pounds. If born, will be able to cry, breathe, and swallow, but is very sensitive to infections and will need highly sheltered environment for survival.

Eighth and Ninth Month

During this time, finishing touches are being put on the various organs and functional capacities. Conditioning can be demonstrated, indicating the readiness of the organism for certain kinds of learning. Fat is formed rapidly over the entire body, smoothing out the wrinkled skin and rounding out body contours. Dull red color of skin fades so that at birth pigmentation of skin is usually very slight in all races. Activity is usually great, and he can change his position within the somewhat crowded uterus. Periods of activity will alternate with periods of quiescence. Fetal organs step up their activity. Fetal heart rate becomes quite rapid. Digestive organs continue to expel more waste products, leading to the formation of a fetal stool (called the *meconium*) which is expelled shortly after birth. Violent uterine contractions begin (though milder ones have been tolerated earlier), and the fetus is eventually expelled from the womb into an independent physiological existence.

* This is adapted largely from *Biography of the Unborn* (8), by M. S. Gilbert. Material from other sources has been added where relevant.

The process of development

The theme of development was made central in introducing the history of the study of the child. We will now examine directly and specifically the concept of development. First, the process of development will be examined in general and then certain major trends in development will be identified. Subsequently, manifestations of development, with particular attention to the reciprocal influence of maturation and learning, will be considered.

Within every living organism, whether composed of one or myriads of cells, there occurs a constant process of change. When this change is orderly and harmonious and enhances the ability of the organism to adjust to its environment, it merits the label of development. When the pattern of change is of such a nature that loss of function and decreasing ability to cope with the environment are signified, the process becomes one either of chaotic growth, as in the production of certain tumors, or of decline, as in old age. Throughout the life span, from conception to death, there is a constant interplay of the forces of development and decline, with the former far more significant and more readily observable during the period with which this book is concerned.

This development is observable in every phase of life. Whether or not the field of observation is at the level of the cell, the organ, the organism, or the person, it is still safe to generalize that some development is always occurring. Development does not begin at birth. Much that is of significance has occurred during the interim between conception and birth. But, if one is to understand the process in its entirety, even the moment of conception would mark a tardy entrance on the observational stage. The birth of a baby and the changes which will manifest themselves in all its future behavior represent in one sense a condensation of the entire history of life up to the time of the observation. Reflected in every act will be the evolution of the entire biological drama as performed within the confines of a complex physical and social world.

The fact that development is a *process* rather than a thing makes reliable (that is, repeatable) observation difficult. In other words, development does not sit and wait for precise measurement of any kind to be made; the organism is constantly changing, and prior conditions can never be exactly duplicated. In actuality no one can claim to have observed the process itself, for the term development refers to a change detectable from observations made at two or more points on a time continuum. No matter how fine or how gross the temporal units, development itself remains an abstraction, an inference from incremental differences detected by the chosen method of observation. For example, one might take sequential pictures of the metamorphosis from caterpillar to butterfly, project them continuously as motion pictures, and thus apparently compress the development in such a way as to make the *process* itself appear to be the unit of observation. But no matter how much, for purposes of more careful study, we either accelerate or retard representations of development, we can do no more than infer the process from more or less discrete observations made at different temporal points.

Observation of the process of development in young children is a fascinating enterprise and one which never ceases to delight and amaze parents and other participants. The addition of two ounces to the weight chart, the sudden ability of the baby to hold his head in the midplane rather than turned always to one side, the momentous transfer of a rattle from one hand to the other, or the solemn embarking on the first solo step or articulation of the first distinct word—all provide manifestations of this potential for development. Furthermore, within certain rather broad limits the development is orderly and sequential. Just as a flower proceeds from bulb to stalk to leaf to bud to blossom and never, except under certain artificial conditions, modifies this sequence or short-circuits one or another stage, the development of the child proceeds in a lawful manner according to certain rules established by the fact that he is a living organism and, specifically, a member of the human species. For example, every parent knows that, in general, a child will sit before he stands, walk before he talks, gain control of his bowel movements before the ability to regulate bladder functioning, and so on. On the other hand, it is likely that not every parent or interested observer has noted other important, if more subtle, aspects of the developmental process. One of the purposes of this chapter is to call to the student's attention some of these less readily observable trends in child development.

Trends in Development

Development refers to an orderly change, either in the status of the organism or in behavior exhibited by an organism, which occurs during the interval between successive observations. One major aspect of the scientific study of child development may be conceived as a search for the variables of which that change is a function. For example, changes in weight and height may be shown to be in part a function of the child's nutrition; acquisition of new motor skills might be a function of such things as age of the child and opportunities for practice.

A fundamental prerequisite to an understanding of the process is a recognition of the interaction of all developmental phenomena. While we can observe a great variety of changes which may appear to be unrelated to one another, it is unlikely that this is ever the case. For the only functionally discrete unit of observation *is the whole child reacting to his total environment.* Only with acceptance of the unitary nature of the entire drama of growth and development can we hope to gain understanding of the dynamics of development. This integrative view does not, however, assert that the forces acting upon different organisms are completely identical in their patterning; for, as will be seen, the factors which influence and shape the developmental patterns in each individual child are diverse. Furthermore, it may well be that these forces do not operate evenly in different individuals. Consider, for instance, a mentally retarded child whose condition is clearly caused by some organic deficit (such as brain damage, insufficient thyroid during fetal life, and so on). Equal exposure of this child and of another whose nervous structures are conducive to maximum sensitivity to external stimuli will undoubtedly yield different results. While the former may be relatively impervious to such influences, the latter could be significantly affected because of his heightened responsivity.

In selecting a locus for studying the developmental process, one might choose to observe certain physical properties (for example, the size of a muscle) or attributes which will be exhibited only when the organism is in action (such as strength of grip on a hand dynamometer). This is the traditional distinction between *structure* and *function.* In order to understand the complex process of human growth, one should know something about each of these aspects of the process and at the same time recognize that they are not completely separable from one another. That is, structure can often be best understood in relation to the function or behavior which it makes possible, and function obviously does not magically occur independently of a particular structure or set of structures. To place the terms in a developmental framework, it can be said that maturity of structure—that is, the size and complexity of organization of component parts at a given time in relation to the corresponding organization when maximum development has been attained—has relevance only with respect to the functions which will be subserved. It is frequently necessary to use functional criteria to define maturity of structure (for example, the sex organs are "mature" when the individual is capable of reproduction). Furthermore, even the terms themselves are relative, for those organs which we ordinarily think of as providing the structures upon which certain functions depend are in turn composed of a group of functioning molecules themselves possessing a characteristic atomic structure.

From a study of the development of physical structures, we can learn much about behavior, and vice versa. Indeed, the emergence of certain behavior patterns provides tangible evidence that the destiny of certain physical structures has been fulfilled. In ordinary usage the term *morphology* is used to designate the total process of structural development. Gesell (7) reminds us, however, that the term morphology pertains only to form and that behavior as well as physical substance has shape and form. Thus, we would use the term *morphology of behavior* to designate the orderly patterning of behavior which can be observed in the process of child development.

After this declaration of faith in the inseparability of developmental phenomena, it is perhaps safe to mention that in the present exposition we will by choice highlight the development of function or behavior rather than that of structure. However, this emphasis does not imply that these features are, for an understanding of the general process of development, any more important than others and certainly not that they occur independently. It merely reflects the necessity of adopting a point of view for the sake of exposition.

It would be desirable in a scientific description of the process of child development to formulate a set of precise laws which would enable us to make predictions about final conditions from initial ones. A scientific law requires that a relationship between phenomena can be demonstrated to be invariable under a given set of conditions. This stipulation of constancy of external conditions is difficult to guarantee and the formulation of invariant relationships are accordingly troublesome. To attempt it on a grandiose scale at this time would undoubtedly be premature. For while a great deal is known about the development of living organisms and, specifically, the process of human development, it is impossible to state with finality all the factors of which this development is a function and the interrelationships among them. Even though one might know everything relevant about the undifferentiated young organism, accurate prediction from initial to final state (or simply from prior to remote subsequent state) would depend upon equally complete knowledge of the environmental conditions within which development is to occur. Since we cannot be sure about the extrinsic influences, we could make gross errors in prediction, called the "error of potentiality." Thus on the basis of a certain pattern of structure and concomitant function observable in a one-year-old we might infer a potential for the development of mature forms of language behavior. If, however, we attempted to make specific predictions about the kind of speech the child would exhibit at the age of five, we might err extensively unless certain facts could be known about the nature of the child's later experiences. There would be no way of determining whether he would speak English or Swahili or what modes of expression he might employ in his vocalization. Anyone willing to make such a prediction would be as injudicious as a broker advising a prospective investor about the value of a particular kind of stock 20 years in the future. Undoubtedly, there are good developmental risks, just as some stocks are more stable than others, but even so it is impossible to estimate precisely the future of either until many external conditions, themselves as yet unformed, can be assessed.

At times a capricious and paradoxical irregularity may appear to be the only predictable feature of development. This impression will most likely arise from a unit of observation too narrow to permit an event to reveal its contribution to the total pattern. But despite the vagaries of chance which may appear to toy with the growing organism and defeat precise prediction, there is apparent in every aspect of development an orderliness which, within broad limits, permits predictability. Some of the patterns which represent the orderliness in development shall be dealt with in this section.

Developmental direction. The general direction of growth moves in fairly steady progression from the head region of the organism downward. This directional gradient has been labeled the *cephalo-caudal* (literally, head-to-tail) sequence. A correlated type of directionality is the *proximodistal* (near-to-far) pattern, which means that development will proceed from the axis of the body toward the periphery. That growth should so proceed rather than in any other fashion seems determined by the fact that the most rapid embryological development occurs in or near those parts of the cells destined to be nervous structure. There appears to be a heightened sensitivity in these areas which facilitates more rapid growth. As the center of the body houses the neural axis, this accounts for the superiority of the axial structures to those at the periphery. And, furthermore, as the focus of nervous activity occurs in the area of the neural structure which is to become the head region, the precocity of upper as opposed to lower extremities is logical. In connection with the directionality, it is relevant to note that the metabolic activity of the cells diminishes steadily from a region of highest intensity in the head to one of least intensity in the lower extremities. Undoubtedly, this distribution of metabolic activity is an aspect of this directionality.

This directionality is characteristic of both structural and functional change. That is, observation of the human embryo reveals that at any given temporal point, the head is relatively more developed than the legs and feet. At the functional or behavioral level, this means that the baby will gain control of his eye muscles before those of the trunk or legs, and that he can coordinate gross arm movements prior to precise and refined finger manipulation. Further exemplification of this trend in development will be found in subsequent chapters.

Differentiation and integration. When one pauses to reflect that the complex human organism was once a microscopic unit of relatively undifferentiated protoplasm, the process of development seems miraculous indeed. But somehow the potential for every phenomenon later to be observed must exist in that original cell from which the organism developed. To a large extent, therefore, development must be the creation of differences, or differentiation, and the continuous reorganization into a unitary whole of the differences which thus emerge.

The original cell from which a child develops may be thought of as *totipotent,* that is, as possessing the capacity to become any structure which will later be found in the embryo. But if growth is to occur, the cell must abandon its totipotency for individuality, its versatility for specialization. As cell division continues, a milestone is eventually reached at which point a parent cell gives birth to a particular kind of offspring—nerve, muscle, or gland—and these resulting cells will in turn produce only their own kind and no other. Coincident with the increased differentiation, however, is an integration which enables the organism at any stage of development always to act as a coordinated whole. That is, if the rigid differentiation into muscle or nerve cells signified true independence among the cell groups, then it is unlikely that any organismic advantage would have accrued as a result of the division of labor. The integration of the ever increasing specificities, however, increases the adaptivity of the organism by assuring harmony among the interacting parts of the total structure.

A similar process of differentiation and integration can be found at the behavioral level. In some notable experimental and observational work on the development of aquatic locomotion in the salamander, Coghill (3) observed that the first movements were gross flexions of the entire trunk initiated in the head region and progressing toward the tail. The flexions may occur either to the right or to the left, and as the reaction becomes more complex a second contraction in one direction may occur before a contraction in the opposite direction has dissipated itself. When these alternating coils occur rapidly enough, pressure upon the water is exerted and the animal propelled forward. Walking on land follows a similar pattern, although of course this cannot proceed until anatomical development has progressed to the point at which limbs have emerged. There are at first only mass movements of the trunk succeeded by gradual differentiation or individuation of action of the limbs as they become able to function relatively independently of the movement of the trunk. Some of these activities are depicted in Figure 2. McGraw (15), who has studied intensively the acquisition of prone locomotion in infants, aptly remarks on the close similarity between this description by Coghill and that which occurs in the human infant.

While generalization from the behavior of lower animals may often be justified, it is never judicious to do so when a direct check at the level of human behavior is possible. Some authorities have challenged the explanation in terms of differentiation, stressing the point that individuation from a generalized response may be too simple an explanation of the development of similar patterns of human behavior. Carmichael (2), for example, reports that in the human fetus no observations have been reported of trunk movements in the absence of associated arm movements. Certain local reflexes (isolated behavior independent of functioning in other parts of the organism) can be observed at a very early stage in the development of the embryo, and more complex patterns of behavior may represent simultaneous individuation from a generalized response potential and a knitting together of specific local movements. Hooker (12) asserts that as early as 14 weeks the human fetus has largely abandoned the generalized response, and, instead, acquired a variety of discrete responses which can appear either singly or in combination.

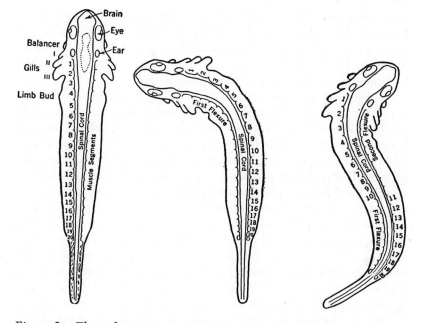

Figure 2.   Three diagrams of Amblystoma.   *(From Coghill* (3).   *Copyright 1929 by Cambridge University Press, and published with permission.)*

Perhaps the most adequate summary of the conflicting points of view would be one which emphasized the coaction of refinement of a generalized responsivity and a process of integration of isolated reflexes into a total pattern.   These in turn differentiate into behavior patterns which enable the organism to adjust to environmental conditions to be encountered later.   There would seem to be little doubt that both processes, integration and differentiation, are simultaneously operative in the morphogenesis of behavior.

Another example of this constant interweaving of differentiation and integration can be found in the development of voluntary prehension in young babies.   The infant possesses at birth a grasping (sometimes called Darwinian) reflex.   Place your finger in a baby's palm and his fingers will close around it with what sometimes appears to be a viselike grip.   This is a clear illustration of a specific response to local stimulation.   After about six weeks, however, this reflex begins to disappear or lapses into a relatively static phase during which an object, once grasped, will not be released until the hand makes contact with another surface which relieves the pull on the tendons. When attempts at voluntary prehension begin, this precise gesture is of little or no assistance, and the new skill must be refined gradually by the perfection of ever more precise movements which become differentiated out of gross movements.

In observing the development of voluntary prehension in infants, Halverson (9) noted how the development proceeds from a crude, pawing closure to a closure of the finger tips in a refined, nipping fashion. To observe this in process, put a tiny pellet of candy on a table top in front of an eight-month-old baby. The chances are that he will observe it, but perhaps not even try to pick it up. At nine months his attempt to pick it up will consist of a forward raking palm, culminating in an ineffectual effort to engulf it in the fingers. Around ten months he will undoubtedly approach the same object with greater precision and will perhaps for the first time bring the thumb into the act, capitalizing on the increased efficiency gained by opposing the thumb and forefinger. However, the approach will still be a cautious one, with palm flat against the surface of the table and the pellet apprehended with a scissorlike movement of the thumb and forefinger. Around one year, however, an entirely new level of skill is likely to have made its debut, as with elevated palm and a precise plucking motion the pellet is grasped with no waste motion (and, it should be added parenthetically, almost invariably thrust immediately into the mouth). Historically one might find roots of the eventual precision in the unfailing appearance of the initial reflex grasp, but observation of the entire sequence reveals that much simultaneous integration and differentiation must be accomplished before such refined movement is possible. Thus it would appear that the almost infinite array of behavioral acts of which the human adult is capable cannot be completely explained in terms of a simple process of differentiation from global, generalized performance. Rather there occurs a constant interlacing of differentiation and integration. As soon as a new pattern emerges it will be absorbed into the total, ever-expanding tapestry of development.

Cumulative influence. Behavior at any moment is a function of the life history of an organism and of the stimuli acting upon it. A significant alteration of either the life history or of the stimulating conditions is likely to produce a different type of behavior. The very concept of development makes it necessary to stress the fact that change is one of the essential attributes of all living organisms and thus by implication that the life history is constantly being altered. Although the events or experiences in the life of the child may themselves be ephemeral and transient, the effects may be stable and permanent. A tornado may last only a few seconds, but its brief visit may leave a permanent scar on the geography of a region.

Each event of significance in the life history of a child leaves him a slightly different person from the one he was prior to the occurrence of that event. The event may be an increase in neuromuscular coordination sufficient to enable him to grasp a bottle when he reaches for it. Or, the event may be an accidental reinforcement of some random movement—such as turning to one side in his crib and finding his mother more consistently visible—which leaves him with a stronger predisposition to behave similarly in the future. Thus, as the child responds to and assimilates the important experiences occurring in his life, a new intrapersonal organization emerges which will be involved in all subsequent reactions.

New patterns of stimuli to which a child has an opportunity to respond are constantly replacing older ones, and whatever effect the new ones have must be upon an organism which has already felt the impact of historically prior stimuli. Thus, the same stimulus—that is, one possessing identical physical properties—occurring at two different times may have entirely different effects. Consider, for instance, the eagerness of some parents and grandparents to give to their children all sorts of toys and play equipment. The presence of a shiny tricycle under a Christmas tree when the child is only one year old will perhaps evoke no response at all. The same vehicle hopefully placed under the tree a year later is likely to elicit a vigorous response, such as exploratory manipulation and excited verbalization. The life history of the child has changed, and his behavior in the situation has shown correlated change.

Of course, not all new experiences will be equally relevant to a particular type of behavior. If, in the above example, some sort of developmental arrest relevant to his capacity to react to a tricycle had occurred (for example, blindness, orthopedic handicap, mental deficit, and the like), there may have been no essential change in response. Thus, only when the change in life history is significant for a given form of behavior will it invariably produce a new response.

An especially effective statement of this pyramiding of influences in all manifestations of development is found in the following quotation from Gerard:

Development, we have seen, consists of a continued sequence of individual reactions, chemical and structural. Specific substances are synthesized and properly organized in cells; totipotent cells subdivide, differentiate, and migrate to form their appropriate structures of particular composition. Each new step is based upon the preceding one; and what will happen at any temporal cross section of the developmental process seems to be determined by the past history and the current situation, by the reacting system and the stimuli playing upon it. Having responded, the whole moves on to a new state of being, which will react again in the next step according to its now determined character and the new environmental situation. If the past history of the system be considered its heredity, then, indeed, much environment is woven into this in the course of development.

The same situation obtains at the behavior level. What one does at any moment depends on what he is and the situation to which he is responding. But what he is at this moment is itself compounded from his previous experiences and his reactions to them as well as from the initial structural endowment received at birth. Or, at the strictly chemical level, the same again holds, for the final products of reactions depend on the initial reagents present but no less on the surrounding temperature, pressure, illumination, and the like; and, of course, the secondary reactions depend on the products of the first ones and, therefore, on the reaction conditions as well as the ingredients of the initial mixture (5, 403).[3]

This formulation clearly recognizes the cumulative effects of experience. The significant events in a child's life history leave some sort of residual that will influence his manner of dealing with future experiences. The residual may be a structural modification or simply a greater probability of responding in one way than in another. A brief if somewhat oversimplified statement of the principle might be as follows: what one does affects what one is, and what one is in turn influences what one does. The child is modified by certain stimuli to which he responds, and the new individual will now behave differently toward subsequent stimulating conditions in his environment. One way in which the change may manifest itself is in selective responsivity. That is, certain stimuli will be attended to or even sought out, while others will be ignored. This means that not every stimulus acting upon the organism will have an equal likelihood of influencing behavior. After the child has learned to ride his tricycle, for example, he may for a long time pay no heed to other toys in his collection. In a choice situation he may try to create opportunities to perform this kind of behavior and no other. The chances of improving his skills

[3] From Gerard (5). Copyright 1940 by Harper and Brothers, and published with permission.

in this one area are increased, but at the same time the likelihood of improvement in unrelated types of behavior is decreased. Another way in which crucial change is revealed is in a unique, individualized response to the stimuli in the environment. That is, not all children of a given age will respond in the same way to the appearance of the tricycle. To one child it may signify gratification of a fervent wish and evoke jubilation; to another who has been injured in earlier unsuccessful attempts to ride a similar vehicle, it may call forth avoidance behavior and evidence of intense fear. Thus previous experiences affect both the choice of stimuli to be responded to and the way in which those present in the environment will be structured. This is a broader statement of what was identified in Chapter 2 as the projective hypothesis.

Related to this cumulative process is what might be termed the *internalization of experience*. Whenever any external influence leaves a permanent residue so that the future pattern of the child's response is altered, then this experience has somehow become part of his intrinsic response mechanism and has thus been internalized. At the same time, a rciprocal process is in operation, also with cumulative effects, which we might call an externalization of influence. Suppose, for instance, that in his efforts to achieve some objective, a two-year-old behaved very aggressively toward his mother—bit her, kicked her, and lashed out violently with his fists. Suppose further that this response pattern met with immediate success and his mother yielded to his demands. His behavior may produce more than her overt response of capitulation; it may at the same time develop in the mother an anticipation that he will act the same way in the future on similar occasions. This anticipation alerts her to any similar manifestations of such aggressive behavior and may lead to the establishment of a pattern for dealing with such behavior whenever it appears—she may resolve to punish severely any such acts in the future, or she may become somewhat afraid of him, and so on. In the sense that the child's probability of responding in the future has now changed, he has internalized an experience (the mother's way of responding to his behavior); in the sense that the mother's probability of future response toward him has been altered, there has been an externalization of influence. Of course, when individual development is the topic of interest, the internalization process is perhaps of greater relevance. The constant reorganization of the life history occurring as a result of this process is the equivalent of what is ordinarily termed the development of personality, a topic to be discussed in greater detail in later chapters.

The principle of cumulative influence is a prosaic way of recognizing the wisdom in the poetic reminder that "The child is father of the man." Development is an irreversible process, just as the flow of time itself is irreversible. The importance of early experiences arises not so much because of their immediate impact but because of whatever residual they leave. A traumatic experience or series of experiences in the life of the child—a serious illness, desertion, or rejection by the parents, consistent favoritism shown to another child in the family—should be evaluated in terms of the possible change in the potential for future adjustment as well as the immediate effects. Likewise, favorable early experiences become important not only because they supply immediate need gratification for the child but also because of their contribution to a life history which will be conducive to continuing good adjustment.

Critical periods. In the Biblical reminder that there is "A time to be born, and a time to die; a time to plant, and a time to pluck up that which is planted," one finds a concise statement of much that is implied in the principle of critical periods. That is, it does provided one interprets it to mean that attempting to plant during the periods when one should be harvesting or vice versa is unwise. Many colloquialisms, such as "Life is just one thing after another," also recognize that any life history is characterized by a sequence of "crises," events sharply etched against a background of seemingly less significant experience which occurs in a formalized time pattern. Furthermore, within any given culture, the critical events will show a high degree of similarity. For example, for the American child there are such memorable occasions as the first day of school, loss of the first baby teeth, being permitted to walk to school alone, the first date, graduation from high school, and many, many more. Most of these events will be retained in the memories of the individual; other significant ones (such as the first solo step, the first use of comprehensible speech, and so on) may be remembered only by other family members, but are nonetheless important items on the developmental chart. Another notable thing about such developmental crises is that an inversion in the time schedule is almost invariably a conversation piece. The fact that Mary talked before she walked was long a subject of family discussion; that Harold had not had his first date at the time of graduation from high school identified him as deviant from the developmental pattern followed by most of his contemporaries.

Thus, it appears that there are some events in the life history which are of relatively greater significance than others, and, furthermore, that within a certain range of variability, a fairly rigid time schedule is followed in the appearance of these events. But the critical period hypothesis goes one step further; it suggests that interference with certain developmental phenomena occurring at one point in the life history rather than at another may be of greater significance for establishing future trends. Evidence for this hypothesis will be sought in a variety of developmental phenomena.

One can find support for the critical period hypothesis at virtually every level of observation. We have already discussed some of the developmental changes occurring at the cellular level—the transition from an undifferentiated totipotency to a regimentation and constant regrouping of the growing multitude of cells. During this transition certain critical mileposts appear which demarcate the limits of cellular versatility. Up to a point the individual cells are apparently susceptible to diverse influences and, as it were, reveal a chameleonic adaptability. Evidence on this point comes from transplantation experiments on lower animals during the embryonic stage of development. In such experiments the timing of events is all important. Suppose some of the cells from the section of the embryo which, if unmolested, would develop into the digestive tract were removed operatively and anchored in the vicinity of the developing heart. If this were done early enough in the life history of the embryo, the cells would develop into a type associated with circulatory functioning, namely, liver cells. Their status at maturity then seems controlled largely by the situation in which they find themselves. Had the same operation been performed only a day or two later, when the cells of the digestive system had made further headway in their initial surroundings, then transplantation would result only in the juxtaposition of heart and intestines.

Similar evidence on this hypothesis can be found in the development of nervous tissue. Spemann (22) established that there is a critical period for the formation of that which will be the neural plate (the forerunner of the later nervous system) and that transplantation past this time will result in neural tissue regardless of location. This crucial period is apparently correlated with periods of intense physiological activity (heightened metabolism) when cellular differentiation receives additional impetus. Regardless of the electrochemical basis, it is apparent that there are crucial periods in embryonic morphogenesis during which a prospective structure is most sensitive to extrinsic stimulation and beyond which it is relatively resistant to such influences.

Fascinating though these experiments may be, we are less interested here in molecular than in molar phenomena, that is, less in chemical than in behavioral changes. What is the significance of such a principle when we divert our attention from anatomical data and look at overt behavior? The answer to that question would require first of all some specification as to the type of behavior and also a defense of the position that a timetable is likely to be followed in any dimension of development. With respect to motor behavior there is some experimental data bearing directly on the question.

It has been demonstrated (17) that salamanders kept in an anesthetic solution during the time when aquatic locomotion should be developing can later acquire precise swimming movements after removal from the solution. However, if left in the anesthesia for longer than a certain length of time (about 13 days), the animals are unable to learn to swim normally. This suggests a critical duration beyond which recovery of normal function is impossible. Likewise, in a famous study of motor development, McGraw (14) found that attempts to accelerate the acquisition of certain muscular skills were likely to be ineffectual unless introduced at a propitious time in the child's developmental cycle.

Evidence for the vitality of the concept of critical periods can be found in the wide variety of approaches to the study of development which have led to such a formulation. From sources as diverse as the animal laboratory, the classroom, and the psychotherapeutic session have come data relevant to the hypothesis. While these approaches differ in terminology, in the extent to which hypotheses have been put to experimental test, in the populations to which generalizations can be made, and in the kinds of phenomena selected for observation, all nonetheless show an undercurrent of similarity. That is, they all stress the importance of certain events in relation to the time at which these occur and the constellation of experiences in which they are embedded.

Although the explicit label has not always been applied, the concept of developmental crises has figured prominently in several theories of the genetic aspects of social behavior. Attention will now be turned to some of these theoretical formulations.

From a laboratory concerned primarily with comparative (interspecies) animal behavior has come a recent description of social behavior calling attention to the special significance of certain periods in development (20). Most of their research has been carried out with dogs, sheep, mice, and other lower mammals, and they have been careful to avoid unwarranted generalization to human behavior. Nevertheless, the implications for an understanding of the behavior of children are so profound that closer examination of their hypothesis is warranted. Their point of view asserts that the development of social behavior of various mammals falls into several natural periods and that in certain of these a particular type of social experience may have lasting effects, while during others the same event may occur without leaving any appreciable impression on the organism.

The five natural periods outlined by these authors are: (1) *neonatal period*, during which patterns essential for survival and useful in early life are learned, such as the ability to take in food and to begin moving about independently; (2) *transition period*, during which adult loco- motion and ingestion patterns are developed in rudimentary form; (3) *socialization period*, at which time the young organisms come into significant contact with individuals other than the parents and litter mates; (4) *juvenile period*, which marks the interim between the disappearance of infantile patterns and the emergence of the capacity for mature sexual behavior; and (5) *adult period*, which is characterized by the appearance of adult patterns of sexual behavior.

According to this formulation, the crucial periods are those during which important new social relationships are being formed. At such times, an adverse experience is likely to be especially potent for in- fluencing later development. Periods one, three, and five should theoretically be most significant. However, because the animal prob- ably does not learn and retain much during the neonatal period, the influence of the first period is almost completely discounted. At the beginning of period three, however, there is sufficient maturation of the nervous system to permit retention of significant experiences and the stabilization of patterns of social response.

In order to confirm or refute some of these assumptions, a number of tests have been designed to measure the behavior of puppies, such as reaction to being handled by humans, "dominance" in relation to other dogs, responses to a barrier, performance in a maze, and so on. Experimental animals (and comparable control animals from the same litter which had received identical treatment except for the experi- mental condition) were evaluated on these tests after they had been subjected at different times to a variety of presumably traumatic events. For instance, puppies that were castrated or had their tails clipped during the neonatal period showed no residual behavioral effects when tested at later times. Likewise, removal of puppies from their mother during periods one and four had no adverse effects, while those dogs removed during period three later exhibited an atypical reaction to other dogs as well as to humans.

On the basis of normative data regarding social development in the human organism, Scott and Marston (21) speculate that in man the neonatal period extends from birth to four weeks, the transition period to 15 months, the socialization period to three years, the juvenile period to about 12 years, and the adult period from that time onward. While recognizing that considerable experimental work needs to be done before generalizations to human behavior are warranted, these researchers propose that the critical period hypothesis has much to offer students of child behavior. Scott, Fredericson, and Fuller state in this connection, "The possibility exists that critical or danger periods in human development may eventually be delineated in such detail that parents and educators may know when to be especially careful to avoid psychologically damaging experiences" (20, 182).[4] Of course, such refined prediction and control must await preliminary labors of considerable magnitude and intricacy. At the same time, their formulation of natural and critical periods as applied to social behavior can be stated in such a form that direct experimental test of the hypothesis is possible. For this reason if for no other the provocative scheme deserves attention.

Another description relevant to the critical period hypothesis is that of Havighurst (11). He uses the term *developmental task* to convey the notion of crises in development with which the growing individual must inevitably cope. A developmental task is defined as "a task which arises at or about a certain period in the life of the individual, successful achievement of which leads to his happiness and to success with later tasks, while failure leads to unhappiness in the individual, disapproval by the society, and difficulty with later tasks" (11, 2).[5] These tasks may arise from physical maturation, from cultural forces, or from the emerging personality which must somehow integrate the forces emanating from the other two sources. Examples of such tasks which must be faced in early childhood are learning to

---

[4] From Scott *et al.* (20). Copyright 1951 by Grune and Stratton, and published with permission.

[5] From Havighurst (11). Copyright 1953 by Longmans, Green and Co., and published with permission.

walk, to talk, and to comprehend and manipulate letter and numerical symbols. Inadequate achievement in any one of these tasks handicaps the individual to a certain extent in his efforts to cope with later contingencies. Consider, for example, the handicap of the child who cannot talk when he begins to try to establish rewarding social relationships. These learning tasks represent an approach toward integration of the demands made on the child by his physical organism and those of the society in which he must develop. They will obviously differ in various social and cultural groups with respect to the acceptable manner in which they will be expressed. At the same time, there should be considerable similarity from culture to culture with respect to the tasks themselves if not to the exact manner in which they are revealed.

The Freudian or psychoanalytic description of character development (in which the meaning of the term "character" is actually closer to that ordinarily ascribed to "personality") could legitimately be labeled a critical period hypothesis. Psychoanalysts postulate several major developmental stages during which the major focus of biological and psychological energy is to be found in one or another bodily zone of development. For example, during the early weeks and months of life, the major source of gratification and, accordingly of potential frustration, resides in those activities associated with the intake of nourishment. Calling attention to the importance of these incorporative activities, Freud labeled this the "oral" stage. Later the focus of energy was presumed to shift to other bodily zones, such as the anal and eventually the genital, at which time the primary source of gratification or satisfaction of important biological and psychological needs was similarly shifted.

While it is undoubtedly apparent that these are "periods" in development, it may not be so apparent that the timetable is stringent enough to warrant calling them "critical" periods. The answer to this question provided by psychoanalytic theory is that insufficient gratification at any one of the periods in effect "freezes" a certain amount of mental energy (Freud's term for this was fixation of libido) and hampers subsequent normal development. That is, the child who does not receive sufficient gratification of his oral needs may be destined to continue to seek substitute (or direct) gratification of such needs and thus be unable to effect smooth transition to the next developmental stage. In line with this theory one might postulate that a child weaned prematurely or too harshly, or for that matter indulged too long in sucking activities, might become fixated at the oral level and be unable to move on freely to more mature developmental levels. We will forego examination of the evidence concerning their contention until later chapters. Enough has been indicated to show that a critical hypothesis is implicit in their formulation.

In discussing the importance of timing in the developmental process, it is easy to make the hypothetical timetable sound too rigid, with lengthy barren intervals existing between the crisis points. Such an alarmist point of view is far from the intent either of these theorists or this writer. Variability is just as likely to be present in the time schedules of different children as it is in the manner in which patterns of overt behavior are expressed. In order to avoid this implication, it must be mentioned here that the critical period for the development of any form of behavior will be to a certain extent unique for each individual and, furthermore, that there is likely to be some overlapping of the periods no matter the conceptual scheme being considered. Only within broad limits can the time schedule be formulated, and prediction for an individual child on the basis of group norms can be fraught with error.

Under the rubric of critical periods, several apparently disparate theoretical formulations have been brought together in the foregoing analysis. Considerable space has been devoted to the topic, as it is regarded as a most useful scheme with which to orient research data to be presented in subsequent chapters. Also the hypothesis is congruent with the general approach of this book, in which material has been organized developmentally. In each of the major sections to follow (infancy, the preschool period, the elementary school years), there will be a focus of attention on those activities regarded as relatively crucial for each period. The present account hardly touches upon the evidence. In later chapters this evidence will be considerably expanded.

Manifestations of Development

The terms generally used by psychologists to characterize the spontaneously appearing and the externally instigated forms of behavior development, respectively, are *maturation* and *learning*. The discussion will center on manifestations of development, in an elucidation of these concepts.

Maturation and learning. Many definitions have been proposed for both of these concepts. Of the two, learning has been defined with much less equivocation and with greater community of meaning and will therefore receive first mention here. Munn offers the definition "Learning may be said to occur whenever behavior undergoes incremental modification of a more or less permanent nature as a result of activity, special training, or observation" (19, 374).[6] Some of the crucial terms in this definition differentiate learning from fatigue (which would involve a performance decrement rather than an increment), from sensory adaptation (relatively impermanent modification), and from maturation (which should not depend upon special activity or training).

Definitions of maturation have not revealed uniformity of thinking. In its original scientific usage the term maturation was used by geneticists to denote the development which occurs within the immature germ cell prior to the process of fertilization. Gesell (6) was one of the first writers to use it in a broader sense, applying it to those developmental phenomena which appear to develop in an orderly fashion without the intervention of any known external stimuli. This usage applies the term to *behavior* as well as to changes in the nerves, muscles, and glands which provide the necessary implements for the execution of behavioral activities. In a recent publication, Carmichael (1) avoids the formulation of an explicit definition by proposing three criteria by means of which changes attributable to maturation can be distinguished: (1) the behavior should be demonstrated as developing universally in all or almost all apparently normal organisms of similar physiological endowment; (2) the behavior change must occur in an organism too immature to be able to form stable habit patterns; and (3) the behavior should appear in an organism that has had no opportunity to observe the act in question in another member of the species. Rigid adherence to these criteria, especially the third, would virtually preclude application of the term to any type of human behavior. Howells offers the definition, " 'Maturation' is simply development in which commonly observed differences between individuals are correlated with previous differences in the inner organism rather than in the environment." (13, 29).[7]

The generally unwieldy nature of the concept of maturation and its resistance to precise definition have led some writers to favor abandonment of it altogether and to encourage instead the adoption

[6] From Munn (19). Copyright 1954 by John Wiley and Sons, and published with permission.
[7] From Howells (13). Copyright 1945 by the American Psychological Association, and published with permission.

of what has been called a *convergence* definition. This approach would recognize the inseparability of the maturational and learning processes. Some writers have objected to such attempts on the grounds that fusion of the two concepts makes scientific investigation of the developmental process difficult and shuns precise explanation in favor of global description. Marquis has thus asserted that the two concepts can be separated and proposes as the distinguishing criteria the following: "Both processes, it is true, represent an interaction of organism and environment, but learning is distinguished from maturation by this fact: It represents a modification of the organismic pattern in response to specific stimuli present in the external environment at the time of the modification. Maturation, on the other hand, is a modification of the organismic pattern in response to stimuli present in the inter-cellular and intra-cellular environments which at the given moment are independent of external influence" (*16*, 347–348).[8] Although at first glance this definition may appear to emphasize a fundamental distinction, the ambiguity of such concepts as "organismic pattern" and "internal and external environments" soon becomes apparent. Thus one is left with the inevitability of defining both maturation and learning in terms of each other—behavior change not attributable to learning is said to be due to maturation, and vice versa. This is a rather ineffectual way of establishing the independence of either concept. Nevertheless, maturation will be found to be demonstrated primarily through studies in which there is little or no opportunity for learning to take place. Chapter 6, concerned with psychological development in infancy, is replete with illustrations of this way of studying maturation. Admittedly imperfect and unclear as distinguishing characteristics, they will serve as an introduction to the problem of manifestation of development.

It has often been said that progress in any field of scientific inquiry is made less by finding the right answers than by asking the right questions. An integrative approach to the developmental process seems to facilitate phrasing questions in such a way that meaningful answers can be found. Viewed in this way, the proper question becomes one *not* of the priority of maturation or learning. Rather it seems more appropriate to inquire into the extent to which the process of development can be influenced or modified by *intervention*. Is development an inexorable, immutable process which will attain reali-

---

zation regardless of the kind of environmental influences to which the organism might be exposed? Or, if it is modifiable, to what extent is this possible? And, as might be predicted from our previous discussion of critical periods, are there times at which modification is more feasible than others? Likewise, if emerging functions are interfered with, is this likely to have a deleterious effect on the total development? To these questions considerable attention will be devoted in later chapters.

Summary

At conception the genetic history of the individual is fixed. During the ten lunar months between conception and birth the development that is taking place is that from cell to organism. During this and later prenatal periods, the organism-to-be is given an environment, a sequestered one to be sure, but, nevertheless, an environment. The state of this environment becomes the conditions for and modifiers of development.

The normal sequence of prenatal development is predictable to a high degree. The zygote begins the process of cell division with increase in number, size, and weight of the cells of the so-called ovular or germinal stage. Specialization of function of these cells begins during the embryonic stage. This stage, in turn, gives way to the fetal period which ends with birth.

The process of development is made central for the remainder of the chapter. The concept of development—orderly and harmonious change which enhances the ability of the organism to adjust—is examined in its myriad ramifications. A discussion of trends in development leads to emphasis upon the fact that the unit of observation is the whole child reacting to his total environment. There is also the recognition that we must break down this unity for purposes of some of the discussions that follow. This is the case in the distinction made between structure and function. This is also the case in discussing the more prominent trends in development—developmental direction, differentiation and integration, cumulative influence, and critical periods. Although all of these trends are important, that of critical periods has been emphasized.

Manifestations of development are seen in forms of behavior development, called maturation and learning. These two forms of behavior development are distinguished hereafter, although they are but aspects of the same fundamental process.

For Further Reading

An excellent discussion of the prenatal development of behavior in infrahuman as well as human mammals is Davenport Hooker's *The Prenatal Origin of Behavior* (Lawrence, Kan.: University of Kansas Press, 1952). Leonard Carmichael in a chapter, "The Onset and Early Development of Behavior," in the book edited by him, *Manual of Child Psychology: Second Edition* (New York: Wiley, 1954) gives a detailed account of development written by a psychologist, for psychologists.

References

1. Carmichael, L.   Ontogenetic development.   In S. S. Stevens (Ed.), *Handbook of experimental psychology.*   New York: Wiley, 1951, 281–303.
2. Carmichael, L.   The onset and early development of behavior.   In L. Carmichael (Ed.), *Manual of child psychology* (2nd ed.).   New York: Wiley, 1954, 60–185.
3. Coghill, G. E.   *Anatomy and the problems of behavior.*   New York: Macmillan, 1929.
4. Corner, G. W.   *Ourselves unborn: an embryologist's essay on man.*   New Haven: Yale University Press, 1944.
5. Gerard, R. W.   *Unresting cells.*   New York: Harper, 1940.
6. Gesell, A.   Maturation and the patterning of behavior.   In C. Murchison (Ed.), *A handbook of child psychology* (2nd ed., rev.).   Worcester, Mass.: Clark University Press, 1933, 209–235.
7. Gesell, A.   The autogenesis of infant behavior.   In L. Carmichael (Ed.), *Manual of child psychology* (2nd ed.).   New York: Wiley, 1954, 335–373.
8. Gilbert, Margaret S.   *Biography of the unborn.*   Baltimore, Md.: Williams and Wilkins, 1938.
9. Halverson, H. M.   The development of prehension in infants.   In R. G. Barker, J. S. Kounin, and H. F. Wright (Eds.), *Child behavior and development.*   New York: McGraw-Hill, 1943, 49–65.
10. Hamburger, V.   *A manual of experimental embryology.*   Chicago: University of Chicago Press, 1942.
11. Havighurst, R. J.   *Human development and education.*   New York: Longmans, Green, 1953.
12. Hooker, D.   Reflex activities in the human fetus.   In R. G. Barker, J. S. Kounin, and H. F. Wright (Eds.), *Child behavior and development.*   New York: McGraw-Hill, 1943, 17–28.
13. Howells, T. H.   The obsolete dogmas of heredity.   *Psychol. Rev.*, 1945, 52, 23–34.

14. McGraw, Myrtle B. *Growth: a study of Johnny and Jimmy.* New York: Appleton-Century-Crofts, 1935.
15. McGraw, Myrtle B. Maturation of behavior. In L. Carmichael (Ed.), *Manual of child psychology.* New York: Wiley, 1946, 332–369.
16. Marquis, D. G. The criterion of innate behavior. *Psychol. Rev.,* 1930, 37, 334–349.
17. Matthews, S. A., and Detwiler, S. R. The reactions of Amblystoma embryos following prolonged treatment with chloretone. *J. exp. Zool.,* 1926, 45, 279–292.
18. Montagu, M. F. A. Constitutional and prenatal factors in infant and child health. In M. J. E. Senn (Ed.), *Symposium on the healthy personality.* New York: Josiah Macy, Jr. Foundation, 1950, 148–210.
19. Munn, N. L. Learning in children. In L. Carmichael (Ed.), *Manual of child psychology* (2nd ed.). New York: Wiley, 1954, 374–458.
20. Scott, J. P., Fredericson, E., and Fuller, J. L. Experimental exploration of the critical period hypothesis. *Personality,* 1951, 1, 162–183.
21. Scott, J. P., and Marston, Mary-'Vesta. Critical periods affecting the development of normal and mal-adjustive social behavior of puppies. *J. genet. Psychol.,* 1950, 77, 25–60.
22. Spemann, H. Some factors of animal development. *Brit. J. exp. Biol.,* 1925, 2, 493–504.

Socialization, Personality, and Behavior Theory

THE PICTURE OF THE CHILD THAT HAS EMERGED IN THE previous chapters still is incomplete. We need to consider further the nature of the process through which the infant becomes a person. Equally necessary to that which went before is consideration of how his unique characteristics emerged which mark him as different from other persons, and consideration of how his common characteristics come about which he shares with other persons. We also need to consider him as living in a world of other persons who influence his development. In short, we must examine socialization and personality. Socialization will be considered first after which a general discussion of personality will follow. Two major approaches to personality will be utilized—behavior-social learning theory and psychoanalysis. The former is to be considered in the last section of this chapter, the latter in the next chapter.

Socialization

Elements of the social situation in which a human infant finds himself at birth are universal. Everywhere infants are born helpless and dependent upon adults. Everywhere infants are suckled, subjected

100

to restrictions for their protection, and provided with care and training. In carrying out this training, the parents in a particular culture or subculture select for the infant those forms of stimulation which they consider desirable for his socialization. In addition to the parents, other agents of socialization come into prominence with the widening of his social horizon. Thus, his siblings, his peers, his teachers, and in varying degrees, other adults become part of each child's social scene and serve to encourage and to discourage specific activities.

This direction from others is demonstrated for what it is through representatives of educational and religious institutions dedicated to inculcating certain behaviors. It is also carried on by agents who are not aware of their functions. Countless little acts must be done in a "right" or "proper" way and are learned without either the agent or the child being aware of their roles as teacher and learner. Socialization takes place whether we know it or not. Often socialization is imparted implicitly and learned incidentally. We have some difficulty in seeing the process of socialization as separate from ourselves— at a distance as it were. We "know" that, of course, breakfast starts with orange juice and ends with the last sip of coffee. Of course, we have eight (plus or minus one) hours of sleep. Of course, babies use potties. But in other societies, of course, you would not be a man until you have had a vision, and, of course, twenty varieties of ice formation are obviously distinguishable, each with their right name, and no other.

Socialization (4, 30, 31) refers to the process of helping children become the adult members of the society to which they belong. It is a process whereby an individual becomes a member of a society by achieving ways of experiencing and behaving which are in conformity with that society's values. Within the limits of what is considered customary and acceptable in his society, the infant, and the child he is to become, is encouraged by his parents to perform certain activities, other activities are viewed neutrally, while still others are actively discouraged. The child is led by the individuals in his social environment to develop an actual behavior repertoire considerably narrower in range than that of which he is capable. A homely example of this process is the difficulty children in an English-speaking culture have with the French "u." In learning to speak French this letter gives English-speaking students considerable difficulty. It seems to be an unnatural sound that is very hard for us to say correctly. And yet, as a basic speech sound our infants have had it in their repertoire to the same extent as do infants in French families. It dropped out with us because it does not appear as a sound in English. In a broader view, all cross-cultural studies in the field of cultural anthropology stand witness to differences among groups of individuals due to the influence of this process of socialization. For example, the various studies of Margaret Mead aim at showing the ways socialization varies from one society to another.

We are justified in speaking of socialization without being mystical in any sense. Socialization is always mediated by individuals, but it does rise above individuals in that you can detach the teaching from the teacher. Illustrative is a comment from Kluckhohn and Mowrer (although they were talking about something slightly different): "If a random third of the parents of Cambridge, Massachusetts, were to die tomorrow and their children were to be socialized by their surviving relatives and friends in Cambridge, it may safely be predicted that what these children would learn—would be approximately the same taking the group as a statistical whole as if their parents had survived" (*19*, 15).[1]

Constitutional Factors and Socialization

Constitutional factors are subject to socializing influences. The infant's maturational equipment for eating, defecating, and sleeping are at birth faced with a series of social pressures (9). He is expected to eat certain things at certain times in a certain manner, to eliminate waste in a prescribed place and manner, and to sleep at certain times in a prescribed object and even for a prescribed length of time. For each of these functions his particular society prescribes what is right and proper, although differing radically one from the other on what this might be. Eventually his eating is regulated not only by a changing blood sugar level but also by the family meals, his elimination not only by internal pressures but also by the aforementioned time and place, and his sleep behavior not only by biological demands but also family schedules.

One research example will suffice. The experiment of Dorothy Marquis (23) is described on page 184. In the context of the present discussion, what she demonstrates is that variation in feeding schedule during the first ten days of life leads to a learned modification of the restlessness accompanying hunger on the part of the infants she

[1] From Kluckhohn and Mowrer (*19*). Published 1944 by the American Anthropological Association, and used with permission.

studied. The onset of restlessness in these infants becomes associated with their feeding time etablished by other persons. Thus, her study illustrates the modification of constitution by socialization practices.

The Agents of Socialization and Learning

Socialization, a process by which conventional patterns of behavior are acquired, is a process of learning. Through socialization a child learns to fit in with the manners and customs of the family, the neighborhood, the community, and the society in which he finds himself. Since we are concerned with learned behavior, it follows that social influences on the child's personality can eventually be understood in terms of learning theory. To be sure, the patterns of socialization in terms reducible to the details of learning theory remain to be worked out, but there is nothing insuperable about this as a task for the psychologists of today and tomorrow.

Children learn from certain individuals and not from others. Insofar as these persons are sources of learning for a particular child we can speak of them as agents of socialization. The mother serves as the major agent through which the infant and younger child learns. He learns through the reinforcements he receives in the course of her care. On the basis of learning theory Bishop summarizes the kinds of behavior the mother shows in socialization as follows:

> She can offer rewards, incentives, or punishments; she can facilitate or inhibit certain activities; and she can influence behavior by direct or indirect means. These three general ways of classifying her behavior overlap, and each is subject to further categorization. For example, if the mother wishes to stop a specific act, she may present a direct interference, she may provide the stimulus for an alternative response, she may punish the unwanted activity or reward the substituted behavior, she may arrange environmental conditions to obstruct the behavior, she may offer incentives to change the child's motivation, and so on.
>
> The child learns to react in certain ways to these various forms of stimulation. The mother's behavior provides stimulus cues which are generalized from previous situations to the present and thus serve to call forth a similar response. In addition, the types of stimulation which are employed by the mother present the child with a model for his own behavior in controlling individuals. Through the mother's response to these stimulus aspects of his behavior he is also learning which techniques are most successful in goal-attainment.
>
> The child, then, is developing patterns of behavior both as an indi-

vidual response to the particular behavior which the mother evidences in her relationships with him and as a direct incorporation of certain aspects of her behavior (3, 29–30).[2]

What happens to the infant and younger child in this learning situation can be ascertained by examining maternal behavior as is done in Chapters 7, 10, and 12.

Other agents of socialization are present. Even in infancy the father is a major source of learning, as are other individuals in the immediate family, such as siblings. As he enters early childhood, the agents of socialization with which he comes in contact increase in number. Neighborhood children and preschoolmates enter the picture as do adult supervisors such as nurses, baby sitters, preschool teachers, and the like. It is in late childhood that the peers become very important. In fact, Chapter 12, concerned with psychosocial development in later childhood, is devoted mainly to consideration of their significance.

Socialization Practices in Different Societies

Socialization practices differ from society to society. In one a given practice may be condemned, in another not even seen as a "practice" and hence accepted. There is abundant evidence that in the absence of determining organic bases, a given problem does not develop in children unless the conditions for its formation are present in the environment. To use an obvious example, in a primitive culture there are no schools and hence no truancy. Somewhat less obvious is the absence of stealing in certain cultures. Stealing as a symptom occurs only in cultures where there is a strong emphasis on property rights. Among the Kaingang Indians of Brazil there is no such emphasis and thievery is absent (13). Other behavior problems show this relation as well.

Enuresis (bed wetting) is not uncommon in the American culture, but in many primitive groups it is nonexistent. Consider the Pilaga Indians of the Amazon area. From the standpoint of our group, they have no toilet training. A quotation from Henry is appropriate:

> Before Pilaga babies can sit up, no attention is given to elimination other than to wipe off the baby or the mother when the child soils. If the child soils his hammock, it is wiped off and the child is put back.

[2] From Bishop (3). Copyright 1951 by the American Psychological Association, and published with permission.

They have no toilets and no "potties." When the child is well able to sit up, his mother places him on her own outstretched legs when she thinks he wishes to move his bowels, and the child defecates between them. When he is able to stand, the mother takes him with her to the bush when she goes to defecate. Before the third year no stress is laid on defecating outside the house; after that, the child who soils inside the house is scolded. No attention is given to nocturnal incontinence, since Pilaga sleep on the ground on untanned hides, which are easily dried. The complete lack of concern about regularity, constipation and soiling (there is practically nothing to soil!) is, from our point of view, one of the most striking aspects of Pilaga culture. The absence of enuresis as a factor in anxiety is to be ascribed partly to Pilaga indifference to urine, partly to the fact that they have no sheets, mattresses, or beds to dirty (*14*, 629).[3]

It is no wonder that enuresis is not present among the Pilaga, since the conditions for its appearance are not present.

There is present in each society a whole series of attitudes about what is desirable and undesirable. One of these is the general attitude that members of these societies hold toward children as such. In some societies, a child is desired and tenderly cared for. In others, he may be considered a nuisance and treated as such. Other societies fall between these extremes of indulgence and severity.

An illustration of socialization in different societies may be drawn from the work of Whiting and Child (*31*), who studied comparatively the literature available about a large sample of societies including one from middle-class families in our own society. The task to which they put their judges was for each independently to read the same material about each of the societies and then to arrive at ratings on certain selected variables. Among other categories that they developed for their raters were a considerable number concerning various aspects of child training. For each society they selected for study, ratings were made on such matters as age at, and severity of, both weaning and toilet training. The ratings with which we are concerned at the moment, though on a variety of topics, have in common the fact that they run from one extreme of indulgence to the other of severity.

One source of variation in child training they investigated was the extent to which each society allowed the child initial indulgence in nursing. They included in this category factors such as the duration of the nursing behavior permitted, the freedom the infant was per-

---

[3] From Henry (*14*). Copyright 1947 by the American Orthopsychiatric Association, and published with permission.

mitted in the performance of nursing, and the encouragement the mother gave to the infant to nurse. They found that about half of the societies showed typical high oral indulgence, while the other half showed gradually decreasing degrees of oral indulgence. The lowest (most severe) rating on indulgence was given the Marquesans. To illustrate the attitude in this culture, Linton says they believe nursing contributes to difficulty in raising since the children will not be properly submissive if given too much breast feeding. Moreover, women take great pride in the shape and firmness of their breasts which are important in sex play. Nursery periods are short and feeding times irregular, dependent upon the convenience of the mother rather than the needs of the child. It was on the basis of this and similar evidence that the raters marked this particular society as severe in their attitudes toward nursing.

The sample from our own society was the next most severe in nursing after the Marquesan. This rating in the direction of severity was influenced considerably by the short duration of nursing in the American middle-class group and the low degree of indulgence of oral interests these American infants were permitted. In the other sources of variation on child training studied, the American group was not necessarily as severe as in the instance just given. Characteristically, however, the American group was on the severe rather than the indulgent side. There is a current widespread impression that the practices of the American middle-class are changing in the direction of greater indulgence; thus the results they used which were obtained in the early forties may not adequately represent this group at the present time. Further discussion of this question of the degree of severity in classes in our society is given in the next section.

Even within a given society there is no necessary consistency of attitude and practice throughout the time encompassed by childhood. In connection with this problem, Goldfrank (11) has proposed a fourfold categorization of societies. They are: (1) societies where both infant and later discipline are weak; (2) societies where both are severe; (3) societies in which infant disciplines are severe and later disciplines are weak; and (4) societies where infant disciplines are weak but later disciplines are severe. An illustration of application of this classification is given in Chapter 7. Although this fourfold classification is a step in the right direction of appreciation of the complexity, it does not bring out all ramifications of the prob-

lem. It is sufficient to show, however, that broad patterns of socialization may be identified.

Different attitudes towards socialization practices in our society.
There is no universal American pattern of socialization practice.
Some conception of the diversity can be obtained from the findings
of Sears, Maccoby, and Levin (28), who report comparative data
on three communities. Two of these were small New Mexican villages, just a few miles apart: Homestead, with a population drawn
mostly from the dust bowl areas of Texas and Oklahoma, and the
other, Rimrock, containing mostly old American stock with Mormon
traditions. The third community was from a suburban metropolitan
area of New England. In a sample of 20 homes each from Homestead and Rimrock, 50 per cent of the Homestead mothers had completed weaning before the child was eight months old, while none
had in Rimrock. In the New England sample, 37 per cent of a sample
of about 400 had completed weaning by this age. In questioning
about which parent had the chief responsibility in deciding child-
rearing policies, the mother said the father did in eight per cent of
the New England sample, in 22 per cent of the Homestead group,
but in 67 per cent of the Rimrock group. These findings at least
indicate some of the diversity to be found.

In our society there has been considerable controversy concerning
the proper way to bring up children based upon two different conceptions of what is healthful and socially useful in socialization.
Escalona, in commenting upon child-rearing practices, contends that
a remarkable change has taken place recently. The older, disappearing point of view she characterizes as follows:

> Bodily and mental health is based on an orderly, strictly scheduled
> existence from early childhood onward. Prescribed formulae are su-
> perior to breast feeding, chiefly because the ingredients are known and
> nutrition becomes, therefore, a controlled process. When babies or
> children cry without recognized legitimate cause it is best to let them
> cry it out. It is the responsibility of adults to teach children what is
> "right" and what is "wrong" in regard to meal times, sleeping hours,
> play interests and most other activities (8, 158).[4]

She comments that this point of view is one which is highly rational, largely based upon a combination of adult patterns of living
and of knowledge of the scientific facts of physical growth. She

[4] From Escalona (8). Copyright 1949 by the Society for Research in Child
Development, and published with permission.

could also have added that the prevalence of behavioristic teachings, so ably advanced by John B. Watson (who wrote a popular book on child care), was also influential in stressing the use of impersonal practices of child care.

The point of view about child care just sketched was in keeping with the belief in a spirit of stability of our society that was characteristic of the early decades of this century. In recent years, this spirit of certainty and belief in stability has diminished. The atom bomb, and all that goes with it, has forced upon us a reluctant belief that our main source of danger is human nature itself. An appreciation of the irrationality of man has come upon us. The considerable influence of psychoanalysis in shaping newer views about socialization Escalona considers to be a consequence, not a cause, of our loss of a stable value system.

The view that there has been a shift in attitude in recent years is supported by the findings of Radke (26). She found that parents showed significant differences in behavior toward their children as compared with what they had experienced previously from their parents. In the younger generation, there was a less dictatorial quality to discipline, a greater participation on the part of the fathers, and a greater consideration for the child's interests and needs. These shifts from one generation to the next, if they hold in the present population, would indicate a degree of improvement of parent-child rapport in the present over that of the past generation.

What is this newer point of view about socialization? Only a few representative illustrations need be given. Quoting Escalona's account:

> It is now thought that it is up to us as adults to meet the needs of the younger child, rather than to expect early adaptation from him. To wit, self-demand schedules and all that goes with them. . . . Among the needs of the young child we recognize the need for affection and for an intimate relationship with the mother as of very great importance, tending to evaluate it as more crucial than the need for good physical care. We prize self-expression, sincerity of feeling and spontaneous interest above good manners, self-restraint, or intellectual accomplishment (8, 160).[4]

Two characteristic procedures arising from this point of view that she mentions are self-demand feeding and rooming-in. Self-demand feeding refers to allowing the infant to express his need for food himself and set his own rhythm of feeding rather than being fed by the clock and by the ounce. "Rooming-in," a term first used by

Gesell and Ilg (10), is a hospital arrangement wherein a mother and her newborn baby are cared for together in the same room, rather than having the infant cared for in the hospital nursery, except for his visits to the mother for feeding. However, the procedure signifies more than this. It goes beyond rearrangement of physical facilities to a recognition of the importance of the mother and child as a physical and psychological unit from birth onward.

The two general points of view have never been given commonly agreed-upon, identifying names. For convenience, they will hereafter be referred to as the "regulatory" and "permissive" points of view, respectively. The quotation marks serve to remind us that these terms are tentative.

The very fact that contrasting child care practices are held in our society and the further fact that protagonists of both points of view are able to point to supporting evidence drive home the realization that the empirical data we have at our command must be too scanty to bring about stabilized practice. It may even be that change from one to the other point of view reflects changing biases in the subcultures in which it takes root, rather than mirroring new, firmly established knowledge.

Research workers in the field of child personality are also parents and citizens. The contrasting regulatory and permissive views inevitably influence their thinking. Their attitudes expressed through this influence may serve to some extent as a guide for the research problems they choose to formulate and investigate. The relation is reciprocal; their research and clinical findings influence attitudes of the general public toward problems of socialization.

By and large, workers of a psychoanalytic orientation hold to a "permissive" point of view (although not to all of the excesses about their views which are attributed to them). They tend to stress the importance of the relationship of the child to his mother during his early years. If the relationship is satisfactory, it is believed that there is every likelihood that the child will develop similar satisfactory relationships in later life with other people. Conversely, if the relationship develops unsatisfactorily, it is considered likely that the child will become disturbed emotionally to a greater or lesser degree and that he may be confronted throughout his life by difficulties in personal relations.

Child specialists subscribing to the regulatory point of view are more heterogenous. It would seem that those who stress constitutional and biological factors tend to be in this group. In general members of this group tend to see the infant and child as more capable of self-regulation and more able to stand viscissitudes and come through unscathed than do representatives of the permissive point of view.

At Yale University School of Medicine, a research project has been organized to investigate the two rival positions. It is too early for their answers on the major issue to be definitive, but some relevant results have already been published (*15, 16, 17*). One study (*17*) adopted the hypothesis that either extreme rigidity (regulatoriness) or permissiveness would be associated with problem child behavior. Case records of 50 mothers and infants were chosen from their files for analysis. They were mostly families in which the infant's father was of the professional, managerial, white-collar occupations. Data from the case records concerning the child when he was one, two, and three years of age were reduced by rating scales to a statistically manipulative form. The children's behavior was rated in the areas of feeding, sleeping, toileting, and socialization. The ratings given each child were in terms of degree of problem behavior shown. Evidences of emotional maladjustment in the child in areas other than these four were also sought from the records. The mother's behavior was defined as to degree of rigidity-permissiveness in her dealings with the child. Either extreme on the scale of maternal behavior was taken to represent deviant handling. Those falling in the middle area of the rating scales were considered as representing optimal and flexible handling. Reliable ratings in terms of interrater agreement were found.

In their first analysis of results, they found that comparing the rigid against the overpermissive parents showed there to be non-significant differences in the problem behavior of their children. Thus, the question of whether regulatory or permissive parental behavior is superior in avoiding problem behavior in children, so far as this study is concerned, is answered that extremes of either is equally pernicious.

For final analysis of results they divided the mothers into optimal and deviant (rigid and overpermissive being classed together). To quote their own words on the results:

> The following statistically significant relationships were found: within the first year, deviant maternal practices in sleep were associated with problem behavior in the child, though no relationships were found between practices and behavior in the areas of feeding, toileting, and socialization. In the second and third years, significant relationships

were found between deviant maternal practices and problem behavior in the child in all four areas. Deviant adjustment to the maternal role was found to be related to deviant practices in sleep and socialization during all three years. Similarly, children showing other evidences of emotional maladjustment were found to have a significantly higher proportion of sleep and socialization problems (17, 93).[5]

Evidently, optimal practice, as distinguished from either extremes of rigidity or overpermissiveness, makes for less problem behavior in infants and young children. Important though this finding may be, it still leaves unanswered the question as to the relative superiority of the regulatory or of the permissive points of view. The results do suggest that an extreme position of regulation expressed in rigidity and an extreme position of permissiveness expressed in overpermissiveness are both to be avoided in the interest of the child's adjustment.

Social class differences in socialization practices. In contemporary thinking concerning our own culture, three divisions of social class are generally accepted—upper, middle, and lower—with each of these three subdivided into an upper and lower group, thus making six groups. Acceptance of the concept of social class when approached scientifically is not a form of snobbery. It is rather a recognition that people live, think, work, and play in different ways. One of the forms of differences among social classes which has been seen as worthy of investigation is the possibility of differences in parent-child practices at these social class levels. Presumably the effects of differential socialization on child behavior and development may be, at least in part, mediated through the different child-rearing practices in different social classes.

A representative report (7) investigating class differences involved interviewing 100 mothers who were almost equally divided between lower- and middle-class groups. The interviews concerned practices of weaning, thumb sucking, cleanliness training, environmental exploration, and the age and sex roles the children were expected to play. Middle-class families were generally found to be more exacting in their expectations. Training was begun earlier, more emphasis was placed on responsibility, and closer supervision was observed in the middle-class families. In these families, fewer children were breast fed, and when breast feeding did occur, it was carried on for a shorter time. Three times as many middle-class children as lower-

---

[5] From Klatskin *et al.* (17). Copyright 1956 by the American Orthopsychiatric Association, and published with permission.

class children were reported by their mothers to be thumb suckers. Bowel and bladder control were begun earlier in the middle-class families, although the children did not achieve control any earlier. This study which indicates more rigid child care practices in middle-class groups was conducted before the permissive point of view became as prevalent as it is today.

In a study conducted in 1951 and 1952, Maccoby and Gibbs (22) reported that middle-class parents are more permissive than lower-class parents, thus disagreeing with the earlier studies. Sears and his associates (28), in a more detailed examination of the data used by Maccoby and Gibbs, demonstrate that the middle-class mothers were gentler than the working-class ones. They were more permissive in toilet training, in allowing dependency, in sex training, toward aggressiveness, and seemed to impose fewer restrictions and demands on their children. Only in infant feeding was there no significant difference in the direction of greater permissiveness on the part of the middle-class group. It may be that their results reflect an increasing change toward permissiveness over the years. Or it may be the "lower-class" group that they studied were not as far down the socio-economic scale as the samples in earlier researches. They had used a somewhat different way of classifying their subjects and may have included in their "lower" group a considerable number which earlier investigators would have placed in the middle group. Moreover, Maccoby and her associates themselves raise the question concerning the upper middle-class mothers they interviewed as to whether or not they were telling what they actually do or what they believed would be the appropriate thing to say. With recognition on their part that considerable professional opinion seems to be inclined in the permissive direction, this might have been the socially acceptable way to state their answers. Hence, they might have seemed more permissive than they actually were. The working-class group, who were also the less well-educated group, might have been less exposed to these newer opinions about permissiveness and hence not as subject to such slanting of their opinions.

The evidence in these matters could be further extended by a considerable number of studies. It probably would be fruitless to do so. At present no clear-cut or definitive conclusion concerning the relatively greater permissiveness of lower- or middle-class groups would appear to be possible. It may be that no such differences will be established. There is, however, general agreement that there is heterogeneity and individuality within all social classes. Havighurst (12), who has devoted considerable research effort to this topic, indicates that he finds "middle-class" and "lower-class" personalities in the same families, irrespective of their social stations. Whether this way of conceptualizing the problem in terms of types should be accepted even in the tentative way he advances it is problematical. His presentation does serve to call forcefully to our attention that individuality still exists within social classes.

Differences in degree of permissiveness are capable of modification by training. In a New Haven hospital a study (15) was conducted using prospective mothers drawn from various social classes. These mothers participated in an elaborate teaching program which stressed leniency and flexibility. One year after exposure to the program, the participating families were studied as to their practices in regard to feeding, toilet training, strictness of regime, and the degree of the father's participation in the care of the child. On the whole, there was a shift in the direction of greater leniency in *all* classes although with different degrees of leniency. When related to social class (upper-middle, lower-middle, and upper-lower) differences in the direction of earlier date of beginning of toilet training and in greater strictness of regime were found in the lower-class families. However, significant differences were not found among the social class samples in duration of breast feeding, leniency, in the feeding practices, or the extent of father's participation. The results indicate that parent-child care practices *are* capable of modification and also that education may result in a reduction in so-called social class differences.

Familial and Individual Differences in Socialization Practices

Parents try to develop certain forms of behavior in their child. They draw upon general attitudes of permissiveness or regulativeness which they express in their individual way. They also draw upon their heritage of social class behavior in their individual fashion. But differences aside from those created by their philosophy of child care and their social class are present in familial and individual differences.

Whether the arrival of the baby is, in general, satisfying or frustrating depends upon (1) the personality of the parents; and (2) the personality of the child.

(1) To the parent the child may be frustrating or satisfying according to his or her own particular makeup. If the mother receives

satisfaction from gratifying the needs of the helpless (nurturance), then motherhood serves as a satisfying outlet. If she is a dominating person, her relationship to her child may be rewarding. If she needs to have a feeling of belonging, then the addition of the child to her family may serve to gratify this feeling. But, on the other hand, if she requires an orderly scheduled environment, or a great number of social contacts, or a freedom from responsibility, then a baby might be seen as a nuisance or as a restriction. Another even more pervasive factor in determining how she views motherhood is her concept of the role and significance of motherhood. A mother may place a high value upon motherhood, feeling that it is a fulfillment of her personality; another mother may place a low valuation upon it, seeing motherhood as a series of monotonous routines.

(2) The characteristics of the child contribute to determining parental reactions. His physical appearance, whether pleasing or displeasing, is one such characteristic. His development, whether advanced or retarded, may be another. But often the particular characteristic is not, in itself, decisive in how he is received in the family. Any one characteristic may be pleasing or displeasing according to its reception by the parents. To some parents an active child would be a joy; others, he would drive to distraction. Similarly, mischievousness or obedience may be reacted to differently, sometimes serving as endearing characteristics, sometimes as repelling ones. In any case, personal characteristics of the infant help to determine the parents' attitudes. Chronologically, the parents' personality comes first and starts the sequence of interactive behavior. But once the infant is perceived by them, no matter the nature of their perception, he becomes a stimulus to them and influences their behavior toward him. The relationship is circular, the cause-effect relation reciprocal.

Parent behavior, moreover, is not fixed and unchanging, even within a specific family. Not only may parents vary in their responses toward different children, they will also vary with respect to their handling of the same child. Nowlis (25), for example, found some mothers who were highly punitive in regard to property destruction, but quite the opposite regarding sibling aggression. Some attention to such variations must be paid in the discussion of socialization. Within this welter of differences—societal, social class, familial and individual—we must search for the regularities of personality as they relate to them and interact with them. Since our interest is primarily in the personality of the child that emerges from the process of socialization it is appropriate now to turn more directly to the question of personality of the child.

Culture, socialization, and personality

Socialization is the mechanism of cultural transmission. These man-made patterns of behavior which we call culture are conveyed to the young through socialization. In this sense, culture is a precipitate of the history of the group which is kept alive by transmittal to the next generation. In even more abstract terms, culture is a logical construct used by anthropologists and other social scientists to refer to, in the words of Kluckhohn, "a network of abstracted patterns generalized . . . to represent the regularities distinctive of the group in question" (18, 942).[6] It is in this sense that we can speak of a given culture such as the Trobriand, Samoan, or American.

Aspects of the culture become part of the child. One of the figures of speech of Park, the sociologist, is apt. Man is like an oyster, he built a shell which has become a significant part of him. Man, too, builds his culture which is a part of him. According to Kluckhohn (18), this introduces a second meaning to the term culture, namely, culture as norms of behavior internalized by the individual. Since we focus on the individual, our greatest emphasis is upon this latter meaning rather than on culture as the knowledge we transmit to the next generation.

No one individual bears the impress of all aspects of his culture In socialization he internalizes certain aspects only. Moreover, he is the product of specific situations in which this internalization takes place—particular parents, teachers, and peers. Inevitably he shows individuality in his behavior. At every stage of development the individual selects from among the socialization variables available to him. He is not passively molded by the processes and agents of socialization. Instead, he chooses according to his past experience and his constitutional background. What emerges from these interactions is his personality—his own unique pattern of tendencies supplied by constitution and culture but modified by the particular situations and adventitious circumstances of his experience. In this

[6] From Lindzey (18). *Handbook of social psychology*, 1954. Addison-Wesley, Reading, Mass.

process the personality itself meets the new situation as a dynamic organization which in turn modifies his particular way of reacting to that new situation.

The definition of personality offered by G. W. Allport is considered to be in the spirit of the point of view just advanced. He defines personality as "the dynamic organization within the individual of those psychophysical systems that determine his unique adjustments to his environment" (1, 48).[7] This definition stresses the uniqueness and dynamic character of personality organization previously indicated as imperative.

We need, however, an inclusive term for the "psychophysical" systems that determine his "adjustments." We follow White (29) in using *tendencies* as this generic term. By tendencies we mean traits, habits, dispositions, drives, needs, interests, attitudes, and related psychological terms. Psychological science has not yet reached a stage of development which permits us to give precise meanings to these terms, much less allowing us to state unequivocally relations with one another. In this setting a *personal pattern of tendencies* is a convenient shorthand way of referring to this aspect of personality.

The needs of the organism and person are one important category of tendencies. Needs are basic tendencies irrespective of whether they are conscious or not. To be sure, their conscious aspects will receive considerable attention, but awareness is not essential for such forms of basic tendencies to operate. Certain basic needs such as temperature regulation or oxygen needs are recognized for what they are when something interferes with their smooth-running functioning. Lest there be confusion it is well to emphasize that the term, tendency, is broader than drive or need. It has the advantage of referring not only to the drive itself but also the associated behavior organized around it.

One important consideration in the selection of the various tendencies for discussion has been the availability of research evidence. Research as a means of advancing knowledge always shows a ragged edge in its advance guard. Certain areas later found to be important may, at any one moment, be relatively neglected. Important personality tendencies may have been neglected by us to the extent that this criterion of available research was applied as a basis for inclusion.

Certain tendencies are emphasized in the account to follow. Since feeding and toilet training are so important, oral and anal tendencies are made central to the discussion of psychosocial development in infancy. Dependence-independence and aggressive and sexual tendencies also are expressed in infancy and in later periods and consequently merit attention.

The Self and Personality

The personality when subjectively viewed is referred to as the *ego* or *self*. These terms will be used interchangeably, except in a setting such as in psychoanalytic theory where one term is preferred or used in a special sense.

The concept of self, as Allport (2) has indicated, although central to the study of personality has been neglected in recent years. This neglect stems mainly from the difficulty of coming to grips experimentally with the phenomena subsumed by this concept. But as Allport says, "The existence of one's own self is the one fact of which every mortal person—every psychologist included—is perfectly convinced" (2, 451).[8] It follows that such an important problem as the beginnings of self in infancy and its development in childhood cannot be ignored merely because of an embarrassing lack of evidence. The task which is being set is the delicate one of dealing with a topic on which there is little or no definitive research. Much of what is written about this topic in the chapters to follow is highly speculative.

The terms self and ego both are used in two distinct senses by different specialists. First, there is the self-as-object, which refers to the person's attitudes and feelings about himself. In this sense, a self is what a person thinks of himself. This is first expressed in the issue of self-awareness. Although awareness is a unitary thing simultaneously involving the "I" and, "not I," it is convenient to distinguish self-awareness from awareness of others, that is, social awareness. Not only are we individuals, we feel ourselves separate from others as well. Hence, self and social awareness are but two sides to a shield. Self-awareness and social awareness are a unity which for matters of stress we may separate. Thus, in addition to personal awareness, there is social awareness—the attitude the individual holds about the world and by which he interprets it. Second, there is the self-as-executor, the self as engaged in thinking, remembering, and perceiving. Here the self is the doer.

[8] From Allport (2). Copyright 1943 by the American Psychological Association, and published with permission.

Approaches to Personality

A great variety of approaches to personality are extant. From time to time men from the fields of psychology, psychiatry, anthropology, and sociology have attempted to bring together knowledge of their own and related fields in an attempt to give an integrated psychological perspective on personality. An adequate theory of personality gives attention both to the structure and to the development of personality. The former aspect of personality has to do with the organization of the personality, how it is put together, as it were. The units or patterns in the pattern used vary from theory to theory, but there are always present certain elements of structure. The second aspect of personality has to do with how the individual develops, the processes by which the infant becomes the man. Thus, the vicissitudes of the individual's journey in time occupies the personality theorist as well as the cross-sectional view of his personality at a given point in time.

Some of the more prominent views of personality are orthodox psychoanalysis, neo-Freudian modifications of psychoanalysis, trait theories, organismic theories, field theories, and type theories. Each of these approaches to personality has its proponents and adherents. Each quite possibly has its modicum of truth and each is in some measure relevant to child psychology. Certain views, however, either have had more profound effect upon child psychology or are potentially of considerable importance. Most prominent are psychoanalysis, neo-Freudian derivatives of psychoanalysis, and behavior-social learning theory.

Many psychoanalytic statements, particularly in the classic or orthodox formulation, make no clear distinction between maturation and socialization as a matter of learning. Psychoanalysis, although it does not formulate the problem in this fashion, has contributed a considerable number of specific hypotheses about how socialization influences personality. But these formulations, in turn, suggested to others, especially the so-called neo-Freudians and the anthropologists and sociologists, related ways of viewing socialization. A reconciliation among and integration of psychoanalytic and socialization and behavioral concepts would appear to be quite a fruitful approach to the personality of the child. Before proceeding further, it is necessary to examine in some detail behavior-social learning theory and psychoanalysis. The remainder of this chapter is concerned with learning theory, while the next chapter is devoted to psychoanalysis.

Behavior-social learning theory

A theory of learning is an attempt to account for the acquisition and retention of new forms of behavior and of the extinction of these or other forms of behavior. In learning there is a tendency for some responses to occur with increasing frequency, strength, or efficiency with repeated experience in a situation, while there is a tendency for other responses to drop out. There are various points of view held by responsible and respected investigators about the nature of the process taking place in learning.

The point of view most fully developed and most directly capable of being related to the present concern with socialization of the child is a derivative of Hull's reinforcement theory, referred to as behavior-social learning theory. This particular point of view will be utilized whenever an account of the dynamics of learning is necessary. Both conditioning, from which Hull derived his point of view, and behavior-social learning theory, as conceived by Dollard and Miller (6, 24), have been described in historical context in Chapter 1. It appears to be desirable to offer a succinct statement of the various facets of learning which are essential aspects of the theory. Fortunately, some prior acquaintance with the psychology of learning may be assumed on the part of readers and only the bare essentials of the theory need to be indicated here. Application of this theoretical position to specific problems will be left for later chapters.

Fundamental Factors

Dollard and Miller (6) make four factors fundamental to their presentation of learning. These factors are drive (motivation), responses (act or thought), cue (stimulus), and reinforcement (reward). All of these factors are interrelated, but it will be found that reinforcement is made central in their conceptualization of learning. Consequently, before examining the interrelationship of the four factors, some preliminary approximation of the meaning of reinforcement is appropriate. As Dollard and Miller (6) indicate, reinforcement is any event following a response which strengthens the tendency for a response to be repeated. Reward is a synonym for the same factor, although, for various reasons unnecessary to go into, reinforcement is the preferred term.

An experiment by Dorothy Marquis (*23*) may be used to illustrate these factors. She was interested in whether or not infants could learn immediately after birth. Eight infants were studied over a period of time extending from their first to the tenth day of life. Hunger was used as the *drive*. Ringing of a buzzer was the *cue*. Amount of activity was the *response*. Receiving the bottle was the *reinforcement*. These were interrelated in the following fashion. Each infant at his feeding time was placed in a stabilimeter (an apparatus for measuring amount of bodily activity described on page 172) and observed for other forms of behavior. After the lapse of a few minutes to establish a base line, the experimenter sounded a buzzer for five seconds. Immediately afterward the bottle was inserted in the infant's mouth. After a period of three to six days, seven of the eight infants began to show changes of behavior on the sounding of the buzzer. A given infant would differ in some respect from the others, but, in general, he would now show, after the buzzer sounded, an increase in mouth opening, sucking movements, and a decrease in bodily movements. It will be noted that these are reactions which accompany food-taking, but that they occurred *before* food-taking.

To summarize in terms of the four factors, with hunger serving as the *drive,* the *cue* of the buzzer now brought forth *responses* of sucking, mouth opening, and cessation of movement, with the *reinforcement* of food-taking occurring after these responses. That the drive factor is important may be illustrated by what happened to the eighth infant who did *not* show these responses. This infant had the cue of the buzzer and the reinforcement of the bottle, but "he never seemed hungry" (*23*, 483).[9] In other words, the absence of *drive* accounts for the failure of the responses to occur. The absence of learning when *reinforcement* is not given is shown by her control group. They received identical treatment to that given the experimental group except they were not fed at the sound of the buzzer. In these infants learning did not take place. If an infant who was deaf had been used, he would not have learned because the *cue* of the buzzer would have been missing. In all three instances above the responses were not given, so nothing would have been learned. We are now in a position to examine each of these factors, one by one, as Dollard and Miller (*6, 24*) conceived them.

[9] From Marquis (*23*). Copyright 1931 by the Journal Press, and published with permission.

Drive. Drives are any strong stimuli which impel to action. Certain drives are not dependent for their appearance upon learning and consequently are primary or innate drives. In Chapter 6 the primary drives or needs of the newborn infant will be classified as hunger and thirst, sleep, elimination, sex, temperature regulation, and need for oxygen. There are, then, strong stimuli which we cannot ignore; they are those to which we must act. The utilization of certain drives and no others, however, is not in any sense fixed or immutable and the theory does not demand that only certain specified primary drives be considered. Dollard and Miller in addition to discussing several of the aforementioned drives also speak of pain and fatigue as primary drives. Primary drives are those which are unlearned and consequently do not require the presence of reinforcement.

Cue. A drive, by definition, must be responded to. But when and where the individual responds and which particular response he will make are due to the cues to which he is exposed. Just as a cue to an actor is a signal for his lines, a cue is a stimulus which guides the response of the individual. Simple illustrations of cues are the class bell, the stop sign, and the instructions, "Go ahead." Each in his own way helps to determine when and where the individual responds. If cues are obscure or absent, if these "guide posts" are not present, learning becomes more difficult or impossible.

Response. Before a particular response can be linked to a given cue, the response must occur. That is, before a response can be reinforced (rewarded) and learned, the response has to occur. The production of appropriate responses becomes a crucial stage in the individual's learning. In any given situation which the individual has not encountered before, a number of so-called trial and error responses are likely to occur. Owing to innate factors or to past learning in similar situations, certain responses are more likely to occur than others, while certain other responses are less likely to occur. Their order of probability of occurrence is called the initial hierarchy of responses. The most likely response to occur, the dominant response, as it is called, is the strongest response. If this response, once given, is *not successful,* that is, not reinforced, then the next most dominant occurs, and so on.

If learning is to occur, the correct response must ultimately be made and be followed by reinforcement. This reinforcement makes the response more likely to occur earlier the next trial, until eventually, the correct response is the first one made. Thus, this learning changes the probability of occurrence of the initial hierarchy of responses, yielding what is called the resultant hierarchy of responses. This is because a certain response is reinforced, making it more likely to appear, that is, it shifts its position from that which it had in the initial hierarchy of responses. The reinforced response, initially weaker, now occupies the dominant position. Operationally, this is shown by decrease in the number of responses from learning trial to learning trial which do not result in reinforcement. Thus, if 16 errors are made on the first trial before the reinforced response is made, this position of being the seventeenth response was expressive of the position in the initial hierarchy of the response followed by reinforcement. After, say, ten trials, the reinforced response is given first, showing a shift in the hierarchy of responses of this response to a position of primacy in the resultant hierarchy.

The correct response, it will be noted, occurred *before* it was rewarded. It was made before it was reinforced. What, then, is new in the learning? It was that the response in question occurs when a specific cue is present, whereas its previous occurrence in this situation may have been very infrequent. The product of learning, then, in this context, is a connection between a cue and a response.

Although it is something of a digression from the main theme of relating factors of learning to one another, for the sake of economy of space, it is desirable to relate at this point cues to generalization phenomena. As is well known, the effects of learning in one situation transfer to other situations. This is called generalization. An illustration given in the first chapter was Albert's fear of white, furry objects. After fear responses had been conditioned to the white rat, fear could now be elicited by a white piece of fur or white rabbit, despite the fact that he had not feared them before nor was any reason known why he should. To state it more precisely in the present theoretical context, reinforcement for making a specific response to a given set of cues strengthens the tendency not only for the response in question, but also for other *similar* patterns of cues to elicit these same responses.

One of the central areas of research efforts concerning generalization is that of the shape of the gradient of generalization. By a gradient of generalization is meant the change in the strength of the response as the test stimulus changes. As one makes the stimulus less and less similar to the conditioned stimulus, there is often found to be a weakening of the strength of the response as similarity decreased. The less the stimulus is similar to the original stimulus, the weaker the response. Or to state it again in terms of cues, the less similar the cue, the less the generalization. Thus, in research described in some detail in Chapter 10, it was found that children punished for being aggressive in the home were also inhibited from being aggressive in the school setting, which is very similar to the home. However, the less similar cues of doll play were sufficiently dissimilar for the same children to release aggression.

There are a number of ways in which the responses to be connected to a given cue as a new habit may first be elicited. In other words, there are different ways of producing responses likely to be reinforced. To name some of the ways mentioned by Dollard and Miller, there is conditioning, trial and error, insight, and imitation. In view of our previous acquaintance with conditioning, conditioning itself will not be discussed in any detail. It is important to point out that in classical conditioning the presence of the unconditioned stimulus (the food or noxious stimulus) insures that the response to be learned will be made. Learning in this instance consists of "connecting" the old responses to a new stimulus, the conditioned stimulus. The presence of the unconditioned stimulus insures that the subject will be reinforced independent of what he does. In all other ways of producing responses there is no guarantee that the correct response will occur. Obtaining a reinforcement is dependent upon the occurrence of the correct response. These other ways of producing responses likely to be reinforced merit a brief review.

In trial and error learning the drive elicits one response after another in an order decided by the initial hierarchy of responses. If a response is nonrewarded, it is extinguished and the next response in the hierarchy occurs. When the desired response takes place, it is rewarded and the learning begins to be established. This process is generally a gradual one.

Insight learning in this perspective becomes learning in which a relationship is perceived, which leads whenever this occurs almost immediately to a solution. Instead of there being gradual improvement, there is a solution because the individual held a verbal hypothesis (or some other cue-producing response) and quick learning thereafter resulted. Sometimes there is little preliminary fumbling and the correct response is made quickly. But this need not be the case. Fumbling may be long or short. The essential feature is that, instead of gradual improvement, the preinsight period (which may be of any duration) gives little or no indication of progress toward the solution, but is followed by a rapid solution. Thereafter, the correct response tends to be made "full strength," as it were. To put it graphically, insight learning is "step-shaped." If the initial practice before might be compared to the floor, then insight is the riser (or vertical part) of the step, with the step itself representing the level of learning thereafter. It would seem that the function of ". . . insight seems to be to produce a response which might otherwise not be made. If this response is rewarded, it will be learned as the response to that situation. If the insight is not rewarded, it will be abandoned" (6, 38).[10] Insight learning differs from trial and error learning in that in an extreme case the correct response is the dominant one in the hierarchy of responses to the unconditioned stimulus. This causes the individual to make the correct response.

Imitation is a way of learning in which similar acts are brought about in two (or more) people and connected to appropriate cues. According to Miller and Dollard (24), imitation appears in two forms—copying and matched dependent behavior. Copying is deliberate in the sense that the copier tries to bring his response to approximate that of a model. Learning to write by copying from the blackboard would be an illustration. In matched-dependent behavior the follower is not directly aware of the cues present in the environment, but is dependent upon the leader for signals as to which act is to be performed and where and when it is to occur. He need not be aware he is imitating, as in a crowd moved by its leader or leaders. Naturally, both copying and matched-dependent forms of imitation required conditions favorable to learning, that is, the operative presence of the factors of drive, response, cue, and reinforcement.

These different ways of producing responses have in common that they are different ways of producing responses likely to be rewarded. These responses when they occur follow the same fundamental laws of trial and error learning which result either in rejection or selection on the basis of reinforcement or nonreinforcement.

Reinforcement. When a response has occurred, what happens thereafter depends upon whether or not it is rewarded or reinforced. It is important to note in this connection that repetition does not always strengthen the tendency for a response to reoccur. When a "mistake" is made in connection with learning something, say a maze pathway, the tendency to repeat a blind alley entry is weakened. As mentioned before, this weakening of a response is called extinction.

[10] By permission from *Personality and psychotherapy* by Dollard and Miller. Copyright 1950. McGraw-Hill Book Company, Inc.

But when the action results in a correct response, the tendency of the subject to repeat the response is strengthened. Any event following the response which strengthens the tendency for a response to be repeated is called reinforcement.

The drive is maintained until it is reinforced. This reinforcement may be expressed through reduction in the strength of a drive. For example, eating is a reinforcement of hunger which reduces the drive. As Dollard and Miller put it ". . . reduction in the strength of a strong drive stimulus acts as a reinforcement" (6, 40).[10]

An important question in child psychology is the presence of a great variety of needs and motives which appear in the child but with which he was not equipped during early infancy. For example, the young infant is not aggressive, nor in need of self-esteem, nor in love in the adult sense; nor is the infant fearful in situations which, later in life, seem to upset him emotionally and from which he strives to escape without apparent cause. From where do these needs and motives come?

In learning behavior-theory, these derived needs or motives are said to arise from several sources. In some instances, these learned motivational states are aroused by originally neutral situations which have been consistently experienced in conjunction with a primary need state. For example, a young child who is ill may be taken on a number of occasions to a doctor's office for rather painful medical treatment. Pain, of course, is a primary motivational state which the child attempts to reduce by escaping. After a number of such visits, the child may begin to cry, show other evidences of being emotionally upset, and endeavor to get away merely at the sight of the doctor or his office. The capacity of such previously neutral stimuli to arouse needs, after repeated pairings with primary needs, seems to occur most frequently, as in our example, when the primary motive is evoked by some unpleasant kind of stimulation.

Still other secondary needs arise from secondary reinforcement. However, it is first necessary to explain secondary reinforcement before dealing with derived needs based on them. A crying infant who is hungry or wet may cease to cry, at least temporarily, at the sight of his mother. His mother has consistently been associated with a primary reward, for example, being fed or changed, and has as a result taken on the properties of a secondary reinforcement. Thus, derived or secondary reinforcement is the partial reduction in a need occurring upon the presentation of a stimulus which has previously been associated with the specific stimulus that reduces the need more directly.   Often, but not always, we learn to "need" these secondary reinforcers for themselves and in the absence of any primary rewards. Thus, the child comes to seek out his mother's company, even in the absence of hunger, pain, or the like.   Many needs are said to come into existence in this way: through persistent conjunction with objects that reduce primary needs (primary reinforcers); previously neutral objects or events themselves take on reinforcing properties.   In many instances, we begin to strive for these secondary reinforcers for their own sake and hence are said to have learned to have a need for them.

If a response is not reinforced (rewarded), thus not reducing the drive, this response tends to drop out.   If, instead, the response is reinforced and the drive reduced, the connection between the stimulus pattern and this response is strengthened.   Consequently, the next time this same drive and the other cues are present this particular reinforced response is more likely to occur.

The emphasis in this account has been upon the *process* of development.   Some attention is nevertheless given in behavior-social learning theory to the *structure* of the personality.

The Structure of Personality

When we consider the structural elements of the personality, we are referring to the nature of its relatively stable unchanging aspects. The structural elements are the characteristics which endure, to some extent, with the passage of time.   In a sense, when viewing the personality structurally we are taking a cross-sectional view of the personality.   In behavior-social learning theory, habit is the basic unit in the structure of personality (6).   Consequently, we must relate habit to the previous discussion of the process of development.   This can be done through the definition of habit.   Habit is a stable stimulus-response connection.   Much of our behavior is made up of simple automatic habits in which we respond directly to cues and internal drives without taking thought.   This is one level of learned behavior habits.

There is another level of learned behavior in the higher mental processes in which instead of responding immediately and automatically we take time to think.   In other words, instead of being guided by a cue or cue situation, they are mediated by internal processes though still based on habits.   In thinking, cue-producing responses are important.   Cue-producing responses are those whose main function is to lead or mediate for still other responses.   Their nature may be made clearer if a distinction is made between these cue-producing responses and those which are referred to as instrumental responses. Instrumental responses are those which have some immediate effect on the environment. Responses which have this instrumental character include opening the mouth, closing the door, jumping the puddle, and so on. They change one's relationship to the external environment directly and immediately. They do not serve to produce a cue that is a part of a pattern leading to another response as do cue-producing responses. Cue-producing responses obviously include language although it may or may not necessarily be spoken language. Cues of this sort allow labeling and other processes of reasoning. In addition to habits and higher mental processes, response hierarchies making one cue response more available than another also contribute to the structure of personality.

Relation of Learning Theory to Other Hypotheses

Behavior-social learning theory is related to various other hypotheses used in this book. It is, therefore, appropriate to examine the relation of behavior-social learning theory to socialization, to frustration-aggression, and to the critical period hypothesis. Its relation to each of these hypotheses will be considered in turn.

Socialization. Socialization as a field of study arose from work in social anthropology and psychoanalysis (4). The position is taken here that socialization may be fruitfully related to behavior theory. Socialization has been influenced by and is capable of being reconciled with behavior-social learning theory. The same intellectual climate and locus for behavior-social learning theory gave us the contributions of Irvin L. Child and J. W. M. Whiting on the process of socialization. Socialization centers on the question of how the infant and child becomes an adult in his own society. Socialization involves the conditions of learning which exist for the child. Learning theory provides us with the principles of learning; socialization provides us with an important facet of the conditions of learning.

That Dollard and Miller relate their analyses of learning to the structure of the social environment, although without relating it to the socialization hypothesis, is brought out in the following quotation:

> No psychologist would venture to predict the behavior of a rat without knowing on what arm of a T-maze the food or the shock is placed. It is no easier to predict the behavior of a human being without knowing

the conditions of his "maze," that is, the structure of his social environment. Culture, as conceived by social scientists, is a statement of the design of the human maze, of the type of reward involved, and of what responses are to be rewarded. It is in this sense a recipe for learning. This contention is easily accepted when widely variant societies are compared. But even within the same society, the mazes which are run by two individuals may seem the same but actually be quite different. . . . No personality analysis of . . . people can be accurate which does not take into account these cultural differences, that is, differences in the types of responses which have been rewarded (24, 5–6).[11]

Stated in learning theory terms, socialization provides us with a way of understanding the types of responses which have been reinforced.

The frustration-aggression hypothesis. A hypothesis frequently utilized by behavior-social learning theorists is the frustration-aggression hypothesis. The frustration-aggression hypothesis has received considerable attention in connection with both child and adult behavior. Frustration and its consequences are to be analyzed in the account to follow in terms of their stimulus-response consequences. In brief, the hypothesis states that frustration instigates aggression. Frustration itself arises from interference with a goal response. Aggression, of course, is not an invariable consequence of frustration. Anticipation of punishment may inhibit aggression, even according to those workers who have placed the most emphasis on frustration leading to aggression (5). Many other reactions to frustration can be mentioned. These include dependency, fear, guilt, anxiety, lowering of performance level, removing oneself from the scene of frustration, or "goes out of the field" to use Lewin's (20, 90) [12] phrase, or increased effort to mention but a few.

Differential responses to frustration are to be attributed to differing situational or personal-individual circumstances. For example, Whiting (30) found that children of a particular age responded to frustration by younger children with aggression but responded to frustration by older children with fear or avoidance. Other situational or individual circumstances would explain differential responses to frustration. Nevertheless, despite exceptions, in many instances frustration does produce aggression. In the following account, aggression will

[11] From Miller and Dollard (24). Copyright 1941 by the Yale University Press, and published with permission.

[12] By permission from *A Dynamic Theory of Personality*, by Lewin. Copyright 1935. McGraw-Hill Book Company, Inc.

be treated as a behavior tendency which is evoked by frustration. Research evidence bearing on this topic will be offered in later chapters.

The critical period hypothesis. The critical period hypothesis has already been described. Relatively little use has been made of this hypothesis in behavior-social learning theory. Dollard and Miller (6, 24) do speak of four critical training situations in a way not incompatible with the hypothesis. These problems are feeding, cleanliness training, sex training, and the treatment of anger in the child. Since they speak of them as having long-lasting effects on the individual, they would seem to be expressing the problem in a fashion compatible with the critical period hypothesis. In child psychology we are very much concerned with development over time, and the critical period hypothesis supplies us with a further determination of the conditions of learning—the condition presented to the child at a given temporal point in his development. To put it in bold outline, the critical period hypothesis allows us to specify the reinforcements crucial to healthy individual development at a particular stage of growth. Consequently, the critical period hypothesis is considered to be a valuable adjunct to behavior-social learning theory.

Summary

The fact that the infant becomes a person with his own unique characteristics while sharing with other persons certain common characteristics necessitates our examination of socialization and personality.

Socialization is the term applied to the process whereby the children in a given society are encouraged or discouraged from certain activities by their parents (or other agents) because these older members conceive these activities as reflecting or not reflecting that society's values. In short, socialization is the process by which children by the time they are adults learn to share in varying degrees the values of their society. In shaping this process, constitutional factors, although present, are so poorly understood as to be capable only of illustration. Learning the process is consequently emphasized. Evidence that socialization practices differ from society to society is then adduced, as is evidence concerning class differences within our own society and differences within familial settings. In extra-, intra-society, and familial settings the dimension of permissive (indulgent)-regulatory (severe) seems to be one which includes within its scope a considerable portion of the phenomena covered under the heading of socialization practices.

In a different perspective, socialization becomes the mechanism of cultural transmission. The child internalizes aspects of his culture. From the specific situations he faces and from the broader cultural forces that are operative, there emerges the infant's personality—his own unique patterns of tendencies. These tendencies, traits, habits, drives, needs, interests, and attitudes embrace those dynamic pressures to action which all human beings share, though with wide differences based on cultural expectancies prevailing at that particular time and in that particular place. Although basic needs, such as temperature regulation and oxygen, are not neglected, selected for special emphasis are certain tendencies—oral, anal, dependence-independence, aggressive, and sexual tendencies.

Personality has a subjective aspect, the self, which also merits attention. Just as there is an emerging awareness of self as a person, there is a social awareness of other persons. The self is conceived as intimately intertwined with its social aspect. Self-awareness and social awareness are aspects of a unity, which for heuristic purposes we may separate.

In an attempt at an integrated view of the structure and development of personality, various approaches have been advanced. Behavior-social learning theory is presented in detail because, along with psychoanalysis considered in the next chapter, it is considered to be a fruitful approach to the personality of the child.

Behavior-social learning as a process of the development of the personality rests upon four fundamental factors: drive, responses, cue, and reinforcement. All are essential for learning to occur, but reinforcement is made central. The reinforcement is any event following the response which strengthens the tendency for the response to be repeated. Derived needs are learned on the basis of the pattern of factors operative. In addition to the development of personality, the structure of personality receives attention. Habit is the basic unit, but there are other levels of learned behavior in the higher mental processes and in response hierarchies.

For Further Reading

In their book, *Personality and Psychotherapy* (New York: McGraw-Hill, 1950), John Dollard and Neal E. Miller give a clear and concise statement of what has been called behavior-social learning theory. The chapter by Irvin L. Child on "Socialization" in the book, edited by Gardner Lindzey, *Handbook of Social Psychology* (Cambridge, Mass.: Addison-Wesley, 1954) is recommended as a systematic account of this topic.

References

1. Allport, G. W. *Personality: a psychological interpretation.* New York: Holt, 1937.
2. Allport, G. W. The ego in contemporary psychology. *Psychol. Rev.,* 1943, 50, 451–478.
3. Bishop, Barbara M. Mother-child interaction and the social behavior of children. *Psychol. Monogr.,* 1951, 65, No. 328.
4. Child, I. L. Socialization. In G. Lindzey (Ed.), *Handbook of social psychology.* Cambridge, Mass.: Addison-Wesley, 1954, 655–692.
5. Dollard, J., Doob, L. W. *et al. Frustration and aggression.* New Haven, Conn.: Yale University Press, 1939.
6. Dollard, J., and Miller, N. E. *Personality and psychotherapy: an analysis of learning, thinking, and culture.* New York: McGraw-Hill, 1950.
7. Ericson, Martha C. Child-rearing and social status. *Amer. J. Sociol.,* 1946, 52, 190–192.
8. Escalona, Sibylle. A commentary upon some recent changes in child-rearing practices. *Child Develpm.,* 1949, 20, 157–162.
9. Frank, L. K. Culture control and physiological autonomy. In C. Kluckhohn and H. A. Murray (Eds.), *Personality in nature, society and culture.* New York: Knopf, 1948, 119–122.
10. Gesell, A., and Ilg, Frances L. *Infant and child in the culture of today.* New York: Harper, 1943.
11. Goldfrank, Esther. Socialization, personality, and the structure of pueblo society. In D. G. Haring (Ed.), *Personal character and cultural milieu: a collection of readings,* (Rev. ed.). Syracuse, New York: Syracuse University Press, 1949, 247–269.
12. Havighurst, R. J. Social class and basic personality structure. *Sociol. soc. Res.,* 1952, 36, 355–363.
13. Henry, J. *Jungle people.* New York: Augustin, 1941.
14. Henry, J. Environment and symptom formation. *Amer. J. Orthopsychiat.,* 1947, 17, 628–632.
15. Klatskin, Ethelyn H. Shifts in child care practices in three social classes under an infant care program of flexible methodology. *Amer. J. Orthopsychiat.,* 1952, 22, 52–61.

16. Klatskin, Ethelyn H., and Jackson, Edith B.   Methodology of the Yale rooming-in project on parent-child relationship.   *Amer. J. Orthopsychiat.*, 1955, 25, 81–108.
17. Klatskin, Ethelyn H., Jackson, Edith B., and Wilkin, Louise C.   The influence of degree of flexibility in maternal child care practices on early child behavior. *Amer. J. Orthopsychiat.*, 1956, 26, 79–93.
18. Kluckhohn, C.   Culture and behavior.   In G. Lindzey (Ed.), *Handbook of social psychology.*   Cambridge, Mass.: Addison-Wesley, 1954, 921–976.
19. Kluckhohn, C., and Mowrer, O. H.   "Personality and culture: a conceptual scheme."   *Amer. Anthrop.*, 1944, 46, No. 1.
20. Lewin, K.   *A dynamic theory of personality.*   New York: McGraw-Hill, 1935.
21. Linton, R.   Marquesan personality.   In A. Kardiner, *The individual and his society.*   New York: Columbia University Press, 1939.
22. Maccoby, Eleanor E., and Gibbs, Patricia K.   Methods of child-rearing in two social classes.   In W. E. Martin and Celia B. Stendler (Eds.), *Readings in child development.*   New York: Harcourt, Brace, 1954, 380–396.
23. Marquis, Dorothy P.   Can conditioned responses be established in the newborn infant?   *J. genet. Psychol.*, 1931, 39, 479–492.
24. Miller, N. E., and Dollard, J.   *Social learning and imitation.*   New Haven, Conn.: Yale University Press, 1941.
25. Nowlis, V.   The search for significant concepts in a study of parent-child relationships.   *Amer. J. Orthopsychiat.*, 1952, 22, 286–299.
26. Radke, Marion J.   The relation of parental authority to children's behavior and attitudes.   *Univ. Minn. Child Welf. Monogr.*, 1946, No. 22.
27. Sears, R. R.   Personality development in the family.   In R. F. Winch and R. McGinnis (Eds.), *Selected studies on marriage and the family.*   New York: Holt, 1953, 215–240.
28. Sears, R. R., Maccoby, Eleanor E., and Levin, H.   *Patterns of child rearing.* Evanston, Ill.: Row, Peterson, 1957.
29. White, R. W.   *The abnormal personality.*   New York: Ronald, 1948.
30. Whiting, J. W. M.   *Becoming a Kwoma.*   New Haven, Conn.: Yale University Press, 1941.
31. Whiting, J. W. M., and Child, I. L.   *Child training and personality: a cross-cultural study.*   New Haven, Conn.: Yale University Press, 1953.

chapter 5

The Psychoanalytic Theory
of Personality Development

IN KEEPING WITH THE TOPIC OF CHILD PSYCHOLOGY, presentation of psychoanalytic theory will be made in a developmental framework. The development of personality according to the psychoanalytic approach will now be sketched. Biological determinants are first examined. Thereafter, the various stages of personality development, as the psychoanalyst views them, will be outlined starting with those of infancy, and then proceeding through childhood, adolescence, and adulthood.

Biological determinants

In using a developmental framework [1] in the presentation of psychoanalytic personality theory, it is appropriate to begin with the biological determinants. In the felicitous phrase of Blum, concern is

---

[1] In considerable measure this account of developmental stages leans heavily upon Blum (1), Fenichel (3), and Munroe (11). Their statements are considerably more detailed and complex and I may have misread the argument as they present it. Grateful acknowledgment is made, but the responsibility for the presentation is my own.

133

with the "neonate's personality potential" (*1*, 14).[2]   These potentials
for personality are those with which the human organism is equipped
at birth.

Infantile Sexuality

The cardinal assumption of psychoanalysis is that sexuality is the
basic human motive.   The orthodox psychoanalysts state that various
manifestations of infant and child behavior are of a sexual nature.
Oral activity of the infant, for example, is considered as qualitatively
continuous with adult sexuality through other intervening stages.
These pregenital stages are considered as the forerunners of adult
heterosexual behavior (the genital stage), with nearly as much sexual
energy employed as later when full psychosexual prowess emerges
with the physical changes of adolescence.   In sexuality is to be found
the biological determinant of personality.

Freud and his followers never attributed adult sexuality to the
infant or child.   Child sexual behavior is not equated with adult
sexuality.   Instead, they insisted that there is a direct continuous
connection between the behavior of the child in oral and other pregenital stages and his behavior in the genital (adult heterosexual)
stage.   Infantile sexuality foreshadows but does not completely define
the adult pattern.   Josselyn states it very well:

> If one looks at a tulip bulb, he does not see the shape, color, or size
> of the ultimate blossom.   However, the blossom would not exist were it
> not for the bulb.   Growing out of the bulb first comes the leaves, again
> an inherent part of the total plant, but still not the blossom.   Finally
> the bud shapes, and ultimately the flower.   Infantile sexuality and its
> vicissitudes of development determine the final successful blossoming
> or failure of fruition of heterosexuality (*10*, 38–39).[3]

Just as the ovum contains the adult potentialities, so infantile sexual
behavior foreshadows genital behavior.   Sexual factors are accepted
as the fundamental motivation; nonsexual motivation stems from the
sexual.

[2] By permission from *Psychoanalytic Theories of Personality*, by Blum.   Copyright 1953.   McGraw-Hill Book Company, Inc.

[3] From Josselyn (*10*).   Copyright 1948 by Family Service Association of
America, and published with permission.

The Libido

Psychoanalysis posits as energy for the sexual drives, the libido. Almost any impulse to receive pleasure would be an expression of libido, and, hence, considered sexual. In one sense this energy is nonspecific in that it energizes any activity, but in another sense it is quite specific in that the natural expression is sexual. The libido may be defined as that fixed quantity of sexual energy available to an individual from birth onward. Simple physical needs, such as hunger and thirst, are accepted as having drive energy (3), but these needs are considered relatively uncomplicated and of minor importance. Instead, stress is placed on the course of development of libido.

In the course of each individual's development, libido goes through various vicissitudes. The expression of libidinal energy in behavior is characteristically different at each of the various psychosexual stages. For example, during the oral stage the mouth is the center of libidinal pleasure. Libido has the capacity to change, to be attached to different objects and persons and then to be diverted to others, to disappear from consciousness, and to appear in various guises.

Freud at one time postulated a second class of drives, the self-preservative drives. In the development of psychoanalysis in still later years, he spoke of life and death instincts in which the latter was invested with a self-destructive quality, including the direction of destructive tendencies upon other persons as expressed in aggressive acts toward them. Neither of these two conceptions of energy postulates need concern us further in this discussion.

The Id

Freud, early in his clinical work, was struck with the ever-recurring phenomenon of his patients failing to be aware of certain significant aspects of or events in their lives which, nevertheless, he found had affected them profoundly. Since they behaved as if they were unaware of these determinants of their behavior and aspects of mental life, he referred to them as unconscious. Consequently, in his theoretical formulation he stressed the unconscious aspects of mental life. Freud likened the mind to an iceberg, only its summit of consciousness being above the surface, while its great mass lay below the surface.

Originally Freud adopted a threefold classification of mental life—conscious, foreconscious (capable of becoming conscious but not attended at the moment), and unconscious (repressed, that is, actively excluded from consciousness or instinctual drives which were never conscious). Later, while preserving these distinctions he preferred, on the grounds of greater dynamic possibilities, to speak of structural divisions of personality—the id, the ego, and the superego.

In his conception of the structural divisions of personality, the deliberately neutral term id (it) was given to the source of unconscious energy. In his earlier formulation Freud had referred to unconsciousness in much the same manner as he now used the term id. Some psychoanalysts continue to use id and unconscious more or less interchangeably. However, it is more exactly considered as one segment of the unconscious because, although all of the id is unconscious, not all unconsciousness is id.

Other characteristics of id are important. Freud said of it, "It contains everything that is inherited, that is present at birth, that is fixed in the constitution" (7, 14).[4] The id's aim is the gratification of its impulses with no sense of morality, logic, or unity of purpose. The major function of the id is to provide free uninhibited discharge of energy. Its activity is in the service of the pleasure principle, that is, the seeking of pleasure and the avoidance of pain with no other considerations entering the picture. This is a kind of animal-like existence with satisfaction only of bodily desires. There is no vestige of "reasonableness" or consideration for the rights of others.

The child is born with id. The other two structural constituents of personality, the ego and the superego, are developed from the id in the course of his daily life. Hence, as infancy begins, we need be concerned only with id.

The Birth Trauma and Anxiety

It is appropriate to conclude this discussion of the biological determinants with a mention of birth trauma. Birth itself is certainly an environmental event, not a biological or constitutional determinant. However, Freud suggested that the sudden flooding of excitation striking the newborn organism brought about in the newborn the prototype of later anxiety. After the calm of uterine existence, the neonate is, at birth, faced with an overwhelming situation he cannot

[4] From Freud (7). Copyright 1949 by W. W. Norton and Company, Inc., and published with permission.

handle. He reacts with what is later to become anxiety. Since his reaction occurs without learning, it is appropriate to speak of a pre-disposition to anxiety shown at birth as one of the biological determi-nants of personality.

The oral stage

Psychoanalysis posits several stages in psychosexual development. In brief, their view is that the infant shows the capacity to receive erotic pleasure from stimulation of various erogenous zones which assume successive centrality in sequence through the various stages of psychosexual development. An erogenous zone is an area of the body which is sensitive to stimuli and is capable of being stimulated in such a way as to arouse pleasurable feelings. The lips and oral cavity form one such erogenous zone, the anal region another, and the genital organs still another. Each of these in turn becomes the center of focus of erotic pleasure in the course of psychosexual devel-opment. Table 3, suggested by one in Healy, Bronner, and Bowers (9) but considerably enlarged and modified, will expedite under-standing of these stages.

Although the sequence is fixed, these stages are not separated one from the other in any rigid fashion. All stages overlap and pass gradually one into another. For example, while phenomena and problems of the oral stage are still very much in evidence, the anal stage has begun, and, as we shall see, the satisfactions of one stage are not entirely given up when the child has moved on to another stage.

In the light of this table it is possible to state another important contention of the psychoanalyst. This is their insistence upon the tremendously important effect of these early years upon later person-ality structure. It will be noted that Table 3 gives most space to infancy (here taken by the psychoanalyst to be the first five years or so), a small amount to latency, and a still small but somewhat larger amount to adolescence and concluding with only a passing reference to adulthood. Since psychosexual development is crucial to psycho-analysis and its vicissitudes seem to become stabilized in an individual characteristic fashion with adolescence, this underscores the relative unimportance of later years. Actually, events in adult life are given attention in psychoanalysis, but there is no doubt that orthodox psy-choanalysis considers a lifelong personality structure to be decided by

TABLE 3

THE COURSE OF PERSONALITY DEVELOPMENT ACCORDING TO PSYCHOANALYSIS

Infancy Period

Areas of Libidinal Localization	Modes of Pleasure Finding	Object Relations	Structural Organization	Mechanisms
1. Oral stage				
Early oral phase	Sucking, swallowing (incorporating)	Mother as first object	Id present. Beginnings of ego emerges in awareness, but it is essentially passive.	Fixation Regression Introjection Projection
Late oral phase	Biting (devouring, destroying)	Ambivalence		
2. Anal stage				
Early anal phase	Expelling (rejecting, destroying)	Continued ambivalence	Ego strengthened and more active by mastering of motility and development of judgment. Anxiety appears. Forerunner of superego.	Denial
Late anal phase	Retaining (controlling, possessing)			
3. Phallic stage	Touching, looking at and exhibiting genitals	Oedipus complex	Superego develops out of reaction to Oedipus complex. Ego emerges in full form.	Beginning of mechanisms of defense of ego. Sublimation Repression Reaction formation Undoing Isolation Displacement

		Latency Period		
No new area	All previous modes, but relative general drop in sexual interests	Extension to peers, sublimation of affection toward parents	Consolidation and strengthening ego and superego. Struggle quiescent among ego, superego, id, and external environment.	No new mechanisms, but sublimation and reaction formation are prominent.
4. Genital stage		Adolescent Period		
Prepubertal phase	Revival of infantile modes of pleasure finding	Reactivation of love objects of childhood	Disruption of truce among units of structural organization.	Asceticism
Pubertal phase Heterosexual-genital	Adult modes of pleasure finding	New nonparental object relations	Reorganization of units in adult personality.	Intellectualization

the experiences of these earlier stages. Indeed, Freud was convinced from his experiences with his patients that personality is rather completely formed by the end of the fifth year and that further development primarily consists of elaborating the basic structure.

We are now in a position to turn to the oral stage itself, the first area of libidinal localization reported in Table 3. In the discussion to follow, we are interested both in how libido manifests itself in the oral stage (mode of pleasure finding) and in what psychoanalysts call *object relations*. By this term is meant the relationship of the individual in question to other persons. According to psychoanalytic theory, the first object of every infant is the mother. Hence, in the account to follow we are examining how libido manifests itself in oral activities and the infant's relation to the mother.

The area of greatest sensitivity and pleasure for the young infant is not the genitals, but another erogenous zone, the mouth. In the oral stage, the libido centers in the act of sucking both at the mother's breast and on other objects. Successful adjustment requires both satisfaction of hunger and satisfaction of the desire to suck of and for itself. Sucking thus not only satisfies hunger, but it also gives libidinal pleasure. Excitation of the lips, mouth, tongue, and cheeks is exciting in and of itself. An illustration would be thumb sucking which stimulates the membrane of the mouth. If hunger alone were the motivation of thumb sucking, psychoanalysts insist, the infant would soon cease sucking since milk is not forthcoming. Infants sucking *after* a meal is a common observation, as is babies going to sleep sucking a thumb. Sucking is pleasurable and thus is a manifestation of libido.

During the first year or so, the mouth is the most important area for the baby. He spends a large part of his waking life in oral activity. In sucking, the milk flowing into his mouth causes pleasurable feelings. A mother soon becomes familiar with the all-absorbing passionate quality of mouth play, the sucking, the gurgles, the bubble blowing of the contented infant. This mouth-centeredness carries over into other activities than feeding. "He puts everything in his mouth," she complains. This mouthing not only includes all sorts of miscellaneous objects from the environment but also parts of his own body—fingers, thumbs, and toes.

The first aim of autoerotic stimulation, the bringing about of pleasurable sensations from the mouth, is followed during this early oral phase by another aim, the desire to incorporate objects. The mother is not only viewed as food, but as Blum puts it, "the infant fantasies being united with his source of supply by swallowing or incorporating it, thus making the object a part of himself" (*1*, 38).[2] Fenichel (3) cites as evidence for this incorporative phase in later personality development, phenomena extending from fondness for animal crackers to the rites of communion, "becoming the same substance." "You're so cute I could eat you up," is an expression indicative of this same idea of incorporation.

Following this early oral phase, centering on sucking pleasure and on oral incorporation is the late oral phase called the "oral-sadistic" phase. This phase commences with the eruption of the infant's teeth. The name "oral-sadistic" refers to the frustration engendered by the pain of their eruption against which the infant retaliates by biting. This biting is interpreted by the psychoanalyst as a desire to injure or destroy, even to annihilate utterly the bitten object (the mother). In contrast to the relatively passive first phase, this late phase of the oral stage is relatively aggressive.

Weaning, which often occurs at this age, results in hostility toward the mother. The infant is faced with his first important human problem—acceptance of frustration. Some infants work the problem through without too much trouble; others are not so successful. Trouble is to be anticipated when weaning, either from breast or bottle, takes place before the infant is ready to relinquish this form of oral gratification. As a consequence of this frustration, a new relationship between infant and mother develops. This new relationship is termed ambivalence which signifies that two disparate feelings, one friendly and the other hostile, exist concurrently. The infant longs for incorporation of the mother, but now he also wishes to destroy her through biting. This is a new type of object relationship in which friendliness and hostility toward the mother exist side-by-side. Instead of having only a positive, friendly, loving feeling, the infant now has mixed feelings toward the mother. She is both "loved" and "hated" at the same time. The infant "wants" his mother, but also wishes that harm would come to her, even her destruction, when he is frustrated in the weaning process.

Weaning inevitably produces this effect, but too abrupt or too early weaning can intensify it. Something has been removed which the child is not yet ready to do without. One of the important props of his existence has been knocked out for reasons he cannot understand. The mother, as the agent of this frustration by her removal of the breast or bottle, has failed the infant. Both anxiety about the mother and hostility toward the mother are natural consequences. Digestive disturbances, refusal to eat, diarrhea, sucking of the thumb, and a host of other oral symptoms may appear. If frustration is prolonged or severe, the child may become severely disturbed.

The oral stage presents certain problems to the infant. According to the degree of success in handling the problems of the oral period, there is a relatively greater or lesser degree of fixation. Fixation refers to the prolongation of habits of pleasure seeking beyond the age for which they are appropriate. Fixation is an investment of libido at a level characteristic of a given developmental stage. In all of us, progress to the next psychosexual stage is never complete; characteristics of an earlier level still persist. In other words, some measure of fixation always takes place. The retention of oral characteristics (kissing, biting, and so on) in normal adult heterosexual behavior is illustrative. But to the extent that fixation has occurred, the individual is thereby weakened in meeting the problems of the next level, since some of the libidinal energy available, fixed in quantity, is now fixated at the earlier level. Freud (6) used the simile of advancing troops; the more occupation troops that must be left behind, the less the remaining army has as it marches on. Hence, though a certain amount of fixation is inevitable, too great a degree is conducive to later personality difficulties in that the individual is impoverished in the amount of libido at his disposal.

The factors responsible for fixation at the oral (and other) stages have been developed by Fenichel (3). He categorizes these factors as: (1) experiencing excessive satisfaction so that the stage is given up with reluctance; (2) excessive frustrations leading to a demand for the withheld satisfaction; (3) alternation between excessive gratification and frustration; and (4) simultaneous oral satisfaction and reassurance for some anxiety. Illustrative of the latter category would be giving the infant a bottle of milk whenever he is frightened or otherwise disturbed.

Since undue frustration or too great indulgence can, under many circumstances, have a pernicious effect on personality, as findings on disturbed infants and children will later attest, it is appropriate to comment on the optimal proportion of deprivation to indulgence. According to Hartmann et al. (8), the optimal proportion for normal development is a large amount of indulgence combined with a small amount of frustration. If this optimal proportion is supplied, no more than the normal amount of fixation takes place.

Besides fixation, another way oral phenomena are manifest in life is through regression—the reactivation of behavioral patterns appropriate to an earlier stage of development after they have been given up. Faced with difficulties in later life, some individuals are predisposed to return to the behavior characteristic of earlier stages. A child of six may suck his thumb when he is frustrated; an adult may smoke excessively or eat compulsively when he is exposed to difficult situations; or, in a more general fashion, his social relations may show the problems of a particular earlier stage. He may be chronically homesick with a longing for the old and familiar. Regression characteristically occurs after the oral stage, as the illustrations attest. But nevertheless it can occur within the confines of the oral stage itself. For example, an infant may regress from the late to the early oral phase.

An individual does not regress in all characteristics so that he behaves just like a child or that age level. Rather his behavior is focused upon the type of libidinal gratification characteristic of the stage. But how he reacts will be attributable not only to his oral experiences but also to the complication and individually differential effects of the experiences in later stages. These experiences, moreover, may also be more generalized and complicated in nature than these specific introductory "indications" of oral regression might be taken to indicate.

The Emergence of the Ego

The infant at birth has no appreciation of the distinction between world and ego. Libidinal energy is directed upon himself. This state is referred to as primary narcissism, a term derived from the legend of Narcissus who fell in love with his reflection in a pool. The infant loves himself with supreme egoism because he is unaware of anyone or anything else. Sexual aims are autoerotic, that is, they are concerned with self-love.

At birth and shortly thereafter, before the infant begins to distinguish between himself and his environment he has, asserts Freud, an infantile sense of omnipotence. The world is not his oyster; he *is* the world, oyster and all. The signal of his needs, the cry, seems almost invariably to produce the mother who does all she can to relieve his tension. Small wonder then that psychoanalysts call this the period of omnipotence.

In considering the emergence of the ego we are, in terms of Table 3, returning to the problem of structural organization of the personality. In discussing the emergence of the ego in the oral stage, we can lay stress on ego as self- and social awareness, leaving, until a later, more appropriate age, the question of the ego as an executor or director of activity.

At birth, the infant does not have an ego. Out of the undifferentiated unconscious state of the id, consciousness of self begins to emerge. In this process, libido originally in the service of id functions can now be diverted to ego functions. Before this, the infant cannot distinguish himself from others. He has, for example, no idea of the mother as an individual. The infant originally makes no distinction between the mother's breast and his own body. The process of "primary identification" is reflected in the infant's perception of the mother as part of himself. When the distinction is made and the mother is shifted to the "outside," this process carries with it part of the original "self-love," or narcissism, which is now applied to the mother. As the process continues, she gradually emerges as a person, and as a person he loves in his own fashion. Hence, libido is directed toward the mother.

The ego of the infant as a sense of self-awareness becomes differentiated when his needs are *not* met. If all of the infant's needs were to be gratified, he would continue to have no sense of ego as differentiated from the world. Anna Freud (5) offers an explanation in these terms. She maintains that the inner world of the infant at birth consists essentially of the contrasting feelings of pleasure and pain. Pain arises under the impact of bodily needs from within or irritations from without; pleasure comes when the needs are satisfied or the irritants removed. The contrasting nature of frustration and gratification leads to the beginning of the ego. True, under the ministrations of the mother, the painful tendencies of the infant give way to relief. But his needs are not always met immediately. For example, when feeding is delayed, the inability to summon the breast or bottle immediately helps the infant to differentiate self from nonself. The mother's failure to meet his needs, the inevitable delays in ministering to his wants lead to his growing recognition of "I" and "not I." Awareness comes that for his needs to be met, to have his tensions reduced, something must be done by "mother." Thus, awareness of the mother's presence comes when she is not there! This leads to his losing the sense of omnipotence and the recognition of his dependence upon others. He begins to realize that "others" must do something before his needs can be met.

There is social awareness, too, in the beginnings of ego development as indicated in discussing the "separation" of child and mother.

The quality attributed to this other person is also produced in emerging social awareness. Taking feeding as central to this stage, what happens when the infant is fed? If the mother fondles him, is gentle in the process, helps him learn to suck, his first adjustment to what, as ego-awareness continues, is his first perception of another person is experienced as good. Consequently, he expects other people to be friendly as well. To use a term of Erikson (2), a sense of trust is developed. But what if she is unfriendly and rough, forcing the bottle or breast? He does not "think" of her as an enemy; his mental processes are not yet developed to this extent. But he does react with fear, tension, and psychosomatic upsets, such as inability to suck, vomiting, random bodily movements and, in extreme cases, the difficulties sketched later in connection with psychological disturbances in infancy. The little world for him, which is the here and now of the mother-child interaction, is bad and hateful in the primitive beginnings of these terms.

The Mechanisms Emerging During the Oral Stage

Two mechanisms have already been discussed, fixation and regression. We found these mechanisms were used to describe how the individual, in this case, the infant, characteristically operates or behaves. This is the general meaning of mechanism as the psychoanalyst uses the term. Two mechanisms other than fixation and regression emerge during the oral stage, as mentioned in the last column of Table 3 where they are called introjection and projection.

You will remember that in the later phase of the early oral stage, incorporation became important. This is relevant to the questions both of how a developing ego emerges and of the mechanisms that emerge during the oral stage. Incorporation, or as it may be called in this context, introjection, along with identification begin to develop in this stage. Projection appears as well. The relation among them is very well stated by Blum:

> The first judgment of the ego is said to be the distinction between edible and nonedible objects; the first acceptance is swallowing; the first rejection is spitting out. Introjection is a derivative of the former, projection of the latter. In the early stage of development of the ego, everything pleasurable is experienced as belonging to the ego (something to be swallowed), while everything painful is experienced as being nonego (something to be spat out).
>
> Originally, then, introjection or incorporation is an oral mechanism aimed at instinctual satisfaction. Later, when the infant no longer feels

omnipotent, oral introjection of the powerful adult serves to regain the feeling. Still later, when incorporation is seen as destroying the independent existence of the outside person, the mechanism functions in a hostile manner as the executive of destructive impulses.

At this point it might be well to attempt to clarify the terms "introjection," "incorporation," and "identification." Introjection and incorporation are generally used synonymously; some also employ identification in the same way. However, identification usually connotes a type of relationship to objects, in other words, a state rather than a process. Thus, oral introjection is said to be the executive of the "primary identification." By introjecting or incorporating, one achieves a state of identification. Primary identification refers to the first relationship to objects, whereas secondary identification is a later repetition of the earlier one.

Projection starts as a primitive method of getting rid of pain, by attributing unpleasant stimuli to the outside world. It is a sort of reverse introjection—instead of the ego's being perceived as having the object's characteristics, the environment is perceived as having the ego's characteristics. In these early phases of development, the mechanism can function without difficulty. Later it requires a serious impairment of the sense of reality for it to play a major role (1, 46–47).[2]

Thus introjection and projection, along with fixation and regression, are the mechanisms emerging during the oral stage.

The oral stage comes to a close some time after the end of the first year of life. But this does not mean that oral activities cease or become unimportant. They continue as long as life. Some individuals bear a greater impress of the stage than do others. We will return to this topic when we consider the "oral character" in adult personality structure after a discussion of the other psychosexual stages.

The anal stage

Somewhere in the second year of life the child shifts libidinal interest to the anal region. Following the oral stage, Freud postulated that the anal region was the next to be libidinized, that is, the next to become a center with high satisfaction value and interest.

The anal stage is bound up in our culture with toilet training. From about the age of a year and a half (or before) to three years, the anal region receives a great deal of attention. Proper evacuation becomes a matter of much attention and considerable ceremony.

For a moment, let us look at anality as the child might (10). The infant has no feeling of repulsion for his excreta as does the adult.

He has created it, its odor, texture, and color are not inherently unpleasant. The infant senses that his mother seems to prize his excretion by the pleasure she shows when he has a movement and by her disappointment at his failure to do so. According to Freudian thinking, defecating is "perceived" by the infant as giving something to the parent. Defecating is the giving of a gift. But what happens when he makes the gift by having a movement? The mother flushes it down the toilet! This is just as confusing to the infant as the husband would be if his wife, on receiving a highly prized fur coat, proceeded to throw it down the incinerator. Illustrative of the concern the infant shows about this confusing behavior is his throwing toys in the toilet, only to retrieve them.

How rapidly and in what form adult disgust will develop depends upon many circumstances. The infant's attitudes which begin to form at this time certainly owe much to his parents' particular attitudes and their strength.[5] In varying degrees all parents in our culture emphasize cleanliness. Attitudes toward cleanliness vary to be sure, but there is inevitably a conflict between the child's wishes in the matter and parental standards. In some homes, cleanliness has a moral aspect so that the dirty child is a bad child. In any case, a great deal of pressure is put upon the child in regard to toilet training.

Consulting the chart on pages 138–139 shows that, as with the oral stage, there are two phases—the expelling and retaining phases. Libidinal attachment is, in the early anal phase, centered on expelling and, in the late phase, on retaining of feces. Extending over both phases is a sadistic overlay—an emphasis on the use of anal behavior by the infant for hostile purposes. Hostility at this age is so common that psychoanalysts often refer to the "anal-sadistic," rather than merely to the anal stage.

As Blum (1) states it, the aim of the early or expelling phase is the pleasure in the act of excretion. The sadistic element of this

---

[5] It might be well to interject the question of how adult attitudes toward matters of the anal stage affect our consideration of psychoanalytic theory. In much greater degree than do the phenomena of the oral stage, experiences of this stage undergo repression in the course of the person's development. In fact, in the adult, "disgust" predominates. This attitude inevitably colors our attitude toward the phenomena under discussion and practically invites a rejection of any theory which says our personality is, in part, determined by how eliminative functions are handled. This very human tendency, then, to reject that which we find repugnant is one which only to a minor degree we can guard against.

phase is derived from excreta being "viewed" by the infant as objects destroyed by elimination. Later, the child may use the expulsiveness as a means of defying the parents who wish to train him to be clean.

The aim of the later or retentive phase is the enjoyment of the intense stimulation of the mucous membrane which accompanies a full lower intestine. But there is also an appreciation by the infant of the high value placed by parents on excreta. The child may wish to keep, rather than give them! Again a sadistic element appears in that he can withhold excretion as a gesture against his parents. By withholding, he can reduce parents to distraction, or by choosing his own time and place of expulsion he can create annoyance, if not more. Thus the element of control now supplements that of destroying which appeared in the oral-expulsion stage.

Ego and Superego Formation

In the oral stage, emphasis was upon the ego as self-awareness. Even in infancy a sense of appreciation of what is real and unreal is also developing. It will be remembered that id impulses of the newborn infant are directed by the so-called pleasure principle. The reality principle comes into play when the infant has contact with frustrating experiences. During the oral stage, the infant learns to distinguish between his perception of reality and his fantasies. This testing of reality wherein he recognizes fantasy products as unreal is demanded for normal adjustment. The bare beginnings occur in early infancy with the emergence of the ability to tolerate delay and to substitute future for immediate gratification. The infant becomes not only aware of changes in his environment but begins to regulate his behavior in line with these changes. Here we have the beginnings of ego as *executor*. In following the reality principle, the infant could "restrain" himself for short periods of time from discharge of tension. Instead of immediate discharge, there is the beginning of the tolerance of tension. For example, an infant can resist grabbing an attractive object for at least a short time.

As he begins to control toilet activities (and other dawning motor skills), the infant manifests one of the requisites of ego as doer. This, as Blum (1) views it, depends upon active mastery. During the oral stage, the infant was predominantly passive, inducing adults, particularly the mother, to do things for him. During the ages of one to three years, he becomes gradually less dependent upon others.

This is possible because he begins actively to manipulate his environment through (1) mastering of his motility in walking, talking, and keeping clean; and (2) the growth in judgment. He can actively manipulate his environment when he can walk and control, albeit for short times, his bladder and bowel. Thus, he can begin to be independent. In learning to talk, he introduces anticipation into his activities in that events can be planned in terms of words. The development of speech is important for the development of the ego not only because of the increased ease and accuracy of communication with others, but also because it increases ease and flexibility in self-communication. Not only can the infant better handle the external world, he can better handle himself. According to Freudian thinking, advances in regard to communication give rise to a belief in the magical power of naming. If one can name something, one can master it. In this connection, it is a common observation that children demand incessantly that objects be named for them. Illustrative of the magical power of words is the plea for reassurance that children find in the old saying, "Sticks and stones may break my bones, but names can never hurt me."

Thinking during the anal stage has another characteristic—extensive symbolism. Blum, in this connection, writes:

> Comprehension of the world originally comes from viewing objects as sources either of gratification or of threat, so that stimuli which provoke the same reactions are looked upon as identical. One illustration is the common symbolic equation of "departure" with "death." A less obvious tie is between "money" and "feces." Both represent possessions which are alike for everyone (not individualized) and thus are in danger of being lost as one's own. In other words, both are deindividualized possessions which are in constant danger of losing their ego quality (1, 65).[2]

Judgment, which in turn is partially dependent upon speech, is a function technically already referred to as "reality" testing. By this is meant that one can explore the solution to a new situation by trying it out and seeing what the consequences are. This allays anxiety. The tentative, quickly withdrawn touching of the "kitty" by the child is an illustration. Another illustration, even earlier in time, would be the fixed alert stare of the infant who watches the "stranger" to see what he may do. If he remains quiet, he may be accepted, but if he moves too quickly or talks too loudly, the infant cries, shows fear, and attempts withdrawal. Reality testing as the child grows older emerges as a process in realistic thinking. A plan of action is formulated and then carried out. A hungry person thinks where he may find food and seeks it out in that place.

With the further development of the ego during the anal stage, the child also gradually comes to exercise another function of the ego as executor—the ability not just to postpone but actually to forego impulses. This is another defensive function of the ego. The ego gradually learns to ward off impulses that are dangerous and not to perform certain acts. But details of how this comes about must be postponed until discussion of the next stage.

As the ego matures there is an increase in the ability to judge events and to anticipate the future. With this increase comes a more realistic perception of danger and a consequent anxiety. Although a prototype for anxiety existed before, as a consequence of the birth trauma, anxiety as such develops when the child can perceive a situation as threatening or dangerous. According to Freud, anxiety is a consequence of the danger of object loss. In this case, the object which might be lost is the mother, so we have a fear of loss of love developing in the infant. He learns that the environment in addition to offering satisfaction can also threaten. It has the power to produce pain. Anticipation of this pain gives rise to anxiety. If the child cannot cope with a situation he becomes anxious.

A forerunner of the superego appears during the anal stage. To avoid detailed discussion at this point, the superego may be described approximately as the equivalent of the conscience. This antecedent of the superego appears when the child begins to conform to the concepts of the parents concerning "right" and "wrong" in toilet matters. It appears because he internalizes parental prohibitions. As Blum puts it:

> The introjection of prohibitions arises from the fear of punishment and the fear of losing parental affection. A portion of the ego becomes an "inner mother," signaling the approach of situations which threaten loss of love. A common sight is the child who, on the verge of performing a forbidden act, looks at his mother, shakes a finger, and cries, "No, no!" Since toilet training is a frequent arena for such battles, Ferenczi designated superego forerunners as "sphincter morals" (synonyms are "toilet-training superego," "visceral ethics," etc.).
>
> These internalized prohibitions, while strong in their threat of punishment, are weak in that they may be easily disobeyed when no one is looking. Also, they can readily be projected onto other individuals like policemen and bogeymen, who are said to stand for "externalized presuperegos." In general, there is no unified, organized character to the prohibitions (1, 66).[2]

Detailed discussion of the superego is reserved for the discussion of the next or phallic psychosexual stage.

The Mechanisms Emerging During the Anal Stage

During the anal stage, the mechanisms which had emerged in the oral stage continue to operate.   Thus, fixation, regression, introjection, and projection are still operative.   Although present in a very primitive form during the oral stage (1), a new mechanism emerges during the anal stage as important as the other mechanisms.   This is referred to as denial.

Along with a gradually opening sense of reality comes a contrary tendency, the denial of reality.   Reaching full form in the second year and continuing in subsequent years, this is the process whereby a child (or an adult) can close his eyes, as it were, to an unpleasant truth and behaves as if it isn't there.   "If we close our eyes, it will go away," a not uncommon theme in cartoons, is illustrative.

Denial is certainly an important facet of children's play.   This denial of reality, or this fantasy, is enthusiastically fostered by the child in his play.   Toys, cops and robbers, the playing of the TV or movie hero of the moment, all breed this tendency at later ages. In infancy it is more primitive and simple but essentially the same. This tendency to use fantasy is abetted by an adult "conspiracy" to foster this mode of behavior.   What child hasn't heard from us, "Oh it doesn't hurt," when, as a matter of fact, it does!   However, this tendency of the adult to encourage denial wears thin or vanishes when the child fails to make the transition back to reality readily—on call, as it were.   All children, on occasion, show denial—for example, reluctance to come back from the wide open prairie or the high seas merely for the sake of eating lunch.   Much more serious is the child who confuses reality with fantasy in such a fashion as occasionally to be unable to separate the two.   Reality testing must, for normal adjustment to take place, exist side-by-side with the occasional mild use of denial of that reality in "play."

The phallic stage

At about the end of the third or the beginning of the fourth year, and continuing roughly to the age of six, libidinal energy is shifted to the genital zone.   In other words, libidinal localization is displaced from the anal zone to the genital zone, and new modes of pleasure finding become prominent. This does not mean that genital interests and activities have been absent before this stage—erections occur, and masturbation and sex play are not unknown before this age— but that emphasis is now centered on the genital organs instead of the other erogenous zones. To distinguish it from the genital stage of adolescence, this early aspect of genitality which cannot come to fruition in reproduction is called the phallic stage.

The child now finds the centering of erotic pleasure in the sexual organs themselves. Occurrence of the shift of libidinal localization is made possible by the new degree of maturation of the sexual organs which occurs at this age. Consequently, the sexual organs become richer in sensations than they have been before. Interest in them is greater; masturbation increases; a greater desire for physical contact takes place, especially with members of the opposite sex; and exhibitionistic tendencies appear. At this age, sexual fantasies as well as these behavioral manifestations are found. The young child places a high value on the sex organs, in the case of the boy on the penis and in the case of the girl on the clitoris. This high valuation, as much as the pleasure obtained, marks the phallic stage.

One consequence of the phallic stage is that the boy and the girl learn sexual identifications appropriate to their own sex. In normal development the boy becomes more masculine and the girl more feminine during this stage. Up to this stage it has been possible to refer to the infant without distinguishing the sex. The convention of language in using *he* where *she* would have done as well must be foregone in the description of phallic development. In describing the phallic stage, *he* will refer only to the boy.

Phallic Development and the Oedipus Complex in Boys

The mother as the love object is already established for the boy. From a Freudian point of view, with awakening phallic sex interest there is an inevitability that the attitudes the boy holds toward the mother will be sexual. True, these sexual tendencies toward her appear in fumbling childish ways. Nevertheless, his sexual emphases are that of an adult although he has no grasp of their implication, nor is he capable of adult practices. Thereafter, as Munroe puts it:

> Sooner or later, the mother rebuffs behavior in her son that is dimly recognized as "sexual." The social taboo begins operating in a variety of ways. It is especially important that the little boy observes that the

father enjoys privileges with the mother from which he is excluded.   It may be that the privilege of creeping into mother's bed is revoked when father is home.   The child may have witnessed the primal scene (that is, his parents in intercourse) or have suddenly remembered such scenes witnessed at a time when he was too young to "understand" them even in the confused way typical for infancy.   Freud suggests that phylo-genetic memories of the primal horde in which father and sons were in open competition of sexual possession of the women (mother and sisters) may also be a factor in the attitude of the little boy toward the father (11, 200).[6]

The tensions which this situation creates between father and son, at least those of the demands of the son for his mother's love, are interpreted in terms of what is called the Oedipus complex. Oedipus, of Greek legend and drama, is the central character of the tragedy in which Oedipus murders his father and marries his mother.   In symbolic terms, Freud says, this is the drama the boy must play. Every boy is fated to have death wishes toward the father (to kill the father in fantasy) and to desire to "marry" his mother. This is an inevitable step in the course of libidinal growth.[7]

On this matter society is at its firmest in forbidding such desires being put into practice.   Mother-son incest is unthinkable in our culture and, indeed, may be so in all other cultures as well.   The social taboo, then, is massive and uncompromising.   In a sense, every boy at this stage of development is at war with society (as expressed at the family level) as well as a rival of his father.   If this were not enough to create an intolerable impasse, there is the fact that he is dependent upon his father and under his authority.   Small wonder he develops anxiety and fears loss of love of both his parents as a consequence of the Oedipus situation.   But in addition to the anxiety engendered by this fear of loss of love there is a more specific anxiety. It will be remembered that the penis is overvalued.   Consequently, this given rise to what is known as castration anxiety.   Castration anxiety refers to anxiety about implied or actual injury to the genital organs, especially the penis.   Some parents actually do threaten harm to the penis to stop masturbation.   The anatomical lack in the girl, once the boy notices such differences, can reinforce the idea that

[6] From Munroe (11). Copyright 1955 by The Dryden Press, Inc., and pub-lished with permission.

[7] To the statement that introspectively one cannot remember these stirring times in his own childhood, Freud would reply that the psychoneurotic manages to get along by repression of his Oedipus complex, while the normal person who has worked it through has amnesia for these early longings and incidents.

castration does take place. Even without this specific threat (which was probably more common in Freud's time than it is now) other factors are operative. Hartmann, Kris, and Loewenstein put it as follows:

> While in many cases the child in our civilization is no longer being threatened with castration, the intensity of the veiled aggression of the adult against the child may still produce the same effect. One might say that there always is "castration" in the air. Adults who restrict the little boy act according to patterns rooted in their own upbringing. However, symbolic or distant from actual castration their threats might be, they are likely to be interpreted by the little boy in terms of his own experiences (8, 21–22).[8]

In the boy, castration anxiety, along with the other anxieties of the situation, is so great that he gives up his desires for the mother. Repression both of sexual desires for the mother and of the hostility toward the father takes place. Repression (discussed in more detail later) refers to the excluding from consciousness some unacceptable impulse. With the sexual and hostile impulses now unrecognized for what they are, as the result of repression, a new interrelationship with the mother and the father becomes possible. With the resolution of the Oedipus complex, object choices are replaced by identification, that is, sexual attractions are replaced by wanting to be like someone. The state of affairs now existing permits an identification to be made by the boy with his father. His dangerous erotic feelings or object choices for the mother are converted into harmless, tender affection. Thus the Oedipus situation is "smashed," but residuals remain because repression results not in eradication of the impulses but merely in their not being consciously experienced.

Phallic Development and the Oedipus Complex in Girls

The problem of the Oedipus complex is more complicated in the girl than in the boy. The boy, after all, maintains a positive relation with his pre-Oedipal object, the mother. The girl, however, must switch affections from the original love object, the mother, to the father and also learn to "hate" the mother.

Along with an awakening interest in her own sex organ is an interest in the sex organs of others and the discovery of anatomical differences.

---

[8] From Hartmann et al. (8). Copyright 1947 by the International Universities Press, and published with permission.

According to Freudian theory, she notices that she lacks a penis and feels she would like to have one. This envy of the male for his possession of a penis is referred to as penis envy. The envy she experiences is accompanied by a feeling that the lack of a penis is, somehow or other, a punishment inflicted upon her. Penis envy is the powerful source which brings about a shift in libido away from the mother and toward the father.

This tendency to shift is reinforced by the ambivalences already established in her relationship with the mother. Frustrations because of weaning and toilet training make more possible this shift in object in the girl. What happens thereafter Munroe describes as follows:

> Freud goes on to consider what happens in the life of the little girl after the crucial "discovery of her castration" and the development of her *penis envy*. We saw that for the boy the Oedipal phase is a natural elaboration of existing attitudes and is given up because of the threat of castration. The same threat, already fulfilled in the case of the girl, drives her *into* the Oedipal situation. She now wishes to regain a penis via the male (in early childhood, the father) and develops the equation of the penis with a child so frequently observed in psychoanalysis. It is having a child by the father that will, she fancies, restore the lost organ. Having renounced much of the activity involved in clitoric masturbation because of the inadequacy of the organ, . . . she is now dominated by the passive aims of the vagina in the development of normal femininity.
>
> From this point on it is not difficult to understand how the girl's Oedipus complex will have much the same contours as the boy's although the sexes are reversed. She will love the father and hate the mother because the mother is a rival for the father's love, as well as because of earlier resentments. And the girl will tend to *identify with the mother* as a means of handling the problem, just as the boy identifies with the father.
>
> It will be noted, however, that the castration complex has for the girl prepared the way for the Oedipus complex during the period of superego formation, instead of destroying it, as in the case of the boy. Under these circumstances, there is less motive for her to overcome it as sharply as the boy, and according to Freud it tends to remain operative far longer—in fact, indefinitely (*11*, 218).[6]

Formation of the Superego

The formation of the superego is a direct consequence of the Oedipus situation in both boys and girls. Before proceeding with the relation of the superego to the events of the phallic stage, a brief review of what has already been said is indicated. The forerunner

of the superego was established during the anal stage through internalization of parental prohibitions about toilet matters.

During the phallic stage, parental views continue to be respected
and these include identifications with their prohibitions. The boy
and the girl incorporate their views concerning these matters as their
own partly on the basis of these positive factors. The child's parents'
views become internalized. As Blum states:

> The frustrations of the Oedipus complex are said to cause a regression
> from more differentiated types of object relationships to introjection and
> orality, and the sexual longing for an object is replaced by an asexual
> alteration within the ego. The introjected parents do not fuse with the
> rest of the ego because of the feeling of distance between parents and
> child. Instead they combine with the previously existing parental intro-
> jects or superego forerunners to form a precipitate within the ego. These
> later identifications differ from the forerunners in the following way: the
> child, in order to escape conflicts revolving about love, hate, guilt, and
> anxiety, does not identify with the parents as they are, but with the
> idealized parents. He purifies their conduct in his mind, and the iden-
> tification proceeds as if they were consistently true to the principles they
> explicitly profess or aspire to observe. According to Freud, the child
> identifies with the superego of the parents. Idealization was present
> earlier in terms of attributing magical powers to parents, but now for
> the first time the idealization concerns moral behavior (1, 97).[2]

The superego has now come into being. On the basis of its origin
it is now easier to see how it has a "drive" quality and why it is so
irrational and punitive.

The superego, in one of its aspects, functions as the conscience.
However, it is broader since, in part, it functions unconsciously.
Its unconscious aspects arise because it was incorporated by the child
without awareness on his part during those early years which are
the phallic stage. Anxiety was already operative before the appearance of the superego. Now that the superego is present, anxiety
becomes expressed in guilt, that is, the superego is the internalized
agency which punishes the child by making him feel guilty when
he violates the social sanctions of his culture. No longer is external
danger alone conducive to anxiety. An inner representation of that
danger, the superego, takes over some anxiety and expresses itself
in the child's experience and behavior as guilt.

There is also another more positive aspect to the superego—the
ego-ideal. The ego-ideal is the child's conception of what his parents
consider to be morally good. The child assimilates his parents'
standards of what is good and virtuous. Internalization of parental

approval and reward allows him to control his behavior in line with their wishes. Instead of relying upon parental approval, he now secures self-approval and pride through the superego's functioning.

To speak more generally concerning the functioning of the superego, moral demands, ideals, and the like are expressed through it. The superego serves the purpose of controlling those sexual (and aggressive) impulses which, if permitted uncontrolled expression, would endanger social stability. The inner restraints imposed by the superego permit man to live in society—but at a price.

The Interrelation of Ego, Superego, Id, and the Environment

With the formation of the superego, the last major constituent of the topographical organization of the personality has come into being. The superego with the id and the already established ego form the constituents of personality structure. Consequently, at about the age of six, the fundamental structure of the personality has assumed in major outlines the form which it will hold throughout life. The basic personality, for good or for ill, is established to be modified only slightly thereafter. It is, therefore, appropriate to summarize the interrelations among the components and the relationship between the total personality.

Contact with the world modifies a portion of the id which emerges as a small area of consciousness, the ego. Only a small part of the ego is conscious at any time. A great portion of the ego exists outside of awareness but can be called into consciousness when needed (the preconscious). Still another part of the ego is unconscious, consisting of those aspects which have been repressed. The self is not identical with the ego. Knowledge of the self in the sense of awareness is immediate. This is not so with aspects of the ego. While each individual recognizes himself, he has no immediate knowledge of ego defense mechanisms (to be discussed in a moment) which arise unconsciously.

The ego, as we have seen, refers both to an awareness of self and to carrying on of executive functions. In connection with the latter, as a representative of reality, the ego serves to mediate among the pressures arising from the id (libidinal pressures), the superego (the conscience and "ego-ideal"), and the demands of external reality. Evaluation of an existing situation, which the individual faces, whatever it might be, and anticipation of the future by him are functions of the ego. Obeying the reality principle, as was outlined earlier, the ego operates through realistic thinking. Plans are formulated for the satisfaction of needs and carried out (reality testing). The ego in evaluating a situation and in anticipating the future must reckon with the demands of reality as they exist.

Anxiety serves as a signal to the ego, alerting it to danger, internal or external. Anxiety, strictly speaking, cannot exist except in conscious awareness. It is an affective state experienced by the ego, not by the id or superego. In the face of danger or threat of danger, anxiety develops. Although often considered synonymous with fear, Freud preferred the term anxiety, because fear is often interpreted as related to something in the external world. Anxiety refers to perception of internal as well as external dangers. The internal conditions giving rise to this anxiety expressed by the ego have to do with unacceptable id impulses or superego demands.

The superego is differentially related to the ego according to whether or not it is in opposition or in harmony. The superego serves, from the first point of view, as a pressure upon the ego. In brief, the superego behaves toward the ego as the parents once did toward the child. The superego makes the child feel guilty just as did the parents. The reproaches of the superego function as did the reproaches of the parents. The prohibitions of the superego must be reckoned with by the ego in expressing id impulses. When the ego and the superego are in harmony, the relationship between the two is felt as pride in accomplishment. The ego in this case measures itself against the superego and finds its accomplishment does not fall short of its demands.

The interrelation of the ego, superego, and id with reality may be summarized by a graphic illustration from Josselyn:

> On a dark night one walks down a street passing a jewelry store. No one is around. In the window showcase is a beautiful diamond ring. The id says: "I want that diamond. I want it because I love myself, because it would make me beautiful and would thus make other people love me, because I am angry at others having what I have not, and because I am uncomfortable under the tension of wanting what I do not have." The superego says, arbitrarily, "No, you can't break the window and take it." The ego solves the impasse by advising, "But you shall have it if you will save your money until you can buy it" (*10, 24*).[3]

Neither the earlier discussion nor Josselyn's analogy should be taken to imply that the id, ego, and superego are to be thought of as *dei ex machinae* which operate the personality, as a puppeteer would his puppets. They are constructs for psychological processes, each operating upon its own systematic principles.

One aspect of the interrelationship among personality structures has been reserved for special consideration; this is the way in which the ego uses the so-called mechanisms of defense.

The Ego and the Mechanisms of Defense

The ego may master problems and anxiety by using realistic methods or it may alleviate anxiety by various methods that distort reality. The conflicting demands of superego, id, and external environment are handled through the unconscious employment by the ego of certain mechanisms of defense. These characteristic ways in which the ego functions in order to avoid pain and anxiety are called defense mechanisms of the ego. Each ego meets these demands of superego, id, and environment in its characteristic fashion. This makes for an endless variety of personality structures.

Some mechanisms have already been discussed but without direct relation to the problems of ego defense. Fixation, introjection, projection, regression, and denial have been identified as existing before the full emergence of the ego's functions. All of these chronologically earlier mechanisms begin to operate as ego defense mechanisms during the phallic stage, but illustrative material will be drawn from new mechanisms emerging during the stage itself.

Repression as an ego defense has been made central in Freudian thinking (11). It is therefore appropriate to stress it in illustrating the operation of ego defenses. Essentially, repression is the keeping of some unacceptable impulse, thought, or motive out of consciousness. This is not voluntary suppression as in "counting ten." Repression is fleeing, psychologically speaking, from something unacceptable without conscious awareness of doing so. An example has already been given concerning the resolution of the Oedipus complex. Other examples might be given. It may be necessary for the child to repress anger at the mother, a feeling of rivalry for the father, or a memory of some traumatic event. These and other tendencies which are unacceptable to the ego must be handled as if they did not exist. But that they *do* exist can be shown in other behavior and experience which the child does not himself relate to the repressed material. He may hit his brother instead of his mother, break his father's razor, or be afraid of something otherwise innocuous which stands for the traumatic event. In none of these instances does the child see the connection between these defensive maneuvers and the emotional situations which gave rise to them. Indeed, he would deny vehemently that there could possibly be any connections.

Other mechanisms of ego defense arising during the phallic stage are reaction formation, or conscious attitudes of the ego which are the exact opposite of repressed impulses; undoing, or doing the opposite of what which unconsciously the person wishes to do; isolation, or depriving an experience of its emotional significance so that the person consciously is not aware of any feelings concerning the traumatic situation or sphere; and displacement or shifting of emotion from one object to another.

All of these mechanisms of defense are, according to Fenichel (3), unsuccessful in the sense that they do not really succeed in their warding-off process but must continually be operative to prevent an eruption of the impulses. They do not settle the battle. At best they maintain a stalemate—a stalemate which drains away libido in a fruitless fashion. Or in more severe form, these mechanisms become the basis of neurotic manifestations.

The successful mechanisms of ego defense are the various forms of sublimation which bring about a cessation of the warded-off impulses by allowing discharge of the impulses. Sublimations have a common characteristic of being socially approved ways of discharging libido without anxiety; they are redirected object libido. That is to say, sublimated activities have aims other than sexual gratification. Since it is a form of desexualized expression, socially approved activities are made possible through sublimation (12). For example, oral pleasures may be sublimated by the child in pleasure of speaking, and later he may go into politics. The child may sublimate his interests in anal matters by playing with fingerpaints and later by becoming a sculptor, or the child may seek knowledge of nature study, and later carry on as a biologist as a sublimation of his phallic interests. Often there is not as obvious a connection between the phenomena of a psychosexual stage and a given form of sublimation. In fact, sublimations characteristically show a more complicated pattern than can be presented here. Friendship, achievement, positive social feeling, law and order, social progress, and interaction are all areas in which sublimation is the mechanism through which the individual functions. Sublimation, therefore, stands in contrast to the other defense mechanisms of the ego in that it is successful and socially approved.

The latency period

The latency period, starting at six or thereabouts and lasting until prepuberty at about ten, is different from the psychosexual stages as such in that no new area of libidinal localization develops. Originally, it was considered that sexual impulses remained latent, accounting for the name the period bears. It is now recognized that during the years of latency there is no necessarily true recession of sex impulses, but that repression and a renunciation of erotic activity are taking place.

During the latency period there is a consolidation of already existing ego, superego, and id relationships. The strengthened ego and superego make the latency period possible. There is a slackening of pace and changes take place slowly and follow the already laid-down patterns. Sexual interests are quiescent and to some extent dormant, but by no means nonexistent. There is, however, a degree of adjustment to the demands of the environment in such a fashion that social feeling is extended to others. So far as object relations are concerned, there is significant extension in this regard on the child's part to his peers, especially to children of his own sex. In terms of relationship to others the libidinal desires for parental love "are replaced by sublimated expressions of affection—tenderness, devotion, and respect" (1, 129).[2] There is a reaching out toward others, a desire for companionship of peers, schoolmates, and neighbors. As a result, the parents are seen more objectively and less blindly. The child may even be more influenced by the opinions of his peers than those of his parents. The child is developing standards which he accepts as his own (superego development) and developing mental and physical skills which serve the purpose of adaptation (ego development).

From among those already established mechanisms, sublimation and reaction formations are prominent. Thus, he redirects his libidinal desires by sublimated affection for his parents. He also uses reaction formations to hold in check forbidden impulses. For example, curiosity about sexuality, may now be sublimated in an interest in how things work and how things were in other times and places. There is thus a realistic orientation to the child's interests.

The genital stage

The genital stage may be conveniently subdivided into the pre-pubertal and pubertal phases. The first phase, beginning at about age ten, is preparatory to physical sexual maturity. Theoretically, there is considered to be a sharp increase in libidinal energy. Libido is again directed toward the love objects of childhood. Oedipal fantasies reappear. Anna Freud in describing the changes from latency to prepuberty puts it vividly:

> Aggressive impulses are intensified to the point of complete unruliness, hunger becomes voracity and the naughtiness of the latency period turns into the criminal behavior of adolescence. Oral and anal interests, long submerged, come to the surface again. Habits of cleanliness, laboriously acquired during the latency period, give place to pleasure in dirt and disorder, and instead of modesty and sympathy we find exhibitionistic tendencies, brutality and cruelty to animals. The reaction-formations, which seemed to be firmly established in the structure of the ego, threaten to fall to pieces. At the same time, old tendencies which had disappeared come into consciousness. The Oedipus wishes are fulfilled in the form of fantasies and day-dreams, in which they have undergone but little distortion; in boys ideas of castration and in girls penis-envy once more become the centre of interest. There are very few new elements in the invading forces. Their onslaught merely brings once more to the surface the familiar content of the early infantile sexuality of little children (4, 159).[9]

In short, there is a reactivation of earlier modes of pleasure finding. There is also a general disruption of the balance among the structural aspects of personality. The truce between the ego and the id, prevailing in the latency stage, is now torn asunder. When id impulses predominate, lapses into pregenital gratifications take place and aggressive, even criminal, behavior may result as has been described in the quotation from Anna Freud.

When the ego dominates, there is an increase in anxiety, and neurotic symptoms may appear. Ego defenses of all sorts are called into play and new ones, such as asceticism and intellectualization, appear. Asceticism may be expressed through a distrust of enjoyment, avoiding company of other individuals of his own age, cold showers, getting up early, and so on. Asceticism as a defense is an attempt by the ego

---

[9] From Freud (4). Copyright 1946 by the International Universities Press, and published with permission.

to keep the id in bonds by use of general prohibition. Intellectualization is the defensive use of abstract, lofty (but empty) discussions and thoughts on love and marriage, philosophy, religion, and so on. In intellectualization, in contrast to asceticism, there is an attempt by the ego to make id impulses conscious by cloaking them in these abstractions and thus to control them.

With the arrival of bodily sexual maturity in the second or puberty phase itself, there tends to be a dropping away of the "sloppiness" of the prepubertal phase. Greater refinement, even fussiness, may appear in general behavior and dress. Sexual interests are again extended beyond the family. Thus nonparental object relations appear. Not only is there this positive force pulling him away from home but there is also the necessity of overcoming the prepubertal Oedipal fantasies. There is uneasiness over displays of affection received from the parents. The adolescent typically behaves almost like a stranger with members of his family. In many cases, strong friendships with people of his own age and "crushes" on older persons appear. The latter are of course substitutes for the parents. In this reaching out toward others there is a whole-hearted (but narcissistic) absorption in the subject of his affection. Nevertheless, these affairs are of short duration and, once over, are rather quickly forgotten as far as his conscious life is concerned. The *form* of the relation is, however, preserved in the inevitable next episode. The disruption of the prepubertal structural organization of personality gives way during the pubertal phase to a new reorganization which normally leads to the genital character of adulthood.

Adult personality structure

The psychoanalytic theory of normal adult personality structure is a description of types of personality arising from differential childhood experiences. Major kinds of personality structures, or "character structures" in psychoanalytic terminology, are attributed to events characteristic of each of the psychosexual stages. In effect, there is a carry-over (or reversal) of certain characteristics in adult life, the origins of which are to be found predominantly in the experiences of a particular psychosexual stage.

The Oral Character

It is possible to speak of the "oral character" in an adult as arising primarily from the experiences of the first year or so of life. Fixations produced during this oral stage have remained strong throughout the life of such a person and have assumed the position of major characteristics. As might be expected, oral preoccupations loom large with him. Eating, drinking, smoking, and kissing are seen by him as more important than they are to other individuals. He may even equate love with food.

In this person, there is not merely a locus of satisfaction in the oral area in adulthood such as the various oral habits just mentioned. His modes of functioning in satisfying any needs may also show these oral fixations as resulting from experiences during the oral stage. Thus, he shows not only what might be called mouth habits, but also he is prone to exhibit general attitudes of dependence-independence in later life.

A major characteristic, depending upon whether frustration or indulgence predominated during the oral stage, is shown in his basic attitude of assurance. The infant frustrated or ungratified in oral drives is apt to become the adult dependent upon others for his feeling of esteem. He wishes to be taken care of, but he does not actively seek this care. He hopes it will come his way without effort on his part. He is passively dependent. When emotionally upset, he eats to overcome the emotion. A pessimistic attitude may prevail. These feelings of dependency tend to persist throughout life, especially when the individual feels anxious and insecure. On the other hand, oral overindulgence in infancy, according to Fenichel (3), leads to the presence of adult feelings of optimism and self-assurance, even to a point beyond which this trait is desirable. Such a person may be so sure that everything is going to "turn out all right" that he feels no need to work toward his goals. This unperturbable optimism is often manifested in lofty ambitions accompanied by a sanguine expectation that the future will somehow take care of itself.

Frustrations arising during the second or late oral stage lead to a host of ambivalent adult attitudes: friendly-hostile, aggressive-submissive, and so on. For example, such a person may be aggressive and given to "biting" remarks, but have periods in which he tries to make amends by swinging in the opposite direction and becoming overfriendly and submissive.

The effect of oral experience on adult personality must, of necessity, be but briefly sketched. Enough has been said to bring out the psychoanalytic contention that experiences during the oral stage are supposed to be important in the formation of adult personality.

The Anal Character

Just as with the child who bears a greater impress from the oral stage, so, too, the child who has developed disproportionate fixations in and tendencies toward regression from the anal stage develops in later life an "anal character." Before the full development of their anal characteristics these individuals may show difficulty in learning to control the bowels. When this problem is finally overcome, certain anal character traits appear. In short, toilet difficulties are replaced by character traits.

The three more prominent personality traits supposed to occur in the anal character are orderliness, parsimony, and obstinacy. Sometimes they are referred to as the three P's: pendantry, parsimony, and petulance. Orderliness in this context refers both to bodily cleanliness and to conscientiousness in the performance of petty duties. Parsimony refers to "tightness" about money and other matters even to the point of avarice. Obstinancy refers to unmovableness even to the point of defiance and irritability. Certain Scrooge-like characters in comic strips carry all three of these as prominent characteristics. A sadistic overlay of hostility and/or desire to control other persons are also present in the anal character.

According to psychoanalytic theory, these characteristics are an extension of the child's compliance with his parents' wishes in regard to excretion. True, they may in this process become too compliant to their parents' wishes as extremes of these traits would suggest. Anal characters often show reaction formation, that is, the defensive transformation of a trait into its opposite. Thus, an undue interest in anal matters may be consciously paraded as a vociferous disgust with such matters. Orderliness of a compulsive character may reflect this defense mechanism. Sometimes there is a continuation of a childish desire to defy the parents in toilet training which shows itself as adult obstinancy. Parsimony as a characteristic is a more direct continuation of the habit of anal retentiveness itself.

The Phallic Character

Castration anxiety and penis envy produce the particular character-istics which typify the phallic character.   In later childhood and adulthood, the boy showing disproportionate effects of the phallic stage in the form of castration anxiety gives an impression of being a reckless, strutting daredevil who behaves in an aggressive, firm, self-assured fashion.   Overvaluation of the penis and confusion of it with the whole body produce intense vanity, exhibitionism, and sensitiveness.   In keeping with expectation of assault he is prone to attack first.   Professional wrestlers, "beach" athletes, weight lifters, and motorcyclists at least fit the stereotype of the picture, even though all such individuals are not necessarily phallic characters.   A similar process takes place in the girl who is motivated by strong penis envy. She tries to assume a masculine role and strives for superiority over men.

Basically, the phallic character, male or female, is dependent and narcissistic, unable to form mature relationships, and contemptuous of the opposite sex.   Sexual conquests, for example, are attempts to demonstrate masculinity or femininity, and are not based on any real feeling for their partners.

The Genital Character

It must be emphasized that the forms of adult personality structure that have been described fall within the normal range.   Character structures of those suffering from personality disturbances cannot be presented.   Of necessity, the descriptions paint an extreme picture of each kind of character structure.   Most individuals do not stay at these extremes, but instead vary in degrees and proportions.   There is, perhaps, just enough preponderance of one to enable placement in a given category.

The genital character is, in a sense, an ideal, imperfectly achieved even by those considered deserving of being referred to in this fashion. The mature or genital personality is the culmination of the sequence of psychosexual stages of development.   Adequate heterosexual ad-justment is the *sine qua none* of the genital character.   Full, non-neurotic satisfaction through genital orgasm in heterosexual relations is a pragmatic test.   Sublimation is extensively used.   Emotions, in-stead of being reacted to by the use of ego defense, are thus used constructively by the ego. To be sure, such a person shows the effects of the previous psychosexual stages but in proportion and form conducive to an effective and happy life. Pregenital impulses are in the main sublimated, though vestiges still appear in the love-making preceding the sexual act.

Summary

Psychoanalysis has been considered in the setting of a developmental sequence beginning with the biological determinants and proceeding through the various stages of psychosexual development.

Sexuality is the basic human motive from which others are derived. However, it is expressed differently at different ages and sexuality in general is not to be equated with adult sexuality. Sexual behavior is qualitatively continuous throughout the life span with its manifestations changing from infancy through childhood into adolescence and adulthood. The energy for the sexual desire is the libido. The source of this energy, to a great extent manifested unconsciously, is the id. Both libido and id are present at birth and hence may be referred to the biological determinants.

The psychosexual stages through which the child passes are characterized by differing areas of libidinal localization, differing modes of pleasure finding, and differing object relations. At each stage there is a characteristic structural organization of the personality and the emergence of certain characteristic mechanisms of adjustment.

The oral stage is characterized by libidinal localization in the mouth area, first in the act (mode of pleasure finding) of sucking and swallowing and later in biting. The mother is the first love object. Following this period of exclusively positive attachment, ambivalence develops in the later oral stage. There is beginnings of the ego through awareness. The mechanisms of fixation, regression, introjection, and projection appear.

The anal stage in its early phase centers in its mode of pleasure finding upon expelling of feces, whereas in the later phase there is a shift to their retention. Ambivalence toward the mother continues. The ego is strengthened during this stage and takes on a more active form with the mastering of motility and the development of judgment. Denial of reality as a mechanism of adjustment appears.

The phallic stage has as its area of libidinal localization the genital region with the means of seeking pleasure centering in these organs. It is during this stage that the Oedipus complex arises, reaches full flower, and is destroyed by the anxieties attendant upon the situation. The superego develops as a reaction to the Oedipus situation, and the ego emerges in final form. Hence, the constituents of personality, the id, ego, and superego, have, at this age, assumed their final form and structure to be modified only in relatively minor ways thereafter. The earlier mechanisms and the new mechanisms of sublimation, repression, reaction formation, undoing, isolation, and displacement now become means whereby the ego defends itself against pain. Hence, hereafter they are referred to as mechanisms of defense.

Latency, ushered in about the age of six, is not a psychosexual stage but a period of relative quiescence so far as sexual activity is concerned. Object relations are extended to one's peers and sublimated affection toward the parents becomes prominent. There is a consolidation and strengthening of the ego and superego. No new mechanisms appear.

The genital stage has a prepubertal phase beginning at about age ten. Libido is again directed toward the love objects of childhood and there is some disruption of the structure of organization of the personality, characterized by variation in dominance of ego and id. When the ego dominates, there is an increase in anxiety and the development of the new mechanisms of asceticism and intellectualization. When the id predominates, lapses into sources of pregenital gratification occur, and aggressive, even criminal, behavior may result. With the arrival of bodily sexual maturity in the pubertal phases, adult modes of pleasure finding are sought, including new, nonparental object relations.

Adult personality structure is interpreted in terms of the various normal types of personality arising from the experiences of childhood. Thus we have oral, anal, and phallic characters arising from disproportionate fixation and tendencies to regression to these modes of pleasure finding on the part of adults. The genital character is an ideal, imperfectly achieved by almost all adults, with adult heterosexual adjustment of a nonneurotic sort being its major characteristic.

For Further Reading

For an account of both psychoanalytic and nonpsychoanalytic approaches to personality, the book by Calvin S. Hall and Gardner Lindzey, *Theories of Personality* (New York: Wiley, 1957), is recommended.   Gerald S. Blum has written an excellent summarization of psychoanalytic theory in developmental terms, *Psychoanalytic Theories of Personality* (New York: McGraw-Hill, 1953).

References

1. Blum, G. S.   *Psychoanalytic theories of personality.*   New York: McGraw-Hill, 1953.
2. Erikson, E.   *Childhood and society.*   New York: Norton, 1950.
3. Fenichel, O.   *The psychoanalytic theory of neurosis.*   New York: Norton, 1945.
4. Freud, Anna.   *The ego and the mechanisms of defense.*   New York: International Universities Press, 1946.
5. Freud, Anna.   Some remarks on infant observation.   In Ruth S. Eissler *et al.* Eds.), *The psychoanalytic study of the child*, Vol. 8.   New York: International Universities Press, 1953, 9–19.
6. Freud, S.   *Introductory lectures to psychoanalysis.*   New York: Boni, 1920.
7. Freud, S.   *An outline of psychoanalysis.*   New York: Norton, 1949.
8. Hartmann, H., Kris, E., and Loewenstein, R. M.   Comments on the formation of psychic structure.   In Anna Freud *et al.* (Eds.), *Psychoanalytic studies of the child*, Vol. 2.   New York: International Universities Press, 1947, 11–38.
9. Healy, W., Bronner, Augusta F., and Bowers, Anna M.   *The structure and meaning of psychoanalysis.*   New York: Knopf, 1930.
10. Josselyn, Irene M.   *Psychosocial development of children.*   New York: Family Service Association, 1948.
11. Munroe, Ruth L.   *Schools of psychoanalytic thought: an exposition, critique, and attempt at integration.*   New York: Dryden, 1955.
12. Sterba, R.   Introduction to the psychoanalytic theory of the libido.   *Nerv. ment. Dis. Monogr.,* 1947, No. 68.

part **II**

Infancy

chapter 6

Psychological Development in Infancy

AT LONG LAST WE ARE READY TO STUDY THE INFANT and child from a developmental viewpoint. We are now going to consider the infant, first as he appears at birth and shortly thereafter, and then as the developmental flow moves through time during the first two years of life. Since emphasis is placed upon research findings, infancy will be introduced by consideration of some research techniques used in its study.

Techniques of studying infants

A distinction may be made between techniques used for controlling the stimulus situation and those used for recording responses. This distinction was made by Richards and Irwin (50) in their review of techniques used in infancy. A few techniques that they mention as used in controlling visual stimuli will serve as illustrations. In the study of color vision, representative methods of controlling stimuli include colored cards, yarns of known saturation, hue, and brightness, and colored light stimuli. For the study of brightness and form, light without color, two and three dimensional forms on paper and spheres, and cubes and cylinders have been used. They go on to offer a similar description for the other sense modalities. With respect to the recording of responses, work with infants has included the use of recording drums, timing devices, conditioning apparatuses, galvanometers and, indeed, the gamut of laboratory devices developed over the years for investigating psychological phenomena. Control of stimuli and means for recording both render the situation more objective.

Cinemanalysis

This technique was developed and refined by Gesell and his co-workers (21). Cinemanalysis refers to an analytic study of a motion picture film either as a sequence or individually, frame by frame. Exactitude of original observation and accurate recording can be no more vividly illustrated than by this type of motion picture study. What the infant or child did is available on photographic film long after the original moment and thus may be studied and restudied. The work of Gesell on the development of behavior, frequently referred to throughout this book, is based primarily on cinemanalysis. Figure 3 shows a drawing of his cinemaphotographic observation unit. The observer records the entire behavior, later studying any selected portions which meet his particular research needs.

Stabilimeter

Measuring general activity of the infant is often done through a device called the stabilimeter. The infant is placed upon a platform which is so arranged as to be sensitive to the slightest movement. The movements of the platform are recorded by pens writing upon a moving tape. To control other unintended sources of stimulation, the apparatus is frequently enclosed in an observation cabinet so that temperature, humidity, sound, and light can be regulated in order to keep them constant.

The neonate

The infant during the first period of life is referred to as a neonate. This period lasts until the end of the first month, according to the generally prevailing view (47). The neonatal period, then, is a stage

Figure 3.   Schematic drawing of the Yale Cinemaphotographic Unit.

preceding infancy proper.   For our purposes, the neonatal period will serve as a means against which to sketch the behavior repertoire of the newborn.   As our base line, we use this band of one month rather than a narrower time interval.   It would be fruitless to try to state the sensitivities and activities of which the infant is capable only at the moment of birth.   Instead, that which appears in his behavior during the first month of life will be discussed, even if we know that a particular function appears earlier or later during the neonatal period.   Those studies of the newborn infant which are developmental in character, for example, a study of the changes in motor activities day-by-day during the first few days of life, are not discussed now but in a later section of this chapter which is concerned with motor development in infancy.   The neonatal period will provide a base line of behavior against which to see the effects of maturational-learning development.

Physical Appearance and Bodily Proportions

Even a fond mother may experience a sense of shock at the first sight of the tiny, wizened, red creature that is her offspring. (The "newborn" babies of the advertisements are apparently about two months of age.) The eyes are approximately one-half their adult size, while the body as a whole is only one-twentieth of its adult dimensions. The head is about one-fourth of body length as compared to the adult's one-seventh. As a consequence of these proportions he appears all head and eyes. Figure 4 below shows something of the neonate's general appearance. At birth, the average infant weighs 7 or 8 pounds and measures about 20 inches. The range, however, is from 3 to 16 pounds and from 17 to 21 or 22 inches. Boys are generally slightly larger and heavier than girls.

The Neonate as an Organism

We may speak of the neonate as an organism as distinguished from the person he is to become. The human being may be viewed on various levels. He may be seen as a molecular aggregation, an or-

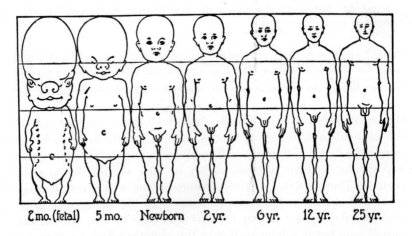

2 mo. (fetal)   5 mo.   Newborn   2 yr.   6 yr.   12 yr.   25 yr.

Figure 4. Changes in body form and proportion during prenatal and postnatal growth. (From C. M. Jackson (Ed.), Human Anatomy, 9th ed. Copyright 1933 by Blakiston Division, McGraw-Hill Book Company, and published with permission.)

ganism, a person, as an aspect of a diadic unit of two or more persons, and as an aggregate in a group. In other words, he may be viewed in order of expanding perspective at a physical-chemical level, a biological level, a psychological level, a social psychological level, and a sociological level.

The scientific laws which have been laboriously worked out at one level are not necessarily suitable for application at a different level. In scrutinizing the child at a given level, we view him in a different light and see different phenomena than we would if another level were applied. The physical-chemical level is too far removed for direct concern; the psychological level has not yet come into being. We shall look at the neonate as a biological organism viewed in cross-sectional perspective. We take our vantage point at the biological level because in the neonate there has occurred a minimum of psychological interaction with others. Psychological laws either of the individual person or of the diadic (social) sort are not relevant as the material is organized in this examination of the neonate's behavior repertoire.

In the light of these principles our organization of the findings on the neonate becomes clear. We must consider reactions to various forms of stimuli and the motor responses of which he is capable.

Sensory Stimulation [1]

Reactions to various forms of sensory stimuli in the neonate will be briefly sketched. There is no question that the neonate can see, hear, smell, and taste. What we need to know are some of the particulars about his prowess with respect to these sensory processes.

Reactions to visual stimuli. The neonate reacts to light, but it is not certain whether he distinguishes color as such. In other words, at birth he may be temporarily color-blind. He does, however, respond to different degrees of brightness. Closing the eyes spontaneously to a flash of light and to objects moving toward the eyes has been noted. Within a day or two after birth the pupillary reflex (widening or narrowing of the pupil in response to light) has been observed. Eye movements of various sorts have also been found. These include: pursuit (following a visual stimulus with movement of the eyes); saccadic (quick jerky fixations as in adult reading); coordinate (eyes moving together); and coordinate compensatory (head quickly mov-

---

[1] The present account leans heavily upon that of Pratt (47).

ing in one direction, with eye movements in opposite direction). The eye movement responses just defined are either reflex in character or, at least, of a circumscribed nature. More gross muscular patterns or general mass behavior has also been elicited. Practically any visual stimuli, if sufficiently intense, will release circulatory and respiratory (for example, "catching" the breath) responses in the neonate. The startle response involving coordination of many parts of the body is also elicited by intense visual stimulation. Thus, both reflex and mass activity are reactions to visual stimuli.

Reactions to auditory stimuli. There is some question as to whether or not the neonate can hear immediately at birth. Certainly neonates vary in sensitivity, with some showing an imperviousness to the influence of sound, despite later normal hearing. Neonatal infants fail to make pitch discriminations, but they do respond differentially to differential intensities of sound. As in visual responses, both specific reflexes, such as blinking the eyes and gross muscular patterns of response, appear.

Reactions to other sensory stimuli. Both taste and smell are well developed at birth. The neonate responds to odors even during sleep by squirming, crying, and sucking. As for taste, sugar solutions tend to elicit sucking which is maintained; acid solutions evoke sucking which lasts for a shorter period; salt solutions, after being tried a bit, are not sucked; while bitter solutions, such as quinine, are seldom sucked. However, wide individual differences among neonates to taste thresholds are found. The neonate's skin is sensitive to touch, temperature, and pain. Concerning skin sensitiveness, there is a general principle that with increase in intensity there is a progression from more localized to more general bodily movements. A light touch may bring about a slight withdrawal of the part touched and no more, a heavy pressure brings out much more violent and widespread activity. Sensitivity to being moved or changed in position, which stimulates the static receptors, is shown in postural or "balance" responses, by which the neonate rights himself when not too far off-balance. Reactions to internal (organic) stimuli are present. Although the respiratory and circulatory system supply some of these, the preponderance of the internal stimuli come from the digestive and excretory systems. Regurgitation, hiccoughing, urination, and excretion are illustrative.

It is apparent, even from this brief summarization, that the neonate exhibits a varied repertoire of reactions to sensory stimuli. His sensory capacities allow him to be sensitive to his external and internal environment. Although sensory capacities will increase in sensitivity and scope, a considerable variety is still available to the human organism during the neonatal period.

Motor Responses

The distinction between reactions to sensory stimulation and motor responses, although clear enough in some respects, is nothing more than a matter of emphasis. In the preceding section, focus was on the sensory modality originating the response. Nevertheless, sensory stimulation was known to occur through the responses that were elicited. We now group responses by the motor areas served. Naturally, many of the same kinds of responses appear again, but they are now in the setting of such areas as the eye, mouth, and trunk to name but three of those considered.

Representative motor responses. A succinct indication of some of the motor responses of the neonate adapted from the summary by Dennis (*11*) will first be presented.

1. EYE RESPONSES—opening and closing eyelids, pupillary, pursuit, saccadic, and coordinate compensatory responses (described in reactions to visual stimuli).

2. FACIAL AND MOUTH RESPONSES—opening and closing mouth, lip movement, sucking, pushing objects from mouth, yawning, and grimacing.

3. THROAT RESPONSES—crying, swallowing, coughing, gagging, vomiting, hiccoughing, cooing, and holding the breath.

4. HEAD MOVEMENTS—upward and downward, side to side, and balancing in response to change of bodily position.

5. ARM RESPONSES—closing hand, arm flexion, rubbing face, grasp reflex, and "random" movements.

6. TRUNK REACTIONS—arching back and twisting.

7. FOOT AND LEG RESPONSES—knee jerk, flexion, extension, kicking (both legs simultaneously), stepping (when neonate held upright with feet touching surface), and toe flexion.

8. COORDINATE RESPONSES OF MANY BODY PARTS—resting and sleeping position (legs flexed, fists closed, upper arms out straight from shoulder with forearms flexed at right angles parallel to the head), springing position (infant held upright and inclined forward, the arms extend forward and legs are brought up), stretching, shivering,

trembling, unrest with crying, creeping, bodily jerk, Moro reflex (throwing arms apart, spreading of fingers, extension of legs, and throwing back of head).

Despite the incompleteness of this account of the neonate's behavior repertoire, the list may still appear surprisingly long. Only to the uninitiated eye is the infant a mass of twists and squirms. The neonate, after all, starts life with a rather large number and often complicated repertoire of responses. The potentialities for both differentiation and integration are present in the neonate's behavior repertoire. There are both specific movements and mass activity present in his behavior. He also starts life with a series of needs. To an account of these needs we next turn.

The Needs of the Neonate

Certain coordinated responses present in the neonate are so vital for his survival and so demanding in their necessity of being satisfied that they may be conceptualized as needs. Therefore, their presentation is organized around the needs which bring forth responses from the neonate.

Hunger and thirst. Certain responses such as sucking, swallowing, and head movements that form parts of the feeding (and drinking) responses have already been mentioned in connection with representative motor responses. We are now concerned with feeding responses as coordinated activities, expressive of hunger and thirst needs. As Pratt (47) indicates, neonatal feeding involves three activities which form a series: (1) head-mouth orientation—contact stimulation of the neonate's cheek evokes head turning toward the source of stimulation, followed by opening of the mouth and snapping movements; (2) lip reflexes coordinated with head-mouth orientation appear—pursing the lips to contact with the nipple; and (3) sucking and swallowing movements which form a rhythm. Swallowing imparts its rhythm upon sucking; this combined rhythm is in turn imposed upon respiration so that breathing is not interfered with. General activity is reduced when sucking starts, the neonate becoming relatively quiescent.

When viewed in the perspective of the neonate's day-to-day behavior, hunger and thirst are clearly seen not to be automatic reflex activities. To be specific, although based upon a reflex pattern, sucking is influenced by repeated reinforcement in securing nourishment. If the infant's hunger and thirst are not reduced, and reduced quite quickly, tensions mount and provoke a considerable amount of bodily activity. Consequently, they are important in his learning activities.

These responses, although they form a coordinated series, are not reflexlike in that, once started, the chain is not invariably completed. Jensen (34), for example, has found that sucking of air may occur without swallowing. It is well known that sucking of some substances, instead of being followed by swallowing, results in spitting out or rejection. The newborn infant frequently sucks in air when he is swallowing, causing him to choke or to develop colic pains.

Neonates show individual differences in the efficiency with which they carry out any or all of these coordinated activities. Although some authorities insist, as did Ribble (49), that a large number of infants show such feeble sucking movements as to require adult help, the weight of evidence appears to indicate that only a small proportion of infants need assistance or prompting. Whatever the proportion may be, there is considerable variability among neonates in this respect as well as in other facets of feeding responses.

A neonate must give his active cooperation if the feeding process is to be carried out smoothly and efficiently. In a modern version of the saying about a horse and water, Escalona comments, "You can put him to the breast, but you can't make him swallow" (16, 14).[2] If he is tired, in pain, drowsy, or not hungry, to name some few instances, he simply does not suck. In general, if the situation is a pleasurable one, he will do so. To bring about this state, the cooperation between mother and neonate, a coordination of their efforts is necessary. Discussion of the significance and ramifications of this social relationship is, however, deferred until the next chapter which is concerned with psychosocial development.

As prerequisites for arousal of hunger and thirst, the neonate needs to be awake and approaching in time a nursing period. The neonate shows his hunger and thirst by crying and restless movements until he is fed. He then tends to quiet down and most often falls asleep. This cycle of feeding and sleeping is the major cycle of activity that neonates show—restless when hungry, quiescent or asleep when fed (4).

Healthy neonates demand food about every three hours. Gesell

[2] From Escalona (16). Copyright 1953 by The Josiah Macy, Jr., Foundation, and published with permission.

and Ilg (23) report that, on the average, newborn babies take seven or eight feedings per day. But, nevertheless, there is wide individual variation. Some neonates may reach a peak of maximum activity in as short a time as two-and-a-half hours, while others may go as long as five hours between peaks. Moreover, neonates who regularly show a given cycle, say, three hours, may have some intervals shorter or longer than the usual interval. It should come as no surprise by now that individual differences among infants in the number of feedings should vary both between infants and in the same infant from time to time, making relative and tentative these seemingly precise statements. Using as an example, one neonate fed on self-demand was studied by Simsarian and McLendon (55) each day between the second and tenth day of life; it was found that on one of these days he demanded to be fed eleven times but on another day, only six times. But there is apt, nevertheless, to be a sort of consistency as shown by the fact that this same neonate five days out of nine demanded nine feedings. Variability, but still with some degree of consistency, seems to characterize the feeding behavior of the neonate.

Sleep. Sleep is very much a need. Without its nourishing restorative function, the organism would die. As Gesell (23) reminds us, sleep is behavior. It is not the cessation of behavior; it is a kind of behavior in which certain forms of waking behavior are minimized or modified.

Sleep conceived in terms of a gradient of motility seems to fit the situation of the neonate most adequately. We do not have available for use the cultural criteria of adult sleep such as going to bed, closing the eyes, assuming a restful posture, and inability when wakened to give an accurate account of the time intervening. For the neonate the application of these criteria simply is not possible. What is present is a gradient of motility extending from considerable activity with eyes open to "inactivity," regular breathing and absence of eyelid and mouth movements. It is generally agreed (47) that during sleep irritability, in its general sense, is decreased and reaction times lengthened. Responses decrease as depth of sleep increases. Indeed, it is difficult, even for trained observers, to agree in some intermediate stages whether or not the infant is asleep or awake. Consequently, lacking verbal response, we cannot always be sure.

Despite these difficulties in measurement it would appear that the neonate sleeps about 20 hours in a 24 hour period (48). Duration of each sleep period is approximately three hours in length. Much of the neonate's time, then, is spent in sleeping. Gesell (23) reports that the neonate averages seven or eight sleep periods in 24 hours. During this period the distinction between the night as the time for sleeping and the day as the time for wakefulness is, of course, non-existent.

Elimination. Waste products must be eliminated from the body. Three processes are available—sweating, urination, and bowel movements. These elimination processes are involuntary and automatic in the neonate. Increased pressure in the bladder and in the bowel results in relaxation of muscles and the contents are involuntarily released. The neuromuscular apparatus for voluntary control has not yet developed.

Temperature regulation. In the fetal period, the environment of the mother's womb supplies a constant temperature. After birth, the neonate faces a fluctuating temperature in the environment. He is exposed to these changes and to drafts. Within certain limits his automatic physiological mechanisms maintain body temperature. However, when these limits are exceeded, adjustment through external assistance by the parents is needed. The neonate, of course, is not "aware" in any true sense of his need for temperature regulation. He, like adults, is aware of it only when something goes wrong. But, unlike the adult, he does not know what he needs when pain and discomfort arise.

Oxygen needs. Vital to the preservation of life is an adequate oxygen supply. In the neonate this need is intensified by the fact that although respiration is a reflex activity, it is not necessarily stabilized in rhythm and efficiency at the time of birth. In a few days, however, it reaches a level of efficiency quite adequate for ordinary needs. Its relative instability dramatically calls attention to respiration as serving a need of the organism. As in the case of temperature regulation it becomes noticeable as a need only when not met.

Precursors to sexual needs. It is a matter of some controversy whether or not we can speak of sexual needs in the neonate and infant. Discussion of this issue will be given in the next chapter. The path of conservatism at this juncture is to speak of forerunners or precursors of sexual needs and leave the matter unsettled until later discussion.

Susceptibility to external genital stimulation in very young infants has been established. Infants are quite responsive to stimulation in the genital area. If an infant is having a crying spell, such stimulation tends to quiet him. Lustman (*40*), in research described in more detail later on page 256, found that newborn infants were quite sensitive to both manual and air pressure stimulation of the genital region, as shown by temperature increase in this area. In another study (*29*) nine male infants were observed for eight-and-a-half consecutive hours per day for ten days. Tumescence (erection) occurred at least once every day in seven newborn infants, while the other two showed such behavior on nine and eight days, respectively. These responses were primarily to internal stimulation—strong sucking or a full bowel or bladder setting off the reflex response. Great individual differences were noted, with the actual number of instances of tumescence varying from a median of four to a median of 35 per day. Tumescence was, in general, accompanied by what can be referred to as unpleasantness—restlessness, crying, fretting, and stiff legs—to name the most prominent concomitants. Detumescence, in contrast, was apparently pleasurable—crying, during it, for example, was almost nonexistent.

Homeostasis and neonatal needs. We have examined the neonate as a biological organism. Like all organisms it is found to be equipped to survive and to develop. Its behavior repertoire demonstrates its ability to relate to its environment. It shows homeostasis, a maintenance of stability in its biological functioning. Given certain assistance from its environment (particularly from the mother), it maintains its organism through meeting its needs, particularly hunger and thirst, sleep, elimination, temperature regulation, oxygen content, and possibly sexual needs. It preserves its equilibrium in the manner and within the limits sketched in the earlier presentation.

Developmental changes in needs during infancy

In concluding the discussion of needs of the neonate, we also conclude the discussion of the neonate as a base line and turn to developmental changes during infancy. We shall begin with a discussion of developmental changes in feeding, sleep, and elimination. The other neonatal needs do not show enough important developmental changes to warrant consideration.

Developmental Changes in Feeding

You will remember that neonates are reported by Gesell and Ilg (23) as requiring about seven or eight feedings per day. By the time they are four weeks old typically the number of feedings has been reduced to five or six. The number of feedings is reduced further to three to five feedings in the following weeks. Beginning at 16 weeks this number of feedings, or a little less, is maintained until toward the end of the first year, by which time the three meals a day regime of our culture is fairly well established (along with one or two snacks).

Supplementation by solid foods has been going on from about 20 weeks of age. Cup and spoon feeding takes place during this time and by 40 weeks the infant helps himself in feeding, incidentally making a fine mess of it in the process. Even preference for certain foods is well defined at one year, for example, certain vegetables, hot as compared to cold cereals, and so on.

Scheduling and self-demand feeding. Scheduling and self-demand feeding will be discussed first in terms of some normative findings in order to place the problem in perspective; next will be a discussion of some of the evidence that led to the use of self-demand feeding; and, finally, consideration of the question of whether scheduling in very young infants is learned or not learned by them.

In general, the large group of mothers interviewed by Sears and his associates (51) used neither a self-demand system nor a rigid schedule but something in between. (This study is described in more detail in the next chapter on page 249.) Only 12 per cent of the mothers always fed the infant when he cried and permitted him to eat as much as he wanted. Only eight per cent fed him by the clock, waking him for feedings. The remainder followed practices that were somewhere between these extremes.

It was the pioneer study of Clara M. Davis (9) in 1928 which probably served as the original scientific impetus for changing adult attitudes in the direction of greater permissiveness toward infant feeding and self-regulation in the scheduling of infant feedings. In her study 15 infants of about weaning age were presented with a variety of foods from which to choose as to kind and amount. In the first few days of free choice, there were great individual differences among the infants as to what and how much they ate. All of the infants gradually selected diets which, according to adult standards, were well-balanced and nutritious. Moreover, none of them developed feeding problems.   In a later study (10), she permitted infants a free choice of different formulas at a single feeding and found that highly variable amounts and kinds were taken at different meals.   Davis's studies and those that followed after helped to usher in an era of greater trust in the infant's capacity to select how much to eat, at what times, and how often.   But this does not mean he cannot learn to adapt to a schedule instituted by his parents.

Infants are fully capable of learning to adapt to the feeding schedules introduced by adults.   This was neatly demonstrated by Dorothy Marquis (43) who studied the learning of a feeding schedule by infants during the first ten days of life while they were still in the hospital.   Two infant groups, experimental and control, were placed on different feeding schedules.   The experimental group was on a three-hour feeding schedule, except during the last day in the hospital when these infants were shifted to a four-hour schedule, while the control group was on a four-hour feeding schedule throughout its hospital stay.   She measured in both groups the activity patterns (restlessness) by a mechanical device supporting the bassinets in which the infants lay.   Their activity was the criterion of adaptiveness to the schedule.   When the interval of feeding was changed from three to four hours in the experimental group on the tenth day, these infants showed a sharp rise in their activity during this extra hour between feedings.   At the end of three hours, their heretofore habitual feeding time, body movements increased abruptly and continued throughout the fourth hour.   Apparently, the infants had learned to respond to hunger cues at the end of three hours.   Failure to receive their accustomed feeding markedly increased restlessness.   Those control infants fed on a four-hour schedule from birth to what was now the tenth day showed only their usual gradual increase in activity as their feeding time approached.   Marquis suggests that this adaptation to a schedule, as shown by the experimental group with their increased activity when the schedule was disrupted, is an instance of the earliest form of socialization.   It made a difference for these infants to have to wait an extra hour for feeding, showing in a definitive fashion the learning of the newborn infant in the process of adapting to the external demands of a feeding schedule.

Breast and bottle feeding.   In the Sears, Maccoby, Levin study (51) they found 40 per cent of the infants were breast fed, of which the majority received breast feeding for but three months.   In view of the large number being fed by bottles and the relative shortness of breast feeding by those who did receive it, it is of interest, despite the somewhat digressive character, to examine the reason the mothers gave for not breast feeding. Over 40 per cent claimed they were unable to breast feed for physical reasons, such as not having enough milk or the presence of inverted nipples. Another 16 per cent reported that the doctor advised against breast feeding without specifying any physical difficulty. Thirty-five per cent did not want to breast feed, some for emotional reasons, others because they did not want to be tied down, and still others for unspecified reasons.

The two groups who gave "physical reasons" or "doctor's advice" seem quite large, too large in fact for the reasons given to represent actually the true state of affairs. There is a strong possibility that the objections they offered to breast feeding were rationalizations and that they did not want to for reasons other than the ones given. For example, "inability" may have been dislike of breast feeding.

Weaning. The sucking movements of the infant are adapted for taking liquid foods from breast or bottle. With increased maturation at about the third or fourth month, mouth movements begin to change in a direction suitable for eating solid food and biting movements begin to appear. By seven to nine months these movements have become stronger.

Repeated reinforcement of sucking has occurred during these early months and sucking has become a well-established habit in securing nourishment. The process of weaning means these habitual patterns must be eliminated and new activities learned.

It cannot be overemphasized that, while weaning at first glance may appear to be a simple straightforward practice, it is, in reality, a very complicated one. Even the term is used in more than one sense. Sometimes, weaning refers to a shift from breast to bottle feeding. In the sense used here, however, it means the process of giving up sucking for a new mode of food-getting through eating of solid foods and drinking (not sucking) of liquids. As Sears, Maccoby, and Levin indicate, weaning involves five tasks:

> The child must learn *not to want* to get his food by sucking. He must learn to *like* to *drink* the same food he formerly got by sucking. He must learn to *want solid foods*. He must learn the *manipulative skills* required for eating them—biting, chewing, and the use of fingers and utensils, as well as drinking from a cup. He must learn to do *without being held* while he is eating (*51*, 69).[3]

[3] From Sears, Maccoby and Levin (*51*). Copyright 1957 by Row, Peterson, and published with permission.

Now each of these tasks may be presented to the child in an endless variety of ways. For example, solid foods can be thrust at him all at once or their presentation can be spaced almost from birth, long before the process of weaning. Frustrations arising from weaning will depend upon many things, not precisely summed up as "weaning."

In their sample of mothers, Sears *et al.* (*51*) found that two-thirds had started the weaning process by the time the infant was 11 months old. For the majority, the process of weaning took four months to complete. Nevertheless, at least 12 per cent took a year or more.

Developmental Changes in Sleep

As the infant grows older, his general activities increase while his sleep decreases. By the end of infancy he may be sleeping as little as 11 hours at night with one or two naps during the day. Gesell (*23*) offers a detailed description of sleep behavior at various ages. At four weeks he reports that typically the infant gradually drops off to sleep toward the end of the nursing period. At this age the infant has four to five sleep periods in 24 hours. By 16 weeks he has established something of a night sleep rhythm, falling asleep after the six P.M. feeding and waking between five and six A.M. He does not fall asleep immediately after each feeding and has about three naps during the day in addition to his sleep periods. At 40 weeks he tends to fall asleep after his six P.M. feeding and sleeps through to five to seven A.M. There may be one long midmorning nap or as many as four short nap periods.

While the total number of hours of infant's sleep is decreasing, the hours are increasing in length (*48*). While hunger and pain may awaken him at any time, loud sounds and other stimuli are decreased in our culture at night and consequently, during this period he is less disturbed by environmental stimuli. This plus other socialization practices cause the interrupting of sleep to be less frequent at night. As the infant grows older, increasing stimulation from its surroundings competes with the biological demands for sleep. We arrange these in terms of cultural expectancies with emphasis on more stimulation during the day than at night. Part of the pattern is, nevertheless, that of daytime naps. He learns sleep habits in relation to the time patterns of his culture.

As Gesell (*23*) indicates, the infant must learn to sleep in the same way he learns to creep, stand and walk, and grasp a spoon. He must also learn to stay awake! Although learning is undoubtedly important, maturation is also important. As he grows older he is not so subcortical (without the service of the highest nerve centers of the brain) as Gesell puts it. Millions of cortical cells, previously non-functional because they had not matured sufficiently, are beginning to make connections between eyes, ears, and the muscles of the eyes. Their maturation serves to keep his cortex "awake" and thus for him to be more receptive to his surroundings. Staying awake for longer periods of time (with increasing amounts of time spent in acts other than those associated with hunger and feeding) is an important part of the process of early development (4). These longer periods of waking afford opportunity for more intensive and varied experiences with the environment.

There are, of course, individual differences in sleep requirements among infants and in the same infant from one time to another. By and large, however, we are not too demanding in our culture and allow the child during infancy to express his individuality in this regard. He generally may be said to sleep as much as he needs to, and to wake when rested. Consequently, sleep is not a vehicle upon which extremes of social pressure are practiced, which accounts for its omission from discussion in the chapter on psychosocialization following this one.

Developmental Changes in Elimination

Gesell's normative findings (23) will again be appealed to in connection with elimination changes. At four weeks the infant tends to have three or four bowel movements in a 24 hour period. He may now cry when his diaper is wet and he quiets when changed. At 16 weeks there are one or two movements, most commonly after a feeding. By 28 weeks there is apt to be only one movement, usually at nine to ten A.M. Urination is still occurring at frequent intervals. At 40 weeks the infant may be dry after an hour's nap and sometimes an infant may respond to the pot. Changes hereafter will be described in the context of the problem of toilet training which this need engenders.

Social demands in our culture require that the child learn voluntary control of bladder and bowel so as to void at an acceptable time and place. Changes in eliminative processes under ideal conditions await the age at which neuromuscular mechanisms have sufficiently matured for them to be voluntarily controlled. As a neonate he cannot do so, even if by some miracle, he "wanted" to do so. Punishment, bribes,

and scolding may go on relentlessly, but the learning remains incidental and sporadic until he is maturationally ready for voluntary
control.

Both bladder and bowel control are extremely complicated processes, neurologically and psychologically (23). Not only are there
complicated neural pathways which must mature, but also the processes and paths change from age period to age period. Moreover,
they involve the entire organism, not just isolated organ systems. For
example, it is not until about 15 months of age that postural immaturi-
ties have lessened sufficiently to allow the infant to sit on the toilet.
Language enters into the process in that he can communicate his
needs in this area at about 18 months.

The importance of maturation in bladder control is shown in a
study by McGraw (42) on twin boys. With one of them, bladder
training was started at about 50 days by placing him on the toilet
every hour. Until about 600 days there was little evidence of learning. After 600 days the curve of success increased sharply, and by
700 days successes were close to 100 per cent. No training whatsoever was started with the other twin until 700 days. His performance
was almost immediately as good as that of the twin with the longer
period of training. This rather startling difference is not an isolated
phenomenon as another record of twins by McGraw shows. Evidently, training started later rather than earlier takes advantage of
maturation and is more effective than trying to train earlier.

The results found by McGraw, however, should not be taken as
definitive concerning the *date* to begin training or to expect its ending.
This is subject to individual variation. Moreover, only one rather
rigid method of training was used in her study. It is quite possible
that if a more flexible schedule had been used, different data concerning timing would have been found. Her data is indicative merely
of *relative* relationships in these twins and is in no way an index of
what happens in sample groups. This normative question is considered in a moment.

Toilet training is a learning situation (15) in which whatever reward may accrue to the child it is not in the satisfaction of the basic
need. His social eliminative needs are, if one may slip into the
vernacular, learned the hard way.

The infant is not repelled by his bodily products. He will play
with them when the opportunity arises. Parents vary in their reaction to this situation, but having to face it is inescapable. They
may arrange to direct attention elsewhere by diverting the child

from this interest, become angry and repressive, or show any other of a hundred other responses, but deal with it they must. They must also deal with the entire problem of cleanliness. In dealing with the problem they train their infants whether this be formal avowed training as it always is in some aspects or in the unacknowledged unintentional facets of their teaching.

As Dollard and Miller (15) indicate, the learning of toilet training practices proceeds without verbal aids because the infant does not have either the active verbal repertoire or understanding to deal with training in this fashion. As a consequence, training in cleanliness proceeds by a process of trial and error. To quote Dollard and Miller:

> The child must learn to wake up in order to go to the toilet, though sleep seems good. It must learn to stop its play even when social excitement is strong. It must learn to discriminate between the different rooms of the house—all this by crude trial and error. In this case, "trial" means urinating or defecating in an inappropriate place, and "error" means being punished for the act so that anxiety responses are attached to the cues of this place. In the trial-and-error situation this must be repeated for each inappropriate place—bed, living room, dining room, kitchen, "outside." The function of this training is to attach anxiety responses to the defecation drive so that they win out over the immediate evulsion response. These anxiety responses also motivate and cue off the next responses in the series, such as calling to the parents, running to the bathroom, unbuttoning the clothes, and the like (15, 138).[4]

This process naturally arouses strong emotional reactions in the child. Anger, defiance, stubbornness, and fear appear in response to this situation. The effects of this process, occurring as it does in a social setting, will be discussed in the next chapter.

We are now in a position to examine in our culture the question of scheduling of toilet training by parents. The pattern study of Sears, Maccoby, and Levin (51) will again be referred to for data about this training. For their group the average age for beginning bowel training was about 11 months and for completion about 18 months. For any two-month period the greatest percentage started between nine and 11 months. Almost 75 per cent were trained between ten and 24 months. A few (eight per cent) were trained between five and nine months and 15 per cent took longer than 24 months. Some mothers claimed it took only a few weeks, while others found it took a year-and-a-half to carry out the process of training. Generally

[4] By permission from *Personality and Psychotherapy,* by Dollard and Miller. Copyright 1950, McGraw-Hill Book Company, Inc.

speaking, if begun later it took less time. For example, if begun at five months it took, on the average, ten months. But if it were begun at 20 months only about five months were required, again pointing up the importance of maturation.

Physical growth during infancy

Just as the psychological development cannot be understood without consideration of social factors, so too some appreciation is necessary of the effect of physical on psychological development. As Thompson (56) indicates, it is his physical maturity which limits the infant's or child's physical and social environment. His size, physique, and agility all affect the psychological environment in which he is to be found. Consideration has already been given to the physical appearance and bodily proportions of the newborn infant. Attention will now be directed to the physical growth which takes place during infancy.

During the first year of life the infant increases his length by over a third and his weight almost triples. Owing to the greater weight than height gain, the infant at one year appears more thick-set. Changes in bodily proportion occur. The "top-heaviness," characteristic at birth, gradually decreases as legs and trunk increase. Although physical development is still proceeding rapidly in the second year, it is at a slower rate than in the first year. At age two, the average child is 32 or 33 inches tall and weighs about 25 pounds (51).

Changes in form and proportion are illustrated in Figure 4 on page 174. It can be seen that parts of the body do not grow equally and at the same rate. Each organ may be said to have a different rate. As Thompson (56) indicates, during the prenatal period growth proceeds cephalocaudally and proximodistally. In other words, to illustrate these two trends successively, head precedes neck development and this in turn precedes chest growth, and so on; meanwhile, upper arm (or leg) growth precedes lower arm (or leg) growth which in turn precedes hand (or foot) growth. Thereafter until puberty, once these trends are established, the greatest growth takes place at the extremities. Hence, head growth is slow, limb growth is rapid, and trunk growth is intermediate.

Changes in height and weight are taking place as Figure 5 attests. In general, height increases at a rapid rate during infancy and then

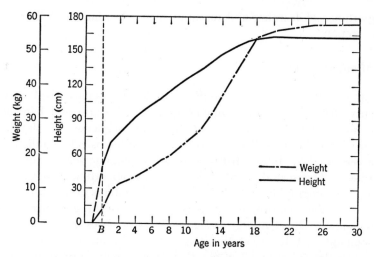

Figure 5. Growth curves for height and weight. (Adapted from Thompson in Carmichael, Manual of Child Psychology (56). E. Boyd, Growth of the Surface Area of the Human Body. Copyright 1935 by the University of Minnesota.)

slows down during childhood and still more later. Weight, after an initial spurt in infancy, slows down thereafter. Fairly large variations in both height and weight are common and considered to fall within normal limits.

Growth and maturation of parts of the body are basically the products of hereditary biological determiners. Nevertheless, the body cannot increase in size and weight without nutritional supplies from the environment. For example, nutritional intake affects weight and height, with infants from poverty-stricken environments tending to be smaller (2). Neither can there be neuromuscular coordination without opportunity for practice. Both learning and maturation are necessary for physical growth.

Motor development in infancy

Motor development during early infancy will be discussed in terms of manipulation and of grasping. Motor development in later infancy is shown through various other skills. Consideration of the

importance of learning and maturation in sensorimotor skills closes
the section.

Manipulation

Manipulatory activity is confined to local, circumscribed movements during most of the infancy period. The arm and hand are
the major means of manipulation. The sequence of development of prehension (grasping) has been intensively studied by
Halverson (28). Infants between 16 weeks and one year of age were
studied. The seated infant was given an opportunity to grasp a
cube. Photographic recordings of various infants were studied to
arrive at the developmental sequence which had grasping as its
culmination. Preceding grasping itself was a series of stages of development. At 16 weeks the infants generally made no contact at
all with the cube; at 20 weeks they made contact, or squeezed it
without grasping. From 24 weeks onward, grasping developed.
Grasping at first is a clawing type of activity with the thumb inactive, followed later by a nipping pressing kind of closure in which
thumb and forefinger dominate, but which is still a form of manipulation which involves much palming. At about one year this immature
form of grasping gives way to a delicate forefinger-tip grasp with
precise placement of the digits on the cube.

Locomotion

The neonate has no effective means of movement from place to
place. From its supine ("face up") or prone ("face down") position
it may shift about a bit, but this movement can hardly be called
locomotion in the sense of movement from place to place. Shirley
(53) has carefully studied the development in posture and locomotion of a group of 25 infants. Figure 6 shows the steps which she
found in the motor sequence. The very fact that one can use the
sequence in this figure to represent changes in locomotion shows that
there is a progressive regularity of development despite some variability from infant to infant. The five major stages are very uniform
and involve the following order: (1) passive postural control; (2)
active postural control; (3) active efforts toward locomotion; (4)
creeping and walking with support; and, finally, (5) walking alone.
The last stage occurred on the average at 64 weeks or about 15
months. Each major stage has within it several steps. Although

Figure 6. The motor sequence. (*Mary M. Shirley,* The First Two Years, *Vol. II: "Intellectual Development." Copyright 1933 by University of Minnesota.*)

these steps may vary in sequence from infant to infant, there is no transposition of the major stages. Each separate stage is a prerequisite for the immediately succeeding stage. Walking is the climax of a long series of activities that are not directly locomotor in themselves but which proceed in an orderly fashion in each infant.

Beginning to walk has profound psychological consequences. The infant is more able to bring himself in contact with "people, places and things." This he does because *he* wants to. Others do not have to come to him. To a much greater degree he now may be independent of adult control. He may walk into areas of which his parents approve, but he may also walk into those of which they emphatically do not. To modify a saying, "Fools, and little children, rush in where angels fear to tread." Thus, beginning at about the age of 15 months and continuing to roughly the age of four, there is a period of great locomotor activity. The period, a strenuous one from the parental point of view, is brought about by the simple fact of walking.

Motor Development in Later Infancy

Motor development in locomotion has been discussed up to the advent of walking at about 15 months, while manipulation has been discussed as it takes place during the first year of life. This means that both other areas of motor development and development in the second year have not been mentioned. Some motor behaviors with characteristic age of appearance according to Gesell and Amatruda (22) are given in Table 4. Both the older infant's versatility and his steady gain in motor skills are exemplified. Other activities such as language and feeding, too, have their motor components which are progressing rapidly.

TABLE 4

MOTOR DEVELOPMENT IN THE SECOND YEAR [*]

Age in Months	Characteristic Motor Skill
15	Creeps up stairs
	Makes a two-cube tower
	Helps turn book pages
18	Walks upstairs, one hand held
	Climbs into adult chair
	Hurls ball
21	Squats while playing
	Walks upstairs holding rail
	Kicks large ball
24	Runs well, no falling
	Walks up and down stairs alone
	Makes a six- or seven-cube tower

[*] Adapted from Gesell and Amatruda (22). Copyright 1947 by Paul B. Hoeber, Inc., and published with permission.

Learning and Maturation in Sensorimotor Skills

During infancy a considerable repertoire of skills is developed by which the infant manipulates and orients himself to his environment (45). Both learning and maturation play a part in this development. Some of these skills, as Munn (45) asserts, are probably more a function of maturation. These include crawling, walking, and finger-thumb opposition. Although we customarily speak of "learning" to walk, neuromuscular maturation seems to be the chief antecedent.

Just as one short illustration, Hopi Indian babies who are bound to cradle boards, thus suffering a good deal of movement restraint during their first year of life, nevertheless walk independently as early as do infants who have much more previous practice (*14*).

To illustrate more specifically the importance of maturation in motor development, the study by Gesell and Thompson (*24*) may be used. They compared the behavior in stair-climbing and cube-building of 46 week old identical twin girls. Use of identical twins meant they were using the method of co-twin control. The choice of age 46 weeks for initial study was dictated by the fact that this is the age at which infants are at the threshold of stair-climbing and cube-building responses. Twin T (trained) was given a ten minute practice session each day for *six* weeks. Twin C (control) was given no training until the end of the six week period at which time she was given *two* weeks of practice.

At the end of this practice period, Twin C was performing these activities as well as Twin T who had four more weeks' practice but at an earlier age. Gesell and Thompson concluded that the time of appearance of stair-climbing and cube-building was not influenced by practice but by the ripening of neural structures. Other related motor activities show the same negative effects of special practice and appear to be primarily determined by maturational factors.

When learning is shown to be involved it is often autogenous, to use a term of Dennis (*12*). That is, such learning arises from the infant's own self-initiated activities, and not because of the influence of specific training by others. There are, Munn (*45*) states, many other skills which would fail to develop unless specific training or opportunity for imitation were provided. These activities include talking, writing, and buttoning clothes.

It is perhaps worth while to call specific attention to the fact that we are considering not motor activity alone, but sensorimotor activity. In the process of learning and/or maturing of these skills a sensory or perceptual aspect is present. Although stressed only in connection with manipulation in the previous discussion, it plays a not inconsiderable part in all motor skills.

Emotional development in infancy

Tension arises in the infant when he is placed in a stress situation such as that described in elimination training. Tension in infants is manifested by such phenomena as heightened muscle tonus, thumb sucking, crying, temperature increase, alteration in respiratory rate and rhythm, gastrointestinal upsets, and disorganization. These conditions may be referred to as emotional states. Tension is the characteristic common to all kinds of emotionality.

In tension states disturbances of smooth on-going functioning occur. Infants show varying degrees of susceptibility to tension. In the last section of the chapter concerned with individuality Fries speaks of varying types of activity patterns in infants. Hyperactive infants, as she uses the term, would be particularly vunerable to tension, while hypoactive infants would be at the other extreme. The former are those sensitive, irritable infants who show tension to stimulation which for the ordinary infant is not tension producing. As will be discussed in Chapter 8, if the stress is severe or prolonged, tensional indices of profound disturbance in the form of psychosomatic symptoms may occur. In the present chapter, emotional factors normal in infancy are considered.

Frustration and Enhancement of Needs

The tension of emotion is aroused when the needs of the infant are frustrated. The relation of frustration and emotional responses in infancy has already been discussed incidentally in connection with earlier topics—for example, frustration expressed in crying and restlessness when hungry, or during toilet training. Hunger-thirst are heightened tension states. It is not conceding too much to agree that hunger is accompanied by displeasure, as manifested in restlessness, labored respiration, tenseness, and failure to sleep. Moreover, the changes following feeding expressed by the other extremes of these just-mentioned changes (less restless, and so on) indicate that a relative state of quiescence follows. A clear illustration of the relation of frustration to emotion is contained in a study by Dorothy Marquis (44). Frustration was investigated in seven newborn infants as it occurred during the delay before feeding. This was done by recording the amount of crying, general bodily activity, and mouth activity the infants showed. The amount of formula to be received at a given feeding was divided into fourths and amount of activity shown during each of these fourths was recorded separately. In other words, amount of activity was recorded for the infant's behavior for each fourth as well as for a fixed delay period without feeding which followed each of the feeding "fourths." As amount of milk consumed increased, there was a decreased amount of activity and increased tolerance of the delay period. To put it succinctly, as frustration from hunger decreased, emotional reactions also decreased. The same general relation of frustration of needs and the appearance of emotional reactions may also be observed when considering needs other than hunger. In toilet training the relation to frustration of doing that which comes naturally, namely wetting and soiling, is especially noteworthy.

The tension of emotion is also aroused by conditions which enhance the gratification of an individual's needs. Not only frustration but also that which furthers or facilitates meeting his needs is provocative of emotion. Delight and affection are emotional responses illustrative of enhancing emotional responses. They are in themselves tension producing. In fact, if this tension is prolonged or intense it may bring about displeasure. Too many toys can bring about an excited delight which readily passes over into displeasure and tears (37). Crying spells at Christmas or on birthdays in early childhood also exemplify the situation.

Differentiation

It is hardly likely that the infant is capable of intense emotional experiences as *adults know them*. It is even debatable that "emotion" in the discrete units language forces upon us is a suitable term to apply to very young infants. We may, for example, see a newborn infant squirming, kicking, and crying. We may infer that the infant is experiencing that which we would feel if we were in his place. But we are not in his place. In support of the position that there is considerable difference between infantile and adult emotional experience several points can be offered. We know that neural maturation is still incomplete in the infant, particularly in the cerebral cortex. We also know that there is little if any knowledge of self on the infant's part and that personal reference, so characteristic of our adult emotional responses, must be lacking with him. We are not even sure to what extent his very early experiences are conscious. Most important perhaps, we know also that certain research studies, described in a moment, show that we can be fooled by what we read into the situation when observing "emotional experiences" of infants. So when such terms as "excitement," "distress" and "delight" are used, they should be viewed as if they carried quotation marks to indicate only a tentative similarity to those which adults experience.

The anthropomorphic tendency of interpreting the behavior of an infant as we would experience it is at the root of methodological difficulties that have been found concerning certain early studies of the emotional reactions of infants. John B. Watson (58) performed in 1919 a classic study of what he called the primary (original) emotions of fear, rage, and love in the neonate. Fear in newborn infants, he claimed, was produced by loud sounds and loss of support. Rage was brought about by hampering of movements. Love was released by stroking and petting. All other emotional reactions, he went on to state, were the consequence of conditioning of these three primary emotions. The simplicity and straightforwardness of the theory had a great appeal, and for some years this was a widely accepted view of the nature of primary emotions in infants.

The validity of Watson's theory rests upon a matter of fact—whether or not the emotions he described could be identified by others in such a fashion that the three patterns of emotion would be found to be separable and identifiable. Sherman (52), in 1927, demonstrated that experienced adult observers could not agree in naming emotional patterns of behavior of infants except when the stimuli which produced the reactions were also shown to them. The situations he used to bring about emotional responses—delay of feeding beyond the usual time, sudden loss of support, restraint of head movements, and pricking with a needle—were first presented to the observers as preludes to the emotional reactions of the infants. Under these conditions the observers were generally able to offer "correct" identifications of the emotions with considerable interobserver agreement, though some disagreements existed. Thus, observers who saw the infant lose his support and then the emotional reaction which followed tended to label the emotional reaction "fear." But when they saw motion pictures of the infant's emotional reactions cut so that the preceding stimulation period was eliminated, they failed to agree on what emotion was being expressed. Moreover, when the film was so spliced as to give the impression that the stimuli preceding the infant's emotion was the actual one to which the infant was responding, the observers tended to ascribe the emotion of the infant as that appropriate to that stimulus, and not to the one for which it was actually the response. In general, Sherman could find no characteristic emotional patterns of the several emotions which would allow one emotion to be distinguished from another. Rather, there were uncoordinated, unspecialized, and diversified responses with no particular patterns of differentiation. Situations which at a later

age arouse a variety of emotions produce the same general undifferentiated emotional reactions in these infants.

Bridges (5, 6, 7), on the basis of observational studies, offered what
appears to be an adequate account of the development of emotional
patterns. She stated that at birth the infant does not have differentiated emotional responses, but instead a general excitement characterizes his behavior. She observed 62 infants from two weeks to two
years of age in an institutional setting. A convenient summary of
her results is to be found in Figure 7. Undifferentiated excitement
(or agitation) is found initially, shown by uncoordinated overt and
visceral reactions to intense stimulation of any sort, internal or external. The vigorous but ill-coordinated movements of the infant's
body show little discernible relation to the stimulus. It will be
noticed that her general contention seems not only to be in general
agreement with the findings of Sherman but also with the descriptions of excitement–quiescence found earlier to be characteristic of
infant behavior. Her contention also receives support when one
remembers that it is generally conceded (5) that there are no distinctive unique patterns of visceral or physiological responses each
corresponding to a different emotion. In fact, in older individuals
what appear to be identical visceral patterns may be associated with
fear responses in one situation and with anger responses in another
setting.

Despite the presence of generalized excitement it is also an inescapable fact that in the older infant and child finer nuances of emotion
are readily observable. Other emotions do emerge. It was to the
study of the emergence of emotional patterns that Bridges addressed
herself.

Emotional differentiations in the infant she found to begin at about
three weeks of age when distress characterized by muscular tension,
trembling, crying, and checked breathing can be distinguished from
excitement. At about two months of age delight, manifested by
smiles and cooing when nursed or petted, emerges from excitement.
As Figure 7 brings out, she considers distress and delight to be the
two emotional patterns first differentiated from excitement. Each
of these two patterns in turn become further differentiated as the
infant grows older. Fear, anger, and disgust are differentiated from
distress before the age of six months. The differentiations of distress
which are called anger and fear are closely related to one another
at this time and continue to be with the passage of time. Fear can
change into anger and anger can change into fear. Elation, as dif-

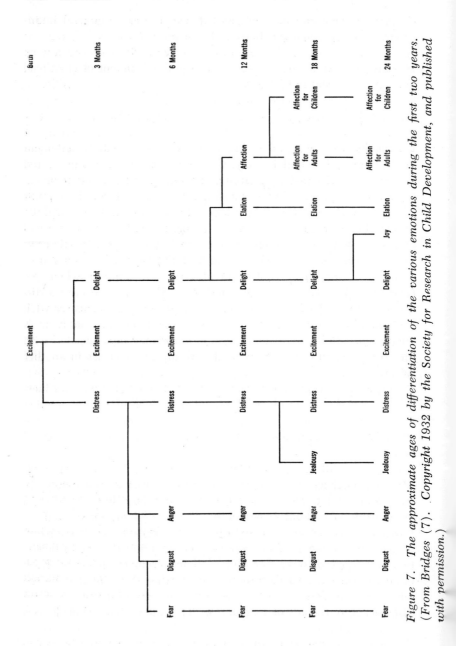

Figure 7. The approximate ages of differentiation of the various emotions during the first two years. (From Bridges (7). Copyright 1932 by the Society for Research in Child Development, and published with permission.)

ferentiated from delight, emerges at about nine months. Subsequently, affection emerges before 12 months, jealousy before the age of 18 months, and joy shortly after that age. Thus, at the age of 18 months a rather extensive repertoire of differentiated emotional reactions is present in the infant.

Changes of Mode of Responses and of Sensitivity

In addition to the progressive differentiation of emotions as the infant grows older there is another process of change with age. That is, within a given emotional pattern gradual changes in the mode of responses are taking place—changes in the way the emotion is expressed. Fear of the twenty-month-old, for example, is different from the eight-month-old infant. The former now can move away from the feared stimulus, not merely cry. As the infant grows older, more nuances of an emotional situation are capable of being perceived. As intellectual development proceeds, new situations become capable of eliciting the emotion. Emotional reactions are intimately bound with the intellectual stages of maturation reached. An individual reacts emotionally only to situations in which he is able to discriminate in some fashion between their disturbing or satisfying qualities. To respond emotionally he must "interpret" the situation in some fashion. For example, a bright two-year-old may show fear of a strange room or of a snake that leave blithely oblivious a child of the same age who is of average intelligence (30).

The Role of Maturation and Learning

The differentiation of emotions, changes of mode of responses, and of sensitivity in emotions with increasing age are related to maturation and learning. Our task now is to examine the roles of maturation and learning, insofar as they can be separated. An illustration was just given in the differential responses of fear stimuli of a bright and an average two-year-old. Presumably both maturation and learning were operative. These processes cannot be separated too clearly. The bright two-year-old in responding to stimuli which his age peer did not sense not only was expressing a faster maturation, but also that he had learned to perceive that which his age peer had not.

It is generally agreed that learning has a profound influence upon the development of emotions. Learning effects are easily demonstrable. For example, there is considerable evidence that some emotional expressions as a means of communication are learned as are our gestures, oaths, and exclamations that accompany them. It is neither as commonly accepted nor as readily observable that maturation plays a role. Consequently emphasis will first be placed upon demonstrating that maturation, too, is present in emotional development.

Emotion as a product of maturation is shown in studies in which there is no opportunity for the usual learning to take place. This may be studied either through differential studies where restriction on infants or children had already taken place or through experimental arrangements to restrict their learning. As an example of differential restriction, a child blind and deaf since birth is not in a position to learn facial or general emotional behavior from others. Goodenough (26) studied such a girl when she was ten. Her facial expressions and general behavior under conditions that usually arouse anger, fear, or pleasure in other children were very much like those exhibited by seeing, normal children. Her forms of emotional expression had arisen through maturation without opportunity for imitation through auditory or visual channels.

Goodenough, although considering the primary forms of emotional expression as determined by maturational factors, did admit that a socialization veneer may appear. This was confirmed in a later study by Thompson (57). This study involved a considerably larger number of subjects, both blind and seeing, of ages ranging from seven weeks to thirteen years. Their varying ages made it possible to study the effect of socialization with increasing age. In addition to confirming Goodenough's general finding concerning maturation, the investigator found also that beyond two or three years of age the blind subjects showed a decrease in facial activity in smiling and laughing. Among seeing children this did not take place. Social reinforcement which was lacking with the blind children was operative with them. The influence of a learning factor thus was apparent.

Let us now turn to an experimental study which demonstrates the influence of maturation. Dennis (13) reared two infants from one month of age until the age of seven months in such a way that the adult voices they heard were not associated with other smile-provoking stimuli. Under these conditions the human voice never caused smiling. Nevertheless, smiling upon *seeing* the adult developed to a marked degree, occurring more markedly when the adult bent over to minister to their needs.

The appearance of different emotional responses to stimuli which previously did not elicit them demonstrates the importance of learning (35, 36, 58, 59). The classic pioneer study of the conditioning of infant fear responses was performed by Watson and Raynor (59). It will be remembered from Chapter 1, that Albert, an infant slightly less than a year old, was found originally to have no fear of furry objects but rapidly was conditioned to be afraid of them. Thus a fear response was given to stimuli which formerly did not elicit them. This fear response persisted for a considerable period of time afterward. The conditioned fear also generalized to other furry objects. He was retested with a rabbit and a dog and then, although no conditioning through sound took place with these animals, he was found to fear them as well. In other instances (60) of similar pairings of sound and animals, however, when the same experiment was tried, various responses were elicited. Some youngsters just turned and scowled at the source of the noise and returned to playing with the pet as if they understood the noise had nothing to do with the animal.

Jones (36) followed up Watson and Raynor's study, reasoning that if the crying and withdrawal could be elicited by previously neutral stimuli, they could also be unconditioned or eliminated through a conditioning procedure as well. An infant, Peter, previously conditioned to fear furry objects, was placed in a room with three other youngsters who did not react in this way to a tame rabbit. Over several days playing in the room, Peter's fear both of the rabbit and other furry objects was reduced gradually. Thus social imitation, as Jones called the procedure, seemed to have an effect on Peter's fears. However, Peter at this point fell ill, and was also accidentally reconditioned to fear the rabbit. When he was returned for further study, a different procedure, direct reconditioning, was carried out. When Peter was eating, the rabbit was introduced first at a considerable or "safe" distance from him and then moved closer and closer from trial to trial. Peter's fear of this and other furry objects was found to be reduced. On the basis of this and another study (35, 36) with other children of different ages, Jones concluded that social imitation and direct reconditioning provided satisfactory means of eliminating children's fears.

Language development in infancy

All societies have languages. In fact, language is perhaps our most peculiarly human characteristic. Out of the vocalization of babes emerges our most powerful vehicle of thought, expression, and communication. Moreover, learning the language of the particular society in which the child is born is a vehicle of socialization. He not only learns through language other aspects of socialization, but also through language is expressing already established socializations. For these reasons it is important to examine the process of language development. Language includes within its scope speaking and comprehending vocalization, reading, and writing. Emphasis will be placed upon spoken language.

In the infant's earliest vocalizations a considerable variety of basic sounds, called phonemes, appear. The delimitation and isolation of the phonemes were arrived at in the course of many investigations by listening to infant vocalizations and recording them phonetically. Some phonemes appear in these vocalizations more often than do others, with vowel sounds predominating (33). Some of these phonemes are said to appear later in English, but many are not elements of any language, let alone English. The infant also uses phonemes destined to be used in languages other than English. Thus, an infant in our culture uses sounds roughly corresponding to the German ü, the Danish ö or the French u and the guttural r. This "initial hierarchy" of basic sounds changes as the infant grows older. Consonant sounds increase, non-English phonemes drop out, and the resultant hierarchy of English sounds comes into being.

There is the possibility that a recently developed method of analysis of phonemes make obsolescent the findings of these earlier studies which had used the method of phonetic transcription of what the investigator heard his subjects say. Lynip (41), after recording the sounds made by an infant, used the Sound Spectrograph developed by the Bell Telephone Laboratories to analyze pictorially the sound samplings. The pictorial representations on this instrument of the infant's vocalizations could then be compared with those for the various letters used in our adult speech. His results illustrate very vividly why phoneticians disagree so much among themselves in their phonetic translations of what they have heard in the speech of infants. The visible patterns on the Spectrograph of early infant sounds were blurs, utterly unlike the pictorial representations of the adult vowel sounds. As the infant grew older, the sounds that he made soon came to resemble adult vowels, so far as hearing them was concerned, but the Spectrograph showed that they were still quite different from adult sounds. Many studies of basic speech sounds of infants have been performed, but in view of the uncertain state of affairs created by the findings with the Sound Spectrograph it is fortunate that further elucidation of phoneme development is not essential for our development of the topic of language in infancy.

Language development starts, then, not with the emergence of the first words, but much earlier with the first vocalizations. In a sense, it starts with the birth cry. So far as the differential use of sounds which characterizes language is concerned, it is at about one month of age that Gesell and Thompson (25) have established that infantile cries of discomfort, pain, and hunger are differentiated by the observer. Mothers claim discriminatory ability along those lines at even younger ages. Vocalization in the form of small throaty noises also appear at about four weeks. This and other representative findings of normative age for kinds of vocalizations, as established by Gesell and Amatruda (22), are given in Table 5. Their results will be supplemented by some of the findings of Shirley (54) in her longitudinal study.

TABLE 5

NORMS OF VOCALIZATION *

Age in weeks	Behavior
4	Small throaty noises
8	Single vowel sounds—ah, eh, uh
12	Coos, chuckles
16	Laughs aloud
20	Squeals
24	Grunts, growls
28	Polysyllabic vowel sounds
32	Single syllables—da, ba, ka
36	Dada (or equivalent)
	Imitates sounds
40	Mama, and one other word
52	Four words
78	Ten words, including names
104	Jargon discarded
	Three word sentences
	Uses I, me, you
	Names various objects

* Adapted from Gesell and Amatruda (22). Copyright 1947 by Paul B. Hoeber, Inc., and published with permission.

Consideration will now be given to the appearance of the first word. Gesell and Amatruda, as shown in the table, place the first word at 40 weeks. On the average, Shirley's babies used their first word in her presence at about 60 weeks. In some of these infants the first word appeared as early as eight months and its appearance in others was delayed to as late as two years of age. The mothers themselves credited their infants with a vocabulary of two or three words at 52 weeks which corresponds to the findings of Gesell and Amatruda. With due allowance for individual variation, it would appear that the average child says his first word at about the end of the first year. Gifted children may do this at an even earlier age, while other children are retarded to the point of not using words until after their second year.

The fact that these findings about the first word seem to vary according to the observer is perhaps due to the fact that some observers, especially mothers, may have a strongly developed tendency to credit the child with speaking words based on utterances, which, as a matter of fact, are quite far removed from the word in question. It will be remembered that Lynip found that the sounds of the infant he studied, although interpreted as being adult vowels, were still a blur on the Spectrograph. Moreover, the word or words for which they are credited by their mothers may be part of a private language wherein a certain sound, perhaps having no resemblance to the word (such as "yo-e" for water), functions as a word in that particular family.

The growth of spoken vocabulary during infancy will now be discussed. Shirley found that at 66 weeks her infant subjects spoke seven comprehensible words. There was little improvement until 86 weeks (she believed that probably this lag was due to the infant's preoccupation with locomotion during this period). By two years of age the average number of words used by her infant subjects was 32. Her findings may be supplemented by returning to those of Gesell and Amatruda as reported in Table 5. At two years of age, not only has jargon been discarded but three word sentences have made their appearance as well as the beginnings of the use of pronouns. Considerable development of language ability during the second year has evidently taken place.

There is another aspect of language development which has not been mentioned so far—the understanding of language, or passive language. Passive language begins when the infant learns to tease out, from the total mass of impression of sounds to which he is exposed, those which are the spoken language of other persons. Actions going hand in hand with language are the language units that are probably learned first. Thus, "pat-a-cake," "bye-bye," "here's your bottle" are accompanied by appropriate actions on the part of adults and thereby more readily learned by the infant than is more abstract language. This aspect of understanding language probably precedes spoken language. The infant obeys simple commands (25) at about 12 months. For example, it is at this age that on command he will place a cube in a cup. This is a relatively complex activity. Compared to his command of active language, which reference to Table 5 will show is only about four words at this age, this is illustrative of his relatively greater passive language comprehension.

The development of understanding in infancy

When considering older children, we will have occasion to use terms referring to perception, conceptualization, and thought with some degree of precision. In infancy, though they will be used, their degree of exactitude of meaning is much less than it will be later. No attempt will be made at distinctions among them at this point. As descriptive of this state of affairs, we will use the more amorphous word, "understanding," to indicate the area of development in infancy with which we are concerned. In its most general sense, understanding has to do with the development of meaning; what an event, object, or person signifies.

The development of understanding is originally dependent upon sensory-conceptual development. If deprived of one or more senses, to that extent the infant is handicapped in the development of understanding. If severely handicapped in several major sensory areas, as was Helen Keller who was deprived of both hearing and vision shortly after birth, the task of "interpreting" the world becomes a very difficult one. Perforce he must learn to interpret the external world through the remaining senses. If completely deprived of all senses, he would have no way of interacting with the world.

Fortunately, in the first few weeks of life the sensory apparatus of a typical infant is in good working condition, but his understanding of what is going on around him is negligible. When something breaks through his hazy awareness, it produces excitement. Otherwise, when he is satisfied—when his stomach is full, digestion is proceeding smoothly, and he is warm and snug—awareness fades out and he drifts into sleep. Gradually, his periods of wakefulness increase. As he grows older, the infant's understandings come from his active sensory exploration of his environment. He tastes, looks at, smells, and handles objects (and persons) that come his way. He discovers the qualities of objects—their particular tastes, contours, warmth, and other qualities. The infant's perception of people and objects, his pleasurable recognition of the familiar and his displeasure at the strange, show that objects and persons are beginning to be perceived. In short, development of understanding begins to take place. Much of what is written about the emergence of the self and social perception in the next chapter shows the beginnings of understanding. It must be emphasized that the infant understands emotional significances as well as intellectual ones. It is even probable that these affective understandings actually precede and are more important for the young infant than are the nonaffective meanings for which he is developing an understanding.

As formulated in behavior-social learning theory, perceptions and conceptualizations serve as cue-producing responses (15). It follows then that they should be modifiable by further learning. This modification of perceptions and conceptualizations is borne out in a general way throughout this section. No matter the specific point being made, cue production is implied in the discussion of the growth of understanding. Language is, of course, a series of cue-producing responses. The study of the influence of verbalization on form conceptualization of Gellerman, described in a moment in this context, would be rephrased as a study of the influence of verbal cues on form discrimination. Perceptions and conceptions come about as a result of learning.

Thus, understandings on the part of the infant emerge as a result of learning. Consequently, the phenomena of learning are present in perception. In the understanding of the infant, one of the most important learning phenomenon is generalization. Because objects, situations, or persons have cues in common which he has not learned to distinguish, he confuses them. As most mothers know to their embarrassment, an infant able to use the word "daddy" may apply it on occasion to any male he sees. Or having learned to use "kitty" for a cat, he is apt to apply it to a dog, a squirrel, or even when playing with the fur collar of his mother's coat. Generalization is operating here as it was in other situations we have examined. It is characteristic of the infant that he assimilates the new aspect of a situation to what is now old and familiar to him by a process of generalization. As he grows older, his cues for discriminatory decisions increase in precision. Illustrative of his growing discrimination is the use by a somewhat older child of an expression such as "funny kitty" for a squirrel. No longer is it a "kitty" alone but a "funny" one. Some of the cues for kitty are present but also something else. The new is seen for what it is, assimilated with the old, and the way prepared for cue discrimination. Attaching distinctive cue-producing responses to heretofore similar stimuli tends to increase their distinctiveness.

Words, too, are cues. As soon as the child discovers that words have meaning (are cues for something else) and that for every object there is a word (cue), he has made a tremendous step forward in understanding. Words also exist for conceptions which are independent of objects. Thus qualities of objects, which may be understood without referring to a particular object, also come to be understood. Roundness, independent of round apples or round balls, is illustrative.

Conceptual discrimination rests upon language in the sense that language discrimination improves conceptualization. Nevertheless, conceptualization may appear without language. For example, conceptual discrimination of forms is possible by infants without their verbalization of the concepts. Ling (38) demonstrated this in an ingenious study in which the infants showed their conceptual discrimination of a correct form by licking it, instead of other forms which were also present. He did this by presenting to six to fifteen months' old infants blocks differing in form, including circles, crosses, and triangles. Successful selection of one form was rewarded by a coating of saccharine it had on its surface. Discrimination shown by licking the correct form was found as early as the sixth month of life. Changing the position of the correct form relative to the others or varying its size had only a slight effect upon accuracy. Another investigator, Long (39), has shown through a manual response setup that somewhat older subjects in the preschool years also can discriminate forms without being able to name them. He was able to demonstrate that very young children formed a given concept, as shown by going through a test series without error, and yet thereafter were quite unable to give anything approaching a verbal formulation of what they were doing. Thus, form concepts precede ability to verbalize these concepts.

It is significant, however, that some, but not all, of Long's older subjects did use such words as "balls" in talking to themselves in the course of their selections.

Language naturally aids a child in concept formation. This may be illustrated by a study of form discrimination by Gellermann (20) in which he compared two-year-old children and chimpanzees in dis-

criminating triangularity. The investigator gave no verbal instructions to the children. Some of the children formulated the problem,
which he had been careful not to verbalize for them, by gestures and
verbal behavior instructions to themselves. He found that the children were definitely superior to the chimpanzees in discriminating
triangularity. In part, at least, this seemed to be due to their greater
verbal facility. Though they did not yet show a high level of verbal
sophistication, their verbalizations did seem to help in arriving at
conceptualizations as shown by higher percentages of correct responses in those using them.

Concepts, such as those just discussed, have their beginning in
infancy, but they are so grossly inaccurate and so primitive in nature
as to hardly deserve the name concepts. The studies of conceptualization which have been described, with the exception of Ling's, either
used infants just barely at its upper limits as did Gellermann or
actually used preschool-aged children as did Long. It is possible that
these studies may have given too mature a cast to the concepts of the
infant. Rather than space concepts, we have poor orientation in space
shown in often reaching for an object in the wrong direction. Rather
than inaccurate concepts of weight, it is more parsimonious to speak
of his making mistakes in weight, such as his being forced to drop too
heavy objects when he attempts to hold them.

Intellectual development in infancy

Some aspects of sensory-perceptual processes including language,
understanding, and intelligence are in many respects very similar.
When used for adaptive purposes, they are used intelligently.

The same active strivings described in the development of understanding are operating in intelligence. Perception of objects outside
of himself is a spur to intellectual functioning. His tasting, smelling,
looking, and feeling show intelligence in action. Without this preliminary but all-important active exploration, intellectual development will be stunted. The work of Goldfarb and others described
in the next chapter stands witness to what happens to intellectual
functioning when the incentive to carry on this active exploration is
stunted.

There is considerable progress in adaptive behavior during infancy.
At the youngest ages, the intellectual tasks expected of the infant are
primarily perceptual-motor in nature. At later ages, adaptive be-

havior of a more abstract nature will be sampled, but for the young infants this is impossible. Indeed, we cannot be sure he is capable of such behavior until at least later infancy.

One of the more widely used infant scales will be utilized to demonstrate the changes in performance expected of the younger and older infant. The Cattell Infant Intelligence Scale (8) is a downward extension of the Revised Stanford-Binet Intelligence Tests (see page 484), and is similar to them in that the items are grouped according to age levels. It is suitable for children as young as two months and, for those thirty months of age, it merges with Stanford-Binet tests. At the youngest levels, the tasks are often perceptual-motor in nature. For example, to receive credit for an item at the two-month level, the child may be expected to show head and eye movements in following a moving stimulus. Beginning at about five months the scale contains a gradually increasing number of manipulatory items. Prior to the age of about 12 months, administration of the items involves neither imitation of the examiner's behavior nor response to verbal requests. Rather, a controlled stimulus is simply presented to the child and his response observed. For example, does a four-month-old infant become more active at the sight of a toy? When a small one-inch block is placed on the table in front of him, what does he do? Chances are if he is an average three-month-old, he will focus his eyes on it; if he is six months old, he can probably pick it up and even reach for another one. If he is seven months old, he can probably hold two blocks simultaneously. But not before the age of 14 months is he likely to be able to hold three such blocks at one time.

Upon reading this description of the items, one may reasonably inquire if this is not expecting stereotypy rather than originality of response. And yet, no matter how unreasonable it may seem to expect the majority of infants to behave in the same way to a given stimulus, developmental studies have revealed that to a great extent they do just that—certainly up to the age of one year—even though an original twist to the responses which would not nullify the score may be present as well.

After the age of one year, the items become increasingly dependent upon verbal factors. Either the child himself must demonstrate the emerging ability to use speech (be able to say one word at 11 months, two words at 12 months, combine words at 22 months, and so on) or at least be able to respond to verbal instructions given by the examiner. Despite this gradual increase in the use of spoken or comprehended language, manipulatory items still predominate until approximately the two-year level.

With items similar to those in the Cattell Scale, Bayley (3) found that the mental growth curve was of the sort given in Figure 8. The rapid increase in scores during the first year and a gradual leveling off thereafter seem to characterize the changes over the two-year period.

It has been generally found that tests given in infancy are not very predictive of later intellectual prowess as measured in preschool ages or later. Despite the standardization of the Cattell test as a downward extension of the Stanford-Binet, even the Cattell Scale is essentially nonpredictive, especially that between measures administered during the first twelve months and testing by the Stanford-Binet. For example, the correlations found between Cattell measures for three, six, and nine months and the Stanford-Binet at 36 months are respectively 0.10, 0.34, and 0.18 (8). For older ages the correlations become progressively greater. Using the same standard of 36 months on the Stanford-Binet, those for 12, 18, 24, and 30 months are, respectively, 0.56, 0.67, 0.71, and 0.83. Predictions of intelligence measures obtained before the age of one year against measures in later years are so low as to be essentially meaningless, but are more adequate thereafter.

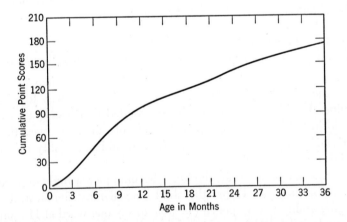

Figure 8. Mental growth curve in terms of cumulative point scores. (From Bayley (3). Copyright 1933 by the Journal Press, and published with permission.)

It is not easy to give psychological tests to infants, especially young infants (27). The young infant is not interested in his own performance because he is not even aware of it as a performance. He cannot be guided by verbal instructions to any great degree, and his attention is not easily directed to the tasks selected. The behavior repertoire which he demonstrates is much more restricted in breadth than is the case with the older child. Most important of all is the still unsettled question as to whether intelligence, as we conceive of it in the adult, can be said to have emerged before the symbolic language processes, which we have just referred to, have been established. Since motor performance is stressed in the testing of intelligence of infants, his repertory may well include very little which is directly related to later intelligence. For these reasons, it is hardly surprising that the results obtained with infant tests of intelligence are not as highly correlated with later performance as are tests given at later years.

These remarks about the relatively poor predictive prowess of infant tests were made concerning a representative or typical sample of infants. In the case of markedly deviant infants where there is gross retardation, as clinicians indicate, tests given in the first year may be of considerable value. As Escalona (17), for example, comments, infant tests may be used to advantage here.

Individuality in the neonate and infant

One of the most obvious sources of individuality among neonates is the degree of maturity at birth. With normal full term being 40 weeks, neonates who are capable of remaining alive vary as widely in birth age as from 26 to 46 weeks (22). Infants before full term are usually referred to as "premature" babies. But infants born after equal periods of gestation may also show considerable degree of developmental prematurity or postmaturity as well. More or less than full development occurs in children even of the classic term of 40 weeks.

Premature children whether because of being born earlier than usual or because of other factors have in common the fact that they are not as fully equipped for the business of living an "independent" life as infants of normal term. In them the physical characteristics of the newborn are accentuated, their nervous systems are less developed, and instability of vital functions such as breathing are more precarious than they are in normal infants. Hence, it is customary to use incubators to simulate as closely as possible the conditions of the mothers' wombs.

Considerable research has been concerned with the measurement of general activity of infants during periods when no external stimuli are applied (31, 32). To study this, the infants are placed on a stabilimeter and their activity measured. In one of these studies (32) the amount of activity between two nursing periods of 73 infants, almost all of neonatal age, was investigated. Variations among infants and for temporal units within the activity period are reported and found to be considerable. In the other study (31) where observation extended over ten days, some infants were five times as active as others.

Individuality has been studied by various investigators, who, following their theoretical predilections, have stressed one phase or another of this individuality. Shirley (54) who closely studied 25 babies from birth to three years describes characteristics distinguishing one infant from another in terms of irritability, tone, and timbre of crying, and motility and tonicity of muscles. This individuality in expression of emotion tends to be maintained within particular gross limits as the infant grows older. Shirley (53), for example, described certain infants in which timorousness and irritability had appeared earlier and persisted throughout the ensuing months of her study. Moreover when "profile charts" were prepared involving a variety of characteristics they differed so much from one infant to another that the examiner could identify the infants from the charts alone. Fifteen years later these same individuals were restudied by Neilon (46) who indicates that there is a strong likelihood that the temperamental qualities present in infancy still characterize these particular individuals.

There is variability in emotional reactions from infant to infant. Even at birth, infants may be distinguished by their differences in crying at different times. Variability in amount of crying among infants is also considerable. Aldrich, Sung, and Knop (1) found that within a 24-hour period time sample, infants varied in amount of crying from 48 to 243 minutes. Among the infants studied by Marquis (44) and referred to in connection with the relation of frustration to emotion, one infant showed five times as much bodily activity in the frustrating situation as did another infant in the same situation.

In her works on individuality in infants, Fries (19) was concerned with degree of activity. On the basis of many years' observation she would categorize the differences among infants in this regard in terms of activity types. She found five types with the normal range including quiet, moderately active, and active with two pathological groups, one at each of the extremes, the hypo- and hyperactive. Fries observed these same children as they grew older and concluded that markedly active infants are markedly active at later ages and that neonates who are relatively quiet tend to remain relatively inactive individuals in childhood.

Escalona and Bergman (18) described unusual sensitivities to external stimuli among infants. They noted that one sleeping infant may be disturbed by sounds through which other infants sleep undisturbed. In sensitive infants, a startle to sound may appear and the infant may seem to "wince" as if stimuli only moderately intense by usual standards are actually painful. Escalona and Bergman consider that these sensitivities may be conceptualized as showing in these infants that there are weak barriers between the stimuli of the external world and the infant. If ordinary stimuli are overwhelming, the sensitive infant may have to withdraw from stimulation to a greater degree than the ordinary infant. We know very little about the relationship of these differences to later personality differences, but it is evident that they may have considerable importance.

Each infant sets his own developmental pace. Despite the enormous amount of normative work that has been done, no timetable can catch precisely what happens to any given child. He will be found to follow the same general order of all human beings but will give it his individual stamp. The *order* of major developments will be the same, the *timing* and the combinations of behavior will be different.

Summary

The neonatal period of the first month of life provides the baseline against which to compare the developments taking place in infancy. Consideration is given to both sensory and motor responses. It was impossible, even in the more detailed statement given in the chapter, to do full justice to the multiplicity of responses which the neonate exhibits. It is suffice to say here that the evidence indicated a much broader repertoire both of specific and mass responses than casual observation would make one believe possible.

The coordinated responses of the neonate that are necessary for his survival, here conceptualized as needs, received the most detailed attention. Hunger and thirst illustrated the coordinated series of activities that are necessary for satisfaction of these needs. Cooperation of the neonate with the mother and vice versa are seen as part of this pattern. Other needs—sleep, elimination, temperature regulation, oxygen, and the forerunners of sexual needs—are also reported as they are observed in infancy.

On turning to development in infancy, changes in number of feedings, in supplementation by solid foods, scheduling and self-demand feeding, breast and bottle feeding, and weaning are all found to take place. Permissiveness by parents and self-regulation by infants were found to exist in varying degrees. Learning by the infant to adapt to feeding schedules was demonstrated. On examination of weaning as a product of both maturation and learning, a quite complicated process was found to exist.

A progressive increase in waking activity, as contrasted with sleep, was found to characterize the changes over the two years of infancy. An increase in sheer length of sleep periods was also noted.

Developmental changes in elimination take place during infancy. Both bladder and bowel control were found to be complicated processes. The neuromuscular maturation essential for adequate control is found to be important for bringing about failures to achieve as early control as some parents would like. Learning of control proceeds without benefit of verbal aids since the infant is so limited in passive and spoken vocabulary. It is hardly surprising that, by and large, toilet training begun later in infancy rather than earlier takes less time to be accomplished.

Physical growth and motor development may be conveniently considered together. Changes in size, strength, and agility are very evident in infancy, perhaps showing greater changes during these two years than during any similar span of years. In motor development, the effects of both maturation and learning reveal themselves with clarity and sharpness.

The infant faces, as do all of us, the stresses of daily living. He reacts by tension which is an invariable characteristic of emotionality. Emotionality arises from the frustration or enhancement of needs. When considering the phenomena of infant emotionality it is found that young infants lack differentiated emotional responses. Instead, under emotional stress the young infant reacts with generalized excitement. As the infant grows older, distress and delight are differentiated-out from this excitement. As still further time passes, both distress and delight become further differentiated. Fear, anger, and disgust, for example, are differentiated from distress. By the age of 18 months, the human infant has a rather extensive repertoire of emotional responses. Along with sheer differentiation goes progressive change in the modes of responses—the ways in which the child reacts to emotion provoking stimuli. Improvement in muscular abilities and gain in appreciation of the meaning of situations contribute heavily to these changes.

From the phonemes of the infant emerges the language the child learns in his particular culture. Language thus begins with the first vocalizations, not the first words. Development proceeds rapidly. From the small throaty noises at four weeks to the three word sentences of two years of age is a remarkable development, with tremendous yet predictable strides being taken in the learning of one's language by the infant. Hand in hand with language development goes the development of understanding. If handicapped in sensory development, the infant is handicapped in language and in understanding. An account of how language and understanding develop in terms of behavior-social learning is a consequence. Special emphasis is placed upon perception and conceptualization serving as cue-producing responses.

Intellectual prowess, too, shows a steady rate of growth during infancy. It is significant that after about one year of age verbal factors are considered more and more responsible for growth in intelligence. Despite predictable changes, however, the instruments developed for the measurement of infant intelligence still lack any great efficiency in predicting intellectual developmental standing at older ages.

In all of these areas of psychological development, individual differences from infant to infant are very obvious. Relating these differences to a scale of activity, ranging from excessive activity to passivity, seems to account for many of these observed differences. Despite the similarity of the order of major behavioral developments from infant to infant, the timing differs from infant to infant. Each infant has his own developmental pace.

For Further Reading

A convenient summarization of the norms of development through 36 months is contained in Arnold Gesell and Catherine S. Amatruda, *Developmental Diagnosis: normal and abnormal child development* (New York: Hoeber, 1947). A fuller account by Gesell and Frances Ilg may be found in *Child Development: An Introduction to the Study of Human Growth* (New York: Harper, 1949). For most of the specific topics covered in this chapter, authoritative, encyclopedic statements may be found in the book edited by Leonard Carmichael, *Manual of Child Psychology: Second Edition* (New York: Wiley, 1954). The articles on the neonate by K. C. Pratt, on physical growth by Helen Thompson, and on learning by N. L. Munn are especially recommended.

References

1. Aldrich, C. A., Sung, C., and Knop, C. A. The crying of newly born babies: II. The individual phase. *J. Pediatrics*, 1945, 27, 89–96.
2. Bakwin, H., and Bakwin, Ruth. Growth of thirty-two external dimensions during the first year of life. *J. Pediatrics*, 1936, 8, 177–183.
3. Bayley, Nancy. Mental growth during the first three years: a developmental study of sixty-one children by repeated tests. *Genet. Psychol. Monogr.*, 1933, 14, 1–92.
4. Bayley, Nancy. Normal growth and development. In P. H. Hoch and J. Zubin (Eds.), *Psychopathology of childhood*. New York: Grune and Stratton, 1955, 1–14.
5. Bridges, Katherine, M.B. A genetic theory of the emotions. *J. genet. Psychol.*, 1930, 37, 514–527.
6. Bridges, Katherine, M.B. *The social and emotional development of the preschool child*. London: Kegan, Paul, 1931.
7. Bridges, Katherine, M.B. Emotional development in early infancy. *Child Develpm.*, 1932, 3, 324–341.
8. Cattell, Psyche. *The measurement of intelligence of infants*. New York: Psychological Corporation, 1940.
9. Davis, Clara M. Self-selection of diet by newly-weaned infants. *Amer. J. Dis. Child.*, 1928, 36, 651–679.
10. Davis, Clara M. Choice of formulas by three infants throughout the nursing periods. *Amer. J. Dis. Child.*, 1935, 50, 385–394.
11. Dennis, W. A description and classification of the responses of the newborn infant. *Psychol. Bull.*, 1934, 31, 5–22.
12. Dennis, W. The effect of restricted practice upon the teaching, sitting and standing of two infants. *J. genet. Psychol.*, 1935, 47, 17–32.
13. Dennis, W. An experimental test of two theories of social smiling in infants. *J. soc. Psychol.*, 1935, 6, 214–223.
14. Dennis, W., and Dennis, Marsena G. The effect of cradling practices upon the onset of walking in Hopi children. *J. genet. Psychol.*, 1940, 56, 77–86.

15. Dollard, J., and Miller, N. E. *Personality and psychotherapy.* New York: McGraw-Hill, 1950.
16. Escalona, Sibylle. Emotional development in the first year of life. In M. J. E. Senn (Ed.), *Problems of infancy and childhood: transactions of the sixth conference.* New York: Macy, 1953, 7–92.
17. Escalona, Sibylle. The use of infant tests for predictive purposes. In W. E. Martin and Celia B. Stendler (Eds.), *Readings in child development.* New York: Harcourt, Brace, 1954, 95–103.
18. Escalona, Sibylle, and Bergman, P. Unusual sensitivities in very small children. In Phyllis Greenacre *et al.* (Eds.), *The psychoanalytic study of the child,* Vol. 3. New York: International Universities Press, 1949, 333–352.
19. Fries, Margaret E., and Woolf, P. J. Some hypotheses on the role of the congenital activity type in personality development. In Ruth S. Eissler *et al.* (Eds.), *The psychoanalytic study of the child,* Vol. 8. New York: International Universities Press, 1953, 48–62.
20. Gellermann, L. W. Form discrimination in chimpanzees and two-year-old children: 1. form (triangularity) *per se. J. genet. Psychol.,* 1933, 42, 3–27.
21. Gesell, A. Cinemanalysis: a method of behavior study. *J. genet. Psychol.,* 1935, 47, 3–16.
22. Gesell, A., and Amatruda, Catherine S. *Developmental diagnosis: normal and abnormal child development* (2nd cd.). New York: Hoeber, 1947.
23. Gesell, A., and Ilg, Frances L. *Child development: an introduction to the study of human growth.* New York: Harper, 1949.
24. Gesell, A., and Thompson, Helen. Learning and growth in identical infant twins. *Genet. Psychol. Monogr.,* 1929, 6, 1–124.
25. Gesell, A., and Thompson, Helen. *Infant behavior.* New York; McGraw-Hill, 1934.
26. Goodenough, Florence L. Expressions of the emotions in a blind-deaf child. *J. abnorm. soc. Psychol.,* 1932, 27, 328–333.
27. Goodenough, Florence L. *Mental testing: its history, principles, and applications.* New York: Rinehart, 1949.
28. Halverson, H. M. An experimental study of prehension in infants by means of systematic cinema records. *Genet. Psychol. Monogr.,* 1931, 10, 107–286.
29. Halverson, H. M. Genital and sphincter behavior of the male infant. *J. genet. Psychol.,* 1940, 56, 95–136.
30. Holmes, Frances B. An experimental study of the fears of young children. In A. T. Jersild and Frances B. Holmes (Eds.), Children's Fears. *Child Develpm. Monogr.,* No. 20, 167–296.
31. Irwin, O. C. The amount and nature of activities of newborn infants under constant external stimulating conditions during the first ten days of life. *Genet. Psychol. Monogr.,* 1930, 8, 1–92.
32. Irwin, O. C. The distribution of the amount of motility in young infants between two nursing periods. *J. comp. Psychol.,* 1932, 14, 415–428.
33. Irwin, O. C. Research on speech sounds for the first six months of life. *Psychol. Bull.,* 1941, 38, 277–285.
34. Jensen, K. Differential reactions to taste and temperature stimuli in newborn infants. *Genet. Psychol. Monogr.,* 1932, 12, 363–479.
35. Jones, Mary C. The elimination of children's fears. *J. exp. Psychol.,* 1924, 7, 382–390.

36. Jones, Mary C.   A laboratory study of fear: the case of Peter.   *Ped. Sem.*, 1924, 31, 308–315.
37. Leitch, Mary, and Escalona, Sibylle.   The reaction of infants to stress: a report of clinical observation.   In Phyllis Greenacre *et al.* (Eds.), *The psychoanalytic study of the child*, Vol. 3.   New York: International Universities Press, 1949, 121–140.
38. Ling, B. C.   Form discrimination as a learning cue in infants.   *Comp. Psychol. Monogr.*, 1941, 17, No. 2.
39. Long, L.   Conceptual relationships in children: the concept of roundness.   *J. genet. Psychol.*, 1940, 57, 289–315.
40. Lustman, S. L.   Rudiments of the ego.   In Ruth S. Eissler *et al.* (Eds.), *The psychoanalytic study of the child*, Vol. 11.   New York: International Universities Press, 1956, 89–98.
41. Lynip, A. W.   The use of magnetic devices in the collection and analysis of the preverbal utterances of an infant.   *Genet. Psychol. Monogr.*, 1951, 44, 221–262.
42. McGraw, Myrtle B.   Neural maturation as exemplified in achievement of bladder control.   *J. Pediatrics*, 1940, 16, 580–589.
43. Marquis, Dorothy P.   Learning in the neonate: the modification of behavior under three feeding schedules.   *J. exp. Psychol.*, 1941, 29, 263–282.
44. Marquis, Dorothy P.   A study of frustration in newborn infants.   *J. exp. Psychol.*, 1943, 32, 123–138.
45. Munn, N. L.   Learning in children.   In L. Carmichael (Ed.), *Manual of child psychology* (2nd ed.).   New York: Wiley, 1954, 374–458.
46. Neilon, Patricia.   Shirley's babies after fifteen years.   *J. genet. Psychol.*, 1948, 73, 175–186.
47. Pratt, K. C.   The neonate.   In L. Carmichael (Ed.), *Manual of child psychology* (2nd ed.).   New York: Wiley, 1954, 215–291.
48. Pratt, K. C., Nelson, Amalie K., and Sun, K. H.   *The behavior of the newborn infant.*   Columbus, Ohio: Ohio State University Press, 1930.
49. Ribble, Margaret A.   *The rights of infants.*   New York: Columbia University Press, 1943.
50. Richards, T. W., and Irwin, O. C.   Experimental methods used in studies on infant reactions since 1900.   *Psychol. Bull.*, 1934, 31, 23–46.
51. Sears, R. R., Maccoby, Eleanor E., and Levin, H.   *Patterns of child rearing.*   Evanston, Ill.: Row, Peterson, 1957.
52. Sherman, M.   The differentiation of emotional responses in infants.   I.   Judgments of emotional responses from motion-picture views and from actual observations.   *J. comp. Psychol.*, 1927, 7, 265–284.
53. Shirley, Mary M.   *The first two years: a study of twenty-five babies*, Vol. 1.   *Postural and locomotor development.*   Minneapolis: University of Minnesota Press, 1931.
54. Shirley, Mary M.   *The first two years: a study of twenty-five babies*, Vol. 3.   *Personality manifestations.*   Minneapolis: University of Minnesota Press, 1933.
55. Simsarian, F. P., and McLendon, P. A.   Feeding behavior of an infant during the first twelve weeks of life on a self-demand schedule.   *J. Pediatrics*, 1942, 20, 93–103.

56. Thompson, Helen. Physical growth. In L. Carmichael (Ed.), *Manual of child psychology*, (2nd ed.). New York: Wiley, 1954, 292–334.

57. Thompson, J. Development of facial expression of emotion in blind and seeing children. *Arch. Psychol., N. Y.*, 1941, 37, No. 264.

58. Watson, J. B. *Psychology from the standpoint of a behaviorist*. Philadelphia: Lippincott, 1919.

59. Watson, J. B., and Raynor, Rosalie. Conditioned emotional reactions. *J. exp. Psychol.*, 1920, 3, 1–14.

60. Woodworth, R. S. *Psychology* (4th ed.). New York: Holt, 1940.

chapter 7

Psychosocial Development in Infancy

In the previous chapter, the behavior and experi-ence of the infant from birth to about two years of age were explored. The regularities and variabilities of infant development were pre-sented normatively. Age was the principal source of anchoring the various facts about infancy in a fashion which permitted an answer to the question, "What is the baby like at this age and what can he do?" General behavioral development during the course of infancy was described. For convenience of presentation, the infant was examined almost as if he existed in isolation, not, as is always the case, in a *matrix of other persons*. Actually, all of the behavior repertoire of infants which has been reported took place in a social setting. Many of the behavioral items can be modified, accelerated, and retarded by the persons who served as the agents of socialization. The infant is now to be examined in this social setting.

The mother as the agent of socialization

Various persons serve as agents of socialization. As indicated in Chapter 4 the first and most important of these agents is the mother or mother surrogate. The most obvious thing about the behavior of

222

any newborn infant is his complete helplessness. He is unable to coordinate his movements to meet his needs. When a need arises, his only effective means of tension reduction is random motor discharge. Unable to move about, to keep warm, to feed himself, to avoid danger, the infant is entirely dependent upon his mother or some other person who takes her place. Since he is unable to cope with his needs, she ministers to him. The infant is a member of a household or an institution which forms his universe. The infant's universe is mediated to him through the one who fulfills his needs— his mother or his nurse. Other individuals are to be found in his social environment, but they are as a shadowy background to the emerging foreground of the mother figure.

At birth the infant spends almost 90 per cent of the day in sleeping or dozing and even at the age of 12 weeks he spends about 70 per cent of the day in this fashion (28). During the early three or four months, the remaining time is concerned with the mother's ministrations to his needs for food and hygiene.

The average infant is in continuous contact with his mother. "Fed," "fondled," "talked to," "changed" and "carried about" express only a few of these forms of contact. As Goldfarb (31) indicates, this contact is a constant source of stimulation. He is encouraged to babble, to form words, to move about, and eventually, to sit up, to stand up, and to walk. He is carried about through a house, filled with many interesting objects and persons. In this atmosphere of contact between mother and child, the infant learns to reach out to his environment, to make his wants known, and to become a social creature.

It should be apparent by now that what a mother does in caring for an infant is more than simple carrying out of a series of acts. She is also communicating something of herself. Contact between infant and mother is, of course, partly verbal. Sometimes overlooked because of its nonverbal character is the important socializing factor of empathy (51). Sensitivity on the part of both mother and infant to one another's touch, bodily tensions, and (later) expressions are an important source of communication between them.

Escalona (21) distinguishes between communication, a purposive attempt to convey information, and contagion. By contagion she means the process by which a feeling state is transmitted from the mother to the infant. A tense and anxious adult may engender crying in an infant who, if shifted to a relaxed adult, may quiet down. Contagion is not entirely subject to voluntary control. A worried mother trying to convey assurance to her infant may find that he responds to her actual feeling state and not to that which she wants him to feel.

A writer who has aroused considerable interest by her plea for the necessity of mothering is Margaret Ribble. In her volume, *The Rights of Infants* (61), and in other publications, she pleads that an infant needs psychological mothering because he has such inadequate and unstable physiological organization of primary bodily functions. Her book, whose sale approached the level of a best seller, has been one of the more popular to advance in support of the plea that the infant needs psychological mothering because of the alleged delicate, precarious balance of the infant's physiological functioning.

Her evidence on the infant's instability and inadequate organization in circulation, oxygen supply, digestive functioning, nervous system, and muscle tonus are very effectively challenged by Pinneau (57). It would appear from his review that the evidence she advanced is contradicted by an even more impressive array of contrary evidence. Stone, in analyzing Pinneau's critique, indicates that the demolition of Ribble's evidence is "a kind of hydrogen bomb perfection of destructive criticism; not a paragraph is left standing for miles around" (72, 14).[1] It is necessary, then, to reject her evidence.

At first glance, since her evidence is rejected, it might appear that discussion of her work was unnecessary. This is not the case. In view of her popularity, the inadequacies of her work as shown by Pinneau and others have been used by some antagonists as evidence to throw suspicion on the point of view that maternal interaction with the infant is of any psychological importance. Such a sweeping conclusion is similar to the well-known cliché about throwing out the baby with the bath water because the water is dirty. What Pinneau conclusively demonstrated was that Ribble's argument that psychological mothering is necessary because of physiological instability is untenable. This is different from demonstrating that other reasons cannot be advanced to support Ribble's contention concerning the importance of infantile experience. As, in substance, Kubie (42) puts it, she was right for the wrong reasons.

[1] From Stone (72). Copyright 1954 by the Society for Research in Child Development, and published with permission.

Parental behavior influencing socialization in infancy

Each mother behaves toward her child with sufficient consistency from situation to situation to differentiate her from other mothers. Moreover, there is enough evidence available to render it fairly certain that her characteristic parental behavior is significantly related to some of the characteristics that the infant and child develop. There is a causal relationship between the child-rearing practices of the mother and the behavior of children. The task before us is to examine these attitudes, specific practices, and behavior patterns which show sufficient consistency to be characteristic maternal behaviors. We wish to find those general trends in maternal behavior that help us to understand the personalities of children. Before examining these trends in the framework of the interaction of mother and child, behavior of prospective mothers before the birth of their children will be examined.

Prenatal Maternal Attitudes Influencing Socialization

A moment's consideration will show why it is appropriate to examine the question of maternal attitudes as they exist before the birth of the child. Inescapably, the mother must adjust her manner of living to the coming infant. Necessarily this has ramifications in all aspects of her customary behavior. The mother has some conception of what she would like the infant to be. These attitudes will carry over into her relationships with the child in that they will help to direct her behavior as she strives to guide the infant's behavior. Before the birth of the child she has developed a pattern of characteristic attitudes. Does she look forward with eager anticipation to the coming child? Does she hate the very thought of the new stranger? Or, as is more likely, is her attitude a mixed one? A mother who was never irritated with her child or the thought of his coming would be more (or less) than human.

Sears, Maccoby, and Levin (66) in the "pattern" study, the procedure for which is described on page 249, found that in a group of about 400 mothers, 50 per cent were rated as delighted with the coming child, another 18 per cent as pleased but with no evidence of enthusiasm, while 25 per cent had either mixed feelings or were displeased. Those mothers having only their first child included more who were pleased than those reporting on later children as well. The mothers with more than one child tended to be more pleased the greater the distance between their pregnancies, and to be more pleased if their existing children were girls rather than boys only, or were both boys and girls. Consciously at least, few of the mothers carried over their doubts or displeasure into the period after the child was born. For example, although a mother might have "wanted to wait," once the child was born, her doubts tended to disappear.

To express this question of attitudes in more general terms, we may designate a continuum extending from enthusiastic acceptance of the child at one end to rejection of the child at the other. Even a so-called rejecting mother almost always shows some positive reaching-out, accepting behavior as well. Mothers reject some trends in their children and accept and stimulate others. These attitudes and behaviors of the mother also shift with changes in the mother, the child, and in the situation. To speak of rejection means merely that negative feelings are dominant in a particular mother at a particular time. Levy's findings on mothering, to be reported in a moment, can be interpreted as consistent with this dimension—with the more maternal subjects toward the accepting end of the continuum and the less maternal subjects toward the rejecting end of the continuum.

There is a suggestion that a constitutional prenatal factor is related to maternal behavior. Levy (46) related favorable attitudes toward mothering to the duration of menstrual flow. He found that the longer the duration of menstrual flow, the greater the amount of mothering behavior. This was expressed in a correlation coefficient of 0.58. Signs of "mothering," used in making the rating, included playing with dolls in childhood, taking care of babies, "baby carriage peeking," number of children wanted, and anticipation of care and breast feeding of their babies. For a statistically significant relationship to be found between such attitudinal material and the physiological function of days of menstrual flow implies that there may be a constitutional basis to maternal attitudes or, alternatively, that attitudes are able to bring about actual physiological differences among potential mothers. Irrespective of which relationship ultimately proves to be correct, a close relationship has been demonstrated between this psychological function of mothering and a physiological factor.

Zemlick and Watson (81) were interested in knowing whether attitudes of acceptance-rejection had an effect upon the prospective mother's psychological and physical adjustment during pregnancy.

In other words, they wished to know whether a prospective mother who tends to reject her coming child also shows psychological and physical differences from a mother who adopts a positive accepting attitude toward her child-to-be. Mothers expecting their first child were the subjects. Each mother was studied by means of: (1) a selection of Thematic Apperception Test cards (TAT), through which was established her level of anxiety; (2) a psychosomatic inventory in which she reported her psychological and somatic symptoms (PS); and (3) a Pregnancy Attitude Scale composed of items which supplied information about her attitudes toward pregnancy, such as the degree to which she wanted the child (ZAR). Independently of these data, her adjustment to pregnancy, in terms of physical and emotional symptoms, was rated by the obstetrician who saw each mother, on the average, ten times. He also rated the mother's behavior during labor and delivery in terms of adequacy in meeting this crisis (delivery adjustment rank).

Some of the obtained relationships among these measures are reported in Table 6. Both in early and late pregnancy, the physical

TABLE 6

CORRELATION OF RATINGS OF MOTHER'S ADJUSTMENT DURING PREGNANCY AND
HER ANXIETY, SYMPTOMS, AND ATTITUDES OF REJECTION *

		Physical Symptoms	Emotional Symptoms	Delivery Adjustment Rank
Early Pregnancy (2 to 5 months)				
Anxiety	(TAT)	0.17	0.44 †	0.54 †
Symptoms	(PS)	0.56 †	0.74 †	0.51 †
Attitudes	(ZAR)	0.30	0.64 †	0.66 †
Late Pregnancy (7½ months)				
Anxiety	(TAT)	0.41	0.52 †	0.47 †
Symptoms	(PS)	0.51 †	0.79 †	0.50 †
Attitudes	(ZAR)	0.11	0.53 †	0.40

* From Zemlick and Watson (*81*). Copyright 1953 by the American Orthopsychiatric Association, and published with permission.
† Significant at least at 0.10 level.

symptoms found by the obstetrician (the first entry at the top of the table) did not correlate too highly with the predictors of anxieties, symptoms, and attitudes (down the table). Correlations at both early and late pregnancy, significant at the ten per cent level, were found only between the report of the physical symptoms by the obstetrician and the scores on the psychosomatic inventory. Emotional symptoms and delivery adjustment rank (the second and third entries at the top of the table), as judged by the obstetrician, showed substantial positive correlation with the anxiety these mothers displayed, the symptoms they recognized, and the attitudes of rejection they exhibited. This positive correlation between attitudes of rejection-acceptance verbalized by the mothers on the attitude scale on the one hand, and emotional symptoms exhibited and delivery adjustment rank on the other, is particularly noteworthy. Mothers with acceptant attitudes tended to have fewer emotional symptoms and higher delivery adjustment, whereas mothers who exhibited rejecting attitudes tended to have more emotional symptoms and lower delivery adjustment. The more the mothers reject their coming child, the more stormy pregnancy they have.

It is important to note that the mothers who were studied were not emotionally disturbed or abnormal individuals. None was neurotic, psychotic, or mentally retarded. And yet, in these more or less normal mothers varying degrees of acceptance and rejection were found, thus disposing of the allegation sometimes made that only abnormal mothers reject their children.

We now turn to the broader issue of the effect of the mother's behavior upon her infant's adjustment. In this discussion it is convenient to distinguish among: (1) specific maternal practices such as weaning; (2) general maternal attitudes; and (3) patterns of maternal behavior. We do this because variations among them would be expected to be associated with different ways of behaving toward children, and consequently to have different effects on these children. Practices, attitudes, and patterns will be discussed in turn.

Maternal Specific Practices Influencing Socialization

A wealth of literature has appeared concerning breast versus bottle feeding, short versus long breast feeding, gradual versus abrupt weaning, self-demand versus scheduled feeding, gradual versus abrupt toilet training, and the effect of these infantile experiences upon subsequent development in later childhood and adulthood. In his careful review, Orlansky (55) demonstrated that many of these studies were inadequate in research design. in the small number of subjects used, and in the control of other variables which might affect the results. Even the apparently more carefully conducted studies are shown to be contradictory in their findings. An illustration from one area of the studies he reviewed will make the contradictory nature of the findings clearer. Several studies investigated whether or not the duration of breast feeding was related to later adequacy of personal adjustment. In one of the studies he reviewed, children breast fed less than six months or more than ten months showed more behavior problems than did children who had been breast fed between six and ten months. But in another study that he describes, a measure of security showed that the most secure college students were those either breast fed little if at all or breast fed for over a year, thus flatly contradicting the first study. The evidence is meager and contradictory and consequently unconvincing concerning any hypothesis which relies upon a specific form of early experience as an explanation of gross and important personality differences in subsequent years.

Since the Orlansky review, Sewell and Mussen (69) have published a study concerned with infant training practices used with about 160 five- and six-year-old children. They hypothesized that better adjustment and fewer oral symptoms would be found in (1) children who were breast fed as compared to those bottle fed; (2) children who were fed on a demand schedule as compared to those on a regular schedule; and (3) children who were weaned gradually as compared to those weaned abruptly. Data on infant training practices were obtained from an interview with the mother. Indices of adjustment were also obtained from this interview as were personality test scores and teachers' ratings of adjustment. In all, there were 26 adjustment or symptom items showing adjustment of these children. Each of these items was compared with gratification or nongratification (frustration) with respect to each of the three criteria (breast versus bottle fed, self-demand versus regular schedule feeding, and gradual versus abrupt weaning). No direct relationship between any method of feeding gratification and later good or poor adjustment was found in the study.

A recent study (70) indicates that there is little relationship between the mother's permissiveness in one aspect of socialization, such as feeding, and later aspects, such as toilet training. This finding suggests that we must look somewhere else than in specific practices for whatever commonality of influence there may be from the mothers which affects the personality adjustment of infants.

It is probable that the matter of the interrelationships reviewed by Orlansky and studied by Sewell and Mussen are of a more complicated nature than the designs of the studies allowed for. Specific techniques of infant care and training do not have an invariant relationship with specific consequent personality variables. Some techniques may produce more unfortunate consequences than others. However, it appears likely that the specific discipline is not ordinarily of critical significance in and for itself. More plausibly a specific practice may be regarded as part of a larger pattern in which it is imbedded. Practices and consequent personality development may be indirectly related in that, say, self-demand feeding and gradual weaning reflects a warm reaching-out for the infant on the mother's part. It may be that practices are but facets of a general attitude toward the infant. Consequently, attention will be given to the relation of maternal attitudes and personality development.

A specific practice of a mother such as breast nursing, self-demand feeding, and gradual weaning may or may not reflect a warmly accepting attitude on her part. A failure to use one or another of these techniques may come about because of reasons quite apart from accepting attitudes. The data of the study of Newton and Newton (54) bear this out. About 100 mothers in a maternity ward were interviewed shortly after delivery. The investigators classified these mothers into three groups on the basis of the attitudes they expressed toward breast feeding their infants. In those whom they judged had positive attitudes, 74 per cent were found later to breast feed their infants successfully. For the mothers they originally classified as having doubtful and negative attitudes, respectively, 35 and 26 per cent breast fed successfully. Let us suppose that these mothers were now studied in the fashion of the "practice" studies described earlier and that they had been divided into breast feeders and nonbreast feeders with no knowledge of their attitudes. In studying later personality adjustment, the breast fed group would have included not only 74 per cent of the positive attitude group but 35 and 26 per cent of the doubtful and negative attitude groups, respectively. Similarly, the nonbreast fed group would have included 26 per cent of those showing positive attitudes. If later study of the personality adjustment of individuals in the two groups had been made without this information, it would not have been known that each group contained individuals judged in terms of *attitudes* who belonged in one or the other group. This observation does not demonstrate that attitudes are more important than practices. It does, however, illustrate that studies based on specific practices may not take sufficiently into account the attitudes held by the mothers.

Maternal Attitudes Influencing Socialization

To anticipate the research studies discussed in a moment, they suggest very strongly that it is not specific practices but general maternal attitudes which most profoundly influence later personality development. If one asks how these broad general attitudes can be communicated to an infant, one must remember that attitudes are *constructs*. The infant still is stimulated by maternal behavior that manifests the attitude she holds, not the attitudes themselves. The evidence presented earlier in the chapter on prenatal maternal attitudes would seem to bear this out. Similarly, the discussion in the next chapter on the effect of pernicious attitudes in creating psychological disturbances lends weight to this contention.

The results of the study of Behrens (4) are relevant and important because she studied both specific practices and general attitudes in the same group of mothers. Her subjects were 25 Jewish, urban, lower middle-class families who were coming to a mental health clinic. Her small sample and other selective factors make suspect wide generalization of the results she obtained, but the results she found are clear-cut and apparently unequivocal. She investigated infant-rearing practices in feeding, weaning, and toilet training in their relation to adjustment of these children at the age of three. She found no correlation between the three infant-rearing practices and the children's adjustment. So far, this study bears out the previous studies using the same approach in that the findings were negative.

Behrens went another step. She investigated what she called the "total mother person," her term for general maternal attitudes and conduct. This was divided into three components based on what she considered to be the mother's underlying attitudes (character structure), the manner of meeting the maternal role demanded of her (maternal role), and observed conduct toward the child (maternal conduct). This last has reference to consistency, overprotection, and adaptation of her discipline to the child's needs rather than to specific practices.

The results in terms of correlation are reported in Table 7. She now obtained highly significant correlations between child adjustment and maternal attitudes with this same group of children that showed no correlation between child adjustment and specific ma-

TABLE 7

COEFFICIENTS OF RANK CORRELATION BETWEEN TOTAL MOTHER PERSON AND ITS
COMPONENTS AND CHILD ADJUSTMENT *

	Child Adjustment
Total mother person	0.75
Character structure	0.80
Maternal role	0.69
Maternal conduct	0.93

* From Behrens (4). Copyright 1954 by the Society for Research in Child Development, and published with permission.

ternal-rearing practices. She was still concerned with the behavior of the mother, but not specific practices. It was something more fundamental, expressed attitudinally, which was found to be positively related to child adjustment. It would appear that positive and negative attitudes are more predictive of the nature of the child's later adjustment than the nature of the specific practices followed by the mother in the infant's socialization.

Maternal rejection and acceptance. An attitude dimension observable in interactions of mother and infant is that of acceptance-rejection. From the investigation of maternal attitudes by Zemlick and Watson (81), there is another phase to be reported. This has to do with how each of the mothers reacted *after* the birth of her child. A new investigator, who had no knowledge of the previously reported findings on prenatal anxiety, symptoms, and attitudes, studied the interaction of mother and the newborn child while they were still in the maternity hospital. She was interested in the mother's evaluation of the baby (approval, solicitude, and contentment, or their opposites), her cooperativeness in meeting the needs of the infant in feeding, and so on. The specific ratings of these factors were summarized in general ratings for the mothers in a sequence extending from the most solicitous to the least solicitous. These general ratings were correlated with the measures of prenatal anxiety, symptom, and attitude. Conceivably, the resulting correlation coefficients could have turned out in any one of three ways. There might have been found low, nonsignificant correlations, implying a lack of relationship between prenatal indices and the mother's behavior with her baby. Or positive correlations might have been found, implying that mothers who "accept" their coming children behave in a very solicitous fashion toward their children after birth. Neither of these results was found.

Instead, *negative* relations were found between indices of care of the child after birth and prenatal anxiety, symptoms, and attitudes of rejection. At first this might seem to imply that mothers who reject their children before birth treat them with greater devotion after birth! Fortunately, this is not the only conclusion open. The investigators summarized their interpretation as follows:

> Mothers who subjectively and objectively display the greatest degree of symptomatology express their rejection through psychosomatic avenues during pregnancy and later exhibit overindulgent, oversolicitous and compulsive behavior (maternal persistence) with respect to the child. In their extreme forms the criteria for the mother-child adjustment used in this study are indicative of maternal overprotection. A qualitative, clinical analysis of the personal data on the subjects shows that two women had been sterility cases, one had had a previous miscarriage, three were obviously ambivalent about the pregnancy, and one had verbally acknowledged she did not want pregnancy. Clinically these factors are to be found in mothers who reject and overprotect their children. In an overwhelming majority of instances these seven mothers achieved the highest, "most accepting," post-partum ranks. An alternative hypothesis, that instead of being "overprotecting" the mothers are showing protection within normal limits, is rejected because it requires the assumption that mothers without a stormy pregnancy are less protecting of their infants. Therefore, fairly convincing qualitative evidence is at hand to support the statement that symptom-oriented mothers who generally are rejecting frequently show their rejection through an overprotecting attitude toward the child (*81*, 582–583).[2]

The mothers, then, who *appeared* most solicitous were really oversolicitous and overprotecting. Maternal overprotection refers to excessive maternal care. Levy (*47*), a pioneer in studies of overprotection, describes the maternal characteristics which are indicative of this excessiveness. Three which he mentions are prolongation of infantile care, excessive contact, and prevention of independent behavior. Naturally, these newborn infants in the study under consideration were not old enough for the mothers to show these characteristics. Rather, their behavior appeared to be within normal limits because their children were so young. These results strongly suggest, assuming no change in the mothers, that as the child grows older, overprotective attitudes will emerge.

Acceptance within optimal limits, in contrast to overprotection, is something healthy and healthful. Porter (*58*), in constructing a *Parental Acceptance Scale,* paid particular attention to this point.

[2] From Zemlick and Watson (*81*). Copyright 1953 by the American Orthopsychiatric Association, and published with permission.

He defined parental acceptance in terms of unconditional love, recognizing that the child has rights as a person, the right to express feelings, the right to uniqueness, and the right for the child to become an autonomous individual (58). Infantilization, excessive contact, and prevention of independent behavior or the overprotecting form of the accepting attitude are specifically repudiated. There is no reason to believe that most mothers do not tend to fall somewhere within these optimal limits. Nevertheless, the evidence of Zemlick and Watson does suggest that some mothers do not accept their children in this healthful way even at birth.

Sewell, Mussen, and Harris (70), whose study was previously referred to, found no general factor [3] reflected in training practices. Thus in their sample, acceptance-rejection was not a pervasive, underlying attitude. Nevertheless, the first two factors they found were permissiveness in early feeding and permissiveness in toilet training. After a parent-child interaction factor, there was a nonpunitive treatment factor and then a factor of promotion of independence. Both of these latter two factors along with the first two can easily be subsumed under the concept of acceptance. Nevertheless, acceptance and rejection cannot be seen as accounting for all maternal attitudes in infancy.

Variations in maternal attitudes. There are variations in maternal attitudes in infancy, the nature of which have not yet been fully understood. Coleman and her associates (15) at the Yale Child Study Center have begun to study some of the variations in early parental attitudes. Only snatches from some of their findings may be given in the form of characteristic vignettes.

1. A mother who held an initially close relationship with her infant was negatively influenced when he was ten months old by his striving toward lessened dependence although this is normal at this age. Now he was no longer so close, not so much "a part of her." As a consequence she became less accepting, although not to the extent of rejecting the infant. She was merely less "in tune" with him.

2. Originally somewhat negative, because the infant was active, hypertonic, easily startled, and sensitive to external stimuli, another mother

[3] Their findings were obtained through the use of what is known as factor analysis. Briefly, this is a statistical technique based upon analyzing the intercorrelations among data, finding those data that seem to be related to one another and then giving the "factor" a name which seems to capture the meaning of the interrelated measures. In this study it can be seen that they did not find a single factor which they could label "acceptance-rejection," but rather the factors that are mentioned.

lost confidence in herself. She regained her confidence and became more accepting of the infant when she could recognize the social responsiveness of the infant to her, and the infant's obvious need for her.

In the illustrations of mother-child interaction from Coleman (15), it will be noted that the characteristics of the child influence the attitudes of the mother. Variations in attitudes were found as the infant changed. Fries (24), whose work on activity types in infancy was described in Chapter 6, suggests that the infant's behavior is one of the factors which influence the parent's attitudes. One infant's early-formed quiet pattern, shown by his rarely crying and by his tendency to sleep more than the usual infant, was welcomed by the parents since it did not disturb their work. Another baby who was very active in her motor achievement was approved by her compulsive intellectualizing mother who wanted signs of her child's advanced state and found them in the motor area. Turning to an instance where there was an increasingly poor mother-child relationship, a third very active infant drove her compulsively overconscientious mother to seek treatment because she could not keep up with the child in his "all-day" running in the park.

In these illustrations of variations in attitudes, an attempt has been made to show that our earlier account oversimplifies the relation of mother and infant. With increasing age of the child, nuances of maternal behavior become more prominent and open to identification. Further amplification of maternal attitudes in connection with older children will be presented in later chapters.

Maternal Behavior Patterns Influencing Socialization

Relatively recently, some attention has been paid to the *patterns* of maternal behavior. One may study the interrelation of various kinds of observed behavior that the mother performs in interacting with the infant. For example, a mother's feeding behavior, cleaning, caressing, and moving the infant about may be studied as they are interrelated to see if they form a pattern, instead of one at a time as is done in specific practice studies.

In connection with this point, Escalona indicates that it is appropriate to "think of all the different variables which constitute a given situation as mutually interrelated in such a way as to form a constellation (or pattern, or whole, or Gestalt) which will alter the manner in which each of the single variables is related to the phenomena in question" (20, 159).[4]   Breast versus bottle feeding, for example, is never in life the single factor which will shape the course of the mother-child relationship.   She goes on to add that what we need to know is the circumstances under which breast feeding may be (1) a medium for a wholesome relation; (2) a deterrent to such a relation; and (3) an irrelevant feature.   The factors entering the situation which determine the responses of a given infant are many and complex.   At times certain factors may reinforce one another, at other times they cancel one another, and always they are in a state of dynamic flux.   Such studies of infant socialization in terms of patterns of behavior are in their barest beginnings.

Brody (12) has carried on a very detailed study of behavior patterns of mothers of infants between four and 28 weeks of age.   The setting was an observation room containing a crib and other baby things.   The 32 mothers who participated were informed that the investigators wished to learn more about how normal infants are able to develop in perfect health.   Each mother was asked to come to the observation room for a four hour period with her baby and while there carry on with him as she would at home, feeding him, changing his diapers, putting him to sleep, and so on.   The mother took care of the infant in any way she saw fit, combining her activities with chatting, reading, needlework, or just sitting.   Carefully planned-for notes were taken by the three women observers.   The observer who functioned as interviewer also served as "hostess," making the situation as natural as possible, but also questioning the mother concerning child-care practice according to a prearranged general plan.

The investigators had selected six kinds of overt maternal activities to be observed during the sessions.   These activities were (1) feeding, for example, offering, withdrawing, forcing food; (2) cleaning, for example, skin care, wiping saliva, hair combing; (3) moving (of whole body), for example, hugging, bouncing, standing-up; (4) touching, for example, minor contacts, stroking, kissing, fingering; (5) offering objects (playthings, pacifiers, empty food utensils); and (6) speaking.   Scales of maternal response were developed for each kind of activity.   These scales were designed to measure the sensitivity with which the mother responded to the needs of the infant.   Each scale had a mid-point of smooth, effective response to the infant.   In one direction away from the mid-point it extended to

---

[4] From Escalona (20).   Copyright 1950 by the American Orthopsychiatric Association, and published with permission.

TABLE 8

GROUPS ISOLATED IN STUDY OF MOTHER-INFANT INTERACTION *

		N
Group A	Sensitive, consistent, attentive	7
B	Less sensitive, less consistent, somewhat overactive	4
C	Insufficiently sensitive, moderately inconsistent, adequately attentive	6
D	Hypersensitive, inconsistent, and hyperactive	11

* Adapted from Brody (*12*). Copyright 1956 by the International Universities Press, and published with permission.

reluctant or perfunctory answering of infant's needs and, in the other direction, to control or domination of the infant. Each unit of behavior in the protocols they obtained from their observations was evaluated and coded against the scales. The investigators grouped the results separately for each mother and for each of the six kinds of activity. For each mother and each kind of activity three measures were calculated: (1) the frequency, a measure of absolute amount of sensitivity each mother exhibited; (2) the mean, a measure of the average degree of sensitivity each mother demonstrated; and (3) the standard deviation, a measure of the consistency of sensitivity each mother showed. The frequency was the measure of how often each of the six kinds of activity appeared; the mean was the measure of the average amount of sensitivity she showed, with a middle value showing optimal sensitivity; and the standard deviation was the measure of how much she varied in her behavior from the average amount of sensitivity she showed in each activity.

The next step in analysis was to inspect the results for each of these mothers and to group together those for whom the means for the six kinds of activity fell at roughly the optimal, middle position. The group of mothers selected in this fashion were found to have small standard deviations and thus to be consistent. They were found also to be moderate in the frequencies of their activities with the infants and thus to be attentive, or active. In short, the mothers of this group were sensitive, consistent, and attentive. This group, numbering seven mothers, the investigators called group A. By a similar procedure of case selection, each time starting with the measure of degree of sensitivity (the mean), three other groups were isolated, accounting for all but three of the mothers. Their frequencies and standard deviations were then examined and characterized.

Table 8 presents a summarization of the groupings that emerged from the total group of mothers.

It would appear that these groupings give us a first approximation of meaningful types of maternal behavior. A summary of the types of maternal behavior is quoted:

> The mothers of group A were conspicuous for their ability to accommodate to the needs of their infants. By virtue of the kind of physical and emotional support they provided and the steadiness of their interest in and communicativeness toward their infants, they gave them freedom to move about, to vocalize, feed, rest or play with a minimum of interference. More regularly and with more ease than all the other mothers they recognized and tried to relieve passing discomforts in the infants. The mothers themselves were not without tension, but most of the time that tension appeared to heighten their intimacy with the infants.
>
> The mothers of group B were conspicuous for their conscious willingness to accommodate to their infants. At first glance some of their behavior resembled that of the A mothers, but on the whole they were more tense, less communicative and less steadily attentive. At times they tried more actively to stimulate their infants and at other times they were mildly distant or insensitive to the infants' immediate needs. The quality of satisfaction with the infant and of enjoyment of their mothering tasks, outstanding in the A mothers, was much less evident, although B mothers were generally positive toward their infants.
>
> The mothers in group C were conspicuous for their lack of spontaneity and their intentions to be efficient above all else. Physically and socially they were detached from their infants. Some reduced their attention to the carrying out of a minimum of essential details of infant care, and showed a low degree of interest in any activity with the infant of a non-physical nature.
>
> The mothers of group D were conspicuously active but also erratic in their attentiveness, efficiency and sensitivity. They quite sedulously governed their infants' actions by stimulating, restricting or instructing them, apparently hardly aware of the possible effects of their behavior on the infants' condition (12, 265–266).[5]

Brody objects to giving the groups specific descriptive names on several grounds, but particularly on the basis of the fear that such terms, for example, permissive, would carry moral connotations. Although there is some danger of this, her stand runs counter to present-day trends. So this writer, with apologies to Brody, would suggest that group A might be labeled as permissive, group B as less permissive, group C as restrictive, and group D as inconsistent.

These four groups were formed on the basis of the behavior dis-

---

[5] From Brody (12). Copyright 1956 by the International Universities Press, and published with permission.

played in taking care of their babies in the observational session. In these same sessions the mothers verbally expressed to the observers many opinions and attitudes about child care. Considerable consistency was found between the behavioral group in which a mother fell and the attitudes she expressed. The permissive mothers were confident in their role, planned their training practices in keeping with the infants' behavior, preferred to use verbal forms of discipline, and expressed tolerance of adjustment difficulties. The less permissive showed attitudes and planned practices somewhat less adequately than did those in the permissive group but, just as in patterns of behavior, were rather close in their attitudes to that group. The restrictive group, although confident, showed some mothers whose confidence was vulnerable, who were explicitly nonindulgent toward their infant in their attitudes, and a little more inclined to consider resorting to corporal punishment in the future. The inconsistent group was nonpermissive in spirit of conscious attitudes to the contrary, planned to institute weaning and toilet training at earlier ages than the other groups, and more inclined to use corporal punishment. Thus a regularity of attitudes that corresponded to regularities of patterns of behavior was found. This adds credence to the belief that both attitudes and patterns of behavior are promising approaches to the study of infancy socialization practices and of the development of personality.

In the diadic unit of mother and infant, one aspect of the relationship, the mother, has been emphasized. Now the focus shifts. The child is brought into the foreground, with the mother in the background. Infant social relationships from the perspective of *his* behavior and experience come to the fore. An "infant's-eye" view of this business of infancy is stressed in the remaining sections of this chapter.

The development of self and social awareness in infancy

One may begin by examining the dawning of self and social awareness. As stated earlier, the nucleus of self appears to be what is experienced as "I" or "me" as distinguished from everything else that is "not me." The newborn infant does not have this awareness of "I" and "not I." There is no awareness of the outside world and, therefore, no self-awareness by which to distinguish himself from that world. The whole world is wet or hungry or cold when he is wet, hungry, or cold. "I" and the "rest of the world" are one.

One particular approach to the differentiation of the ego has already been discussed. This is the psychoanalytic theory of the emergence of the ego. What was said concerning that position is not contradicted by the discussion to follow. Rather, the classic psychoanalytic picture of the emergence of the ego may be supplemented by a statement of other factors which also appear to make for self and social awareness. These other considerations are added in order to get as full a picture as possible of the development of awareness.

The intertwined factors of maturation and learning are operative in the development of self and social awareness in the manner described in the previous chapter in connection with the development of understanding. In fact, the topic now under consideration is a special aspect of understanding—the understanding of the self and of others. Its first phase is the emergence of an understanding of the sheer existence of self and of other selves. Maturational effects may be illustrated by the change in the sensory apparatus in the first few months of life. Awareness (consciousness) itself, quite apart from *self*-awareness, is rudimentary in the neonate. The infant's lack of awareness of what is going on around him could be expected from the relatively undeveloped state of his sensory apparatus, particularly the eyes and ears. The ability to perceive differences among objects requires the maturation of the perceptual systems taking place during the early months and in the integration of visual, motor, and tactual functions. His first contacts with his environment are blurred, fluid, and global (52). People are probably right when they speak of the consciousness of the infant as a "blooming, buzzing confusion." Fenichel (22) offers some interesting speculations concerning the nature of infantile perceptions based on his observations of regressed psychotic adults. He suggests that in the infant objects are not sharply distinguished, images are inexact, and perceptions of the various sensory modalities overlap. The more primitive sensations such as the kinesthetic predominate. By the very nature of the problem, clinical evidence of a rather nebulous sort is the only source of verification that he can offer. Lacking other evidence, this conception has a certain plausibility.

In this connection, Piaget (56) speaks of the infant as functioning at the sensory-motor level. At this level the infant "assimilates" external realities. Realities are not yet entities; they are only functional elements—something to be sucked, to be handled, or to be moved. Objects do not yet exist as objects. "Out of sight, out of mind" might be said to characterize the view of the infant. He behaves as if objects which have disappeared from view have ceased to exist. For example, Piaget tells us that an infant of five to eight months of age, already old enough to seize a solid object, will lose interest and turn away if a cloth be thrown over the object before his hand reaches it. At a slightly older age he is capable of seeking an object behind a screen and thus shows the beginnings of the notion of the real exterior permanence of objects. Nevertheless, he is still functioning at the more primitive level.

An infant at the just-mentioned level was given the experience of retrieving an object which he saw placed under the left of two pillows. On the next occasion, he sought the object where he had found it before, despite the fact that the examiner, in full view of the infant, had placed it under the *right* pillow. As Piaget indicates, it is as if his action in reaching under the left pillow was decided by the success of his actions by which he had secured it previously and not by the reality of its external placement under the right pillow on this new occasion. At the sensory-motor level the world to the infant is not that of permanent objects with an autonomy of their own but a series of perceptive views which periodically disappear into nonexistence only to be brought back as the function of the proper action on the infant's part.

How does the infant "construct" a world of permanent objects in space independent of himself? It is his sensory-motor intelligence which permits this distinction to take place. He learns to distinguish objects as realities independent of himself through his experience with them. In so doing he shifts the center of space and its objects from his action to himself. He is still the middlepoint of the world, but it consists of stable objects with independent existences. What happens at this new level will be described in Chapter 10.

Whether interpreted as Piaget does or not, it is evident that the task before the infant is to mark off the separate specific objects in his environment from himself. He is learning to specify the contours of his body, the sound of his voice, and to identify the various sensory kinesthetic processes from his own body. Simultaneously he also has the task of perceiving or learning to know other persons *as* persons. The mother's gentle voice, soothing touch, and warm body emerge from the fog of his impressions. Also emerging from this total matrix is a sense of the unity of his own person. Gradually, it is not pain but *my* pain, not hunger but *my* hunger, not hunger being fed but *mother feeding me.*

Behavioral indices related to the emerging of self and social awareness may be observed in infancy. Examination will show that some of the items concern the beginnings of the perception of other persons, others concern a recognition of the need for cooperation and communication, and still others concern the use of words which have self-reference. It has been observed that at about age of four weeks responsiveness to social surroundings begins to appear (*26*). The infant reacts to social overtures by a reduction of bodily activity. For example, the infant ceases crying, at least for the moment, if held in someone's arms. At eight weeks his face shows signs of animation on seeing other persons and at 12 weeks he may vocalize his reply to their speech. A spontaneous social smile is reported by Gesell (*26*) as being present at 16 weeks. By the beginning of the sixth month, Spitz (*71*) found a smile on seeing the experimenter for the first time present in 98 per cent of his rather large sample.[6] A dramatic change was found by Spitz when these infants were observed again, this time in the last half of the first year. The indiscriminate smiling responses both to the mother and to a stranger give way to smiling sometimes at one person or another but not indiscriminately at everybody. One of the early signs of what is popularly called "self-consciousness" appears at about the end of the first half year when an infant tries to hide himself when in the presence of strangers.

Murphy *et al.* (*53*) stress the importance of the infant's contact with the mother for the development of the self. During this interaction of mother and infant he forms a vague conception of her as a person carried over to his observation of himself. They write:

> What with seeing himself in the mirror, noticing the similarity of his voice to that of others or observing the whole body as he sits or lies, he forms an idea of himself, partly on the analogy of other selves. The analogy is rough and vague and the child does not know that it is an analogy. Whatever the mother is, thinks and feels, and whatever he is, thinks and feels, tend to be more or less confused. As Piaget so well shows, the child of three or four assumes that others see the world as he does; his mother feels about things as he does. All the more painful is the shock of discovery that this assumption makes trouble. For a long

---

[6] The smile appears in rare cases as early as the twenty-fifth day. It may be that its appearance at this young age is due to visceral changes, which are known to produce a "smile."

time, however, it is inevitable and natural that he "identify" himself with the mother or with whatever other persons are near and dear. It is quite fatuous to ask whether he really "believes himself to be his mother" when he does as she does, or "believes himself to be his daddy" when he puts on daddy's hat and announces "I am daddy," or to ask whether he "half believes" this or "just pretends" it. The child does not live in any such world as the one of disjunctive realities which we try to force upon him. Analogies come and go; the world is a phantasy and has its own reality; it is not clear reality *plus* make-believe (53, 208).[7]

Murphy *et al.* (53) also express the opinion that the self is based in part upon experience the infant has in the use of proper names and when parents hold him responsible or reward him for his behavior. The attainment of the pronoun, "I," and related terms such as "me" and "you" are characteristic, according to Gesell (28), at about 24 months of age. In language, then, we find evidence of an emerging sense of self.

Another means whereby the self emerges in the infant is found in the development of independent oppositional behavior (48). At age 18 to 24 months he is "into everything." He knows where things are kept and gets them out in what appears to some mothers an alarming profusion. He darts everywhere, and refuses to allow his arm to be held. If restrained, he often resists strenuously and vocally. A specific illustration from Levy is appropriate.

> A two-year-old tries to fill the sink with water. He struggles to turn the faucet. His efforts are persistent, exhausting, and fruitless. . . . The father silently turns the faucet. The two-year-old bursts into a loud scream. He runs out of the bathroom. He is angry and in tears. He refuses to be washed or bathed. For him, everything is spoiled. An obstacle was thrown in the path of progress towards his own goal: his own job, to be done by himself alone, without the slightest help, or suggestion, or interference (48, 114).[8]

Mothers can supply countless similar illustrations of behavior having this flavor of opposition which seemingly serves to sharpen the child's sense of being an individual person. These same ways of behaving show the pronounced influence of what later is to be described as independence tendencies. His growing self-awareness leads to demands for independence.

[7] From Murphy *et al.* (53). Copyright 1937 by Harper and Brothers, Inc., and published with permission.

[8] From Levy (48). Copyright 1953 by Charles C Thomas, and published with permission.

Behavior tendencies in infancy

In a later section of the chapter concerned with evidence for the psychoanalytic theories of infancy, oral and anal tendencies are examined. Other major behavior tendencies are important in infancy as well. Dependence and independence, aggressive and sexual tendencies require examination. They are now presented and evaluated.

Dependence and Independence Tendencies

One aspect of dependence is a tendency to rely upon the help of others in striving to reach one's goals. Or to put it another way, dependence is the tendency to seek to obtain nurturance from other people. Dependent behavior has its beginning in infancy: each infant must be dependent because of his helplessness. He may be, as the psychoanalysts say, in the period of infantile omnipotence, but he is learning to be dependent, not all-powerful. He is not born with a need for dependency: helplessness thrusts dependence upon him.

The mother is the agent for meeting his needs despite his helplessness. His mother satisfies his needs and, in terms of learning theory, becomes the agent of drive reduction. She is the configuration or pattern of stimuli that is consistently associated with the reduction of his needs—she feeds him when he is hungry, changes him when he is wet, and warms him when he is cold. He learns to be dependent upon her as the instrument for meeting his needs. This aspect of dependence occurs when the infant learns to seek help from others. He is learning, to use a term of Heathers (37), *instrumental* dependence.

There is another aspect of dependence—*emotional* dependence. This may be illustrated by considering what happens after instrumental dependent tendencies have begun to be learned. After the first few days or weeks it is observed that an infant will cease crying when picked up *before* he is relieved of his hunger or other discomfort. Her mere presence has acquired reward value for him. Her comforting presence has become a secondary drive in itself. Receiving from others comfort, love, notice, and praise becomes a secondary drive on his part. Instrumental dependence leads to emotional dependence.

It is in this perspective that the need for mothering is interpreted.

The rocking, stroking, cuddling, and being fussed over in countless ways are what is meant by mothering. Instead of the need for mothering being innate as Ribble contended, this need is interpreted by this writer as a secondary drive based upon learning emotional dependence in the fashion just described.

The infant learns not only to discriminate among persons, but he also shows differential reactions to them. One facet of his differential behavior toward persons can be referred to as affectionate behavior. (The other facet, hostile behavior, will be described in connection with aggressive tendencies.) He learns to find pleasurable responses in his relations with others, to have affection for various people, and to wish to be near them. What are the antecedents of this affectionate behavior? It may have a sexual component, but the greatest stress can be placed upon emotional dependence. The mother's presence has acquired reward value. The infant reacts with affection because of emotional dependent tendencies.

One investigator (2) has studied the development of affectionate behavior avowedly and directly. She observed 900 infants who were between four weeks and two years of age. These observations were made incidental to the giving of intelligence tests and, consequently, she reports in an anecdotal, qualitative fashion. Although her results are not gathered in as carefully controlled and specified conditions as one would like, they are reported because of their original nature.

The infant's affectionate behavior is first shown at about four months by outgoing strivings and approach—his smiling gaze fixed on the person's face. He waves his arms and tries to rise from the crib. Without coordination or too much success, he strives to get closer to the attractive person. At about six months, he reaches out to pat the person. This is roughly the same age as when he begins to discriminate between persons. This is also the age when he responds to affectionate cuddling. As memory develops, so, too, does anticipation. Toward the end of the first year he shows anticipation of the mother coming for feeding, and laughs, squirms, and wiggles with delight on her approach. During the second year affection extends by the process of generalization to objects—his toys, clothes, chair, favorite blankets, and the like. These then are manifestations of affection in infancy.

Frustration and dependency. Intruding upon the idyllic scene so far sketched is the fact that there is discomfort and pain in the life of the infant, too. He becomes hungry or experiences a pain of one sort or another. In other words, as Dollard and Miller (17) put it, a goal response is interfered with. In the course of learning to be dependent, the infant is inevitably frustrated. The mother is not always there at the instant he wants help. Frustration results. The process is very well illustrated by Whiting in discussing frustration in a primitive group, the Kwoma. He writes:

> Kwoma infants are cared for almost exclusively by their mothers. For approximately the first three years of his life a Kwoma infant sits in the lap of his mother during the day and lies by her side at night. It is the Kwoma mother's duty to care for all the needs of her child during this period. When, despite this constant care, Kwoma infants suffer frustration, crying is the response which becomes most firmly fixed. A Kwoma mother, whenever her infant cries, does her best to comfort him. If he is hungry she feeds him; if he is cold she warms him; if he is sick or in pain she tries to soothe him. Thus by removing the source of frustration or pain the Kwoma mother rewards crying as a response to these conditions. Toward the end of infancy, when the child begins to talk, he responds to frustration or pain by asking for help, and his mother complies with his request whenever it is possible for her to do so. Thus during infancy a frustration-dependence sequence is established (77, 138).[9]

This relation of frustration and dependence is continued and strengthened as the child becomes less dependent, when adult care is withdrawn as he becomes older. For example, learning to keep clean, to care for himself, and to take responsibility inevitably brings about frustrating situations.

Determinants of dependence tendencies. A variety of reasons have led psychologists to postulate that a relation would be found between the severity of frustrations in infancy and later magnitude of dependence tendencies infants exhibited. Although the dependence tendencies under consideration are those learned in infancy, their effects are apt to be more evident when the child is somewhat older, that is, when he is of preschool age or older. In other words, to study the antecedents of dependency in an infant we examine what sort of preschool child he has become.

The clearest evidence of infantile antecedents of dependency is to be found in a study of preschool children by Sears and his associates (67). Since they were interested in the antecedents of both dependency and aggression in infancy and in early childhood, this study

[9] From Whiting (77). Copyright 1944 by the Royal Anthropological Institute of Great Britain and Ireland, and published with permission.

will be referred to at several points. For convenience it will be referred to as the "antecedent" study. The children in the antecedent study were rated by their nursery school teacher on a scale of dependency based on instances of seeking help, praise, physical contacts, and nearness. These same categories were used to find (1) dependency toward the teacher; and (2) dependency toward other children. A trained observer also obtained the number of instances of dependent behavior in a time sample with the same children. Through an interview, material concerning infant socialization, particularly about feeding and weaning and toilet training practices, was gathered from the mothers.

Amount of dependent behavior in these children at preschool age was found in their sample to be positively correlated with the rigidity of their feeding schedule in girls, but not in boys; and, especially, with the severity of weaning they had experienced in infancy in both boys and girls. Both rigidity of feeding and severity of weaning are frustrating. Their prediction, that "degree of early infant frustration will vary positively with later overt dependency behavior" (67, 187) [10] was borne out. Frustration in infancy expressed through rigidity of scheduling and severity of weaning tended to be related to extent of dependency in early childhood. In other words, the greater the rigidity of scheduling and the severity of weaning during infancy the greater the amount of dependency during early childhood. Infantile frustration leads to later dependent strivings.

Severity of toilet training, another source of frustration in infancy, was found *not* to be related to dependency during the preschool years. It becomes necessary to consider how this finding of a form of frustration not correlated with dependency may be reconciled with the substantial correlation of severity of weaning and subsequent dependency. A clue is obtained from the fact that weaning takes place in the first year; toilet training does not take place until later. If toilet training frustration is unrelated to dependency in nursery school while severe weaning frustration is, it suggests that the critical period for the development of dependency is the last part of the first year of life, that is, during weaning but before toilet training. This would imply that for the present findings to make sense, as Sears and the others (67) point out, the dependence drive was formed during the first few months, that is, when rigidity and scheduling were operative.

[10] From Sears *et al.* (67). Copyright 1953 by The Journal Press, and published with permission.

They state this and a related point as to why severity of toilet training and dependency are not correlated as follows:

> It may be suggested, then, that the child begins to develop dependency actions and drive from birth. The actions change continuously as new understanding of how to get help occurs, but dependency drive reaches an asymptote early in infancy. Only in cases of severe deprivation of parental nurturance will the dependency drive fail to develop. Once the drive is developed, non-nurturance and other social frustrations will serve not to weaken the dependency drive, but to strengthen the reactions designed to gratify it. Hence, degree of early infant frustration will vary positively with later overt dependency behavior.
>
> Another point worth considering is the lack of correlation between severity of toilet training and dependency. The feeding process involves the mother in a diadic relationship in which her main function is to give the child help. She acts in a supportive manner, giving, providing, bringing to him. In toilet training her role is quite different. She does nothing *for* the child, only *to* him. He has no initial desire to use the potty; her putting him on it is not a reward, as is her giving him food. Only gradually does he learn to *want* to have approved toilet habits, and the desire comes at the end of the mother's training activity; it is not there while she is teaching. Thus, toilet training fills no need, satisfies no initial drive; it is nothing but a modifier of behavior, a frustration, mild under the best procedure and dreadful under the worst (67, 187).[10]

Thus, both positive relation between events in early infancy and dependency in the preschool years and the lack of relation of events in later infancy and dependency in the preschool years are satisfactorily accounted for.

According to theoretical expectation and according to our introductory paragraphs in the present account of how dependence is formed, dependency should be positively related to gratification of nurturance. That is, the child who received a great deal of gratification through nurturance should show considerable dependency. In the same study, the interview with the mother included data about the amount of nurturance she gave the child. It had been hoped that information on self-demand feeding would supply the index of nurturance, but this proved disappointing since no clear relation between it and dependency was found. Instead, the other end of the scale of nurturance, that of rigid scheduling, was found to be an index of frustration correlated with dependency as mentioned earlier. Although admittedly there was difficulty in measurement, the investigators suggest that the lack of relationship between nurturance and dependency is due to all the children in the sample receiving enough reinforcement of dependent behavior so that what became crucial in creating individual differences were the differences in frustration, not nurturance. If the last part of the first year of life be crucial for establishment of dependency then it was the nurturance *offered then* which would be important in the formation of dependency. Measurement of nurturance thereafter would be too late. Nurturance had already served its function.

The pattern study of Sears, Maccoby, and Levin (66) supplies much valuable data about infants, including some bearing on the present topic. Both as background for their findings concerning dependency in infancy and for the sake of future reference to their findings, a somewhat detailed statement of their procedure and subjects will be given. Hereafter it will be referred to as the pattern study. The mothers studied were chosen from those living in two suburbs of a large metropolitan area in New England. One suburb was primarily residential and the occupants were mostly of middle-class occupational level, while the other suburb contained considerable heavy industry with the population mostly working-class people. Eight schools supplied the sample. Standardized, but not completely structured interviews were conducted by ten trained women interviewers with nearly 400 mothers of five-year-olds. These interviews were recorded for later analysis. Information about both mother and child was secured. The investigators chose for description various dimensions which will be referred to as they become relevant in the topics considered here. These were based on interview schedules, or rating scales. Analysis of the interviews was made to decide on the ratings to be given and ratings made by ten advanced graduate students. Each interview was rated independently to test the reliability of rating. Final scores were on pooled judgments of the two raters. Dimensions concerning the mother had to do with (1) her disciplinary technique; (2) her permissiveness; (3) her severity in applying techniques; (4) her temperamental qualities; and (5) her positive inculcation of more mature behavior in her child. We are at present concerned with their findings on dependency in infancy.

The Sears pattern study (66) did not verify the earlier antecedent study. Either negative or even diametrically opposite results were found. No general connection between severity of weaning and dependency could be elicited. Instead of girls showing a relationship of scheduling and dependency, none was found, but boys fed on self-demand (nonrigid) scheduling were more dependent.

From the conflicting results of the two studies, it would appear that the relation between frustration and dependency is not unequivocal. One may either take the position that the evidence is contradictory and that no clear relationship between infancy training and dependency has been established, or decide on the basis of the merits of the designs of the two studies which should be tentatively accepted as the more valid. The latter course is recommended.

A tentative conclusion may be drawn that the earlier antecedent study focuses more sharply and precisely on the problem at hand. In the later pattern study, mothers gave their opinions about infancy practice at least two more years removed from actual weaning experience than was the case for the mothers in the earlier study. This time lapse may have distorted their perception of the situation. Moreover, it should be noted that in the pattern study the mothers themselves were the ones supplying information about dependency. Sears and his associates comment on how the mothers' attitudes, favorable or unfavorable, influence their perception of their children's dependency. In the antecedent study, trained observers sampled dependence reactions, on the spot as it were. Presumably, they were more free from the effects of this distorting factor. Therefore, more credence is placed on the positive results of the earlier study, which showed a relationship between the frustrations of weaning and scheduling and later dependence reactions. Frustration from rejection leads to greater dependency. Although this is offered as a generalization, it is subject to qualification. In the next chapter, Goldfarb's results with severely rejected institutionalized children leads to the conclusion that massive rejection leads to lessened, not greater, dependency. Therefore, it is necessary to add that frustration leading to greater dependency holds only within normal family settings. For a more detailed discussion the reader is referred to page 297.

In the Sears study of normal children, frustration from rejection produced *more* dependency. Emotionally deprived children were shown by Goldfarb (*29, 30, 31*) to have more "independence" than those not deprived, even though they paid for it at the cost of being unable to develop adequate emotional relationships with others. True, the children Goldfarb studied showed an exaggerated need for affection and attention, but the rest of their behavior belied these as indices of dependency. In short, frustrations arising from rejection produced in these children *less* emotional dependency.

This disagreement can be explained through a consideration of differential amounts of reinforcement of dependency the normal children received as compared to the disturbed children. The children in the Sears nursery school group, although perhaps under the care of somewhat neglectful and indifferent parents or guardians, did receive many reinforcements for dependency. They were fed, bathed, dried, dressed, and otherwise cared for, if only in a perfunctory manner. Even a neglected child received enough reinforcement to have strong dependence tendencies. With the dependnce tendencies established, if the mother is then rejecting, the child's dependency needs are unfulfilled and he will increase his efforts to secure the desired behavior on her part, that is, his dependency is increased. In contrast, the massively rejected children studied by Goldfarb received so little reinforcement for dependency that dependence tendencies failed to develop. Hence, the results are not contradictory. Frustration due to strong rejection leads to lessened dependency, while less strong frustration from rejection leads to greater dependency.

Relation of Dependence and Independence Tendencies

In infancy, dependency looms large. But the account would be incomplete if something were not said about another and contrary tendency. Almost as fast as an infant learns to seek help, he learns to get along without it (66). Independence becomes an end in itself.

Independence like dependence is the result of socialization. Dependent habits over and over again must be interfered with in this new phase of socialization. As Dollard, Doob et al. put it:

> Under normal circumstances each child may also be said to decrease steadily its dependence on its parents. It must learn to walk where it has formerly been carried; and being carried is, of course, a *response* in this situation. It learns not to be picked up when it has experienced some small disaster. It must give up much of the cuddling, holding, and petting which is the prerogative of the smallest darling. Childish approximations of table manners and etiquette must be altered in favor of the customs preferred by adults. The child must learn to wait for its food, to keep its face clean, to submit to having its hair combed, to eat in the regular stages designated by our table techniques. At some time or another all of these lengthened sequences involve frustrations and elicit protest from the child (17, 64–65).[11]

In his second year, the infant is now able to move about. In doing so, he shows the overwhelming importance of independence. He

[11] From Dollard, Doob et al. (17). Copyright 1939 by the Yale University Press, and published with permission.

is enthusiastically everywhere and as much as possible doing so on his own. He walks, climbs, jumps, and trots, he pushes his stroller instead of riding in it, he carries things, wants to put on and take off his own clothes. Most of the time he does what he is told, but he shows his dawning independence in saying, "no," "no," to anything and everything persistently and vehemently. This tendency toward independence is also brought out when one reconsiders the evidence about the emergence of self during infancy. He has the sense of being a person, a bit fuzzy as to the boundaries to be sure, but a person for all that and *he* wants what *he* wants when *he* wants it. It will be remembered that one of the factors making for the emergence of the self was the oppositional quality of many of the infant's activities. In emerging as a person, he wants to be independent. In addition to protesting against help, there is the obvious pride he takes in doing something on his very own, which also points to independence tendencies.

But in all of this pushing out into the world, in his seeking of independence, there is vacillation. He takes two steps forward and one step backward, sometimes literally. Off on some gallant adventure, but just out of mother's sight, he bursts into tears and flees back. Most of our research evidence has been secured on independence tendencies of children of the preschool age, so further discussion will be foregone until a later chapter. Nevertheless, it was important to note that independence tendencies appear to exist even in infancy.

Aggressive Tendencies

It will be remembered that Bridges (11) in exploring the emotional process in infancy found that both undifferentiated and ill-defined positive *and* negative feelings were prominent. As the infant grew older, they gave way to the emergence of focused positive and negative feelings directed towards specific persons. Important in aggression are anger responses—the vigorous reactions of crying, hitting, screaming, thrashing, and striking out—described in the previous chapter. Constitutional and hereditary factors seem to give us these anger responses to restraint and to discomfort. Frustration was found to be an antecedent of anger. Anger comes about when the infant is frustrated. But this does not relate it to aggression as such. Frustration gives rise to striking out, which in turn results in satisfaction of a need. That is, expression of anger is successful in bringing maternal aid which results in gratification or relief from tension. Thus they, too, are reinforced and acquire reward value. From anger responses emerge aggressive tendencies.

This occurs in what Sears and his associates (67) refer to as instrumental aggression—hurting someone to obtain some goal. Certainly, a newborn infant cannot be charged with being aggressive in this sense. At this stage there is no clear knowledge of person as person as previous discussion of the emergence of self demonstrated. By doing what he does he secures compliance with his wishes without recognition of any intent to hurt. Later, as the infant grows older behavior operative as aggressive tendencies includes as an essential component the *intent* to attack, injure, or destroy. As these distinctions emerge, the child, instead of striking out blindly because he did not know what produced the success of his instrumental aggressions, begins to discover that it is by hurting other people that he secures his own way. Gradually, this learned instrumental action becomes a drive, and a drive practiced for its own sake.

It should be noted that this emphasis on injury distinguishes aggression from such assertive behavior as competition or dominance. While aggressive tendencies may easily be an accompaniment or even be the source of assertive tendencies, they should not be confused.

As was the case with dependence, aggressive tendencies are also secondary drives. The same secondary drive character seems to be indicated. The secondary drive character of dependency was explained as coming about from the infant's learning that his mother met his needs. The secondary drive character of aggression arises from a similar discovery that he secures compliance with his wishes by hurting (67). Success of his aggression reinforces this drive. At first, it is more or less crude striking out, but with age he becomes more skilled and more sophisticated forms of aggression appear. A special form of aggressive activity emerges—fighting. Other nuances, sarcasm, destructiveness, and noncooperation also appear as means of control. The discovery that he can, if he chooses, not give his cooperation to his mother, not turn his head when she wants a kiss, make his body stiff when clothing is being removed, does not require striking out but is nevertheless aggressive in character.

Some aggressive responses may appear divorced from anger as when an individual coldly and calmly carries out some act which is intended to injure another person. Partial divorce of the emotional involvement from aggression is not uncommon in our culture. After all, fighting in the physical or literal sense is not our most common form of aggression. Many motives of others can be thwarted by aggressive activities on our part without our fighting. As the quality of aggression is attenuated so, too, is our emotional arousal.

Determinants of aggressive tendencies. Sears and his associates (67) in the antecedent study were concerned with aggression as related to infantile experience. Aggressive behavior was investigated through nursery school teacher ratings and time-sampling observations in the already familiar fashion. Total ratings on aggression were obtained by summing ratings on such items as attacking, threatening or quarreling with other children, threatening the teacher, or destroying property of the other children.

They found no stable definitive relation between preschool aggressive behavior and infantile feeding frustration. There is enough evidence to suggest that if there is a relationship it is between aggression and severity of toilet training. The exception to the trends of this relationship was a minority of highly aggressive children who had experienced not average or severe toilet training but very little frustration from this experience. Aggressive tendencies will be further considered in connection with children of preschool age in a later chapter.

Sexual Tendencies

One of the most important of Freud's discoveries was the presence of sexual needs in infancy despite the absence of genital maturity. Before Freud, sexual tendencies in infants were almost completely ignored. It was his work that opened up this important area to psychological investigation. He himself was so impressed with this fact that it contributed materially to his developing of the concept of the libido. Nevertheless, it is possible to consider sexual tendencies as present in infancy without use of the concept of the libido. Instead, sexual needs may be conceived as one among several basic organic drives which give rise to tendencies. The organic drives, on environmental interplay, speedily give rise to second order drives. If this modification be accepted, then the findings of psychology concerning learning may be seen to be compatible with many of the psychoanalytic contributions concerning sexual tendencies. This theme will be further developed in the last section of this chapter which is devoted to a neo-Freudian interpretation of infancy.

Sexual behavior in infancy was described in Chapter 6. Sexual tendencies are subject to socialization pressure during infancy, but the effects of socialization become more apparent during early childhood. Indeed, during the first year of life there is little evidence that sex behavior is socially oriented. During the second year social contexts of sexual tendencies become increasingly prominent, but no great violence to the facts is done in foregoing further discussion at this point. Most research on sexual behavior in the nonpsychoanalytic sense has centered on childhood. Consequently, further exposition is deferred until later chapters.

Evidence concerning the psychoanalytic theories of infancy

We now examine the research evidence, other than clinical, which is relevant to the psychoanalytic theories of orality and anality. The psychoanalysts insist that verification of their concepts be within the framework in which they are conceived. Despite this, it is desirable that their concepts be submitted to controlled research even if one has to go outside their system to do so. This is essential if psychoanalysis is not to remain a capsulated system divorced from the main stream of psychology.

In previous sections of this chapter, an exposition was presented of the effect of specific maternal practices and of maternal attitudes upon the infant's subsequent personality development. Now the concern is not with general later adjustment but with the specific constellations of oral and anal personality characteristics which are supposed to appear during infancy.

From the comments earlier in the chapter regarding the relation of specific practices to general personality development, one would be prepared to take a skeptical view of the studies based upon specific practices. Some of the studies to follow did attempt to relate specific maternal practices to psychoanalytically predicted outcomes. Specific practice studies which do not support psychoanalytic contentions need not be construed as evidence against psychoanalytic theory. A single factor, for example, that the child was (or was not) breast fed, cannot be interpreted meaningfully except in the context of the enormous reaches of mother-child interactive behavior about which the single behavioral item tells us nothing.

Only recently have infants themselves been studied in the light of psychoanalytic theories by controlled research methods. The research findings today most often are *not* a direct or a crucial test of the validity of their theoretical position. Rather, they are tests of whether or not the facts on the basis of which the propositions have been advanced do or do not hold when checked by controlled research methods. It must also be noted that even if the facts do hold, it does not follow that their theoretical explanation is correct. Other assumptions may account for the facts equally well or even better. The evidence relevant to the oral stage will first be examined. The evidence concerning the anal stage will then be discussed in a similar fashion.[12]

The Oral System

The dominance of the oral zone is said to characterize the so-called oral stage. Anyone even cursorily observing an infant during his first year will vouch for the importance of the mouth. But this does not give us a clear indication of oral dominance. One research study has attempted to do this. Lustman (*49*) stimulated 32 three-day-old babies both by massage and by air stream on the lips, the skin of the abdomen, the genitalia, and the anus. Response was measured by temperature increase in the stimulated area. Massage of the lips showed the greatest change in magnitude and air pressure in the same area was third in magnitude. The hyperresponsiveness of one infant was largely responsible for air pressure stimulation of the genitalia falling in second place. Dominance of the oral zone in early infancy is suggested. But variability is also suggested by the infant's sensitivity in the genital area mentioned above. Oral primacy is a relative not an absolute one, and sensitivity in other areas is also present. In specific infants, sensitivity in another area may be even greater than mouth sensitivity.

It will be remembered that the psychoanalytic theory of the libido as manifested in the oral stage proposes that erotic pleasure arises from stimulation of the mucous membrane of the mouth. Sucking is the universal way this is expressed. If libidinal theory is correct, then sucking pleasure must be in large measure independent of sucking as related to hunger. Fenichel (*22*) contends that if erogenous stimulation did not occur, the infant would not suck his thumb since

[12] In this and subsequent discussion the research evidence concerning the psychoanalytic mechanisms will be referred to only insofar as it is crucial to other issues. Limitation of space prevents direct attention.

by so doing he produced no milk. This position follows from regarding the sexual drive (libido) as primary, hunger being regarded as merely one of the tissue needs of little importance to personality development.

Let us first consider some more general observational findings. The obstetrician has even reported finger sucking to be present before birth, as shown by a swollen thumb inserted in the mouth following the birth cry (27). Several observers (8, 36, 59) have reported sucking very shortly after birth. Gesell states that finger sucking is commonly evident in the first few weeks of life. He significantly adds that this is the case especially when the infant is hungry. This evidence for the early appearance of sucking behavior indicates strength of this form of behavior.

David Levy was among the first to offer controlled research data on this topic. In 1928 Levy (44), through a questionnaire, found from mothers that the frequency of thumb sucking in infancy was higher among those infants who took less time at breast or bottle. The finger suckers finished eating more quickly, because they were forced to by a time-limited feeding, because there was a very rapid flow of milk, or because they were fed by dropper. Those taking greater time turned out to be nonsuckers.

Levy (45) also found that when the sucking of puppies was interfered with, they engaged in nonnutritional sucking. Four puppies were taken from one litter and placed on bottle feeding. Amount of food was constant for all puppies. One pair sucked from nipples in which the holes were small, the "long-time feeders." The other pair was fed from nipples with large holes, the "short-time feeders." The latter tended to suck all kinds of objects between meals—towels, straws, their own and each other's bodies. Levy argued that thumb sucking in human infants could be similarly explained because of inadequate opportunities to satiate the sucking impulse. His results were substantiated by independent studies. Ross (63), for example, also in studying puppies found essentially the same results. Roberts (62) found that finger-sucking human infants during feeding actually sucked fewer minutes than those infants who were nonsuckers except at feeding. Yarrow's research (80) also supports this view. Using the carefully collected data of a longitudinal research program, he found that children having short feeding times developed severe thumb sucking. It is well established, then, that nonnutritional sucking is greater in those who do less nutritional sucking.

These studies of Levy and the others lead easily, though not necessarily, as we shall see in a moment, to the conclusions that (1) the oral drive, expressed in sucking, is largely constitutional and the infant needs sucking satisfaction; and (2) the researches could be offered as support of the Freudian contention of the libidinal (drive) character of this oral behavior.

Probably no one would insist that sucking is completely independent of hunger. Freud himself postulated that there was an association. He considered sucking as related originally to one of the self-preservative functions (taking food) but later becoming independent of it (23, 586). Nevertheless, many Freudians interpret nonnutritional sucking, occurring because of less nutritional sucking, as evidence that the sucking need is innate and as evidence for the libido concept. The question now arises whether or not this is so. The alternative position with which it may be contrasted is that sucking behavior is "a secondary drive established (or strengthened) through the almost universal rewarding of the sucking act by food getting" (65, 107).[13] Hence, the libido and the secondary drive interpretation are contrasted in terms of research findings.

A well-controlled study relating to the drive properties of oral activity and the reinforcements accompanying cup, breast, or bottle was performed by Davis, Sears, Miller, and Brodbeck (16). The investigators took the position that if sucking was an inherent biological drive, then cup babies, lacking opportunity to reduce their sucking drives during feeding, would show *more* nonnutritional sucking. On the other hand, if sucking were a secondary learned drive, cup-fed babies, having little opportunity to associate sucking with hunger reduction, would show *less* nonnutritional sucking. In their study, nonnutritional sucking strength was measured by length of time each infant sucked a nipple-covered finger. At the end of ten days, thus measured, infants who sucked at the breast developed a stronger sucking reflex than did those who either sucked bottles or were fed by cup. This clearly supports the learning hypothesis. Cup feeding provided no reinforcement of the sucking response and bottle feeding, in view of the "open" type of nipples used, provided relatively little reinforcement. Breast feeding, on the other hand, provided repeated reinforcement. Thus the oral drive appears to be influenced by experience and the results suggest that spontaneous sucking activities may be a by-product of the almost universal method of feeding by letting the infant suck. Sucking acquires habit strength

[13] From Sears (65). Published 1950 by Annual Reviews, Inc., and used with permission.

and thus becomes gratifying in its own right through primary reinforcement of hunger.

Another test of the effect of different amounts of rewarded practice
in sucking was performed by Sears and Wise (68). If the oral drive
is, in part at least, a product of the sucking act during food-taking,
its reinforcement strength should vary with the number of opportunities for reinforcement. Thus, the longer a child feeds by sucking,
the stronger his oral drive should be. Drawing upon the private
practice of a pediatrician, the investigators secured data on mothers
and 80 normal children, aged two to seven, concerning child-rearing
practices and the behavior of the children. The children were divided
into three groups on the basis of information concerning the age of
weaning. These groups were: (1) the early weaned (cup from birth,
or weaned before two weeks); (2) the middle weaned (weaned between two weeks and three months); and (3) the late weaned (after
four months). Thus, the groups differed in the amount of rewarded
sucking experience, extending from the early weaned who had little
rewarded sucking experience to the late weaned who had a great
deal. One measure of drive strength used was the number of frustration reactions to weaning (disliking meals, refusal to eat, irritability, and crying). Another measure of drive strength was the amount
of thumb sucking. This was considered as a manifestation of oral
drive strength on the basis of the reasons advanced earlier. It was
hypothesized that if the strength of the oral drive increases with
reinforcement, the more reinforcement, the stronger the drive will be,
and the greater the frustration at weaning. Put simply, the stronger
the drive to suck, the more the child will be upset by weaning. The
late-weaned children were found to have (1) the greatest number of
frustration reactions to weaning; and (2) slightly greater incidence
of thumb sucking. Thus the children whose sucking had been rewarded more frequently (the late weaned) were found to have the
strongest oral drives. Put another way, the oral drive gets stronger
with age because sucking is rewarded.

If libidinal derivation be disregarded, the relationship between
sucking and nourishment can be described in terms of instrumental
acts and goal responses. As will be remembered, an instrumental act
consistently leading to a goal response develops, in its own right, the
properties of a goal response. Sucking is an instrumental act in infant
feeding. Sucking, therefore, becomes a secondary goal response in
infancy.

Sears, Maccoby, and Levin (66) in their pattern study of child rearing found evidence corroborating the finding that the later the weaning, the stronger the upset. About twice as many of their children showed "some upset when weaning was begun after eleven months of age as when it was begun under five months" (66, 86).[14] This group, it will be noted, were in general weaned later than those of the Sears and Wise study (whose "late" weaned were all weaned after only four months). This helps allay the suspicion arising from the criticism sometimes brought against the Sears and Wise study that the so-called late weaning at four months is really still early weaning.

Whiting and Child (14) also found evidence that is relevant in their cross-cultural comparisons among the societies they studied. Up until 13 to 18 months, age of onset of weaning increased as amount of emotional disturbance increased, but thereafter as age further increased emotional disturbance decreased. Weaning frustration increases with age and then decreases. But within the age range of the controversy over its libidinal character, weaning frustration increases with age.

The results obtained in the studies just presented must be discussed from two points of view: their relation to the results of Levy, Roberts, and the others and their implications for libido theory.

It must be emphasized that the Sears and Wise study in no way contradicts the results of Levy, Roberts, and the others. These other workers reported on puppies and babies *whose earliest feeding had been achieved by sucking.* In these instances when sucking during feeding was interfered with, nonnutritional sucking occurred. Sears and his colleagues reported, in part, on babies *who did not have sucking experiences at all.* For these babies who have not learned to suck, not sucking does not necessarily mean frustration.

The Sears studies show that it is possible to interpret sucking behavior in terms of a secondary goal response. If there is a sucking drive postulated, the data may be interpreted as indicating that this drive is increased by practice. The experiments discussed are not a direct test of libido theory. The Sears studies do not prove there is no primary oral drive or libido. It is even plausible to believe that no direct test is possible. The results do, however, seem to weaken the necessity of postulating a libido to account for such behavior. The more parsimonious explanation of nonnutritional sucking being

[14] From Sears, Maccoby, and Levin (66). Copyright 1957 by Row, Peterson, and published with permission.

a secondary learned drive makes libido theory less convincing so far as the oral stage is concerned.

This interpretation that the research evidence makes libido theory less plausible does not imply that oral phenomena are unimportant. It must be remembered that these same data used as critical of the libido concept have also demonstrated that babies possess strong oral tendencies, even if they are secondary learned ones. The presence of strong oral tendencies postulated by psychoanalytic theory (and expected on the basis of learning theory) has been verified.

The oral character. The various kinds of character structures are habitual and characteristic adult ways of meeting the problems of life when the psychosexual problems of infancy or childhood are not worked through optimally. They are psychoanalytic formulations of indices of constancy of the later personality to be expected because of certain kinds of experience at one of the earlier psychosexual stages.

The essence of the concept of the oral character is that if unusual deprivation or gratification in infantile feeding behavior and experience occurs, a constellation of personality characteristics will be present in adulthood. An adult oral character will show undue oral fixations and tendencies to regression. According to psychoanalytic theory, orality is blurred and modified by admixtures arising from later stages. The events in the time elapsing between infancy and the time its effects are evaluated create research hazards if they are not taken into account. In current research, these influences are often ignored, hence, methodologically weakening the studies.

Research studies on the oral character are almost nonexistent, despite the relatively straightforward nature of the theoretical position that the psychoanalytic conception postulates. The presently available research findings either do not support the contention concerning the oral character or are rather difficult to interpret because of ambiguities or omissions in the account given.

The findings of Thurston and Mussen (75) clearly do not support the psychoanalytic position. Using male college students as subjects, they collected information through their mothers about the presence or absence of breast feeding, the age of weaning, the duration of bottle feeding, and the strictness of the feeding schedule. The subjects themselves were given selected cards on the TAT. The TAT protocols thus secured were scored for various oral personality traits (dependency, pessimism, and so on). Tests of relationships between these traits and the criteria of gratification in infancy showed only chance relationships. Thus, no support was found for the concept of oral character structure. But it should be noted that the study did not take into account the interrelationships among, or the effects of, the various other stages of psychosexual development intervening between the subjects' experiences with these practices and the evaluation of their effects. Psychoanalysts might justifiably argue that the study is irrelevant.

Blum and Miller (9) found with third grade children that the psychoanalytic traits attributed to the oral character did, in fact, cluster. They found that their measures of food intake, food interest, concern over giving, need for being liked, social isolation, and tolerance for boredom were correlated above chance expectation. But other measures, theoretically expected to be correlated with the others, such as the children's need to be ingratiating, did not fall in this cluster. Thus, a partial agreement and partial disagreement with Freudian theory seems indicated by their results.

Goldman (35) has also reported a factor analytic study which was based on self-ratings of adults. As subjects, she used 115 middle-class men and women—college students, personal friends, and neurotic patients in psychoanalytic treatment. She developed a variety of rating scales relevant to oral characteristics which each subject filled out. Examples are groups of items designed to measure optimism, pessimism, passivity, desire for the unobtainable, ambition, and dependence. In these instances, the correspondence to traits alleged to be shown by oral characters is obvious. The 19 scales she developed were standardized through various statistical tests of consistency. Reliability was checked and found to be adequate. She extracted two factors from the intercorrelations of ratings on these traits— pessimism-optimism and impatience-aggression-autonomy. She interprets these two as factorial aspects of the oral character.

The major results of Goldman's studies (33, 34), which will now be explored, also favor accepting the conceptual validity of an oral character structure. She was interested in relating the characteristics of the oral "optimist" and of the oral "pessimist" to experiences of gratification or frustration in feeding in the oral stage. She did this by finding out the length of breast feeding of each of her subjects and relating it to the findings on the optimism-pessimism factor she had isolated in the previous phase of her study.

In this phase of the study with a group of adults, she found by correlation techniques how closely each of 100 subjects corresponded to the oral pessimist type. She also obtained from the mothers of these subjects information on the age at which they were weaned. Defining early weaned as those weaned at not later than four months, and late weaned as those weaned at nine months and more, she found significant differences between the two groups on oral pessimism scores. The correlation she found between early weaning and oral pessimism was .30. She also found that the early weaned tended to be located toward the oral pessimistic end of the scale, while the later weaned showed a tendency to develop oral optimistic characteristics.

There were certain ambiguities in her presentation which make her rather complex procedure difficult to follow and evaluate. It is not at all clear just how she separated her two extreme groups for factor analysis or whether she did or did not use the same subjects on the two phases of the study. This weakens the confidence one can place in her results. She herself concludes that there are factors other than duration of feeding involved in oral pessimism, as yet uninvestigated. This is told us very graphically by the relatively modest correlation of .30 she found, since this leaves 91 per cent of the variability unaccounted for. On the other hand, it will be remembered that the nature and extent of oral fixation according to Freudian theory depends not only upon many other oral phenomena but events in later stages as well. In the light of other specific practice studies and the fact that only weaning was used by her to supply information, any significantly positive correlation at all is somewhat surprising. Other neglected oral phenomena might supply the unaccounted-for 91 per cent of variance. We simply do not know.

Although the psychoanalytic theory of orality and oral character receives some support from the literature surveyed, it is not particularly impressive. Again the relation of specific practices to personality characteristics can, at the most, be said to receive only slight support. It is clear, however, that oral behavior is important in spite of the fact that sucking would appear to be a secondary learned drive.

The Anal System

It will be recalled that the psychoanalytic position calls for libidinal interests at this stage to be directed toward anal matters—particularly expelling and retaining feces. The task now before us is to examine the research evidence relevant to the psychoanalytic interpretation of the anal stage.

Unlike the oral stage, there is no direct research evidence, other than clinical experience, on the issue of whether the pleasures of the anal stage are to be considered as subsumed under an "anal" primary drive or whether they might be considered as arising from learning. It is clear that infants are as interested in feces as they are in other objects or parts of the body. Knowledge of anality is found in studies in which there has been interference with functioning in this area. For example, there is some evidence concerning the pernicious effects of coercive bowel training.

As a preliminary step toward the objectification of clinical evidence, Huschka (38, 39) made a study in child guidance clinics of the incidence of emotional disturbances as related to bowel and bladder training. She was interested in whether the training these disturbed children received showed immediate emotional consequences and whether later difficulties in personality adjustment in the same children could be attributed to these frustrations.

Over half of the children had been started on bowel training "prematurely," or the training had been accomplished by coercive methods, such as the use of shaming, a rigid schedule, or unduly frequent placement on the toilet. Many of the children reacted immediately during or following training in that they showed a history of constipation, diarrhea, fear, negativism, excessive cleanliness, and guilt. In the individual histories of their later difficulties, she could trace a direct connection between events in toilet training and subsequent maladjustment. She concluded that coercive training is an important determinant of personality disturbance.

Methodologically, the study is weakened by the absence of a control group. Without a sample of normal children studied in the same manner, we cannot know whether coercive training and later personality are in fact related beyond chance expectancy. True, the percentages are high, but without knowledge of comparable figures in normal children, it may be a noncausative purely incidental relationship. The results are suggestive in that they support the contention that severe practices in this area are followed by immediate temporary upset and (less certainly) by later problem behavior. Her findings, too, are in line with clinical experience which would predict that socialization in this area is accompanied by strong emotional reactions and sometimes by personality disturbances. Definitive studies have not yet been carried out.

Amount of emotional upset created by toilet training was studied in the Sears "pattern" study (66). It was found that emotional disturbance of their normal child subjects was most prevalent (in about

45 per cent of the cases) if the age at beginning of training was 15 to 19 months. Training beginning both before and after these ages produced the least amount, with 5 to 9 months' onset or after 20 months' onset of training conducive to the least number of children showing upset. Severity of training (scolding and punishing for deviation, frequent taking to toilet) by these mothers did not succeed in completing training any sooner, but it did produce emotional upset. Over half of the most severely trained children showed some disturbance, while no more than one-sixth of the least severely trained showed disturbances. These findings, it must be remembered, are based upon the mothers' opinions, not upon independent verification by outside sources. Hence, the results are not as conclusive as one would like.

It is clear that their results are not incompatible with general psychoanalytic theory, but the evidence does not demonstrate conclusively the psychoanalytic position. The evidence is compatible, but not definitive. Their findings are also compatible with both learning theory and frustration theory.

The anal character. It will be remembered that the anal character in adult life shows a certain constellation of personality characteristics which are traced back in origin to his experiences in the anal stage. There are undue or unusually strong fixations of libido in adult life which express themselves in characteristics traceable to experiences in, or extensions of, events at this age. This pattern of interrelated characteristics includes orderliness, parsimony, and obstinancy. Each of these characteristics may have a sadistic overlay. Concerning this point, it is not strictly accurate to equate sadism with aggression. Nevertheless, findings concerning aggressiveness as related to toilet training will be considered as relevant.

A major group of research investigations concerning the anal character represents attempts to find out whether or not the alleged anal characteristics are actually interrelated. In these studies, there is no attempt to study the infancy or childhood of the subjects. Naturally, the studies tell us nothing about the *origin* of the triad of characteristics mentioned above, merely whether they are interrelated. Three studies will be described.

Sears (64) had the members of a college fraternity, who knew one another well, rate each other on the three characteristics of obstinancy, parsimony, and orderliness. He then calculated the intercorrelations of these ratings. They were all about .37. showing a positive interrelation of the three characteristics.

Barnes (3) performed a factor-analytic study involving material selected as being appropriate for the oral, anal, and phallic stages. The research is reported at this juncture because insofar as he found corroborative findings they apply at the anal stage. From the psychoanalytic literature, he first derived a number of trait adjectives, such as "stingy," associated with each of these stages. A large number of college students rated themselves on these trait adjectives. The trait scores thus derived were intercorrelated and a factor analysis was performed. He found an anal factor including meticulousness, orderliness, reliability, law abidance, and cleanliness. This factor is clearly in lines with psychoanalytic theory. Two of the remaining factors he found offered some, but less, support at the other two psychosexual stages. Five other factors which he found, however, could not be explained by any Freudian hypothesis. The nonsupportive factors had clustering of tests which included in their composition some theoretically placed at the oral, anal, and phallic levels. For example, the factor of "externalized aggression," as he named it, was made up of "phallic" tests of aggression but also included sadism (anal), biting (oral), and several others from each of the three psychoanalytic levels. He concluded that the Freudian theory of levels of psychosexual development was not, as a whole, supported by his results.

Rappaport (60), in still another investigation, first developed a self-rating scale consisting of items relevant to experiences of the anal stage. Items were developed to measure obstinancy, orderliness, and parsimony. One type was multiple-choice items concerned with preferences, interests, and reactions to social situations. Representative are the items which ask about hobbies which are appealing, or interest in saving money. Responses showing interest in collecting were interpreted as showing anal interests, as was emphasis on the saving of, or the spending of, money. The second type of item involved selecting from pairs of proverbs the one of the set which expressed the person's feelings. A typical item would be the choice between "A wise man turns chance into good fortune," and "A bird in the hand is worth two in the bush." In this instance, the one with the anal slant should be obvious. The third type of item was similar to those used by Goldman-Eissler and consisted of descriptions of a habit on which the subjects were to rate themselves. Typical items included saving odds and ends, operating according to a system, and disinclination to lend money. The items he constructed were submitted to three psychoanalytically-oriented psychologists with a request that they judge their applicability to the problem of anality.

Items judged unsuitable by them were eliminated. The remaining items considered applicable were administered to college student subjects. An item analysis was then performed. Reliability was also checked and found satisfactory. The "purified" items were administered to a cross-validation group and intertrait correlation calculated. The results in terms of intertrait correlations involving orderliness, obstinacy, and parsimony yielded only one statistically significant correlation, instead of three, which would have been predicted on theoretical grounds.

So far this study resembles other intertrait studies, but Rappaport went beyond this. By means of TAT protocols he now investigated the extent of felt aggression, feeling of persecution, preoccupation with financial matters, and obsessive compulsive concerns with cleanliness and with control of the environment. In each instance, it was hypothesized that anal characters would tend to show to a greater extent the end of the continuum suggested by these terms than would nonanals. The "anal" person would be expected to show more aggression, more feelings of persecution, and so on, than would the nonanal person. Subjects were college students who were at either extreme on the anality scale previously developed. To these subjects he administered the TAT and had judges score the protocols obtained against the criteria mentioned previously. Although the majority of obtained differences were in the predicted direction, none of them was statistically significant. So, again, we have a study showing some slight support for the psychoanalytic point of view, but not with sufficient decisiveness that psychoanalytic contentions were verified conclusively.

Another method of research attack on the problem of the anal character involves trying to relate the nature of the toilet training experiences the subjects received in infancy to their later personality characteristics. The most definitive evidence available is found in research studies which relate experiences in infancy to aggressive tendencies in childhood.

In the course of a much more extended study dealing with other issues, Wittenborn and his associates (79) secured information concerning the relation of aggressiveness in children to the severity of their toilet training. Severe toilet training (early placement on toilet, ridicule or hitting for soiling, disgust on part of mother for child's messes) was significantly correlated with the child's aggressiveness (anger with the mother or other children, calling names, having a temper tantrum, and doing spiteful things). At age five in one group the correlation was .36 and at age eight or nine in another group the correlation was .30. Sears and his associates (67), in the antecedent study, also found that severity of toilet training in boys had a positive relation to later aggression. This was not the case in the girls they studied.

A more extended study of the relation of toilet training to later characteristics was performed by Bernstein (6). Drawing upon a sample of children attending a public well-baby clinic, he studied the relation between coercive toilet training and certain of their characteristics in later childhood. Information on 47 children, about five years of age at the time of the study, was obtained from the clinic records, play interviews, and observations which he carried out. Sixty-six per cent of these children were considered to have been coercively trained. The criteria of coercion which he used were training begun before six months of age, or training begun later which was accompanied by punishment if the child failed to comply. The non-coercively trained children were so classified if they were started in their toilet training after they were six months of age and they received no punishment for their mistakes. A variety of measures were used to supply information about the children's behavior at the time of the study. Information on their tendency to collect stamps, coins, and so on (collecting) was obtained from the interview. They were observed on how much smearing of fingerpaints and cold cream occurred (smearing). Their willingness to leave the mother to go into the play room for the interview was measured by the time consumed in getting them to do so (separation anxiety). Their willingness, or lack of it, to perform six tasks at the request of the investigator during the session was observed (negativism). Information on constipation, uncommunicativeness, and immaturity was also obtained. There was a statistically significant relationship between coercive toilet training on the one hand and separation anxiety, negativism, uncommunicativeness, and immaturity on the other. But no relationship was found between coercive training and collecting, constipation, or smearing. Again the results he found sometimes favored the psychoanalytic contention, sometimes not.

A neo-Freudian interpretation of infancy

There is another possibility of interpretation which does not require either sweeping acceptance or rejection of orthodox psycho-

analytic theory, but instead makes it possible for there to be a reconciliation and an integration of some psychoanalytic contentions with
those found in academic psychology and anthropology. For example,
this has already been done in this chapter in connection with the
extension of the discussion of the emergence of the self as a supplementation to the statement of the psychoanalytic theory of the emergence of the ego. These attempts at modification and extension are
customarily referred to as neo-Freudian positions. A great variety
of individuals impressed by the orthodox psychoanalytic position
have, nevertheless, offered what they considered to be needed modification of the original orthodox psychoanalytic doctrines. These
changes, involving some major segments of the general psychoanalytic
position, are called neo-Freudian. As might be guessed, the label
neo-Freudian is applied to a wide assortment of theoretical positions.

The psychoanalyst tends to stress the realities he finds in the therapeutic hour; the psychologist tends to stress the realities he finds in
controlled research. Many neo-Freudians attempt to reconcile, so far
as possible, these two realities. If they cannot be reconciled, they
make a revision, restatement, or rejection in line with their interpretation of the evidence. This neo-Freudian course is followed here.

What is to follow is in no sense to be considered as being agreed
upon by all neo-Freudian workers. In spite of specific acknowledgment of certain of these contributions in this section, what is written
is merely the way this writer would reconcile the theory and the
research findings without eliminating the psychoanalytic findings or
ignoring these researches. There is, however, no necessary agreement
on the part of others with the position presented here.

The psychosexual stages of orality and anality are interpreted here
as socialization tendencies in the sense described earlier. They are
so considered because the behavior subsumed under each of them
meets the criterion of tendencies; namely, interrelated responses and
response tendencies which share roughly comparable drives and goals.
Their dynamic character is thus stressed. No *a priori* decision is
reached concerning their innate character. Along with other tendencies they are considered as due to both constitutional and learning
factors.

Neo-Freudians tend, in general, to minimize the sexual aspect of
development. Often libido theory, as such, is rejected. No special
energy is found to be necessary to account for oral and anal behavior,
and the results of the various investigations reviewed earlier in which
oral and anal behavior were interpreted as secondary learned drives

are easily assimilated if this view be accepted. Indeed, it is more congruent with the cultural emphasis than is the concept of a blind primordial force. The concept of libido as the driving force may thus be rejected.

Acceptance of the concept of infantile sexuality in its all pervasive form is not required. The analogy to the flowering from a tulip bulb put so poetically by Josselyn as quoted in Chapter 5 is seen as a bit forced and broad. One can define a life instead of a flower in such a fashion, too, so that relationship between ameba and man, which does exist, is there for all to see. But man and ameba are discriminable, one from the other. Scientific progress is seldom served by subsuming discriminable variables under this same conceptual category. Infants are intensely emotional, and derive pleasure from sucking and elimination. But there are emotions and sucking and eliminatory pleasures separable from adult sexuality, even though personality being all of a piece will show relationship in adulthood between such behavior and adult sexually motivated behavior. Sensory pleasure and sexual pleasure are interwoven in adult life. In infancy, the sensual predominates.

None of the evidence so far discussed detracts from the Freudian insistence, now accepted quite generally, that much of an infant's interests are occupied with oral and anal matters. That which absorbs so much of his time and energy (as well as that of his parents) cannot be disregarded. Consider the number of repetitions of feeding and toileting experiences facing the infant. Conservatively estimating an average of from four to six feedings a day, he is fed nearly 4000 times during the first two years of life. Soiling occurs, say, from six to ten times a day. In the first year alone somewhere around 2000 changes of diapers take place! Repetition of the two problem situations over and over again is certainly present during infancy. It is plausible to infer that many habitual attitudes and behavior patterns will be acquired during these repetitions. The terms orality and anality are still considered very appropriate for the ages under scrutiny. They are seen as important features of the total situation which the infant faces at this age. Nevertheless, certain modifications may be suggested.

Freud developed what he considered to be a picture of *innate* instinctual development. Most orthodox psychoanalytic statements concern behavior imbedded in developmental sequences with little emphasis on the socializing facets as separable from the maturational. It is, however, possible to relate the phenomena he observed more closely and coherently with the research findings just described if modification be made which leads to an emphasis upon social factors.

The oral and anal stages function as critical periods. Child psychologists of many different theoretical persuasions, other than psychoanalytic, accept certain child situational relationships at a particular age as being of crucial importance. In the earlier discussion in Chapter 3, these were conceptualized as critical periods. In the course of socialization, the infant typically faces certain problems. If the conflicts and difficulties of a period are surmounted, the child proceeds toward adequate adjustment. Failure to meet the demands of the period through unsatisfactory resolution of the conflicts will in varying degrees mar personality development and the sense of self. The particular susceptible age at which socialization pressures in connection with a given tendency are applied form a critical period. It is the age limits in each tendency where its effects are most pronounced. Although critical periods are not generally considered to be a part of psychoanalytic thinking, the concept may be appropriately applied to what the psychoanalysts call the psychosexual stages. In brief, the present writer would consider that the phenomena of infancy occurring during the psychosexual stages may be interpreted as instances of critical periods.

The very concept of critical periods suggests that the significance of socialization pressures should vary with the age of the child to whom they are applied. The effects should vary in that critical periods vary with age, and socialization pressures are capable of being applied too early, optimally, or too late. Thus the psychoanalytic findings concerning psychosexual stages which stand research scrutiny may be subsumed under the rubric of critical periods. This introduces a flexibility that the psychosexual stage theory lacked. The psychoanalytic position called for certain fixed stages, and no others. In terms of critical periods, the ones psychoanalysts identify are found to be important. But there may be others that also deserve consideration, not included in their scope.

Illustrative anthropological evidence will now be offered which suggests that factors other than anality or orality should be given stress that are either ignored completely or given little emphasis in orthodox psychoanalytic thinking. Goldfrank (32) has made a study of Hopi and Zuni societies which is relevant. In connection with this study, she used her classification of consistency of socialization referred to in Chapter 4. She shows by her study of Hopi and Zuni societies that they fall in category four (societies where infant disciplines are weak and later disciplines are severe), and that different patterns emerge because of this temporal relation of early weak discipline and later severe discipline. The Hopi and Zuni are, according to all observers, indulgent toward their offspring. The Hopi infant is invariably breast fed, seldom weaned before one year and frequently not before two years, is nursed as soon as he cries, and there is little adherence to predetermined routines. Yet, "mass maladjustment" insecurity and apprehensiveness characterize the adults who experienced this infancy.

Possible sources of this change are present in infancy. The cradleboard with its enforced period of inactivity is still in extensive use. A fear of witchcraft runs throughout all ages. This arises from a process of learning from which the young child and infant cannot be immune. Anyone, even one or both of his parents, may be a witch. In early childhood, and later, comes a variety of customs which are probably relevant. Although not nagged about personal cleanliness or sexual behavior, the child in these cultures is exhorted about habits of frugal eating and the need for industry. Stories with the suggestion of threat through them are told as aids to training. But bogey man tales are not enough. The Hopi and Zuni bring them to life. Once a year "kachinas" visit the villages to perform a dance expressly to frighten the children. Previously acquainted with all of their naughtiness the kachinas threaten the children while brandishing their weapons. After an agonizing delay they are appeased by the children's gifts. It is not surprising that whipping by the parents is superfluous. Later in childhood, initiation rites, painful and fear-provoking, are carried out. At one of these ceremonies, it is revealed to the child that the kachina he has so feared are his own relatives and elders of the village. The shock is sometimes very great and always seems to make a deep impression. The mass insecurity of the adult Hopi and Zuni may plausibly be interpreted as being related to these traumatic factors occurring both *during* and *after* infancy independent of oral and anal phenomena.

Concerned with discrepancies between Navaho childhood experience and their adult personalities, in a culture closely related to those of Zuni and Hopi, Kluckhohn (41) offered an explanation which admirably summarizes not only the situation raised by the illustration, but also offers a general conception of the importance of the anal and oral stages as well. He writes:

> But the main point is probably not that the theorists are utterly wrong but that they claim too much for the earliest years and do not pay enough

attention to later events and to the total situation in which the mature person finds himself. Infantile indulgence very probably does constitute the firmest foundation upon which, if later circumstances are reasonably favorable, a secure and confident adult personality can be developed. But it affords only a possible basis; it does not, in and of itself, promise fulfillment (41, 485).[15]

With this, the present writer is in hearty agreement.

Now that a general neo-Freudian interpretation of orality and anality has been offered, it is appropriate to consider more specific interpretations of oral and anal tendencies.

Oral Tendencies

The oral tendencies arise from their relations to the hunger drive. Many oral phenomena become in themselves secondary drives. Among the more important of these already discussed is sucking. Orality is important because the mouth provides the means whereby the infant contacts the world. In the words of Thompson, a prominent neo-Freudian:

> The oral stage seems to be chiefly determined by biological development. The newborn infant is chiefly a mouth. The most developed part of the cortex at birth is that which governs the oral zone. We are justified in assuming that the infant contacts the world and comprehends it in the beginning primarily in terms of the mouth. We, however, question whether the erotic satisfaction obtained is the determining factor. It seems more likely that he contacts the world by mouth because it is the most adequate organ. Thus the oral stage is organically determined but not primarily because of its pleasure value (74, 35).[16]

Orality is the major determinant of the infant's reactions to other people. If the situation is a pleasurable one, hunger tensions and secondary drives, such as sucking, become attached through identification with the mother figure. Thus, emphasis may be placed upon the relation of mother and infant in which the latter uses the mouth as a means of contact, rather than orality as a drive.

Behavior-social learning theory may be used to account for the development of this relationship between mother and infant. By responding to his needs, she is associated with tension-reduction experiences and thus acquires reward value. But if her mothering is

---

[15] From Kluckhohn (41). Copyright 1949 by Geza Roheim, and published with permission.

[16] From Thompson (74). Copyright 1950 by Clara Thompson, and published with permission.

inadequate, either expressed through negative factors such as rejection or through dilution of the relationship as in an institution, then the infant will not have these pleasant tension-reduction experiences and the first reaction to other people will be frustrating.

A general, though perhaps implicit, hypothesis held by many neo-Freudian investigators and practitioners is that gratification in the infantile feeding aspects of the oral tendencies generalize to other situations. Thus, satisfaction and security in relations with the mother generalize to other social situations. One way this is expressed has already been mentioned; what Erikson (19) refers to as a sense of trust—a sense that the world can be approached confidently and handled adequately. Similarly, dissatisfaction and insecurity will also generalize. The infant and child builds his attitudes toward the world from his experiences with his own little world. How well his needs are met, how secure he feels will help to establish his later attitudes, not only towards himself, but also towards the world and toward other individuals. Orality is one of the ways these attitudes are learned.

Anal Tendencies

The middle part of the second year of life is critical in that parents may credit the child with more ability than they should. The child walks and talks a bit, and seems to "understand" much of what is going on about him. Therefore, discipline is instituted by parents. In our culture the form of discipline stressed at this age is toilet training. Such training sometimes begins some months before the first birthday in spite of the fact that control is not ordinarily achieved until about 18 months or thereafter (28).

To make the matter specific, just what is toilet training? Certainly, it involves the child's learning to withhold expulsion of feces and urine until the "proper" time and place. Thus expulsion and retention appear as facets of the learning process. Aside from these essential similarities there are wide differences in how parents and children work out the problem. Some parents may emphasize regularity—the child should defecate at regular intervals. If he fails to have a movement during the day, the mother may worry or resort to enemas. With still other parents, the emphasis may be on cleanliness rather than schedules. The child should not wet or soil himself. No matter what pattern of emphasis may develop, there is little question that toilet training is an important experience in the life of children in our culture.

A plausible neo-Freudian interpretation would place the emphasis in the anal stage on the struggle with the parents, rather than the pleasure from expelling and retaining of feces. Thus, emphasis may be shifted from the erotic pleasure to the interpersonal situation. The infant does not originally want to develop the habits which are the goals for our methods of toilet training. His wishes are quite different from those of his parents. In fact, we have here the first major source of conflict between the infant's needs and the parent's wishes. Unlike the case of the feeding situation, what he wants to do and what the parents want him to do are not the same. Toilet training is not a need and satisfies no drive in the infant of this age. This, however, does not mean that there are no anal interests on the part of the infant. They are there, but the emphasis can be placed on the relinquishment of something originally pleasurable to the demands of socialization.

Toilet training demands the substitution of voluntary control for involuntary or reflex action. This makes toilet training a function of learning. In learning terms there must be a "reversal of a strong innate connection between a cue and a response" (18, 137).[17] A full bowel originally produces automatic evacuation. This original sequence is broken by toilet training given the child. The automatic discharge must be held while a definite sequence of behavior gradually develops. The child must learn to call his mother and go through the usual steps of waiting until undressed and placed on the potty. Then, and only then, may evacuation take place in a socially approved manner. He also learns loathing and disgust for these originally pleasurable objects. He also learns, if he is to be conventional, to restrict verbal reference to the process of defecation to medical consultations and to humor.

If trained coercively (too early or punished severely), it would be predicted on the basis of learning principles that this would both generalize and produce personality disturbances in much the same way as rats faced with an insoluble problem. Huschka's results reported earlier are a case in point. Moreover, studies confirm the prediction that early imposition of training delays the acquisition of control (50). Enuretic problems were found to follow in normal boys who were slow maturing physiologically and who had been started on training too early to be followed by success.

[17] By permission from *Personality and Psychotherapy*, by Dollard and Miller. Copyright 1950. McGraw-Hill Book Company, Inc.

The child during this period learns not only from his struggles for independence with the parent over toilet training but also from conflicts with the parents in other areas of his daily life. For example, he is at an age where he can crawl and walk. He can get into prohibited areas, for example, the sidewalk or road. He can break precious objects and grasp dangerous ones. These, too, enter the picture as part of his "training" period. How he is encouraged or prohibited in these areas as well as in toilet training probably also influences his personality development.

Toilet training practices in our own subculture also show considerable variety as earlier discussion indicates. Outside of our own culture there is much evidence of even greater variability. The nonchalant attitude of the Pilaga of the Amazon River country described in Chapter 4 may be contrasted with the extremely severe and punishing attitudes concerning cleanliness training shown by the Tanala of Madagascar (40). The Tanala begin infant training at two or three months and expect it to be completed by six months. Severe punishment is meted out for accidents. This age of complete training may be compared with the conception among some in our culture of complete bladder and bowel control not being possible until 18 months (28).

If learning to conform to parental authority is accepted as crucial to the anal stage, the so-called anal characteristics, such as cleanliness and orderliness, can be seen as among the goals of socialization, or, as Kardiner puts it, "forms of acquiescence to cultural demands" (40, 44).[18] In our culture, these characteristics are highly prized virtues. In another culture, such as Pilaga, they would hardly apply and the "anal" stage may take quite a different course and have radically different outcomes.

If cultural factors are important and causative in the patterns of personality which emerge from this or other stages, then we are in a better position to understand the exceptions found in the research. For example, *sometimes,* the "anal character," in a classic pristine sense, may emerge from the viscissitudes of this period. But more often, other, perhaps as yet unrecognized, characteristics may be acquired precisely because the anal stage involves more than the orthodox psychoanalytic position would postulate. Specific maternal practices and attitudes will enter the situation in such a fashion as to

[18] From Kardiner (40). Copyright 1939 by the Columbia University Press, and published with permission.

make it impossible methodologically to account for the effect of these other variables.

Other Behavior Tendencies

In a sense, the earlier discussion of other behavior tendencies in infancy is also a neo-Freudian extension. This arises from taking the position that anal and oral tendencies are not the only ones which are operative during infancy. Dependence-independence, aggression and sexual (nonlibidinal) tendencies have been discussed as arising in infancy and of being of considerable importance in personality formation. There may be others which also have beginning patterns in infancy deserving the term, tendency, which the present status of research has not unearthed. The six tendencies—oral, anal, sexual (nonlibidinal), dependence-independence and aggression—conveniently and parsimoniously encompass a considerable segment of infantile behavior. Undoubtedly, other ways of patterning infantile behavior will be found. It is even conceivable that some, or even all, of the present tendency groups will disappear as constructs.

Summary

The infant has now been examined in the setting of a matrix of other persons. Because the mother serves as the principal agent of socialization, she is the most important of these other persons. The evidence shows that there are varying degrees of causal relationship between the child-rearing procedures of the mother and the behavior of her children. Classification into specific practices, attitudes, and patterns of maternal behavior allows us to see the degrees of relationship between child rearing and children's behavior more clearly. Specific practices in maternal behavior have not been found to show invariant relationships with consequent personality development. Maternal attitudes were found to be much more closely related to behavior in the children. The use of attitudes as a conceptual framework supplied us with a means for understanding of the mother's part in the socialization of the infant. Basically, this was because behavior expressed in terms of attitudes allows one to embrace within one construct many specific behaviors. It would appear from the discussion that this same advantage accrues to patterns of maternal behavior. Both attitudes and patterns allow one to see maternal propensities to behave in general ways which are then related to later adjustment in their children. Moreover, maternal attitudes and maternal patterns of behavior were found to be interrelated.

It would appear that maternal attitudes of acceptance-rejection and the maternal pattern of behavior in terms of the amount and the degree and the consistency of sensitivity mothers exhibit are significant and important approaches in the understanding of the effects of infant socialization and personality development.

Shifting perspective from the mother to the child, the infant's behavior and experience in the development of self and social awareness is indicated. The emergence of the beginnings of a sense of self and of social awareness has been presented as based upon learning and maturation. A considerable variety of experiences is found to be responsible for the appearance of self and social awareness. These are: the objectification of objects, the perception of persons both as friendly and strange, the recognition of the need for cooperation and communication, the closeness yet separateness from the mother, the use of proper names and pronouns, the fact of being held responsible for actions, and the development of independence tendencies. The psychoanalytic position that awareness arises from the infant's experience of his needs not being met takes its place as one of the factors making for the emergence of the beginnings of a sense of self.

In considering behavior tendencies in infancy, dependence tendencies are first examined. Dependence is found to be a secondary drive learned through social experiences. The helplessness of the infant demands his dependence upon the mother. Dependence takes the form of both instrumental dependence and of emotional dependence (which includes considerable of the behavior ordinarily referred to as "affectionate"). Frustration is found to be related to dependency, although the literature is somewhat equivocal on this point. It is tentatively concluded that frustration arising from rejection during infancy leads to greater dependence on the part of children. Some evidence is offered that independent tendencies also appear during infancy. Aggression also appears in infancy—hurting someone in order to gain some goal. During infancy aggression begins to take on the character of a secondary drive. Success of aggression reinforces that drive. Despite these findings, knowledge of specific determinants of aggressive tendencies in infancy is very meager.

Sexual tendencies, although present to some degree, are considered as assuming greater importance in the preschool period. Socialization pressures concerning sexual tendencies are not as great as they are later.

Controlled investigation gives some support to psychoanalytic theories of the oral and anal stages. The results, however, are predominately negative. It may be, when negative results are found, that we are in the position of pursuing a delicate, finely spun theory with unsuitable and clumsy tools. Chasing butterflies with a meat-axe comes to mind as an analogy. Whatever the reason, positive research evidence is scanty. If the orthodox psychoanalytic theories of orality and anality be accepted in their entirety, it must be on the basis of clinical evidence obtained in psychoanalytic hours, and not on the basis of controlled research evidence.

The realities of oral phenomena and anal phenomena *have* been established. Before psychoanalytic propositions were advanced, these realities would have been denied. These advances in knowledge are due to psychoanalytic efforts. However appreciative of their efforts one may be, it does not follow that their explanations of these phenomena need be accepted.

This is also substantially the position taken in regard to some of the interpretations suggested by the writer in a neo-Freudian perspective. The psychosexual stages of orality and anality are interpreted as expressive of socialization tendencies, centering upon feeding and toilet training problems, respectively. The oral and anal stages are also conceived as representing critical periods. Libido as a special energy source is rejected as unnecessary and nonparsimonious. Hence, sexual aspects of behavior are considered as somewhat narrower in scope and significance during infancy than psychoanalysts would argue. Conversely, other influences than those they suggest are considered operative as illustrated by some anthropological evidence.

More specifically, oral tendencies are deemed important because the mouth is a sensitive means of contact with the world, particularly with the mother. Gratifications learned in infantile feeding are conceived as generalizing to other life situations. As for anal tendencies, emphasis is placed upon the struggle with the parents rather than upon the pleasures of expelling or of retaining feces. This struggle takes the form of the infant acquiescing to cultural demands in the learning of voluntary control as a substitute for involuntary action.

These struggles also concern other areas of his daily life at this age and not merely those occurring as a result of toilet training. Moreover, behavior tendencies other than oral and anal, such as those shown in dependence-independence, aggression, and in the narrowly sexual are considered as operative during infancy.

For Further Reading

The diversity of topics covered in this chapter make recommendation rather difficult. From among the references that follow, the publications of Brody (12), Levy (45), Sears, and his associates (66, 67) are especially recommended.

References

1. Baldwin, A. L., Kalhorn, Joan, Breese, Fay H. Patterns of parent behavior. *Psychol. Monogr.*, 1945, 58, No. 268.
2. Banham, Katherine M. The development of affectionate behavior in infancy. *J. genet. Psychol.*, 1950, 76, 283–289.
3. Barnes, C. A. A statistical study of Freudian theory of levels of psychosexual development. *Genet. Psychol. Monogr.*, 1952, 45, 105–175.
4. Behrens, Marjorie L. Child rearing and the character structure of the mother. *Child Develpm.*, 1954, 25, 225–238.
5. Beller, E. K. Dependence and independence in young children. *J. Genet. Psychol.*, 1955, 87, 25–35.
6. Bernstein, A. Some relations between techniques of feeding and training during infancy and certain behavior in childhood. *Genet. Psychol. Monogr.*, 1955, 51, 3–44.
7. Bishop, Barbara M. Mother-child interaction and the social behavior of children. *Psychol. Monogr.*, 1951, 65, No. 328.
8. Blanton, Margaret G. The behavior of the human infant during the first thirty days of life. *Psychol. Rev.*, 1917, 24, 456–483.
9. Blum, G. S., and Miller, D. R. Exploring the psychoanalytic theory of the "oral character." *J. Pers.*, 1952, 20, 287–304.
10. Bowlby, J. *Maternal care and mental health.* Geneva: World Health Organization, 1951.
11. Bridges, Katherine, M.B. Emotional development in early infancy. *Child Develpm.*, 1932, 3, 324–341.
12. Brody, Sylvia. *Patterns of mothering: maternal influences during infancy.* New York: International Universities Press, 1956.
13. Buhler, Charlotte. *From birth to maturity.* London: Kegan, Paul, 1937.
14. Child, I. L. Socialization. In G. Lindzey (Ed.), *Handbook of social psychology.* Cambridge, Mass.: Addison-Wesley, 1954, 655–692.
15. Coleman, Rose W., Kris, E., and Provence, Sally. The study of variations of early parental attitudes: a preliminary report. In Ruth Eissler, *et al.*

(Eds.), *The psychoanalytic study of the child:* Vol. 8. New York: International Universities Press, 1953, 20–47.

16. Davis, H. V., Sears, R. R., Miller, H. C., and Brodbeck, A. J. Effects of cup, bottle and breast feeding on oral activities of new born infants. *Pediatrics,* 1948, 3, 549–558.

17. Dollard, J., Doob, L. W., *et al.* *Frustration and aggression.* New Haven, Conn.: Yale University Press, 1939.

18. Dollard, J., and Miller, N. E. *Personality and psychotherapy.* New York: McGraw-Hill, 1950.

19. Erikson, E. *Childhood and society.* New York: Norton, 1950.

20. Escalona, Sibylle K. Approaches to a dynamic theory of development: round table, 1949: 3. discussion. *Amer. J. Orthopsychiat.,* 1950, 20, 157–160.

21. Escalona, Sibylle. Emotional development in the first year of life. In M. J. E. Senn (Ed.), *Problems of infancy and childhood: transactions of the sixth conference.* New York: Macy, 1953, 7–92.

22. Fenichel, O. *The psychoanalytic theory of neuroses.* New York: Norton, 1945.

23. Freud, S. Three contributions to the theory of sex. In A. A. Brill (Ed.), *The basic writings of Sigmund Freud.* New York: Modern Library, 1938, 553–632.

24. Fries, Margaret E., and Woolf, P. J. Some hypotheses on the role of the congenital activity type in personality development. In Ruth S. Eissler *et al.* (Eds.), *The psychoanalytic study of the child:* Vol. 8. New York: International Universities Press, 1953, 48–62.

25. Gesell, A. *An atlas of infant behavior.* New Haven: Yale University Press, 1934.

26. Gesell, A., and Amatruda, Catherine S. *Developmental diagnosis: normal and abnormal child development: clinical methods and pediatric applications* (2nd rev. ed.). New York: Hoeber, 1947.

27. Gesell, A., and Ilg, Frances L. *Feeding behavior of infants: a pediatric approach to the mental hygiene of early life.* Philadelphia: Lippincott, 1937.

28. Gesell, A. *et al.* *The first five years of life: a guide to the study of the preschool child.* New York: Harper, 1940.

29. Goldfarb, W. Infant rearing and problem behavior. *Amer. J. Orthopsychiat.,* 1943, 13, 249–265.

30. Goldfarb, W. Psychological privation in infancy and subsequent adjustment. *Amer. J. Orthopsychiat.,* 1945, 15, 247–255.

31. Goldfarb, W. Effects of psychological deprivation in infancy and subsequent stimulation. *Amer. J. Psychiat.,* 1945, 102, 18–23.

32. Goldfrank, Esther. Socialization, personality and the structure of pueblo society. In D. G. Haring (Ed.), *Personal character and cultural milieu: a collection of readings* (Rev. ed.). Syracuse, New York: Syracuse University Press, 1949, 247–269.

33. Goldman, Frieda. Breast feeding and character formation. *J. Pers.,* 1948, 17, 83–103.

34. Goldman, Frieda. Breast feeding and character formation, II. *J. Pers.,* 1950, 19, 189–196.

35. Goldman–Eissler, Frieda. The problem of "orality" and its origin in early childhood. *J. ment. Sci.,* 1951, 97, 765–782.

36. Halverson, H. M. Mechanisms of early infant feeding. *J. genet. Psychol.,* 1944, 64, 185–223.

37. Heathers, G. Emotional dependence and independence in nursery school play. *J. genet. Psychol.,* 1955, 87, 37–57.

38. Huschka, Mabel. The child's response to coercive bowel training. *Psychosom. Med.,* 1942, 4, 301–308.

39. Huschka, Mabel. A study of training in voluntary control of urination in a group of problem children. *Psychosom. Med.,* 1934, 5, 254–265.

40. Kardiner, A. *The individual and his society.* New York: Columbia University Press, 1939.

41. Kluckhohn, C. Some aspects of Navaho infancy and early childhood. In D. G. Haring (Ed.), *Personal character and cultural milieu: a collection of readings* (Rev. ed.). Syracuse, New York: Syracuse University Press, 1949, 472–485.

42. Kubie, L. S., Margaret A. Ribble. The rights of infants: comments. In O. Fenichel *et al.* (Eds.), *The psychoanalytic study of the child:* Vol. 1. New York: International Universities Press, 1945, 415–416.

43. Lewin, K. *Field theory in social science.* New York: Harper, 1951.

44. Levy, D. M. Finger-sucking in and accessory movements in early infancy: an etiologic study. *Amer. J. Psychiat.,* 1928, 7, 881–918.

45. Levy, D. M. Experiments in the sucking reflex and social behavior of dogs. *Amer. J. Orthopsychiat.,* 1934, 4, 203–224.

46. Levy, D. M. Psychosomatic studies of some aspects of maternal behavior. *Psychosom. Med.,* 1942, 4, 223–227.

47. Levy, D. M. *Maternal overprotection.* New York: Columbia University Press, 1943.

48. Levy, D. M. The early development of independent and oppositional behavior. In R. R. Grinker (Ed.), *Mid-century psychiatry.* Springfield, Ill.: Thomas, 1953, 113–121.

49. Lustman, S. L. Rudiments of the ego. In Ruth S. Eissler *et al.* (Eds.), *The psychoanalytic study of the child:* Vol. 11. New York: International Universities Press, 1956, 89–98.

50. Macfarlane, Jean W., Allen, Lucile, and Honzik, Marjorie. *A developmental study of the behavior problems of normal children between 21 months and 14 years.* Berkeley, Calif.: University of California Press, 1955.

51. Miller, D. R., and Hutt, M. Value interiorization and personality development. *J. soc. Issues,* 1949, 5, 2–30.

52. Murphy, G. Social motivation. In G. Lindzey (Ed.), *Handbook of social psychology.* Cambridge, Mass.: Addison-Wesley, 1954, 601–633.

53. Murphy, G., Murphy, Lois B., and Newcomb, T. M. *Experimental social psychology.* New York: Harper, 1937.

54. Newton, N. R., and Newton, M. Relationship of ability to breast feed and maternal attitudes toward breast feeding. *Pediatrics,* 1950, 5, 869–875.

55. Orlansky, H. Infant care and personality. *Psychol. Bull.,* 1949, 46, 1–48.

56. Piaget, J. *Factors determining human behavior.* Cambridge, Mass.: Harvard University Press, 1937.

57. Pinneau, S. R. A critique of the articles by Margaret Ribble. *Child Develpm.*, 1950, 21, 203–228.
58. Porter, B. M. Measurement of parental acceptance of children. *J. Home Econ.*, 1954, 46, 176–182.
59. Pratt, K. C., Nelson, A. K., and Sun, K. H. The behavior of the newborn infant. *Ohio State Univ. Contrib. Psychol.*, 1930, No. 10.
60. Rappaport, G. M. A study of the psychoanalytic theory of the anal character. Unpublished doctoral dissertation, Northwestern University, 1955.
61. Ribble, Margaret A. *The rights of infants.* New York: Columbia University Press, 1943.
62. Roberts, E. Thumb and finger sucking in relation to feeding in early infancy. *Amer. J. Dis. Child.*, 1944, 68, 7–8.
63. Ross, S. Sucking behavior in neonate dogs. *J. abnorm. soc. Psychol.*, 1951, 46, 142–149.
64. Sears, R. R. Experimental studies of projection: I. attribution of traits. *J. soc. Psychol.*, 1936, 7, 151–163.
65. Sears, R. R. Personality. *Annu. Rev. Psychol.*, 1950, 1, 105–118.
66. Sears, R. R., Maccoby, Eleanor E., and Levin, H. *Patterns of child rearing.* Evanston, Ill.: Row, Peterson, 1957.
67. Sears, R. R., Whiting, J. W. M., Nowlis, V., and Sears, Pauline S. Some child-rearing antecedents of aggression and dependency in young children. *Genet. Psychol. Monogr.*, 1953, 47, 135–236.
68. Sears, R. R., and Wise, G. W. Relation of cup feeding in infancy to thumb-sucking and the oral drive. *Amer. J. Orthopsychiat.*, 1950, 20, 123–138.
69. Sewell, W. H., and Mussen, P. H. The effect of feeding, weaning, and scheduling procedures on childhood adjustment and the formation of oral symptoms. *Child Develpm.*, 1952, 23, 185–191.
70. Sewell, W. H., Mussen, P. H., and Harris, C. W. Relationship among child training practices. *Amer. sociol. Rev.*, 1955, 20, 137–148.
71. Spitz, R. The smiling response: a contribution to the ontogenesis of social relations. *Genet. Psychol. Monogr.*, 1946, 34, 57–125.
72. Stone, L. J. A critique of studies of infant isolation. *Child Develpm.*, 1954, 25, 9–20.
73. Symonds, P. M. *The psychology of parent-child relationships.* New York: Appleton-Century, 1939.
74. Thompson, Clara. *Psychoanalysis: evolution and development.* New York: Hermitage, 1950.
75. Thurston, J. R., and Mussen, P. H. Infant feeding gratification and adult personality. *J. Pers.*, 1951, 19, 449–458.
76. Whiting, J. W. M. *Becoming a Kwoma.* New Haven: Yale University Press, 1941.
77. Whiting, J. W. M. The frustration complex in Kwoma society. In C. Kluckhohn and H. A. Murray (Eds.), *Personality in nature, society and culture.* New York: Knopf, 1948, 137–145.
78. Whiting, J. W. M., and Child, I. L. *Child training and personality.* New Haven, Conn.: Yale University Press, 1953.
79. Wittenborn, J. R. *et al.* A study of adoptive children. *Psychol. Monogr.*, 1956, 70, 1–115.

80. Yarrow, L. J. The relationship between nutritive sucking experiences in infancy and non-nutritive sucking in childhood. *J. genet. Psychol.*, 1954, 84, 149–162.

81. Zemlick, M. F., and Watson, R. I. Maternal attitudes of acceptance and rejection during and after pregnancy. *Amer. J. Orthopsychiat.*, 1953, 23, 570–584.

chapter 8

Psychological Disturbances in Infancy

P SYCHOLOGICAL DISTURBANCES OF INFANCY AND CHILD-
hood are exaggerations and distortions of normal development.
Deviating children highlight the process of normal functioning. Consequently, consideration of psychological disturbances helps to en-
large understanding of the process of development. If we can understand what goes wrong in development, we can more accurately
predict and control it and thus work toward helping correction, or
avoidance. The study of disturbed children leads to a better understanding of the reactions of the normal child, just as the study of
diseases promotes our understanding of the normal functioning of
the body.

Illness is to be expected as part of the developmental process. To
quote Halliday, "Illness is regarded, not as a fault in the parts but
as a _reaction_, or a mode of behavior, or vital expression of a living
unit in response to those forces which he encounters as he moves and
grows in time" (_12_, 369).[1] It is appropriate, then, to draw upon
the contributions of various medical specialties for information about
psychological disturbances in infancy.

By and large, psychological disturbances are studied by the differ-

[1] From Halliday (_12_). Copyright 1943 by the _British Journal of Medical
Psychology_, and published with permission.

ential method. That is to say, they are already in existence when studied. They are not produced by the manipulations of an experimenter for the reasons given in Chapter 2. The use of the differential method in connection with psychological disturbances does not prevent reliable and valid findings any more than it does with other problems. Only in various forms of treatment, where change is sought deliberately, can the experimental method be brought to bear upon this aspect of child development.

The nature of psychological disturbances in infancy

Many psychological disturbances in infancy are psychosomatic disorders. Before considering them, it is necessary to gain some conception of the nature of a psychosomatic disorder. From the very word itself, it is evident that the "body" and the "mind" are jointly considered. In a way, "psychosomatic" is a curiously inept term to convey the meaning intended. Actually, it means that the psychological and physical components of a disorder are so intermingled as to make precise separation impossible. And yet the term "psychosomatic" might be taken to connote a dichotomy of body and mind which its proponents wish to eliminate. Essentially, the psychic and somatic aspects represent one and the same process. As a working definition for present purposes, the one by Halliday has much to recommend it. He defines a psychosomatic disorder as a "bodily disorder whose nature can be appreciated only when emotional disturbances (that is, psychological happenings) are investigated in addition to physical disturbances (that is, somatic happenings)" (13, 692).

An actual case history is introduced here in order to illustrate subsequent points.

J. B., an eighteen-month-old child, developed diarrhea which lasted with varying severity for six weeks. No fever was present, nor any laboratory or physical findings which would explain the conditions on an infectious basis. The child, son of a soldier, was born two months after his father sailed for England, only ten months after his parents' marriage. His mother, an extremely insecure woman, had always expressed her anxiety over her husband's absence and safety quite overtly. During the child's eighteen months of life, he had had every opportunity to feel very strongly his mother's insecurity. The period of his diarrhea coincided with anxiety on his mother's part resulting from her conviction that her husband was a member of the invasion troops then landing on the Normandy beachhead. Premonitions that her husband would never return, plus the conviction that he was participating in a terribly hazardous operation, raised her expression of anxiety to a high level. Her child, too young to understand the dangers, and without any direct emotional attachment to the father, expressed this reflected anxiety somatically through hyperactivity of his colon (*21*, 288).[2]

In the remainder of this section, this case will be referred to parenthetically to make concrete the points being made. In this instance, in view of the relatively brief duration of the child's disordered functioning, we were dealing with something close to the level of generalized tension, described in Chapter 6 as a normal reaction to stress. A disturbed infant does not recover from tension as quickly and as easily as do normal infants. In this instance, the infant showed psychosomatic difficulties only for a short period of time and there may even be some doubt as to whether he should be referred to as disturbed. Nevertheless, since the infant was sick, he will be identified as showing a psychosomatic disorder.

Another form of behavior appears which may be described as lethargy. At first glance this seems to indicate complete absence of tension. (This is in contrast to the infant whose tension was expressed through his diarrhea.) Thus, the infantile depression described on page 291 showed an infant in the later stages who was quiet, dejected, passive, and unobservant. Nevertheless, heightened tension in the form of frantic behavior was originally present. This later lethargy may arise either because the child is so fatigued as to give this appearance or because he resorts to a kind of withdrawal as a mode of protection against tension-arousing stimuli (*16*). The effects of tension, in one form or another, are prominent in psychosomatic disorders in infancy.

An exhaustive discussion of psychosomatic disorders in infancy would have to include almost all aspects of bodily function. Physiological and psychological processes are even less divisible in the infant than in the adult. Lack of differentiation is one of the identifying marks of the infancy period. The infant's relative lack of verbal facility, general immaturity, lack of human experience, and lack of self and social awareness all cooperate to make him signal *psychological* disorder through *physiological* channels.

This point may also be illustrated by a consideration of anxiety.

---

[2] Lester W. Sontag, "Psychosomatic Aspects of Childhood" in *Contributions toward Medical Psychology*, edited by Arthur Weider. Copyright 1953. The Ronald Press Company.

In adult anxiety, there is apt to be felt a more or less conscious threat to one's sense of self-worth and identity as a desirable person. To be sure, there is a somatic component in anxiety, reflected in changes in the autonomic nervous system and in the musculature. In the infant, however, due both to a low degree of development of the sense of personal awareness, including awareness of danger, and to a lack of verbal facility, the somatic component—the tenseness—would appear to predominate. (The infant expressed his anxiety by diarrhea.)

The infant is in a close dependent relationship with adults, especially the mother. It is on the basis of this dependence that psychosomatic relationships may be considered. When feeding problems occur in an adult, they are usually of great concern only to the adult. This is not so with feeding problems in an infant or child. There the parents are a part of the pattern of tension these difficulties create. The psychological ties between infant and mother make it a family matter. (The whole case illustrates this point. The infant developed diarrhea in response to his *mother's* anxiety.) In addition to the repercussions psychosomatic difficulties in the infant create in adults, there is a still more significant facet to the intertwining of child and other family members. This is the possible causative relationship that is operative. The mother and other significant adults in the infant's environment, by their ways of dealing with the child, precipitate the development of psychosomatic disorders. (The mother's anxiety brought on the infant's disturbance.) Often the symptoms are a direct emotional expression of the child's relation to the parents. Other examples might be given. Feeding problems, such as the refusal of food, are interpreted as simply expressions of hostility, or as a means of getting more of the mother's attention. Constipation, because of deliberate withholding of feces, is a way of disturbing the mother either as an expression of hostility or in securing further solicitude from the mother. Instead of a specific symptom appearing in response to parental attitudes and behavior, increased general tension may be the way the infant expresses his reaction to the stress existing in the relationship.

Psychosomatic disorders in infancy illustrate the point made in the previous chapter concerning empathy. (Nonverbal communication is evident in the case where diarrhea in the infant seems related to anxiety in the mother.)

Normal responses to tension as a result of stress were explored in an earlier chapter. Now concern is with tension when it is symptomatic of psychosomatic disturbances in infants. In such instances, not only are the disturbances both more profound and more lasting than in normal babies, but they also form rough and recognizable patterns. (The case was too simple to illustrate this.) They appear when stress is severe or when it is operative over a long period of time. In fact, stress may leave the infant in a state of chronic tension. (This infant recovered after six weeks, too short a period for this to develop.)

The importance of the mother–infant relationship shows itself with particular clarity when something acts to disturb the positive, on-going sort of relationship described in the previous chapter. These negative attitudes and practices may be due to long-established attitudes which make child rearing unpleasant; or they may be due to situational or growth difficulties in caring for the child itself. Thus, marital difficulties may arise or difficulties in feeding may be present. Whatever the sources of these tensions, they seem to be communicated to the infant and mother. There is a markedly high concomitance of the anxious mother and the restless infant. Tenseness in infant or mother, no matter the point of origin, creates a vicious circle which further exacerbates the situation.

It should come as no surprise that classification of disorders of infancy might conceivably center either in learning theory or in psychoanalysis. Interpretation of psychological disturbances in infancy in terms of learning theory, although possible, has not yet been exploited to the point of gaining any real acceptance. Clinical workers have generally chosen to interpret difficulties in terms of psychoanalytic premises. Two psychoanalytic classifications will be used. The first, which might be referred to as neo-Freudian, is based upon the quantity and quality of parent-infant relationships. The second, although drawing upon mother-child relationships, stresses in more orthodox fashion the disturbances arising from the psychosexual phases of the oral and anal stages. These two ways of schematizing disturbances in infancy are not mutually contradictory. Both can be accepted without creating logical incompatibilities. It is merely that different aspects are chosen for emphasis—on the one hand, the mother as the instigating agent, and on the other, psychosexual stages of infancy in which infant-mother interaction takes place.

Interpretation in terms of mother-infant relationships

A classification [3] developed by Spitz (25) which has much to recommend it is based on the division into two major etiological classes. The first category involves those cases in which there is the wrong kind of mother-child relationships and the second category involves those in which there is an insufficient amount of mother-child relations. Since in an instance of the first category the mother's personality serves as a disease-provoking agent, a psychological toxin as it were, Spitz refers to the *psychotoxic* diseases of infancy. The second category, since partial or complete absence of mother-child relations is focal, he identifies as *emotional deficiency* diseases.

Psychotoxic Diseases

Some of the psychotoxic patterns will be described both in terms of the disorder and of the alleged etiological factors provided by the maternal attitudes. Only one of these, overt rejection leading to coma, will be described in any detail. In these instances, there is a massive, all-embracing rejection of the child dating perhaps from the onset of pregnancy, but certainly present at delivery. In extreme cases, infants react to the frustration engendered by this rejection by becoming stuporous; falling into deep sleep with shallow, fast breathing; extreme pallor; and diminished sensitivity. A case history follows:

> The mother was a 16 year old, unmarried, Catholic girl who had been seduced by the son of her employer. The child was undesired and severe guilt feelings were present. Delivery was uneventful, and the attempts to nurse were uneventful although milk could be produced only by manual pressure. During nursing the mother behaved as if the infant was a complete alien; she withdrew from the baby which she held in a rigid and tense way. After five days, the baby was observed in the coma previously described. Energetic methods including tube feeding were necessary to bring the baby out of the condition. Equally vigorous, very directive and authoritarian methods were used with the mother so that nursing thereafter went on relatively successfully. (Adapted from 25, 260.) [4]

[3] Although this classification was advanced only to deal with the first year of life, it can be extended, without much violence to the facts, to include the second year as well.

[4] Adapted from Spitz (25). Copyright 1951 by the International Universities Press, and published with permission.

Relations have also been traced clinically between frustrations brought about by anxious overpermissiveness and "three month colic"; hostility (appearing to be merely anxiety) leading to rash; and an oscillation between pampering and hostility leading to hypermobility, particularly in the form of rocking.

Emotional Deficiency Diseases

These diseases are traced to maternal deprivation. The deprivation pattern to be discussed must be distinguished from the rejection pattern previously discussed (10). In deprivation there is a meagerness of stimulation permitting no specific identification. That is, there is no older person from whom to draw inspiration as to attitudes, thoughts, feelings, and behavior. There are no meaningful reciprocal relations with other people. Thus, motivations to normal maturation and differentiation of personality are stunted. Poverty of content of intellect and emotion follow. Passivity is exaggerated by adjustment to the routine demands of group life which leave little or no room for individuality. Maternal deprivation is quite different in atmosphere and in effect from that experienced by the rejected child. When he is rejected, hostility is directed toward the child by one or both parents. He is made to feel unwanted. There is a severity rather than a lack of stimulation. He meets adults, and, although they may block him, he may also be stimulated to meet and solve problems even though his solutions are distorted.

A number of different situations is covered by this term, emotional deficiency. It may be that a child is frustrated by being deprived even though living at home with his mother, or he may be someone looked after by a relative stranger in a foster home, or he may be almost completely deprived, as in many institutions such as residential nurseries. The differences in degree of maternal deprivation are signalized by distinguishing between partial and total emotional deprivation.

Partial emotional deprivation is used in the present context to refer to those children who, after establishing a satisfactory emotional relationship with the mother for the first six months of life, are thereafter frustrated by being separated from her. This leads to a condition which Spitz has called anaclitic depression. A general case description derived from Spitz (24) follows:

> There is first what is described as a "search" for the mother. Such infants cannot be quieted, some cry bitterly, others less vehemently but

they cannot be soothed. Nevertheless, at this stage they cling to the available adult.

The picture changes on failure of the mother to return. He becomes quiescent, does not look up when adults enter the room, does not play and does not grasp at objects. Along with passivity and dejection he develops eating difficulties, loses weight and shows sleep disturbances. In general, the level of development does not proceed normally or even drops.

As a reaction to the loss of the mother after establishing a satisfactory relationship, an infant develops a pattern of behavior which is a fairly characteristic response of infants to such a situation. It occurs often enough, according to Spitz, to be considered a disorder of infancy attributable to frustration brought about by partial deprivation.

In total emotional deprivation, the infant does not have, early or late, anything resembling emotional ties with a mother figure. The importance of these maternal contacts for normal development is dramatically illustrated through infants almost completely deprived of these experiences.

In infancy, a condition called marasmus is said to develop from the frustrations of total emotional deprivation. The following case adapted from one described by Ribble (20) illustrates not only the conditions but also something of the general situational background from which it is said to come.

The child was full-term and weighed six pounds, three ounces at birth. The two weeks' stay in the hospital was uneventful. On returning home the mother discovered her husband had deserted her. Thereafter her milk did not agree with the baby. Since the infant refused the breast and began to vomit he was hospitalized. The mother did not come to see him at this time or later, thus deserting him.

He was in a crowded ward, and received little attention or handling. He became a finger sucker and a ruminator (regurgitating food). At two months of age, he weighed about five pounds and had an appearance of a seventh month fetus with arms and legs wasted, large head and large protruding abdomen.

He was transferred to a small children's hospital, where a thorough physical examination revealed nothing of an organic nature. Concentrated nursing care was given him, with his being held in the nurse's lap for a feeding of one half hour duration, his position changed frequently and his being carried about whenever possible. After some slow improvement, a volunteer "mother" began to come to the hospital twice daily. Her visits were gradually lengthened until she was spending an hour with him on each visit. She had been told the infant needed loving care and physical contact which she gave him.

The results were such that by five months of age he weighed nine pounds without rumination. He was now alert and vigorous, although some remnants of his difficulties remained, such as retarded motor co-ordination and finger sucking.

Research on Emotional Deprivation

The question of maternal deprivation will now be examined in terms of the relevant controlled research studies. It is appropriate to begin by considering a study sometimes cited as evidence that there is no ill effect from minimal social stimulation. This is the study of the twins, Rey and Del, by Dr. and Mrs. Dennis (6).

They reared the two babies from one month through six months under conditions of social isolation. Human contacts were kept at a minimum, with the intent of not fondling, playing, or talking to them during their first six months of life. Thereafter, conditions of social isolation were eased for the remainder of their first year.

These babies showed a record of early development very much like that of infants reared in an environment with the usual social contacts and experiences of fondling, play, and talking. They even responded affectionately when an observer attempted to preserve a pronounced stolidity. These infants emerged from their first year as healthy, alert, and happy.

It is hardly surprising that others have seized upon their general finding as evidence against the position stated earlier concerning the effect of emotional deprivation. Fortunately, the "lack" of stimulation the twins received is capable of rather precise statement. In this connection, Stone may be quoted.

Let us see now precisely *how* isolated the infants were; how minimal was their social stimulation—since, for our purposes, the whole story hinges on this. First, we observe that the period of most marked isolation was when we would expect it to be least injurious: after the first six months most restrictions were removed. All the evidence to date from other studies is that the *latter* part of the first year is crucial with respect to damage produced by isolation.

Second, we find that the babies, by Dennis's own statement, were not "isolated." . . . Basically, I suppose the trouble was that the Dennises are decent human beings and could not bring themselves to impose restrictions of the sort that are apparently involved in Spitz's study or in the occasional accounts of illegitimate children hidden away in attics. Another trouble was that the Dennises were just too interested in the babies to leave them alone very much. According to their report, the babies were visited on the average of twelve times a day and one, or both, experimenters were in the room during two hours of the day. They also point out that during this period of the first half of the first year all ". . . infants are awake but little longer than is required for feeding, bathing, and dressing." And how much attention did these babies receive? "The subjects were taken from their cribs only for feeding, bathing, cleaning, and dressing *and* for a few experiments." . . . Moreover, "We did not smile at the subjects nor did we speak to them, romp with them, or tickle them *except* as these actions occasionally were incorporated into routine experiments. We talked to each other when in the nursery *but* did not direct our remarks to the infants." . . .

In addition to entrances into the room which were made in order to care for the infants and experiment with them, several entrances per day were made solely to note down the condition and activities of the babies. . . . When either infant cried insistently, we entered the room and corrected whatever condition seemed to be the cause of the cry. We did not adhere rigidly to the feeding schedule. . . .

Incidentally, beginning the twenty-seventh week the Dennises allowed themselves to smile back at the twins and to speak to them, and even permitted themselves to fondle and play with them. This was done in such a way as not to reward the performance of any specific act. "We romped with the children, as by shaking or rolling them only when they were indifferently employed with some response that was already well established." . . . But this does not throw a sidelight on the Dennises' regrettably human responsiveness to the infants (*26*, 16–17).[5]

Stone goes on to conclude that the condition under which the studies were conducted was "minimum *adequate* social stimulation" (*26*, 17). The Dennis study contributes valuable information on what is probably close to the lower limit of adequate social stimulation. Our present concern is with deprivation more severe in degree.

Another study by Dennis and Najarian (*7*) is more crucial in evaluating the effect of emotional deprivation. Their study was performed in a foundling home in Beirut, Lebanon, the staff of which was unable to offer the infant little more than essential physical care. Mothering and other forms of child-adult interaction were necessarily at a minimum since the adult-child ratio was one to ten. Contact with the mother ceased shortly after birth. For the first four months the infant was swaddled and on his back in a crib with a covering around the sides. He remained in a crib until about one year of age. From about one to three years of age, he spent most of his waking hours in play groups of about 20 children with a supervisor and assistant. Equipment was limited to a very few toys. From three to four years, he spent most of the day seated at a small table occupied with

[5] From Stone (*26*). Copyright 1954 by the Society for Research in Child Development, and published with permission.

slates, beads, and sewing boards. At about four, he was placed in a kindergarten within the home. For a comparison group they had infants of comparable age from the poorer sections of Beirut.

They had as subjects about 50 foundling infants and 40 comparison infants. The Cattell Infant Scale (5) was given these infants. In addition, they had 30 four-and-a-half to six-year-old children from the foundling home. They were given a drawing of a man test (Goodenough, Draw-A-Man-Test), a maze tracing test (Porteus Maze Test), and a cube tapping test (Knox Cube Test). The foundling children of four-and-a-half to six were assumed to be similar to the foundling infants on the basis of the fact that the policy and child care of the foundling home had not changed over the years involved.

There was little difference in intelligence between the infant groups tested at two months, the means for foundling and comparison groups being 97 and 107. For older infants up to those tested at one year of age, there was significant inferiority in the foundling infants with a mean of 63 as compared to 101 for the comparison infants. On the performance test, the four- to six-year-old foundling children were only about ten per cent below the norms of American home-reared children. In terms of their own summary, Dennis and Najarian regard the foundling home children as normal during the second month, greatly retarded from three to twelve months of age, and almost normal on performance tests between four-and-a-half and six years of age.

The finding of normality at two months is not uncommon and might be expected, no matter the position one takes concerning the effect of stimulus deprivation thereafter. The infants are either simply too young to be affected by stimulus deprivation or their environment simply is not a restricted one for so young an infant. Their explanation of retardation between three and twelve months of age is that it was owing to lack of practice in being held in a sitting position (which is a requirement of Cattell testing) and lack of opportunity to practice visual-motor coordination. In short, lack of learning opportunities is the basis for the retardation. They attribute the lack of retardation in the four- to six-year-old children to the selection of tests where their environment would have less effect than other factors. They admit that on language tests the foundling children would have been retarded, perhaps to a marked degree.

Emotional factors were not measured, but in terms of impression they felt the foundling infants and children were approachable and not shy of strangers. Some of the older babies did develop automatisms such as arching the back or hitting themselves. In their opinion, there was nothing to suggest that the infants suffered from loss of mothering. They feel that specific kinds of restriction of learning opportunity account for the results.

On the other side of the argument, though most, if not all, research studies show methodological weaknesses, the diversity of studies both here and abroad which leads to the same general conclusions concerning the pernicious effect of maternal deprivation is impressive (4, 9, 10, 11, 22, 23, 24, 25). The studies are in agreement that frustration arising from deprivation leads to serious emotional and intellectual retardation. Impetus to this view was furnished by observation of infants in adverse conditions, particularly those in Great Britain who were evacuated to the country during World War II and those living in institutions. In general, it has been found (9) that infants living in their own homes suffer from considerably fewer personality difficulties than those living in the impersonal environment of an institution. Almost needless to add is the fact that the extent and quality of the damage vary with the age of the child, the specific kind of deprivation, the severity of deprivation, the length the deprivation continues, and other relevant factors.

The differential research studies of human infants under institutional care by Spitz (22, 23, 24, 25) often have been referred to as offering evidence concerning the deleterious effect of maternal deprivation. The criticisms presented in the devastating review by Pinneau (18) preclude the use of these studies as supporting evidence. Other studies of the effect of emotional deprivation directly upon infant behavior are also similarly weak methodologically. Perforce, major attention is directed to studies of older children and adolescents who have been frustrated by being deprived in infancy.

A study which will be used to illustrate the effect of institutional deprivation is one of the series by Goldfarb (11). Adolescents in foster homes were studied who, as infants, had lived in an institution. The case workers who supervised the children in the foster homes rated the children in terms of adjustment. The subjects were then divided into two groups. Those rated as showing good adjustment formed one group, and those showing severe problem behavior or extreme emotional difficulties formed the other. The two groups were then equated for age and sex. All that was known about the children at this point was that they had been in a particular institution some time during the first three years of life. This institution had an unusually complete physical plant and a thorough program of medical care. The infants were kept in their own isolation cubicles until nine months of age. The nurses had neither the training nor the time to give their charges love and affection. Instead, each baby was given a few hurried moments for changing, dressing, and bathing.

The poorly adjusted children were found to have entered the institution at a significantly younger age (mean—6 months) and to have spent a significantly longer time in the institution (mean—34 months) than the well-adjusted group who entered at an average age of 11 months and spent 25 months in the institution. Even on the first placement after leaving the institution, the two groups differed, with poor adjustment predominating in one group and good adjustment in the other.

In an earlier, closely related study, Goldfarb (9) compared adolescents reared in an institution until an age of three and then placed in foster homes with a group placed in foster homes in early infancy. The children who were reared until three in the impersonal environment of the institution were definitely handicapped. They showed significantly more forms of problem behavior, lower IQ's, and lower scores on social maturity as measured by the Vineland Social Maturity Scale. On both the intelligence and social maturity scales the foster home children were nearly at the average for the general norms, while the institutional children were seriously retarded.

An older child or adolescent frustrated from institutional deprivation shows as major characteristics, emotional imperviousness and shallow, superficial relationships with other persons (10, 11). Although insatiable in demanding affection, he seems to lack a capacity for being dependent upon others. He cannot be reached by others, including the foster parents. He can leave a foster home where he has been reared for years, even from the time he left the institution, and seem to have no feeling about leaving. Frustrations engendered by the deprivations of institutional living produced a freedom from dependency tendencies. The results obtained by Goldfarb would, at first, seem contradictory to the findings of the antecedent study by Sears.

There can be no question that differences were established by Goldfarb which conform to the hypothesis that frustration coincident with institutional life has a pernicious effect upon child development when compared to children placed in foster homes. There remains, however, the possibility that sometimes the socially undesirable char·

acteristics on which differences were found between the groups of children were the very basis for the decision *not* to place the child in a foster home. Of course, some reasons for not placing institutionalized children have nothing to do with the characteristics of the child in question. But retardation or problem behavior observable in infancy might have been the reason for longer institutionalization before eventual placement.

An exception to the statement that research on this issue which involved the study of infants directly has been poorly controlled is to be found in the study of Rheingold (*19*). Her infant subjects were drawn from an institution where, insofar as possible, they were given personal care and contact. From her description it is evident that considerable effort in giving this care was expended. Volunteers and hospital personnel were encouraged by the Sister in charge of the floor to talk to the babies and to hold them. Her research situation, then, was unlike the more impersonal institutional situations, and did not, by any means, represent the extremes of emotional deprivation that may be found. She was using a situation which was somewhat closer to that normally prevailing in an infant's home. Hence, if she were to find differences in the infants because of the increased "mothering" she introduced, she would be submitting her hypothesis to a more difficult test than if she had used a more impersonal institution for her study.

On the basis of previous studies she inferred that institutional babies depart from normal development by being less interested in and responsive to people and less sensitive to changes in an adult's facial expression and tone of voice.

Sixteen infants between five and seven months of age were her subjects. She cared for the experimental subjects four at a time for nearly eight hours per day, five days a week for eight weeks. She repeated the procedure for the second group of four. A control group, each time numbering four, was cared for in the usual hospital routine.

Observation by an independent observer showed that she gave the experimental group much more in the way of care than the control subjects received. For example, for the first experimental group caretaking acts were recorded for 23 per cent of the observations, while in a comparable period of time with the control infants caretaking acts involved only 7 per cent of the observations with these acts performed by 14 different persons.

This established a situation in which one "mother" gave more intensive care than did many "mothers." The effect of this differential situation on social responsiveness of the infants was assessed. Among other results she found that the experimental infants to a greater degree than the control subjects (1) were more socially responsive to her; (2) were more responsive to another person (the examiner); and (3) made slightly higher scores on postural tests, cube manipulation, and on the Cattell Infant Intelligence Scale. That "mothering" has a considerable effect upon the infant's social development has been neatly demonstrated by Rheingold.

Cautions in Interpretation

It is well to emphasize that knowledge of the etiologies of the psychosomatic disorders of infancy in terms of mother-infant relationships is relatively nonspecific and incomplete. A case in point would be the illustration of marasmus presented earlier. Ribble, from whom the case was drawn, has been criticized in referring to this disorder as being due to inadequate mothering (17). Evidence is adduced by others that marasmus may be due to malnutrition, adrenal hormone insufficiency, or cobalt deficiency. It is thus argued that marasmus has a physiological basis rather than a psychological one as postulated by Ribble. It may be that each of these explanations is equally correct (or incorrect). In her interpretation, Ribble has support from various authorities. Such conservative and respected pediatric-psychiatric textbooks as those of the Bakwins (1), Gesell (8), and Kanner (15) speak of a condition of hospitalism, marasmus, or "environmental retardation" which bears considerable similarity, if not identity, to what she is describing. Invariably they describe the condition in question as arising from psychological factors. This fact in itself does not, of course, provide proof. It may be that "psychological" marasmus is a matter of misdiagnosis, but there is a great deal of clinical evidence to be marshalled in support of the existence of the condition. Whatever the outcome of this matter, it serves to illustrate the necessity of caution in evaluating psychosomatic conditions in infancy.

The research evidence is contradictory. On the one hand, we have the study of Dennis and Najarian (7) in which they found no evidence of intellectual or emotional retardation due to emotional deprivation. On the other hand, we have the considerably larger array of evidence that lack of mothering does have an effect. Adherents of this latter point of view would charge that selection by Dennis and

Najarian of the particular tests they used masked effectively the intel
lectual effects of development and that they did not thoroughly or
expertly investigate the emotional ones. The weight of evidence
supports their view, but future advance may show that a certain corrective is necessary to what may be a rather extravagant acceptance
of the influence of emotional deprivation on infants and children. In
this advance, the study of Dennis and Najarian may be a pioneer one.

The alleged relationships just described are by no means as simple
and as unequivocal as this short and therefore bald summarization
might be taken to imply. It may well be that other attitude and
reaction patterns exist which differ from those described and that
a given maternal attitude or relationship may instigate any or all
of the reactions in different circumstances.

Interpretation in terms of psychosexual stages

Psychosomatic disorders of infancy interpreted in terms of psychoanalytic theory and therapy will now be presented. Although Spitz,
the source for the previous classification, is a psychoanalyst, his way
of approaching disorders of infancy may be presented without direct reference to psychoanalytic theory. Interpretation of disorders
of infancy in terms of psychosexual stages depends directly upon
psychoanalytic theory. In terms of symptoms, the disorders of infancy considered in this fashion are essentially similar to the so-called
psychotoxic disorders of Spitz. However, explanations are couched
in terms of the infant's stage of development rather than in terms of
the mother's attitudes. That these points of view are mutually complementary rather than contradictory is evident. The case chosen
for presentation deals with difficulties originating predominantly in
the anal stage. A case might just as appropriately have been
chosen to highlight difficulties in the oral stage.

The boy described by Huschka was three-and-a-half and was seen
in treatment sessions six times a week for two-and-a-half months. (The
age of the child may cause some confusion. It was chosen because it
illustrates how what happens in infancy may influence later development.) Psychoanalytically oriented play therapy was used. The play
equipment included dolls, household furniture, trains, modeling clay,
water, and at the window a Japanese dirt garden mentioned because it
was incorporated into therapy. The boy was brought for treatment as
a last resort because of a long history of constipation treated by diet,

cathartics, and drugs. When seen, he was unable to have a bowel movement without an enema. Hereafter Huschka is quoted directly.

He was the older of two children, the younger being a girl of 1½ years. . . . The mother, a petite, superficially gracious intellectual, was very tense; she obviously rejected the child and she was the type who quietly but relentlessly dominated those about her. In giving the history, the parents stated that the child had always been "regular" with respect to his bowel movements until the age of 2½ years. At that time his nurse, who had cared for him since birth, and to whom he had been devoted, returned to her home in England. One week before she left he became constipated and he had remained so ever since. . . . In telling about the child's presenting symptom, the parents remarked incidentally that he also had a difficult personality. He was unhappy, petulant, irritable, and exceedingly stubborn, these characteristics being precipitated by the birth of his sister which occurred when he was two years old. As the father put it, "The little fellow sometimes acts as if he hates the whole world."

With regard to development, it was learned that in infancy there was difficulty with feeding. The child took the breast well but, because the supply of milk was inadequate, got only about three ounces at each feeding. Complementary feedings were therefore necessary. The mother said she disliked the nursing experience, the nurses making her feel inferior because she had so little milk. The child never seemed satisfied, and at three months he was taken off the breast altogether and fed by bottle. Although slow at emptying the bottle, he took it fairly well, and he seemed happier and gained weight. At five or six months there was a gradual addition of soft solids to the diet. This he did not like. The age at which the bottle was given up was not recalled.

Toilet training was effected by the nurse who cared for the child for the first 2½ years of his life, and to whom he was devoted. She was an exceedingly neat, meticulous, strict woman. She began his toilet training when he was between three and four months old by holding him on a pot in her lap. The parents did not recall the length of time which it required, but it was "very short" and the nurse took pride in achieving quick toilet training. She was also fastidious about the child's general cleanliness, washing his hands many more times than was necessary. Obviously such training was coercive.

Clinical findings: The patient was a good-looking, blond-haired, blue-eyed, intelligent boy. The day he was seen for psychiatric examination he looked serious, unhappy, and harassed. Only once in the first session did he smile. A bit pale, he was fairly well nourished though not robust. He talked very little; usually he declined to respond to conversational leads, and when he did speak, his voice was low and conspicuously lacking in childhood enthusiasm. Negativism, an outstanding feature of his behavior, was demonstrated by his declining to have his wraps removed, refusing to come into the office and rebuffing all overtures to interest him in the toys. His need to control those about him was seen in the play with the truck when he ordered the physician about, also in the tea party play when he made her wait for her tea. Because of the child's refusal to enter the office, most of the treatment during the first few weeks had to be carried on either in the waiting room or in the hallway leading from there to the office. Significantly, on the day of his initial visit, the toy which he first began to play with was a truck with an automatic dumping device in the rear end, and throughout the entire treatment period this dump truck was one of the chief implements of his play. On leaving the office that day he asked if he might take the nursing bottle home, but on discovering the toy toilet, chose that instead and according to his mother, "He kept it in his hand all day."

The second day he suddenly picked up a piece of modeling clay and saying, "Want me to make something?" piled up a mass of clay, grunting and panting as he added blobs to it and pounded them into place. When he was asked what it was, he replied, "A castle." The castle, too, was a theme present throughout the treatment. He always guarded it and for some time he would not let the physician or any of the dolls come near it. In his play he crossly ordered the analyst about: "Make something," he shouted, or "Get up!" "Stay in that room." "Open the door" (in rear of truck). "Give me that dirt!" (from garden at window). As the treatment proceeded, hostility toward the analyst and toward each member of his household in turn became an outstanding feature of the play. Calling one of the dolls his sister and describing her as a "teeny, weeny baby," he said sweetly that she was "very nice," but simultaneously drowned her in a tub of water. In riding the dump truck he always backed into the office and he became anxious whenever the plasticine was about to pass through the hole in the rear, abruptly giving up his play and unloading it. Also he showed anxiety whenever his hands became slightly soiled, immediately having to wash them. After about two weeks of treatment, his mother telephoned that he was beginning to show "rage and temper" at home, screaming at his nurse and telling his mother to "Shut up!" He developed great interest in the messes which the new puppy made on the floor. At this time it was learned that his term for defecation was "making a dump." In the twentieth hour of treatment, when the child's hostility toward the physician was at its height, he expressed great hatred toward the doll whom he called "the mother," twisting off her head, crushing her and saying, "Bang! She's dead. She's all burned up. She's all dead now!" And he threw her across the room. His face during all this was vicious and there was clenching of fists and teeth. Shortly afterward he picked up the nursing bottle and threw it across the room, exactly duplicating the movements used in the earlier destruction of the mother. At this point in the treatment, friendliness toward the analyst began to appear from time to time, accompanied by verbalizations such as, "Would you like some presents?" Coincidently the child introduced play having to do with proffering gifts. A doll of plasticine, which he identified as his first nurse by a reference to her glasses—the nurse who had managed the toilet training—came in for a great deal of harsh treatment. "Crinkle her up! . . . Hit her with the gun." He pushed her across the room, then twisted off her head and broke her body in two. Suddenly he smiled sweetly and said, "She wears glasses and she's very funny," but quickly added, "Bang her on the ground. . . . Take that stone and bang her on the ground." He then began playing "the boy (doll) is sick," and decided to give him an enema. Holding "the enema thing," a colored crayon, to the doll's anal region, he shouted in a vindictive tone, "Give him a lot! How much has he got now?" The father, represented by the Beccasine (amputation) doll, came in for destruction, too. In the fortieth hour the child tore him to pieces, saying, "He's a bad man." (What did he do that was bad?) "He slept with his mother last night. I'm going to spank him." He then spanked the doll and added, "And he hit his mother with his hand." This theme involving the father floated in and out of the treatment during the subsequent sessions. About two weeks later when the child again called the father "bad" and was again asked what the father did that was bad, he replied, "He gave his mother a kiss, he gave his mother a dump." A few days later, "He gave his kiss to his mother." (What else?) "He brought a birthday present to his mother." At that he pounded the father so viciously that he broke the neck of an unusually strong doll.

Coincident with all this release of anger at his family, the child's stubbornness gradually disappeared, he became amiable, and there was reduction of his uneasiness about dirt to the extent that the day following a particularly active session of aggression toward the physician, he spontaneously began playing in the mud from the Japanese garden. A little later (fifty-fifth hour), following play involving the inter-change of gifts which was stimulated by his sister's birthday party, he started taking the "castle" to pieces, and a few days later began smearing the sides of the dump truck with it. One day during this phase of treatment, on chancing to see a crib in the psychologist's examining room, he said, "I want to be a baby." In the baby-play period of regression that followed he passed flatus, gurgled and babbled in unintelligible monosyllables and he pawed the air with the poorly coordinated movements of an infant. Shortly afterward, when he began making mud pies, he let down completely with respect to his rigid cleanliness and enjoyed an ecstatic bout of smearing (*14*, 301–303).[6]

At this point treatment was terminated by the mother who felt that she could no longer defer hospitalization. Just before treatment at the hospital the boy had a normal bowel movement and after a complete intensive study was pronounced well.

The case was selected because of the classic picture it paints of a psychoanalytically interpreted and treated infantile neurosis. Deprived in early infancy because of unsatisfactory breast feeding, the infant then met coercive bowel training at the hands of an excessively demanding nurse who started training during his third month. Frustrated again at the age of two-and-a-half by the permanent loss of this nurse, he showed the classic symptoms of persistent constipation

[6] From Huschka (*14*). Copyright 1942 by The Williams and Wilkins Company, and published with permission.

on the basis of what was now an irritable stubborn negativism. Behind this stubbornness was marked hostility which, in the safety of the therapy sessions, found release in destructive aggression. It was concluded by Huschka that there is a relationship between the coercive bowel training and the type of symptomatology through which the neurosis expressed itself.

A hazard common in the clinical situation is the invariable selection of factors considered significant which are presented as evidence. The case history of this boy with anal difficulties may be used as an illustration. First, Husckha, it is evident, did not report *everything* which went on in the approximately 65 hours of treatment. She had to select, and she undoubtedly did so on the basis of her theoretical preconceptions of what was significant. She looked for certain factors and perhaps ignored others. There is no reason to believe that this sort of thing is done intentionally. Rather, the clinical situation makes selection inevitable. This weakness, of course, is not specific to disorders of infancy. It is mentioned now rather than later because the weakness is evident here just as much as with older children. The only safeguard we have against omissions of significant factors is the clinical experience of the investigator and the criticism of colleagues with whom he consults.

Treatment

Knowledge of effective methods of treatment for disorders of infancy is as incomplete as is knowledge of etiology. The major reason for the lack of knowledge is not difficult to identify. Verbalization and other forms of symbolic communication such as play are the principal vehicles of therapeutic activity and understanding. With an infant who cannot even tell "where it hurts," the sources of information are closed. Through observation and inference, certain principles of treatment can, nevertheless, be offered.

Interpretation and treatment in terms of orthodox psychoanalytic theory, which call for emphasis upon psychosexual stages, have been illustrated in the case history from Huschka. Case studies in other parts of this chapter incidentally refer to treatment. Other ways of treating psychosomatic disorders, which include modifying the attitude of the parents through psychotherapy, are examined in Chapter 13.

If many instances of disorders of infancy are brought about by either the wrong kind or by an insufficient amount of mother-child relations, it follows that treatment, too, must take into account this relation. Preventive therapy often takes the form of removing environmental conditions likely to lead to difficulties. Generous dosage of TLC, otherwise known as tender, loving care, appear prophylactic. Separation of the parents from the infant for any long periods of time should be avoided whenever possible.

It is also appropriate to consider what may be done to help prevent maternal deprivation at the social as distinguished from the individual level. Bowlby (4), in his report on behalf of the World Health Organization, outlines several interrelated approaches toward this goal. For example, there could be prevention of family failure through direct and indirect economic and medical aid. Reduction in illegitimacy should be sought together with more realistic and humane methods of handling the problem when it occurs. There should be wiser methods of handling adoption. Also, he feels that we need to develop more boarding homes which reflect what knowledge we have of the effects of maternal deprivation and that do what they can to minimize these effects. Discussion of putting such principles into operation is beyond the scope of this book, but emphatically not beyond the concern of all those interested in optimal development of the child's personality.

Summary

Psychological disturbances in infancy are discussed as exaggerations or distortions of normal development. By understanding what makes for pathological development, we can better understand normal development.

Psychosomatic disorders, in other words, disturbances in which the psychological and physical components are intermingled, are characteristic of infancy and have been stressed in this presentation. These disturbances, moreover, are also social in the sense that disturbed mother-child relationships are often seen as related to these psychosomatic disorders.

Two approaches to interpretation of infantile disorders are presented. The first approach stresses the nature and quality of the parent-child relationship. In this approach, a distinction is made between psychotoxic diseases and emotional deficiency diseases. In psychotoxic disease, there is the wrong kind of mother-child relationship; in emotional deficiency diseases, there is an insufficient amount of this relationship. The second approach stresses the relation of the phenomena of the oral and anal psychosexual stages to the disturbance in the infant. There is nothing logically incompatible between the two approaches, emphasizing as they do different facets of the psychosomatic, psychosocial disorders of infancy.

For Further Reading

It is somewhat difficult to suggest further readings on psychosomatic disorders in infancy because the material is scattered in clinical reports in the professional journals. A. Maslow and B. Mittelmann, *Principles of Abnormal Psychology* (New York: Harper, 1951) gives an account of disorders in infancy which is of considerable value. For an account of the literature on maternal deprivation, the review by John Bowlby under the auspices of the World Health Organization makes vivid reading. An edition of his report prepared for general reading, *Child Care and the Growth of Love*, is published in a paperback edition in London by Penguin Books, 1953. The article by J. E. Anderson entitled, "Personality organization in children," and published in *The American Psychologist* (1948, 3, 409–416), is suggested for reading because of its vigorous portrayal of the infant and child as a hardy resistant creature able to take many of the viscissitudes of life with great aplomb.

References

1. Bakwin, Ruth M., and Bakwin, H. *Psychologic care during infancy and childhood.* New York: Appleton-Century-Crofts, 1942.
2. Benda, C. Psychopathology of childhood. In L. Carmichael (Ed.), *Manual of child psychology* (2nd ed.). New York: Wiley, 1954, 1115–1161.
3. Bliss, M. The homogeneity of the mentally subnormal: a fallacious concept. *Train Sch. Bull.*, 1953, 50, 152–156.
4. Bowlby, J. *Maternal care and mental health.* Geneva: World Health Organization, 1952.
5. Cattell, Psyche. *The measurement of intelligence of infants and young children.* New York: Psychological Corporation, 1940.
6. Dennis, W., and Dennis, Sena G. Development under controlled environmental conditions. In W. Dennis (Ed.), *Readings in child psychology.* New York: Prentice-Hall, 1951, 104–131.
7. Dennis, W., and Najarian, P. Infant development under environmental handicap. *Psychol. Monogr.*, 1957, 71, No. 436.
8. Gesell, A., and Amatruda, Catherine S. *Developmental diagnosis* (2nd ed.). New York: Hoeber, 1947.

9. Goldfarb, W. The effects of early institutional care in adolescent personality. *J. exp. Educ.*, 1943, 12, 106–129.

10. Goldfarb, W. Psychological privation in infancy and subsequent adjustment. *Amer. J. Orthopsychiat.*, 1945, 15, 247–255.

11. Goldfarb, W. Variations in adolescent adjustment of institutionally-reared children. *Amer. J. Orthopsychiat.*, 1947, 17, 449–457.

12. Halliday, J. L. Principles of aetiology. *Brit. J. med. Psychol.*, 1943, 19, 367–380.

13. Halliday, J. L. Concept of a psychosomatic affection. *Lancet*, 1943, 245, 692–696.

14. Huschka, Mabel. The child's response to coercive bowel training. *Psychosom. Med.*, 1942, 4, 301–308.

15. Kanner, L. *Child psychiatry* (2nd ed.). Springfield, Ill.: Thomas, 1948.

16. Leitch, Mary, and Escalona, Sibylle. The reaction of infants to stress. In Phyllis Greenacre *et al.* (Eds.), *The psychoanalytic study of the child*, Vols. 3–4. New York: International Universities Press, 1949, 121–140.

17. Pinneau, S. R. A critique on the articles by Margaret Ribble. *Child Develpm.*, 1951, 21, 203–228.

18. Pinneau, S. R. The infantile disorders of hospitalism and anaclitic depression. *Psychol. Bull.*, 1955, 52, 429–452.

19. Rheingold, Harriet L. The modification of social responsiveness in institutional babies. *Soc. Res. Child Developm., Monogr.*, 1956, 21, No. 2.

20. Ribble, Margaret A. *The rights of infants: early psychological needs and their satisfaction.* New York: Columbia University Press, 1943.

21. Sontag, L. W. Psychosomatic aspects of childhood. In A. Weider (Ed.), *Contributions toward medical psychology: theory and psychodiagnostic methods.* New York: Ronald, 1953, 275–289.

22. Spitz, R. A. Hospitalism. In O. Fenichel *et al.* (Eds.), *The psychoanalytic study of the child*, Vol. 1. New York: International Universities Press, 1945, 54–74.

23. Spitz, R. A. Hospitalism: a follow-up report. In O. Fenichel *et al.* (Eds.), *The psychoanalytic study of the child*, Vol. 2. New York: International Universities Press, 1946, 113–117.

24. Spitz, R. A. The importance of the mother-child relationship during the first year of life: a synopsis in five sketches. *Ment. Hlth. Today*, 1948, 7, 7–13.

25. Spitz, R. A. The psychogenic diseases in infancy: an attempt at their etiologic classification. In Ruth S. Eissler *et al.* (Eds.), *The psychoanalytic study of the child:* Vol. 6. New York: International Universities Press, 1951, 255–275.

26. Stone, L. J. A critique of studies of infant isolation. *Child Develpm.*, 1954, 25, 9–20.

part

Early
Childhood

chapter 9

Psychological Development
in Early Childhood

With the close of infancy comes the period of early childhood. We now turn to psychological development during the years from after two through five years of age. Psychological development is considered in terms of practically the same general rubrics as were used in discussing infancy. The sections that follow are devoted, respectively, to motor development, emotional development, language development, the development of understanding, and intellectual development.

Motor development in early childhood

It is during the preschool period that the child coordinates the motor skills he has already established as well as learning many new ones. In summarizing the motor skills of the five-year-old, Gesell (27) speaks of his being poised and controlled, with economy of movement, able to maintain one position for relatively long periods, and adept with hands and fingers. He has come a long way from the clumsy, not too well-coordinated two-year-old. At that earlier age, his way of getting upstairs may be regarded as epitomizing his motor development. He did get upstairs unaided (27), but he did so in mark-time fashion, without alternating his feet on successive steps. The two-year-old "got around," but not in a fluid, smooth, or efficient fashion as does the preschool child.

By the age of three most of the traces of the clumsiness of the infantile patterns in motor behavior have disappeared. Gesell and his associates (26) mention as characteristic of the three-year-old his ability to accelerate and decelerate in walking and running, to turn sharp corners, to go upstairs alternating his feet, and to stand on one foot even though only for short periods of time. From the child's perspective, being three years old is being at the age when he is ready to leave behind the infantile "kiddy car" with its primitive, shoving form of propulsion for a tricycle with its complicated means of movement. Jumping, climbing, and riding tricycles occupy a not unconsiderable portion of the preschool child's time. Such activities are derived essentially from the simpler ones of infancy but with considerably greater ease and efficiency. New skills also appear.

Learning and Maturation in Motor Skills

During the preschool age many motor skills are learned. There is a wealth of studies identifying learning in this process. The influence of learning may be readily seen in such skills as talking, writing, and buttoning clothes. These particular skills do not develop unless training or opportunity for imitation is provided.

Maturational influences are not confined to infancy, but are also operative during the preschool period. Since several studies (for example, those reported in Munn (56)) produce substantially similar results, only one illustrative study, that of Hicks (36), will be reviewed. Sixty children between two-and-one-half and six-and-one-half years of age were divided by Hicks into two groups on the basis of their initial ability in throwing balls at a moving target. The experimental group practiced ten throws once a week for eight weeks. Thereafter, both groups were retested and found to have made gains. However, the experimental group was not significantly better in performance than was the control group who received no practice. It would appear that improvement in skill did not result from the specific practice in throwing balls, which the one group had, but resulted from maturation, general practice, or autogenous learning. Autogenous learning refers to the fact that undoubtedly the children in both groups, whether or not they were actually throwing at a moving target, were, in the course of their daily living, practicing many of the coordinations of body, eye, arm, and hand that are utilized in the complex skill of hitting a moving target. As far as clarity of results is concerned, this complicating factor of autogenous learning appears to be an insuperable obstacle to a clear demonstration of maturational effects with children. Specific practice may be instituted by the experimenter or parent, but the child continues to live and learn (practice) in ways which probably affect the results obtained. Nevertheless, it is plausible to believe that some effects of maturation are still present after allowance is made.

Stages of Motor Development

It should be evident that a given motor skill may be considered as passing through stages beginning with nonachievement, or absence of skill, through various degrees of proficiency. In examining motor development in young children, the nature of its stages will be considered first. Gutteridge (31), in connection with some research to be considered in a moment, developed a rating scale defining steps of motor development. Specific motor skills of a child may be evaluated against this scale, one by one. Table 9 is adapted from her work.

TABLE 9

DEGREES OF MOTOR SKILL *

Stage	Degree of Motor Skill
No attempt made	1. Withdraws or retreats when opportunity is given.
	2. Makes no approach nor attempt but does not withdraw.
Skill in process of formation	3. Attempts activity but seeks help or support.
	4. Tries even when not helped or supported, but is inadept.
	5. Is progressing but is still using unnecessary movements.
	6. Is practising basic movements.
	7. In process of refining movements.
Basic movements achieved	8. Movements coordinated.
	9. Easy performance with display of satisfaction.
	10. Evidence of accuracy, poise, and grace.
Skillful execution with variations in use	A. Tests skill by adding difficulties or taking chances.
	B. Combines activity with other skill or skills.
	C. Speeds, races, or competes with self or others.
	D. Uses skill in larger projects such as dramatic play.

* Adapted from Gutteridge (31). Copyright 1939 by the Archives of Psychology, and published with permission.

Four general stages of major motor development are indicated: the first stage in which no attempt is made to carry out the motor skill in question; the second stage in which the skill is the process of formation; the third stage in which the basic movements have been achieved; and the fourth stage in which there is skillful execution with variation in its use. Within each stage there are various degrees of skill. The use of initial letters beyond the first ten numbered degrees of skill indicates her recognition that beyond the point in the scale which indicates skilled performances the child uses his skills in all sorts of variations of the activity executed, despite no further increase in proficiency. Hence, it is only in the first three stages that we have degrees of increase in skill in any strict sense. A rating of eight or better on her scale is considered as indicating the child is proficient in the particular motor skill. Although another investigator might use another way of formulating the stages and degrees of motor skill, her scale has enough generality to be of significance quite apart from the research in which it has been used. These four major stages and their related, more precisely defined degrees of motor skill are considered applicable to the motor skills of childhood in general.

Some changes in motor skills. Gutteridge (*31*) used ratings of these degrees of motor skill in an investigation of various activities of nearly 2000 children, most of whom were four, five, and six years of age. The motor activities which she studied were climbing, jumping, sliding, tricycling, hopping, galloping, skipping, throwing, bouncing and catching balls. Teachers, trained as raters, made the necessary observations in the natural settings of classroom and playground. No attempt at special training in these motor skills was given; the children's own "methods of attack" were studied. The degree of proficiency exhibited by the children at each age level was ascertained for each activity. Four of these activities have been selected as exemplifying her results.

Climbing is already proficient (in the sense of the term as earlier defined) at the end of the third year in nearly 60 per cent of the children. By the end of the sixth year, 97 per cent were proficient. Among the children there was considerable variability; a child or two in the sample were proficient before reaching two years of age, while 3 per cent of them were still not proficient even at the end of the sixth year. The children she studied climbed on every conceivable piece of equipment whether it was designed for this purpose or not. Anything with height might become a challenge to climb. Most of them climbed as high as opportunity afforded. Some "stunting" occurred even at as young an age as two years.

Jumping was proficient in 40 per cent of the children by the age of three-and-a-half, while about 85 per cent were efficient by the age of six. There was a sharp rise in the percentage, showing proficiency from the youngest aged child to that of the four years, six-months-old children for whom the median rating was nine. From this age on, there was relatively little rise in proficiency since for the oldest or six-year group the median rating was only a little over nine. Variability was considerable at all ages. In the five-year group the range covered nine of the ten possible points, while even in the six-year group it still covered six points.

Tricycling was an accomplishment in which at three years of age, 63 per cent of the children were proficient, while by four years of age 100 per cent were proficient. Stunting with a tricycle was very evident as most mothers know; riding backwards, turning corners, and navigating narrow spaces were common.

Ball-throwing was a motor skill in which even some of the two- and three-year-old children showed proficiency. By the end of the sixth year, about 85 per cent were proficient. Range of achievement at all ages, even the oldest, extended from awkward to excellent.

These, then, are some representative findings on the development of some motor skills in preschool children in relation to chronological age. It is pertinent to consider comparative skill among the activities at a given age. In general, her study indicates that a fair proportion of children are proficient in some motor activities before the age of three years, ranging from 17 per cent in tricycling to 50 per cent in sliding. However, proficient use of balls and control of movements in such activities as hopping, skipping, and galloping do not appear before age four or five.

Sex differences and variations with individual children were found. Boys are ahead of girls in climbing, jumping, sliding, skipping, and ball-throwing; girls are more proficient in tricycling, galloping, hopping, bouncing and catching balls. Variation within each child from one skill to another was also noticeable, although Gutteridge states there is some evidence of consistency of pattern. This consistency appeared to be tendencies for each child to use certain kinds of motor movements to the relative exclusion of other kinds. This question of consistency or interrelation among motor abilities needs more detailed consideration.

Interrelation Among Motor Skills

There is some question as to whether or not it is appropriate to speak of motor skills as showing a considerable degree of interrelation, one skill with another. Some workers would argue that there is a high and positive interrelation among motor skills. For example, Ames (1), as a consequence of studying manual and locomotor behavior in infants, stated that slow creeping means slow climbing and slow prehending. Bayley (5) found considerable evidence of substantial correlations among infant motor abilities. However, she suggested there is a possibility that motor functions at later ages are more discrete and independent than in infancy.

The evidence would tend to bear out Bayley's suggestion that there is greater functional independence of motor abilities at the preschool ages than is the case during infancy. A representative study is that of Hartman (34) who studied a variety of gross motor coordinations in about 60 boys and girls who were between four and six years of age. The motor tests she used were the hurdle jump, jump-and-reach, standing broad jump, baseball throw, and the thirty-five-yard dash. After establishing the proficiency of each child, she intercorrelated the achievement scores of the children. She found intercorrelations ranging between only 0.36 and 0.56. Hartman concluded (correctly in the writer's opinion) that different motor abilities were being sampled rather than a general motor ability. A child who is high in one motor skill may not be high in another motor skill. A child may even be quite unskilled in one motor performance and still do quite well in others. Or, to put it in terms of specific skills, knowing a child's skill in baseball throw does not enable one to predict with any degree of certainty what he would do on the hurdle jump. One cannot speak of "motor ability"; rather there are motor abilities with a child excelling in one not necessarily excelling in another.

This point of view receives support from factor analytic studies. If motor ability were a unitary matter, then factor analysis should show the existence of a general motor factor. Instead, often several group factors emerge when this matter is studied in children. For example, using 250 children from the first three grades, aged six through ten as subjects, Carpenter (12) applied a battery of motor tests. She intercorrelated the measures she obtained with the children and then performed a factor analysis. She found three factors—a strength factor, a speed factor, and a factor of sensory-motor coordination that was associated with ball-handling. Disregarding this last more limited group factor, a speed factor and a strength factor are often isolated as they were in this study. It would seem that at least two of the major components of motor ability are speed and strength. Strength measures seem to be interrelated and speed measures seem to be interrelated, but there appears to be much less relation between those for strength and those for speed.

Presumably other factors, perhaps not yet isolated, are operative in determining motor ability. At any rate, one would expect that more elusive possible determinants such as interest or lack of interest, willingness or unwillingness to take a chance, intrepidity or timidity in the face of a challenging activity, and self-confidence or the lack of it might influence proficiency in motor skills. However, the evidence concerning the influence of these determinants is either nonexistent or confusingly contradictory. Thus, little more is possible than the guess that it may be established that they do influence motor skill. Speed and strength, at any rate, are factors in the motor skills of early childhood.

Emotional development in early childhood

The emotional patterns of early childhood continue the process of change which was found in infancy, and the emphasis in the present discussion will be upon the developmental changes taking place. These patterns, although showing some effects of maturation, are primarily acquired through learning. In fact, each of the patterns may be considered learned drives since they can motivate behavior and their reduction can reinforce learning.

In discussing emotional reactions in infancy, it was indicated that Bridges found that there were two streams of emotional differentiations arising from the original state of excitement. One of these led through distress, the first to emerge, then to anger, disgust, fear, and jealousy. Emotional patterns from this stream are unpleasant, disruptive emotional states. Out of excitement also emerged delight, and later, elation, affection, and joy. These emotional patterns are pleasant and integrative. The distinction between unpleasant and disruptive emotional states on the one hand and the pleasant and integrative emotional states on the other will be continued in the present discussion. Anger and fear, the most important of the unpleasant, disruptive states, will be discussed first. Then the pleasant, integrative emotional states receive consideration.

Anger

In anger, the physiological responses in themselves, such as change in heart rate and blood pressure and tenseness and crying, are not learned, but appear to be innately determined. The relationship, however, between these responses and what at one time in the history of the child were neutral (nonemotional) cues is a matter of learning. Stimuli which originally did not elicit the physiological responses now do so. The child learns to be angry about certain situations which previously did not arouse these responses.

In a now classic study, Goodenough (30) investigated anger in 50 children (most of whom were of preschool age) in such a definitive fashion that her results merit detailed discussion. The cooperation of the mothers of these children was secured in gathering information about anger. The mothers kept daily records of the anger incidents that occurred, noting the time, the place, and the duration of the outburst, the immediate cause, and the kinds of behavior the children exhibited. Records were kept for periods extending from about one to four months. In this fashion, Goodenough collected over 1800 instances of anger outbursts. The results she found from the analysis of these anger outbursts will be used in the following sections to demonstrate a variety of findings about anger in young children.

Developmental changes in expressions of anger. Goodenough classified the expressions of anger in these children in two ways. The first approach was more global and consisted of classification in terms of the direction the energy was expended. She found she could classify the direction of energy in the anger outbursts into three major categories: (1) undirected energy—anger not directed toward any end except that of an emotional outlet, such as in kicking randomly, holding the breath, and screaming; (2) motor or verbal resistance—anger expressed in opposing doing what was asked, such as verbal refusal or resisting being held; and (3) retaliation—anger expressed in motor or verbal attempts at revenge, such as biting the agent or giving him a verbal scolding. With increasing age, there was a steady decline in expression of anger in undirected energy, no consistent trend in connection with expression through motor or verbal resistance, and an increase in expression through retaliating behavior.

These age trends appear to verify common observations concerning undirected discharge of anger as characterizing younger, immature children and an increase in retaliative behavior with increasing age. Failure to separate motor from verbal resistance may have obscured the possibility that motor resistance decreased with age as verbal resistance increased. Goodenough concluded that, as the child grows older, there is an increase in anger overtly directed toward a source of anger and a decrease in mere random discharge. Thus, with increasing age expressions of anger are less random and more directed towards something or someone.

The second approach that she used took the form of study of the various specific acts associated with anger in younger children. Crying was the most frequently encountered form of vocal behavior up to about four years of age. Nevertheless, crying decreased fairly regularly with increase in age. Kicking decreased as well, but stamping increased slightly, whereas striking increased regularly and throwing self on floor increased until age three and four and then decreased. She found that these were the major specific acts during anger. Contrary to popular opinion, jumping up and down, stiffening the body, making the body limp, refusing to budge, and glaring "defiantly" were some of the less common forms of expressing anger at these ages. Holding the breath also belongs in this less common category since only four instances occurred in the 1800 outbursts that she studied.

Developmental changes in frequency and duration of anger outbursts. Goodenough also studied developmental changes in frequency and duration of anger with the same children. Figure 9 presents her findings on age and sex differences in the frequency of anger outbursts. Omitting the findings for children under one year of age because of the small number of cases (two children), rapid decrease is found in anger outbursts with increasing age from the initial high point at the age of one-and-a-half years. The sharp decline in anger with increase in age probably reflects the older child's increasing sensitivity to social demands and increasing ability to meet frustration by forms of behavior other than anger. A consistent sex difference, with girls showing less anger outbursts, is also apparent. The results support the contention, often made, that boys are more difficult to raise than girls. It also represents a difference in the sex roles, with boys showing the expected greater amount of aggressiveness. Further discussion of sex roles will be deferred until the next chapter.

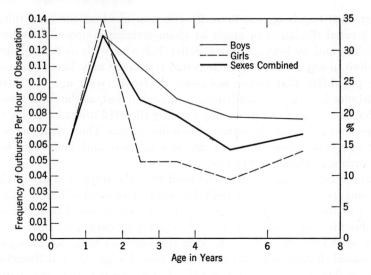

Figure 9. Frequency of anger outbursts as related to age and sex (Florence L. Goodenough, Anger in Young Children. *Copyright 1931 by the University of Minnesota.)*

According to Goodenough's findings, the duration of specific anger outbursts underwent little change during the first eight years of life. In other words, there was no particular evidence of decrease or increase in duration as age increased. It is noteworthy that of the over 1800 outbursts she studied, fewer than one-third persisted for as long as five minutes.

Developmental changes in the immediate causes of anger. During this age period, Goodenough found certain categories of immediate causes of anger to encompass adequately her findings. Before dealing with developmental changes, these categories will be described. Three are especially prominent. These she categorized as anger produced in connection with: (1) *conflicts over routine physical habits,* such as objection to going to the toilet, to bed, to coming to meals, or to having the face washed; (2) *conflicts with authority,* such as the child's negative response to being refused permission to carry out some activity, to being forbidden some on-going activity, to being punished, and to having to take the logical consequences of his own act; and (3) *problems of social relationship,* such as being denied attention, inability to make desires understood, a blocking of desires to share in the activities of others, an unwillingness to share, or a desire for someone else's possession. In terms of the percentage of the total number of anger outbursts at all ages, those in connection with routine physical care made up over 20 per cent, conflicts with authority nearly 20 per cent, and problems of social relationship nearly 30 per cent. These three immediate causes of anger totaled nearly 70 per cent of all the incidents the mothers reported.

Developmental changes in anger with age will now be considered. A few of her children were under two years of age, making possible a comparative account involving later infancy as well as childhood. During the second year, she found the major source of anger to be conflict over establishment of routine physical habits. Almost equally prevalent was anger brought about by conflict with authority over matters other than routine physical habits, such as their objections to going to bed, coming to meals, or brushing their teeth. Together, these two conflict categories included over 50 per cent of anger outbursts at this age. Problems of social relationship represented still another important source of frustration. She found at this age that problems arising from provocations to anger, from matters of self-help, minor physical discomforts, and "fears" or restriction of bodily movements were relatively infrequent. In children between the ages of three and four, social difficulties, particularly difficulties with playmates, reached their maximum, accounting for nearly 45 per cent of all outbursts. Conflicts with authority and over routine physical habits account for an additional 35 per cent. In children four years and older, social problems continue to be the largest single category. Conflict with authority account for 35 per cent of the anger outbursts. A heretofore unmentioned category, problems of self-help, in which the child becomes angry at his own ineptitude, accounts for over 10 per cent of the outbursts at this age.

It will have been noted that Goodenough studied anger in the home situation only. Anger, even at these ages, may appear in other social settings, particularly the nursery school. A study by Landreth (48) investigated anger in this setting as well as in the home. At home, nearly 40 per cent of the anger outbursts she found were related to conflicts with persons and about the same per cent related to personal care routines (where a parent was present in the situation). In the nursery school, on the other hand, about 75 per cent of all outbursts involved social conflicts with other children or with adults. A more detailed breakdown shows that in the home conflicts were most often with adults, but that in the nursery school they were most often with other children.   In another study, Ricketts (68) found similar results concerning the relative differences in the source of anger in nursery school and in the home.   These two studies, as well as that of Good-enough, attest to the increased importance as age increased of social conflict as the immediate cause of anger in younger children.   More detailed examination of the social facets of anger will be considered in Chapter 12 in connection with conflict behavior.

General conditions for the appearance of anger.   In examining the circumstances under which anger arises, two major factors must be taken into account—the nature of the immediate disturbing circum-stances and the general conditions prevailing at the time.   The former factor has just been considered, the latter now merits attention.   The activity which the child is engaged in at the moment affects his re-sponse to the immediate disturbing circumstance.   In other words, it is not simply some stimulus to anger alone which we must consider, but also the on-going activity and state of the child at the time the immediate cause for anger occurs.   A hungry child playing desultorily is not angered by the call to lunch, but a child not so hungry and engrossed in his play as well may be angered by this same call.   In this instance, the appearance or nonappearance of anger may be pre-dicted as a resultant of the relative strength of hunger and of a desire to play.   Other factors, such as his general physical condition, may also enter in such situations.   For example, a hungry child who has a cold may react angrily to the call to lunch even if not particularly wrapped up in his playing.

Goodenough in her study found that general conditions that lower the threshold for anger include amount of sleep, general physical con-dition, special unusual occurrences in the home, the size and com-position of the family, the hour of the day, and the like.   When these conditions were related to the frequency of the anger outbursts, she found that the frequency of anger outbursts was positively related to: (1) *the time of day,* in the sense that more anger outbursts occurred at certain hours, namely, either before mealtime or after eight in the evening when fatigue had set in; (2) *condition of temporary poor health,* such as the child having a cold or being constipated; and (3) *atypical social conditions,* such as the presence in the home of visitors (both adults and children or a family in which there were several adults rather than only the mother and father).   A comment by Goodenough in connection with these factors is quoted here.

It should be noted that the establishment of a relationship between any or all of these factors and the frequency or duration of anger outbursts does not always afford evidence as to the essential nature of the relationship. An increased number of outbursts may be due either to the increased irritability of the child himself, causing him to become disturbed over minor conditions that would ordinarily be ignored, or to external factors involving an increase in the irritating conditions to which the child is subjected. Variations in the frequency of anger may thus be brought about either by internal conditions resulting in differential responses to constant stimuli or by external conditions affecting the frequency and intensity of the annoyances to which the subject is exposed. Although the nature of the factor under consideration in many instances enables us to infer with a fair degree of certainty whether its major influence is external or internal, there are other cases in which either or both types of influence may be at work (30, 84–85).[1]

Her findings on the general conditions for the appearance of anger were not related by her to developmental change at specific ages because of technical difficulties. That is to say, what she reports are findings about general conditions for the appearance of anger during the preschool age in general, rather than as anger shows change with increase in age during that period.

Individuality in anger. In discussing anger in young children it must not be lost sight of that each child will give an individual stamp to his behavior when angry. He would differ in proportions of anger as to direction, frequency, duration, and susceptibility to general conditions. Consider Goodenough's classification of specific forms of angry behavior. Goodenough in her study of anger lists *among others* kicking, stamping, jumping up and down, throwing oneself on the floor, holding one's breath, pulling, struggling, pouting, frowning, throwing objects, grabbing, biting, striking, crying, and screaming. No child would be "talented" enough to display all these forms of becoming angry in one or in many settings. He would have his own particular repertoire with a definite preference for some and not for others. Moreover, with the passage of time, he would show his own unique changes in his repertoire of the acts used in expressing anger.

Anger and frustration-aggression. The most general conclusion to be drawn from the over-all results of the Goodenough study is that the most common source of anger she found are situations which interfere with the goal-seeking behavior of the children. In short, anger

[1] Florence L. Goodenough, *Anger in Young Children.* Copyright 1931, University of Minnesota.

is produced by frustration. In discussing this point Sears may be quoted:

> The theoretical derivation of aggression suggests that its origin lies in the effectiveness of producing pain in others as a method of removing their interference with goal-directed behavior. For example, if the mother fails to provide the child with food when he is hungry or with attention when he is seeking affection, he may strike her or cry loudly enough to make her uncomfortable.
>
> In order to eliminate this pain or discomfort, she may then give the child food or offer it affection. This reward act not only reinforces the early, and perhaps more or less random, acts of injuring the mother, but it does two additional things. First, it establishes the act of hurting, as exemplified by the mother's expressions of dislike or pain, as a secondary drive. Increasingly thereafter, with continuing reinforcement, the child therefore secures pleasure from injuring other persons. Second, the immediate stimulus situation that accompanied the rewarding act becomes an effective stimulus for eliciting the acts he used at that time. In other words, the child who is rewarded for his injurious acts develops a secondary drive of aggression (*i.e.*, to make a goal response of injuring others, the necessary environmental event being to see the expressions of pain), and he learns to repeat the act when he is frustrated.
>
> Goodenough also found, as have a number of other investigators, that not every aggressive or angry act was immediately preceded by a discernible frustration. This suggests that other stimulus aspects of the frustrating situation besides the fact of frustration itself, *i.e.*, the mother, mealtime, cross talk between parents, are sufficiently often associated with frustration to become the instigators to aggression (*71*, 230–231).[2]

This indirect relationship between anger (aggression) and frustration asserted by Sears is not in all instances demonstrated to exist. Until this rather unlikely possibility has occurred, it is probably the path of caution to accept the possibility that there are multiple causes of anger. True, children may show anger when needs are frustrated, but the general conditions that lower the threshold for anger found by Goodenough such as poor health also appear to be operative as aspects of the dynamics of anger.

Fear

Fear in young children will be discussed in almost the same topical format as was anger. Developmental changes in the expression of fear will be discussed first. Presentation of developmental changes in

[2] From Sears (*71*). Copyright 1953 by Henry Holt and Company, and published with permission.

the frequency of fear, in the immediate causes of fear, and in the general conditions of fear arousal will follow. Discussion of the relation of fear and anxiety will close the presentation.

As a means of centering discussion, the studies of fear by Jersild and Holmes (45) will serve in the same fashion as did Goodenough's study of anger. In their work there were two major phases to be referred to, the observational and the experimental study, respectively. In the first study they had parents record on observation forms all situations in which their children displayed fear during a 21-day or longer period. The nearly 140 children who were observed for fear incidents ranged in age from under one year to slightly over 12 years of age. The procedure in this study was much the same as Goodenough's. In the second or experimental study, other children, aged from two to six years, were invited to enter into situations, such as coming into a dark room, which were known to be effective in causing fear in at least some children of this age. How they behaved when they participated or when they refused to participate in these situations was studied.

Developmental changes in expressions of fear. In Chapter 6, in discussing emotions in infancy, it was indicated that fear was found by Bridges to differentiate from the "distressed" pattern at about six months of age. Since no systematic discussion of fear has been given, it is appropriate to consider fear as expressed in later infancy as well as later manifestations. As might be expected on the basis of our knowledge of the work of Bridges (8), fear in later infancy is expressed in a global rather than a specific fashion. Crying, along with general bodily distress, characterizes fear at this age. In older infants, fear resembles more what we would call a state of panic in adults. Generally, the duration of this pattern is short in infants. They also show a remarkable resiliency in recovering from fear attacks.

As children become older, fear responses become increasingly specific. With increasing maturity fear becomes more often expressed in a withdrawing from the fearful situation. The preschool child runs away, avoids fear-provoking situations, or, when faced with such situations, uses verbal responses such as, "Take it away."

Developmental changes in frequency of fear. In the Jersild and Holmes parent-observation study they had mothers report any fears which they had noted in their children during a 21-day period of observation. The number of fears in the observation study shows a sharp decline with age after two years. For the group of two-year-olds, the average number of fears on the 21-day record was about six, but for the next year group the average number of fears was only 3.7. For the four-to-five-year group only two fears per child were reported. Variability, however, at any one age level is so great that some children at all ages deviated considerably from the average.

Since their experimental study was based on the study of *selected* fears, there may have been an inclusion of fears to which children of certain ages were relatively more susceptible. ⌐Consequently, all we can say from examining Table 10 is that for the fears included in

TABLE 10

PERCENTAGE OF CHILDREN AT YEARLY AGE LEVELS WHO SHOWED FEAR IN RESPONSE TO THE VARIOUS EXPERIMENTAL FEAR SITUATIONS *

	Age in Months			
	24–35	36–47	48–50	60–71
Situation	Percentage Showing Fear	Percentage Showing Fear	Percentage Showing Fear	Percentage Showing Fear
Being left alone	12.1	15.6	7.0	0
Falling boards	24.2	8.9	0	0
Dark room	46.9	51.1	35.7	0
Strange person	31.3	22.2	7.1	0
High boards	35.5	35.6	7.1	0
Loud sound	22.6	20.0	14.3	0
Snake	34.8	55.6	42.9	30.8
Large dog	61.9	42.9	42.9	0
Average	32.0	30.2	18.1	4.5

* Adapted from Jersild and Holmes (45). Copyright 1935 by Teachers College, Columbia University, and published with permission.

this study the two- and three-year-olds showed about an equal amount of fear, whereas the four- and five-year-olds showed a considerable decrease. The two aspects of their study consequently show no particular discrepancies.

⌐The decrease in frequency of fear must be related to developmental changes in the expression of fear. The diminution of overt signs of fear—the characteristic crying, trembling, shrinking away or retreating—does not necessarily mean that there is no longer as much fear as before in the life of the child. The decline in fear that they found may be a decline only in overt expression of emotion similar to that already noted in the case of anger. In our culture social pressures against displaying fear are operative. Moreover, many of the more symbolic fears to be found characteristic of the older child leaves him with nothing to "flee" from, since such fears do not have as definite a locus as do the earlier more specific fears. Transitory feelings, a minor tremor soon concealed, a slight trembling of the lip, clammy hands, and the like may be the only expressions of fear now displayed. These manifestations of fear are easier to overlook than are the more frank, obvious, open ones shown at a younger age. Fear is still shown; the overt manifestations produced have declined in frequency.

In the experimental study of Jersild and Holmes, intelligence and sex differences were found to be related to the number of fears the children expressed. There was a correlation of .53 between intelligence and number of fears for the children in the 24 to 35 months' range. In other words, the smarter the child at this age, the greater the instances of fear that he showed in their standardized situations. This relation may be seen as to be expected if one considers that fear arises in part after appraising a situation for its dangerous qualities. Some children, more advanced intellectually than the others of the same age, were able to perceive danger where the other children did not. Since intelligence is at least partly a matter of maturation, it suggests that maturation plays a role in children's fears. A precocious child is afraid of situations that do not disturb other children of the same age until they are older. For the specific situations they studied, the correlation between fear and intelligence declined to almost zero by the age of five. By that age all of the children were able to perceive each of the fearsome aspects of these situations, so intelligence was no longer a factor. Note that this may hold only for the specified situations. Other situations might be found where the relation between intelligence and number of fears again became a positive one.

In almost every situation of the Jersild and Holmes study the percentage of girls of a given age who showed fear was found to be higher than the percentage of boys. This finding of greater fear in girls is in keeping with general observation that girls tend to show more fear than do boys.

Developmental changes in the immediate causes of fear. The immediate causes of fear in the experimental study have already been presented in Table 10. Those selected, namely, fears of being left alone, falling boards, a dark room, a strange person, the possibility of falling from high boards, a loud sound, a snake, and a large dog, with one exception, show a decrease with age. Indeed, in all except one of these situations, no child between five and six years of age showed fear in any of them. Undoubtedly, some children could be found who showed fear in these particular situations but, presumably, they would be a small minority. Fear decreased for the situations studied. Only the fear of snakes was manifested by roughly the same percentage of children throughout the ages studied with no tendency to decline.

The findings concerning the fear situations found in the observational study are reported in Table 11. Many fears show either a steady fall (noises and falling) or an irregular fall (animals, sudden rapid motion, and strange objects) with age. Except for fear of strange objects, no child older than five years of age showed fear in any of three situations just mentioned. Other fears (pain, the dark, harm, and being alone) show an increase with age.

Those fears that decline and those that increase with age form two roughly distinguishable groups. Fear of tangible immediate situations decline with age. This includes fear of noises, specific objects, falling and danger of falling, strange objects, and the like. Fears of a more symbolic kind, such as fear of imaginary creatures, of the dark, of being alone, and so on, increase with age.

In the experimental study only selected situations were used. They were of tangible, immediate situations and again a decline with age was found. More symbolic situations are by the nature of the situations harder for an experimenter to arrange. Even the dark room situation does not qualify in this instance. Experimenters found that fear of the dark room declined with age, but here it was a dark room with the presence of an adult not more than about 18 feet away whose presence would be more reassuring to the older children. So, fear of the dark, which increases with age in the observational study, is not contradicted by their finding in the experimental study. The fear of the infant and younger child is of the tangible events and situations in his immediate environment (43). As he grows older, his perceptual and intellectual prowess increases. The preschool child is afraid not only of more things but of different things than is the infant. As intelligence increases, he begins to recognize

TABLE 11

SITUATIONS IN RESPONSE TO WHICH FEAR WAS SHOWN *

Situation in Response to which Fear Was Shown	Per Cent of Fears Occurring at Each Age					
Age in Months	0–11	12–23	24–35	36–47	48–59	60–97
Number of children	8	23	45	46	22	9
Number of fears	25	75	151	99	49	17
Animals (not including imaginary animals)	8	10.7	11.9	21.5	18.4	0
Sudden rapid motion, lights, flashes, shadows, reflections	8	5.3	11.3	6.1	4.1	0
Noises, events associated with noise, and noise plus motion	24	18.7	17.2	19.4	12.2	0
Falling, heights, danger of falling, sudden or gradual displacement	12	10.7	9.9	6.1	6.1	0
Pain, persons, objects, situations inflicting or associated with pain and tactual shock	8	16	6	7.1	6.1	29.4
Strange objects, situations, and persons	16	16	15.9	14.3	8.2	5.9
Harm, danger of bodily injury, falling	12	10.7	9.9	16.2	14.3	17.6
The dark and being alone in the dark	0	2.7	3.3	4.1	4.1	11.8
Being alone or abandoned by parents	0	4	2.6	4.1	4.1	5.9
Imaginary creatures	0	4	2.6	2	10.2	5.9

* Adapted from Jersild and Holmes (45). Copyright 1935 by Teachers College, Columbia University, and published with permission.

potential, real, and imaginary danger which he had not recognized before. Meanings, not before open to him, become part of his behavior reportoire. As stressed by the psychoanalysts (see Chapter 5) fantasy life becomes increasingly prominent at about age four or thereabouts. As his symbolic linguistic and conceptual prowess increases, the nature of his fears changes; hence, the increase in fears of imaginary creatures, the dark, and of being alone. By the same token, an increase in intelligence and in general knowledge renders him less susceptible to fears of tangible objects, noises, and falling. The fear of strangeness decreases in that not so many things are strange any more. The bell of the ice cream vendor may startle the infant but is known for what it is by a five-year-old.

General conditions for the appearance of fear. Up to this point fear has been examined as if its expression was independent of any other aspects of the situation (with the exception of the discussion of intelligence). This omission has painted too simplified a picture. Aspects of the situation other than the "fear" stimulus itself help to determine whether fear will or will not be shown. Consider for a moment the percentage changes with age found for fear of snakes. The fear of snakes rises substantially from what it was before between three and four years of age. Then this particular fear declines. At first (in infancy) there is no fear of snakes, then at the age of two or three a snake is perceived as a potentially dangerous, noxious stimuli which increases to a peak at three or four. With increasing experience the still older child recognizes that the snake is non-dangerous *in the particular situation in which it is seen.* A similar explanation could be offered of the situation, "being alone," which shows a similar rise and fall. Both seeing a snake and being alone might, under other situational circumstances, bring about fear in these same children. The study of Arsenian (2) described on page 417 shows the fearsomeness of a strange situation when the child was alone. With the mother's reassuring presence the child was not afraid in an otherwise identical situation.

These considerations of the effect of the general situation have implications for the findings concerning the immediate causes of fear discussed in the preceding section. As Jersild and Holmes (45) indicate, the circumstances eliciting fear often include considerably more than the immediate stimulus, such as a noise. If the child hears a noise when accompanied by an unfamiliar adult or when alone, the response may be fear, whereas if he is in the company of a trusted adult, the same noise may produce no emotional response whatsoever.

Since most fears are learned, it is plausible to believe that some fears that children show are acquired from the behavior of their parents. Hagman (32), on investigating this hypothesis, found a relationship between the nature of the fears of the mothers and those of their children. He interviewed the mothers of 70 preschool-aged boys and girls about their own and their children's fears. There was a distinct tendency for the child to have the same fears as his mother, particularly fears concerning dogs, insects, and storms. To give more point and meaning to this positive correlation, let us consider a specific example of what might be happening in the situations which give rise to these complementary fears. Suppose a child unexpectedly hears a barking dog. No matter what, he will be afraid for just a moment if the situation is new or strange. But if the mother handles the situation calmly, the fear passes rapidly. But suppose she, too, is frightened by dogs. Consequently, she cries out and makes a fuss. His fear may then persist thereafter to the extent that it contributes to a correlation that has just been given between the fears of children in relation to those of their mothers.

Jersild (44), in a summarization of the studies of fear with which he has been associated, considers that there are three major ways in which fear is aroused in relation to the fear situation. In each instance he is considering how the child learns to be afraid. First, there is a specific relation in which persisting fears can be traced to the event itself. For example, a child is bitten by a dog and thereafter fears that dog. Second, the child may respond with fear not only to the specific stimulus, but also to aspects of the situation in which the fear took place. A child bitten by a dog not only fears the dog, but also is afraid to go into the neighborhood where he was bitten. Or he may be afraid, not only of the dog who bit him, but of other dogs as well. Third, the child may respond in an indirect and generalized way. Bitten by the dog, he has a bad dream that night, and, thereafter, is afraid to go into his bedroom in the dark. This formulation of the ways in which the child learns to be afraid appears to be both plausible and adequate.

Fear and anxiety. Anxiety is related to fear. Although we will have occasion later to use more specific and technical applications of the term, anxiety may be conceived as fear in which the source of the fear is vague or somehow obscured. In other words, the person, child or adult is not clearly aware of what he is being fearful. In this sense the source of the fear, but not the emotional state itself, may be said to be unconscious. Since this awareness of the source is not present, it follows that the situation about which one is fearful is not directly and immediately present to consciousness (at least not in the form which generates the emotion). Hence, anxiety is anticipatory. The child is anxious about the visit to the dentist and fearful in the dentist's office. It is this anticipatory element which Mowrer (55) stresses. He argues that anxiety is a learned response that enables individuals to face potentially harmful events in the advance of their occurrence. Sometimes, then, anxiety is adaptive in that it permits us to do something about the situation in time to deal with it before it happens. A student anxious about an examination may consequently study. But often anxiety is debilitating, causing avoidance of the situation or fruitless anticipation of situations which are not really dangerous. In such cases, anxiety becomes pathological. In such instances, anxiety is even more generalized than it is in less pathological forms. Anxiety may pervade almost all aspects of one's life. Anxiety is sometimes described as "free-floating," which catches this latter aspect of the meaning of the term quite aptly. Anxiety is "in the air," the fear is related to something or somebody which cannot be precisely specified and which is not yet being directly encountered. Since anxiety is of great significance for the social and psychopathological aspects of the development of the child, it will be considered again in later chapters.

The Relation of Fear and Anger

Anger and fear are related in a variety of ways. Clinical observation often demonstrates that an apparently anxious or fearful child on closer examination will be found to be one in whom his anxiety is a mask for considerable anger and aggressiveness. Conversely, an apparently "cocky" (angry) child may be found essentially to be a very frightened child. Quite apart from such admixtures, sometimes an individual vacillates between fear and anger as when he faces a disagreeable situation first by attack but, on this failing, flees from it only to return to attack later. Or, on "being cornered," a child previously afraid may find himself angry and therefore attack.

This intimate relationship between fear and anger is useful in describing conflict in learning on the part of children. Dollard and Miller (22), for example, trace how fear becomes attached to anger cues. Anger on the part of the adult produces punishment, and hence the situation becomes one in which the fear of punishment may outweigh the anger. It is their contention that this often happens during the period of toilet training. Presumably, anger may become attached to fear cues as well, as in an instance where a child who is originally afraid of an older child finds his fear unnecessary and now finds himself angry.

The relative frequency of fear and anger in preschool children has been investigated by Felder (24). He found that anger outbursts were far more frequent than were displays of fear. It is plausible to believe that we live in a society in which we protect our children from fear situations while exposing them more to anger-provoking situations. Also it is probable that the higher incidence of observed anger is due to our relatively greater emphasis on a child concealing his fear while permitting him to express his anger more openly. At any rate, it is not uncommon to find greater instances of anger than of fear in preschool children.

The physiological changes occurring in anger cannot clearly be differentiated from those of fear (11), but the overt behavior of these emotional patterns is dramatically different in direction. As Goodenough puts it, "Fear is emotional avoidance; anger is emotional attack" (30, 48–49). In general, fear behavior takes the form of avoidance or escape, while anger is characterized by approach-attack in motor or verbal aggression.

Both anger and fear are disruptive emotions. Despite their behavior directional difference, they are related as outlined earlier. They are similar in that they are unpleasant and represent the disruptive aspects of emotional development. There is no doubt that much unhealthful psychological development is attributable to their disruptive character. Indeed, physical changes as well as psychological can be attributed to their functioning. To some extent this has already been made clear in discussing psychosomatic relationships in disturbed infants in Chapter 8. To this theme we will return in Chapter 13 in connection with psychological disturbances of early and late childhood.

Jealousy

Some more complicated emotional patterns also involve an intermingling of anger and fear. Jealousy, a compounding of anger and fear along with more positive emotional components, illustrates this intermingling. Jealousy is a socially oriented emotional response compounded of anger, fear, and love. It is discussed now because there is evidence (43) that jealousy is most common and most pervasive in its effects during this age period. It comes into being when the child is threatened by loss of love because of the presence of someone who apparently or actually diverts love from him. The classic instance of jealousy in young children is the presence of a newly born sibling because of the mother's preoccupation with the infant. There is no question that a loss for the older child does take place. Baldwin (3) in a study of 46 expectant mothers applied the Fels Scale for child centeredness and found a substantial loss in this centeredness of the older sibling during and after pregnancy. Loss of her time and attention is equated by the child with loss of love and he becomes jealous, seeing the younger sibling as a rival. The young child, already experiencing the presence of a struggle over antithetical needs of dependence and independence, now has the additional burden of a rival. He witnesses the infant enjoying a dependency which he is struggling to outgrow. It is hardly surprising that regressive behavior is not uncommon in a child faced with a new brother or sister—lapsing into baby talk, stuttering, bed wetting, night terrors, and negativism (50).

Aggression toward the young sibling is not uncommon. Siblings are in close contact and in a rivalry position. One might say aggression is inevitable in the socially maladroit child. Tipping the bassinet, accidentally or otherwise (73), may occur. This aggression, however, is often admixed with genuine affection toward the brother or sister. Ambivalence is the result. An excerpt from a doll-play study by Baruch is illustrative. It is drawn from the play of Flora, two years and nine months old, who has a six-weeks-old baby sister. She had been supplied with the usual familiar dolls. To quote:

> After the worker has helped her to identify the dolls, Flora picks up the baby and places it in the bed. She puts the mother next to the baby. Lays the father down on the couch and puts Flora next to him. Takes the mother out of bed and puts her with the father on the couch. . . . Puts the baby on the toilet. Shoves her down into the toilet and tries to shut the toilet lid on her. Then takes her out rather vigorously. . . . Pulls the baby's arms and legs and then puts her in the bed and puts herself next to her.
>
> She then moves the mother into the bed next to herself, and the father into the bed next to the baby. After a few seconds, she takes the father out of the bed. Then takes the mother out of the bed. Takes Flora out of the bed, too, thus leaving the baby alone in the bed. Then picks up the baby and again puts her in the toilet, stuffing her vigorously in.
>
> Flora next puts the father and the mother back into the bed and places the doll representing herself between them. Shoves the baby into the toilet further. Tries to shut the lid of the toilet, but the baby doll is too large for it to go entirely down. Finally she takes the baby out of the toilet and puts her in bed between the mother and the father, moving Flora to the father's side.

Next she puts Flora quickly on and off the toilet and puts her back into the bed, in between the parents, lifting the baby out as she puts herself in.

She violently crams the baby into the toilet. Again tries vigorously to shut the lid. . . . Presses the baby further down into the toilet. Presses more. Then takes the baby out of the toilet and moves her toward the bed. Hesitates as though she were going to put her into the bed. Then finally does put her in, placing her—not lying down with the others as before—but at Flora's feet. Leaves her there for only an instant. Then she grabs the baby up and throws her into the box, which is empty and which stands at the far end of the couch. Goes back to the bed. Pets the Flora doll. Then stands and smiles down at the arrangement of Flora lying between the two parents. Nor does Flora retrieve the baby again. She leaves her in the box, where she had got rid of her, until the end of the play (4, 573–574).[3]

The play brings out vividly how at one moment she is trying to give the baby a place in the home and the next to get rid of her.

Aggression, regression, and ambivalence do not exhaust the reactions of jealousy. Vollmer (73), for example, illustrates with case excerpts how confusions in identification may occur, withdrawal from the beloved person may take place, repression of any feeling of jealousy may come about, sublimation may predominate, creative competition may be carried on, and even masochism may result.

We now turn from the disruptive unpleasant emotions to the affectively pleasant emotions.

Affectively Pleasant Emotions

It will be remembered that Bridges found that delight was the first of the affectively pleasant emotions to differentiate from excitement. This she found to occur somewhat before the third month. Before the infants reach 24 months of age, she also observed elation, affection, and joy. It is to these positive emotions that attention is now directed. Unfortunately, not very much research attention has been devoted to the study of emotional changes with growth in the affectively pleasant emotions. Perhaps this, in part, is because they have a less dramatic character than do anger and fear. Certainly, they are not marked by as severe or as extreme behavioral signs. Often their expressions are less spectacular, partaking more of the character of pleasant feelings than of the pronounced changes of fear and anger. Indeed, anything resembling the pronounced visceral

[3] From Baruch (4). Reprinted from *Mental Hygiene*, 1940, 24, with the permission of the National Association for Mental Health.

changes accompanying the disruptive emotions is not generally apparent. The visceral changes, although present in the affectively pleasant emotions, are often of so mild a character that they go unnoticed.

Smiling and laughter are the major external behavior indices of the pleasant emotions. Since these indices are observable and quantifiable, research has tended to focus on them. Smiling and laughter, however, are not always indicative of affectively pleasant emotions. One may smile or laugh as a social gesture, as an expression of scorn, or because of manifold other reasons not directly related to the pleasant emotional states. Since not all smiling and laughter are the results of pleasurable emotions, it follows that the available studies must be scrutinized carefully to see that one is really considering the affectively pleasant emotions and not some other source of these behavioral indices. Fortunately, children are not so given to these other uses of smiling and laughter as are adults.

Before turning to the research on laughter and smiling, it is pertinent to indicate that it is neither necessary nor profitable to present the many theories that have been offered for their explanation. In general, these theories are attempts to find one or few causes for laughter by analysis of the various more specific causes. Often they are offered in a philosophical vein, with but anecdotal evidence for their validity. For our purposes, there is no necessity of trying to reduce further the causes of smiling and laughter as demonstrated in the research studies by trying to find a superordinate level which reconciles and integrates them. In the presentation to follow, discussion of causes is at the specific level of the categories adopted by the research investigators themselves with merely some added comment on commonalities among their findings.

Incidental brief reference has already been made to smiling and laughter in the account of infancy. That account, however, by no means exhausted the important relevant research literature. Consequently, one or two studies will be briefly described so as to make it possible to consider the results on infants in indicating commonalities among the causes of laughter and smiling. Leuba (49), studying laughter in his own two infants, found that at about six or seven months smiling and laughter appeared in response to mild, intermittent tickling. Before the end of the first year, the laughter and smiling had been conditioned to the sight of the moving fingers (preparatory to tickling). Washburn (74) observed the development of laughter and smiling of 15 infants from eight weeks to one year of age at monthly intervals. By means of a check list, facial responses to a standard set of stimuli were obtained at each monthly observation. Some of the "stimuli" she used were (1) smiling, "chirruping," and talking to infant; (2) peek-a-boo; (3) threatening head (lowering of head toward infant and saying "ah boo"); (4) hand clapping; (5) sudden reappearance from under table; and (6) tickling. All of the stimuli she used were effective in producing smiles at one or more of the monthly age levels. However, some were more effective in producing laughter than others. Laughter in one-half or more of the subjects was produced by peek-a-boo, the threatening head, and hand clapping. Before commenting on the significance of these findings about infants, consideration will be given to some of the studies of laughter and smiling in preschool children.

The study of Justin (46) was specifically designed to test the various major theories of laughter that she had culled from the literature on the topic. The situation groupings depicting this classification of theories of laughter may be summarized as (1) surprise-defeated expectation; (2) superiority-degradation; (3) incongruity and contrast; (4) social smile as stimulus; (5) relief from strain; and (6) play. She devised test situations for each class of theory and then applied them all to nearly 100 children between the ages of three and six. She found that *some* children laughed in *all* of the situation groupings. Insofar as the situation she devised were tests of the theory on which it was presumably based, each theory accounted for some laughter. Some situation groupings were more effective than others, but as she indicates, she may have been more adroit in preparing situations appropriate to one theoretical position than she was in another. At any rate, the most effective were the social smile and the surprise situations which produced laughing in more than 90 per cent of the children, while the least effective was the relief from strain situation, which, however, still produced laughter in about 50 per cent of the children. Quite apart from the groupings by theory, she noted that situations in which the children were active participants, instead of being spectators, were the most effective in producing laughter.

Three other relevant studies of laughter were based on the observation of younger children in the nursery school-kindergarten situation. No attempt was made in any of them to direct or change the already on-going situations from which they derived their findings. Instead, the observers unobtrusively, but systematically, observed the children with particular attention to laughter-provoking situations.

Both Brackett (7) and Ding and Jersild (21) found that laughter occurred most often in social situations—situations in which the children were interacting with one another. Laughter was much less frequent when the children engaged in solitary play or parallel play (the latter being play in which both children use the same material, such as a sandbox, but did not apparently pay attention to or react with one another). To illustrate the importance of the social factor, Brackett found that almost 85 per cent of the laughter of her groups occurred in social settings. Moreover, laughter in a given child was predominantly found when laughter occurred in the other children who were present.

Ding and Jersild (21), in addition to noting the social setting of laughter, also collected considerable evidence that laughter occurred predominantly in connection with physical activity on the part of the children. The children they studied laughed most often when they were engaged in active physical play. Laughter, then, seemed to be related to having a motor outlet.

Blatz and his associates (6) also studied laughter in the nursery school setting. They were particularly interested in laughter associated with performing certain activities—falling, using the swing, climbing on the jungle gym, going down the slide, and the like. They found that almost always the laughter occurred *after* the completion of an event, that is, after the child had reached the bottom of the slide, after he had jumped into the pool, after he had fallen, after a toy he had thrown actually landed in the water, and so on. They consider that their results indicated that laughter comes when a conflict of some sort has been resolved. That is, the activity the child was engaging in had reached a solution and the conflict about whether or not the desired result would happen was resolved by its completion. At the top of the slide, for example, there is a tiny element of danger. When a child arrives at the bottom unhurt, he laughs. Their other results, in the main, permit this interpretation although some are more complicated to interpret, involving as they do anticipation of the completion of the act. At any rate, they would emphasize the solution to the activity, rather than the activity itself, as being the cause of laughter.

It is now necessary to summarize the major findings of these studies concerning the sources of pleasurable emotions in infants and young children. It should be emphasized that the summarizing statements to follow, although perhaps plausible, are not in any way the result of definite research. Some of the findings are those of but one study.

No one research study has submitted all of the sources of these pleasant emotions to joint scrutiny; nor is there any precise way of delimiting relative importance of each source. Even granting that each of the alleged sources of the affectively pleasant emotions to follow has some validity, the results of these studies tell us nothing about whether a given source is important or unimportant, central or peripheral. In the summary to follow, the source or sources will be given in the parenthetical mention of the name of the investigator or investigators whose results led to the statement in question.

The sheer presence of sensory stimulation, especially sudden stimuli, seems to be important in infants (Leuba, Washburn). As sources for the pleasurable emotions in both infants and preschool children, physical activity seems to be very prominent (Brackett, Ding and Jersild, Blatz, and probably Leuba and Washburn). The presence of others in the social situation, the parents in the case of the infant (Washburn) and other children in that of the preschool child (Justin, Brackett, Ding and Jersild), seems to be operative in producing pleasurable emotions. Another source seems to be the resolution of conflicts (Blatz). It seems that relief from strain (Justin) may be related to this same source. Other sources, such as surprise-defeated expectation, superiority-degradation, incongruity and contrast (Justin) may be operative as well.

The account of the sources of pleasurable emotions cannot be left without indicating that some of these same sources in other circumstances can produce other than the affectively pleasant emotions. Consider the production of laughter and smiling in infants by sudden stimuli. Just a few pages before it was indicated that sudden stimuli produce fear. In fact, this source of fear was a prominent one. It would appear that situational factors must be operative in which sudden stimuli under some circumstances produce fear and under others produce affectively pleasant emotions. What these situations may be cannot be specified with any degree of precision; however, it is plausible to consider that the foreground stimuli (such as the sudden ones just mentioned) are pleasant or unpleasant just as the general background for the stimulation are pleasant or unpleasant (a trusted adult versus a strange person). In any event, the situation helps to determine whether laughter and smiling do or do not appear.

Language development in early childhood

In Chapter 6 normative landmarks in language development in infancy were pointed out. Little was said about the functions of language nor was the importance of learning indicated. Both of these topics will now receive consideration, although normative findings about language development in early childhood will not be neglected. The growth of vocabulary will be sketched as will the growth of other language skills. Individual differences in language development will also receive attention.

A study by Dorothea McCarthy (51) is emphasized in the following discussion because she investigated several important related aspects of language development through securing 50 consecutive verbal responses made by each of a large group of children. She studied language development in this fashion in 140 preschool-aged children divided more or less equally between boys and girls. To secure their verbal responses, she observed them in their homes and in nursery school, using 20 children at each of seven age levels from 18 to 54 months. The mean IQ of her sample was 109, showing it was more or less typical in intelligence of the population at large. Her analyses of data will be presented at appropriate points in later discussion. Hereafter, her study will be referred to as the McCarthy preschool study.

The Functions of Language

In language development, the most important single step taken by the infant is the intertwined discoveries that words have meaning and that their meanings may be used in communication with himself and with others. Since the work of Piaget (59), communication with self and with others has been referred to, respectively, as the egocentric and the socialized functions of language. Piaget was interested primarily in the thought processes of children. In pursuance of this interest, he studied their language. He did this through noting the vocalizations of children between the ages of two and eleven who were students in a private school in Switzerland. By American standards, his work is unsystematic and poorly controlled. Even his classification of the speech of his subjects bore within its very structure contradictions from one part to another (52). Nevertheless, his classification of the egocentric and socialized functions of speech has had a profound effect on studies of language. In fact, the fundamental distinction in function between egocentric and socialized speech has been generally accepted since his work, despite disagreements about their definition, relative proportion, and nature and age of appearance of these functions.

As he described it, egocentrism refers to the infant's isolation within himself. In an infant egocentrism is epitomized by his inability to distinguish the self from the world as expressed in the discussion of this problem in Chapter 7. In a preschool child it is shown in egocentric speech—in his talking without knowing to whom he is speaking or whether or not he is being listened to. Egocentric speech may be expressed in any one of three forms: (1) repetition, or talking for the sake of talking; (2) monologue, or talking to oneself as though thinking aloud; and (3) collective or dual monologue, or the other person serving both as stimulus and as recipient of the speech, although that person's point of view is not being considered. Extending the concept of egocentrism beyond its manifestation in language, it means that an egocentric individual shows no consideration of the other person's point of view. This is in contrast with socialized speech in which the talker addresses the listener, considers his viewpoint (at least to some degree), and tries to communicate with him. Piaget seems to regard adult speech (and thought) as highly socialized and egocentrism as a characteristic of immaturity. In fact, for him the proportion of egocentricity becomes an index of immaturity in the individual. The more egocentricity in speech and thought the greater the degree of immaturity of that individual.

In studying egocentric speech in the manner mentioned earlier, Piaget found that the speech of children showed considerable egocentricity but with a decrease in the proportion of egocentricity and an increase in sociocentric speech as age increased. His major source of data were about 1500 remarks made by each of two children, six-and-one-half years of age. He classed 38 per cent of these remarks in the egocentric category with about 45 per cent classed as spontaneous social speech. (The remaining 17 per cent was made up of answers to remarks or questions and thus not spontaneous.) He found even higher percentages of egocentric speech for less intensively studied children ages three to five as well as lower percentages for children ages seven and eight. It is only at about age seven or eight that he considers true social maturity to appear simultaneous with the virtual disappearance of egocentric speech.

This work of Piaget has stimulated the carrying out of a considerable number of research studies both here and abroad. These investigators were motivated by a desire to explore more thoroughly and with larger samples of children these intriguing distinctions between egocentric and socialized speech. McCarthy (52), in summarizing these investigations, found that the studies which try to follow Piaget's approach literally, or at least very closely, found considerably less instances or proportions of egocentricity than did those other investigators who defined the meaning of egocentricity differently from Piaget. Usually the definitions of egocentricity adopted by the latter group of investigators were based upon considering the sentence egocentric or not on the basis of the grammatical subject of the sentence. If the sentence had the self as subject, it was considered to be egocentric in nature (for example, 25). Paradoxically, in studies using these other definitions of egocentricity, they found percentages which agreed rather closely with those Piaget found following his own definition. Others using his definition found much less egocentricity. In her preschool study McCarthy (51), with due attention to reliability and objectivity, followed Piaget's meaning of egocentricity closely in classifying her sentence samples. She found the percentage of egocentric speech to range only between 1.3 and 6.5 per cent for children aged one-and-a-half to four-and-a-half. The average for all ages was 3.6 per cent, a proportion considerably less than that claimed by Piaget.

Rather than explore other specific research findings concerning egocentric speech in children, an attempt will be made to offer a summary. It would appear that there is general agreement among investigators that a certain proportion of the young child's speech is egocentric. There is similar agreement that a decrease takes place in this proportion with increasing age. Turing now to the magnitude of this proportion, even if one accepts as more valid those studies finding the highest percentages, they never reach 50 per cent. So the remark sometimes heard that egocentric speech predominates in that of young children is unfounded. Egocentrism in the speech of young children does exist, but it does not predominate. The present evidence indicates that the percentage of egocentric speech in children is less, perhaps considerably less, than that reported by Piaget.

In view of the stress on the immaturity of egocentric speech, it is sometimes lost sight of that it does also serve a useful function. By naming things to himself the child is learning to communicate with *himself*. He is learning the names of objects and properties. His first active use of words—omitting the use of interjections, "bye-bye," "hi!" and so on—is learning to name people, acts and things such as "mama," "doggie," "baby," "milk," "eat," and the like. He develops a great interest in names and is always demanding (in his own version, of course), "What's that?" Talking to himself does not mean he is not still learning. Is it any wonder, then, that he repeats words to himself? Naming seems to make an experience his very own. If he can name what he is doing to himself in egocentric fashion, he can use them better later for social communication. Despite this, egocentric speech is primarily an indication of immaturity.

The increase in socialized speech with increasing age is the complement of the decrease of egocentric speech. From the point of view of socialization of the child, it is interesting to explore the various forms that socialized speech may take. McCarthy in her preschool study (51) followed Piaget's classification of sociocentric speech with only minimal modifications. Consequently, giving her classification serves two purposes—preparation for giving her findings and the presentation of Piaget's classification of socialized speech. The first major category of socialized speech was called (1) adapted information. Adapted information categorizes the child's speech when he "exchanges" his thought with others. Subcategories of adapted information include naming, remarks about the immediate situation, remarks associated with the situation, or irrelevant remarks. The other major categories were (2) criticism; (3) emotionally toned responses, including commands, requests, and threats; (4) questions; (5) answers; (6) social phrases such as "please" or "thank you"; and (7) dramatic imitations of adult conversation and imitations of animal sounds, and the like. These categories are considered to encompass socialized speech.

In her speech samples, adapted information was by far the largest single category of socialized verbal responses. At most ages it made up as much as 40 to 60 per cent of the total verbal responses. There was a definite trend of an increase with age in adapted information. Questions, and especially answers, also showed an increase with age in her sample. On the other hand, emotionally toned responses showed a decrease. The other categories included few responses and no age trends could be noted.

The shift from egocentric to sociocentric speech with increasing age reflects the influence of socialization. The socially oriented verbalizations which the child learns bring with it rewards. Through sociocentric speech rather than egocentric speech he can manipulate his environment. Moreover, everyday observation would indicate that egocentric speech is actually discouraged as the child grows older and hence not rewarded. As McCarthy (52) indicates, it is more than accidental that a marked degree of socialization occurs in the behavior of the older preschool child. Language is becoming a more efficient means of communication and it plays a considerable role in the socialization taking place during the period. When he can understand instructions, when he can ask and answer questions, when he can defend a course of action, when he can tell what he is doing, then he is in a position to profit expeditiously from socialization efforts of those around him. Every parent knows how much more facility there is in controlling a child's behavior when his understanding of spoken language improves. We will now examine the growth of vocabulary and other language skills during these years.

Growth of Vocabulary

A number of normative studies of the growth of children's vocabularies have been performed (52). For a variety of reasons the figures that are reported on the average size of a child's vocabulary vary considerably from study to study. Some of the reasons for this variation from study to study are not hard to isolate. First, there is difficulty in getting agreement on what is meant by "knowing" a word, that is, one investigator may ask only that a word be recognized in context, another that it be used in a sentence, and still another that it be defined. Although all of these methods have some claim to legitimacy as indices of the growth of vocabulary, they would and do yield different size vocabularies. Second, quite apart from how it is to be measured, there is the ambiguity created by the various meanings a given word has, that is, the same word is apt to have different meanings as anyone consulting a dictionary knows. Differing standards toward the variety of meanings to be counted also result in differing estimates of the size of the vocabulary.

Fortunately, there seems to be agreement (52) that a study performed by Smith (72) is, to some extent perhaps, more definitive than are most of the other studies. Smith standardized a vocabulary test on children who were one to six years of age. She did so by selecting words from a list developed by Thorndike containing the 10,000 words most frequently encountered in writing samples. The meanings of these words were elicited by Smith from her subjects by carefully probing for their meanings by using objects, pictures, and questions. Consequently, more than usual care was taken by her to find out whether the child did or did not know the word meanings. The vocabulary sizes she obtained for various ages are reported in Table 12. It will be seen that at first the vocabulary increases slowly and then more rapidly and then again more slowly.

TABLE 12

AVERAGE SIZE OF VOCABULARIES OF CHILDREN IN RELATION TO AGE *

Age			Number of	
Years	Months	N	Words	Gain
	8	13	0	
	10	17	1	1
1	0	52	3	2
1	3	19	19	16
1	6	14	22	3
1	9	14	118	96
2	0	25	272	154
2	6	14	446	174
3	0	20	896	450
3	6	26	1222	326
4	0	26	1540	318
4	6	32	1870	330
5	0	20	2072	202
5	6	27	2289	217
6	0	9	2562	273

* From Smith (72). Copyright 1926 by the University of Iowa Press, and published with permission.

According to Smith's findings, the one-year-old has a vocabulary of three words, the two-year-old nearly 300, the four-year-old about 1500, the five-year-old about 2000, while the six-year-old has about 2500 words. A really pronounced increase occurs during the period from two years six months to three years of age when 450 new words become known. Many authorities (for example, 52) believe that the most pronounced increase occurs *after* mastery of the motor skills of locomotion, especially walking. When younger, he is so busy mastering these motor skills that, until they have been achieved, less emphasis on learning new words occurs. The relatively great increase at this particular age thus becomes plausible.

From a variety of lines of evidence, summarized by McCarthy

(52), these findings of Smith seem to place the size of vocabulary at any given age somewhat too low. The most important of the reasons for this low estimate is that her selection of words came from a specific and, therefore, limited list of words. No credit for knowing words not on the Thorndike list could possibly occur. In view of these considerations, it is probably most accurate to consider that her findings represent the minimal size of the vocabulary of the average child of the ages studied. Her findings, in other words, although probably reflecting growth trends quite accurately, tend to be somewhat too low at any one age.

With increase in age beyond the preschool period, estimates of the size of the vocabulary become even more hazardous (52), so that no attempt will be made to present figures for later ages. It is probably safe to say that the vocabulary never stops increasing until past maturity.

Developmental Changes in Other Language Skills

Developmental changes in language skills, other than vocabulary, have been studied. Growth in clearness of articulation, in the integration of words into sentences, in the sheer length of sentences, and in the relative usage of the grammatical parts of speech are taking place during the preschool period.

Ability to give the sounds of their language correctly increases as children grow older. Wellman, Case, Mengert, and Bradbury (80) report that the correlation between age and clearness of articulation is 0.80. In their study the average two-year-old child was able to articulate correctly only about 32 per cent of the sounds he made. At age three the most marked increase was made to an average correct of 63 per cent. As age continued to increase, the percentage increased steadily, at age four it was 77 per cent, at age five it was 88 per cent, and at age six it was 89 per cent. These results are confirmed by Davis (14) who extended their results by the finding that in six-and-a-half-year-olds 91 per cent have essentially "perfect" articulation. In the McCarthy preschool study (51) similar, although somewhat greater, improvements were found. In her two-year-olds, 67 per cent of their vocalizations were comprehensible, and by age of three-and-a-half practically all their vocalizations were comprehensible.

Growth in language skills is shown in changes with age in the integration of words into sentences. In this connection, Nice (58) outlines four major stages of sentence development. Stage one, the single word stage, begins at approximately the end of the first year and lasts from four to twelve months. The second is the early sentence stage. Only one or two words are used by infants, with a preponderance of nouns. This stage lasts until about 28 months of age. Even if he uses but a single word, he still uses it to convey differences of meaning to others. This single word may function as a sentence, although not yet having its grammatical form. Mothers soon learn of single words functioning as whole sentences. Even the same word may, on different occasions, serve as several sentences. For example, the single word, mama, used with varying inflections and gestures means "mama look," "mama is here," and "mama come quickly." A small vocabulary, using one word at a time, may still go a long way. The next stage, the short sentence stage (three to four words), is one in which nouns and verbs are used by the young child, but tenses, comparatives, and other inflections are not mastered. This stage beginning at about 28 months of age lasts until approximately the fourth year. The last stage, the "complete" sentence stage, involves six to eight words and is also characterized by a fairly precise use of inflections. This stage does not appear until after four years of age. Although, as McCarthy (52) remarks, the study by Nice from which she arrived at this classification was an early one in which few subjects were used, it remarkably foreshadows what later, more painstaking work was to establish about the pattern of growth in sentence development.

Closely related to the integration of words into sentences is the sheer length of the verbal response which also increases with age. In the McCarthy preschool study, at 18 months of age the average response they gave was slightly more than one word, at 30 months it had increased to about three words, while at 42 months it was over four words with only a slight increase thereafter. The most rapid increase was therefore between 18 and 42 months of age. The sheer length of the verbal response thus increases with age.

Changes in relative usage of the different grammatical parts of speech also change with age. In the McCarthy preschool study she found that nouns which constitute about 50 per cent of the speech of the eighteen-month-old children decrease to about 19 per cent in the 54-month-old sample. Verbs increase from 14 per cent to 25 per cent over the same age range. Although this is an increase, it is relatively slight as compared to that for adjectives and pronouns which almost double during the age range in question. Prepositions do not show up at all until about 24 months of age and connectives are hardly found until children are 30 months old.

These various developmental differences in the speech of children help to explain its particular so-called childish quality in the younger preschool child. This is most apparent in their usage of grammatical parts. Relative to adult speech the younger preschool child uses many nouns, a fair number of verbs, but very few pronouns and adjectives, and hardly any prepositions or connectives. Speech is direct and bald without the later nuances he learns with increasing age. It is essentially disconnected and lacking in, what to adult ears is, rhythm and fluency. When to this differing grammatical usage is added three properties of relatively poor articulation, shorter sentences, and a small vocabulary, we have the speech of the younger preschool child. Over the years of this period profound changes take place, the nature of which have just been sketched. These changes have taken the five-year-old, on his leaving the preschool period, a great distance in the direction of adult speech. Certainly, the preschool years are the period of the greatest changes in speech development of the child. By the same token he has advanced in the degree of his socialization.

Individual, Group, and Sex Differences in Language Development

Children of five years of age differ considerably in their facility with oral language. Some are chatterboxes, talking from the moment they wake up in the morning until they fall asleep at night. Others are quiet, almost silent children, economical with words, speaking only when spoken to and often using a nod or a shake of the head where a flow of words would be forthcoming from another child. Some children speak with a variety of good and poor articulations, a sparse or rich vocabulary, and so on. To put the matter in terms of the specific aspects of oral language previously discussed, there are individual differences among children of the same age in size of vocabulary, clarity of articulation, ability to integrate words into sentences, length of verbal responses, and the relative usage of different grammatical parts of speech. In fact, from time to time in these preceding sections attention was drawn to these differences. Nevertheless, stress was then placed upon changes with age. Attention was focused on individual differences, but differences in speech brought about by differences in age. In one sense, age was tacitly treated as the source of differences although it is, of course, recognized that changes were a matter of maturation and learning concomitant with age, not age itself. It is only in this sense that age is a source of differences. Attention will now be focused on other sources of individual, group, and sex differences in speech skills during the preschool period.

Individual differences among children in language skills reflect the importance of practice and reinforcement. Several lines of evidence may be mentioned. Factors making for impoverishment of language skills owing to lack of reinforcement of language responses will first be indicated. Studies of institutionalized children by Goldfarb (28, 29), reported in detail in Chapter 8, show vividly the importance of lack of reinforcement. Because of lack of contact with others, the institutional children he studied did not have as many reinforced speech responses as compared to the other children— those living in foster homes which he also studied. The speech of the institutional children was found to be impoverished. Other sources of evidence for the effect of lack of reinforcement may be cited. For example, twins and triplets are slower in learning speech than singletons (52). Presumably, they are not so highly motivated to learn language because many of their reciprocal social needs may be met by means other than verbal communication which results in less language reinforcement.

There are also some situations which increase exposure to reinforcement of language responses. Increased vocabulary development is associated with vacation travel (23). In this instance, there would be exposure to the words for new objects and new processes seen. Thus "tractor" or "harvesting" may be learned from a visit to the farm. Upper (or upper middle) socio-economic circumstances (51) appear to increase vocabulary. Exposure to the material things that go with upper socio-economic circumstances, such as the magazines and the encyclopedia, help to broaden the language horizon (14, 15, 16, 17, 18). Only children are also more advanced in vocabulary than are others. They tend to associate more with adults than do other children and are thus exposed to more opportunities for reinforcement of new language responses.

Sex differences in language skills uniformly have been found. The evidence is quite clear in demonstrating that girls show superiority over boys in nearly all aspects of speech development (52). One aspect of speech development, length of response, will be used to illustrate this contention. McCarthy (52) summarizes 14 major, carefully controlled studies of length of speech responses at preschool ages. Of the 64 comparisons, 43 favor the girls. Moreover, some of the comparisons showing superiority in boys can be criticized as involving material in which they would tend to be more interested, while relatively few such biasing selections could be found to favor girls. In the McCarthy preschool study, to take one research study of the seven age comparisons for different age groups, six showed superiority in girls. There is no definitive evidence as to why girls show this superiority. It is plausible, however, to speculate that differential reinforcement of girls as compared to boys may take place. In contrast to the boys receiving relatively greater reward for motor accomplishment, girls are more likely to be reinforced for verbal accomplishments. If this be the case, then the obtained differences would fit in with learning theory expectations.

Differences in intelligence is another potent factor related to differences in language ability. In fact, size of vocabulary as measured by the Stanford-Binet Intelligence Scales is generally considered to be the most important single test of intelligence among the scales. Indicative of the popularity of the vocabulary section is the common practice that when a relatively short intelligence measure is wanted, the vocabulary test is used alone. The correlation between the vocabulary test and the total Stanford-Binet Scales is about 0.70 or 0.80 (53), thus showing a remarkably high degree of relationship between the two. To give an illustration from studies of language development, in the McCarthy preschool study approximately the same degrees of relationships to language indices were found with mental age as was the case when chronological age was used. In other words, mental age could be substituted for chronological age in stating any of the previous findings from this study with about equal results. A high degree of relationship between language ability and intelligence has been established. This degree of relationship, it must be emphasized, does not indicate that intelligence "causes" language ability or language ability "causes" intelligence. We must be content with knowing that there is a relationship, not precise knowledge on which causes the other.

Learning and Speech

That speech is learned is already evident. When internal processes (the higher mental processes) are involved in the child's interactions with his environment, these internal processes are mediated by cue-producing responses. Language is most often, though not always, involved in cue-producing responses.   Hall and Lindzey in discussing behavior-social-learning theory summarize so well the position of Miller and Dollard (54) concerning cue production and language that they are quoted at length as follows:

> One of the most important cue-producing responses is the labeling or naming of events and experiences.   The individual may immediately increase the generalization or transfer between two or more cue situations by identifying them as having the same label, for example, by identifying two completely different situations as "threatening" the individual may greatly increase the likelihood that he will behave in the same manner in both situations; or he may build up a sharp discrimination between two similar situations by giving them different names, for instance, two individuals who are objectively very much alike may be labeled respectively as "friend" and "enemy" with the result that they will be responded to in a highly individual manner.   Within any culture there will be critical generalizations and discriminations which are emphasized and thus made easier by the structure of the language.   The often repeated examples of tribes where a given commodity, such as cattle or coconuts, is of great importance and where the language contains a tremendous number of differentiated labels for such objects illustrate this principle.
> Not only may words serve to facilitate or inhibit generalization, they may also serve the important function of arousing drives.   Further, words may be used to reward or reinforce.   And, most important of all, they serve as time-binding mechanisms, permitting the individual to instigate or reinforce present behavior in terms of consequences which are located in the future but susceptible to verbal representation in the present.   It is clearly the verbal intervention in the drive-cue-response-reinforcement sequence which makes human behavior so complex and difficult to understand and at the same time accounts for much of the difference between man and lower species (33, 438–439).[4]

Language as a product of learning can be seen as an important aspect of development.   Without the learning of language much of our characteristically human prowess would be lost.

The development of understanding in early and late childhood

In Chapter 6 the beginnings of understanding in infancy were sketched.   It was pointed out that in infancy perceptualization, con-

[4] From Hall and Lindzey (33).   Copyright 1957 by John Wiley and Sons, and published with permission.

ceptualization, and thinking (and even intelligence) could not be sharply separated from one another. In early and late childhood these aspects of understanding can be separated with a greater degree of validity and clarity. In the account to follow, thinking, with special emphasis upon the work of Piaget, will first be presented. Since it is almost impossible to make meaningful the distinction between early and late childhood, attention to the entire age range of childhood will be given in presenting his and other views on thinking. This will be followed by a discussion of a particular way in which understanding is expressed in childhood, namely, concept formation.

Thinking in Early and Late Childhood

Attempts to state the stages of the development of thinking will first be presented with particular attention to the work of Piaget. One of these stages, so-called animistic thinking, will then be singled out for special attention. Lastly, a critique of Piaget's work will be offered.

Stages of the development of thinking. The child's processes of understanding have been illuminated more by the work of Jean Piaget (*59, 60, 61, 62, 63, 64, 65*) than that of any other one person. We have already examined in this chapter his conception of language as serving egocentric and socialized functions. Cognitive processes, so important in language, are regarded by him as also being expressed in thought and intelligence. Thought and intelligence, between which he makes no sharp distinction, are aspects of the same central cognitive process. In his various works mentioned above, he deals with this problem of thought process in different ways. No matter which one is chosen for exposition, there are differences in phraseology and sometimes even difference in the sheer number of stages of development to which he alludes. The account chosen for exposition was one he considered as presenting the principal factors determining intellectual evolution from childhood to adulthood (*64*). In this account he said that there are three "planes" of intellectual evolution: (1) sensory-motor activity; (2) egocentric thought; and (3) rational thought. This formulation, it now becomes evident, is related to the earlier formulation of egocentrism in language. Indeed, Piaget says explicitly that following these three levels allows us also to trace thought from egocentric perception to objective reasoning.

The first, or sensory-motor activity plane, has already been described in Chapter 7 in connection with the emergence of self in infancy. To recapitulate briefly, the sensory-motor stage is the period in which the infant adapts to the external world by "creating" it from his experiences in assimilating external realities. He learns that there is a world "out there" quite apart from his actions.

About the time the outside world has been "created" he begins to learn language and must now adapt not only to the external material world but also to the thoughts of others. He now faces the same problems he encountered in the sensory-motor stage all over again. In early childhood he has passed to the level of egocentric thought. Although knowing the permanence of concrete objects, he has as yet no fully developed concepts such as of matter, weight, movement, number, or logic. He has passed from initial egocentricity of the sensory-motor stage to logical and social egocentricity. Piaget illustrates this new level of egocentricity in the existence of the inability of a preschool-aged child to take the perspective of another person. A child in this age range was shown a model of three mountains and asked to select from a number of pictures of these mountains the one which showed the way it looked to the *doll* who was placed in the mountains. The child, instead of selecting from the perspective of the doll, selected the one showing how it appeared from his own vantage point. As the doll was shifted from one place in the mountains to another, he persisted in selecting the picture which showed his own view of the mountains. He did not understand that an observer sees the same mountains quite differently from various points of view. An everyday example of the same phenomenon is the difficulties children have with personal pronouns. To put it in doggerel, "I am I and you are you, and how can you be I and I be you?" The young child's own personal perspective is absolute, not relative.

As the child grows older he gradually learns the relativity which is necessary for objective conceptions to emerge. The third phase of rational coordination appears in later childhood. To quote Piaget:

> The essence of rational coordination is then to be sought in the "logic of relations"—that is, in this fundamental group of operations which assures the reciprocity of individual perspectives and the relativity of the facts of experience. To refer again to the example of space, on which we have already insisted, it is the logic of relations which makes the child come gradually to understand, between seven and eleven years, that the left and the right are not absolute, but that his own left corre-

sponds to the right of an individual opposite him, and that an object between two others is at one and the same time at the left of the first and the right of the third. It is then the logic of relationships which permits the formation of the idea of a conceptual space by the coordination of the different perspectives possible, and which also allows the imposition of this upon practical space, whose relationships, however well coordinated they may be among themselves, are always limited to one's own perspective.

Now this logic of relations, which thus maintains on the level of thought the "groups" of operations outlined by sensorimotor intelligence, and which gradually eliminates intellectual egocentricity, finally succeeds, in the realm we are trying to analyze here, in forming invariables which represent for the reasoning mind so many principles of permanence applicable to the physical world (64, 45).[5]

This stage emerges during the seventh to the eleventh years. According to Piaget, only now is the child capable of logical thought. It will be noted that this, in effect, means that during early childhood and a not inconsiderable portion of later childhood, the child is not considered to be capable of logical thought. In fact, it would appear that if a specific age must be chosen, it would be about eight years of age that the child is capable of thinking on the adult type of rational coordination.

It is now appropriate to turn from Piaget's general theory of levels of development to consider a more specific aspect of his views. The emergence of conceptions of physical causality is chosen for detailed exposition (62). It was his work on physical causality which stimulated widespread interest in the manner in which children developed these conceptions. In studying physical causality various phenomena of nature were mentioned or demonstrated by Piaget and children asked to explain them. Thus he would ask, "What makes the clouds move?" After the child had responded he would further question him until satisfied he had understood the child's conception. From work along these lines he arrived at a classification of 17 types of causal thinking. Five of these types moving from relatively great to less egocentricity as one moves from one type to another are defined by Deutsche as follows:

Phenomenistic Causality.—Two facts given together in perception, such that no relation subsists between them except that of contiguity in time and space. Pebble sinks to bottom of water because it is white. No concept of relations. . . .

[5] From Piaget (64). Copyright 1937 by The President and Fellows of Harvard College, and published with permission.

Animistic Causality.—An internal biological tendency that is both alive and conscious. Clouds move because they are alive. . . .

Dynamic Causality.—Animism gone, but still sees in objects forces that are capable of explaining their activity and movements. . . .

Mechanical Causality.—Explanation by contact and transference of movement. No internal force at all. Wind pushes the clouds. Pedals make bicycle go. . . .

Explanation by Logical Deduction.—Explanation by the principle of sufficient reason. Water flows into the second of the connected tubes because water can go equally well in both directions. Uses concepts of density, specific weight, etc. (*20,* 51–52).[6]

The first three are definitely precausal (and egocentric), while mechanical causality may be considered as transitional, with explanation by logical definition belonging in the category of rational coordination. According to Piaget these (and the remaining 12 levels) are discrete in that children's thinking proceeds during the course of development from one level to the next higher level with relatively little overlap. In terms of the previously defined type levels, a child would be phenomenistic in his thinking rather than animistic, then animistic, and so on, until logical deduction developed. A child, say at the level of dynamic causality, would when at that level be incapable of logical deduction.

This view of conceptualization as a series of discrete levels is in sharp contrast with another view prevailing among a considerable number of students of children's thinking. They take the position that, instead of there being separate levels, thinking emerges gradually. They would also argue that younger children were capable of logical thought—that the youngest child's thought, though limited by sheer inexperience, is not qualitatively different from adult thought.

Representative of this point of view is the study of Deutsche (*20*), whose definitions for certain of Piaget's types of causal thought were just quoted.

She performed one of the better controlled studies of children's thinking which tested Piaget's contentions. Several hundred children aged between eight and sixteen were tested both through their reactions to demonstrations of physical phenomena and the completion of a questionnaire. The demonstrations included placing a jar over a lighted candle and asking why the candle went out; dropping blocks and asking what made the noise; adding to beakers containing blue and yellow solutions some colorless acid which changed the colors,

[6] Jean M. Deutsche, *The Development of Children's Concepts of Causal Relations.* Copyright 1937, University of Minnesota.

respectively, to yellow and red and asking why a colorless substance changed the colors; and playing different keys on a musical instrument and asking why different sounds were heard. The questionnaire included items about what makes the wind blow, what makes a rainbow after rain, what makes airplanes stay in the air, what makes boats float, what makes shadows, and what causes thunder. For both demonstration and questionnaire items, the children wrote their answers and were not further questioned.

Classification into one or another of Piaget's classifications was made by three independent observers. Table 13 shows the per-

TABLE 13

PERCENTAGE OF ANSWERS FALLING IN SEVERAL OF
PIAGET'S CLASSIFICATIONS *

Type of Causality	Age, Years								All Ages
	8	9	10	11	12	13	14	15–16	
Phenomenistic	37.3	32.5	29.5	22.4	16.1	11.9	12.4	10.3	20.8
Animistic	0.6	0.2	0.6	0.3	0.3	0.2	0.0	0.0	0.3
Dynamic	8.3	5.8	6.3	6.2	7.1	6.7	2.9	5.7	6.3
Mechanical	32.5	33.2	37.4	40.5	41.1	41.0	39.5	42.9	38.9
Logical	10.7	11.8	14.1	19.8	28.1	32.0	35.6	31.6	23.4

* Jean M. Deutsche, *The Development of Children's Concepts of Causal Relations*. Copyright 1937, University of Minnesota.

centage by age of the five types previously defined. The other types omitted from this table made up the differences between the totals for each age column of about 90 per cent and 100 per cent. Since the remaining types made up only about ten per cent of the total, for the sake of economy of presentation they may be disregarded.

It can be seen from the table that only four of the types of causal thinking advanced by Piaget were found in large enough frequencies to permit study of age trends. Phenomenistic causality declined with age and mechanical causality and logical deduction increased with age, while dynamic causality showed no age trend. It might be said the findings on the first three supported Piaget's contentions so far as the direction of expected age trends are concerned. However, discreteness of levels of thinking age by age was emphatically not found. Each type of thinking was found to extend over the entire age range studied, suggesting that causality does not develop in saltatory stages. She found many more naturalistic explanations of physical causality than one would expect from Piaget's account. This would seem to indicate that children even as young as eight carry on logical thinking. Moreover, children even as old as fifteen or sixteen continue to use phenomenistic, dynamic, and mechanical types of causal explanation. A variety of other studies, for example, those reviewed by Huang (38), supports similar conclusions to those of Deutsche.

Factors other than sheer age affect children's concepts of personality. Nass (57) investigated the effect of personality, experience, and the form of wording of the questions asked upon Piaget's types of thinking. The effect of personality was investigated by contrasting the responses of normal and withdrawn eight- to ten-year-old children, matched as to school attendance, age, sex, and intelligence test scores. The withdrawn children were selected from those referred to a child guidance clinic for this problem. The hypothesis was advanced that withdrawn children would be hampered in developing an objective point of view in Piaget's terms. In other words, they would be expected to function at a less mature level than normal children. This hypothesis was verified in that the withdrawn children displayed significantly more nonnaturalistic responses to a series of questions, akin to those used by Piaget and Deutsche. Thus, they functioned at a less mature level than did normal children. The effect of experience was investigated in subgroups of the normal and withdrawn matched groups by comparing their responses to items dealing with phenomena with which they were likely to have had direct experience, for example, radiators getting hot or a clock ticking, as contrasted with items dealing with phenomena with which the children could not have experienced the causal process directly, for example, thunder or the stars shining. The more remote phenomena with which the children had no direct experience produced more nonnaturalistic responses. The effect of the wording of the questions was studied through similar subgroups, the members of one of which were asked "Why" as in "Why does a car move?" The members of the other subgroup were asked "How" as in "How does a car move?" It was hypothesized that the first form of question would be more suggestive of dynamic or animistic forces than would the second form. Significant differences in the expected direction were obtained. Thus, personality, experience, and the form of the question were all found to affect the degree of naturalistic and nonnaturalistic explanations of physical causality in the thinking of children.

Although emphasis has been laid upon Piaget's types of thinking as applied to the development of concepts of physical causality, it is important to note that roughly these same types of thinking appear in other aspects of the child's thinking although going through different stages. This will be illustrated by a further consideration of one particular type of thinking—animism.

Animistic thinking. Animistic thinking, it will be remembered, consists of attributing life to nonliving things. Piaget (59, 63) distinguishes four definite stages. As summarized by Russell (69), they are as follows: in the first stage, everything is alive (unless broken or damaged) for children between four and six years of age; in the second stage, everything is alive which moves for six- and seven-year-old children; in the third stage, everything which moves by itself is alive for eight- to ten-year-old children; in the fourth stage, life is reserved for animals and plants, or animals alone, by children aged eleven or older.

Deutsche's results on animistic thinking have already been presented. It will be seen from Table 13 that at no age from eight through sixteen does animistic thinking reach as much as one per cent. If only her results were discussed, they would be misleading because her findings concerning the relative paucity of animism seem to be contradicted by a relatively large number of studies as, for example, those summarized in (38). In general, these other studies indicate a considerably greater amount of animistic thinking in children.

It has not been the practice in this book to make very much reference to studies on adults. At this point it is considered worth while to do so since, if studies of young adults of relatively high educational status show that animistic thinking is present, it demonstrates quite forcefully that children may also be expected to show it. Dennis (19) conducted a survey asking groups of both college and graduate students whether certain common objects presented or referred to one by one were living or nonliving, along with their reasons for saying so. The objects about which they were queried were an unlighted match, the same match when lit, an electric clock on the wall, the sun, the wind, a five-cent piece, a pearl, gasoline, and the ocean. In one group made up mostly of graduate students in education, 45 per cent said one or more of these objects were living (with special emphasis on the lighted match, the sun, and the ocean). In two other groups, 37 and 48 per cent, respectively, gave one or more animistic answers. Dennis now searched deliberately for a group that would *not* be expected to be animistic, finding it in students just completing an integrated science course in which there had been strong emphasis on biological matters that included the distinctive characteristics of living things. Even in this group 12 per cent attributed life to one or more of the objects.

If the reader is inclined to come to the conclusion that in giving animistic answers these students were clowning, poetically fanciful, or not aware of the implications in their answers, two replies may be given. One, the presentation of detailed responses in which one can reach their own conclusions, Dennis proposes himself. He quoted some of the detailed responses of which the following is but two of the samples:

> *The lighted match:* "Living, because it has flames which indicate life." "Living because it is burning brightly, giving forth something." "Dying— I saw it being burned."
>
> *The sun:* "Living because it gives forth energy. Gives us power, warmth, light, and energy. Makes things—living things—thrive and exist." "Living because it gives off heat." "Yes! Living! Without breath, but living, scientifically living, changing" (*19*, 248–249).[7]

The other answer is given by a follow-up study by Crannell (*13*) using a multiple choice questionnaire wherein the student chooses the best answer from alternatives of animistic and nonanimistic nature. Two groups totaling 163 college students were given the questionnaire. In the quotation of one of the items that follows, the two percentages in the parentheses after the alternatives refer to the percentages in the two groups giving that response.

> 7. ( ) Is the sun alive?
>   A. Yes, because it gives off flames, which indicate life. (0.0– 0)
>   B. Yes, because it gives forth energy. (5.5–0)
>   C. Yes. It is not breathing, but it is pulsating, scientifically living and ever changing. (22.1–11)
>   D. Probably not. It is doubtful that the sun is really alive. (6.1–15)
>   E. No. It is not a living thing. (66.3–75) (*13*, 2) [8]

[7] From Dennis (*19*). Copyright 1953 by the American Association for the Advancement of Science, and published with permission.

[8] From Crannell (*13*). Copyright 1954 by the American Association for the Advancement of Science, and published with permission.

Although this is the item producing the highest percentage of animistic responses, the percentages he obtained on the other items showed that there were at least a few college students who accepted an unequivocally animistic answer. The presence of animistic thinking even in adults seems to be definitely demonstrated. It would follow that animistic thinking occurs in children as well. Although there is some doubt as to how much animistic thinking in adults and children occur, it does not appear that the percentage is so small as to be dismissed as negligible.

Despite this demonstration of the reality of animistic thinking, it is pertinent to examine the question of the levels of animism in children. On the basis of a standardized method, nearly 800 children six to fifteen and one-half years of age were interviewed by Russell (69). Ninety-eight per cent of their answers could be classified into one or another of the stages of animistic thinking presented earlier. Furthermore, examination of the classification by stages at each chronological and mental age showed that probably individuals passed through the series in the sequence suggested by Piaget. Although the fundamental validity of Piaget's classification was accepted by Russell, he could find no evidence that the age range for each stage was limited in the sharp fashion thought by Piaget to exist. Instead, each of the concept stages was found throughout the entire chronological and mental age range covered in the study. The question of whether or not these results might merely be an artifact of the child's usage of the terms "living" and "dead" was also investigated by Russell (70). In other words, a child might be saying something was living because he was not familiar with the essential meaning of the term itself. Some of the children on whom he had information about animistic thinking from the previous study were now questioned whether the same objects as used in the earlier study were capable of "knowing" and "feeling." Classification by Piaget's stages of "knowing" and "feeling" and then correlating them with the findings on animistic stages for the same children showed a substantial degree of relationship among animism, knowing, and feeling. This would seem to be rather convincing evidence—that if confusion about the meaning of living did exist, it also extended to the most specific meanings of knowing and feeling. In general, it would appear that the children do know what "living" means when they give animistic answers.

Despite this impressive array of evidence, there are some studies whose findings are negative and thus support Deutsche's findings. Representative of these studies is that of Huang and Lee (39). They asked children aged three-and-a-half to eight years of age not only whether the objects in question were living but also whether they had life, felt pain, were capable of wanting, and comparable questions. They found only a slight tendency to attribute life to such objects as a tree, river, pencil, bicycle, and watch. Knowledge of the traits was more advanced (correct) than was their judgment concerning animation. In other words, the children did not attribute feeling pain or wanting, and the like to these objects to as great a degree as they said they were living. The term "living" was applied more loosely than "having life." Evaluation of these disparate results will now be considered in the setting of a general critique of Piaget's conceptions.

A critique of Piaget's stages of development and animistic thinking. In some psychological circles, Piaget is dismissed because his own research rightly is not considered as sufficient evidence. This dismissal on this basis is essentially short-sighted and incorrect. The scanty data he has presented were meant to illustrate, not to prove. It is his ideas which are stimulating, not his evidence. Hence, for evidence we turn to the work of other men who have tested his formulations.

Some of the differences between Piaget's findings and the studies which support him and those of other investigators whose findings are in disagreement are to be found in the differing methods they used. Piaget used (as did Russell and Dennis) a clinical method of adroitly questioning the children he interviewed. The method had the advantage of allowing him to trace down the particular meaning the child was giving to a word. Children, as Piaget's own work so ably shows, are in the process of developing sharpness and clarity in their use of words. There certainly is an advantage of this approach over using a group-written test where there is no follow-up of what the child meant by his answers. In a group test, the response obtained for each object or demonstration is equivalent only to the unfollowed-up first response in the interview procedure. The group method, too, has advantages. It permits a larger sampling of subjects and the application of a series of controls. Although not intrinsic to the group testing method, the use of independent observers to measure reliability was a distinct advantage. These differences in procedure undoubtedly go far in accounting for the differences in the results obtained. Despite this, it is mandatory that some sort of reconciling summary be offered, tentative and uncertain though it may be.

Piaget's sharp contrast between childish and adult thinking is an overrevaluation of verbal expression as a measure of thinking and an exaggeration of the logical nature of adult thought (35). This contention suggests that just as children's thinking is not so different from adult thinking because the child is more adult than pictured by Piaget, so, too, is the adult more childish. A child's thinking does not differ fundamentally from an adult's by differing in kind, but rather seems to differ in degree.

It is important to note that Piaget did not claim the entire absence of one form of thinking and then the full-blown appearance of another, with no residue of the earlier stage. For example, socialized speech in early childhood is recognized and accepted by Piaget. He claimed only that egocentric speech clearly predominated. Nevertheless, much more than did others, he argued for relatively abrupt shifts in thinking on the part of the children at different ages.

It would seem as if the weight of evidence (38) is against the saltatory shifting from one stage of conceptualization to the next. The almost universal finding of research studies is that, instead of there being leaps from one kind of thinking to another, there is a gradual orderly change in the child's conceptualization (no matter how defined). This forces disagreement in emphasis with Piaget on this point. For example, most studies, whether of physical causality or of the narrower problem of animism, find that the categorizations of thinking they used, whatever form they may take, extend over the age range of the subjects they studied. Trends of change in stages of conceptualization are found to be sure, but they are progressive and not of an "all or none" variety.

Children's thinking cannot be as sharply distinguished from adult modes of thought as Piaget would have it. There is confusion of fantasy with reality, as the psychoanalysts as well as followers of Piaget argue, but there is not a qualitative difference between the thinking of children and that of adults. Reality limits the child despite his creation of make-believe situations; fantasy enlivens and yet distorts the thinking of adults.

There is little reason to question that animistic thinking does occur, and in adults as well as in children. But it is not an all-or-none affair. An adult may be animistic about some matters and not others as the studies of Dennis (19) and Crannell (13) show. So far as adults are concerned, it should be remembered that questions concerning matters outside one's fields of interest sometimes may show an individual, no matter how much an expert in his own field, to be as naive as a child. One form of naiveté is animism.

Piaget described a vivid fantasy life that arose from the nature of childish thinking. Although he considered thinking as arising from the child's modes of thought, little was said about the effect of experience or motivation upon their arousal. It is characteristic of Piaget's point of view that, although accepting an affective life in his systematic presentation, he makes little reference to it. In contrast, the psychoanalytic view gives, if anything, too much emphasis upon the need or drive facet of experience. Autistic thinking—vicarious gratification of unconscious motives by wishful fantasies—is closely related to egocentric thinking. They differ, according to Piaget (59), in that autistic thought is undirected or unconscious, while egocentric thought is directed in the sense that it carries out a conscious aim of the thinker. A child's needs, conscious or unconscious, undoubtedly influence the nature of his thinking. He is still profoundly influenced by what Freud calls the pleasure principle. In this context, egocentric thinking is thinking in which the pleasure principle predominates.

Concept Formation in Early and Late Childhood

It is sometimes said that a concept is a perception that has been given a meaningful label. By giving it a name, a concept has been formed. Concepts develop as language develops, despite the evidence that concepts may be acted upon before the appearance of language (see Chapter 6). It is certainly true for most concepts beyond its beginnings in infancy that by naming it we have given it a meaningful label; we have implicitly said that it is like other things having the same name and different from things having other names. There are varying degrees of naming, or levels of development, in the process of concept formation.

Granting that the beginnings of conceptualization are in infancy, what are some of the conceptual tasks which the young child emerging from infancy has before him? He enters early childhood with but very hazy conceptions of space, time, weight, number, form, color, and size. It is during early and later childhood that he makes his greatest strides in mastering these concepts.

Concepts as shorthand devices become the means whereby reasoning or problem solving is most economically carried on. Indeed, without abstract concepts many of the higher accomplishments of man would be impossible. The most generalized concepts of man, those of mathematics and symbolic logic, allow us to indicate a great variety of antecedent conceptual operations in an economical intelligible form that more concrete operations would not permit.

It is impracticable to discuss all major classes or aspects of concepts. Instead, discussions of time and space concepts will serve to illustrate conceptual development during early childhood.

Development of time concepts. Some development of appreciation of the nature of time takes place during infancy. Gesell and Ilg (27) find that the child of 18 months lives very much in the present. It is characteristic that he finds it difficult to wait and the only time word that is used is "now." Only the slightest indications of any sense of timing have yet appeared, as for example, the sight of juice and crackers may bring him to the table. At two years of age although he still lives chiefly in the present, he has begun to use words denoting the future, as for example, "gonna" and "in a minute." He is also beginning to comprehend simple time sequences as implied in "have dollie after juice." By the age of three years most common basic time words are now in his vocabulary. He can be persuaded to wait for things. Although he shows only pretense of telling time, the very fact that he does so shows a dawning conceptualization in this area. During these years he is still living very much in the here and now, as shown by the fact that even at five years it is very difficult for him to conceive of not being alive, of dying, or of anyone living before him. At this age he can name the days of the week and is interested in clocks and calendars, although by no means adroit in handling these time phenomena.

Development of space concepts. Similar developments are taking place for space concepts (27). Even at one year of age there is enough appreciation of space dimensions to perform gestures for up and down and to play "peek-a-boo." By two years of age he has in his vocabulary such expressions as "up high," "in," "out," and "go away." By the age of three he can tell what street he lives on, but usually not the number. At the age of five he is still very much literal and factual, although capable of taking simple routes through the immediate neighborhood. He is beginning to appreciate the significance of maps and even may make simple maps indicating the route he takes to school, and so on.

The development of other concepts in early childhood could also be traced, but enough has been said to illustrate the nature of age changes in conceptual development. We will now examine concept formation more systematically through consideration of levels of development in concept formation.

Levels of development in concept formation.   Various attempts have been made to specify the levels of development in concept formation as related to age.   Two of these formulations, those by Reichard and Rapaport (66) and Welch and Long (75, 76, 77, 78, 79) will be presented here.   Reichard and Rapaport consider there to be three levels—concrete, functional, and abstract.   Welch and Long speak of a concrete level and a number of differing levels of abstractness according to the concept involved.   To make these two approaches to levels of development of concept formation clear, they will now be examined in detail.

Reichard and Rapaport (66) formulate concept formation, in general, as seeing the common essential factor in a variety of things.   All tables are contained in the concept "tables."   The content of the concept is an abstraction independent of the form, color, material, and structure of tables.   The most common everyday manifestation of concept formation is calling a thing by its name.   The use of nouns, in fact, is a conventionalized conceptualized device.

Reichard and Rapaport distinguished three levels of the development of analyses in concept formation.   In this connection they write:

> Many investigators have found that one can distinguish crudely between three levels of development of concept formation.   The first is that called concretistic, in which things are considered as belonging together because of non-essential, concrete features possessed by them (e.g., an orange and a banana are similar because both have peels); the second usually is designated as functional, and refers to the belonging together of objects which have a common use or function (e.g., an orange and a banana are similar because one eats them both); the third is that abstract conceptual level on which two things are considered as belonging together because they are associated in a well-known and defined abstract category (e.g., an orange and a banana are similar because both are fruits) (66, 100).[9]

The intimate relation between intelligence and concept formation is evident here since distinctions among these concrete, functional, and abstract levels are actually used in scoring vocabulary tests of intelligence tests.

Reichard, Schneider, and Rapaport performed a developmental

[9] Reichard, Suzanne, and Rapaport, D. (66). The role of testing concept formation in clinical psychological work. *Bull. Menninger Clin.*, 7:100, May 1943.

study (67) which exemplified these levels and showed the changes occurring with age. Subjects were 234 children, aged four to fourteen. Two tests were used, the Color-Form and the Sorting Tests. The Color-Form Test consists of 12 figures of different forms and colors—four circles, four squares, and four triangles in which each form was in red, green, yellow, and blue. The task which the children were to perform was to put together those that belonged together. After performing a sorting based on either form or color, they were asked to sort them another way. Afterwards, they were asked to tell why that which they put together belonged together. Success was shown in shifting from color to form or form to color, while failure was represented by inability to sort, repetition or mixed groupings, and the inability to verbalize. Thus, the children made none or one or two groupings. The Sorting Test consists of 32 objects including a real knife, fork, and spoon, pliers and screwdriver, and miniatures or toys of each of the foregoing, sugar cubes, a matchbook, pipe, cigar, cigarette, a rubber ball, a rubber eraser, a rubber sink stopper, a white filing card, a green cardboard square, and a red paper circle. In the first phase of the test, with these and all of the other objects in view, he was handed one object at a time and told to put with it all that belonged with it. The material he was handed had been selected so as to permit (among others) sorting on the basis of use (eating utensils, smoking equipment, toys, tools); material (metal, paper, rubber); shape (round, rectangle); color (red, white); and size (regular, miniature). In the second phase of the test, the examiner placed several of the objects at one time before the subject and informed him that now he was to verbalize the principle of sorting involved in this group of objects. In this, as in other sortings to be placed before him, the preorganized groupings were such that the groupings involved common use, form, material, or the existence of pairs. It is these principles, one sorting at a time, which the subject had to discover. Considerable space was given to a description of their procedure in order to bring out what is meant by measures of concept formation with children. Space does not permit as detailed attention to their results.

It is suffice to say that concretistic definitions prevailed in the youngest children as shown by failure to sort in any one of the acceptable ways. The second, or functional stage, occurred when the somewhat older children made their first creditable responses by classifying in terms of what use the objects were to them. This functional level of concept formation reached its peak at the eight- or nine-year level, giving way to the more abstract level which reached a static point of maturity at about the age of eleven.   In other words, concrete definitions decreased with age, giving way to functional definitions, and, these in turn decreasing with age, giving place to abstract definitions.   Abstract explanations of the groupings steadily increased with age.

Welch and Long present another view of the levels of concept formation as summarized by Welch (77).   They sketch conceptualizing ability as extending from simple to complex levels.   There is, first, the concrete or object level of, for example, "this dog."   Beyond this concrete level there are varying degrees or levels of abstractness, each referred to as a hierarchy.   This may be illustrated by considering the five levels of abstractness of the concept from the concrete level of "this dog."   The first hierarchy level is that of "collie"; the second, "dog"; the third, "animal"; the fourth, "living sustance"; and the fifth, "substance."   These are levels of increasing abstractness on a logical basis.   The logical order is based on the fact that the next higher hierarchy includes the lower and so on to the highest level.   The first order, "collie" is included in the second, "dog," and this in turn in the third, "animal," and so on.

The developmental order, however, may be quite different from the logical.   Indeed, this is what has been found.   To quote Welch:

> The child in learning a language may begin to use some of the words which are found at the second or third hierarchy level in the logical order.   This does not necessarily imply that the child is using second or third hierarchy concepts, but rather that he is erroneously applying to concrete objects, a term used by the mature organism to designate classes at a higher level of abstractness.   If the child has not grasped the fact that animals may be thought of as cats and as dogs, he will be using the class animal as a first hierarchy concept only.   Unless he thinks of a class as including another class, he is not using a second hierarchy concept, and unless he thinks of a class which includes a class which in turn includes a class, he is not making use of a third hierarchy concept.
>
> If dog is his first class concept, then dogs, cats, cows and horses, in fact, all four-legged animals will be regarded by him as members of this class, while as yet, he will be unable to divide this class into subclasses, such as the class of dogs, cats, etc.   The child will have comparatively little difficulty in learning other *1st hierarchy* concepts such as cat.   He may have greater difficulty, however, in learning that dogs and cats belong to the class of animals.   The relationship between the class of animals and the classes of dogs and cats is what is known as a genus-species relationship.   It appears to be quite simple, but it is really very complex.   The child does not understand this relationship until he

is aware of the fact that this thing over here is a dog and that other thing over there is a cat and that both are animals. To the under-developed mind this seems to be a paradox or even a contradiction. If the child in his confusion could verbalize he might complain by saying:

> You call all of these things animals. That means they are the same. Then you turn around and call one a dog and another a cat. That means they are different. Why don't you make up your mind! Are they the same or are they different?

The answer is quite obvious! They are the same in some respects and that is why we think of them as a class of animals; still, they are different in other respects and that is why we think of them as dogs and cats. Things *can* be similar in some respects and different in others, but the task of considering their similarities one moment and their differences the next is much more difficult than considering the similarities without the differences. In other words, it is much simpler to think of things which are *either* dogs or cats under the circumstances, and never mem-bers of a more inclusive class, animals (77, 203–204).[10]

He goes on to indicate that there are two kinds of abstract con-cepts—(1) those representing classes as, for example, a chair; and (2) some characteristics divorced from any object, such as number or justice. The second kind of abstract concept is shown in the learn-ing of arithmetic. Progressing from two apples and two apples equal-ing four apples to $2 + 2 = 4$, the child is also moving from the first to the second kind of abstract concept (77).

Welch and Long have carried on a whole series of studies showing the psychological development of concepts with a wealth of detail that, of course, cannot be indicated here. One or two illustrations may be given. Welch (76) investigated when children normally begin to learn abstract concepts and their increase with age. He found that at the age of 21–26 months a group of children manifested an average of little more than one abstract concept (in the particular setup he used to measure it). The trend of development with in-creasing age was linear with an average of about six concepts at age 34–39 months, an average of about 14 concepts at 53–58 months, and 20 concepts at 65–72 months. Abstract concepts develop in a gradual orderly manner with increase in age. There appears to be an evolu-tion of concepts with gradual changes rather than a saltatory discrete series of levels.

In addition to investigating the sheer number of abstract concepts at various ages, he also investigated (77) the hierarchical level of

[10] From Welch (77). Copyright 1947 by The Journal Press, and published with permission.

concepts. Findings on first order abstract concepts, it is not surprising to observe, correspond to the findings on number of concepts. In other words, first order concepts (for example, men and women are all people) are grasped at about the twenty-sixth month. This is followed about the middle of the fourth year in the ability to grasp second-hierarchy concepts (apples are fruit and potatoes are vegetables). As ages increase, children develop abilities to grasp concepts at still higher hierarchical levels.

In this process of the development of abstract concepts, Welch considers that discrimination, generalization, and memory are the major factors involved. He illustrates this by the following:

> The behavior of a normal child of 12 months would indicate that he understood the difference between foods and non-foods, and that, at the same time, he could distinguish between one species of food and another. For instance, such a child seems to know at mealtime that the milk and pabulum, let us say, are what go down his throat, and when he manifests a preference for one or the other, he is demonstrating that he has discriminated between these two species of food; still, such behavior, at the linguistic level, where the parts of genus species phenomena are associated with words, requires much greater mental development (76, 360–361).[11]

He does not deny that motivation is also important, but pertinently observes that the development of learned motivations also depend upon discrimination, generalization, and memory. As evidence he advances such matters as the teaching of children below two years of age to verbalize differences from one stimulus situation to another when different color and size objects are presented. Again learning is found to be important.

Intellectual development in early childhood

As a consequence of developments in language and conceptualization during early childhood, there arises the greater possibility of using verbal materials for measurement of intelligence. This is reflected in the contents of the California Preschool Schedule, an intelligence test especially developed for use with children of this age. Although it includes items on block building, manual facility, and drawing, it also includes conceptual material such as spatial relations

[11] From Welch (76). Copyright 1940 by The Journal Press, and published with permission.

and size and number discriminations; also included are verbal items on language comprehension, language facility, and immediate recall of verbal materials (41). As can be seen from this listing, conceptual and verbal materials are not neglected. It will also be noted that a relatively wider array of abilities has been included than was the case with infant tests. As might be expected from its greater weighting with verbal-conceptual materials and from its wider sampling of abilities, intelligence tests administered during the preschool years are better predictors of later intelligence than are scores on tests administered in infancy (37).

As part of the Guidance Study of the University of California Institute of Child Welfare described in Chapter 1, 250 childen were given periodic intelligence tests beginning at the age of one year nine months, and continuing for a 16 year period (37). The California Preschool Schedule was given to each child during early childhood, while the Stanford-Binet (described on pages 484–488) was administered during later childhood. The correlations they found between intelligence test scores in early and later childhood are given in Table 14. As the children became older their test scores became increas-

TABLE 14

CORRELATION BETWEEN INTELLIGENCE TEST SCORES IN
EARLY AND LATER CHILDHOOD *

Age	Correlation with S-B Age 8	Correlation with S-B Age 14
2	43	21
3	49	35
4	61	54

* Adapted from Honzik et al. (37). Copyright 1948 by the *Journal of Experimental Education*, and published with permission.

ingly more related to scores obtained in later childhood and hence increasingly more predictive. This continues a trend, mentioned in Chapter 6, for intelligence test prediction to become increasingly more accurate the older the child is when tested. It will be remembered that group predictions of later intellectual development based on measures administered before one year of age were so low as to be meaningless, and that predictions based on later ages in infancy, although improved in accuracy, still were not very predictive. This was true even for the short intervals of one and two years elapsing between early and late infancy, or late infancy to early childhood. Correlations of intelligence test scores of preschool-aged children with those obtained in later childhood are relatively more predictive even over much longer periods of time. However, the correlations are not high enough to eliminate the possibility of large differences in the scores of individual children from test to retest. Individual children may still differ markedly from age to age in intelligence test scores, despite these substantial correlations.

Summary

The preschool years are a period of considerable psychological development for the young child.

In his motor development he progresses from the clumsy two-year-old to the graceful, smooth, efficient five-year-old. Both learning and maturation contribute to this development. For a given motor skill, stages may be traced beginning at the level where no attempt is made, progressing through the stage in which skill is in the process of formation, to the point where the basic movements are achieved. Illustrative changes in these degrees of motor skill are given. The isolation of a strength and of a speed factor has been achieved on studying the interrelation among motor skills.

Emotional patterns of anger and fear in early childhood show developmental changes in expression, frequency, causes, and general conditions for their appearance. Although fear and anger differ from one another in regard to all of these characteristics, they are related in a variety of ways, including their being simultaneously aroused and their intermingling in the form of jealousy. In contrast to anger and fear which are the disruptive emotions, the affectively pleasant emotions have received less systematic attention. Although smiling and laughter are found to be their major external behavior indices, there was relatively little in the way of agreement on the nature of the sources which brought about their arousal.

Language development in early childhood brings out clearly that both egocentric and socialized functions are being served. Although there is disagreement on the proportion of the speech of the child serving each of these functions, there is general agreement that both functions are present and that a decrease in egocentric speech takes place with increasing age. The growth of vocabulary size continues during these years. Other developments during this age period are changes in clearness of articulation, in the integration of words into sentences, in the length of sentences, and the relative use of the grammatical parts of speech. All are found to show greater maturity as the child grows older. Despite these similarities, there are individual, group, and sex differences in language development. Speech, it is found, rests firmly upon the learning processes.

The development of understanding in early and late childhood has been expressed through consideration of thinking in general and concept formation in particular. The stages in the development of thinking are examined in the setting of Piaget's formulation of these stages as sensory-motor activity, egocentric thought, and rational thought. His views on conceptions of physical causality and animistic thinking are more specific aspects of thinking. In general, it was found that there is perhaps not as sharp a contrast between adult and child thinking as Piaget would have it, and that there is no saltatory shifting from one stage of conceptualization to the next. Animistic thinking does occur, but probably not in as extensive a fashion as Piaget believes. Discussion of various concepts closes the discussion of understanding. Time and space concepts serve as illustrations. Specification of the levels of conceptual development is given in terms of two classifications; the first in terms of three levels—concrete, functional, and abstract; and the second in terms of a concrete level and a number of levels of abstractness.

Intellectual development, as differentiated from language development and the development of understanding, is only briefly considered since in a later chapter considerable attention is devoted to this facet of development. Verbal-conceptual materials are increasingly used for intellectual measurement as age increases during this period. With increase in age intellectual measures become increasingly predictive of intellectual status at still older ages.

For Further Reading

Exhaustive reviews of emotional and linguistic development appear in the *Manual of Child Psychology: Second Edition*, edited by Leonard Carmichael (New York: Wiley, 1954). These are the chapters by Arthur Jersild and Dorothea McCarthy. Many of Piaget's books have been translated. For a general review, although somewhat outdated, his book, *Factors Determining Human Behavior* (Cambridge, Mass.: Harvard University Press, 1937), has much to recommend it.

References

1. Ames, Louise B. The constancy of psycho-motor tempo in individual infants. *J. genet. Psychol.*, 1940, 57, 445–450.
2. Arsenian, Jean M. Young children in an insecure situation. *J. abnorm. soc. Psychol.*, 1943, 38, 235–249.
3. Baldwin, A. L. Changes in parent behavior during pregnancy: an experiment in longitudinal analysis. *Child Develpm.*, 1947, 18, 29–39.
4. Baruch, Dorothy W. Doll play in preschool as an aid in understanding the child. *Ment. Hyg., N. Y.*, 1940, 24, 566–577.
5. Bayley, Nancy. The development of motor abilities during the first three years. *Monogr. Soc. Res. Child Develpm.*, 1935, No. 1.
6. Blatz, W. E., Allen, Kathleen D., and Millichamp, Dorothy A. A study of laughter in the nursery school child. *Univer. Toronto Stud. Child Develpm. Ser.*, 1936, No. 7.
7. Brackett, Catherine W. Laughing and crying of preschool children. *Child Develpm. Monogr.*, 1934, No. 14.
8. Bridges, Katherine, M.B. *Social and emotional development of the preschool child*. London: Kegan, Paul, 1931.
9. Brigance, W. N. The language learning of a child. *J. appl. Psychol.*, 1934, 18, 143–154.
10. Bruce, Myrtle. Animism vs. evolution of the concept "alive." *J. Psychol.*, 1941, 12, 81–90.
11. Cannon, W. B. *Bodily changes in pain, hunger, fear, and rage*. New York: Appleton-Century-Crofts, 1929.
12. Carpenter, Aileen. The differential measurement of speed in primary school children. *Child Develpm.*, 1941, 12, 1–7.
13. Crannell, C. W. The responses of college students to a questionnaire on animistic thinking. *Scientific Mon.*, 1954, 78, 1–2.
14. Davis, Edith A. *The development of linguistic skill in twins, singletons with siblings and only children from age five to ten years*. Minneapolis: University of Minnesota Press, 1937.
15. Davis, Edith A. Mean sentence length compared with long and short sentences as a reliable measure of language development. *Child Develpm.*, 1937, 8, 69–79.
16. Davis, Edith A. The mental and linguistic superiority of only girls. *Child Develpm.*, 1937, 8, 139–143.
17. Day, Ella J. The development of language in twins: I. A comparison of twins and single children. *Child Develpm.*, 1932, 3, 179–199.
18. Day, Ella J. The development of language in twins: II. The development of twins; their resemblances and differences. *Child Develpm.*, 1932, 3, 298–316

19. Dennis, W. Animistic thinking among college and university students. *Scientific Mon.*, 1953, 76, 247–249.

20. Deutsche, Jean M. The development of children's concepts of causal relations. *Univer. Minn. Child Welf. Monogr.*, 1937, No. 13.

21. Ding, Gladys F., and Jersild, A. T. A study of the laughing and smiling of preschool children. *J. genet. Psychol.*, 1932, 40, 452–472.

22. Dollard, J., and Miller, N. E. *Personality and psychotherapy: an analysis in terms of learning, thinking, and culture.* New York: McGraw-Hill, 1950.

23. Drever, J. A study of children's vocabularies: I, II, and III. *J. exp. Ped.*, 1915–1916, 3, 34–43, 96–103, 182–188.

24. Felder, J. G. Some factors determining the nature and frequency of anger and fear outbreaks in preschool children. *J. juv. Res.*, 1932, 16, 278–290.

25. Fisher, Mary S. Language patterns of preschool children. *Child Develpm. Monogr.*, 1934, No. 5.

26. Gesell, A. *et al. The first five years of life: a guide to the study of the preschool child.* New York: Harper, 1940.

27. Gesell, A., and Ilg, Frances L. *Child development: an introduction to the study of human growth.* New York: Harper, 1949.

28. Goldfarb, W. Psychological privation in infancy and subsequent adjustment. *Amer. J. Orthopsychiat.*, 1945, 15, 247–255.

29. Goldfarb, W. The effects of early institutional care on adolescent personality. *J. exp. Educ.*, 1943, 12, 106–129.

30. Goodenough, Florence L. Anger in young children. *Univer. Minn. Inst. Child Welf. Monogr. Ser.*, 1931, No. 9.

31. Gutteridge, Mary V. A study of motor achievements of young children. *Arch. Psychol., N. Y.*, 1939, No. 244.

32. Hagman, E. R. A study of fears of children of preschool age. *J. exp. Educ.*, 1932, 1, 110–130.

33. Hall, C. S., and Lindzey, G. *Theories of personality.* New York: Wiley, 1957.

34. Hartman, Doris M. The hurdle jump as a measure of the motor proficiency of young children. *Child Develpm.*, 1943, 14, 201–211.

35. Hazlitt, Victoria. Children's thinking. *Brit. J. Psychol.*, 1930, 20, 354–361.

36. Hicks, J. A. The acquisition of motor skill in young children: a study of the effects of practice in throwing at a moving target. *Child Develpm.*, 1930, 1, 90–105.

37. Honzik, Muriel P., Macfarlane, Jean W., and Allen, Louise. The stability of mental test performance between two and eighteen years. *J. exp. Educ.*, 1948, 17, 309–324.

38. Huang, I. Children's conception of physical causality: a critical summary. *J. genet. Psychol.*, 1943, 63, 71–121.

39. Huang, I., and Lee, H. W. Experimental analysis of child animism. *J. genet. Psychol.*, 1945, 66, 69–74.

40. Hull, C. L. Quantitative aspects of the evolution of concepts. *Psychol. Monogr.*, 1920, 28, No. 1.

41. Jaffa, Adele S. The California Preschool Mental Scale (form A). *Univer. Calif. Los Angeles Syllabus Ser.*, 1934, No. 251.

42. Jersild, A. T. Emotional development. In L. Carmichael (Ed.), *Manual of child psychology* (2nd ed.). New York: Wiley, 1954, 833–917.

43. Jersild, A. T. Research in the development of children. *Teach. Coll. Rec.*, 1936, 38, 129–143.
44. Jersild, A. T. Studies of children's fears. In R. G. Barker *et al.* (Eds.), *Child behavior and development: a course of representative studies.* New York: McGraw-Hill, 1943, 329–344.
45. Jersild, A. T., and Holmes, Frances B. Children's fears. *Child Develpm. Monogr.*, 1935, No. 20.
46. Justin, Florence. A genetic study of laughter provoking stimuli. *Child Develpm.*, 1932, 3, 114–136.
47. Landis, C., and Hunt, W. A. *The startle pattern.* New York: Rinehart, 1939.
48. Landreth, Catherine. Factors associated with crying in young children in the nursery school and the home. *Child Develpm.*, 1941, 12, 81–97.
49. Leuba, C. Tickling and laughter: two genetic studies. *J. genet. Psychol.*, 1941, 58, 201–209.
50. Levy, D. M. Hostility patterns in sibling rivalry experiments. *Amer. J. Orthopsychiat.*, 1936, 6, 183–257.
51. McCarthy, Dorothea. The language development of the preschool child. *Inst. Child. Welf. Monogr. Ser.* Minneapolis: 1930, No. 4.
52. McCarthy, Dorothea. Language development in children. In L. Carmichael (Ed.), *Manual of child psychology* (2nd ed.). New York: Wiley, 1954, 492–630.
53. McNemar, Q. *The revision of the Stanford-Binet Scale: an analysis of the standardization data.* New York: Houghton Mifflin, 1942.
54. Miller, N. E., and Dollard, J. *Social learning and imitation.* New Haven: Yale University Press, 1941.
55. Mowrer, O. H. A stimulus-response analysis of anxiety and its role as a reinforcing agent. *Psychol. Rev.*, 1939, 46, 553–565.
56. Munn, N. L. Learning in children. In L. Carmichael (Ed.), *Manual of child psychology* (2nd ed.). New York: Wiley, 1954, 374–458.
57. Nass, M. L. The effects of three variables on children's concepts of physical causality. *J. abnorm. soc. Psychol.*, 1956, 53, 191–196.
58. Nice, Margaret M. Length of sentences as a criterion of a child's progress in speech. *J. educ. Psychol.*, 1925, 16, 370–379.
59. Piaget, J. *The language and thought of the child.* New York: Humanities Press, 1926.
60. Piaget, J. *Judgment and reasoning in the child.* New York: Harcourt, Brace, 1928.
61. Piaget, J. *The child's conception of the world.* New York: Humanities Press, 1929.
62. Piaget, J. *The child's conception of physical causality.* New York: Harcourt, Brace, 1930.
63. Piaget, J. Children's philosophies. In C. Murchison (Ed.), *A handbook of child psychology* (2nd ed. rev.). Worcester, Mass.: Clark University Press, 1933, 534–547.
64. Piaget, J. *Factors determining human behavior.* Cambridge, Mass.: Harvard University Press, 1937.
65. Piaget, J. *The origins of intelligence in children.* New York: International Universities Press, 1952.

66. Reichard, Suzanne, and Rapaport, D.   The role of testing concept formation in clinical psychological work.   *Bull. Menninger Clin.*, 1943, 7, 99–105.

67. Reichard, Suzanne, Schneider, Marion, and Rapaport, D.   The development of concept formation in children.   *Amer. J. Orthopsychiat.*, 1944, 14, 156–161.

68. Ricketts, A. F.   A study of the behavior of young children in anger.   *Univer. Iowa Stud. Child Welfare*, 1934, 9, No. 3, 159–171.

69. Russell, R. W.   Studies in animism: II. The development of animism.   *J. genet. Psychol.*, 1940, 56, 353–366.

70. Russell, R. W.   Studies in animism: IV. An investigation of concepts allied to animism.   *J. genet. Psychol.*, 1940, 57, 83–91.

71. Sears, R. R.   Personality development in the family.   In R. F. Winch and R. McGinnis (Eds.), *Marriage and the family.*   New York: Holt, 1953, 215–240.

72. Smith, Medorah E.   An investigation of the development of the sentence and the extent of the vocabulary in young children.   *Univer. Iowa Stud. Child Welfare*, 1926, 3, No. 5.

73. Vollmer, H.   Jealousy in children.   *Amer. J. Orthopsychiat.*, 1946, 16, 660–671.

74. Washburn, Ruth W.   A study of smiling and laughing of infants in the first year of life.   *Genet. Psychol. Monogr.*, 1929, 6, 397–537.

75. Welch, L.   The genetic development of the associational structures of abstract thinking.   *J. genet. Psychol.*, 1940, 56, 175–206.

76. Welch, L.   A preliminary investigation of some aspects of the hierarchical development of concepts.   *J. gen. Psychol.*, 1940, 22, 359–378.

77. Welch, L.   A behaviorist explanation of concept formation.   *J. genet. Psychol.*, 1947, 71, 201–222.

78. Welch, L., and Long, L.   The higher structural phases of concept formation of children.   *J. Psychol.*, 1940, 9, 59–95.

79. Welch, L., and Long, L.   A further investigation of the higher structural phases of concept formation.   *J. Psychol.*, 1940, 10, 211–220.

80. Wellmann, Beth L., Case, Ida M., Mengert, Ida G., and Bradbury, Dorothy.   Speech sounds of young children.   *Univer. Iowa Stud. Child Welfare*, 1931, 5, No. 2.

chapter 10

Psychosocial Development
in Early Childhood

$\mathbf{G}$REAT STRIDES WERE MADE IN PSYCHOSOCIAL DEVEL-
opment from the neonatal period to the end of infancy. The infant's
social behavior repertoire increased enormously. During infancy he
encountered the problems of the oral and anal phases and worked
out some solution to them. He learned social needs. He learned to
be dependent but also took the first steps toward independence. He
learned, to some degree, to direct and perhaps even control his aggression. He encountered sex in its primitive beginning. He began
to recognize himself as a person and to appreciate the presence and
effect of other persons. Above all, he developed a complex pattern
of relationships with another human being, his mother. But at the
end of infancy he was by no means a fully socialized human being.
Allport expresses this point very well when he writes:

> Even at the age of two, the child is, when measured by standards
> applied to adults, an unsocialized horror. Picture, if you can, an adult
> who is extremely destructive of property, insistent and demanding that
> every desire be instantly gratified, helpless and almost totally dependent
> on others, unable to share his possessions, impatient, prone to tantrums,
> violent and uninhibited in the display of his feelings (2, 28).[1]

[1] From Allport (2). Copyright 1955 by the Yale University Press, and published with permission.

The two-year-old is not a completely socialized creature. To put it in Freudian terms, he is still ruled primarily by the pleasure principle although he is beginning to appreciate the reality principle with its demand for sacrificing present pleasures either for future gain or for avoiding subsequent punishment.

Now we need to examine psychosocial development that takes place between the second birthday and the end of the fifth year. The order of presentation used in discussing psychosocial development in infancy will be followed. Psychosocial development in early childhood will be examined in terms of parental behavior influencing socialization, the development of self and social awareness, behavior tendencies of dependence and independence, sex and aggression, the evidence concerning psychoanalytic theories, and a neo-Freudian interpretation of these theories.

Parental behavior influencing socialization in early childhood

The mother's role in interaction with the younger child must be examined because of its importance in his socialization. Concern is with the interactive behaviors she exhibits. The various forms that her specific practices take, such as encouraging or discouraging her child, will first be considered briefly. Subsequently, the significance of parental attitudes and the general atmosphere of the home will be reviewed. The patterns that are found in this review then form the basis for consideration of their relation to the child behavior with which they are associated. Thereafter, the socializing effect of the father, techniques of training used with young children, and changes in parental behavior with age of the children are taken up. The section closes with examining the question of the degree to which the parental behavior and attitudes that have been explored can be considered as causative of child behavior.

Specific Maternal Practices Influencing Socialization

Specific maternal practices were studied by Tucker (76) in the setting of a cooperative nursery school where the mothers participated as helpers. The mother's practices toward the children, including her own, was observed over a period of time and her behavior classified according to a prearranged schedule. Once the behavior samples were collected and classified the investigator calculated the percentage frequency for each of the categories which had been set up. In decreasing frequency the kind and extent of maternal practices she found are reported in Table 15. Directing behavior, that is, the

TABLE 15

KINDS AND EXTENT OF MATERNAL PRACTICES *

Maternal Behavior	Per Cent
Directs	52
Seeks information	11
Offers explanation	10
Impedes	6
Encourages	5
Overlooks	4
Commends	3
Diverts attention	3
Urges	3
Reassures	2
Warns	1
Discourages	0.5
Forces	0.5

* Adapted from Tucker (76). Copyright 1940 by Clara Tucker, and published with permission.

mothers telling the children how or what to do, makes up over half of their activities. At the other extreme, forcing the children regardless of their opposition makes up only about one-half of one per cent of their activities. Individual mothers showed considerable variability in the percentage of their activities that fell within a given category. For example, although the average for directive activities was 50 per cent, one mother's behavior consisted of such activities over 60 per cent of the time; another followed this kind of practice less than 40 per cent of the time. Some mothers never forced or discouraged their own or other children; others devoted two per cent of their activity to these practices.

Tucker found that the kinds of maternal practices varied according to the situation. For example, in a routine situation, such as putting on wraps, forcing and discouraging were not used at all, and in an emergency situation, the mothers did not commend or discourage. Maternal practices also varied according to whether the mother was dealing with her own or some other child. When interacting with her own child, mothers tended more often to seek information, offer explanations, encourage, commend, warn, and overlook. In contrast, when interacting with other children, the mothers tended more often to impede, direct, urge, force, discourage, divert attention, and re-assure. In general, mothers in dealing with their own children tended to be more sympathetic and protective, while with other children they tended to lack empathy and to be more guided by a sense of responsibility.

Merrill (59) studied systematically variation in maternal behavior in different situations. Through a one-way screen, each mother was observed in interaction with her preschool child during two play sessions. From the findings of the first session, behavior categories were developed in terms of facilitative and inhibitory behavior, the methods of control used, and the kinds of response the mothers showed. After Merrill had determined that these categories were reliable, they were used as the basis for dividing the mothers into two matched groups. Each mother in the experimental group was led to believe that her child "had not shown a full realization of his capacities on the first session," as contrasted with the mothers in the control group who received instruction similar to those of their first session.

It was assumed that the relatively mild pressure on the mothers in the experimental group would result in increased motivation on their part for their children to do well. Almost all mothers whose children were thus mildly criticized responded to this pressure, as indicated by increases in some forms of behavior and decreases in others. It was found that the mothers of the criticized children tended to assume more direct control of their children's behavior and to impose their own standards to a greater degree than they had in the first session. Almost all of these mothers showed a significant increase in directing, interfering, criticizing, and structuring changes in activities. As a result of this study it would appear that when their child is criticized by someone else, the mothers tend to become more authoritarian and controlling of their children's behavior. Presumably, other forms of shifting of the mother-child situation would also show consistency of shifts of maternal behavior.

What happens when the situation is substantially the same for two sessions? In another study, this time with no criticism made about any of the subjects, the same investigator (15) demonstrated a considerable degree of consistency in maternal behavior between a first and second session. Mothers were found to show consistent behavior in successive sessions when the situation was substantially the same.

These studies of maternal behavior directed toward younger children are significant for showing the kinds of maternal behavior to be expected. The change of maternal behavior with shift in the nature of the situation and the consistency of maternal behavior when the situation continues to be the same have both been demonstrated.

Maternal behavior has been analyzed without attention to the "intent" of the parent in carrying out a particular activity. For example, "directing" behavior was not identified as to what the mother expected to accomplish by the behavior so categorized. To be sure, it could be conjectured that some socializing aim might have been intended. She might, for example, have wanted him to do a certain thing, say, learn to hang up his coat, and told him to do it. However, a particular behavior episode involving direction might have been engendered out of one of her deep-seated temperamental personality characteristics, or it might have been nothing more than a momentary pique on her part. Or, turning to another example, "Keep quiet!", a form of directive behavior, was not studied in relation to what motivated a particular mother to behave in this way. About these matters we know nothing from these studies.

Even more important, the behavior of these mothers has not been related to what the children did. From our knowledge of what happens when attempts are made to relate specific maternal practices in infancy to subsequent child behavior, this omission is understandable. There is no reason to believe that specific maternal practices during the preschool years would be any more predictively effective than practices in infancy. At any rate, evidence about consequent child behavior is absent. Parental attitudes and home atmospheres have been more fruitful in giving us information about the child behavior with which it is associated.

Parental Attitudes and Home Atmospheres Influencing Socialization

Aspects of socialization broader in nature than specific parental practices have been utilized and related to child behavior. The study of parental attitudes, already familiar from earlier discussion of their influence during infancy, is one such approach. Another approach to socialization of the young child is that of examining the effect of the "home atmosphere." Home atmosphere refers to phases of the familial situation which have been isolated for study, such as the democratic atmosphere or unharmonious family relationships. It will be noted that atmospheres appear to be somewhat more general in nature than is the case with attitudes. Although these two approaches are distinguished methodologically, both often have been used in the same study. Hence, there will be no attempt to discuss the results separately.

Baldwin's approach to patterns. One of the most significant research programs concerning parent behavior has utilized the *Fels Parent Behavior Rating Scales* as the major instrument for the collection of data. These carefully contrived rating scales were designed to measure 30 variables of parental attitudes, parental behavior, and home atmospheres. Each scale was devised because it was concerned with something considered important for its psychological impact on the child. The scales range from such global, all inclusive judgments as "adjustment of the home" to such specific variables as "restrictiveness of regulations."

Baldwin, Kalhorn, and Breese (*11*) investigated the *patterns* revealed by correlating the interrelationships among the 30 variables. The subjects they used were drawn from 124 homes, a major portion of the Fels Research Institute permanent cooperating population. The parents, in the main, were above average in intelligence, economic status, and education. A visitor observed both mother and child in the home and made the ratings on the scales. The intercorrelations of the ratings on each variable with every other variable were calculated. Three syndromes, or groups of homes, were isolated which accounted for the intercorrelations they had obtained. These syndromes, identified in the left-hand portion of Figure 10, are democracy in the home, acceptance of the child, and indulgence. The variables which made up the syndromes and from which they derived their summarizing names are also given and listed in order of their importance to the cluster. (At the moment no attention need be paid to the individual ratings given in the diagram portion of the figure. They are to be considered later.)

Knowing that the homes fall into these three syndromes does not tell us into which category a specific home would fall. It would be too much to expect that these three group categories describing homes in general would be suitable for classification of individual homes. Rather, in specific homes we would expect that there would be not only various combinations of these three dimensions, but also varying positions from high to low on each syndrome. Consequently, the in-

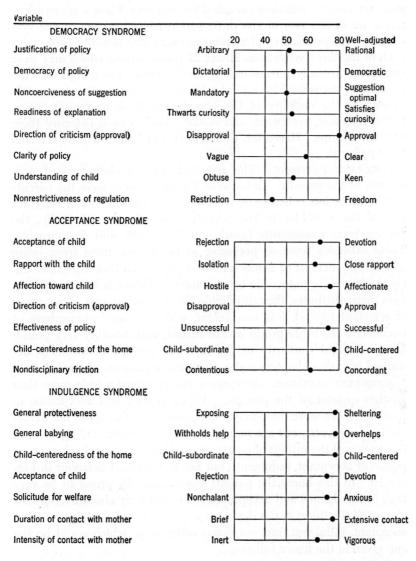

Figure 10. Syndromes of parent behavior and sample profile of indulgent behavior. (Adapted from Baldwin et al. (11). Copyright 1945 by the American Psychological Association, and published with permission.)

vestigators subdivided each of the three syndromes into "high," "low," and "middling," and then classified the homes. Thus, a given home might be in any one of the three subdivisions for each of the syndromes. All possible combinations among three possible choices for each of the three syndromes allows 27 combinations which may have emerged. Actually, a considerably smaller number of groups than the possible 27 accounted for all but a few of the homes. It was possible to classify the majority of the homes into three major categories, called rejectant, acceptant, and casual. Within each category there were subgroups. Hereafter, these clusters of homes will be referred to as patterns.

REJECTANT PATTERNS. The rejectant pattern characterized one-quarter of the parents. In terms of Figure 10 these were the parents who more or less consistently received ratings at the low or rejectant end of the variables in the acceptance syndrome. Basically, the parents were consistently hostile, unaffectionate, and disapproving. These attitudes were so pervasive as to prevent them from being genuinely solicitous or democratic in dealing with their children. Instead, they were autocratic toward them. Although having in common these attributes, they did divide into two subgroups. One group of rejectant parents was *nonchalant,* with a general atmosphere of unconcern; the other group was *dominant,* with hostility very prominent. General similarity of the rejectant pattern to instances described in earlier chapters makes further comment unnecessary.

ACCEPTANT PATTERNS. *Acceptance* characterized a little more than another quarter of the parents. Although they had acceptance in common, there were three major subgroups: *indulgent, but not democratic; democratic, but not indulgent;* and *democratic-indulgent.* An illustration of the ratings of an acceptance home is given in the sample profile of acceptant, indulgent (but not democratic) behavior in Figure 10. In this home the parents were especially prone to be very high in indulgence and acceptance items, but only about average for almost all the items in the democracy syndrome. A description of an acceptant, indulgent, but not democratic, home which could be the one given in the figure follows:

Shirley Ann Harper: Indulgent

Mrs. Harper is extreme in almost every variable of behavior making up the *indulgent* syndrome. Her attitudes and behavior toward Shirley Ann are obvious reflections of her smug, narrow set of values and her complete identification with the child. She is "living again" in her child, in the most literal sense of the phrase—setting her own adult standards for Shirley's behavior, interpreting Shirley's motives as identical with what her own would be, enjoying Shirley as a new and more attractive version of her own self. Seeing Shirley Ann as a replica of herself, she freely gratifies any of her whims with which she can identify. Within the limits of what is "proper" for a little girl, Shirley is granted whatever she wants, no matter what sacrifice may be entailed for the parents. It is only when Shirley Ann's behavior violates Mrs. Harper's strict code of morals and proprieties that it meets uncompromising opposition.

A professional woman, married when she was thirty-three to a middle-aged salesman, Mrs. Harper has become a smug and proper middle-class mother. Her social philosophy is righteous and superior; she looks down on those she thinks of inferior class or of different standards, and her behavior toward them is condemnatory rather than beneficent. Money, morals, and mores are her values. Shirley Ann was a much desired child, and her birth represented fulfillment to both parents. Being attractive and intelligent, Shirley is a social asset to the Harpers, and their appreciation of her unique qualities has led them to be two completely doting parents who make no effort to conceal or rationalize their adoration of the remarkable handiwork they have brought forth.

From Shirley Ann's birth, indulgence and child-centeredness have been the central features of the Harper household. When Shirley was two and a half months old, the home visitor reports: "Mr. and Mrs. Harper have apparently lost all objectivity in dealing with the child. Their treatment of her is a succession of lavish kisses, affectionate conversation, and considerable handling, almost mauling. Baby talk abounds, even when Shirley is not present." In all of her social contacts, Mrs. Harper's description of Shirley Ann is liberally sprinkled with such saccharine phrases as "Shirley is our life"; "She's my little sweetheart"; or, proudly, "At school she's really a teacher's little helper." At the time of the birth of a second child, Mrs. Harper had the delivery at home, saying, "I'd much rather go to the hospital but I just couldn't stand to be away from this little dumpling."

Even in disciplinary situations Mrs. Harper finds it necessary to temper her severity with indulgent sympathy because, as she says, "punishment just about breaks Shirley's little heart." When Shirley was two, we have this report: "Mrs. H's requests are all on an emotional level, usually given in baby-talk. When the mail came, Mrs. Harper let Shirley have it on the condition that she would not tear any of the letters. Shirley proceeded to tear the letters open. Mrs. H. finally took them away from her, then commiserated with her when she began to cry."

Next only to the Harpers' rapture over the "bundle from heaven" they have produced comes their concern with molding this property into an utterly nice, utterly proper child. At three months Shirley was being broken of thumb sucking; at ten and a half months, we find this behavior; "The baby imitated everything that her mother did . . . once, inadvertently, Mrs. H. forced air out of her lips, and Shirley did that too. At first Mrs. H. was amused, then she became worried, saying that she did not want Shirley to have the habit." Muss and clutter are forbidden and from the very earliest age Shirley was subjected to intense restriction as to how many toys she could have out at one time and to rules about picking up one thing before going on to the next. This imposition of adult standards of propriety, neatness, orderliness, reaches into the area of "free play" too, of course, since little of Shirley's life may be conducted according to her own initiative or taste. Another visitor reports: "Mrs. H. remarked to me with some despair after she had fruitlessly tried to get Shirley to arrange the blankets on her doll in correct order (sheet, blanket, quilt, and spread), 'How old do they have to be before they learn to do things *right?*'" The proprieties which Mrs. Harper attempts to dun into the child vary from good manners at the table, including saying grace, to a subservient respect for her elders; this old-fashioned, rigorous philosophy of the docile child who is to be seen but not heard conflicts continually, of course, with the rapt adulation of the parents. Their approval is intense, their punishment halfhearted and full of sympathy for the "poor little thing."

The combination of indulgence and insistence on social graces leads to an extremely restricting form of protectiveness. Throughout infancy Shirley was kept in a condition of "surgical asepsis." When she was three, for example, she had a special doll to take to bed that she couldn't play with at any other time because it was kept laundered, fresh, and supposedly germ free. Her social life is similarly kept free from possible taint. Very few outsiders are permitted more than the most casual relationship with Shirley, all being found "bad for her" in one way or another. The paternal grandfather has all but been forbidden the house, for instance, because he persisted in "spoiling" Shirley Ann (laughed when she sucked her thumb, kept her from a nap to entertain her, etc.); children are uniformly not good enough to play with her—they are dirty, infectious, bad-mannered or contaminating in some other way. A Country Day School was handpicked to exert the proper guidance on Shirley and to set a high moral tone—e.g., the children assemble, give the teacher "a nice smile," recite the Lord's Prayer, sing "America," pledge allegiance to the flag, and then are ready to begin the morning's activity. . . .

Though in reality Shirley is far from being a docile, conforming child, she stays well enough within the limits imposed by the parents to assure a safe margin of approval. Disciplinary crises are rare, but small mischievous types of disobedience are common enough to warrant continual suggestions and nagging. An interviewer summarizing a conversation with Mrs. Harper wrote: "The general impression of the home is that Shirley is the apple of the eye; she has a secure place, but is handled with old-fashioned strictness about routine and 'niceness,' is being brought up 'properly.' I felt that Shirley was on to this and could manage her parents skillfully, crying, loving, being cute, good, independent, etc., within the well-defined discipline limits, and that she is far more dominating and sure of herself, more indulged and self-centered than her parents suspect. I had the feeling that Shirley was well in command of the situation and was keeping her parents happy" (*11*, 37–39).[2]

The acceptant, indulgent, nondemocratic home bears considerable resemblance to the overprotective home described in connection with infancy. The acceptant home, democratic but not indulgent, would appear to be at the desirable end of the continuum and to be related to acceptance within normal limits as described in the chapter on psychosocial development in infancy. The finding by Baldwin and his associates that these two belong in separate groups serves to strengthen the contention made earlier that acceptance and over-protection should be distinguished.

While having the acceptant pattern in common, three subpatterns of democratic homes were found: (1) *pseudo-democratic*—a subpattern in which the parents allow the child to participate in some decisions, but at the same time give no freedom concerning anything fundamental or important; (2) *scientifically democratic*—a subpattern where the parents, although fond of their children, tend not to show it, but conscientiously apply and even force democracy because they know it is "right"; (3) *warm democratic*—a subpattern in which the child is treated warmly, accepted in his own right, and treated democratically. A description of an acceptant, warm democratic home follows:

> The Rampion household represents a rather happy combination of those factors judged by the authors to be productive of a "good environment" for the child. The parents themselves are well-adjusted, vital, outgoing; they enjoy children as such and their own children as individuals. They show a healthy balance between the type of psychological detachment which allows them to appraise the child objectively and a warm emotionality that permits them to exhibit their devotion without embarrassment or artificiality. The child occupies his proportionate place in the household, is a full member of the family group, and is neither catered to nor ignored.
>
> Mrs. Rampion herself is a healthy "farm-woman" type of person, sturdily built, stable, kindly, and good-humored. She was a professional woman before her marriage and possesses to a remarkable degree qualities of tolerance and patience. With a keen sense of humor she embellishes the most mundane situations, making life interesting and flavorful for her family. She is alert and interested in community life, contributes generously of her time and services for a variety of groups and causes. Liberal in her political philosophy, she is a genuinely democratic person in the home and in the community.

[2] From Baldwin *et al.* (*11*). Copyright 1945 by the American Psychological Association, and published with permission.

The maturity Mrs. Rampion exhibits in her personal life and in her general attitudes is also displayed, naturally enough, in her behavior toward the children. Respecting them as individuals, she makes a conscious and conscientious effort to maintain an emotional distance, a detachment giving objectivity to her appraisal of them. An incident which reveals her imperturbability in the area of sex behavior is equally illustrative of her ability in general to see the children's behavior in perspective. "There is some possibility that Leonard masturbates, although Mrs. R. does not know definitely. He likes to stick out his penis and run around the house. Bobby is disgusted with the performance, Carol and Bud think it funny. Leonard also likes to rub himself on a toy horse which the children play on. 'He's very sexy,' Mrs. R. remarked. She had no emotional reaction to it, seemed casual and straightforward about the situation. It is definitely not a problem in her mind."

Her philosophy of nonintervention is further illustrated by the following incident: "The three children were playing well together. Once Carol got too near a ladder the boys were balancing. Mrs. R. called out the window for Leonard to watch her. She remarked that she hated to do it, and only resorted to warnings when she could foresee serious injury." If anything, the parents are too loathe to intervene. In their determination to stay out of the children's disputes they sometimes allow an undue amount of social pressure to be exerted upon the unfortunate culprit who incurs the disapproval of his siblings.

The Rampions, more than any other family in the study, have explicit and formalized techniques for expressing their democratic philosophy of child care. Family council is traditional, with full and equal membership being accorded each child as soon as he can meet the requirement of repeating verbatim and explaining the motion before the group. The agenda may consist of matters ranging from the question of who shall wash and who shall wipe the dishes to the decision as to whether Mrs. R. should take a job offered her. The council convenes at the request of any member, and customarily handles the arbitration of all disputes. For example: "A situation has recently arisen in the Rampion family which is significant in that it shows the technique of settling difficulties among members of the family. While Bobby was combing his hair upstairs, Leonard 'dibbsed' on the wishbones from two chickens. Bobby was furious when he found what L. had done, said that it was unfair because one could never dibbs on more than his share, that he had never done it, etc. As a matter of fact, Bobby had done it more than any of the others. The two argued about it far into the night. Both Mr. and Mrs. R. kept out of the argument, hoping, however, that Leonard would stick to his guns and that Bobby's fallacy in argument would be brought out by him. The night of my visit Bob had called a family council to settle the question, said that he would abide by the council's decision. Mrs. R. said that she was not going to bring up the fact that Bobby was the prize dibbser unless the other children mentioned it first."

In spite of the formality of democratic government and in spite of the emotional distance which the Rampions maintain, the home atmosphere is not bleak or forbidding. The warm tone so evident in all the family's relationships characterized their attitudes toward one another. Without a great deal of fondling or other overt symbols of affection, the parents convey to the children their deep devotion.

It should be emphasized that the Rampion home is not "perfect" nor even optimum in its effect on the child—so far as we can, at present, evaluate the optimum. Mrs. Rampion faces the usual run of disciplinary crises, feeding problems, and general reversals that come to most mothers, although she handles such situations with more than average patience and understanding. In this democratic atmosphere Leonard is, at present, making an excellent social adjustment, although his development in the past has illustrated some of the difficulties peculiar to such a closely knit and satisfying family structure. On the one hand his home background has been so encompassing in its satisfactions that Leonard found the outside world, by comparison, somewhat dull and uninteresting. His social adjustment during the preschool years was marked by shyness and withdrawal. At the same time, Leonard has suffered from his failure to meet the high standards of the Rampion household. He has been the most irresponsible and lazy of the children and, as a consequence, has been subjected to tremendous pressures, not from the parents as much as from his siblings. As a result, he has suffered from rather severe feelings of inferiority which have only been alleviated by his quite remarkable popularity in school. Under the flattering admiration of his classmates, his talents for leadership and organization have blossomed until, at present, he is making a good adjustment (*11*, 49–51).[2]

CASUAL PATTERNS. The third major pattern of parent behavior was the one called casual. This category included nearly 50 per cent of the homes in the sample. These homes could not be as neatly categorized as those in either the acceptant or in the rejectant patterns. They were united only by being mild and casual, not being either acceptant or rejectant. Along with other lesser groupings, there were two which the investigators thought deserved particular mention—the casual autocratic and the casual indulgent. In order to consider the casual autocratic home, it is helpful to refer back to the rejectant pattern. Parents in the rejectant pattern were autocratic in a negative way because of their dislike for children. Autocracy in the parents in the casual pattern is a positive technique adopted either out of policy or out of expediency, without being accompanied by rejectance. An autocrat cannot be warm, but he is not necessarily rejectant. Illustrative is the fact that "old-fashioned" discipline is autocratic as a policy. Some "more modern" parents try to be sympathetic, but when faced with crucial issues become autocratic as a matter of expediency.

The other major casual pattern, the casually indulgent, includes parents who react as the mood moves them, generally in a mild and haphazard way.

OTHER FINDINGS IN PATTERNS. In a later study Baldwin and his associates (12) found somewhat different patterns from those just described. Democracy and indulgence were verified as important patterns, but a new pattern emerged which was "warmth," a combination of what in the earlier study was primarily the acceptance syndrome with some of the characteristics earlier assigned to indulgence. Still another new major cluster they found was intellectuality (striving to hasten development, readiness to explain to the child, and an understanding of his abilities and needs). Without going into detail it is possible to summarize these later findings along with the earlier ones and state that the major patterns of parent behavior, so far as this research has now taken us, are warmth, democracy, intellectuality, and indulgence.

Two of these patterns, warmth and indulgence, were used by Lasko (54) for investigating the problem of whether or not a mother's behavior differed when evaluated in interaction with her first child as compared to her second. It is a common experience to hear from a mother that she "learned on her first child," which carries the implication that she corrected her mistakes when dealing with the second child. It is, therefore, of interest to see what Lasko found in this connection. She studied a first and a second child of the same mother by administering the Fels Scales separately for the two children and then studying the varieties in the warmth and indulgence patterns between them. The first child's initial experiences were found to be much more child-centered (a warmth variable) than were those of the second. At the youngest age it would appear that the first child experiences a somewhat more fervent relationship than does the second child of the same family. There was also a tendency (though not statistically significant) for the mother to have been more solicitous toward the first child and to protect and to baby him more than toward the second child of the same age. However, for both children child-centeredness declined markedly from age two until age five.

PARENTAL PATTERNS AND THE BEHAVIOR OF THE CHILDREN. In the case illustrations presented in the previous section, some hints of the differential behavior of children faced with differing patterns of parental behavior can be discerned. Nevertheless, no systematic examination of the relation between patterns of parental behavior and the behavior of these children has yet been given. It is to this task we now address ourselves. Baldwin and his associates in connection with their original study (*11*) and Baldwin in a later study (*9*) reported on the relation of the patterns of parental behavior to the behavior of the children in these homes. In securing information, trained child specialists observed the children's behavior both in the preschool situation and in their homes and then rated them on a number of characteristics.

They meant their findings about children's behavior in connection with the earlier study (*11*) to be more illustrative than definitive. One group, children from the rejectant homes, was not systematically dealt with in their later research, and hence their earlier report will be drawn upon. The actively rejected children were found to be nonconformists and resistant to adults. Less actively rejected children showed somewhat milder forms of these same characteristics. If one word could be used to describe these children from rejectant homes as a group, it would be aggressive (*62*).

Baldwin, in a more definitive study (*9*), investigated three clusters of home variables—democracy, warmth, and indulgence—as related to the behavior of children from homes with these characteristics. The subjects were 56 nursery school children between the ages of three and five years.

The democratic parental pattern was found to be associated with that for warmth and hence the results of children from these homes are treated together. These children were found to be socially outgoing in both friendly and hostile fashion, to be active participants in school activities, and to be generally assertive. They were also socially successful and popular. In more general terms they may be described as social and assertive.

The children from indulgent homes showed the opposite kind of personality characteristics from those of children from the democratic-warm homes. They tended to be inactive, unaggressive, and socially unsuccessful. In general, they may be described as unsocial and nonassertive.

Radke's approach to patterns. Another approach to the patterns of parent behavior and attitudes in relation to their children's behavior has been followed by Radke (*62*). Her subjects, mothers and fathers of 43 preschool children, completed questionnaires and were interviewed concerning their disciplinary practices and the way in which they carried on authority functions of the family. The items in the questionnaire were grouped into scales which made it possible to make judgments concerning (1) philosophy of authority, extending from autocratic to democratic; (2) parental restriction, extending from strict and firm to lax and easy-going; (3) severity of punishment, extending from severe to mild; and (4) parent-child rapport, extending from good to poor.

What are some of the characteristics of the children who come from homes characterized as autocratic, democratic, restrictive, or severely disciplined? A summary answer to this question may be obtained from information Radke had collected about the children from the preschool and the home.

Children from relatively autocratic homes compared with children from more democratic homes were found to rate as more unpopular with other children, as more given to fighting and quarreling, as more inconsiderate, as more emotionally unstable, as more daring and uninhibited, and as more insensitive to praise or blame. Radke suggests in explaining these results that they come about from the shift of setting which such a child experiences. A child coming from an autocratic home to the presumably less autocratic atmosphere of the school finds himself in the midst of contemporaries whose powers are not as strong as those of his parents. As a consequence, he assumes the behavior of his parents toward the other children, acting without sensitivity or consideration for others. Unpopularity and not getting along well with schoolmates are logical outcomes. In general, the patterns from the restrictive homes and those where severe discipline is used give the same picture as that from autocratic homes.

Children from more democratic homes were found to show a constellation of behavior characteristics opposite those of the autocratically controlled children. Thus, they are more popular, nonquarrelsome, considerate, compliant, emotionally stable, sensitive to the opinions of others, and nonleaders (though not followers).

Sears's approach to patterns. A factor analysis of the ratings on the Sears, Maccoby, Levin child-rearing scales (69) isolated five major factors: (1) permissiveness-strictness; (2) general family adjustment; (3) warmth of mother-child adjustment; (4) responsible child-training orientation; and (5) aggressiveness and punitiveness.

In other words, through the intercorrelations among the measures they used, a lesser number of patterns emerged. Through use of these factors they could summarize their findings. In discussing the effects of child rearing on the children they chose to emphasize the mother's warmth and the effects of punishment and of permissiveness.

The other end of the warmth continuum, maternal coldness, associated in their research with the development of feeding problems and persistent bed-wetting, contributed to high aggression and was an important background condition for emotional upset during severe toilet training and for the slowing of conscience development. The second factor, punishment, and the third, permissiveness, were related primarily to the first factor of permissiveness-strictness and secondarily to the fifth factor, aggression and punitiveness. Since relation to the last factor may not be immediately apparent, it should be mentioned that the scales defining this factor were for use of high physical and severe punishment and low permissiveness for aggression toward parents as well as high demands and permissiveness for aggression toward other children. Punishment was important—mothers punishing severely for toilet accidents or punishing severely dependency in their children tended to have bed-wetting children in the first instance and dependent children in the second. The children who were punished severely for aggressiveness were apt to be more aggressive than those who were punished lightly. Permissiveness, the third quality, had no discernible relation to dependent behavior. But permissiveness for aggression was an important source of continuing aggression and was associated with a low frequency of feeding problems. Permissiveness about sexual matters was less associated with a low frequency of enuresis.

A comparison among the patterns found. The three studies of parent behavior of Baldwin (*11, 12*), Radke (*62*), and Sears (*69*) and their associates supplement one another and permit comparison. It must be remembered, however, that they were derived by different methods, with different populations, and varying scope of content and direction of interest. Consequently, any degree of resemblance may be considered gratifying. By the same token, this comparison is hazardous and not to be given much weight. Certain *possible* relationships among the three studies may be pointed out. Table 16 presents a summary of the major patterns found in their studies. Warmth appears as a major pattern in both the Baldwin and Sears studies, and democracy and permissiveness in all three studies. The autocratic aspect of the autocratic-democratic pattern, as well as parental restriction and severity of punishment, appears to have a counterpart in the strictness end of the permissiveness-strictness factor of Sears. Thus, warmth, permissiveness, and punishment appear to be three major dimensions of parent behavior. Perhaps it

TABLE 16

THE MAJOR PATTERNS OF PARENT BEHAVIOR FOUND BY
VARIOUS INVESTIGATORS

Baldwin	Radke	Sears
Warmth	Autocratic-democratic	Permissiveness-strictness
Democracy	Parental restriction	General family adjustment
Intellectuality	Severity of punishment	Warmth
Indulgence	Parent-child rapport	Responsible child-training orientation
		Aggressiveness and punitiveness

is mere coincidence, but as mentioned earlier, Sears and his associates (69) in summing up their entire pattern study chose as most pervasive precisely these three characteristic attitudes around which to summarize the effects of child rearing.

The Socializing Effect of the Father

The father has not been neglected as much as it might first appear. Both in the Fels series of studies under Baldwin and the study of Radke, the socialization patterns that emerged bore the imprint of the father as well as the mother. *Parents,* not mothers alone, were their subject of study. Nevertheless, very little direct reference has been made to the father as such.

Radke's approach (62) made possible a comparison of the mothers' parental behavior and attitudes with those of the fathers'. On her four scales the responses of the mothers, when compared with those of the fathers, showed only a few relatively specific differences in connection with philosophy of authority, parental restriction, and severity of discipline. In the entire area of philosophy of authority, the only item showing differences was that the mothers more often explained to the children the reasons for the discipline they received than did the fathers. In the area of parental restriction, mothers were more lenient in allowing the child to have his own way. It was in the area of parent-child rapport that differences were more widespread. As compared to fathers, mothers showed greater rapport with their children in the form of confidences shared, a greater amount of time devoted to answering questions, and a greater amount of affection shown their children. In general, mothers appear to be both the chief supervisors and more affectionate and yielding than the fathers.

It would appear not incompatible with Radke's data that, as Kardiner (50) states, the father, although standing in the background, is often the final authority even though executive power is exercised through the mother. Supporting evidence directly bearing on this point is to be found in a later section of this chapter concerned with the child's perception of the situation. To anticipate, investigators have found that children perceive the father as the source of authority.

One direct and crucial way to study the socializing effect of the father is to examine homes in which the father is absent, and thus to see what effect this absence has upon the children. Both in early (70) and later childhood (7), the boys from father-present homes demonstrated much more aggression than did boys from father-absent homes. A girl's aggressive tendencies were not affected by the father's absence. These results are examined in more detail later in connection with the discussion of aggressive tendencies.

The father, it would seem, serves as a model, especially for the boy. This is brought out very clearly in later discussion of identification and sex-typing. Serving as a model is one of the father's major functions. But it is not his only function. Besides being a father, he is a husband, an economic provider, a source of intellectual and social stimulation, an arbiter, and a friend. Not always does exercise of these functions involve the child directly. As a husband, his functional relations are primarily with his wife. Always, however, he is a member of a network of social relations. Affecting one part of that network ultimately affects all parts. So the child in this social complex is ultimately affected by all of the father's functions.

Techniques of Training

The problem of techniques or ways of child training or discipline has not yet been examined explicitly. The mother wants the child to continue certain forms of behavior and to stop others. She may use rewards or incentives on the one hand, or she may use threats, punishments, or distractions. The scales used by Baldwin and his associates included the degree of restrictiveness of regulations, the direction of criticism, the effectiveness of parental policies, and the like which appear relevant to the problem. Similarly, three of Radke's four scales, authority, parental restriction, and severity of punishment, have a distinct disciplinary cast to them. Permissiveness-strictness was one of the factors found by Sears, Maccoby, and Levin. In the three studies, information about discipline in a rather general supervisory sense has already been examined. There is another more restrictive specific and technique-oriented aspect to discipline which needs examination. Before considering the results of specific studies, a short general statement is necessary in order to put discipline in perspective.

Discipline is essential for the child. Without it the world is too "unstructured" to permit his adjustment to it. If there are no rules to the game of living, he cannot learn to play it. A paradoxical condition of social living is that for full development to occur, child and adult alike, one must give up some of his freedom. Without limits by discipline a child cannot learn to deal with the demands set by the environment when they run counter to his own inclinations. A balance or a compromise must be set between his needs and the restrictions placed by the environment. In this connection, it will be recognized that the psychoanalytic formulation of the interrelation of superego demands with external reality as mediated by the ego is, in one sense, a formulation of a solution to this particular problem. Discipline is very much an instrument of the process of socialization in that through discipline the parent guides the child in the direction of what is socially acceptable in his culture.

From the point of view of the child, much of the discipline which he receives is arbitrary. For reasons he often does not understand, he discovers he is expected to behave in certain ways and not in certain others. In fact, it is because of his failure to understand that the imposition of discipline takes place.

With this discussion as background, we are now in a position to turn to the empirical results concerning parental discipline and the young child. Radke's study (62) supplied information about the types of punishment used by the parents of preschool-age children. The kinds and percentage of homes reporting the kinds of punishments are shown in Figure 11. Spanking, isolating, rewards and praises, allowing conduct to bring about its consequences, verbal appeals, and depriving were the most common kinds of punishment. Commenting on the influence these punishments may be presumed to have on the children's behavior, Radke states that most of the kinds of punishment "are aimed at undermining the power of the child or at restricting his freedom, either physical or psychological" (62, 49).[3] Spanking, isolating, and depriving are illustrative of under-

[3] Marian J. Radke, *The Relation of Parental Authority to Children's Behavior and Attitudes.* Copyright 1946, University of Minnesota.

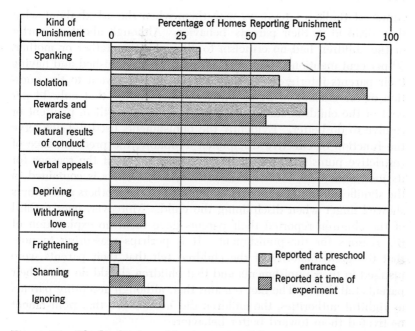

Figure 11. *The kinds of punishment reported by parents of preschool-age children.* (*Marion J. Radke,* The Relation of Parental Authority to Children's Behavior and Attitudes. *Copyright 1946, University of Minnesota.*)

mining or restrictive tendencies. Allowing the child to suffer the natural consequences is also somewhat restrictive. Discipline as practiced by the parents in her sample thus seems to be predominantly restrictive. Quite possibly these kinds of punishment tend to decrease the child's sense of security. Her results as just summarized were stated without regard to changes in punishment practices with changes in age of the children. The reports concerning punishment practice at time of preschool entrance were taken one-and-a-half to three years before the reports collected in connection with the research study data heretofore considered. Changes with ages are also reported in Figure 11. It is apparent that there was an increase in the amount of almost all kinds of punishment as the children became older.

What did the children think of their parents' punishment practices and how effective did they appear to be in the light of their opinions? Information about what the children thought was collected in the course of Radke's interviews with them when she asked about what they disliked in their parents' behavior. Although about a quarter of the children had no criticism to offer of either father or mother, 50 per cent mentioned they disliked most being punished and having their parents interfere with play. Even more relevant to the question of the efficacy of punishment was her finding that only 14 per cent of the children stated that punishments made them penitent or resolve to do better. Evidently the punishments used did not serve the function of effective discipline. Probably, the predominance of restrictive punishments already mentioned is one of the reasons for its inefficiency. A further clue to its ineffectiveness is contained in the significant finding that over 50 per cent of the mothers and fathers showed anger when disciplining the child. Moreover, over a third of the children reported their parents gave them no explanation of the reasons for the punishment. It is perhaps reassuring to note that the great majority of the children felt that their parents were justified in their punishments and that children should do what their parents tell them. The fact remains that, although accepting parents as rightful authorities, the children did not believe that punishment motivated them toward better behavior.

In interviewing their mother sample, Sears, Maccoby, and Levin (69) in seeking information in their pattern study about training used many categories similar to those of Radke (62). They make a distinction between positive and negative sanctions. Those techniques which provide a reward include praise, a symbolic reward, and tangible rewards. Both praise and reward serve as reinforcers of preceding behavior. About 60 per cent of their samples fairly often or frequently used tangible rewards. Only 12 per cent of the mothers claim they never used rewards. Almost 80 per cent used praise fairly often, moderately, or occasionally. No use of praise is claimed by one per cent of the mothers.

Negative sanctions provided punishment including physical punishment, deprivation of privileges, withdrawal of love, and isolation. They used both spanking and slapping as indices of physical punishment. In their sample, about 80 per cent are included in the region extending from those who spanked rarely and only occasionally to those who spanked fairly often, sometimes severely. Only one per cent report never using physical punishment. A little more than 70 per cent of their sample are included in the area extending from occasional use of deprivation of privileges and slight use of isolation to those who fairly often use deprivation and show considerable use of isolation. The extent of use of withdrawal of love deserves a more detailed statement. Three per cent are explicit in saying they never use it, 37 per cent make slight or moderate use, while 10 per cent make considerable or much use of withdrawal of love as a technique of punishment. In 50 per cent its use was not ascertained due to either the reluctance of the mothers to speak of it or because its subtle manifestations could not be detected by the raters.

To summarize their many findings on punishment, Sears and his associates conclude that parental punishment was a dismal failure. To quote: "Our evaluation of punishment is that *it is ineffectual over the long term as a technique for eliminating the kind of behavior toward which it is directed*" (69, 484).[4] Punishment just did not work. It did not eliminate the kinds of behavior for which the mothers used it. As they state, their generally negative conclusion does not mean that punishment might not have been successful in eliminating some specific act, or another, say, a specific aggressive act such as a boy picking on his sister. In the long run and extending over more general forms of behavior, punishment was not effective.

One cannot leave this topic of patterns of parent behavior with its emphasis on authority, restriction, punishment, and control without considering how the children Radke studied "controlled" their parents. In interviews the children had been asked how they got their own way against their parents' requests. Table 17 summarizes Radke's findings. Each figure in the table refers to the percentage

TABLE 17

PERCENTAGE OF CHILDREN USING VARIOUS METHODS
OF CONTROLLING THEIR PARENTS *

	Used with Mother		Used with Father	
Method	Boys	Girls	Boys	Girls
Pay no attention	26	25	39	29
Cries, has tantrums	21	26	17	14
Refuses parent's request	50	26	41	19
Whines, begs, and so on	47	39	53	33

* Marian J. Radke, *The Relation of Parental Authority to Children's Behavior and Attitudes.* Copyright 1946, University of Minnesota.

[4] From Sears, Maccoby, and Levin (69). Copyright 1957 by Row, Peterson, and published with permission.

of the boys or girls who used the method in question. Thus the first entry, "pays no attention," shows that 25 per cent of all the boys used this method with their mothers. This means that the remainder, or 75 per cent, did not. Each entry in the table represents the percentage of the total sample of boys or girls who used the particular method of control with their mother or their father. Naturally, many used more than one technique which accounts for the fact that going down any one column will not give a total of 100 per cent. Whining, begging, and other verbal appeals, and plain refusal appear to have been most successful. Crying and having tantrums worked least well. Girls, it may be noted, "get away" with less than do boys. As Thompson (75) suggests, this table might be studied with some profit by children of this age!

Changes in Parental Behavior with Age

Parental concern about toilet training, eating habits, sex training, and the host of other psychosocially oriented behaviors would be expected to change as the child grows older. In general, there would be expected to be less contact between parent and child and fewer restrictions on his behavior (8). Not only would parents expect different things in the way of appropriate behavior when their child was older, but also they would hold with different attitudes, or attitudes different in degree from those which prevailed when the child was younger.

Baldwin (8), using the Fels Parent Behavior Rating Scales, investigated differences in attitudes of parents toward three- and nine-year-old children. The results are stated in terms of the now familiar patterns. Parents of nine-year-old children were less warm, less indulgent, less intellectually stimulating, and more restrictive than parents of three-year-old children. He stresses that this is due, in part, to changes in cultural standards in handling children. Norms of socialization shift and parents are expected to change as the child grows older. For example, hostility toward a three-year-old is considered more reprehensible in our society than is similar behavior toward a nine-year-old. Presumably other factors are at work as well.

Causation and Congruity in Parental and Child Behavior

Although the relationships that have been reported are not to be taken as evidence that long term patterns of child behavior are inevitably and precisely associated with particular patterns of parent behavior, they do demonstrate that important relationships exist between the behavior of mothers and fathers and the behavior of their children.

Variations in home atmosphere and parental attitudes have been found to vary concomitantly with constellations of behavior in the child. It is tempting to conclude that direct causative relations have been found between parental behavior and consequent child behavior. Unfortunately, the picture is not so simple. There is undoubtedly an interaction effect and a reciprocal relation of child and parent behavior. Future research will help serve to untangle the skein of cause and effect.

Caution must be offered concerning interpretation of these congruities between paternal and child behavior. True, certain characteristic trends in child behavior were isolated for a given paternal pattern. But these characteristics, it must be emphasized, are of a general nature and did not hold for all children from homes with that paternal pattern. Children in any one home pattern may react in many different ways. Children from a rejectant pattern may react as described in the group trends or, as clinical studies demonstrate, they may become overdependent or withdraw into themselves or develop a precocious self-sufficiency, or react in several other ways. In dealing with group trends, as we are, individual exceptions inevitably are lost to view. A second limiting factor in the generality of the findings about parent and child behavior is the fact that the subjects were what might be described generally as "middle-class" parents and children. Generalization of the findings which have been reported to other socio-economic classes with the expectation that identical results would be found should only be done with considerable caution.

The development of self and social awareness in early childhood

We now turn, as we did for infancy, to the issue of self and social awareness—the inner feeling of individuality and the perception of other social beings. As was the case in infancy, we are plagued by a lack of carefully controlled research findings created by the methodological problems that arise when this segment of early childhood experience is examined.

The Self in Early Childhood

It might appear that since we are concerned with self-awareness by definition that we would use this very awareness of self as the method of investigation. If we want to know what a child thinks about himself, it appears that all we should do is simply to ask him. This, however, is a method doomed to failure. The history of the psychology of introspection shows this clearly. Moreover, psychoanalytic investigation has established that there are distortion and deception created by the defensive stratagems of the personality. It is for this reason that introspection failed as a technique of psychological investigation (38). True, by such procedures we may get some crude approximations of what children think they think about themselves, but little more.

Localization of the self. One introspective study cannot be eliminated not only because of its general interest but also because it demonstrates some of the confusion attendant upon use of the method. This is the study by Horowitz (43) on the spatial localization of the self. He asked young children and college students, in terms appropriate to their ages, where the "self" was located. An overwhelming variety of localizations emerged, especially in the replies of the children. The vividness and definiteness of this localization of the self are shown in an illustration taken from the account of Horowitz.

> Conversation yielded that the child's name was Lena; Lena was three years old (accuracy unchecked). Lena localized herself in the body, at first. As we continued exploring, in order to check the consistency of the response, Lena appeared in her lower right jaw. She was not in the hand, arm, or leg, nor in the eye, head, nor other (left) jaw. Lena seemed fixed in her lower right jaw. The definiteness of this localization may be indicated by her petulant response when we touched her right cheekbone and asked, "Is this Lena?" *"What is the matter with you? I told you three times this* (pointing to lower right jaw) *is me"* (43, 483).[5]

The child just mentioned "was" in the right jaw, another in the abdomen, another in the head, and so on. Most adults tended to locate the "self" in the head, brains, face, and eyes, but a few placed it in other parts of the body. Even the locus of the self gives little consistent agreement among children and adults.

[5] From Horowitz (43). Copyright 1935 by The Journal Press, and published with permission.

Memory and the self. In considering the self, one important difference between the infant and the younger child must be noted. The infant has a very poor memory. The pertinence of this fact comes about because the idea of self is partly as a unifying generalization of the continuity of one's personal memories (38). It is necessary for the memory capacity to be better developed for this generalization to take place. During infancy this memory capacity gradually increases. It is probable, however, that this factor of memory as a contributor to self emerges in major importance only during early childhood. Through continuous memories of one's past, a child (and an adult) is led to have a sense of personal identity. He is a person who has done this and that and the other. These are seen as personal and very much a part of oneself.

Self-evaluation in the self-concept. From the discussion of psychoanalytic concepts later in the chapter it will be seen that it is also in early childhood that self-criticism develops. Self-evaluation or self-criticism is considered by Hilgard (38) as the other necessary feature in understanding self-organization. Self-evaluation is shown through guilt feelings. The presence of guilt feelings indicates that the individual considers himself an active agent responsible for what he does. If he fails to do that which he considers worthy and right, he develops self-reproof in the form of guilt. On the other side of the coin is the effort of the self to protect against criticism in order to reduce guilt. In trying to keep a good opinion of oneself we are capable of self-delusion. We try to make our motives acceptable to ourselves. Self-respect (even if we cannot always give it) is important to children and adults. Again the protective function, the mechanisms of defense to use psychoanalytic terminology, comes to the fore. The individual strives but does not always succeed in keeping a sense of self-worth. He values his opinion of himself and goes to great lengths to protect his favorable view of himself.

The self itself is a value. We expect desirable things from ourselves and expect to behave in ways that are admirable. We are ever ready to defend our evaluation of our self. We become aggressive or show other defensive maneuvers when something threatens our self-evaluation. Indeed, the psychoanalytic conception of defense mechanisms is expressly defense of the ego. If something does not fit these values or we fall short of our view of ourselves, we are apt to explain by saying, "I was not myself." We have self-esteem to the degree to which we have self-confidence or satisfaction with our behavior. In short, we value ourselves to some degree. True, there are varying degrees of self-acceptance. Sometimes we do not value ourselves very highly. We may on occasion dislike or even hate ourselves, and we may even be among those who take so jaundiced a view of ourselves that this disparaging view prevails. By and large, our self is something we hold dear.

Parental attitudes contribute to the child's self-evaluation. For example, in earlier discussion considerable emphasis was placed on parental rejection. From the child's point of view rejection is something he experiences. He feels unwanted, despised, unattractive, or somehow found lacking. Fortunately, he also comes in contact with other parental attitudes and atmospheres. The prevalence of positive fostering attitudes helps to establish in children self-evaluations which are of a more healthful nature than the one chosen for illustration. Whatever their outcome, parental attitudes are experienced by the child and affect his self-evaluation.

Children's Standards of Behavior. Values and the self are also related through finding out what values of good and bad the child holds. The younger child's pattern of values of what is good and what is bad throws light on the self as he sees it. Knowledge of his values helps to understand how socialization works through the standards he internalizes as part of himself. The boy or girl is continuously admonished to be "good," and not to be "bad."

Radke (*62*) asked her preschool children what is a "good" and what is a "bad" or "naughty" boy (girl). Each child was urged to continue until four answers were given to both of the questions. Table 18 shows the summarization of her results when she had grouped their answers into categories.

Both goodness and badness at the preschool age appear to have a paucity of moral content. Doing "nice, kind things," and "saying bad words, is cross, isn't nice," are the most moral of the categories respectively in the table. Most of the values these children express may be called utilitarian and practical. A child is good or bad to the extent that he fits in with the family routine, takes care of himself, and avoids arousing maternal displeasure. The father's influence as an authority is strikingly absent.

Boys and girls show certain differences. In terms of the more prominent percentages of both good and bad behavior, girls stress helping, obeying the mother and avoiding being disobedient to her,

TABLE 18

CHILDREN'S STANDARDS OF BAD AND GOOD BEHAVIOR *

	Percentage of Responses		
Bad Behavior	Girls	Boys	Both
Doesn't do what mother asks	28	7	18
Doesn't do what other people tell him	0	14	6.5
Does overt acts of violence (that is, spits, scratches, snatches, hits, breaks windows, throws mud, and so on)	47	55	51
Cries, says bad words, is cross, isn't nice	12.5	17	15
Makes mother sad	0	7	3
Miscellaneous and doesn't know	12.5	0	6.5
Good Behavior			
Helps mother (specific items such as dusts, washes, cleans, and performs other household tasks)	20	40	29
Takes care of own routine (that is, dresses self, goes to toilet, picks up toys, cleans up his mess, and so on)	13	6	10
Plays (that is, plays gently with dolls, colors, and so on)	28	6	18
Does nice, kind things (that is, does good things, does things for people and so on)	13	30	21
Obeys mother (that is, does what mother says, and so on)	8	6	7
Doesn't destroy or break things (that is, doesn't break records, and so on)	3	3	3
Stays out of mother's way (that is, doesn't bother mother, and so on)	3	6	4
Miscellaneous and doesn't know	12	3	8

* Marian J. Radke, *The Relation of Parental Authority to Children's Behavior and Attitudes.* Copyright 1946, by University of Minnesota.

self-help, doing nice, kind things, playing nicely, and avoiding violence. Boys emphasize helping mother, doing nice, kind things, and avoiding violence. These findings express their ideal concepts of a good boy and a good girl. A "good" girl or a "good" boy is one who seeks certain kinds of behavior and avoids other kinds as just sketched. This does not mean that each individual child sees their responses as his own self-concept—that *he* or *she* exhibits these seekings and avoidances. In his or her own estimation he or she may, in varying degrees, fall short of these ideals.

Origin of the self-concept. There emerges in the child a concept of himself—an awareness of what he thinks he is like. It is his conception of who and what he is. From where comes this self-concept of oneself? Stagner (72) has given us a thoughtful analysis of the answer to this question. He considers that the sources of the self-concept (self-image) include the child's (1) real characteristics; (2) descriptions by adults; (3) comparisons with others; and (4) inner pressures. Each will be considered in turn.

(1) "Real" characteristics refer to the objective characteristics of the child—his physique, his manner, his intelligence, his emotionality. (2) Perhaps almost as important are the characteristics which he knows have been attributed to him by adults—his assimilation of what they think of him. To some extent the self is created by what Sullivan (74) called "reflected appraisals." What a child's self-appraisal is, in part, is what others think and feel about him. Both gross overrevaluation or derogation can create harmful effects expressed through his self-image. If "everyone" regards a child as clumsy or naughty or what you will, it should come as no surprise that the child believes them and acts to some degree in a way to correspond to their view. More often than not, however, a child's self-concept is less of a consistent pattern than these illustrations imply. After all, the way he is viewed differs from person to person even in a short space of time. He may be seen as mother's "darling," to the neighbor boy as a "sissy," and to his big sister, a "pest,"—all in the same hour. How he assimilates these pressures and makes his own is contingent not only upon this factor of attribution of traits but also upon the other sources of the self and the effect of past experience. (3) Comparison of the self with others enters through comparison with members of the groups in which the child finds himself. A bright child with even brighter older siblings will think of himself (as will others in the family) as less smart than if he were closer to them in intellectual ability. A child, actually average in height, may perceive himself as rather large if all of his classmates and playmates happen to be short. A child's self-concept is based partly on comparison with other persons. (4) Inner pressure as a determinant of the self-concept acts through the aspirations or ambitions the child holds. A girl with operatic ambitions may distort her inner evaluation to fit more in line with these ambitions. A boy

who conceives himself as an athlete may be under self-pressure to try to fit this conception. These inner pressures may, of course, be reinforced by outer pressures from adults and others who hold similar expectancies for them. Inner pressures also act through his interpretation of the situation. The view he holds may or may not correspond to the situation as others view it. A child may feel that a parent favors a brother or sister or is unduly harsh toward him when from the parent's point of view such is not the case. But the child's inner pressures will influence him whether they reflect reality or not.

Social Perception

In early childhood social awareness may be viewed as the problem of social perception.[6] Emphasis will be placed on the child's perception of parental roles. In brief, the issue at hand is what do children think about parental practices and about their parents as parents.

Differences between the parents' reports of home situations and the children's perceptions are very apparent. It will be remembered that Radke (62) reported the kinds of punishment used by parents of preschool children. Implicitly at least, the assumption was made that the way of reporting and classifying the punishments reflected the reality of the situation. This may be the case, but it does not follow necessarily that the child himself perceives the punishments in the way the adults do. Using a sample of preschool children, Neill (60) as reported by Hawkes (36) found considerable difference between what the parents reported the situation to be in their household concerning punishment as compared to their children's perceptions of the same issue in the same home. Fifty per cent of her children named corporal punishment as what they expected from their parents; parents reported using corporal punishment only as a last resort. Only about 10 per cent of the children seemed aware that their parents expected them to take the consequences of their acts; about 70 per cent of the parents said they used this practice.

[6] Many studies of children's perceptions include as subjects children somewhat beyond preschool age. There is no reason to suspect that the greater age of the subjects significantly changes the findings despite some shifts with age. To be sure, the younger child is not as aware of the nature of his social perceptions as are these older children, but no great straining of the facts comes from reference to these studies at this point.

Twenty-five per cent of the children agreed that their parents might put them to bed forcefully; 50 per cent of the parents said that, if necessary, they would do this. Even from these brief illustrations it is possible to sense the vast difference between parental practices and the ways in which these children perceived the same situations.

It is significant in this connection that Hansen as reported by Anderson (3) has found that while parents emphasized disciplinary and management controls, their children tended to see these parents primarily as sources of frustration. As Brown (18) suggests, it may be the way the child perceives the parent, not his attitude as objectively given, that determines the child's personality adjustment. That the perception, not the real situation, is crucial is rendered at least plausible by Itkin's findings (46) with a sample of about 400 college students. He had a variety of attitude scales completed both by the students and by their parents. Through the attitude scales he had information about the attitudes of these students toward their parents and information about how their parents supervised these students. From examination of the pattern of intercorrelations that the scales provided, he reached the conclusion that if children have a favorable attitude toward their parents, they tend to approve of the supervision they received irrespective of whether the parents are dominating or submissive in their attitudes; conversely, if they have negative attitudes toward the parents, they tend to judge parental supervision as dominating regardless of what their parents' attitudes may be.

Children's conceptions of parental roles were investigated by Finch (28). Subjects were children between three and seven years of age drawn from 20 professional families. Among other techniques, a set of photographs were used, each of which showed both a father and a mother following some child care routine. From each picture the child told a story, at the conclusion of which the boy or girl was asked whether the mother or the father should carry out the task shown in the particular picture. Responses were categorized as mother, father, or both. It was found that, instead of either parent alone, the children spoke more frequently of both mother and father as performing 10 of the 13 roles—bedtime, baths, meals, prayer, companionship, affection, discipline, teaching, illness, and protection. Almost unanimously the father was seen as economic provider and the mother as housekeeper and contributor to the children. Before knowing the children's replies, the mothers had been asked what they expected them to reply. Some roles which the mothers expected the children to consider to be those of the mother—bathtime, meals, and care during illness—were roles for which the children chose both father and mother.   In response to the direct question, "What is daddy?" about 75 per cent of the children replied in terms of his being an economic provider.   To a similar question about the mother, 50 per cent fell in the category of household duties and 25 per cent in that of caring for children.   It would seem that the child sees the roles of the father in the home both as more numerous and as more important than general opinion might lead one to expect.

Which parent is seen as the source of authority and which is seen as the source of affection?   Through interviews Kagan (49) obtained answers to questions from 217 children about whether it would be the mother or the father who would be on their side in an argument (friendliness), who would punish them (punitiveness), and who was boss (dominance).   The majority of both boys and girls perceived their mothers as friendlier, less punitive, and less dominant than their fathers.

Gardner (32) studied the perception of the father and of the mother through about 400 boys and girls.   She used a questionnaire approach which asked them which parent was easier to get along with, who would punish them, and who was the bigger boss.   The correspondence to friendliness, punitiveness, and dominance of mothers and fathers as studied by Kagan is apparent.   Mothers were perceived as friendlier, less dominant, and about equally punitive. The studies, then, are in essential agreement about friendliness and dominance.   Only in connection with punitiveness is there some difference.

This discrepancy about punitiveness is easily accounted for when age differences are taken into consideration.   The children studied by Kagan ranged from six to ten years of age.   The older children of about nine or ten in his sample, both boys and girls, tended to view the same sex parent as more punitive and dominant than did the younger children.   The differential handling of boys and girls as they begin to assume more definitive sex roles is suggested to account for this finding.   The children Gardner studied were almost all 10 through 13, thus extending Kagan's age group.   Kagan found that as age increased within his sample, punitiveness of the same sex parent increased.   In Gardner's group this had increased to such an extent that the parents were equally punitive.   Thus, there is no discrepancy between the results of the two studies.   The answer to the question with which these studies were introduced, which quali-

ties are parents perceived as having, appears to be that the father is
seen as the source of authority and the mother the source of affection, but as age increases the same sex parent assumes more and more
a punitive role.

Behavior tendencies in early childhood

As was the case in considering infancy, discussion of behavior
tendencies in early childhood will center upon dependence-independence, aggression, and sex.

Dependence and Independence Tendencies

Before examining the nature of dependence or independence tendencies in early childhood, it is appropriate to present evidence concerning the extent of the separation of dependence tendencies from
independence tendencies along with a more detailed examination of
what is meant by these terms.

Relation of dependence and independence tendencies. It is
hazardous to assume without evidence that dependence and independence are merely opposite ends of the same continuum. In
an earlier chapter, changes in dependence in infancy were described
as moving from dependence to less dependence rather than from
dependence to independence. The nature of the distinction between
independence tendencies and dependence tendencies will now be
dealt with explicitly. This is justified in that the ages three through
five appear to be the critical period for optimal normal development
of independence. Dependence was a necessary condition of infancy;
independence is a task of the younger child. Certainly, the diminish-
ing dependence of the child as he grows older is a fact. It must be,
in part at least, the result of positive development of more independent ways of responding to the same situations in which, when younger,
dependent reactions were elicited. The preschool child appears to
be motivated to perform independently. There is, as will be developed later, a series of studies establishing the reality of something
we can call independence behavior in preschool children. Hence,
we shall refer to independence tendencies.

As components of independence behavior, Beller (*14*) suggests
the following five: taking initiative, the overcoming of obstacles,

persistence, just wanting to do something, and wanting to do things by oneself. Using these as the crucial components of independence, Beller proceeded to demonstrate the reality of an independence drive. He constructed rating scales based on each of these components. Children about three to nearly six years of age were then rated on these scales by their nursery school teacher. Highly significant relations among the rating scales were found. The five indices of independence were found to "hang together" in that most of the children were consistent from one to another of these scales, thus demonstrating the reality of an independence drive so far as these components are concerned.

The second phase of his study was concerned with the hypothesis that specific behavior components can also be selected which furnish evidence of a general dependence drive. Rating scales were constructed for five such components, namely, seeking help, physical contact, proximity, attention, and recognition. He used the same subjects and raters and procedure as in the previous phase of the study. A highly significant degree of relationship among the components was again found. Children differed consistently from one another in the composite dependency scores. Thus at least for these five components, there was evidence of a dependence drive.

He next performed the third phase of the study which is crucial to the issue of whether or not dependence and independence are separable. The correlation between independence and dependence, as he had measured them, was calculated for this group of children. If dependence and independence were but opposite ends of the same continuum, a correlation approaching (but because of errors of measurement not reaching) a perfect negative correlation of -1.00 would be expected. The correlation he did find was moderately negative, being -0.53. This relatively small correlation suggests that assuming dependence and independence to be merely bipolar ends of the same continuum is not indicated. Instead, they should be treated as separable, although related, tendencies. An additional bit of relevant evidence is to be found in Wittenborn's study reported in more detail on page 414. He found by cluster analysis of children's customary behaviors that dependence on adults was a separate cluster from taking an adult role (independence). In other words, there was no high (negative) correlation between children seeking dependent relations with adults and their desire to take on adult roles.

Still further support for considering dependence and independence as separate tendencies is to be found in a study by Heathers (37) reported in more detail on page 418. He found dependence and independence may be negatively, positively, or noncorrelated, depending upon the specific independence and dependence measure considered.

Dependence and independence seem best conceived as separate components of child behavior. It is proper, therefore, to speak of the child while learning to depend on others as simultaneously learning to be independent. He shows both tendencies. He learns to help himself at the same time as he learns to depend upon being helped. Independence responses and dependence responses acquire habit strength when they are reinforced. As the child begins to explore and to manipulate his environment, his own behavior brings about drive reduction.

Determinants of dependence tendencies. Before examining the determinants of dependence tendencies in early childhood, it is worth while to examine what forms dependence tendencies take at these ages. We already have clues from the work of Beller (14). He was found to define dependence in terms of seeking help, physical contact, proximity, attention, and recognition. Sears and his associates in their pattern study (69) found many indices of dependency in five-year-old children akin to those of Beller. The investigators questioned each of the mothers in their sample about how much attention their child seemed to want, how much and whether he ever followed her about hanging onto her skirt, and his reaction on her going out of the house leaving him with someone else. About 25 to 35 per cent of the children showed quite a bit or a great deal of attention-demanding and following about. Only about 15 per cent objected with any degree of strength to her going out without him.

These aspects of dependency studies by Beller and Sears will be seen to have an obvious inspiration in the early pioneer work of Levy (56), who was concerned with overprotection as a determinant of dependency. He used the method of case sifting described in Chapter 2 to isolate 20 instances of pure maternal overprotection. Hundreds, if not thousands, of case records were examined by him in the process of finding this group. Maternal overprotection is distinguished from overprotection which masks as rejection in that the child is *wanted*. "Pure" maternal overprotection with which Levy was concerned refers to instances in which the child was, consciously at least, wanted by the mother.

Maternal overprotection is the unhealthy exaggerated manifestation of that which within optimal limits has been called acceptance. Even when the child is past infancy, the mother "is always there," "treats the child like a baby," and "won't take any risks." To speak a bit more technically by using Levy's terms there is apt to be present (1) excessive contact; (2) infantilization; and (3) prevention of independent behavior.

Consider the following case history of a four-year-old boy:

> *Excessive contact:* There is still much fondling, sitting on mother's lap, constant kissing. Because she would not leave her children, the mother, until recently, rarely went out with her husband.
> *Prolongation of infantile care:* Mother still dresses him (until modified by treatment) at age 5.
> *Prevention of independent behavior:* The patient refuses to play with other children, preferring always to be where mother is (56, 35).[7]

The first two of these factors, excessive contact and infantilization, reinforce dependent behavior directly; the third factor, prevention of independent behavior, certainly does not reinforce independent behavior. But a fourth factor, excessive maternal control, seems crucial because its presence would appear essential if dependency is to appear. The group of 20 children whose histories showed excessive contact, prolongation of infantile care, and the prevention of independent behavior, sharply divides into two distinct groups because of the differences in the kind of maternal control exercised. One subgroup was dominated by their parents and these children unequivocally showed dependent behavior. The boy, whose case description was just given, had a very dominant mother. He did just as she told him and was considerate and solicitous of her. These dominant, overprotecting mothers of the group were found to be very much intent in trimming their children to a desired shape. The children of these dominant mothers showed docility, neatness, cleanliness, obedience, politeness, and diligence—but with all of these virtues were so timid and submissive as to be called sissies and fools by their playmates. Clearly, these children can be described as dependent. Overprotection combined with dominance reinforces dependence. The other subgroup in which indulgence accompanied overprotection was found to lead to aggression and will be considered later in connection with aggressive tendencies.

[7] From Levy (56). Copyright 1943 by the Columbia University Press, and published with permission.

In evaluating the determinants of dependency, it is appropriate to return to the study by Sears and his associates (71) of antecedents of aggression and dependence. They were concerned with the relation of frustration and dependence. In addition to infantile frustrations considered earlier, they studied the relation of maternal punitiveness directed toward the preschool-aged subjects in relation to their dependence tendencies. To summarize their results, they found a positive relation between the amount of punitiveness in the home and dependence tendencies in boys, but found the opposite relation in girls. By and large the boys' dependency varied positively with the amount of punitiveness of the parents just as did other frustrations in infancy, but with the girls dependency varied to some degree negatively with the amount of punitiveness of the parents.

In both boys and girls the distributions were slightly curvilinear, instead of being straight lines. Figure 12 illustrates this lack of linearity and also serves as a means of conveying Sears and his associates' interpretation of the different findings for boys and girls. In order to explain the different results of boys and girls, they make two assumptions. The first concerns the curvilinear relationship between amount of frustration of a drive and dependence tendencies. The second is that girls are more susceptible than boys to punishment by their mothers. The essence of their complicated argument is so well-caught by Baldwin that he is quoted.

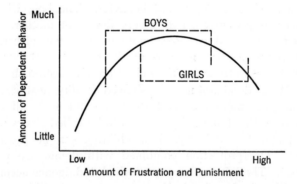

Figure 12. Hypothesized relation between frustration punishment and dependent behavior. (Adapted from Sears et al. (71). Copyright 1953 by The Journal Press, and published with permission.)

The first assumption to be made is that the strength of drive that is formed from the combination of reinforcement and punishment depends upon the severity of the punishment. Whereas a mild punishment or a threat of one may only strengthen the motive that is frustrated, a very severe punishment may inhibit behavior completely. The severity of punishment required to inhibit action may depend upon the strength of the motive. This hypothesis overlaps to some extent an earlier one we have discussed regarding the effect of tension level upon the directedness of behavior. Moderate tension permits directed adaptive behavior; very high levels result in restless undirected behavior. So the theory now hypothesized is that the combination of reinforcement and moderate frustration or punishment establishes a drive of maximum strength. Too much or too little frustration results in a weaker drive.

Now, a second assumption is that girls are more susceptible to punishment by their mothers than are boys. This in turn depends upon the assumption that girls are more identified with their mothers, whereas boys are more identified with their fathers. Thus, when a mother punishes her daughter, the punishment has greater psychological impact than when she punishes her son; it is more likely, therefore, to inhibit than to accentuate the motivation (10, 569).[8]

Sears *et al.* (71) offer evidence that girls have higher identification with their mothers than do boys. Three of their findings in this connection are that girls (1) use the mother doll more often as the agent in doll play; (2) were rated higher by the mothers as emulating adult behavior; and (3) showed significantly higher dependence on their female teacher.

To return now to Baldwin's presentation he goes on to state:

> Putting these two assumptions together, let us suppose that the effect of frustration upon the strength of drive is represented by the curve in Figure . . . [12]. Now, if punishment by the mother were more severe for girls than for boys, then the sample of girls in this study would fall toward the right-hand end of the curve. In this region of the curve, the more punishment, the less drive. The boys, on the other hand, are less affected by being punished, so they would fall along the left-hand end of the curve. Within this region, the more punishment, the more drive. This corresponds to the empirical finding (10, 569).

Current frustration in relation to dependency seems thus to be accounted for. Amount of dependency behavior of preschool children is a curvilinear function of the amount of frustration and punishment of dependency-instigated behavior. Both lesser and greater amounts of frustration and punishment are associated with less oc-

[8] From Baldwin (10). Copyright 1955 by the Dryden Press, Inc., and published with permission.

currence of dependency, while the maximum occurrence of dependency is produced by moderate amounts of frustration and punishment. Girls identify more closely with their mothers than do boys and therefore a given degree of maternal frustration or punitiveness has a stronger effect on girls. This leads to a greater generalized inhibition in the severely punished girls than it does in boys and also to the fact that dependency is positively correlated with maternal punitiveness in boys and negatively correlated in girls.

The positive relation between current frustration and expression of dependency receives support from the research of Wittenborn and his associates (81). A cluster (intercorrelation of variable) approach was used in their study of adopted children. In an interview they asked 100 five-year-old children what they would do in certain familiar social situations. Responses from these children were correlated and certain clusters of positively related items emerged. These clusters they called: (1) dependence on adult; (2) aggression; (3) socialized compliance; (4) taking an adult role; (5) weakness-avoidance; and (6) constructive approach. The items indicative of dependence on an adult had in common that when asked what he would do, a child replied he would tell an adult, for example, he would tell an adult if a toy broke, if he hurt himself, if other children wouldn't let him play with them, or if other children called him names. Interviews with the adoptive mothers provided information on the conditions of child rearing in the adoptive home (81). Using again a cluster approach, they found the clusters of conditions of child rearing to include one cluster concerned with rejection of the child. One of the higher degrees of relationship which they found was that between rejection of the children and the children's expressions of dependency. The correlation, although not high in absolute terms (+0.30), was statistically significant. Since rejection is presumably frustrating, supporting evidence is thus found for the contention that dependency and frustration are related. In this study, data from boys and girls were not treated separately, so sex differences, if they were present, were not obtained.

In a later study, the pattern study, Sears and his associates (69) gave some of the nuances of the relationship between dependency and maternal behavior without contradicting the findings so far offered. In the study in question, the findings on boys and girls were treated as a single group. Opinions about the causes of dependency expressed by the mothers are worth attention. One theory they advanced had to do with the original production of dependency.

Some mothers expressed the opinion that fondling and cuddling would produce overdependence during the period in which these practices were followed. Little support for this view was found by Sears and his associates when the group data were analyzed. Another source of dependency the mothers suggested was that the amount of their child's dependent behavior was related to insecurity and that, therefore, they should give the child more affection and security. This view was, in general, supported by the findings of Sears and his associates. Rejection of the child, withdrawal of love used as a disciplinary technique, and severity of punishment for aggression toward the parents were each positively related to child dependency. The *total* amount of physical punishment was *not* related to the child's being dependent. Only the more specific punishment for aggressiveness toward parents was so related. Sears *et al.* suspect the reason for the greater potency of the latter form of punishment was that aggression toward the parent is an action threatening the bond between them. "If you don't love me, I don't love you." This will cause the child to seek reassurance through his efforts toward increased dependency that his parents really do love him.

The other points of view expressed by the mothers were concerned with the handling of dependency once it had developed. Some mothers took the position that if dependency were punished sufficiently, it would be reduced. Sears and his associates found no evidence whatsoever that punishment for dependency helped to eliminate it. Instead, punishment for dependency only made the children more dependent. Other mothers expressed the opinion that rewarding dependency, such as dropping what she was doing and going to the child's aid, or generally being permissive, would increase dependency. This again did not work out in actual practice. Rewarding dependence was not related to dependence in the child.

They summarize their findings on dependence as follows:

> Mothers who repeatedly demonstrate their affection for children are providing many supports for whatever actions the children have performed in order to obtain such demonstrations. These actions often involve following the mother around, touching her, smiling at her and talking, and keeping some kind of contact with her. These are the actions, of course, that we have labeled dependency. Once the child has developed these habitual ways of acting—and all children develop some— he may be expected to use them as devices for reassuring himself that his mother does love him. That is to say, if she shows signs of rejection, if she uses withdrawal of love to discipline him, and if she is punitive

toward his aggression, he may be expected to double his efforts to secure her affection. This will simply increase the frequency and persistence of the acts we have defined as dependent, and hence the mother will describe more of them.

The influence of affectionate demonstrativeness, if we may suggest a theoretical point, is an influence on the *learning* of dependent behavior. The effect of withdrawal of love, punishment of dependency and aggression, and other behaviors that threaten the child's security, is an effect on performance or *action*. Therefore, the actual amount of dependency observed and reported by a mother is a product of both factors. It follows that the most dependent children should be those whose mothers express openly their affection for the child but repeatedly threaten the affectional bond by withholding love as a means of discipline and by being punitive toward his displays of parent-directed aggression.

These relationships are exactly what we have found, but just which way the cause-and-effect arrows point is impossible to say. We are skeptical that there is any single direction of cause-and-effect relations in the child-rearing process. True, the mother's personality comes first, chronologically, and she starts the sequence of interactive behavior that culminates in the child's personality. But once a child starts to be over-dependent—or is *perceived* as being so by his mother—he becomes a stimulus to the mother and influences her behavior toward him. Perhaps, within the present group of mothers, over-dependency of their children increased the mothers' rejective feelings, made them more angry and hence more punitive for aggression. The whole relationship could be circular. An enormous amount of painstaking research will be required to untangle these phenomena (69, 174–175).[4]

In summarizing the determinants of dependency in preschool children it would appear that domination with overprotection (56), the kind and amount of frustration and punishment experience (69), and rejection (81, 83) were the major determinants. Both dominance with overprotection and rejection are probably frustrating and involve punishment. Hence, emphasis may be placed on the kind and amount of frustration and punishment experience as the major determinant of dependence tendencies in early childhood. Frustration in current parent-child relationships is related to strong dependence tendencies, although differentially for girls as contrasted with boys. Differences in reaction of boys and girls to frustration are attributable to differential identifications with their mothers.

The influence of situational factors upon dependence tendencies. Consideration has been given to factors determining dependence reactions in early childhood. They were examined as they apply throughout this age period. No attention has been given to situational factors which may modify the degree of dependence tendencies in a given child at different times. In other words, although a younger child may show consistent dependence tendencies, they are subject to temporary fluctuation. One of the factors causing temporary fluctuation is situational insecurity which increases dependence upon the mother. In childhood, strangeness evokes fear and is considered to be one of the conditions of insecurity in childhood. In one research study on this problem by Arsenian (4), the insecure situation was a room strange to the children but containing many toys. The investigator observed through a one-way vision screen the influence of the mother's presence or absence on the one- to three-year-old child's reaction to this strange room. He hypothesized that security is a function of the mother's presence. He systematically varied the presence or absence of the mother with the child. Some of the children were accompanied by their mothers, some were not. Children left alone in the room for the first few sessions spent most of their time crying as well as showing agitated nonadaptive movements, hanging around the door, and the like. When children were accompanied by their mothers from the first, they played with the toys in the strange room with little evidence of insecurity. Her presence made it possible for the child to react adaptively to the new situation. Security was felt by the child because of his dependence upon the mother. The situation of being left alone temporarily increased his dependence tendencies.

Changes in dependence tendencies with increasing age. Factors related to dependence tendencies applicable throughout early childhood have been examined. Situational influences were also considered. There remains the task of examining changes in dependence tendencies with increasing age during early childhood.

The mothers' attitudes toward dependency are important in connection with age changes. Parental attitudes about the desirability of dependency are subject to change with time. Mothers expect the infant to be completely dependent but also expect that he will become gradually less dependent as he grows older. The mother, as the principal agent of socialization during infancy, fosters dependence in some degree and manner, but at least in later infancy also introduces training with the aim of decreasing dependence. The infant is expected under his own direction to learn to feed himself, to keep himself clean, and in general to adapt to certain rules of the game of living in the family. The goal of socialization is first to foster complete dependence and then to bring about less and less dependence.

It is probable (though not backed by specific definitive research) that during younger childhood emotional dependence takes a different course from instrumental dependence. The mother wishes to lessen instrumental dependence. But with emotional dependence her goal is not so much to lessen dependence as it is to bring about in her child culturally approved and suitable "mature" expressions of emotional dependence. Consider the two-year-old and his manifestations of affection. He is most direct and open, hugging, kissing, and clinging, and tugging at her dress. But adults believe there is something "infantile" about such behavior. Their goal of socialization, whether they are conscious of it or not, is to bring about a fondness for the mother, a pleasure in her company, and not this embarrassing, demanding, passionate attachment. Above all, his incessant demands for proofs of affection must somehow be curtailed. Modification of emotional dependence rather than elimination is the goal. In addition to modification of emotional dependence upon her, she teaches him to seek affection and attention from other adults and from his peers. If she fails or does not try, then the mama's boy of Levy, who is a social isolate, is one vivid consequence.

Changes with age in dependence tendencies during these years have been investigated empirically. Sears and his associates (69), in their pattern study, found that physical clinging decreases during early childhood but that more verbal forms of seeking attention from the mother were still quite strong at the age of five, the end of the age period.

Heathers (37) studied systematically changes with age in dependence (and independence) tendencies in two different age groups. One was composed of 20 two-year-old children, the other of 20 four- and five-year-old children. Teachers in a nursery school observed the behavior of the children in both age groups toward their teachers and toward other children during play. They recorded their findings on a variety of relevant variables. Included were four emotional dependence categories. For dependence tendencies directed toward both children and adults, the categories were clinging to and seeking affection, and seeking attention and approval. Two hypotheses concerning the relation of age to the development of emotional dependence were investigated. The first hypothesis is that during the early years of childhood emotional dependence upon adults declines relative to emotional dependence upon children. The second hypothesis is that emotional dependence as expressed in seeking reassurance and affection tends to decline with age relative to its expression through seeking attention and approval. By comparing the behavior of the younger and the older groups, he found concerning the first hypothesis a marked significant decline in teacher dependence in both clinging-affection seeking and in attention-approval seeking. He found clinging-affection seeking in relation to children showed no significant decline with age but that attention-approval seeking by children showed a reliable increase. As he hypothesized, there is a shift of dependent behavior away from the teacher. The hypothesis that concerned seeking reassurance and affection as declining relative to seeking attention and approval was also supported though not in as clear-cut fashion. Related to other children they showed no change with age in clinging-affection seeking, but with adults they showed a definite decrease in clinging-seeking affection. In general, there was a declining teacher-dependence and a declining clinging or affection seeking from them. ". . . in the process of socialization, emotional dependence tends to shift away from a passive, 'infantile' dependence toward a more active and assertive dependence on one's peers" (37, 56).[9] Thus, changes in dependence tendencies with increasing age have been established. We now turn to the equally important problem of independence tendencies in early childhood.

Determinants of independence tendencies. As dependence declines and independence increases the child at each point in time must strike a balance. He must learn and relearn the areas of and manner in which he is expected to be independent and dependent. A ratio of dependence-independence must be struck. Conflicted frustration may arise. Either overdependence of the sort described earlier or too great independence may result.

This age of three through five seems to be the period which is critical for the development of optimal balance. Research definition of this assertion still is necessary. Consequently, this statement is not to be considered as anything more than plausible, not definitive. At least, problems of independence-dependence balance appear important to the behavior of the young child.

Resistant behavior towards adults when encountered in a setting of proffered assistance may be interpreted as an instance of the young

[9] From Heathers (37). Copyright 1955 by The Journal Press, and published with permission.

child testing his capacities for independence. Social resistance expressed in saying, "No!", or "Don't" is a way the socially maladroit children have of dealing with attempts of others to direct their behavior. Sometimes their resistance is an essential feature of healthy growth.

It has been observed that resistant behavior, or negativism, reaches a high frequency when the child is about two or three years of age. Ausubel (5) offers the interpretation that this is due to the frustration suffered by the child when his parents slow down their nurturance and begin to make demands for independent behavior. This phenomenon he called "ego devaluation."

Frustrations result from learning independence. As Dollard and his associates put it:

> Under normal circumstances each child may also be said to decrease steadily its dependence on its parents. It must learn to walk where it has formerly been carried; and being carried is, of course, a *response* in this situation. It learns not to be picked up when it has experienced some small disaster. It must give up much of the cuddling, holding, and petting which is the prerogative of the smallest darling. Childish approximations of table manners and etiquette must be altered in favor of the customs preferred by adults. The child must learn to wait for its food, to keep its face clean, to submit to having its hair combed, to eat in the regular stages designated by our table techniques. At some time or another all of these lengthened sequences involve frustrations and elicit protest from the child (24, 64–65).[10]

Whiting and Child (78) investigated in their cross-cultural study what they called severity of socialization out of dependence, independence training, and socialization anxiety. None of the societies they studied seriously tried to begin independence training before the age of two and the median age of serious efforts was about three and a half years. The American group began somewhat earlier at about two and a half years. Severity of independence training in the American group received a rating at the median. Two aspects of severity of independence training were isolated—freedom to act on his own initiative without adult surveillance and responsibility for taking on the adult role. As compared to other societies, ratings emphasizing the former were on the severe side in the American group, the latter on the mild side. The measure of severity of socialization involves the behavior of parents. But from another point of view, and one more fundamental to Whiting and Child's intent in

[10] From Dollard *et al.* (24). Copyright 1939 by the Yale University Press, and published with permission.

connection with this particular problem, it is also an index of socialization anxiety aroused in the child. Consider the four aspects used in arriving at a judgment of severity of socialization or socialization-anxiety—brevity, severity of punishment, frequency of punishment, and signs of emotional disturbance in the child. Each of these is potentially an arouser of anxiety in the child; the briefer the transition, the stronger the anxiety, the more severe the punishment, the greater the subsequent anxiety, the more frequent the punishment, the greater the anxiety developed, and the more signs of disturbance, the greater the anxiety.

In dealing with indices of anxiety in the children of different cultures, the investigators related these indices of anxiety in children to indices of adult anxiety. In their cultures, the adult anxiety index was derived from the explanation of illness as being either loss of soul or spirit possession. Whiting and Child considered such explanations as being projective expressions of anxiety about dependence. When the soul leaves the body, it communes with ancestral spirits. They interpreted this as a metaphorical dependence upon parent-figures. Spirit possession also shows a metaphorical dependence, but its parentlike character is not so clear. Nevertheless, both loss of soul or spirit possession as explanations of illness were positively related to severity of socialization out of dependence. Societies with these explanations were more severe; societies without these explanations were more lenient in socialization out of dependence. The adult anxieties ascribable to dependence phenomena were found to be related to the anxieties they stirred in their children.

Training for and encouragement of independence increase independence. Striving for independence takes place in areas where moderate difficulties still exist for the child. If the activity in question has been thoroughly mastered, neither the parent nor the child sees in it anything of a challenge to striving for independence. Thus, a child strives for independence in areas where his ability is still marginal. In this sense, strivings for independence are reflected as an aspect of level of aspiration, that is, the level toward which a person is striving. Fales (26) studied nursery school children in the course of their activity of putting on and taking off their wraps. The percentage of refusal of help was taken as an index of "rudimentary aspiration." Next, one group of children were trained in taking off their wraps. Afterward, they were compared with another group not so trained. The group receiving the training increased considerably in their percentage of refusal as compared to the control group. In another related study by Fales (26), a group of children were praised (encouraged) in connection with their endeavors while another group was not. The praised group increased considerably in independence. It would appear that both training and praise increase independence. Both of these incentives are probably important in accounting for the learning of independence. Increase in independence tendencies with age probably reflects the effect of both these incentives. Conversely, if the parent and other adults engaged in socialization give no training or actually discourage independence tendencies, then a less independent child may be expected.

Some research studies ostensibly concerned with achievement motivation may in our present perspective be considered as studies of independence. These are the studies where *independent* accomplishment is stressed. Independence is the goal; achievement is a means of accomplishment. This was the case in the Fales study just reported. This is not meant to imply that all achievement socialization is independence oriented; achievement may be neutral in this respect or even dependence oriented.

The mother's role in the development of independent accomplishment was studied by Winterbottom (80) as reported in Child (21). TAT stories were told by boys aged eight to ten. Winterbottom then analyzed them for the achievement-related ideas they expressed in their stories, making it possible to arrange the children from those who expressed high-achievement to those who expressed low-achievement motivation. From the mothers of these boys, the investigator secured information by questionnaires on the nature and extent of the demands for independent accomplishment the mothers used in socialization practices, the rewards she gave for fulfillment of these accomplishments, and the restrictions she placed on independent activity. The results she found support the following conclusions: (1) mothers of high-achievement children make these demands at younger ages than do mothers of low-achievement children; (2) mothers who reward such demands have high-achievement children; (3) the more restrictions the mothers place on independent activity, the less independent the accomplishment.

Changes in independence tendencies with increasing age. Changes of independence tendencies with age will now be examined. Independence, as differentiated from lessened dependence, was also investigated by Heathers (37). His measures of emotional independence included those meant to be measures of self-reliance as evidenced in nondistractibility, namely, the extent to which children: (1) ignored stimuli from teacher; (2) ignored stimuli from a child; and (3) played alone. He also included measures of self-assertion or dominance in social interaction with other children as other measures of independence, namely, the extent to which they: (1) structured another child's play (telling him what to do or showing him how); (2) interfered with another child's play; and (3) resisted another child's interference or aggression. Of all of these measures only ignoring stimuli from teacher and structuring another child's play showed an increase with age. Some support, although meager, is thereby given to the hypothesis that independence increases with age.

Behavior maturity has been found to increase with age. Joel (48) studied what he called the behavior maturity in nursery school age children through ratings. He found that certain items he used showed progressive changes from two- to five-and-a-half years of age. His most differentiating items between his younger and older subjects were those concerned with going to the toilet without help or reminder, removing wraps without help or reminder, facing difficulties without appeal to adults or fussing, being absorbed in an activity, self-sufficiency in play, showing initiative, playing constructively with others, being able to see another child's viewpoint, and initiating group play. All of these behavioral changes with age may be interpreted as changes in increased independence tendencies. From both studies it would appear that in the younger child independence increases with age.

Aggressive Tendencies

The younger child, too, is aggressive. He expresses aggression directly both at home and in preschool and indirectly in his play fantasies. A variety of determinants for this behavior has been established. After consideration of the determinants of overt aggressive tendencies, attention will be directed to the relation of overt and fantasy aggression, and then to the determinants of the latter. Consideration of the influence of situational factors on fantasy aggression follows, and the section closes with a discussion of the relation of aggressive and dependence tendencies.

Determinants of overt aggressive tendencies. The constitutional determinants of aggressiveness are very evident though not isolated as to their exact effect by definitive research. Consider how at the age of four height, weight, strength, and sheer activity may be crucial in determining the winner (and the loser) in preschool "bopping" contests and the consequent reinforcement or failure of reinforcement of aggressive tendencies. These characteristics are, at least in considerable measure, attributable to a constitutional determinant. Be that as it may, they are by no means simple, direct determinants. Other factors soon overlay the constitutional sources of difference, creating a pattern in which they are totally overshadowed by other factors. We need to look elsewhere to examine the determinants of aggression.

From the point of view of socialization, it is immediately apparent that our society encourages aggression in certain forms. Under certain circumstances our society expects the individual to be aggressive and to "defend his rights." Reward for aggression is more apt to occur with the boy than with the girl. Quite possibly, constitutional differences accentuate the greater aggressiveness of the male. When we examine sex differences and sex roles in a later section of the chapter, we will find that the preschool-aged boy has been found by Hattwick (35) to be characteristically more aggressive than the preschool-aged girl. At least in part, this difference would come about because we reward boys more for being aggressive than we do girls. This, of course, does not mean the girls are not subjected to rewards for aggression. They are, but to a lesser degree. Research studies to be considered in other connections show that a permissive attitude toward aggression increases aggression. In effect, this attitude means that the child receives rewards for being aggressive. This determinant of aggression will become self-evident as we consider the research on aggression.

From our knowledge of the socialization process of aggression in infancy, we would also expect the experience of the young child would also contain instances in which frustration would serve to breed aggression. In accordance with learning theory, a child will express aggressive responses to the extent that his past history includes reinforcement or failure of reinforcement for such responses.

The proposition that frustration leads to aggression will now be evaluated. Before examining new evidence, it should be pointed out that the principle already has received support. Discussion in an earlier chapter attests to its operation during infancy. The findings of Baldwin and his associates (11), reported earlier in this chapter that the rejective home pattern breeds aggressive children, are suggestive of the same conclusion, since rejection is a form of frustration.

But we cannot be content with this bald statement that frustration leads to aggression. We must explore the qualifications and inter-relations that accompany this general statement. In each of the following studies it is not so much the general proposition that needs elucidation as it is the further complications and nuances of frustration-aggression relationships which their investigations show.

As was the case in discussing dependence tendencies, one may begin with the evidence from the historic research of Levy (56). His was the pioneer study which demonstrated something about the determinants of aggression in preschool children. It will be remembered that Levy found two patterns of maternal overprotection. One of these, that associated with dominance, was found to be related to dependence in children. The other pattern of overprotection was associated with indulgence. The parents falling in this pattern showed excessive control of their children, prolongation of infantile ways in their children, prevention of independence, and indulgence. The parents always gave the children their own way. These children uniformly showed overactivity, obstructive behavior, fighting, and disobedience. In short, they were aggressive.

Maternal-child interaction as studied by Merrill-Bishop (15, 59) has already been reported in connection with maternal control behavior directed toward young children (pages 378 and 379). It will be remembered that most mothers on the second session increased their controlling behavior after they had been led to believe that in the earlier session their children had not shown their full capabilities. We are now concerned with the children's behavior under these circumstances. For both observation sessions she found that the frequency of maternal restricting and controlling behavior was positively correlated to indices of frustration in the children during these sessions, namely, their irritable or complaining behavior. Or to put it another way, at one extreme were the more controlled children who manifested considerable irritability and complaints; at the other extreme were the less controlled children who showed less irritability and complaints. Not only does the study demonstrate that frustration breeds aggression in the form of irritability, but also that there are individual differences in the extent to which children are exposed to frustrating reinforcements of aggressive behavior.

Another finding emerges from the same study. Generalization of aggressive tendencies to other situations is shown by the finding that the children who were more restricted by their mothers were more complaining when they played in other sessions with an unfamiliar young woman rather than with the mother. This woman had been deliberately trained to be equally neutral toward all children so that her behavior would be as constant and as similar as possible toward them. The children who were more aggressive with their mothers tended to be more aggressive when with this neutral young woman. Habits of aggressiveness established with the mother tended then to carry over into this new situation. Moreover, in a second session when each child was more familiar with her, the child's behavior became even more similar to that he had shown toward his mother. Evidently, experiences with the mother established habits that the child carried over into other situations. The young woman by a process of stimulus generalization elicited similar degrees of aggressive behavior.

Before considering further findings, a brief discussion of the meaning and significance of punishment in relation to aggression must be given. In addition to knowing what makes for aggression, we need also to know how we control aggression in the young child. As Child (21) indicates, the strength of tendencies to be aggressive is but one aspect of aggressiveness in relation to socialization. The other aspect about which we need to know is the nature of control or inhibition of tendencies to be aggressive. All societies and individuals have ways of controlling the expression of aggression. Without such controls on in-group aggression, life in a society could not long endure. Every society and individual have learned ways of controlling or inhibiting aggression. By punishment for aggression we mean the extent to which the child was pained or discomfited because he acted in an aggressive manner. True, punishment, whether for aggressiveness or not, is a kind of frustration, but for the sake of clarity it may be distinguished from other frustrations. Punishment for aggressiveness during infancy seems hardly likely. It is probable that it is during early childhood that the child learns aggressive behavior brings punishment. What happens when this occurs needs scrutiny.

A study investigating aggression in relation to punishment was the Sears's et al. antecedent study (71). They investigated the severity of punishment for the expression of aggression (punitiveness) their subjects experienced. They collected their data by further interviewing the same 40 mothers of preschool-aged children they had used on other phases of the study. Assignment of a high rating on punitiveness meant that a mother used severe forms of punishment and consistently and vigorously attempted to suppress the child's aggressive activity in the home. They also secured information on the overt social aggression exhibited by the children in preschool. For the boys, the correlation between punitiveness and aggression was 0.56. In other words, the more punitive the mothers, the more aggressive the boys were in preschool. For girls, however, the correlation was slightly negative although both low and high punishment were associated with low aggression. In girls, moderate maternal punitiveness is related to higher aggression, whereas low or high punitiveness leads to lower aggressive behavior. These differential results for boys and girls were precisely the kinds of relationships they had found in the dependency phase of their study—a positive correlation between punitiveness and amount of dependence in boys and a slightly negative correlation in girls. It is possible to use again the same arguments to account for their results with aggression. (Pages 412–414 give a full account of the argument.)

A similar interpretation may be made based on the assumption that there exists greater identification of the girl with the mother and consequently, a stronger effect from a given degree of maternal punitiveness; this in turn leads to a greater generalized inhibition of aggression in severely punished girls than it does in boys. Since the girls have taken over (identified with) their mothers' values, they are more self-punitive than are the boys when their mothers reprimand them. Hence, girls actually suffer more severe frustrations than do boys from given amounts of maternal punitiveness. "Severely" punished boys presumably were not punished hard enough for this to happen and, in their case, the more punishment the more aggressive tendencies they showed.

The relation of overt and fantasy aggression. So far the studies of aggressiveness in preschool children that have been reported have used indices of behavioral aggression exhibited in day-to-day situations at home or in preschool or in specially contrived settings as in the Merrill-Bishop study. Other studies have been performed which are dependent upon indices of covert or fantasy aggression expressed in play. The doll play studies used similar procedures and materials since they were the work of Robert Sears or his colleagues. Consequently, their doll play procedure can be described in a general fashion. Pauline Sears (65) has offered a convenient summary of their procedures.

A standardized set of doll play equipment is used with which the child is allowed to play. For each session instances of aggressive behavior that a particular child showed were noted by trained observers. Aggression was defined as behavior having the intent of irritating, hurting, injuring, punishing, frustrating, or destroying a doll or play equipment. Sometimes the aggression was innocuous— a girl doll sneaks out of bed—sometimes it was severe—the father doll after spanking the boy doll has his head bashed in. Verbal aggression, such as the child's threats or scoldings of the dolls, was included in the aggressive behavior.

The relation between overt and covert (fantasy) aggression needs clarification. Let it be stated at the onset that fantasy aggression expressed through play does not have a high, linear correlation with independently derived indices of aggression obtained from interview or observation. This has been found by Korner (53) and Sears (67), to name but two investigators. Correlations in the neighborhood of only 0.13 to 0.21 are found. This lack of appreciable direct relationship, then, is a fact and one not to be ignored. The inference, however, is not to be drawn that overt and fantasy aggression are unrelated. Both are forms of behavior; both tell us something about the child. Since a simple linear relation does not hold, investigators have tried to find out if there are not more intricate ways of relating the two kinds of expressions of aggression.

Let us start with the assumption that some, but only some, of the fantasy aggression reenacts aggression a child would actually display in home or school. Let us make certain other assumptions. Some fantasy expression reflects aggression directed toward him (as when he reenacted some punishment that actually did happen to him). Some of his fantasy aggression represents aggression he feels he would like to indulge in but cannot (as when he stuffs the father doll down the toilet). Moreover, conditions will be present which *inhibit* expressions of fantasy aggression. Although he would like to express them, for some reason he cannot. The most obvious source of inhibition is punishment by the parents for aggression. Their punishment does not necessarily eliminate aggression; it may merely inhibit him in his expression of it in play. So fantasy aggression expressed in play may have several different meanings and implications. These assumptions are subject to empirical investigation.

Sears (67) has related fantasy aggression and overt aggression in preschool as the basis of the following expectations. Child punishment serves to frustrate a child and hence to increase his aggression. More severe punishment at home would tend to inhibit aggression there due to fear of punishment but increase aggression elsewhere. This was the finding of Hollenberg and Sperry (40) in a study reported later, that is, punishment of aggression decreases aggression in the situation in which it occurs and increases it in situations dissimilar to those in which the punishment occurs. We need now to examine this term, "dissimilar." The very term suggests "less similar" which in turn suggests that a *gradient* of similarity may be involved extending from most to least similar. Another more technical way to express it is to speak of a gradient of stimulus generalization (see page 122).

Two response tendencies instigated by the parents have now been established: aggression and fear of punishment for aggression. They operate in opposite directions. Sometimes, if punishment is mild, aggression wins out. Their relative influence will depend not only on the strength of the opposing tendencies but also upon the similarities of the older home situation to a new situation. It will be agreed that the school with its parent surrogate, the teacher, is similar in many respects to the home. The child may make the same response in school as he does in the home because of stimulus generalization. On the dimension of similarity, doll play lies further out on the gradient, that is, it is less similar than is that of the school setting. If anxiety created by inhibition and punishment generalizes less extensively than aggression, then the inhibition of severe punishment would be expected to affect behavior toward the preschool teacher but to leave doll play not only uninhibited but actually increased because of the increased frustration created by the punishment.

This was neatly demonstrated by Sears (68) among preschool children who were divided into three groups based on estimates of the amount of punishment of aggression in the home. The first group came from homes low in punitiveness, the second from homes moderately punitive, and the third from homes highly punitive. The moderately punished group showed the most aggression in school. The low and high punished group were found to be approximately the same in mean frequency of aggression. Both were reliably lower in aggression than the moderately punished group. This corresponds to expectancy outlined earlier. The same children were placed in the doll play situation. In their doll play, the children from highly punitive homes showed more aggression than did either of the other two groups. Thus, the more severely punished group was highest in fantasy aggression but inhibited in overt aggression. Fear of punishment did not show enough generalizations to reach the doll play situation, so aggressive tendencies, inhibited in the preschool situation, were permitted to appear.

To return to the issue of the relation of fantasy and overt aggression, the group in which a linear correlation of only 0.13 was found between the two forms of aggression was now found to show an intelligible high interrelationship when the additional factor of the mothers' punitiveness was taken into consideration in interpreting the results.

Determinants of fantasy aggression. It is now possible to consider the determinants of fantasy aggression when it was studied independent of overt aggression. A phase of the study of Hollenberg and Sperry (40) demonstrated that frustration leads to fantasy aggressiveness, but they went beyond this simple relationship. From interviews they derived a measure of home frustration based on the number and kinds of restrictive rules, forcing of the child, and the like. The mothers interviewed were divided into high and low frustration groups on this basis. Thirty children from these homes were observed in highly permissive play sessions and their aggressive responses were measured. They found that the children highly frustrated in the home tended to be more aggressive in doll play. The differences between the high and low frustration groups, however, although in the predicted direction, were not statistically significant. In general, frustration does lead to fantasy aggression, but it is evident that other factors are at work which also must be considered.

The fact that Hollenberg and Sperry obtained a suggestive, but not statistically significant, trend shows that we must look beyond a simple statement that the greater the degree of frustration the greater the degree of fantasy aggression. The blurred, nonconclusive differentiation they obtained was removed when another factor, the severity of punishment for aggression the mothers inflicted on their children, was taken into consideration. A measure of punishment for aggression based on an interview-rating of frequency, intensity and duration of spanking, threatening, isolating, denying privileges, and derogating the child was also available. Instead of just dividing the children into two groups, low and high frustration, they now subdivided the original two groups each into a low and a high punishment group. Thus a given child might be, to use initials, low P—low F, low P—high F, high P—low F, or high P—high F. When this was done, the difference among the groups, blurred when frustration alone was considered, became more definitive and clear-cut. It would be expected that the high P—high F group would be the most aggressive in doll play and the low P—low F group would be the least aggressive, with mixed groups of low and high P and F in the middle. This was the case in their study. High frustration *and* high punishment led to the greatest doll play aggression, while low frustration and low punishment led to the least aggression.

They also investigated the effect of punishment with another group of preschool children. This time they hypothesized that the young child *inhibits* his fantasy aggression in situations where fear and anxiety have been associated with punishment-producing responses. At first glance this appears contradictory to their former findings that punishment produces aggression. The crux of the matter is the question of the situation in which aggression is expressed. They had previously measured fantasy aggression in a situation *different* from that in which punishment had been inflicted. They now studied both punishment and aggression in the *same* setting.

About 25 preschool-aged children were observed in four consecutive doll play sessions. The control group was treated permissively throughout all four sessions. The experimental group was given the first, third, and fourth sessions under conditions of permissiveness identical with those accorded the control group. However, during their *second* play session the experimental group was punished by verbal disapproval every time they made aggressive responses. That is, if the child kicked the baby doll he was asked if he didn't know that nice boys shouldn't do such things. Turning to the results, in the control group aggressive responses increased steadily from session to session. (Under conditions of permissiveness an increase in aggressiveness through the sessions would be expected rather than maintenance of the same amount from session to session.) On the first session, the experimental group behaved as the control group did, but during the second session when they were verbally punished, there was not the increase in aggression that characterized the control group. In the third session (after the punishment session), aggressive responses decreased. In short, punishment of aggression decreased the frequency and intensity of aggression in the situation in which the punishment occurred. Presumably, this finding in doll play would apply in the home situation as well. If aggressive responses are punished in the home, the child will learn to inhibit aggression in that setting. Neither in doll play nor in the home does this mean that his aggressiveness is no longer present. He merely does not show his aggressiveness because of his fear of punishment.

The parallel argument for both dependency and overt aggression concerning the greater susceptibility of girls to maternal punishment as compared to boys was advanced by Sears and associates to help explain the curvilinear results they had obtained. They had not demonstrated this in the study in question; they had merely advanced it to help explain the results. But their point about identification raises the question of its importance in relation to aggression.

Levin and Sears (55) investigated identification as a determinant of fantasy aggression. They advanced various hypotheses having to do with identification, arguing that fantasy aggression is in part a function of the child's identification with aggressive role models. To test their hypotheses, several other measures than those for aggressiveness were also necessary. First, they found the degree of identification of the children with their parents through questioning about how the child acts when he has done something naughty, for example, "What does he do when he is naughty?" "Does he tell you about it?" "What do you do if he denies something you are fairly sure he has done?" They proposed that identification could be estimated from the stage of development of internalized control the child had reached. An example they give of high control (superego) for this age was a child whose mother recounted that when he does act naughty he holds out for a while, but after a short time comes to her and, without prodding, admits he has done something naughty. Second, the severity of punishment for aggression toward parents was assessed. Third, which particular parent usually punished the child was ascertained from interviews. Two sessions of doll play with 126 boys and 115 girls of five years of age were carried out to provide information on the amount of aggressiveness displayed, through recording the frequency with which it appeared in the play session.

In view of the complexity of their design it is worth while to summarize information they had about these children and their parents. On the one hand, they knew the degree of identification the child exhibited along with related findings and, on the other, they knew the frequency of doll play aggression he or she showed. To test their hypotheses they had merely to relate these two sets of data, treating the data for the boys and girls separately.

Their results supported the hypotheses they had advanced. Boys who were highly identified with the father and had the cue for male aggressiveness by being usually punished by their fathers showed the highest frequency of doll (or fantasy) aggression. The boy's identification with an aggressive male model is then a determinant in the frequency of fantasy aggression. For girls, identification was related to high aggression only when it was associated with the mothers being the agent of severe punishment. In other words, when the girls, as well as the boys, were identified with an aggressive model, then identification was related to high aggression.

The influence of situational factors upon fantasy aggression. Situational factors affect expressions of aggression. Situational factors vary from the transitory, almost momentary incident to the longer maintained situation. The previous discussion of determinants included references to various situations which modify aggression. Those situations with which we are now concerned differ only in degree. By and large, they are less common than are those dealt with earlier which are of the sort that all, or almost all, children must face, though in varying degrees. Situational factors now to be considered are more transitory and relatively more unique.

An illustration of increased frustration due to a transitory factor is shown in a study by Bach (6). The more frustrated group had a nap in preschool of one to two hours, the less frustrated group had one of only 10 to 20 minutes. Using the standardized play technique already described, he found that the group forced to take a longer nap showed significantly more aggressive themes in their play than did the children who had had less frustration. Play fantasies of an aggressive sort appeared significantly more often in the more frustrated group.

Situational factors related to the expression of fantasy aggression include the situation in which actual training is given. Keister (52) studied training as a means of reducing frustration in children between three and six years of age. She placed the children who served as subjects in the mildly frustrating situation of having them attempt to solve a difficult puzzle and recorded their manipulatory and verbal behavior. The children showed crying, sulking, and destructive behavior as a consequence of the situation. She then proceeded to eliminate many of these negative reactions to failure by building up their self-confidence through a series of successes with other tasks of graduated difficulty. After training, they tried longer and manifested more interest in solving a comparably difficult problem. Failure of a control group to show similar gains demonstrated that the success of the trained group was not simply a function of their increased age at the time of the training phase of the study or of longer preschool attendance but of the training situation itself.

The presence or absence of the father in the home as related to aggressive tendencies is another of the situational factors having a possible differential effect upon aggression which have been investigated. If, as later discussion shows, the father is the identification model for the boy and if aggressiveness is a masculine quality, then we would expect the boy to be influenced in his aggressive tendencies by the presence or absence of the father. During the Second World War, this situation was neither so uncommon nor in any sense suggestive that other factors might be making children from these homes otherwise different or atypical. Two major studies were performed. One by Sears and his associates (70) involved preschool-age children; the other by Bach (7) concerned school-age children. Both investigators used substantially similar procedures, with data being collected through doll play procedure of the sort already familiar.

Sears *et al.* (70) studied doll play aggression, as expressed in the fantasy of the play situation, with 63 preschool-aged children whose fathers were absent from the home and 63 comparable children whose fathers were at home. The father's absence had little observable effect on the amount of aggression shown by the girls. Boys from father-present homes demonstrated much more aggression in general than did boys from father-absent homes. As to direction of aggression, these same boys showed both more self-aggression, that is, aggression toward the boy doll with whom they presumably identified themselves, and also greater aggression toward the father than did the boys from father-absent homes. These results are compatible with the interpretations that the father served both as a model for the boy and also as a source of frustration for him. Each interpretation will be considered in turn.

It is reasonable to assume that the adult male is more aggressive than the adult female. Hence, the father in serving as a model is a more aggressive model than is the mother. Boys from father-absent homes lacked this model and hence were less aggressive. Moreover, the father's aggressiveness would operate as a frustration to the son. This view can be held on the basis of the results just mentioned. In addition, even more specific evidence is at hand. When the father is absent, equal aggression toward both parent dolls is shown; when he is present, more aggression is shown toward the father doll. Greater self-aggression (aggression toward the boy doll) when the father is present in the home suggests that the father's control is more rigid than the mother's.

Bach (7) studied the father fantasies of a smaller group of father-separated children and a control group, both six to ten years of age. The fathers in the doll play of the father-absent children were portrayed as affectionate and agreeable, whereas the fathers of the father-present children were portrayed as more aggressive in the sense used in the Sears's study. As far as sex differences are concerned, the fantasies of the father-absent girls and boys are both very similar to those produced by the *girls* in the father-present families. This suggests that father-separated boys of from six to ten years of age under the increased influence of the mother were becoming somewhat feminine in their outlook.

Although speculative only, it might be well to mention that father-absent homes probably resemble those in which the father, though present, is such a cipher as to be psychologically absent and consequently to wield only a negligible effect on the child's socialization. Matriarchal homes have been known to produce feminized sons.

On the basis of research described earlier, it has been established: (1) frustration often leads to aggression, presumably because it has been rewarded, that is, found effective in removing interference; (2) punishment of aggression may produce inhibition of subsequent aggression responses in the setting in which they are punished; (3) permissiveness with regard to aggression may lead to subsequent aggressive responses. When these findings are applied in the setting of a particular situation, the following hypotheses emerge. (1) The extent to which children are likely to manifest aggression in a given situation is partially dependent upon the amount of frustration in that situation. (2) Similarly, it is partially dependent upon the amount of punishment of or permissiveness for aggression.

Studies corroborating these two hypotheses have appeared. One by Yarrow (83) is particularly clear-cut and definitive. Sixty preschool children from lower- and upper-middle class families equally divided as to sex were divided into three groups. In the first session all were allowed to play freely. Immediately before the second session, the so-called, failure group was given a task beyond their abilities—building a difficult Tinker-Toy windmill—which resulted in failure and frustration. The so-called satiation group was given pegboards and encouraged to place the pegs in the board for 20 minutes preceding the play session. The control group received neither frustration nor satiation experiences before the second doll play session.

As would be expected from the permissive character of the first session, all three groups on the second session displayed more aggression than they had in the first session. The permissive atmosphere weakened inhibition against expression of aggression and consequently it increased. The influence of situational frustration and satiation was nevertheless apparent. The frustrated group and the satiated group showed significantly greater increase in aggression than did the control group. Thus, both predicted hypotheses were verified—that amount of aggression in a given situation is dependent both on the amount of frustration and the amount of permissiveness for aggression in that situation.

The relation of aggressive and dependence tendencies. The kind and amount of frustration and punishment experiences are major determinants of both dependence and aggression. Since dependency and aggressive tendencies are both related to frustration, it is plausible to infer that they would be correlated with one another. This raises the question that, if this be the case, are we justified in speaking of them as separate tendencies? Sears and his associates (71) in their study of the antecedents of dependency and aggression did, as a matter of fact, find a high correlation between frequency of aggressive and dependent behavior. That is, if a given child were given to considerable (or little) aggressive behavior he tended to show considerable (or little) dependent behavior as they measured it. Fortunately, there was also available a measure of activity level (an amount of physical movement and frequency and persistency of social interaction). Both aggression and dependence are highly correlated with level of activity. When the effect of activity level was statistically removed or held constant, the relationship between dependency and aggression is considerably reduced, suggesting that they are sufficiently different so that the two tendencies vary independently. Hence, we are justified in speaking of aggressive tendencies as distinct from dependence-independence tendencies.

Sexual Tendencies

Despite the appearance of sexual behavior in infancy, there is a general impression that there is an increase in the scope and frequency of sexual behavior in early childhood over that in infancy. Definitive controlled research on this question of frequency and scope is lacking. One must be content with general descriptions.

Sexual curiosity. Isaacs (45) observed 30 English children (mostly boys) in the setting of a nursery school. Her observations covered a period of three years. She reports her findings in an anecdotal fashion which the quotations below about sexual curiosity exemplify.

When the children were playing a family game with the puppy as baby, Duncan said: "Undress him." Priscilla: "Yes." Duncan: "and then we can see his bim-bom." There was great laughter and excitement among the children and all repeated, "see his bim-bom." Priscilla undid the rug in which he was wrapped and called others to look: "Come on, come on, look underneath." The puppy stood on its hind legs near Priscilla. Duncan: "Oh, he tried to get to your what-d'ye-call-it." . . .

Jane and Conrad went with Mrs. I. to the ethnological museum today. When looking at a human figure made of bamboo, Conrad pointed out the prominent penis, giggling, and saying, "What is that funny thing, sticking out? We know, don't we?" They whispered and giggled about it (45, 141–142).[11]

In addition to sexual curiosity, exhibitionism (exposing genitals) and voyeurism (looking at others' genitals) were frequently observed by Isaacs. The sheer wealth of her observations support the contention that sexual activities are common in preschool children. Her unsystematic method of selection makes this the only conclusion which can be safely drawn from her data. Her results are not capable of yielding quantitative comparison among ages or between the sexes.

In another study Hattendorf (34) interviewed a large number of mothers about the nature of the sex questions their children asked them. Despite the distortion and unreliability brought about by the retrospective nature of the mothers' recall, her results are of some value. For over 800 children from two to five years of age the most frequent questions these children asked their mothers centered on the origin of babies and the coming of another baby. The next most frequent question concerned physical sex differences. Sexual curiosity during preschool ages seems to be established.

Masturbation and related activities. Although reported in infancy it is not surprising that studies reporting male masturbation have centered in early childhood as the earliest age for sufficient frequency to occur to make possible reliable observations. Many studies depend on retrospective report of mothers or of the subjects themselves. This introduces the factors of forgetting, of repression, lack of opportunity of observation, and of dissimulation which presumably would mean that whatever the findings are concerning frequency, there would be a serious understatement. Moreover, some studies finding very small percentages of conscious recall may be based upon the reporting of the presence of *habitual* rather than occasional activity. This is the

[11] From Isaacs (45). Copyright 1933 by Harcourt, Brace and Company, Inc., and published with permission.

explanation that Sears (66) offers of Willoughby's 1937 summary of the literature (79) in which only 5 per cent of men and 18 per cent of women could recall having masturbated before the age of ten.

Later somewhat more adequately controlled studies show higher percentages. About 60 per cent of the mothers interviewed by Sears and his associates (69) in their pattern study reported they had observed masturbation in their children who by then were five or six years of age. Sex play with other children was reported by over half of the mothers. Most mothers were not permissive toward these activities. On the other hand, quite a few were moderately permissive, not making an issue of it although discouraging these practices. Huschka (44) in presenting data on 300 problem children reported about the same percentage of masturbation. These mothers of the problem children dealt with the problem much more destructively than did the mothers in the Sears study. In fact, about two-thirds on detecting masturbation used direct threats predominantly of a physical sort and specifically threats of genital injury.

Awareness of genital differences. A young child can readily identify himself as a boy or a girl. This does not necessarily mean awareness of genital differences on their part. Often children stress, as we shall see, differences in dress or hair arrangement even if they are aware of genital differences. In fact, the situation recalls the old story of the little boy asked about the sex of a baby he had seen in the process of being bathed who replied, "I don't know, it's so hard to tell with the clothes off."

Conn and Kanner (23) interviewed 200 children concerning sex awareness in the setting of doll play. Most of the children were between the ages of five and seven, and thus somewhat older than the age range now being stressed. Nevertheless, it is more appropriate to deal with the study now rather than later. The child spoke about sexual matters, not as himself, but for boy dolls, girl dolls, father dolls, and mother dolls, making the situation a projective one. Several illustrations of how they structured the situation to the child might be given. When embarrassment was strong in a boy, a "tough boy" doll was introduced with the implication that there was no reason that he should be nice and say conventionally approved things. A doll with a dress was introduced to lead up to questions on how to tell boys and girls apart. "Modesty" was investigated through a toy bathroom with a doll on the toilet. The situation and procedure varied from child to child so as to make it as natural and spontaneous as possible. In their sample of 200 children, 140 gave in the first session "certain" awareness of genital differences. To be sure, other differences were mentioned, with differences in clothing, tonsorial distinctions, and differences in urination posture being prominent. Differences were stated in childish terminology and with considerable diversity of names used. Not less than 61 different names for the genital organs were given including some invented for family use. Awareness of sex differences at these ages seems established.

A better controlled study of awareness of genital differences was performed by Katcher (51). It will have been noted that Conn and Kanner's subjects were children referred to a psychiatric clinic and hence they were a rather special population. Katcher used as subjects over 200 normal children of higher and lower socio-economic status in preschool or school settings. Their task was to identify the sex of the drawings of figures of clothed and nude children and adults. Excluding hair, the outline of the figures used was a compromise between that of the male and of the female. The same outline was used in all pictures (adult nude figures were cut off at the waist). Systematically varied cues from which they could make identification were added to the outline figure—hair, clothes, breasts, and external genitals. These figures were presented in pairs in randomized fashion for them to make a choice as to sex.

The errors they made were analyzed by age and socio-economic differences. In general, except for breast cues, errors decreased with age. No significant socio-economic difference was found. The most readily identified sex-differentiating characteristic was clothing, followed in order by hair, genitals, and breasts. So few errors were made in clothing or hair that no detailed breakdown was given.

Genital errors produced several findings of interest. No subject older than eight years made a single error in identifying genitals. Older children were more accurate than younger ones. Girls throughout tended to be superior to boys in identification of both male and female genitals. For ages four and five, by which the phallic stage is said to be in operation, there were still over 50 per cent of the children making mistakes on genital cues. Breasts, presumably theoretically less traumatic in their import than the genitals, nevertheless showed more errors.

Interpreting the over-all results of awareness of genital differences in terms of Freudian thinking is not impossible. However, there is nothing crucial to contraindicate a learning or experience interpretation, quite apart from Freudian thinking. Except in terms of specific details, with some favoring one view, some the other, there is little in the evidence itself on which to base a choice between the alternative hypotheses. Katcher (51) himself considered his results favored the experience hypotheses.

Discovery of genital differences, postulated by Freud to account for much of the subsequent development in the phallic stage, has not been submitted to crucial controlled research. The available evidence does, however, suggest that factors other than discovery of sex differences, such as socialization pressures, also contribute and that undue emphasis has been placed on one of the factors responsible for increased sex differentiation which takes place during early childhood. Increased general maturity and learning experiences of the preschool child over that of the infant may help to account for the results. There is nothing in these researches to show that it is the specific discovery of genital differences which makes for this increase in sex differentiation. On the other hand, the results are not in general incompatible with psychoanalytic hypotheses.

Socialization. Our culture is still hostile toward expression of childhood sexuality. Indeed our culture is more severe in their restrictions on sex behavior in children than in many, if not most, other societies (29, 78). Restrictive efforts by parents take three forms: to avoid or minimize chances of their stimulation, to avoid opportunity for erotic play with other children, and to inhibit sexual impulses toward family members (69). To use but one facet of restriction, the typical parent is still misinformed about the "pernicious" effects of masturbation (47). He does not hesitate to use forceful measures, including threats and coercion, to stamp it out. Since the customs of our group require that self-stimulation be prohibited, the parents must find ways to discourage the child's discovery of his capacity for this particular form of self-enjoyment. All of this means that sexual expression of children is a problem of socialization.

From the child's point of view these parental efforts along these lines are restrictions which must be learned, and, if we may drop into the vernacular, "learned the hard way." He experiences pleasure in touching his genitals and is affectionate toward his parents and his peers. He must learn when to inhibit, to redirect his impulses, or to hide them from view.

Parents in general wish him to inhibit sexual tendencies (69). Unlike feeding and toileting where there are socially approved outlets, no redirection is given for sexual tendencies. No substitutes are offered. Prohibition is stressed. To be sure, arranging conditions to prevent stimulation, such as separate sleeping rooms, separate bathing hours, and closed doors, are used. Distraction is also practiced, moving the child's hand or finding something else for him to do. But prohibition—saying, "No!" in a multitude of forms—is perhaps the principal agent. None of these parental practices offers the child other substitute outlets—they are all restrictive in intent. Punishment may lead to elimination of masturbation, but other effects may follow. Small wonder, then, that seeds of maladjustment in many children can be planted within this area.

It is important to note that observed sex behavior in children is not always evidence that sexual needs are present. Plant (61), on the basis of his clinical experience, indicates that many children in engaging in sex experiences are motivated, not by sex tendencies, but by other factors. There may be a desire to break taboos, including sexual ones, a desire to be "grown up," a desire to be sought after and to gain prestige, a facet of general curiosity, and the like. Thus, various other needs may be expressed through "sexual" behavior that is not motivated by sexual tendencies but by other socialization tendencies.

Sex differences and sex roles. There are present the hereditary and constitutional factors making for sex differences in strength, stature, and speed. But personality differences between men and women in a given culture are largely dictated by the goals of socialization in that culture.

Sexual differentiation in the individual requires consideration of intense and prevalent sex typing which socialization introduces. Sex roles refer to the taking on of behavior that is appropriate to one's sex in a particular society. In our society, the infant is identified at birth by the blue or pink blankets used. From then on sex roles are relentlessly drilled in. It is not surprising that by early childhood distinguishable sex differences are to be found.

Not only are sex differences to be found, but they are of the kind our society expects to find in boys and girls. Let us consider Hattwick's study (35) of sex differences in several hundred nursery school children aged two- to four-and-a-half. Ratings on 60 observable behavior characteristics were made. Statistically significant differences on 27 of these items were found between boys and girls. Eleven of the items showed greater occurrence in boys. These were attacking others, breaking toys, grabbing toys, being hard to reason with, ignoring requests, laughing and jumping around excessively, rushing into danger, handling sex organs, leaving tasks incomplete, tenseness at rest, and wasting time at routines. Girls showed greater occurrence on 16 characteristics. These were avoiding risk, avoiding play with others, bossing, criticizing others, crying easily, fearing strange places, fearing high places, jealousy, misrepresenting facts, refusing food, shrinking from notice, staying near adults, sucking thumb, twisting hair, telling fanciful stories, and seeking praise. These, then, are established differences in behavior characteristics between younger boys and girls.

Her findings do not demonstrate whether these sex-linked behavioral differences are expected in our culture to be characteristic of boys and girls. Social expectations were investigated by the writer (77). The 27 terms used for types of behavior which Hattwick found for differentiating between preschool age boys and girls were arranged on a report form in alphabetical order; then 59 boys and 138 girls in a college undergraduate child psychology class were asked to check whether boys or girls at this age would show more often each particular behavior item. No discussion of this topic had yet occurred in class or in text.

Their opinions concerning what to expect in sexual differences agreed with the empirical results found by Hattwick. For boys, 10 of the 11 observed sex differences were expected by both male and female raters either in statistically significant degree or at least with differences in the expected direction. The only exception was the expectation rating by both males and females of laughing, squealing, and jumping around excessively as more characteristic of girls than of boys. For girls, 13 of the 16 observed sex differences showed statistically significant agreement or with differences in the expected direction by both male and female raters. Those three on which there was disagreement between empirically observed differences and expectation never even approached statistical significance. Indeed, sometimes it was a disagreement of expectation and empirical finding on the part of one sex only, with the other being in the expected direction. Examination of the three behavior characteristics showing exceptions—bossing, misrepresenting facts, and sucking thumb—shows how this could come about. These three characteristics were actually more prominent in girls, but tended to be rated as being expected in boys—at least by girl raters! Combining Hattwick's and the writer's results, they fit the notion that the girl both is and is expected to be timid and more passive; the boy is and is expected to be aggressively forceful in our culture. Expectancy and actuality concerning sex differences seem to agree.

The role of the parent in creating sex differences in roles of the child has been demonstrated in the studies of Sears and his associates (70) and Bach (7) discussed earlier in connection with the role of the father. The father was hypothesized as supplying for the boy the primary patterns and rewards for masculine traits such as aggression. If absent, the child would lack him as a model and be less masculine. He does not serve as the model of sex appropriate behavior for girls and consequently it was hypothesized that his absence would have little influence on them, which was found to be the case. In general, with the qualifications and nuances mentioned in the earlier discussion, boys from father-absent homes manifested less aggression, while girls were not affected.

In the pattern study of Sears and his associates (69), intentional sex typing was investigated. A variety of questions were asked the mothers, the answers to which threw light on this issue. Using the questions about boys as illustrative, the investigators asked about how important she thought it for him to be a real boy, to play or not play with dolls, and differences in ways boys and girls ought to behave, and how he should treat little girls. It was possible to reduce their findings to a single scale on sex-role differentiation. Only about 5 per cent believed little or no sex-role differentiation existed at this age, but only about 4 per cent were at the other extreme of always stressing it. Most mothers did put some weight upon sex-role differentiation.

It was also possible to take up all of the training practices followed by the mothers and compare the ratings of the mothers of boys to that of the mothers of girls. Girls were more warmly treated in infancy, were more often disciplined by their mothers, were more often subjected to withdrawal of love and praised for their conduct. Boys received more physical punishment. It was in the area of aggression where the greatest distinction was made. Boys were allowed more opportunities for aggression, although not permitted to fight with brothers and sisters. It was evident that, to many mothers, being "boylike" implied being aggressive. No particular differences were found in connection with toilet training and, most surprising perhaps, no differences in sex training in the narrow sense. Evidently this latter source of differentiation does not start as early as the pre-school age.

Sex roles are decidedly a matter of socialization to fit in with the expectation of a particular culture. This fact is shown by consideration of how sex roles vary from culture to culture. All sorts of diametrically opposed behavior is expected of males and females in different cultures. An illustration is chosen for presentation which runs counter to some degree at least to the expected trend in our culture. This group, studied by Mead (58), are the Tchambuli of New Guinea. This group, Mead significantly remarks, was the only one of all those in which she has worked where little girls of 10 or 11 were more alert, bolder, and enterprising than little boys. In adulthood, unadorned Tchambuli women with shaven heads are the managers and providers; they fish and go to market. Activity is expected of her—if childbirth is hard, Tchambuli say, "The mother has not gathered enough firewood." The men, decorated with strings of ornaments and bedorned with real or false curls, spend their time practicing dance steps, carving, and painting. They are the artists managed by the strong practical women. They are gossips and easily show hurt feelings in a skittish sort of a way. This culture shows almost a complete reversal of what might be considered a caricature of the roles of men and women in our society. But even in this particular society the male is pursuing the ideal of his society, which happens to be furtherance of the arts, and women are carrying on more pedestrian humdrum tasks. In this as in most societies masculine traits are more prized.

In our culture "masculine" tendencies are prized which are quite different from those which are held as prominent by the Tchambuli. Horney (42) specifically relates so-called penis envy to cultural conditions arising from this prizing of masculine traits. Instead of feminine envy being rooted in a biological difference and in experiences of early childhood, she attributes it to an envy of the qualities which the male has. These qualities such as strength, independence, and relative right to choose sexual partners are at the root of women's envy. This point of view bears strong resemblance to Adler's (1) "masculine protest" wherein women react against inferiority feelings by assumption of masculine roles.

Sex-role preferences. What of the children's preferences in these matters of sex-linked behavior? This question leads us to the issue of sex-linked behavior which a child either would like to adopt or that which he perceives as the preferred behavior.

Brown (17) quantified a scale for the measurement of sex-role preference. It consisted of picture cards showing various objects, figures, and activities commonly associated with masculine or feminine roles.

Some of the cards showed single items such as a necklace, a tractor, a doll, or a purse. Other cards bore paired items such as trousers and shirt with a dress, and cosmetic articles with shaving articles. The last section of the scale was a picture of a girl, a girlish boy (boy dressed as a girl), a boyish girl (girl dressed as a boy), and a boy. A child-figure, unstructured as to sex, called "It," was used by each child who made choices from the cards for It. For the single item cards, each child subject picked eight liked best by It. For each pair and for the four-child figures, one was selected as preferred. Range of the total weighted scores on the sex-role cards was from zero, an exclusively feminine score, to 84, an exclusively masculine score. Seventy-eight male and 68 female middle-class children aged 5 to 4 to 6 to 4 were used as subjects by Brown. Their mean scores respectively were 66 and 38. This resulted in a large and statistically significant difference, indicating definite sex-role patterns in young children.

Further analysis showed that a number of children (twice as many girls as boys) indicated a mixed preference pattern. Some even showed a strong opposite sex-role pattern. Boys showed significantly greater preference for the masculine role than girls showed for the feminine role. The sex-role ambiguity of girls may express her minority status in a culture where the male role has the dominant status. Among the sex-typed toy objects, 70 per cent of all choices of boys are masculine, only 49 per cent of the choices of girls are feminine. On choosing between wanting to be a boy or a girl or a mixture, only one boy in ten expressed desire for the female role, while one girl in three expressed a preference for the male role. In general, there was evidence that the masculine role had greater value and prestige.

Evidence concerning the psychoanalytic theories of early childhood

As was the case in infancy, the reality of sexual behavior in early childhood has been amply proved. Consequently, material, which might have been presented at this point if this had been considered a debatable question, is discussed in the preceding section devoted to sexual tendencies in early childhood. The evidence amassed shows sexual behavior in early childhood exists, but its existence does not prove that the *interpretation* that psychoanalysts make of this behavior is correct. The behavior does exist, this much the evidence shows, but alternative nonpsychoanalytic interpretations of its significance may be made. The extent to which this may plausibly be done is a major theme in that which follows.

Some studies alleged to be evidence, generally negative evidence, concerning psychoanalytic propositions about the phallic stage will be ignored as irrelevant. For example, concerning the Oedipus complex, it will be remembered that psychoanalytic theory holds that attitudes, largely unconscious, arise which are positive and erotic toward the cross-sex parent and comparatively hostile toward the parent of the same sex. Some studies have appeared which use the technique of asking the subjects to designate the preferred parent. The studies depending upon direct questioning and conscious report are not reviewed because they are considered irrelevant. After all, these object choices are according to theory supposed to be unconscious, and deception, unconscious though it may be, would be expected. The results on conscious preferences are irrelevant to the issue at hand, though not to other issues discussed elsewhere in the chapter. Moreover, answering which parent do you like best does not allow for the obvious fact that in some ways and for some purposes one parent may be preferred, but for others the other parent may be preferred. Insofar as typical fathers differ from typical mothers (see Radke's results on page 392) one might expect that the boy would prefer the mother as a source of affection but still esteem the father as a preferred model. Studies based on conscious report are ignored.

Projective studies, although psychoanalysts might object that they do not penetrate the depths of unconscious phenomena sufficiently to be a crucial test, are, nevertheless, somewhat more satisfactory unless it is fairly obvious they are tapping results quite close to the surface of consciousness. This lack of depth is true of most doll play studies of parent preferences. Friedman (30) found that questioning children about which "parent" in the picture was liked best after they had told a story to the picture was the only one of several techniques not yielding statistically significant differences on feelings toward cross-sex and like-sex parents. He interprets this to mean that it was the technique among those he used, although somewhat projective in character, which reflected attitudes too near the surface to include Oedipal material.

The presentation of the evidence concerning psychoanalytic theories of the phallic stage of early childhood will center on identification, castration anxiety, and the Oedipus complex. Evidence concerning the functioning of the ego defense mechanisms must be ignored because of space limitations. Evaluation of the research evidence has appeared elsewhere (for example, 39, 66). Fortunately, psychoanalytic hypotheses concerning the phallic stage do not stand or fall in terms of evidence concerning these mechanisms.

Identification

Identification with the like-sex parent is the means whereby the child learns the behavior considered appropriate to his or her own sex in his or her particular culture. Identification has been defined in Chapter 5 as wanting to be like someone, to take over the like-sex parent's characteristics. Object choice, on the other hand, is what the child wants as a love object. During the course of events of the phallic phase the child is supposed to pass from object choice to identification.

Sears as discussed in (17) has made an important distinction between sex-role preference and identification. As he indicates, sex-role preference refers to sex-linked behavior which an individual would either like to adopt or which he perceives as the preferred or more desirable behavior. Identification, on the other hand, refers to sex-linked behavior which an individual introjects and makes his own. To be sure, in many cases an individual identifies with a given sex model as well as preferring sex roles appropriate to that model—he identifies with what he prefers and prefers what he identifies. But sex-role preference does not prove identification.

According to psychoanalytic theory, the girl is expected to have more difficulties in assuming her feminine role than the boy has in assuming his masculine role. Brown (17), who dealt with this issue quite clearly in his study with sex-role preferences, showed that, in general, this appears to be true.

Brown's results on sex-role preferences are consistent with a theory of identification (and also the theories of penis envy and castration anxiety) of Freudian thinking, but his findings are also consistent with a cultural theory in which the male is seen to have a preferred status.

In connection with the study of Sears and his associates (71), evidence has already been presented that girls have higher identification with their mothers than do boys. In studying the relation between frustration and punishment of dependent behavior, girls were found to be more susceptible to maternal punitiveness. This is in the direction expected by psychoanalytic theory. But there is another facet of the theoretical expectation; boys will identify more with their fathers than will girls. To relate the two facets—boys will identify more with their fathers and girls more with their mothers.

That boys tend to identify with their fathers and girls with their mothers has been substantiated by Blum (16). A subsidiary finding was that identification is less clear-cut in females. The Blacky test was used which consists of cartoons of the adventures of Blacky, a young dog. The frontispiece to the series introduces the characters Blacky, Mama, Papa, and a sibling, Tippy, unspecified as to age and sex. When the test is given to boys, Blacky is described as "son" and when given to girls as "daughter." The cartoons in the series were designed to study stages of psychosexual development. Cartoon VII reproduced as Figure 13 is relevant to the present problem of identification.

Figure 13. A Blacky Card. (Copyright 1950 by The Psychological Corporation, and reproduced with permission.)

Spontaneous stories told to this cartoon, illustrating strong and not strong identification, are given by Blum as follows:

Strong:
Now listen you, you little pooch, when I bark, you jump, do you get that? Blacky feels very superior to this little dog. He is making believe that he's the boss, or maybe pretending to be his father talking to him in a superior tone.
Not Strong:
Blacky has found something peculiar. It looks like a dog, but it doesn't move or bark at her. She's a little afraid of it at first, but later she realizes she's bigger and the toy can do her no harm—so she settles down to enjoy it (16, 32).[12]

After seeing the cartoon, about 100 male and 100 female college students responded to the following questions:

(1) Who talks like that to Blacky—Mama or Papa or Tippy? . . .
(3) Whom is Blacky imitating here—Mama or Papa or Tippy?
(4) Whom would Blacky rather pattern himself after—Mama or Papa or Tippy?
(5) Blacky's disposition, actually, is most like the disposition of which one—Mama or Papa or Tippy? (16, 78).[12]

On all four questions 119 young adult males significantly more often responded "Papa," and 90 young adult females replied, "Mama." Blum thus verified that identification normally occurs with the parent of the same sex.

Identification was less clear-cut in females as compared to males. As mentioned before, males tended to say "Papa" and the females, "Mama" to the question, "Whom would Blacky rather pattern himself (herself) after?" However, the males are significantly more decisive in that a greater percentage of males chose "Papa" than females chose "Mama." Moreover, to another question for the same cartoon, "Whom is Blacky most likely to obey—Mama or Papa or Tippy?" both males and females say "Papa" significantly more often than "Mama." Females seem less sure with which parent they seek to identify and the father is the one most likely to be obeyed—as Blum indicates, this latter is a relevant point in that the decisive frustrating agent is a crucial influence in developing identification.

England (25), too, has found evidence that boys tend to identify with their fathers and girls with their mothers. As material, he used one drawing of two "stick" figures (resembling those that might be

[12] From Blum (16). Copyright 1949 by The Journal Press, and published with permission.

made from match sticks), one seated on a bench by the figure of a man and the other beside the figure of a woman. Another drawing showed the stick figures walking down the street hand in hand, one with "mother" and the other with "father." The task was to identify the stick figures as boys or girls. He also used a drawing which was to be completed. The drawing already showed a woman seated on a bench with a tree immediately on her left. In this instance, the task was to draw a boy and a girl sitting with the mother. The arrangement of the drawing forced the child to place either the boy or the girl closer to the mother.

The three tasks were given to the 134 boys and girls aged five to fourteen. In each instance, scoring for identification was made by assuming that a boy or girl placed the boy or girl figure beside the parental figure with whom he or she identified. In general, girls associated with the mother and boys with the father according to the selection of both boys and girls. For example, 72 per cent of the children drew a girl beside the mother with the boy on the other side of the girl. The girls were found to be more pronounced in the parental identifications, with only 4 per cent saying the boy should be closer to the mother and only 8 per cent saying the girl should be closer to the father. Since no age differences were found, results were given without age breakdown.

Cava and Raush (20) utilized the Blacky pictures in an investigation of the perception that 37 adolescent boys had of their fathers. Several Blacky pictures were selected which were theoretically related to identification, for example, Figure 13 and another card concerned with castration anxiety. Scores were calculated for each picture used. The subjects were then classified as weak (less conflict) or strong (more conflict) for each Blacky picture and for a total combined identification score. To serve as a measure of the similarities the boys perceived between themselves and their fathers, they filled out the Strong Vocational Interest Blank twice, once to describe themselves and then as they thought their fathers would fill it out. The Strong Vocational Interest Blank is a standardized measure of interests and preferences. It is primarily intended to aid in predicting degrees of satisfaction with a variety of occupations. Its items are responded to in terms of likes and dislikes. The score on perceived similarities on this measure was derived from the number of times the subject showed agreement between his own responses and those he attributed to his father. This gave them an operational measure of identification for the amount of perceived similarity. Although "perceived" similarities are not actual similarities between fathers and sons, they are nevertheless of some significance.

The question the investigators raised had to do with whether or not those boys who showed conflict on identification matters also perceived their fathers as less like themselves than the other boys who showed less conflict. The differences they obtained were all in the direction to be expected on the basis of the foregoing hypothesis. Those for Castration Anxiety and Total Identification were statistically significant. The boys showing statistically significantly more conflict over castration anxiety perceived their fathers as less like themselves. This is in line with psychoanalytic theory in that boys with more conflicts about castration anxiety would be expected to have made less "identification" with their fathers.

Gray and Klaus (33) in a study of identification of college men and women with their mothers and fathers used the Allport-Vernon-Lindzey Study of Values as their measure of perceived similarity. The Study of Values is a measure of the relative strength of six values or motives in the personality. Filling out this measure based on the classification of values as theoretical, economic, aesthetic, social, political, and religious gives information about how strongly the individual holds certain values as his own. For example, a person with a high "political" score values power for its own sake. The investigators chose the instrument as one which it could be assumed tapped aspects of personality in which parental influences would be of major importance. Each student filled it out (1) for himself; (2) as his mother would; and (3) as his father would. It was also actually answered by his father and mother. When scored and the various scores interrelated, the investigators were dealing with both actual similarities between child and parent and similarities with his parent as perceived by the child. Without going into their statistical findings it is possible to summarize the results. They found considerable evidence for the following statements: (1) Both boys and girls were more like their same-sex parents in areas of major interest than their opposite-sex parents; (2) both boys and girls tend to perceive themselves as more like their same-sex parents than their opposite-sex parents; (3) girls were more like and perceived themselves as more like their mothers than did boys their fathers. These findings, as they point out, are compatible both with psychoanalytic and general social learning theory.

The study of Cass (19) was also concerned with identification and related factors but differed in one essential respect from the preceding studies of Cava and Raush (20) and Gray and Klaus (33). Unlike Cass these investigators asked subjects to give information of how their parents would answer questions which they also answered for themselves. Cass first asked mothers to answer a questionnaire involving preferences and vocational ambitions and fears as she would herself, and then to answer as her child would. The child also filled it out for himself. A score of the mother's "awareness" of the child's thoughts was made when the items, filled out similarly by her adolescent child, were extracted from the answers to the same questions. Cass went on to define "identification" operationally by the number of the child's answers which were similar to the answers the mother had given for herself (not as she guessed the child would answer). In addition, the adolescent completed another questionnaire concerned with the restrictive and regulatory control practices the mother followed. The children also finished the sentences of a sentence completion test which yielded a score on the conflict between mother and child. There was thus made available measures of (1) "awareness" on the part of the mother of her child; (2) identification of the child with his mother; (3) the restrictiveness of control the mother practiced; and (4) the conflict between mother and child.

In terms of these definitions Cass found that there was (1) a positive relationship between awareness of the mother for the child and identification of the child with the mother; (2) a significantly higher positive relationship between awareness and identification for girls than for boys; and (3) greatest conflict among girls and boys when the mother was low in awareness and high on restrictiveness of control.

It is worth while to explore a bit the meaning of her three major findings, one by one. Evidently, the children identified with their mothers to a greater degree when the mother was more aware of the child's thoughts and feelings. This relationship was greater for girls than for boys. She found in her sample that low awareness on the part of the mother when combined with high restrictiveness of control made for the greatest conflict between mother and child. A mother unaware of her child's feelings and yet intent on closely directing her child's behavior created a setting for considerable conflict between mother and child.

The reality of the process of identification has been demonstrated by controlled research. A variety of interrelationships with sex, conflict, and the like have been demonstrated. But in no way have these researches shown that the psychoanalytic interpretation is to be favored over a general cultural interpretation.

Castration Anxiety

The discovery of genital differences and consequent castration fears and penis envy has been emphasized in Freudian literature. In research exploration castration anxiety sometimes is not investigated directly. Instead, the researcher reasons that if castration anxiety did exist, there would be general emotional disturbances apparent when children discovered sex differences. Even if such disturbances were universally and unequivocally shown to be present, this would not demonstrate the existence of castration anxiety in itself. It would demonstrate that the necessary concomitant for castration anxiety to be present, that is, emotional disturbance, actually did occur. Huschka's data (44) on masturbation threats directed at problem children described earlier, although interpreted by her as evidence of castration anxiety, may be more parsimoniously interpreted as demonstrating emotional disturbance on the part of children who were threatened about masturbation. In other words, problem children are emotional about frustration, but this does not prove they are disturbed because of castration anxiety. Nevertheless, the presence or absence of emotional concomitants of discoveries of sex differences are of interest. Conn and Kanner (23) found that even among children referred to a psychiatric clinic, that most of them accepted genital differences with tranquility. From a population of 200, only 10 boys and 11 girls thought of differences between the organs of the two sexes in terms of absence through loss. Their data collected from parents of the children were obtained in various ways, including projective doll play. Conn (22) also using play techniques found that 17 out of 50 children were disturbed by the discovery of sex differences but that the majority were not. It may be that the relative absence of castration thoughts which they discovered indicates merely that they failed to gain rapport with their subjects or that their research methods failed to get through defenses to deeper levels and consequently that their results were of too superficial a nature to be of great significance. Despite this possibility, lacking other more definitive evidence, it would appear that disturbances over discovery of sex differences (and consequently, castration anxieties) are not universal or inevitable in our culture.

Friedman (30) made an investigation of the castration complex on the assumption that its content is unconscious and most appropriately studied through use of projective materials. The subjects came from a middle-class, white, Protestant background, randomly selected from a school population. His was a cross-sectional, developmental study in that his subjects were 300 five-, six-, seven-, eight-, fifteen-, and sixteen-year-old boys and girls, with each group divided equally as to number (50) and sex. The particular ages studied by him were chosen because psychoanalytic theory calls for a heightened castration anxiety to be present at age five or six (or even a little younger), a diminution at seven or eight during latency, and for a resurgence of castration anxiety at fifteen or sixteen. For testing castration anxiety, he developed three incomplete fables involving animals or a child in which something happened to a projecting organ. The subjects were to complete the fables. They were so structured that they invited the subjects to do so by either cutting-off or not cutting-off the projection. Is the response of cutting-off or not cutting-off a sign of anxiety? A good case could be made for either response. He solved the problem by finding separately the average reaction times of those subjects who cut off and those who did not cut off the projection. Those who ended fables by *not* removing the projection took longer or "blocked" in their reaction times. He assumed that people who "block" are more anxious; he further assumed that the greater anxiety in the face of the castration stimulus exists in this group who did not remove the projection.

Psychoanalytic theory would call for the youngest (Oedipal) and the oldest (pubertal) age groups to be more disturbed by castration anxiety and therefore to end the fables by removing the projecting organ significantly less often than would be the case with the middle (latency) age groups. The members of "Oedipal-pubertal" group failed to cut off the projection significantly less often than did those in the "latency" group, thus supporting the psychoanalytic concept of the castration complex. When responses for boys and girls were analyzed separately, the results for the boys supported the psychoanalytic hypothesis at both Oedipal and pubertal ages, but for girls the hypothesis was confirmed only between the latency and the pubertal ages but not between the Oedipal and latency ages.

Castration anxiety receives little support from studies of acknowledged conscious disturbances of children when they become aware of sex differences. This evidence may be objected to as being superficial and irrelevant since the child may not be consciously aware of his "anxiety." The study by Friedman in which projective materials were used is not subject to these criticisms. He finds results compatible with psychoanalytic theory. Thus, support from one study can be mustered for the reality of castration anxiety, but obviously much more work will be necessary before it can be decided if the psychoanalytic interpretation of castration anxiety is a valid one.

The Oedipus Complex

It is very difficult to evaluate a problem so broad as that of the Oedipus complex. Anthropological evidence gives us the nearest approach to a global test. Through such evidence one can see whether the Oedipus complex seems to take the same general form in all cultures. We now turn to the problem of the universality of the Oedipus complex.

Many anthropologists would argue that the Oedipus complex does not exist in some cultures. After a study of the anthropological evidence, Honigmann (41), for example, concludes that hostility toward the father and rivalry for the affection of the mother (essential characteristics of the Oedipus complex) exist in some, but not all, societies.

One important study is of Malinowski (57) who investigated the Trobriand Islanders. Family organization in this group is quite different from our own. Fatherhood among the Trobrianders is a purely social relationship. The father plays with his children, is affectionate, and watches and cares for them, but he has no authority and never issues orders or forces obedience. Authority and discipline are vested in the mother's oldest brother who, it is agreed among the Trobrianders, is the model for the child to follow. He, not the father, is the source of pride and social ambition, wealth, and social status which comes to the boy. On his death he leaves his worldly possessions to the boy. In this culture, the most important taboo, or restriction upon social interaction, is that concerning brother-sister relationships. Brothers and sisters are separated at an early age and are never permitted to be socially intimate. According to Trobrianders it is common knowledge that a brother or a sister shows not the "slightest interest" in the love affairs of the other. The sister is a mysterious being forever hidden from the boy. When questioned about brother-sister incest, Trobrianders are emotionally disturbed. In general, this and other evidence indicate that the forbidden sex attraction is more apt to exist between brother and sister rather than

mother and son.   Mild amusement, rather than disturbance, characterizes their discussion of mother-son incest.

As Malinowski indicates, the complex of sex attraction and repulsion appears to be quite different from that in our own society.
Hostility is directed against the uncle, not against the father, despite
the fact that Freudian theory says that it is sexual relations between
father and mother which are at the root of the son's hostility.   It is
this and other anthropological evidence that argues against the
universality of the Oedipus complex.

There has been considerable criticism of Malinowski's findings
from the orthodox psychoanalysts (for example, 63) on this matter,
resting upon their charge of the anthropologist's lack of competence
to detect subtle manifestations of Oedipal functioning.   If this criticism is accepted, it means that there is still a possibility that the
Oedipus complex does exist in the Trobrianders (and in the other
groups) in a form analogous to our own.   Nevertheless, it is probable
that this complex does vary.   The classic form which the Oedipus
complex is supposed to take does not appear to be universal.

Other evidence is available.   There are those nonanthropological
research studies that must be referred to in connection with Oedipus
complex.   First, there is a phase of the study of Blum (16) using
the Blacky pictures.   He investigated a hypothesis derived from
psychoanalytic theory that girls would show greater vestiges of pre-
Oedipal attachments after passing through the Oedipal situation than
would boys.   In this connection it must be remembered that his
subjects were all young adults who had thus passed through the
Oedipal stage.   One of the cartoons of the Blacky series (Cartoon IV)
was designed to tap "Oedipal intensity."   It depicts Blacky wearing
an "unhappy" expression, lurking in the bushes and watching Mama
and Papa close together and "holding paws," with the usual cartoon
device of love, a series of small hearts hovering over their heads.

For this cartoon two questions with their respective answers are
relevant to the question of sex differences in the extent of pre-Oedipal
attachments.

Which of the following makes Blacky most unhappy?

(1) Papa keeping Mama all to himself (Mama keeping Papa all to her-
    self).
(2) The idea that Mama and Papa seem to be ignoring him (her) on
    purpose.
(3) He (she) is ashamed watching them make love out in the open.

Which would make a happier picture?

(1) Mama left on the outside watching Blacky together with Papa.
(2) Papa left on the outside watching Blacky together with Mama (16, 42).[12]

For the first question, the first alternative answer is conceived to be the Oedipal alternative, the second, the pre-Oedipal alternative, that is, that which would be the interpretation of the situation if pre-Oedipal object relationships were strongest. Significantly more males than females select the Oedipal alternative and significantly more females than males select the pre-Oedipal alternative. In connection with the second question, significantly more females than males answered that Blacky would prefer to be with the same sex parent, thus indicating a greater pre-Oedipal attachment. Blum concludes that psychoanalytic theory and the results from his test are in agreement concerning the greater retention of pre-Oedipal components in girls than in boys.

Friedman (30), using the children studied in connection with his results concerning castration anxiety, investigated the Oedipus complex. Specially designed projective fables and picture cards were given the children who told stories to them. These stories were then submitted to thematic analysis with special attention to the attitudes that were expressed toward parental figures. He found positive attitudes toward the cross-sex parent and negative attitudes towards the same sex parent. Moreover, the adolescent girls' fantasies retained a more Oedipal character than did those of the boys, which is in line with psychoanalytic theory.

There is, then, some research support for the Oedipus complex, but again this support is from findings not incompatible with theory but not crucial to it. In our own society something resembling the Oedipus complex, if not identical with it, probably does exist. Many clinical workers, including nonpsychoanalysts (for example, 73), agree that many instances of emotional disorders stem from excessive attachment to opposite-sex parents and excessive hostility to same-sex parents. Moreover, the preschool child is still profoundly dependent upon his mother and gives her affection. In fact, this is one of the basic themes stressed earlier in the chapter. But it does not follow that this interpersonal situation is but a disguised version of the Oedipus situation. Acceptance of the reality of these clinical findings does not demonstrate that the Oedipus drama follows the lines laid down for it in psychoanalytic theory. Controlled research evidence has not been found which shows that the Oedipus situation works through the steps ascribed to it, nor does research show that all boys and girls follow the particular patterns ascribed to its course.

A neo-Freudian interpretation of early childhood

Neo-Freudian interpretations of aggressive dependence and sexual tendencies (as such) have already been offered. There remains for discussion the problems for which the evidence for the psychoanalytic position have just been reviewed—identification (and the superego), castration anxiety, and the Oedipus situation.

Identification and the Superego

Identification is a term used in many senses (for example, 64) both within orthodox psychoanalytic thinking and in the broader area of general psychological theory. One does not necessarily accept the Freudian account of its origin to admit that identification does take place. Disregarding Freudian dynamics, identification still may be considered a fundamental mechanism of socialization. It is because the child attempts to duplicate his parents' behavior and that of other adults that socialization is possible. It is through identification with the like-sexed parent that the child learns the responses appropriate to his sex in his culture. Serving as a model for his or her children is recognized as an important function of the father or mother, a function having profound effects upon the socialization of the child.

Identification is a learning process. In learning terms, identification is a tendency to be like or to imitate another person because of emotional attachment to this person. In this sense identification is a variety of imitations. It follows that identification should be investigated as a problem in learning to see the degree to which it follows the usual phenomena of learning—its parameters and interrelationships. Research studies on these matters are at their barest beginnings. Therefore, these remarks about identification and learning must be left at the level of assertions. They apparently are not incompatible with what we now know about learning and socialization, but they definitely have not yet been demonstrated by research. They are our guesses on how the process of identification might be conceptualized until this research evidence is secured.

The process of identification has been divorced from the Oedipus complex in the present context. Instead of identification being considered a consequence of the Oedipal situation, it is interpreted as arising both during and after the age at which the Oedipus drama is supposed to take place.

In earlier stages identification is the process by which a child takes over and makes his own the wishes and demands of his parents. Their values, their thinking, and their behavior become his social values, his way of regarding what is correct thinking and behavior for functioning in his society. For him, parental prohibitions become self-administered inhibitions.

In later stages of identification the child successively (and simultaneously) takes unto himself attitudes, feelings, and beliefs of persons other than his parents or parental surrogates. Healthy growth demands it. If the child did not shift identifications, he would show an unhealthy stultification of personality development. He would be too dependent upon his parents. It can be seen that dependence-independence is closely related to the process of identification. Much of the child's struggle for independence is a struggle for increasing the scope of his identifications. He broadens his social horizon from home to neighborhood and school and beyond. There are identification relationships with parent substitutes (teachers, policemen, athletic coaches, fictional characters, movie and TV heroes), with older siblings, and in fantasy with toys or imaginary companions. Identification as a process is not confined to the domestic setting.

Since there is a continuing series of identifications, individuality in personality is an inevitable consequence. The mother and the father may be the sources for many identifications and to that extent the child resembles them. But other identifications develop from the shifting pattern of other significant individuals with whom he comes into contact.

Self-administered inhibitions, or self-instigated control, arise from parental prohibitions and, thus, what may be described as the superego or conscience is learned. Identification involves learning the values, ideas, and morals of the parents and others and tending to be like them in these respects as well. Once learned, as Whiting and Child put it, he punishes himself ". . . whenever he has done something for which he believes his parents would feel he should be punished" (78, 226–227).[13] This punishment which he inflicts

[13] From Whiting and Child (78). Copyright 1953 by the Yale University Press, and published with permission.

upon himself in the course of the socialization process is guilt. According to Whiting and Child, guilt is not just anxiety; it is a specific type of anxiety created from punishment at the hand of the parents or parent figures. For example, when his parents disapprove of his sexual or toilet behavior, guilt develops. Dependence tendencies, previously discussed, are an integral part of the situation. Guilt arises when he feels anxiety about situations threatening this dependent relationship.

Guilt is one of the more important ways through which the individual becomes socialized. Without the presence of guilt feelings many socializing experiences would become extraordinarily difficult. From child rearing to living in society under the law, our lives would be very difficult without guilt serving as a silent policeman. Consider how difficult child rearing would be if the child did not begin to set up his own prohibitions. Sheer physical force and punishment would be among the major methods applied with unceasing vigilance to a creature with no sense of obligation or accountability. Similarly, adult society would show even more instability than it does today—if it existed at all.

Inner control appears to come about from an acceptance of the parents' standards as one's own (69). Sears and his associates give a vivid illustration. It concerns a bright, lively seventeen-month-old girl on a visit with her mother and father to a friend's home. She explored the living room avidly. One of the floor lamps especially fascinated her. Twice her eager grip on it brought about a teetering and swaying and twice her father said clearly and distinctly, "Martha, don't touch!" To quote hereafter:

> After the second interruption, Martha began a general exploration of the room again. Now she went a little slower, and several times glanced at her father. As she came closer to the lamp, however, she stopped looking his way and her movements were all oriented toward the lamp. Deliberately she stepped toward it, came within a couple of feet of it, and lifted her arm partly, a little jerkily, and then said sharply, commandingly, "*Don't touch!*"
>
> There was an instant of struggling silence. Then she turned and stumbled across the room, flopped down on the floor, and started laughing excitedly. Her father, laughing with her, and obviously adoring, reached out and hugged and snuggled her for several minutes (69, 365–366).[4]

They go on to indicate that it was not simple fear of her father. She didn't look at him furtively, didn't whimper, didn't oscillate on her decision. She clearly looked to herself for guidance, not her father. She had accepted her father's standards as her own.

This incident gave no opportunity to observe the conscience operating in the face of a temptation when no one was present, nor of guilt feelings when the temptation was not overcome. These two characteristics—control in face of temptation when no one is present and guilt—are the characteristics Sears and his associates allege to be those by which conscience control may be recognized. In their pattern study (69) they found a gradual growth in behavior which showed these characteristics. The three-year-old is trustworthy but only to a point, the four-year-old somewhat more, and the five-year-old still more. Even when five or six, the children's age at the time of the study, 13 per cent of the mothers reported no evidence of the development of conscience, that is, the child still hides and denies his infractions and does not seem unhappy when naughty.

Castration Anxiety

Little need be said about castration anxiety. It may well exist in varying degrees in some children. But its role may be divorced from the impetus for the Oedipus situation and seen as one rather numerically infrequent difficulty some children face. No particularly important role need be given it.

The Oedipus Situation

Intensification and prominence of sexual interplay in the family have been repeatedly observed with children in the clinical setting. This is an observation of many workers, whether psychoanalytically oriented or not. It is also a common finding that parents are responsible for many of the personality disturbances in their children. It may be that an intensification of sexuality in the situation is primarily an expression of the *parents'* sexual needs which they work out through the child.

Fromm's neo-Freudian interpretation (31) of the Oedipus complex is in terms of a child's struggle to free himself from the authority of the parents. It is an attempt to emerge from dependency. Sexual factors may be present, but they are not the cause of the struggle with the father. In effect, Fromm places the Oedipus struggle in a framework of an aspect of socialization. This position is obviously compatible with the earlier discussion of dependence-independence tendencies.

Behavior-social learning theory throws an interesting light on the so-called Oedipus drama. In the family structure in our culture the father is probably the major source of punishment of the child. It would be plausible in learning theory terms that the child would react with hostility to punishment at his hands. But adherents of Freudian theory would reply that this hostility is attributable to sexual relations between the parents. Here the findings of Malinowski about the Trobrianders become pertinent. Despite sexual relations between the parents hostility of the child was directed against the mother's brother. In Trobriand culture, it is he, not the father, who is the disciplinarian. It is also in this culture that he is the target of hostility. Thus, behavior-social learning accounts for the hostility in relation to punishment in both our own and in Trobriand culture.

Perhaps more than in any other psychoanalytic hypothesis, the Oedipus complex appears to be due to socialization factors in the child's experience rather than being a universal phenomenon (66). This may be one reason that many psychoanalytic workers, even though more or less orthodox concerning other issues, are apt to take a broader view of the Oedipus complex than prevails in the direct Freudian conception. Innateness, inevitability, and strict pattern of development of the Oedipus situation are not insisted upon. Fenichel (27), for example, speaks of the complex as a product of family influences. Whether this is a neo-Freudian interpretation or not, it is one to which this writer can subscribe.

Summarization of the theory of psychosexual stages

In earlier chapters and in earlier sections of this chapter the theory of psychosexual stages was examined against the evidence of controlled research. Some support was found for the existence of oral, anal, and phallic stages. But evidence was also offered that these stages had neither the generality nor scope claimed for them. Relevant to this is the conclusion already reached that libido as a common energy source is rejected. In the present account "psychosexual" stages have been interpreted as "psychological" stages, and sexual tendencies relegated primarily to the phallic stage and subsequent years.

Freud assumed that the oral, anal, phallic, latency, and genital stages follow one another inexorably and everywhere show the same pattern. There remains for discussion the issues of whether or not psychoanalytic stages follow a strict progression and whether or not each stage is fundamentally similar for all children.

Anthropological evidence may be appealed to in connection with the generality of the sequence of psychosexual stages. In general, it may be stated that evidence from various societies indicates that these stages may be changed and sometimes one or another stage may be nonexistent. The data involving cross-cultural comparison of primitive societies studied by Whiting and Child (78) does not show a rigorous uniformity of progression of psychosexual stages.

To these claims the orthodox psychoanalyst can reply that the data these anthropologists have advanced is inadequate. This, they would claim, is due to their lack of thorough training in the nuances of interpretation of psychoanalytic material. They were not deeply enough versed in psychoanalytic thinking to detect its subtle functioning. Consequently, materials which would have upheld psychoanalytic doctrine were not recognized for what they were. This objection has some cogency. It is also possible to argue, as Mead (58) does, that in various cultures there are different settings and different resolutions to the Oedipus problem. But at some point, that which appears up to then to have been mere secondary elaborations to a basic theme now takes such different form as to be a primary, not a secondary difference.

The weight of evidence demonstrates the importance of variation of cultural factors. Freud may well have described a position which explains the development of *some* children in a *particular* kind of society or within a stratum of that society, but his position is less and less valid as the individuals in the groups one is considering differ more and more in these respects from those in which Freud found his patients.

Summary

Parental behavior was the first major topic considered. Specific maternal practices, although they have been studied, were not related to effects upon the child, and hence are not of any great systematic value. Similar patterns of parental behavior expressed in attitudes and home atmospheres have been found with a certain degree of consistency in different studies using different subjects and procedures. Warmth, permissiveness, and punishment appear to be the three major patterns of parental behavior. Each of these patterns may be related to characteristic behavior in the children exposed to these patterns. Turning to differences between fathers and mothers, the latter are found to be the chief supervisors and more affectionate and yielding. Techniques of training used by parents which stressed punishment were found to be ineffectual. Investigators found that changes in parental behavior with increasing age of the children consisted of older children receiving less contact and fewer restrictions in general; yet parents applied more severe restrictions when situations arose which, in their judgment, required them. The discussion closes with the caution that the parental patterns do not inevitably and precisely predict the consequent child behavior.

Shifting perspective to the child, the development of self-awareness is first considered. The self rests, in part, upon memory continuity and is expressed in the self-evaluation of the self-concept. Knowing what is held to be good and bad throws light on the self as the child sees it. Consistent ideal concepts of "good" boys and "good" girls emerge. As for the sources of the child's self-concept, attention is given to his "real" characteristics, his reflected appraisals of others, his comparisons of self with others, and his inner pressures.

Discussion of social perception centers upon the child's perception of parental roles. He sees his parents as the sources of frustration, with the father being the greater source of authority and the mother being the greater source of affection.

Behavior tendencies in early childhood were first considered in terms of dependence and independence tendencies. Evidence was introduced to show that dependence and independence should be considered as distinguishable, although related behavior tendencies. The kind and amount of frustration and punishment are the major determinants, so far established, for dependence tendencies in early childhood. Differences between boys and girls in dependence tendencies are attributable to differential maternal identifications. The influence of situational factors and age changes are also discussed. Turning to independence tendencies, they are shown to be related to dependence socialization anxiety, to training for and encouragement in independence, and to independent accomplishment. Some support is found for the hypothesis that independence increases with age.

Aggressive tendencies in preschool children are shown to be related in a variety of ways to permissiveness toward aggression, to frustration, and to punishment. Overt and fantasy aggression do not have a high linear correlation, but they are found to be much more interrelated when the additional factor of maternal punitiveness is taken into consideration in the fashion described. Frustration, as such, leads to fantasy aggression, but the relationship becomes considerably greater when the severity of punishment for expression of aggression is also taken into consideration. High frustration when accompanied by high punishment leads to the greatest fantasy aggression; low frustration and low punishment lead to the least fantasy aggression. Identification is also found to be a determinant of fantasy aggression. Boys highly identified with their fathers show the highest frequency of fantasy aggression. For girls identification is related to aggression only when it is associated with their mothers being the agents of their punishment. The effect of temporary situational factors was also explored. It was found that when they lead to increased frustration this in turn leads to increased fantasy aggression.

It would appear that there is an increase in scope and frequency of sexual behavior during the preschool years. Awareness of genital differences in these ages seems established. Socialization pressures from parents directed toward inhibition of sexual tendencies during these years are strong. Sex differences, definitive sex roles, and sex-role preferences are established during these years. Greater aggressiveness in the boys and more timidity and passivity in the girls characterize at least some of these differences.

The psychoanalytic theories of identification, castration anxiety, and the Oedipus complex were discussed. The reality of identification was demonstrated, but the evidence was interpreted as compatible with a general social theory as it was with a more specific psychoanalytic interpretation. Neither approach has been proved to be more valid than the other. Emotional disturbance, a necessary concomitant for castration anxiety, appears in some children, but research evidence is too scanty to allow the conclusion to be drawn that the psychoanalytic interpretation is valid. The Oedipus complex is not found to be verified by controlled research studies.

Neo-Freudian interpretations of identification and the superego, castration, and the Oedipus situation are offered. Identification is interpreted as a process of learning, independent of the Oedipus and as occurring both before and after the phallic age and as taking place with persons other than the parents or parental figures. Self-administered inhibitions do occur through guilt. Guilt, in turn, is one of the important ways the child becomes socialized. Neither a particular role nor much importance is attached to castration anxiety. The Oedipus situation is seen as an attempt of the child to emerge from dependency, and shows, in this as well as in other aspects, compatibility with behavior-social learning theory.

The chapter closes with a brief statement concerning the theory of psychosexual stages in general. It is concluded that these stages exist, but they have neither the generality nor the scope sometimes claimed for them, with variation among children being due primarily to the influence of cultural factors.

For Further Reading

The book by R. R. Sears, E. E. Maccoby, and H. Levin, *Patterns of Child Rearing* (Evanston, Ill.: Row, Peterson, 1957), is recommended. They give an account of their findings on what happens in the process of rearing the younger child in our contemporary culture. The interrelation which forms the various patterns is brought out in vivid detail. The somewhat different approach of A. L. Baldwin is brought out in the monograph he wrote in collaboration with J. Kalhorn and F. H. Breese called, *Patterns of Parent Behavior* (*Psychological Monographs*, 1945, 58, No. 268).

References

1. Adler, A. *Understanding human nature.* New York: Greenberg, 1927.
2. Allport, G. W. *Becoming: basic considerations for a psychology of personality.* New Haven: Yale University Press, 1955.
3. Anderson, J. E. Parents' attitudes on child behavior: a report of three studies. *Child Develpm.,* 1946, 17, 91–97.
4. Arsenian, Jean M. Young children in an insecure situation. *J. abnorm. soc. Psychol.,* 1943, 38, 235–249.
5. Ausubel, D. Negativism as a phase of ego development. *Amer. J. Orthopsychiat.,* 1950, 20, 796–805.
6. Bach, G. R. Young children's play fantasies. *Psychol. Monogr.,* 1945, 59, No. 272.
7. Bach, G. R. Father-fantasies and father-typing in father-separated children. *Child Develpm.,* 1946, 17, 63–80.
8. Baldwin, A. L. Differences in parent behavior toward three- and nine-year-old children. *J. Pers.,* 1946, 15, 143–165.

9. Baldwin, A. L. The effect of home environment on nursery school behavior. *Child Develpm.*, 1949, 20, 49–62.

10. Baldwin, A. L. *Behavior and development in childhood*. New York: Dryden, 1955.

11. Baldwin, A. L., Kalhorn, Joan, and Breese, Fay H. Patterns of parent behavior. *Psychol. Monogr.*, 1945, 58, No. 268.

12. Baldwin, A. L., Kalhorn, Joan, and Breese, Fay H. The appraisal of parent behavior. *Psychol. Monogr.*, 1949, 63, No. 299.

13. Bartemeier, L. The contribution of the father to the mental health of the family. *Amer. J. Psychiat.*, 1953, 110, 277–280.

14. Beller, E. K. Dependence and independence in young children. *J. genet. Psychol.*, 1955, 87, 25–35.

15. Bishop, Barbara M. Mother-child interaction and the social behavior of children. *Psychol. Monogr.*, 1951, 65, No. 328.

16. Blum, G. S. A study of the psychoanalytic theory of psychosexual development. *Genet. Psychol. Monogr.*, 1949, 39, 3–99.

17. Brown, D. G. Sex-role preference in young children. *Psychol. Monogr.*, 1956, 70, No. 421.

18. Brown, F. An experimental study of parental attitudes and their effect upon child adjustment. *Amer. J. Orthopsychiat.*, 1942, 12, 224–229.

19. Cass, Loretta K. An investigation of parent-child relationships in terms of awareness, identification, projection and control. *Amer. J. Orthopsychiat.*, 1952, 22, 305–313.

20. Cava, Esther L., and Raush, H. L. Identification and the adolescent boy's perception of his father. *J. abnorm. soc. Psychol.*, 1952, 47, 855–856.

21. Child, I. L. Socialization. In G. Lindzey (Ed.), *Handbook of social psychology:* Vol. 2. Cambridge: Addison-Wesley, 1954, 655–692.

22. Conn, J. Children's reactions to the discovery of genital differences. *Amer. J. Orthopsychiat.*, 1940, 10, 747–754.

23. Conn, J. H., and Kanner, L. Children's awareness of sex differences. *J. child Psychiat.*, 1947, 1, 3–57.

24. Dollard, J., Doob, L. W., Miller, N. E., Mowrer, O. H., and Sears, R. R. *Frustration and aggression*. New Haven: Yale University Press, 1939.

25. England, A. O. Cultural milieu and parental identification. *Nerv. Child*, 1947, 6, 301–305.

26. Fales, E. Genesis of level of aspiration in children from one and one-half to three years of age. Reported in Lewin, K. *et al.* Level of aspiration. In J. Mc. V. Hunt (Ed.), *Personality and the behavior disorders:* Vol. 1. New York: Ronald, 1944, 333–378.

27. Fenichel, O. *The psychoanalytic theory of neuroses*. New York: Norton, 1945.

28. Finch, Helen M. Young children's concepts of parent roles. *J. Home Econ.*, 1955, 47, 99–103.

29. Ford, C. S., and Beach, F. A. *Patterns of sexual behavior*. New York: Harper, 1951.

30. Friedman, S. M. An empirical study of the castration and Oedipus complexes. *Genet. Psychol. Monogr.*, 1952, 46, 61–130.

31. Fromm, E. The Oedipus complex and the Oedipus myth. In Ruth N. Anshen (Ed.), *The family: its function and destiny:* Vol. 5. New York: Harper, 1945.

32. Gardner, L. Pearl. An analysis of children's attitudes toward fathers. *J. genet. Psychol.,* 1947, 70, 3–28.

33. Gray, Susan W., and Klaus, R. The assessment of parental identification. *Genet. Psychol. Monogr.,* 1956, 54, 87–114.

34. Hattendorf, Katherine W. A study of the questions of young children concerning sex: a phase of an experimental approach to parent education. *J. soc. Psychol.,* 1932, 3, 37–65.

35. Hattwick, LaBerta A. Sex differences in behavior of nursery school children. *Child Develpm.,* 1937, 8, 323–355.

36. Hawkes, G. R. The child in the family. *Marriage & Fam. Liv.,* 1957, 19, 46–51.

37. Heathers, G. Emotional dependence and independence in nursery school play. *J. genet. Psychol.,* 1955, 87, 37–57.

38. Hilgard, E. R. Human motives and the concept of self. *Amer. Psychologist,* 1949, 4, 374–382.

39. Hilgard, E. R. Experimental approaches to psychoanalysis. In E. Pumpian-Mindlin (Ed.), *Psychoanalysis as science.* Stanford, Calif., Stanford University Press, 1952, 3–45.

40. Hollenberg, Eleanor, and Sperry, Margaret. Some antecedents of aggression and effects of frustration in doll play. *Personality,* 1951, 1, 32–43.

41. Honigmann, J. J. *Culture and personality.* New York: Harper, 1954.

42. Horney, Karen. *New ways in psychoanalysis.* New York: Norton, 1939.

43. Horowitz, E. L. Spatial localization of the self. *J. soc. Psychol.,* 1935, 6, 379–387.

44. Huschka, Mabel. The incidence and character of masturbation threats in a group of problem children. In S. S. Tomkins (Ed.), *Contemporary psychopathology.* Cambridge: Harvard University Press, 1944, 49–62.

45. Isaacs, Susan. *Social development in young children: a study of beginnings.* New York: Harcourt, Brace, 1933.

46. Itkin, W. Relationships between attitudes toward parents and parents' attitudes toward children. *J. genet. Psychol.,* 1955, 86, 339–352.

47. Jaques, E. H. Miscomprehensions of parents concerning child health and behavior. *Amer. J. Orthopsychiat.,* 1942, 12, 202–213.

48. Joel, W. "Behavior maturity" of children of nursery school age. *Child Develpm.,* 1936, 7, 189–199.

49. Kagan, J. The child's perception of the parent. *J. abnorm. soc. Psychol.,* 1956, 53, 257–258.

50. Kardiner, A. *The individual and his society.* New York: Columbia University Press, 1939.

51. Katcher, A. The discrimination of sex differences by young children. *J. genet. Psychol.,* 1955, 87, 131–143.

52. Keister, Mary E. The behavior of young children in failure: an experimental attempt to discover and to modify undesirable responses of preschool children to failure. *Univ. Iowa Stud. Child Welf.,* 1937, 14, 29–82.

53. Korner, Anneliese F. Relationship between overt and covert hostility—economy and dynamics. *Personality,* 1951, 1, 20–31.

54. Lasko, Joan K.   Parent-child relationships: report from the Fels Research Institute.   *Amer. J. Orthopsychiat.*, 1952, 22, 300–304.
55. Levin, H., and Sears, R. R.   Identification with parents as a determinant of doll play aggression.   *Child Develpm.*, 1956, 27, 135–153.
56. Levy, D. M.   *Maternal overprotection.*   New York: Columbia University Press, 1943.
57. Malinowski, B.   *Sex and repression in savage society.*   New York: Harcourt, Brace, 1927.
58. Mead, Margaret.   *Male and female.*   New York: Morrow, 1949.
59. Merrill, Barbara A.   Measurement of mother-child interaction.   *J. abnorm. soc. Psychol.*, 1946, 41, 37–49.
60. Neill, B. M.   Perception by preschool children of parental roles in selected home situations.   Unpublished M.S. thesis.   Ames, Iowa: Iowa State College, 1946.
61. Plant, J. S.   *The envelope.*   New York: Commonwealth Fund, 1950.
62. Radke, Marian J.   The relation of parental authority to children's behavior and attitudes.   *Univ. Minn. Inst. Child Welf. Monogr.*, 1946, No. 22.
63. Roheim, G.   Psychoanalysis of primitive cultural types.   *Internat. J. Psychoanal.*, 1932, 13, 2–224.
64. Sanford, N.   The dynamics of identification.   *Psychol. Rev.*, 1955, 62, 106-118.
65. Sears, Pauline S.   Doll play aggression in normal young children: influence of sex, age, sibling status, father's absence.   *Psychol. Monogr.*, 1951, 65, No. 323.
66. Sears, R. R.   *Survey of objective studies of psychoanalytic concepts.*   New York: Social Science Research Council, 1947.
67. Sears, R. R.   Relation of fantasy aggression to interpersonal aggression.   *Child Develpm.*, 1950, 21, 5–6.
68. Sears, R. R.   A theoretical framework for personality and social behavior.   *Amer. Psychologist*, 1951, 6, 476–483.
69. Sears, R. R., Maccoby, Eleanor E., and Levin, H.   *Patterns of child rearing.*   Evanston, Ill.: Row, Peterson, 1957.
70. Sears, R. R., Pintler, Margaret H., and Sears, Pauline S.   Effect of father separation on preschool children's doll play aggression.   *Child Develpm.*, 1946, 17, 219–243.
71. Sears, R. R., Whiting, J. W. M., Nowlis, V., and Sears, Pauline S.   Some child-rearing antecedents of aggression and dependency in young children.   *Genet. Psychol. Monogr.*, 1953, 47, 135–236.
72. Stagner, R.   *Psychology of personality* (2nd ed.).   New York: McGraw-Hill, 1948.
73. Strecker, E. A.   *Their mother's sons.*   Philadelphia: Lippincott, 1946.
74. Sullivan, H. S.   *Conceptions of modern psychiatry.*   Washington, D. C.: William Allison White Psychiatric Foundation, 1947.
75. Thompson, G. G.   *Child psychology: growth trends in psychological adjustment.*   Boston: Houghton Mifflin, 1952.
76. Tucker, Clara.   A study of mothers' practices and children's activities in a co-operative nursery school.   *Teach. Coll. Contrib. Educ.*, 1940, No. 810.
77. Watson, R. I.   Unpublished data, 1956.

78. Whiting, J. W. M., and Child, I. L. *Child training and personality: a cross-cultural study.* New Haven, Conn.: Yale University Press, 1953.
79. Willoughby, R. R. Sexuality in the second decade. *Monogr. Soc. Res. Child Develpm.*, 1937, 2, No. 10.
80. Winterbottom, Marian R. The relation of childhood training in independence to achievement motivation. Unpublished doctoral dissertation. Univ. of Michigan, 1953.
81. Wittenborn, J. R., *et al.* A study of adoptive children: I. Interviews as a source of scores for children and their homes. *Psychol. Monogr.*, 1956, 70, No. 408.
82. Wittenborn, J. R., *et al.* A study of adoptive children: III. Relationship between some aspects of development and some aspects of environment for adoptive children. *Psychol. Monogr.*, 1956, 70, No. 410.
83. Yarrow, L. J. The effect of antecedent frustration on projective play. *Psychol. Monogr.*, 1948, 62, No. 293.

part IV

Later
Childhood

chapter 11

Psychological Development
in Later Childhood

P ROFOUND CHANGES IN PSYCHOLOGICAL FUNCTIONING take place during later childhood. Motor development is approaching adult standards. Emotional expressions and the situations which elicit them take on a new direction and subtlety. Intellectual processes are not only developing, but also taking on characteristics closer to those shown by adults than was the case in infancy and early childhood. It is to these topics of motor, emotional, and intellectual development that this chapter is devoted.

Motor development in later childhood

During the school age period children refine and extend their motor skills. During the earlier years of the period girls delight in such games as jacks and hopscotch which call for more precise use of the musculature than did the large-muscle activities of their earlier years. Boys become interested in such sports as baseball and basketball which likewise call for greater refinement of eye-hand-muscle coordination than did their earlier efforts. Fancy stunts on bicycle and roller-skates occupy both boys and girls. They naturally are not equally adept in all fine-muscle coordinated activities, as any

473

child of six will tell you when asked about his writing skills in keeping his "e's" from looking like "i's." Nevertheless, there is increasing skill with the smaller muscles, such as those of the hand. In fact, it often is said that this is the age to begin learning to play a musical instrument or to type if these skills are to become highly developed.

Most children keenly enjoy motor activities. They delight in constantly being on the go. "Spectators" among them are still very much in the minority. Although considerable advance in motor abilities has taken place during the infancy and preschool years, the psychological significance of motor development takes on even more importance in this period of later childhood. Much of its psychological significance rests upon the fact that children have reached the age when they become aware of what others think of them, including their status in motor skills. A high premium is placed upon motor skills by older children. No adult with any contact whatsoever with children at play can fail to have noted either some child's outright rejection from a play group or his being grudgingly last chosen in making up a team because of his lack of strength, speed, or coordination. Having observed this situation one cannot but be convinced that such discrimination may contain the possibility of some adverse psychological consequences. Those children fortunate enough to be adept in motor abilities are not only more acceptable to their playmates, but because of these skills are more apt to be chosen as leaders. This choice may be made not only in tasks where their motor skills are important, but may generalize to leadership functions essentially independent of motor skills, such as being elected as a class officer.

Growth Trends

In later childhood the regularity of growth continues. It will be remembered from the discussion in Chapter 8 that Carpenter (3) found two motor ability factors of general significance—strength and speed. These two factors will form the basis for discussion of trends in motor development during later childhood.

Growth trends in speed of response show a regular increase with age. A study by Goodenough (12) is relevant in this connection. She had children from age three-and-a-half through eleven-and-a-half respond to a test whereby each made a voluntary movement on hearing a sound. At three-and-a-half years of age they took about five-tenths of a second to respond; at four-and-a-half years of age about four-tenths of a second. This increase in speed continued steadily, until at age eleven-and-a-half the children were responding in two-tenths of a second. This and other evidence indicate an increase in speed with increasing age during these years.

There is a similar increase in strength with increase in age according to a summarization by Metheny (39). Up until the age of puberty boys are superior to girls at most strength tests. In both boys and girls there is found to be a general positive relationship between the indices of strength and height and weight and health status. Thus among measures of motor development there is a tendency for the strong to be taller, faster, and healthier than the weaker child. These relationships are closely related to similar relations between physical and mental ability.

The Relation of Physical and Mental Ability

The interrelationship between mental and physical measures in infancy was discussed in a previous chapter. It will be remembered that there was found to be a relatively high degree of relationship. By the later childhood age this relationship has decreased considerably. There is, however, still some degree of relationship.

In general, there is found to be a low but positive correlation between physical and mental ability. Even physical measures such as height or weight have been found to conform to the same general rule (45). In other words, there is a *slight* tendency for the taller individual to be smarter than the shorter. But the relation is such that a number of exceptions to it are found. This does not mean that the relationship is so negligible in children that it can be dismissed, merely that relationships based on it must be interpreted with extreme caution.

Abernethy (1) studied physical and mental growth in nearly 200 boys and 200 girls. The Stanford-Binet Scales provided the measure of mental ability and a large battery of physical growth measures provided the indices of physical ability. Both kinds of measures were administered at regular intervals over an eleven-year period to the children. Comparable measures were also given college men and women in order to provide measures to serve as a terminal standard of development. Low positive correlations between the physical and mental measures were found. In the case of height and mental ability, the average correlation was 0.26 for boys and 0.22 for girls over the age range of two to eight years. There was a general trend for the correlations to decrease after 14 or 15 years of age, eventuating in negligible correlations in the adult group. This general "togetherness" of physical and mental measures in childhood has been supported by a number of studies, for example, (42, 51). Enough information has been reported here to show that there is a slight positive relationship during later childhood which tends to decrease as the child grows older.

Emotional development in later childhood

As was the case with early childhood, emotional development in later childhood will be centered in a discussion of anger, fear, and the affectively pleasant emotions.

Anger

A systematic study of anger of the scope of the Goodenough (11) study concerning older children (described in Chapter 9) has not appeared. However, it will be remembered that the age range of her subjects extended to over seven years, thus overlapping the ages now under consideration. It will also be recalled that certain age trends seemed to be operative. Some of her major findings were that (1) the immediate causes of anger shifted with increase in age and that the older children showed an increase of problems of social relationships; and (2) developmental changes in expression of anger showed less and less random behavior and more and more such behavior directed toward something or someone.

The continuing prominence of social relationships as causes for anger was studied by Hicks and Hayes (19). In a group of older children and adolescents, 11 to 16 years of age, they found that the social situations most apt to evoke anger were being teased, being lied to, being treated unfairly, being imposed on by brothers and sisters, and other people being bossy or sarcastic. These causes of anger relate to people and the characteristics of people. Even more specifically it was the child's peers who often made him angry.

These "causes" of anger in older children can also be seen, from the perspective of the source of anger, as instances of angry behavior on the part of his peers. Although the investigators did not study the way these children directed their anger, only what made them angry, it is not difficult to see that the instigators of the anger (often older children themselves) were also expressing anger themselves.

If this interpretation be accepted, it means that this study also throws light on how the older child expresses anger. As the child grows older, he learns to show deviousness in his expression of anger. It is a common observation that physical violence decreases and that the form of anger is expressed more subtly and less overtly in older children. They become more roundabout in their aggressiveness, finding that through sneers, sarcasm, and so on they are able to stir up anger in older children. Just as in adults, a whisper may take the place of a blow, an upraised eyebrow the place of a scream, a joke the place of name calling, so, too, in later childhood these and other subtle forms of anger may appear. Consequently, on the basis of general observation and of this study we would expect to find in older children less evidence of motor expression of anger, a greater rise of verbalization as a means of expressing anger, and a general toning down of overtness and violence.

A derivative of anger, annoyance, becomes more prominent in later childhood. Annoyance is an emasculated form of anger and frequently expresses more aptly the general kind of emotional response given during these years than does anger itself. In addition, the older child may be observed to express his anger in sulkiness, quarreling, fussiness, and being generally disagreeable.

Fear

Fear is still very much present in the life of children of this age range. The results of a study by England (8) bring this out dramatically. He asked about 100 seventh and eighth grade children of an average age of 11.8 years to make drawings of the most important events of their lives. Note that nothing in the instructions called for drawings depicting fear. Nevertheless, 88 of the resulting 290 drawings were identifiable as those of fear experiences. Since they were asked for drawings of their most important experiences, the relatively high number of drawings in which fear was the central element is impressive of their awareness of fear situations. Indeed, Pratt (46), in a carefully conducted study of the fears of children living in rural areas, found that children from grades five through eight reported both more fears and more different fears than did children from the four earlier grades.

The study of fear by Jersild, described in connection with preschool-aged children, was extended by him and his associates to school-aged children as well (29, 30). As might be anticipated from the growing subtlety of anger expression in children of this age, fear in its direct open sense was not the only form that was investigated. In fact, in one of the two major studies (29) in which they used a questionnaire check list, they were directly concerned with whether or not each of the children they studied "often," "sometimes," or "never" *worried* about their specified situations. In this study over 1000 fifth and sixth grade children were presented with 25 one-sentence descriptions of fear situations and asked to express the degree to which they would worry about each one. Their particular choice of terminology, worry, aptly expresses the shift away from overt naked fear that takes place during childhood in the direction of more complex derivatives from it.

Apprehensions about commonplace occurrences in their own environmental situations were prominent among their worries. For example, more than four-fifths admitted that they sometimes worried about failing a test, more than two-thirds worried about the possibility of having a poor report card, and about two-fifths sometimes or often worried about being hit by rough children. These findings are, in a sense, practical worries about realistic situations. However, many of these worries were pointless in that those doing the worrying were doing so about what actually was only a very remote contingency. Almost one-fifth worried *often* about being left back in school and many hundred more of the over 1000 children *sometimes* worried about this. Actually, analysis of promotion practices showed that less than one per cent, or less than ten students, was really not going to be promoted. Fear of being attacked by animals was mentioned in an interview by 18 per cent of the children studied, yet, actually less than two per cent of this sample had been attacked by animals. Thus, even what appears on the surface to be realistic fears is found to contain a large amount of fantasy.

An interview study by Jersild, Markey, and Jersild (30) of 400 children aged five to twelve years also bears out their contention that many fears of children of these ages are unrealistic. About 20 per cent of all fears of the children involved fears of imaginary creatures, of the dark, and of being alone. Another 10 per cent dealt with robbers and other criminal characters. Remote dangers, such as fear of wolves or tigers, also loomed large. In general, fears of a mundane sort were relatively low in frequency as compared to those fears of an anticipatory or imaginary sort. Such fears, then, are irrational in the sense that they often occur either when there is no danger or when it is very remote. Many of the fears, then, are

• of an irrational sort, quite far removed from fears of the actual dangers which may threaten one in daily life. This raises the question as to whether or not fear is useful in adjusting to daily problems. It is evident that often it is not. Many fears are restricting and fruitless wastes of energy.

A large proportion of the fears shown in childhood persist into the adult years. This was a finding of Jersild and Holmes (27) through the study of the recall by adults of childhood fears. Over 40 per cent of the fears they had had as children persisted in their later years. To be sure, they may have forgotten the nature of some of their childhood fears and thus failed to report them while reporting proportionately more of those that persisted into adulthood. Nevertheless, although we cannot accept these results without reservation, the study is impressive in its demonstration of an appreciable carry-over or persistence of childhood fears in adulthood. In terms of previous categories used for grouping of fears, those that showed the greatest persistence were fear of animals, of bodily harm through such dangers as fire, illness, or drowning, of fears of the supernatural, of the dark, and of being alone. These fears are presumably kept alive by circumstances in the adult's life that made them in some way indices of his present insecurities and conflicts. Their persistence, however, from childhood is still an impressive indication of the importance of the emotional experiences in these earlier years.

Affectively Pleasant Emotions

Relatively little research has been conducted on the affectively pleasant emotions in the school-aged child. Joy producing experiences have been studied somewhat indirectly through finding out what children consider their happiest experiences to be. Again it is the work of Jersild (28) to which we turn. In collaboration with Tasch, he made a study of children's interests which included inquiring into what they considered to be one of the happiest days in their lives. Table 19 presents the results in terms of the major categories into which their responses to this inquiry could be placed for various age groups. As Jersild (26) indicates, younger children tended to stress a holiday or a birthday or other occasions when they received special attention and gifts more than was the case with older children. Children of all ages were apt to mention visiting friends, the return home of relatives, and the like. Girls much more than boys described joyful events as involving social relationships. The oldest-age boys

TABLE 19

FREQUENCY OF RESPONSES IN VARIOUS CATEGORIES WHEN CHILDREN
DESCRIBED "ONE OF THE HAPPIEST DAYS OF MY LIFE" *

(The values represent percentage of children giving
one or more responses in each category.)

	Grades 1–3 Ages 6–9		Grades 4–6 Ages 9–12		Grades 7–9 Ages 12–15		Grades 10–12 Ages 15–18	
	Boys	Girls	Boys	Girls	Boys	Girls	Boys	Girls
Number	363	331	309	343	282	290	159	171
Receiving or having or otherwise enjoying material things, gifts, toys, money, living quarters	8.7	8.1	10.4	7.2	10.1	4.5	5.6	3.1
Holidays, festive occasions, birthdays, Christmas, etc.	39.1	40.5	32.4	38.9	6.3	10.1	0.6	6.5
Sports, games, hiking, hunting, bicycling, etc.	10.2	6.4	9.1	5.5	12.4	5.8	13.0	7.3
Going to miscellaneous places of recreation, going to camps, traveling, going to resorts, to parks	9.6	9.0	10.1	11.4	9.7	13.9	30.2	6.9
Self-improvement, success in school, educational opportunity, evidence of vocational competence, getting a job	2.4	2.3	2.9	1.9	4.8	4.1	13.6	15.9
Happenings connected with school, including last day, end of school, going to a certain school	3.6	3.4	5.4	4.3	14.0	11.1	7.0	5.4
Relationship with people (explicitly described), companionship, being with certain friends, return home of relatives, etc.	7.7	15.9	8.0	15.8	10.5	22.0	8.7	19.9

TABLE 10 (*Continued*)

	Grades 1–3 Ages 6–9		Grades 4–6 Ages 9–12		Grades 7–9 Ages 12–15		Grades 10–12 Ages 15–18	
	Boys	Girls	Boys	Girls	Boys	Girls	Boys	Girls
Number	363	331	309	343	282	290	159	171
Residing in, moving to a certain city or community	1.3	1.0	0.8	2.9	0.9	2.9	1.4	5.0
Benefits befalling others, or mankind in general, including end of war	0.6	0.8	3.2	2.8	2.2	2.6	7.9	9.7

* Adapted from Jersild and Tasch (*28*). Copyright 1949 by Teachers College, Columbia University, and published with permission.

had a sudden upsurge of interest in literally going places, such as parks and recreational centers and in traveling. Older children placed more emphasis upon the pleasures of self-discovery and self-realization, opportunities for self-improvement, and for vocational preparation. Benefits for individuals other than themselves were mentioned more often by them than they were by younger children.

Many of the results of the Jersild and Tasch study were indirectly verified by still another study by Jersild and his associates (30). This was a study involving interviewing 400 five-to-twelve-year-old children about their wishes, dreams, fears, dislikes, pleasant and unpleasant happenings. The youngest child's wishes, likes, and dislikes were more specific and the older child's more inclusive and social. Girls, again, were more concerned with social relations than were boys.

With increase in age the importance of social relationships and the opportunities for self-realization loom large. The period of later childhood, in terms of the affectively pleasant emotions, is the period of self and social discovery.

Intellectual development in later childhood

Brief reference has already been made in Chapters 6 and 9 to intellectual development during infancy and early childhood. Attention was then devoted to specification of the kinds of intelligent behavior expected at these particular ages and to the predictive value (or lack of it) of later intellectual status made possible by measures of intelligence given at these ages. It is obvious that much more could have been said about intelligence than has been presented. Deferring detailed examination until now allows us to do so from the vantage point of prior acquaintance with these other cognitive processes of which intelligence is a function. Furthermore, the delay allows stress to be placed upon the verbal symbolic nature of intellectual functioning which emerges in full fashion only during later childhood.

The Nature of Intelligence

Intelligence is closely related to understanding as we have used the term in earlier chapters. Intelligence becomes evident through the observing, the thinking, and the conceptualizing that the child carries on. In fact, the work of Piaget referred to in discussing these points indicated that from his point of view these cognitive processes *were* intelligence. Thurstone (62) who studied the problem of intelligence for many years through factor analysis summarized those components which he considered to be most important and more or less mutually exclusive. The eight factors which ultimately met his criteria are (1) verbal comprehension; (2) word fluency; (3) numerical ability; (4) spatial (ability to analyze objects in space); (5) memory; (6) induction (discovering principles or rules); (7) deduction (applying principles or rules); and (8) flexibility and speed of closure (facility in sizing up a problem and moving from less to more promising problem solutions). The intimate relation of these factors to the earlier discussions of perception, language, and conceptualization is apparent.

Intelligence involves all of the cognitive processes but with emphasis upon the efficiency, scope, and level of difficulty of function which is expressed through them. Concepts, for example, are *used* by a child in intellectual activity—with efficiency, breadth, and hierarchical level of capabilities helping to decide what we call the intelligence of the child in question.

As Woodworth (69) contends, intelligence is one of those nouns which should be considered a verb. A child is intelligent insofar as he acts intelligently, stupid insofar as he acts stupidly. Intelligence is always expressed in some behavior, reinforcing the necessity of considering it essentially a verb since the emphasis is upon the be-having. Intelligence is not an entity, but a construct about ways of behavior inferred and measured indirectly. We infer from certain behaviors that are now learned that the individual will behave in this fashion.

Traditionally, if observing, conceiving, and thinking are efficient, broad, and involve higher levels of difficulty, we speak of the individual as bright; if they are the opposite, we speak of the individual as stupid. However, instead of there being a dichotomy into the bright and the stupid, there is a continuum from the highest degree of brightness to the lowest degree of stupidity. It is only for convenience that we break down this continuum into discrete areas.

Since the functioning of intelligence calls for a solution to a problem, there is an implication that the situation in which it functions is a new one in some particulars. Habit carries us through many activities. But before we have a habitual way of behaving, we must at some time have met what is now habitual as a first new situation. Then intellectual application took place. Intelligence, then, is expressed in the application of the higher mental processes in accomplishing a task, particularly new tasks.

Intellectual development is related to learning. From the first explorations of his little world by the infant to the new conception of the universe by the physicist, there is a steady background of learning. One learns more and faster because of more efficient intellectual functioning. To point this up it is only necessary to indicate that we measure intelligence on the basis of things we have learned; for example, vocabulary, common knowledge, and school attainment, to mention but some of the categories sometimes used to classify specific items on intelligence tests. Intellectual development and learning are inextricably intertwined—intellectual development results in gaining knowledge. This is a result of learning.

Intelligence is related not only to the cognitive functions and to learning, it also is imbedded in all aspects of the personality. Consequently, emotional life influences intellectual functioning. Intellectual development stands in a definite relation with emotional development. For example, as Rapaport (47) indicated, knowledge is a threat to some people. In them the natural endowment will become inhibited and refractory to acquisition of new knowledge, or, to put it in our earlier terms, refractory to observing, conceptualizing, and thinking. Children may, in other words, be affectively stupid.

Intelligence is both a unified integrated way of behaving and a combination of these other aspects of personality. Intelligence in this sense is a function of the total personality. Intelligence is used in the adaptation of the person to his changing environment. Intelligence takes its place as one of the interrelated aspects of the psychological processes of the child. It is an interdependent part of the personality. Consequently, intelligence is discussed not only for its own sake as an integrated way of behaving in an important aspect of psychological functioning, but also because it allows us to again stress the interrelatedness of the psychological functions which contribute to the development of the individual child.

With this delimitation of the nature of intelligence completed, we shall now examine a widely used intelligence test, the Stanford-Binet Tests of Intelligence. Thereafter, several interrelated aspects of intellectual growth will be considered. An account of the intellectually gifted closes the discussion of intellectual development.

The Stanford-Binet Tests of Intelligence

Many of the research studies to be described that are concerned with intellectual development used as their basic instrument the Stanford-Binet Tests of Intelligence. A rather detailed description of this measure will be given since this will make possible an analysis of the nature of a typical intelligence test. This analysis will be carried out by considering its description, the related concepts of mental age and Intelligence Quotient (IQ), the distribution of Intelligence Quotients in the general population, and the question of the constancy of the Intelligence Quotient. Although these topics are examined as aspects of the Stanford-Binet, all of them are important and significant in their own right. Except for material purely descriptive of the Stanford-Binet, all other issues apply in general to any adequate test of intelligence which depends upon the mental age and IQ as measures of intelligence. The meaning of the IQ, for example, given on the Stanford-Binet applies at least roughly to any IQ, no matter how derived. Each of these topics is essential as an introduction to the discussion of the growth of intellectual functions which follows.

The Revised Stanford-Binet Tests of Intelligence (57) is the most widely used measure for children in its field both in clinical practice and research. In an earlier revision it clearly dominated the field of intelligence testing and many of the developments and conceptualizations about intelligence arose from its use.

Description. The form and contents of an intelligence test when coupled with its method of standardization to some extent serve as a definition of the nature of intelligence as the test constructor conceives it. Terman and Merrill were operationally defining intelligence by what they chose to include as material in the Revised Stanford Scales. Consequently, its description should be considered as giving information about their definition of intelligence as well as a means of familiarizing oneself with its contents.

There are two complete scales, Forms L and M, each of which contains about 130 tests grouped at the various age levels for which they are suitable. They are designed to be administered individually by an examiner especially trained in their use. On the basis of prior information, he decides to begin testing at some age level appropriate to what he knows about the child. Testing continues until a specified series of failures have occurred. Tests too easy or too hard for the child are not administered.

On the first examination of the material for these numerous tests a sense of bewilderment is apt to appear. Mazes, bead stringing, giving similarities to various words, arithmetic items, memory span for digits, and so on appear as items, but it would be grossly inaccurate to infer that they have been mingled together with no particular rhyme or reason. As consideration of each item comprising the test is impracticable here, we shall instead consider only one of the classifications of the items.

The classification chosen was based upon a factor analysis of the standardization data collected by Terman and Merrill—(to be described on page 487). Jones (32) analyzed factorially the data for the 13-year-old standardization group consisting of 100 girls and 100 boys. Their performance on the items contained at age levels 12, 13, and 14 were submitted to a factor analysis. He carried this analysis on to the point that a complete factorial description of the data was obtained. Once the factors were derived, they were interpreted by him as much as possible in terms of underlying processes rather than in terms of the superficial content of a group of interrelated items. Each of the nine factors he found will be reported in two forms: (1) the general, vague but more inclusive term that was applied; and (2) the precise more specific meaning given it by Jones.

The first is a Verbal factor more precisely defined as *"the process of supplying previously learned linguistic responses, primarily word meanings*" (32, 133).[1]   The second is also a Verbal factor, "*the ability to manipulate words in a manner such that an appropriate meaningful relationship is imposed*" (32, 134).[1]   The third factor likewise is a Verbal factor, "*the verbalization of gross ideas as contrasted with the definition or manipulation of words which serve as elements of these ideas*" (32, 134).[1]   The fourth factor is a Memory factor, "*the ability to reproduce, immediately after presentation, a sequence of disconnected elements*" (32, 135).[1]   The fifth factor is also a Memory factor, "*an ability for verbatim recall of meaningful verbal material*" (32, 136).[1]   The sixth factor is a Space factor, "*visualization of movement within a particular configuration*" (32, 137).[1]   The seventh factor is a Reasoning factor, not found capable of more specific statement by Jones.   The eighth factor was a Closure factor, "*the ability to fuse a perceptual field into a single percept*" (32, 140).[1]   The ninth and last factor was a Carefulness factor, "*the ability to carefully and precisely perceive the details of a spatial configuration*" (32, 142).[1]

The definition of these factors in two forms, general and precise, makes possible the relation of the general factors to previous studies of the factor composition of intelligence tests.   The general factors, Verbal, Memory, and the like, are all ones which have been found in other studies although not necessarily in the form the more precise detailed description gives.   The predominance of Verbal factors should be noted since their predominance shows it is in this region that the Stanford-Binet is most heavily weighted.   The classification arrived at by factor analysis helps us to grasp what is meant by intelligence when we say that the Stanford-Binet measures intelligence.   Evidently intelligence to Terman and Merrill is heavily weighted with verbal functions which was the case with the cognitive processes discussed in earlier chapters.   The relation of the verbal and other factors to the processes of thinking, perceiving, and concept formation should now be obvious.   At the age levels of childhood the tests are heavily weighted with abstract verbal material.   These findings are in keeping with the contention of Terman and Merrill: "At these levels the major intellectual differences between subjects reduce largely to differences in ability to do conceptual thinking, and facility in dealing with concepts is most readily sampled by the use of verbal tests.   Language, essentially, is the shorthand of the higher thought

[1] From Jones (32).   Copyright 1954 by The Journal Press, and published with permission.

processes, and the level at which this shorthand functions is one of the most important determinants of the level of the processes themselves" (57, 5).[2]

At first glance it might appear difficult to reconcile such an apparent heterogeneity of factors with intelligence as a unified, integrated way of behaving which we have claimed intelligence to be. One might be tempted to say that if this classification is correct, that there must either be many "intelligences" or that they are not measures of intelligence at all. However, quite apart from the method of standardization which will be found to help to assure us that the test *does* measure intelligence, there is evidence from other research (35) on the test that whatever it measures it does so with at least some unity. It was found that, in spite of the fact that the tests at each age level overlap only in part those at another level and in spite of the heterogeneity of names with which they may be labeled, there is considerable internal cohesiveness throughout the scale. This stress on underlying unity does not mean that intelligence is necessarily a simple or integrated entity throughout the life span. We know the testings of infants lead to very low correlations with tests in childhood. We shall also find in later discussion of the growth of intelligence that factor analysis shows that intellectual processes show change in organization over the years.

Standardization. Using a representative sample of about 3000 children and adolescents, Terman and Merrill standardized the test in what is known as an age scale. The object of the standardization was to construct scales such that average Intelligence Quotients (IQ's) of 100 were found at each of the age levels covered in the test. Keeping this goal in mind, they tried out in preliminary fashion a much larger variety of tests and items than were ultimately used. The percentage of children passing each item at a given age made it possible for them, by a series of operations of cutting and filling, to arrange the items finally selected so that the goal of average IQ's of 100 at each age level was reached for each age. Once this was done, a child now taking the test could be compared with the results from this standardization sample. If he behaved on the test like an average child of his particular chronological age group, he would receive an IQ of 100; if he showed a performance inferior to that of his standardization peers, he would earn an IQ lower than 100; if

[2] From Terman and Merrill (57). Copyright 1937 by Houghton Mifflin, and published with permission.

he exceeded his peers, he would receive an IQ higher than 100. Thus, an IQ of 100 or 70 or 90 or 110 or 130 has each the same meaning at different age levels. How the quotient is actually derived will be mentioned in a moment.

Mental age. Each test successfully completed earns for the subject a certain number of months of mental age credits, with the maximum possible for any one year being twelve. Some tests, with easier and harder items spread over several age levels, can gain credit for the subject at more than one age level, depending on the percentage of children in the standardization sample who passed a definite number of items. A test which requires the detection of verbal absurdities is credited not only at age level 9 if three of the items are answered correctly, but also at age 12 if all four of the items are answered correctly.

The average performance of subjects of the standardization group of a given chronological age provided the standard for mental age scores; the average child 10 years old would have an MA of 10 years. A given child's mental age is found by crediting him with all the tests successfully passed (plus all those of lower age level tests which were considered so easy as to not be worth while actually giving). Thus, children might earn mental ages of 5 years, 6 months; 8 years, 3 months; 11 years; 13 years, 11 months, and so on.

Derivation and Distribution of the IQ

It is now possible to return to the IQ, mentioned before as the figure in terms of which standardization data were reported. The mental age gives an absolute measure of intelligence, irrespective of the age of the child concerned. In contrast, the IQ gives an index of relative brightness or dullness in comparison with children of similar chronological age. A child might have a mental age of eight years but be six years of age. Another child also might have a mental age of eight but be ten years of age. The formula for calculating the index is MA/CA $\times$ 100 = IQ. In other words, the chronological age of the child translated into months is derived, and this chronological age value is divided into the total of the mental age month credits accumulated on the Stanford-Binet. Multiplying by 100 merely clears the obtained value of the decimal point, nothing more. Three examples below illustrate this calculation.

	John	Bill	Ed
Chronological Age (months)	37	65	96
Mental Age (months)	37	57	126
	$37 \div 37 = 1.00$	$57 \div 65 = 0.81$	$126 \div 96 = 1.31$

Clearing of the decimal points gives IQ's respectively of 100, 81, and 131. John, a child of 37 months of age, earned exactly 37 months mental age credits. His IQ of 100 shows him to be average in intelligence. Bill, although earning 57 months of mental age credits, was considerably older (65 months) and, consequently, his IQ places him at less than average in intelligence. Ed, on the other hand, although oldest (96 months), was, in terms of mental age units, 126 months (or 10 years, 6 months), and consequently earned an IQ considerably above average. The upper limit on chronological age used in the IQ formula is set at 15 years (180 months) because it was found on testing older individuals that mental age increments with increasing age ceased to appear at about this age. Using an increase in CA indefinitely with an increasing age would imply the MA kept pace with the CA indefinitely which is not the case. In other words, using say, 20 years, or more precisely 240 months as chronological age in the denominator for calculating the IQ, could result in impossibly low values. At some age MA levels off. We shall return to a more precise definition of this age of no further increase in mental age, in discussing the growth of intelligence. Whatever this age may be, age 15 is the limit necessary to use when working with the Stanford-Binet. If this adjustment were not made when using this test, older individuals would have spuriously low IQ's. Using chronological age 15, Terman and Merrill found, kept the average IQ of groups of older individuals so that they worked out to be about 100.

The question now arises as to the meaning of these IQ's. Of course, to a person who uses the results of the Stanford-Binet testing in his daily work, such as a remedial teacher or school psychologist, the IQ itself numerically expressed has a direct meaning, especially when this value is supplemented with other information about the child. Thus, knowing that an IQ is 67, 89, 103, 120, or 157 is, in itself, meaningful quite apart from any other interpretation. A moment ago we referred to John, Bill, and Ed as "average," "less than average," and considerably "above average" in IQ. But these are terms which do not necessarily have commonly understood meanings. What we need is some generally agreed-upon classification. One is presented in Table 20.

TABLE 20

DISTRIBUTION OF REVISED STANFORD-BINET IQ'S OF THE
TERMAN-MERRILL STANDARDIZATION SAMPLE *

IQ	N	Per Cent	Classification
160–169	1	0.03	
150–159	6	0.2	Very superior
140–149	32	1.1	
130–139	89	3.1	Superior
120–129	239	8.2	
110–119	524	18.1	High average
100–109	685	23.5	Normal or average
90–99	667	23.0	
80–89	422	14.5	Low average
70–79	164	5.6	Borderline defective
60–69	57	2.0	
50–59	12	0.4	Mentally defective
40–49	6	0.2	
30–39	1	0.03	

* From Merrill (38). Copyright 1938 by American Psychological Association, and published with permission.

Table 20 gives for various IQ levels, grouped by 10 point intervals, the number of cases in the standardization sample, the per cent of cases of the total sample falling in this group, and the verbal classification for each group suggested by Merrill (38). Inspection of the table will reveal that the total distribution of scores is approximately normal (bell-shaped). On studying the table, it will be noted that many of the children had IQ's in the so-called high average, average, and low average range. In fact, IQ's 90 to 120, those in the three groups, include 79 per cent of the cases. From this high point in terms of sheer number of cases there is a gradual falling-off. Between the "average" groups and the two extremes were borderline groups called "superior," with 11 per cent, and "borderline defective," with almost six per cent. At the extremes, the "very superior" make up a little over one per cent of the sample, while a little over two-and-a-half per cent were classified as "mentally defective."

This distribution gives us information on the distribution of brightness in the population. Although this distribution was derived from the testing of children, it also is applicable to adults and thus tells us something about the distribution of brightness in the population in general.

Through the information the IQ reveals, we are in a position to compare one individual with another despite differences in age as we did for the three boys a little earlier. If one child is seven and another thirteen, their IQ's give us indices of relative brightness. We are also in a position to compare an individual to the age group with which he belongs. The IQ permits comparison of a given individual with the norms and placement at a particular point on the curve of intelligence. Thus, we can compare a six-year-old with the general run of six-year-olds through the norms on the test. We are also in a position to compare one group of children with another. For example, we can compare one group of children initially matched with another group who thereafter are given an enriched accelerated school program and see if their IQ's are different on completion of the training.

Constancy of the IQ

As an aspect of intelligence in relation to age, one of the most significant problems is the so-called constancy of the IQ. The average IQ for each age is, by definition, 100. Tests using the IQ method of interpreting their results are designed to have this outcome. Moreover, they are designed to have the same distribution of IQ's for each age if an IQ of 80, 90, 110, or 120 are to have the same meanings at all ages. In this sense, constancy is built into the tests themselves.

As indicated in Chapter 2, in order for a test of intelligence (or a test of anything else for that matter) to be useful, it must be reliable or stable—it must yield reasonably similar scores on repeated testings. Under ordinary conditions with an adequately reliable instrument, we would expect the average IQ to remain fairly constant provided there were no conditions working upon the group to bring about a change. The child's environment is most often apt to be relatively constant, but, nevertheless, there may be factors which affect it. This, then, becomes the problem of whether, under general circumstances, a given child's IQ remains constant from age to age. We would expect a slight margin of fluctuation since no psychological measuring device yet developed is perfect in its precision. Error factors may also affect the results making for changes in scores. Factors intrinsic to the test material affect variability. For example, the test material used at one age may be related little or not at all to that used even on the same test at a different age. This may bring about variability. There may be differences in administrative procedure from age to age. There may be practice effects from repeated administration. There may be shifts in attitude toward taking tests by the children which might affect scores. Negativism, more common at certain ages than at others, might result in a lowered score. These complicating factors are sources of error. For the investigator it is essential to know about them and to control or allow for them; otherwise he might confuse them with true changes in intelligence. Even if they were controlled adequately, we would expect a change of a few IQ points in an individual without assuming it represented a genuine change in functioning intelligence. Under ordinary conditions with an adequate and reliable instrument and with the child's environment remaining fairly constant, we expect some degree of constancy of the IQ. Whether the IQ will be less constant under other conditions is a matter of research investigation.

Constancy is supposed to be relative to the average of the group. Individual children continue to differ as the distribution of IQ leads us to expect, but they should, if there is a constancy, remain in the same position relative to the rest of the group. Individuals may deviate from average growth in intelligence by exhibiting a consistently faster or slower rate. In fact, these deviating individuals may be so consistent in this respect as to delimit some kind of exceptional group to which an identifying name has been applied. This is the case with the gifted group described later on in the chapter.

The Growth of Intelligence

We are now in a position to turn to the growth of intelligence during the years of childhood and beyond. Four related major problems merit attention, in this order: the constancy of intellectual development, the nature of the curve of intellectual growth over time, the organization of the intellectual processes with growth, and the effect of environmental factors influencing the growth of intelligence.

Constancy of intellectual development. In examining this topic we are viewing the question of the constancy of the IQ as it relates to growth constancies and changes, not, as in the previous section, with its relation to sources of error of the test instrument or elsewhere. We are now concerned with the nature and extent of constancy of intellectual development over the years as it works out in a sample of children when a stable instrument has been achieved and the other sources of error controlled.

It will be recalled that tests given in infancy were relatively weak in predicting future intelligence test scores. It will also be remembered that tests given in the preschool years were somewhat more predictive in this respect. In connection with those years, the study by Honzik, Macfarlane, and Allen (25) was described in Chapter 9. It will be remembered that in their study they periodically administered intelligence tests to a group of children for a period of 16 years. Consequently, their findings can now be utilized for information about school-age children. Table 21 presents the correlations

TABLE 21

CORRELATION BETWEEN INTELLIGENCE TEST SCORES IN
EARLY AND LATER CHILDHOOD *

Age	Correlation with Stanford-Binet, Age 14
2	0.21
3	0.35
4	0.54
6	0.67
8	0.85
9	0.87
10	0.87
12	0.92

* Adapted from Honzik *et al.* (*25*). Copyright 1948 by the *Journal of Experimental Education*, and published with permission.

between intelligence test scores obtained at age 14 with those at earlier ages. The trend toward increased degree of relationship as the children become older is very apparent. The relationship becomes relatively stable at the older ages. Along with increasing age the interval between the first and second testings also shortens, which may also serve to raise the correlation. As they indicate, predictions are better over short periods and become increasingly predictive after the preschool years. Moreover, as data shows (not reported in the table), tests given during this period are relatively good predictors of intellectual status in early adulthood at age 18. For example, tests given at eight years of age or later tend to correlate about 0.72 with those obtained at age 18.

It will have been noted that two sources of possible changes in test scores are contained in the data. There is the shift in score of different ages from two to twelve, as compared with the scores at age fourteen. But there is also the fact that as age increases, the constant age, with which it is compared, decreases. It may be that the increases in correlation are a function only of the decreases in interval and that if we had held the comparison as to age to some constant length, we would have to place another interpretation upon the data. Consequently, to find out whether this is the case, comparison using a constant interval of elapsed time is necessary.

Their results at a constant three year interval are reported in Table 22. It will be noted that each entry is based on the lapse of

TABLE 22

RETEST CORRELATIONS AT THREE YEAR INTERVALS *

Ages Compared	Correlation
2 × 5	0.32
3 × 6	0.57
4 × 7	0.59
5 × 8	0.70
7 × 10	0.78
9 × 12(13)	0.85

* From Honzik *et al.* (*25*). Copyright 1948 by the *Journal of Experimental Education*, and published with permission.

three years—ages two and five, three and six, and so on, up to nine and twelve. Thus, the length of interval being compared is held constant. The correlations again show a progressive increase with age, showing that the increases reported earlier were not due merely to shorter intervals.

Many other studies find substantially similar results (*31*). It would appear that there is considerable variability during infancy and then gradually the relationship becomes more stable so that by the age of six or thereabouts there is a relatively high correlation from year to year and over still longer periods. Constancy of intellectual development within certain limits seems established.

It is also possible to examine constancy of intellectual development of individual children through consideration of changes in IQ. Before indicating some of the findings, it is necessary to consider the interpretation of the IQ in this setting.

It was indicated before that the IQ is a means of comparing an individual child with other children, irrespective of age. It is also possible to compare his IQ at one age with that at another age. In the study of Honzik and her associates, the data so far reported involved scores, not IQ's. We shift from score to IQ when we study individuals and variation among individuals. We do this because of the greater precision and fund of meaning it conveys than does a mere test score.

In the study of Honzik *et al.* (25) the extent of changes in IQ for the age period six to eighteen years was specified. The IQ's of almost 60 per cent changed 15 or more points, the IQ's of a third of the group changed 20 or more points, while 9 per cent changed 30 or more points. In 15 per cent of the group, the IQ changed less than 10 points over these same years. Inspection of individual IQ's obtained at various ages showed that some exhibited consistent upward or downward trends. But when *averages* of the group, year by year, were examined, the maximum shift was from a low of 118 to a high of 123 or only 5 IQ points. These findings demonstrate that there was constancy of the IQ for the group over the years despite considerable variability among individual children. There was sufficient variability in the IQ's of individual children to make prediction from a single test administration hazardous. Using statistical techniques, the nature of which need not concern us, Honzik and her associates demonstrate that a prediction based on a single test administration at age six years would be wrong by as much as 20 IQ points in one child out of three by the time he reached the age of 18 years. Variability of this magnitude should make us cautious concerning putting too much faith in the constancy of the IQ's of individual children.

The curve of intellectual growth. The median performance of large samples of children will show a steady improvement in intelligence test scores with increasing chronological age. Moreover, there is agreement that intelligence increases to some age beyond childhood before leveling-off. This increase and an ultimate leveling-off are found in all research investigations on this point. But the shape of the curve of increase and the age wherein the leveling-off takes place are a matter of disagreement. In seeking ways to present the sweep of intellectual growth over time, psychologists have used the graphic presentation to present their data. There is no general agreement about what is the best or most adequate way of doing this. There has been a considerable number of such attempts using different methods of measurement and calculation and based on different assumptions concerning the curve. This has resulted in a considerable variety of such curves. It is unnecessary for us to go into the complexities of development of these presentations. For present purposes, the major three ways of presenting the curve of intellectual growth may be referred to as the logarithmic, the linear, and the sigmoid functions.

The first curve in Figure 14 shows a logarithmic function claimed by Gesell (9) and others to represent the growth of intelligence. This is a curve which is negatively accelerated, that is, shows a rapid rise at first and then a slower rise thereafter. This curve implies that intellectual growth takes place at the younger ages very rapidly and then, as age increases, more and more slowly. It will be noted that intellectual growth is assumed to increase until about 20 years of age where it levels off.

The second curve in Figure 14 is linear and based on Terman's method of measurement of intellectual growth (57). The Stanford-Binet was standardized in a way that meant the curve of intellectual

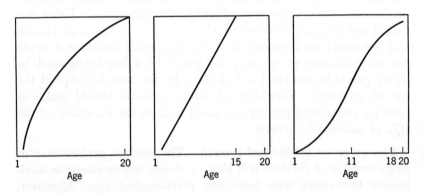

Figure 14. Approximations to various hypothetical statements of the curve of intellectual growth.

growth was essentially linear to age 15. This implies that there are equal increments of intellectual growth throughout these years. It will be noted full mental growth is shown to have been reached at age 15 after progressing linearly to this point.

The third curve in Figure 14 was derived from an inferred scale with equal units and an absolute, not a relative, zero. It is based upon the work of Thurstone and Ackerson (63). Intellectual growth was found by them to be positively accelerated during the first nine or ten years of life, passing through an inflection point around eleven years, and to be negatively accelerated thereafter. This implies that intellectual growth increases slowly at first, then more rapidly and thereafter again more slowly. No attempt was made to establish the exact upper age limit, although they found an increase still taking place at age 18. This is signified in the graph by stopping the curve at age 18 *before* it reaches the upper limit.

Each of these ways of presenting intellectual growth has its adherents. Actually, there is no definitive way of deciding among them. The first or logarithmic curve with its emphasis upon greater intellectual gains at earlier ages would probably be more appealing (and the term is used advisedly) for those who would emphasize the importance of infancy and early childhood. The linear curve of Terman shows mental growth ceasing at age 15. There is considerable evidence that mental age does increase beyond this age and that this relatively early cessation of mental growth found with the Stanford-Binet is due to a limitation of the test. The Stanford-Binet simply does not have enough "ceiling," that is, in the upper intellectual levels there are not enough very difficult tests to reflect mental growth after age 15. The general consensus is that intellectual growth takes place through the teens and perhaps into the early twenties, say 21 or 22.

The linear curve, many would argue, is an artifact of the method of construction of the Stanford-Binet Scales. If you assume mental age increases by equal increments with one year of mental age corresponding to one year of chronological age, then the linear results of equal increments expected every year are inevitable. On the other hand, this curve may be said to be the one which makes the least assumptions about the increase in intellectual growth. In other words, lacking definite information to the contrary, assuming linearity of growth is the most parsimonious way of interpreting the problem in that it involves the simplest function possible. However, it may not be the most accurate. The third or sigmoid curve is based on statistical calculations and an absolute zero and, therefore, is the most sophisticated statistically. It, too, has its adherents. Rather than force a conclusion that is difficult to make, it is felt that the shape of the curve is an unsettled issue about intellectual growth in children.

Changes in the organization of intellectual processes with growth. The relative failure of infancy tests of intelligence to predict what intelligence will be when infants are of preschool and school age suggests the possibility that "intelligence," despite its considerable degree of unity mentioned earlier, has a somewhat different meaning at different ages. In other words, although we may speak of intelligence, thus implying some sort of unity, it may be that it is a series of closely related developing functions. If evidence can be cited about differences in intelligence, other than amount, at different ages, it may be more correct to speak of intellectual processes rather than of intelligence in the singular in this context. It will be remembered that this was the position taken by Piaget in an earlier discussion. It will also be remembered that he considers there to be three levels of intellectual functioning: sensory-motor intelligence, egocentric thought, and rational coordination.

One approach to the investigation of the possibility of changing organization of intellectual prowess with changing age is to factor analyze intelligence data on the same subjects over a period of years. Data collected by Bayley (2) as part of a longitudinal study of intellectual growth over a period of 18 years was factor analyzed by Hofstaetter (22). Three factors were found from the matrix of intercorrelations. Factor I, called by him "sensory-motor alertness," accounts almost entirely for a child's achievement up to the age of 20 months. This factor continues to contribute somewhat to intelligence during the next 20 months, but by 40 months of age it has practically disappeared. From 40 months onward, Factor III, called "manipulation of symbols," accounts for the correlations. It, along with Factor I, contributed to the period from the 20th to the 40th month, but the major factor in accounting for a child's intelligence between 20 and 40 months was Factor II called "persistence." To summarize, sensory-motor alertness accounts for intelligence during the first 20 months; persistence plus sensory-motor alertness and manipulation of symbols, the period between 20 and 40 months of age, and manipulation of symbols from 40 months onward increasingly account for intellectual processes. In the second decade of life, it is practically only Factor III that accounts for the intellectual processes.

Factors I and III seem to reflect what we already know about intelligence. Sensory-motor alertness appears to be very similar to Piaget's sensory-motor intelligence and also reflects the general contention that motor capacities are of crucial importance in infant testing. With different test materials, Richards and Nelson (49) had found two factors in infancy tests, alertness and motor ability, which, when treated as one factor, appear to be very much like sensory-motor alertness. Factor II, persistence, predominates at ages 20 to 40 months. It appears to be something of a transition factor related to the negativism commonly found at this age, and, perhaps, to what Piaget referred to as egocentricity.

It might be thought at first that these findings on a changing organization of intellectual processes are contradicted by those that Jones found from his factor analysis of Stanford-Binet scores and the other evidence reported in the earlier section devoted to these scales. Jones (32), however, used the data of only one year's standardization group, the 13-year-old group. In the perspective of the age sweep now being considered, his results are an analysis of what was referred to as manipulation of symbols in the Hofstaetter study. His results also serve to remind us that not all intellectual processes in these later years of childhood are symbol manipulation alone, as a re-examination of the description of his factors will show. The Space factor, the Closure factor, and the Carefulness factor that he found do not seem to involve manipulation of symbols, at least to the extent that the Verbal factors do. The Verbal factors, the Memory factors, and the Reasoning factors do seem to involve manipulation of symbols directly and avowedly. Jones's study, then, is in a sense a corroboration of that of Hofstaetter's but also a corrective to the idea that intelligence in these years is only a matter of manipulation of symbols. Hofstaetter himself accepts the fact that probably it was limitations in the data which made Factor III, or manipulation of symbols, appear to be of a unitary nature. This implies that he would not be surprised to see it broken down into other factors, some closely related to manipulation of symbols and some not so closely related. At any rate, this is the interpretation being offered here.

This factor represents what most tests of intelligence are designed to measure. Manipulation of symbols is still a convenient summary of the third phase of the development of the intellectual processes.

The probability of changes in the organization of intellectual processes with growth seems established. However, the clarity and validity of the first and third phases of intellectual development, that is, sensory-motor alertness and the manipulation of symbols, seem to be more evident than does the second phase of so-called persistence.

Environmental factors influencing the growth of intelligence. We have just examined the growth of intelligence in terms of its regularities, variabilities, and changes in organization. Environmental factors which may impede or accelerate or change this growth requires clarification.

It is first necessary to consider the native intellectual endowment of the individual. That there are differences in native intellectual endowment is granted. Children are born with differing potentialities for intellectual development. Just as individuals are not born with other aspects of their physique and person equal one to the other, so too intellectual functioning has a biological substratum. There is no doubt also that all degrees of intellectual ability exist in children whose environment is neither bad enough to retard development nor so superior as to accelerate development. The very existence of mental retardation, in spite of a stimulating environment, and the presence of the genius in spite of a barren environment stand witness to this undeniable fact. Individual differences due to constitutional factors cannot be denied.

In Chapter 3, it was indicated that it was appropriate to inquire into the extent to which the process of development can be influenced by *intervention.* The influence of intervention upon intellectual development is now to be considered.

There is a natural endowment unfolding maturationally which sets the limits of the adequacy of intellectual functioning. The maturation process is hindered or helped by the wealth or poverty of stimulation in the environment during the early years. This effect of stimulation produces differential learning. Hence, we are here concerned with the relative influence of learning on the process of the maturation of intelligence. The environmental factors influencing the growth of intelligence will be organized around certain groupings to be mentioned in a moment. Only space limitations prevent attention to the other environmental factors that might be considered, such as education of parents, rural-urban status, racial comparisons, and educational grade achieved. It is sufficient to say that such factors have been demonstrated to effect intellectual development. We have already been concerned with the problem of social deprivation as expressed through institutionalization. General retardation of development was the consequence. But now we need to examine the effect of intervention through schooling, socio-economic status, and emotion-provoking situations. They will be considered in terms of changes observed in groups of children. Thereafter, an illustration of the study of the effect of varying circumstances upon the IQ of an individual child will be examined.

THE EFFECT OF SCHOOLING. The study of the effect of schooling upon intellectual growth has produced considerable controversy. Some responsible investigators have interpreted their results as demonstrating that IQ changes they found are a function of some form of enrichment in schooling; other equally responsible investigators and critics have opposed this view. Consequently, the effects of schooling upon intellectual development will be examined in greater detail than would have been the case if the results of research pointed in one general direction and the task was simply to choose illustrative representative findings with which to convey to the reader the present status of the problem. Since two opposing camps made their appearance over the problem, it is necessary to be somewhat specific about the sources of the information being used.

It was child psychologists at the University of Iowa Child Welfare Station who championed the view that there was a positive effect upon intellectual development from certain schooling or other enriching experiences. Their thesis is that intelligence is not static; it is a phenomenon of development showing growth changes due to learning experiences. They claimed that it was possible to increase permanently the intellectual level of young children by providing stimulating environments. Their studies of children exposed to preschool training (67), mentally retarded children exposed to enrichment through contact with older, brighter (but still mentally retarded) girls (52), and children placed in superior foster homes (53) are illustrative of their varied efforts. In general, they found a tendency for the IQ to increase in the special "enriched" environment. One of the principal methods of study of changes in intelligence as a growth phenomenon is the investigation of the effects of schooling, the topic to which the remainder of this section is devoted.

The preschool offers unique opportunities for the study of the effect of a particular environment. Unlike grade school that nearly everyone attends, it is possible to find two groups that may reasonably be matched, one attending preschool, the other not. This advantage in a particular age group accounts for its popularity in research along these lines. However, the studies involving presumably matched groups of preschool attenders and nonattenders have been so severely criticized as being inadequately matched that the data chosen for discussion concern a group of preschool children tested on several occasions. This means that instead of having a control group, the children served as their own controls by being tested more than once.

In a summarization of the effects of preschool attendance upon IQ, Wellmann (65) presents data on children who were tested and retested in the fall and spring for one or more years. The dates of the tests were so arranged that the intervals between fall and spring and spring and fall were comparable. This is important because the interval between fall and spring is the preschool interval, whereas the interval between spring and fall (the summer vacation period) is the nonpreschool interval (although it does contain some weeks of preschool attendance since the school year is longer than six months). The problem, then, is a comparison of IQ's of children after attending preschool as compared to their IQ's after a period of nonattendance at preschool. (It was because of this alternation of attendance at preschool and nonattendance that we can speak of the children serving as their own controls.) If their special environment made no difference, their IQ's should not differ appreciably between those obtained after a period of preschool or after a period without this preschool. The data for 67 children, who attended preschool three consecutive years, will be reported as a basis for exposition and discussion. Table 23 presents the IQ's obtained in fall and spring over the three years. It shows that during the first year of

TABLE 23

IQ CHANGES OVER A THREE-YEAR PERIOD OF PRESCHOOL ATTENDANCE *

Item	Year	Fall	Spring	Change
IQ, points	First	116.6	124.3	+7.7
C.A., months	First	31.7	37.7	6.0
IQ, points	Second	123.7	128.0	+4.3
C.A., months	Second	45.2	51.0	5.8
IQ, points	Third	125.4	127.1	+1.7
C.A., months	Third	58.1	63.9	5.8

* From Wellmann (65). Copyright 1940 by the National Society for the Study of Education, and published with permission.

preschool attendance the children gained 7.7 IQ points, then over the summer lost 0.6 points (found by subtracting the IQ obtained in the fall of the second year from the IQ at the end or spring of the first year); during the second year gained 4.3 points and over the second summer lost 2.6; and over the third year gained 1.7 points. The over-all gain from the first fall to the third spring was 10.5 points. The hypothesis of the enriching effect of the preschool seems to be borne out. After attendance, the children gained IQ; after nonattendance, they lost, although not as much as they had previously gained. Moreover, this alternative process continued for three years.

A more detailed summary involving many more children might have been presented (66), although not involving as many intervals of attendance and nonattendance. Substantially similar results were obtained. Factors examined as possibly accounting for the results were the revision of the test used, testing conditions, bias of examiners, and certain measured parental characteristics. They did not appear to explain the differences found during times of attendance and nonattendance.

It is manifestly impossible to review here the plethora of critical articles which came forth shortly after the various reports appeared, alleging a positive effect upon IQ from stimulating environment. We will utilize only one critic's comments, that of McHugh (34), who summarized the criticisms of McNemar (35, 36) and Goodenough (13, 14, 15, 17) among others. He writes as follows:

> These writers have criticised the Iowa studies in the following major respects: (1) Failure to present the mental development of the same individual from age to age, and presentation of average I.Q. of rapidly diminishing or changing groups, thus ignoring selective factors operating. (2) No consideration given influence of hereditary factors in accounting for individual differences from group to group. (3) Changing tests without keeping separate records of children given one or the other. (4) Vagueness in reporting the selection of groups under consideration. (5) Errors in tabulation. (6) Failure to make mention of rapport factors which might have operated to depress the initial I.Q. (7) Use of incorrect or inadequate methods to determine statistical significance of obtained differences. (8) No account taken of tendency of re-test measurements to show regression towards the mean of the population with the result that artifactual changes have been attributed to the effect of the environment. (9) Frequent positive conclusions without foundation in facts reported in the studies. (10) The acceptance of the hypothesis "That intelligence tests given to infants and young children have the same predictive value for later mental development as those given after

school age." (11) Overlooking the possibility of systematic error in testing as a result of the examiner's knowledge of previous test results for individual children and for the group (*34*, 3–4).[3]

In the opinion of the writer most of these criticisms do not apply to the particular data reported here. These criticisms were often well-founded and applicable to one or another study that emanated from the University of Iowa during these years. It is the previous evidence of Wellmann that concerns us at the moment. Using the numbers of McHugh's analysis for comparing these data with Mc-Hugh's criticisms, it appears to the writer that: (1) They did use the same individuals from age to age. (2) The same group was used thus ruling out hereditary factors. (3) The tests for all children at a given age were the same. (4) There is a certain vagueness in reporting the nature of the group, thereby weakening the strength of the evidence somewhat. (5) There is no evidence of errors of tabulation for this group. (6) It is difficult to see why, if rapport be accounting for the results, there would be this alternation of greater or less gain coincident with attendance and nonattendance. (7) They do not report statistical tests but calculations would show them to be significant. (8) Regression toward the mean does not apply in these reversible shifts. (9) Conclusion seems to stem from the findings. (10) Infant tests were not included. (11) There may have been systematic error based on the knowledge of previous test results, but this is a possibility in the great majority of studies.

Some studies, other than those performed at the Iowa Child Welfare Station, support the general findings of the increase in IQ under a supposedly enriching environment, for example, Starkweather and Roberts (*55*), others do not, for example, Olson and Hughes (*42*), Page (*43*), and Schott (*50*). In the Olson and Hughes study, in which they found nursery school children from privileged backgrounds did not significantly differ in their intellectual growth from a matched sample of nonnursery school children, they offer an explanation which shows that their results do not necessarily contradict the Iowa studies. They suggest that the home background of the children they studied was already of such a nature that the nursery school could add little to it. There is the suggestion in the Iowa data that the children of highest initial IQ were least affected by their nursery school experience. Their suggestion that the "enrich-

---

[3] From McHugh (*34*). Copyright 1943 by The American Psychological Association, and published with permission.

ment" which in this instance failed to enrich their subject's backgrounds is in keeping with the Iowa position.

Still other "non-Iowa" studies not directly concerned with the preschool situation seem to show the positive effect of a stimulating environment which might be mentioned at this point. These include studies of children who have migrated. Klineberg (33) in an intensive investigation of Negro intelligence, found that the longer the children lived in New York City, the higher was the IQ. Since the subjects had come originally from the South, it seemed that the improved educational opportunities in New York City helped to account for this higher IQ. The alternative explanation that some factor was causing less and less intelligent children to migrate year-by-year could safely be rejected as implausible.

In general, there is today comparatively calm acceptance of the finding that preschool attendance may bring about some increased ability in intellectual functioning. Probably there were exaggerated claims of too sweeping a nature offered originally. For example, there is no conclusive, commonly accepted evidence that mentally retarded individuals can be brought to normal functioning by any amount of enriched environmental experience, although this seemed to be the position taken by some of the Iowa investigations.

After a cautious and conservative review of the literature for an authoritative handbook, Jones states, "It is quite reasonable to expect some IQ gains among children released from a static and unstimulating environment, whether this release is provided by a nursery school, a foster home, or other environmental change" (31, 682).[4] With this, the writer is in agreement. After all, the claims of gain that are accepted as valid need not be of more than relatively modest proportions. It is contended here that the preschool environment does stimulate intellectual growth as shown in a rise in IQ which represents a true gain and that it is not a chance accompaniment of the testing or of the procedure followed. In closing, it might be indicated that the findings of the effect of preschool training are in line with behavior—social learning theory. The children exposed to preschool have had thereby more learning opportunities and have profited from them.

THE EFFECT OF SOCIO-ECONOMIC STATUS. It is generally found that groups of children of higher socio-economic status have an average

[4] From Jones (31). Copyright 1954 by John Wiley and Sons, and published with permission.

higher level of intelligence than do groups of children from less favored socio-economic status. The higher (or lower) the socio-economic class of the groups, the higher (or lower) their average IQ's on the Stanford-Binet or similar verbal tests (*10, 18*). For example, children from professional homes make higher average scores on verbal intelligence tests than do children from homes of unskilled laborers. This has been found often enough by a variety of investigations so that there seems to be little doubt that such a relationship exists (*41*).

However, these differences between higher and lower socio-economic groups may be due to nonintellectual factors. Some of these factors serving to depress intelligence test scores among lower socio-economic groups could be greater resistance to taking tests (*31*), the effect of nutritional deficiencies (*44*), differential attitudes toward education (*20*), and suspicion, lack of rapport, and the like. Although any or all of these factors seem reasonable, there is no definitive research to establish the answer conclusively. They are plausible reasons, nothing more.

An interpretation in terms of differential reinforcement of verbal learning becomes possible. Homes of higher socio-economic status probably offer greater opportunities for verbalization than do homes of lower socio-economic status. To put it for the sake of clarity in a bald fashion, children of higher socio-economic status tend to be taught words; children of lower status tend to be taught things. This, of course, is an overstatement since both groups are exposed to words and things, but in a relative sense the statement seems to have validity. In homes of higher socio-economic status, problems of socialization are handled through words. Consequently, the environment furnished by them is heavily weighted with verbality which the children learn, and in turn they become proficient verbalizers.

This fact, however, has led to an even more serious criticism of most verbal intelligence tests. The question is whether a cultural bias in the direction of differential weighting with items more familiar to the middle- and upper-class children has not created this difference, instead of there being a true difference in intelligence. Perhaps, it is merely that many tests are inappropriate for children of lower status. All investigators of intellectual functioning admit that learning enters intelligence testing, but some claim the material used for this purpose is selected in such a way as to be equally available to all. But this contention has been challenged. In other words, there may be a cultural bias included in the material selected for the intelligence tests. Many of the items in intelligence tests are apt to be more familiar to middle- and upper-class children than to those of lower status. For example, Davis (5) compares two items from one of the tests he used in studying high and low socio-economic groups. On the first item 78 per cent of the higher group answered the item correctly, but only 28 per cent of the lower socio-economic group were able to do so. This item required the child to be familiar with the term, "sonata." On the second, the percentage getting it correct was practically identical in the two groups. This item had to do with a "cutting tool." Davis contends that the first item was more likely to be much more available to the children of the higher status, but the second was subject matter common to all socio-economic groups. He proceeded to amass considerable evidence concerning items which showed socio-economic differentials on a variety of conventional measures of achievement and intelligence. The major research stimulated by the position that there is a cultural bias in much present-day intelligence testing (7) has been subjected to serious criticism (64); thus no conclusion can be reached at this point about the reality of these demonstrated differences in intelligence in different socio-economic groups.

Those objecting to the cultural bias of tests would say this is another source of error in the sense this term was used earlier. Just as a change in score due to practice or to negativism is a source of error, so, too, is the cultural bias of certain or all items of a test a source of error. Those who contend it is not would retort that the usual culture-bound tests, after all, do reflect efficiency of adjustment to the culture for which they are designed. For example, supposing we are using a test of intelligence (with, it is hoped, other necessary measures of information) to select children who are to go on to higher education. We could understand why children from certain subcultures did not do as well on the conventional intelligence test as they might have done under other circumstances when culture-bound items were eliminated. But understanding the reason does not mean these cultural-bound hurdles can be disregarded merely because they are related to culture, provided, as evidence now shows, these conventional intelligence tests do predict academic success in the higher grades. The only satisfactory rebuttal would be for the critics of the conventional tests to produce test materials not only "culture free" but also as equally predictive as the present instruments. As yet, this does not seem to have been done.

THE EFFECT OF EMOTIONAL AND PERSONAL FACTORS. The effect of personal-emotional factors upon the level of intellectual functioning has only been tentatively explored by controlled research methods. Definitive findings of differences due to these factors have *not* been established. Indeed, many responsible investigators of intellectual functioning would take the stand that they will not be established. Tentative though they may be, it is still worth while to review some of the available researches.

In a relatively early study, Despert and Pierce (6) found evidence by tracing relationships between environmental events and shifts in IQ that the individual child's emotional adjustment influenced his intellectual functioning. In no sense were their findings definitive since no crucial experiment or observations were made. Perhaps as a consequence of the tentative character of their findings, they presented no inclusive hypothesis on the reasons for inhibition or acceleration of intellectual functions through emotional factors, although claiming they did occur in various cases.

From the Fels Research Institute has come a preliminary report on the effect of personality factors on intelligence. Sontag and his associates (54) selected from their total cooperating group of 140 children, the 35 who gained the most and the 35 who lost the most in Stanford-Binet IQ over ten years of annual testings from age three to twelve. Thus, they had three groups: the "ascending," the "descending," and the remaining or neutral group. Roughly twice as many boys were in the ascending group and roughly twice as many girls in the descending group. Individual children in the ascending group gained from 18 to 58 IQ points and individuals in the descending group lost from 11 to 27 points from a base IQ consisting of a combination of the first two or three testings. The results of Sontag and his associates, are, so far, in preliminary form and only one or two illustrations of their results will be given. They indicate that debilitating anxiety may account for lowered scores and cite a case. This was a boy who was moved from foster home to foster home, creating a high anxiety level, until finally he was adopted and had for the first time a stable, secure, human relationship. Thereafter, his intelligence test scores rose.

Motivation making for a rise in IQ may be seen in the case of another boy to whom the test situation was a challenging problem to be surmounted for the assurance it gave him; in the same way, his competitive behavior in school, his satisfaction from mastery of school subjects, and his absorption in books, with little dependence on human relationships illustrate the same motivation.

Before considering the effect of decreasing motivation upon intelligence, discussion should be prefaced by a reminder that twice as many girls as boys were in the descending group. Examination of the experiences of many of these girls showed that they had experienced what is called a flight into femininity. Now in their latency period, these girls were approaching the age when they would assume the adult feminine role. Although women's perceptions of their role differ, a not inconsiderable proportion find that competition and achievement are of importance only in being more feminine and charming, whereas school attainment (and the taking of intelligence tests) is of little emotional comfort or significance. In the investigators' opinion, a majority of the girls in the descending group could be thus accounted for.

ILLUSTRATION OF THE EFFECT OF ENVIRONMENTAL FACTORS ON AN INDIVIDUAL CHILD. One of the reasons the search for a relation between fluctuations in intellectual functioning and changes in environmental factors has been so intriguing is that changes of the IQ in relation to the life situation are so often *apparently* observed in disturbed children. This same relationship has been found in normal, nonproblem children. Richards (48) studied the course of development of such a boy with emphasis upon the relation of intelligence test performance at different ages to the child's life situation during the same period. In other words, there were two streams of data, test scores and a history of the individual's current adjustment at the time of each testing. Figure 15 shows his Stanford-Binet performance at various ages. The mean IQ for all the testings was 124, with individual IQ's fluctuating between 117 and 140. There are four trends in the curve he obtained for IQ's between the ages of three and ten, first a rise of 11 IQ points from age three to four, then a drop of 13 points from five to six, a rise again of 25 points from six to eight years, and finally a drop of 18 points from eight to ten years. Space cannot be given to description of all of the environmental data geared to these ages which Richards collected. Instead, concentration will be made on the rise of 25 points, occurring between six and eight years of age.

The boy, called Bobby James, was studied at the Fels Research Institute, and the already familiar Fels Parent Behavior Scales were used several times throughout the years. Projective test results, in-

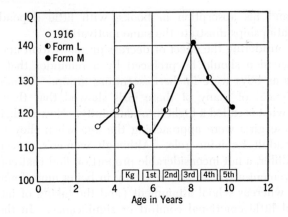

Figure 15. Changes in IQ in an individual child. (From Richards (48). Copyright 1951 by the Society for Research in Child Development, and published with permission.)

cluding those for the Rorschach and TAT were available. Some pertinent comments about Bobby follows:

> Bobby's father was a college graduate with an IQ of 127, and was a business man in moderately good circumstances. His mother had had some college training and had done some secretarial work before marriage. During his first five years, Bobby seemingly led a normal life, perhaps with a greater than usual attachment to the mother although he was also close to the father. The father played with and read to the boy quite frequently. During the period from when he was five to when he was six (immediately preceding the rise in IQ), his father, in addition to active business during the day, started a company which took most of his evenings. Bobby saw less of him but they continued to be congenial.
>
> We now come to the period of age from six to eight when the IQ rose 25 points. In the middle of the second grade he was switched from a teacher who was a stern disciplinarian to one considerably more sympathetic. He continued with her throughout the remaining year and a half of the six to eight period. His father, about the same time, gave up his night work and started spending considerable time with Bobby. Tense and nervous while holding the two jobs, the father now "became a new man," thoughtful and easier to live with. The Fels Parent Behavior Scales applied to their home during this time showed that the home, always "well-adjusted" and "democratic," now accentuated these characteristics. It was during this period his IQ was 140. Thereafter in the later phase, the home was more severe with less devotion, affection and sheltering of Bobby.

In the last phase from eight to ten (showing a drop in IQ of 18 points) Bobby's "understanding" teacher gradually became "tired and inactive," culminating in the necessity of having a tumor removed. Bobby, himself, had been promoted to the fourth grade where he had a severe teacher.

In summarizing this history Richards comments on the following points: (1) the situation fluctuated with the rise and fall in IQ; (2) the role of the father fluctuated with the rise and fall in IQ; and (3) in the period where the highest IQ was obtained, the child-centeredness of the home was at its highest.

This instance of a single boy is, of course, not conclusive. The evidence shows plausible reasons for the shifts in intelligence, but, as Richards himself clearly indicates, no generalization to other children is possible on the basis of a single case. This case is an illustration of a not uncommon finding that shifts in the IQ can be related to shifting environmental circumstances. Honzik *et al.* (25), whose study has been referred to several times, found similar correspondences between shifts in circumstances and shifts in IQ. But there are also instances of failure to find related environmental circumstances coincident with shifts in IQ. Honzik and her associates themselves found a considerable proportion of children whose scores remained constant, despite disturbing circumstances. Goodenough and Maurer (16), in a carefully conducted study involving repeated retests, found some individual cases who exhibited IQ changes as great as 20 to 50 points in an eight or nine year span. Yet, careful examination revealed no associated environmental circumstances which could account for such extensive shifts. The extreme shifts just discussed are exceptional, not typical. In the vast majority of children consistency, not inconsistency, of intellectual development is the rule. Emphatically, acceptance of the thesis that personal factors may affect intelligence does not mean that all children faced with unusual variations in their environment react with changed IQ's.

The Intellectually Gifted

A gifted child possesses intellectual capacities just about as much removed from the average as does the mentally retarded child in the opposite direction. Generally, an IQ of 140 is set as the lower limit of the gifted. But, as is the case with the mentally retarded, the IQ gives but a rough equivocal criterion. Other factors which should be considered will receive attention in this account.

The gifted in infancy and early childhood. Before discussing the gifted in later childhood, the years of infancy and early childhood must be considered. It is appropriate to start with the home into which the gifted child is born. Gifted children are born in homes of all socio-economic classes, but in a nonrandom fashion. In one major research study of 1500 gifted children, Terman (58) found that 31 per cent of the fathers were professional men, 50 per cent were in business or in some semi-professional activities, 12 per cent were skilled laborers, and less than 7 per cent were in semi-skilled occupations. Since professional persons make up about 3 per cent of the population, parents of this class have ten times their proportion of gifted children. Similarly, college training on the part of the parents was much more common than in the general population. Although certain ethnic groups produced more than their expected proportion of these gifted children, this may reflect a biased sampling rather than being the true state of affairs and, consequently, will not be discussed.

During infancy, the gifted child is often, though not always, advanced developmentally. In Terman's group, the "typical" gifted child cut his first tooth at an average of seven months in comparison with a norm range of six to nine months. He talked at 11 months and took his first step at 13 months. These developmental levels may be compared with norms for the average child of talking at 15 months and walking at 14 months. In general, precocious talking is more characteristic than other activities at this age.

During the preschool years, the gifted child ordinarily presents no special problems. He is perhaps a bit healthier, heavier, taller, and more active than the average child. He may show uneven development in the sense that in some ways he is advanced for his age, in other ways he is not. The story is told of a boy who had learned to read at four, expressing three wishes for presents for his fifth birthday—an atlas, a bow and arrow set, and a teddy bear. Each, in its own way, expressed his needs.

It is with later childhood, the period of schooling, that the gifted child comes forcefully to the attention of parents and teachers. He has reached the age that allows unequivocal evidence of his intellectual superiority and he presents the greatest challenge to his elders. Hence, the gifted child will be examined more extensively during this period.

The gifted in later childhood. Before presenting some of the research on the gifted child, a few words about some of his general characteristics seem indicated. The gifted child is often called "old for his age." Presumably, this is because his interests are those which older individuals show and because he expresses himself in a manner beyond his years. In later childhood, a large proportion show an interest in the precise meaning of words. For example, they like to use dictionaries and encyclopedias. Often they read at an unusually early age. Although to some extent restricted by the rules of school age entrance, they are often the youngest in their classes. In characteristics other than intelligence, they exceed the average. Gifted children, as a group, are taller, heavier, and stronger than average children, and their physical health is better (24).

Misconceptions about the gifted. This finding of general superiority runs counter to the popular stereotype of the bright child as thin, intense, small in stature, and wearing the inevitable glasses. The origins of this prevalent misconception are multiple. Undoubtedly, the fact that they are younger in school and play groups is a factor. Gifted children may be smaller and weaker than their classmates, but not their age mates.

The theory of psychological compensation, which holds such a grip on the thinking of many individuals, is also partially responsible for this misconception. According to this view, if superiority is found in one area, then a compensatory weakness in some other area must be present. "Beautiful but dumb," "smart but scrawny," "egghead," and the like are common expressions of this viewpoint. According to this traditional picture, the "child prodigy" is weak, sickly, asocial, and narrowly specialized. To be sure, children showing these characteristics may be found just as they may be found in the intellectually normal child. Expressed as a correlation coefficient, the theory of compensation calls for a negative correlation among desirable traits. Actually, research shows that there is a positive (though slight) correlation among desirable traits. The gifted tend to show not only a superiority of intellectual development over the general run of the population, but also superiority in other spheres as well.

The prodigy. Consideration of what is meant by a prodigy, a term used in connection with a particular kind of gifted child, becomes relevant at this point. It is generally understood to refer to a child who, from the earliest age, showed an unusual capability in one or more fields. With a minimum of educational exposure, this talent unfolded at least to the point where it was recognized for what it was. Prodigies in music are the ones which most readily come to mind, but they are also to be found in the fine arts and in literature and, perhaps, even in the sciences. Although their special talent is naturally stressed, the study of Cox (4), to be referred to in a moment, suggests that general intellectual ability is also superior. Although it may be outstripped by the talent, general intellectual ability is apt to be associated with special talent in the prodigy.

General summary of research findings. The research studies on gifted children made by Terman and his collaborators since 1921 overshadow the work of all others (4, 56, 58, 59). However, it is re-assuring to note that his general findings have been corroborated by many other investigators. Here the works, of Hollingworth (23, 24) and Witty (68) are prominent.

Terman (58) used the California school systems from which to draw his population of gifted children and painstakingly located 1500 grammar and high school children of IQ 140 or higher. The average IQ was 150, and 80 of the group achieved an IQ of 170 or higher. A careful check showed that the sample he studied was close to 90 per cent of all those who could qualify, thus demonstrating the representativeness of his sample. A great variety of physical measurements, medical examinations, achievement, character, and interest tests were given the children and, in addition, trait ratings of these children were secured from parents and teachers.

Their principal findings are summarized by Terman as follows:

> Children of IQ 140 or higher are, in general, appreciably superior to unselected children in physique, health, and social adjustment; markedly superior in moral attitudes as measured either by character tests or by trait ratings; and vastly superior in their mastery of school subjects as shown by a three-hour battery of achievement tests. In fact, the typical child of the group had mastered the school subjects to a point about two grades beyond the one in which he was enrolled, some of them three or four grades beyond. Moreover, his ability as evidenced by achievement in the different school subjects is so general as to refute completely the traditional belief that gifted children are usually one-sided (56, 223).[5]

School progress is important in appraising the gifted child. In Terman's group, three out of five attended kindergarten before start-ing the primary grades at an average age of six years and three months. Immediately, one out of ten was placed in the second grade, and one out of five skipped half of the first year. By the time ele-

---

[5] From Terman (56). Copyright 1954 by The American Psychological Association, and published with permission.

mentary school was completed, about one entire grade had been skipped. They were, in the teachers' opinions, entitled to even additional promotions. None was retarded in terms of age-grade standards, but four per cent actually repeated a grade. If he had been promoted in terms of mental age, the child typical of this group would have been 2.8 years advanced at age seven and by age eleven entitled to placement in the tenth grade. It should not be inferred that such radical advancement as this would be desirable; rather these findings bring out dramatically the serious misplacement of the gifted child in our educational system. The contrast of their school work with that of the average child was most conspicuous in subjects requiring verbal comprehension (history, composition, literature, grammar, reading, and arithmetic) and least in activity subjects (physical training, manual training, sewing, modeling, and penmanship).

The childhood of eminent men. Practically all eminent men have shown evidence of superiority in childhood, though only a small proportion of gifted children attain eminence in adult life. This question of prognosis of eminence has occupied many scholars. The study of Cox and her associates (4) is noteworthy in this connection.

They were concerned with assessing the early accomplishments of 300 eminent men and women. Their study was based on historical material known about them. On the basis of the space allotted in biographical dictionaries, they knew these men and women were of unquestioned eminence. They further selected a sample on the basis of adequate records of early achievement. Cox and her collaborators were also thoroughly familiar with the content and significance of present-day intelligence tests. The task to which they set themselves was to estimate the IQ's of their subjects based on the assembled biographical material. Agreement between independent ratings is expressed in 14 correlations of about 0.70. In their major group, they contend that the average IQ was above 160, with but few individuals falling below 140. A summarization of their account of the life of Goethe will serve not only as a "case history" of the childhood of an eminent man, but also as an illustration of the sort of data they used in arriving at an estimate of the IQ.

Johann Wolfgang Goethe lived between 1749 and 1832. He was fortunate to be born into a family with wide interests. From the age of three until six he attended a day nursery where he learned to read. At about four, if his mother's creativeness failed her in telling him stories, he supplied the gaps from his own inventiveness. When he was four and a half, a puppet theatre was presented him and at six and a half he began to arrange and conduct plays on this miniature stage. When barely six, he began biblical reading and shortly moved into stories such as Robinson Crusoe. At eight he was already acquainted with his father's library and with the German poets of his century, the best Latin and Italian poets, Roman antiquities, and classic works on jurisprudence, travel and philosophy. A little later he secretly devoured modern works.

From his seventh year to his seventeenth he was trained under private tutors. His training in Latin began at seven, and within a few months he was writing free Latin compositions. Among the subjects studied during this period were Latin, Greek, Hebrew, French, English, Italian, history, geography, religion, natural science, mathematics, composition, rhetoric, drawing, music, fencing, and riding. At the age of nine he was doing work at the same level as that taught by one of his tutors to 16 to 22 year old boys in the local gymnasium. During this period he knew and was accepted by his family's friends who were drawn from the diplomatic and artistic world. He entered into current matters of interest with zest. For example, at the time of the Lisbon earthquake he drew philosophical and theological inferences from this catastrophe. At twelve he composed a story written in Latin with a sprinkling of Greek, English, French, Italian, Yiddish and German. Later, he wrote poetry of considerable merit. At fourteen he argued there was no need for a separate study of philosophy since religion and poetry covered the field. At sixteen he entered the university, already a man of the world familiar with all aspects of European culture of his time and place.

It is estimated by Cox and her associates that his IQ was 185 during these early years. Some of their other estimations are given in Table 24. The individuals selected for presentation are drawn from

TABLE 24

ESTIMATED INTELLIGENCE QUOTIENTS FOR SOME EMINENT PERSONS *

Leibnitz	190	Coleridge	175
J. S. Mill	190	Pope	170
Voltaire	180	Chatterton	170
Macaulay	180	J. Q. Adams	165

* Adapted from Cox (4). Copyright 1926 by the Stanford University Press, and published with permission.

those for whom the data were more complete and hence more reliable.

The evidence of superior intellectual ability in their subjects is unequivocal. Not one of the individuals they evaluated was rated as having had below average intelligence in childhood. Nevertheless, wide individual differences in the estimated IQ's for members of the group were found. When grouped according to the field of eminence, soldiers rated lowest and yet had an average IQ not too far from 140. Artists and musicians averaged 160; statesmen and imaginative writers, 165; religious leaders and prose writers, 170; scientists, 175; and philosophers, 180.

Interference with optimal performance. It is not, of course, intelligence alone which makes for superior performance. Motivational and emotional factors channeled in the service of intellectual endeavor are of major importance. Personality mobilization is a term which may be applied to the coordinating of all personality resources so as to allow optimal intellectual performance. The flowering of intellectual superiority under these circumstances is most aptly evaluated when considering the gifted adult. With gifted children it is most appropriate to consider how personality mobilization may be interfered with.

The gifted child may experience great difficulties in finding or creating that special environment suitable for his talents. Out of difficulties in this sphere grow many of the tragedies and misunderstandings to which individuals in this group are subject. Some capsules of cases will give the flavor of the difficulties the gifted child encounters.

A bright girl from an impoverished home had been placed in a domestic-science course, which fitted her neither for further education nor for earning a living commensurate with her ability (*60*, 70).

A boy, who had been taken by an elderly grandmother because his home had been broken by divorce, and who had languished in effeminacy and loneliness in a city school, blossomed into honors and leadership in a suburban town under the care of an intelligent young stepmother (*60*, 73).

The child whose parents expected her to be a genius lived in a haphazard household where everyone was allowed full liberty of self-development. At the age of eight, she had been removed from school after a quarrel about her placement, and had been irregularly instructed by tutors. At the age of sixteen, she had not completed the requirements of the eighth grade, but talked fluently and superficially on philosophy, psychology, and the arts. She was desperately trying to find a short cut to a profession that she considered worthy of her genius, and was becoming pathetically aware of her plight as she began to see the inadequacy of her preparation (*60*, 74–75).

A . . . girl, who had been overawed by a tyrannical older brother, gained self-confidence away from home at a junior college. She was determined to defend herself, and the conflict resulted in a nervous break-down in the mother (*60, 76*).[6]

It is possible to generalize from Terman's work that the gifted child can and is often supplied with a suitable environment for the flowering of his abilities. With the upper reaches of the gifted, the so-called genius, it is more difficult to create or find this proper environment. Goethe's family, as in the earlier illustration, could and did do this, but a certain talent and economic means were necessary which are lacking with some families. It has also been indicated that other factors, more subtle in nature, are operative.

The gifted child in adult life. What happens to these children in adulthood? It would appear that high intellectual status is maintained by some, but not all, of these children. In a careful comparison of Terman's gifted group in adulthood with a sample from the general population, Thorndike (*61*) found that 20 years after the original study they had as a group regressed 40 or 45 per cent of the way back to the population mean. As children, they were on the average three standard deviations above the mean; in adulthood, they were slightly less than two standard deviations above the mean.

Follow-up studies of these children, studied by Terman, took place at several points in time. These have culminated in the 25 year follow-up of this group (*59*). Over 95 per cent of the original subjects supplied information. The results previously reported were sustained. When compared with the general population, they were again superior in general health, in measured intelligence (in spite of the regression mentioned above), in percentage marrying, in graduating from college, in occupational status and in publications, and professional recognition. There was even a slight superiority in mental health as shown by the smaller percentage showing serious maladjustment than the general population did.

A high intelligence quotient does not necessarily mean high crea-tive productivity. Although evidence is not conclusive, a further major quality in addition to intellectual prowess would appear to be something which earlier was called personality mobilization. This, in part at least, is a motivational-emotional matter.

In 1940, Terman and Oden studied those 750 men in the original group who by then were 25 years or older. Three judges working

[6] From Thom and Newell (*60*). Reprinted from *Mental Hygiene*, 29, 1945, with the permission of the National Association for Mental Health.

independently rated each on life success using as a criterion the extent to which each had made use of his superior intellectual ability. In doing this, little weight was given to earned income. When this was completed, the 150 rated highest for success and the 150 rated lowest were compared on some 200 items of information. A variety of differences in academic success, emotional stability, leadership, and marital status in favor of the more successful group was found. But the most spectacular differences between the more and less successful groups were found on certain personality ratings made about himself, by the subject, by his wife, and by a parent. The three independent sets of ratings agreed in finding four person-ality characteristics on which the successful and less successful groups differed significantly. These were "persistence in the ac-complishment of ends," "integration toward goals as contrasted with drifting," "self-confidence," and "freedom from inferiority feelings."

On the basis of these findings, which this writer would summarize as "personality mobilization," there is evidence that nonintellectual factors contribute heavily to creative productivity and may well mark one of the major differences between the "gifted" and the "eminent." As Terman remarks (56), the data lent little support to the theory that great achievement stems from emotional tensions. Success in this group is associated with stability, not instability.

In the older literature, and to some extent in popular opinion to-day, there is said to be an association between intellectual brilliance and "insanity." In earlier years much effort was expended in trying to demonstrate an underlying relationship between the thought processes of the man of genius and that of an insane person. There is no point in reviewing the literary speculations and biographies which purport to demonstrate this relationship. It is mentioned because many people still find satisfaction in the illogical belief that the possession of great talent predisposes one to insanity. This legend meanwhile is kept alive through science fiction and Grade D movies about the mad scientist and by the occasional newspaper account of a childhood prodigy who comes to a "bad end," which, since it is unusual, makes news.

The gifted—especially those in the highest reaches—have diffi-culties of adjustment, but they are more often minimized by their abilities rather than exacerbated by them. In reference to scientists —one variety of superior children grown up—A. V. Hill of Cambridge University made a comment which seems to cover the situation: "Most scientists are quite ordinary folk, with ordinary human virtues, weaknesses and emotions. A few of the most eminent ones indeed are people of superlative general ability, who could have done many things well; a few are freaks with a freakish capacity and intuition in their special fields but an extreme naiveté in general affairs. . . . The great majority of scientists are between these groups, with much the same distribution of moral and intellectual characteristics as other educated people" (*21*, 371).[7]

Summary

During later childhood motor skills continue to develop showing both increases in speed and strength and greater refinement and adeptness. Mental and physical growth are found to have a positive, though relatively slight, relationship.

The evidence concerning emotional development in later childhood attests to the importance of social relationship, especially those with one's peers, as instigators to emotions. Greater subtlety in sources of instigation and less overt and bald expressions of emotion are found with the increase in age of the child.

Despite the importance of motor and emotional development, it is intellectual development which receives the greatest attention. Turning first to the nature of intelligence, it is indicated that it is closely related to the understanding, the observing, thinking, and conceptualizing that the child carries on. Intelligence involves the cognitive processes with emphasis upon efficiency, scope, and level of difficulty of function that the child exhibits. Moreover, it is an interdependent aspect of personality.

In the sections pertaining to the *Stanford-Binet Tests of Intelligence*, a description of the scale is given and also the way it was standardized; the method and meaning of deriving mental age and IQ, and the distribution of the latter in the population are presented; and the significance of the so-called constancy of the IQ as an aspect of the test instrument is considered. Intellectual growth over the years of childhood and beyond is first discussed in terms of the evidence for this constancy as it relates to growth constancies and

[7] From Hill (*21*). Copyright 1951 by the Educational Foundation for Nuclear Science, Inc., and published with permission.

changes. The curve of intellectual development shows a steady increase with increasing age, but the shape of the curve is a matter of dispute. There are changes in the organization of intellectual processes with growth. The first phase, it would appear, may be called sensory-motor alertness, the second, somewhat more doubtfully, the phase of persistence, and the third, with greatest influence of all, the phase of manipulation of symbols.

Environmental factors either impeding or accelerating intellectual growth were examined. In terms of the effect of attendance at preschool upon intellectual growth it was found that it produced some increase in intellectual functioning. In terms of the effect of socio-economic status upon it, results were found which must be characterized as equivocal. In terms of the effects of emotional and personal factors, both accelerating and inhibiting factors affecting intellectual growth could be discerned. These inhibitions and accelerations were further illustrated by a case study.

The intellectually gifted child is examined in his infancy and early and late childhood with special emphasis upon the latter period. The general tendency for intellectual superiority to be associated with other positive characteristics is very striking.

For Further Reading

The article by Nancy Bayley, "On the Growth of Intelligence" (*American Psychologist*, 1955, 10, 805–818) is a masterly summary of this topic. The lengthy chapter, "The Environment and Mental Development," by Harold E. Jones in *The Manual of Child Psychology* (2nd Ed.) (New York: Wiley, 1954), edited by L. Carmichael, is a thorough, painstaking and conservative review of the topic suggested by the title. This volume also contains an excellent general review of the findings on gifted children in the chapter by Catherine Cox Miles. Erika Fromm and Lenore D. Hartman in their *Intelligence: a Dynamic Approach* (New York: Doubleday, 1955) give a stimulating account of how intelligence functions as an aspect of the total personality.

References

1. Abernethy, E. M. Relationships between mental and physical growth. *Monogr. Soc. Res. Child Develpm.*, 1936, 1, No. 7.
2. Bayley, Nancy. Consistency and variability in the growth of intelligence from birth to eighteen years. *J. genet. Psychol.*, 1949, 75, 165–196.

3. Carpenter, Aileen. The differential measurement of speed in primary school children. *Child Develpm.*, 1941, 12, 1–7.
4. Cox, Catherine M. *Genetic studies of genius: Vol. II.. The early mental traits of three hundred geniuses.* Stanford University, Calif.: Stanford University Press, 1926.
5. Davis, A. *Social class influences upon learning.* Cambridge, Mass.: Harvard University Press, 1948.
6. Despert, J. Louise, and Pierce, Helen O. The relation of emotional adjustment to intellectual function. *Genet. Psychol. Monogr.*, 1946, 34, 3–56.
7. Eels, K., Davis, A., Havighurst, R. J., Herrick, N. E., and Tyler, R. *Intelligence and cultural differences: a study of cultural learning and problem-solving.* Chicago, Ill.: University of Chicago Press, 1951.
8. England, A. O. Non-structured approach to the study of children's fears. *J. clin. Psychol.*, 1946, 2, 364–368.
9. Gesell, A. *Infancy and human growth.* New York: Macmillan, 1928.
10. Goodenough, Florence L. The relation of the intelligence of preschool children to the occupation of their fathers. *Amer. J. Psychol.*, 1928, 40, 284–294.
11. Goodenough, Florence L. *Anger in young children.* Minneapolis, Minn.: University of Minnesota Press, 1931.
12. Goodenough, Florence L. The development of the reactive process from early childhood to maturity. *J. exp. Psychol.*, 1935, 18, 431–450.
13. Goodenough, Florence L. Look to the evidence: a critique of recent experiments on raising the IQ. *Educ. Meth.*, 1939, 19, 73–79.
14. Goodenough, Florence L. Can we influence mental growth: a critique of recent experiments. *Educ. Rec.*, 1940, 21, suppl. 13, 120–143.
15. Goodenough, Florence L. New evidence on environmental influence on intelligence. *Yearb. Nat. Soc. Stud. Educ.*, 1940, 39 (I), 307–365.
16. Goodenough, Florence L., and Maurer, Katherine M. The mental growth of children from two to fourteen years: a study of the predictive value of the Minnesota Preschool Scales. *Univ. Minn. Child Welf. Monogr. Ser.*, 1942, No. 19.
17. Goodenough, Florence L., and Maurer, Katherine M. The relative potency of the nursery school and the statistical laboratory in boosting the IQ. *J. educ. Psychol.*, 1940, 31, 541–549.
18. Haggerty, M. E., and Nash, H. B. Mental capacity of children and paternal occupation. *J. educ. Psychol.*, 1924, 15, 559–573.
19. Hicks, J. A., and Hayes, M. Study of the characteristics of 250 junior high school children. *Child Develpm.*, 1938, 9, 219–242.
20. Hieronymus, A. N. A study of social class motivation: relationships between anxiety for education and certain socio-economic and intellectual variables. *J. educ. Psychol.*, 1951, 42, 193–205.
21. Hill, A. V. The duty of the scientist in society. *Bull. Atomic Scientist*, 1951, 7, 371-372.
22. Hofstaetter, P. R. The changing composition of "intelligence": a study in T-technique. *J. genet. Psychol.*, 1954, 85, 159–164.
23. Hollingworth, Leta S. *Gifted children: their nature and nurture.* New York: Macmillan, 1926.

24. Hollingworth, Leta S. *Children above 180 IQ, Stanford Binet.* New York: World Book, 1942.
25. Honzik, Muriel P., Macfarlane, Jean W., and Allen, Louise. The stability of mental test performance between two and eighteen years. *J. exp. Educ.*, 1948, 17, 309–324.
26. Jersild, A. T. Emotional development. In L. Carmichael (Ed.), *Manual of child psychology* (2nd ed.). New York: Wiley, 1954, 833–917.
27. Jersild, A. T., and Holmes, Frances B. Children's fears. *Child Develpm. Monogr.*, 1935, No. 20.
28. Jersild, A. T., and Tasch, Ruth J. *Children's interests and what they suggest for education.* New York: Teachers College, Columbia University, 1949.
29. Jersild, A. T., Golman, B., and Loftus, J. J. A comparative study of the worries of children in two school situations. *J. exp. Educ.*, 1941, 9, 323–326.
30. Jersild, A. T., Markey, Frances V., and Jersild, Catherine L. Children's fears, dreams, wishes, daydreams, likes, dislikes, pleasant and unpleasant memories. *Child Develpm. Monogr.*, 1933, No. 12.
31. Jones, H. E. The environment and mental development. In L. Carmichael (Ed.), *Manual of child psychology* (2nd ed.). New York: Wiley, 1954, 631–696.
32. Jones, L. V. Primary mental abilities in the Stanford-Binet, age 13. *J. genet. Psychol.*, 1954, 84, 125–147.
33. Klineberg, O. *Negro intelligence and selective migration.* New York: Columbia University Press, 1935.
34. McHugh, G. Changes in IQ at the public school kindergarten level. *Psychol. Monogr.*, 1943, 55, No. 250.
35. McNemar, Q. A critical examination of the University of Iowa studies of environmental influences upon the IQ. *Psychol. Bull.*, 1940, 37, 63–92.
36. McNemar, Q. More on the Iowa studies. *J. Psychol.*, 1940, 10, 237–240.
37. McNemar, Q. *The revision of the Stanford-Binet Scale: an analysis of the standardization data.* Boston: Houghton Mifflin, 1942.
38. Merrill, Maud A. The significance of IQ's on the Revised Stanford-Binet Scales. *J. educ. Psychol.*, 1938, 29, 641–651.
39. Metheny, E. Breathing capacity and grip strength of preschool children. *Univ. Iowa Stud. Child Welf.*, 1941, 18, No. 2.
40. Miles, Catherine C. Gifted children. In L. Carmichael (Ed.), *Manual of child psychology* (2nd ed.). New York: Wiley, 1954, 984–1063.
41. Neff, W. S. Socioeconomic status and intelligence: a critical survey. *Psychol. Bull.*, 1938, 35, 727–757.
42. Olson, W. C., and Hughes, R. O. Growth of the child as a whole. In R. G. Barker *et al.* (Eds), *Child behavior and development.* New York: McGraw-Hill, 1943, 199–208.
43. Page, J. D. The effect of nursery school attendance upon subsequent IQ. *J. Psychol.*, 1940, 10, 221–230.
44. Passamanick, B. A comparative study of the behavioral development of Negro infants. *J. genet. Psychol.*, 1946, 69, 3–44.
45. Paterson, D. G. *Physique and intellect.* New York: Century, 1930.
46. Pratt, K. C. A study of "fears" of rural children. *J. genet. Psychol.*, 1945, 67, 179–194.

47. Rapaport, D. with collaboration of Schafer, R., and Gill, M.   Manual of diagnostic psychological testing: 1. Diagnostic testing of intelligence and concept formation.   *Publ. Josiah Macy, Jr., Found. Rev. Ser.*, 1944, 2, No. 2.

48. Richards, T. W.   Mental test performance as a reflection of the child's current life situation: a methodological study.   *Child Develpm.*, 1951, 22, 221–233.

49. Richards, T. W., and Nelson, Virginia L.   Abilities of infants during the first eighteen months.   *J. genet. Psychol.*, 1939, 55, 299–318.

50. Schott, E. L.   IQ changes in foster home children.   *J. appl. Psychol.*, 1937, 21, 107–112.

51. Shuttleworth, F. K.   The physical and mental growth of girls and boys age six to nineteen in relation to age at maximum growth.   *Monogr. Soc. Res. Child Develpm.*, 1939, 4, No. 3.

52. Skeels, H. M., and Dye, H. M.   A study of the effects of differential stimulation in mentally retarded children.   *Proc. Amer. Assoc. Ment. Def.*, 1939, 44, 114–136.

53. Skodak, Marie, and Skeels, H. M.   A final follow-up study of one hundred adopted children.   *J. genet. Psychol.*, 1949, 75, 85–125.

54. Sontag, L. W., Baker, C. T., and Nelson, Virginia.   Personality as a determinant of performance.   *Amer. J. Orthopsychiat.*, 1955, 25, 555–562.

55. Starkweather, E. K., and Roberts, K. E.   IQ changes occurring during nursery-school attendance at the Merrill-Palmer school.   *Yearb. Nat. Soc. Stud. Educ.*, 1940, 39 (II), 315–355.

56. Terman, L. M.   The discovery and encouragement of exceptional talent.   *Amer. Psychologist*, 1954, 9, 221–230.

57. Terman, L. M., and Merrill, Maud A.   *Measuring intelligence: a guide to the administration of the new revised Stanford-Binet test of intelligence.*   Boston: Houghton Mifflin, 1937.

58. Terman, L. M. *et al.*   *Genetic studies of genius: Vol. 1.   Mental and physical traits of a thousand gifted children.*   Stanford University, Calif.: Stanford University Press, 1925.

59. Terman, L. M., and Oden, Melita H.   *The gifted child grows up: twenty-five years' follow-up of a superior group.*   Stanford University, Calif.: Stanford University Press, 1947.

60. Thom, D. A., and Newell. Nancy.   Hazards of the high I.Q.   *Ment. Hyg., N. Y.*, 1945, 29, 61–77.

61. Thorndike, R. L.   An evaluation of the adult intellectual status of Terman's gifted children.   *J. genet. Psychol.*, 1948, 72, 17–27.

62. Thurstone, L. L.   Theories of intelligence.   *Sci. Monthly*, 1946, 62, 101–112.

63. Thurstone, L. L., and Ackerson, L.   The mental growth curve for the Binet tests.   *J. educ. Psychol.*, 1929, 20, 569–583.

64. Tyler, F. T.   Comments on the correlational analysis reported in *Intelligence and Cultural Differences.   J. educ. Psychol.*, 1953, 44, 288–295.

65. Wellmann, Beth L.   Iowa studies on the effects of schooling.   *Yearb. Nat. Soc. Stud. Educ.*, 1940, 39 (II), 377–399.

66. Wellmann, Beth L.   IQ changes of preschool and nonpreschool groups during the preschool years: a summary of the literature.   *J. Psychol.*, 1945, 20, 347–368.

67. Wellmann, Beth L., and Pegram, E. L. Binet IQ changes of orphanage pre-school children: a reanalysis. *J. genet. Psychol.*, 1944, 65, 239–263.
68. Witty, P. A. A study of one hundred gifted children. *Univ. Kan. Bull. Educ. State T. C. Stud. Educ.*, 1930, 1, No. 13.
69. Woodworth, R. S. *Psychology* (4th ed.). New York: Holt, 1940.

12

Psychosocial Development
in Later Childhood

IN LARGE MEASURE, INFANTS AND PRESCHOOLERS ARE confined to the home. Children of the age now under consideration leave home, literally and figuratively, to a much greater degree than they did. This is brought out in graphic fashion in Figure 16. Wright (*110*) studied the average number of hours per day spent by the children and adults in the family and the community settings in a mid-western town. On the average, infants and preschoolers spent only about one hour a day outside the home. An increase to six or seven hours outside the home occurs in the age period now under discussion (referred to as young middle and old middle childhood in the figure). During these hours away from home they are in school and at play. Most of this time they spend in the company of their age-mates.

The psychosocial development of the child between six and twelve is commonly referred to in three different ways. According to the emphasis desired, one may call it the peer group age, the school age, or the latency period. It is called the peer group age to signalize the importance of these years for learning to live with his age-mates. It is referred to as the school age because of the beginning of compulsory school attendance. It is spoken of as the latency period because of the psychoanalytic contention of relative quies-

526

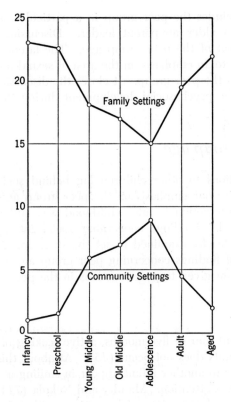

Figure 16. Average amount of time spent on family and community settings. (From Wright (110). Copyright 1956 by the Society for Research in Child Development, and published with permission.)

cence in sexual strivings between the twin storms of the Oedipus situation and of adolescence. In keeping with these three emphases of the peer group age, of the school age, and of the latency period, discussion is to be organized around each of them as the major problems of psychosocial development in later childhood. There is a danger of too sharp a separation in this way of approaching psychosocial development. The peer group age child, the school-age child, and the latency-period child are, after all, one and the same child. It is only for the sake of emphasis that we separate in this fashion these three aspects of his life. The peer group age is the most inclusive grouping for discussion and is presented first. The school age includes the peer group in a particular setting with the addition of an older nonparent leader. Discussion of the school age follows that of the peer group age. The latency period, referring as it does to an emphasis on the area of sexual tendencies, again is expressed in the peer group. It closes the discussion of the major problems of the psychosocial development during these years.

The peer group age

Social reactions to other children lag behind social reactions to adults. Despite our emphasis on the peer group age, the basis for much social interaction in later childhood was laid in infancy and early childhood. Findings concerning social interaction in these ages must be briefly examined to set the stage for a more detailed presentation of findings concerning peer group age itself. Detailed attention is then given to peer reactions in the peer group age.

Infancy

Prior to about four or five months, active seeking of social contact with other infants does not occur (15). At about this age, the first social reactions to another infant appear in smiling at him or crying when he receives attention. Maudry and Nekula (71) demonstrated progressive age changes in social reactions with infants ranging in age from 6 to 25 months. They used the technique of episode sampling at "baby-parties" that they had arranged. Two infants of approximately the same age were placed together in a playpen, first, without play material, then, after a time, with hollow cubes introduced, followed by a drum and a drumstick for each, and, lastly, a ball was given them, preceded by showing them how to roll it between them. Each infant was paired with other infants at different observational periods and the reactions of each infant recorded. The results are presented in terms of specified age periods. For each period, the findings are those for a typical infant at the designated age.

Six to eight months. One-third of the time the infant turns immediately to the surroundings, not to the partner or the play material. Nearly half the attempts of the partner to interact with him are ignored. Friendly contacts, when they occur, are limited to looking, smiling at, and grasping the partner. Games are few and short. Often they consisted of unspecific manipulations of the same object without the partner receiving attention. Fights are equally impersonal, consisting of a blind attempt to get hold of the play material.

Nine to thirteen months. Play material is responded to first. Since the partner often becomes an obstacle to getting it, fighting is at its maximum at these months. Conflicts now become personal; though it is not yet genuine hostility since nonpartner material (his own toys and clothing, hair, and so on) is still much preferred.

Fourteen to eighteen months. This is a transitional period wherein the infant shifts his attention from the play materials to his partner when his desire for playthings is satisfied. There is a pronounced decrease in fighting for material.

Nineteen to twenty-five months. The infant integrates his social interest in the partner with his interest in the playthings. Games show a considerable increase in frequency and length. The play becomes personal with much looking, smiling, and grasping, with a modification of his behavior in adjustment to that of his partner.

Disregarding the transitional 14 to 18 months' interval, Maudry and Nekula found that the infant regards the partner first as play material in itself (6 to 8 months), then as an obstacle to play material (9 to 13 months), and finally as a playmate (19 to 25 months). In other words, the infant has progressed from passivity to social contact, albeit crude, during the first two years of life.

The finding that infants of 19 months typically are more interested in their playmates than in the material suggests a primary social orientation at a very young age. Moreover, cooperation and competition in their crudest beginnings are apparent.

These findings tell us nothing about the factors responsible for the infant's social responsiveness; nor is there other research to which to turn for information. Presumably, the infant's first social relationships in the home, particularly with the mother, play an important part in determining his attitude and behavior in his relations with his peers. Behavioral generalization from the home setting would be expected.

We may lack understanding of their origin, but we do have evidence of individual differences in social reaction. Buhler (15), as a result of observation of infants' social settings, concluded that three patterns could be discerned—the socially blind, the socially dependent, and the socially independent. She describes them as follows:

(a) The socially blind infant behaves in the presence of another child as if nobody were present; he looks at the other without any emotion, he takes toys, plays and moves without any regard for the other child; he does not pay any attention to the other's movements; he is neither impressed nor interested in the other's presence or activities. (b) The socially dependent, on the contrary, is deeply impressed by the other's presence and activities; he can either be inhibited or else be stimulated by the other's presence. In the first case he will not move, will watch the other or copy him, will obey him, and sometimes even give signs of fear in front of him; in the second case, he will display in front of the other, will demonstrate objects and gestures, will try to rouse the other, and sometimes will even get enthusiastic and excited. In both cases all his movements are dependent on the presence of the other child; he observes the effect of his behavior on the other and carefully watches the other's reactions. (c) The third type is still different. The socially independent child is one who—though aware of the other's presence and responsive to his behavior—yet does not seem dependent on him, is neither intimidated nor inspired. He reacts to the other, wards him off when necessary, yet never becomes aggressive himself. He may or may not join the other in play, is not inconsiderate, but sometimes even consoles the other, encourages him, takes part in his activities; yet, with all that, he remains independent in his movements; for instance, he may suddenly turn away and do something for himself (*15*, 393–394).[1]

These types of social reactions in infants are influenced by the social developmental trends reported earlier. Presumably, all infants are first socially blind. Even those who can still be so characterized, when other infants are more "dependent" or "independent," still show change with increased age in the direction of greater outgoingness. Social dependence presumably is heavily influenced by the age of the other child. If the other child is older, dependence through dominance of the older would be expected. By no means can these three characterizations be considered as hard and fast, unalterable by events. The three patterns are, nevertheless, suggestive of the emerging personality differences shown by infants in peer interaction.

Although there were social reactions to peers during infancy, it must be emphasized that social situations are almost completely confined to the family setting. Social interactions with adults far

---

[1] From Buhler (*15*). Copyright 1931 by the Clark University Press, and published with permission.

outnumber peer interactions. The "baby parties" of Nekula and Maudry after all were arranged by psychologists, not by the infants themselves!

Early Childhood

At the outset, a word of caution is necessary. Parental attitudes influence the child's social reactions with his peers. Sometimes this influence is very direct and overt. This can be illustrated from the attitudes expressed by Mrs. Harper toward Shirley Ann (12), which was described in more detail in Chapter 10. It will be remembered that, although indulgent, Mrs. Harper insisted that most children were not good enough for her darling. By her very actions in this connection she directed Shirley's acquaintance with other children into certain channels. Instances of direct and deliberate channeling of the child's social interactions are certainly common. The effect of other parental influence is not directly planned in that a specific result is expected. This is presumably the case with the young children studied by Baldwin and his associates (11, 12). It will be remembered that they found children from rejectant homes tended to be aggressive, children from democratic homes to be socially outgoing and popular, and children from indulgent homes to be inactive and socially unsuccessful. Children from each home pattern had characteristic ways of reacting in social settings, including social settings with their peers.

Social participation. Social participation with a child's peers increases in versatility and complexity between the second and fifth years. These increases with age are shown by the more cooperative nature of their participation. Parten (84, 86) studied social behavior in nursery children by a technique of time sampling. The sizes of the groups in which the children played and the nature of their play activity were focuses of her sampling. Playing in groups of two occurred 30 per cent of the time for the children two- to two-and-a-half years of age, whereas at the other extreme, groups of five children occurred only 9 per cent of the time. For children aged four- to four-and-a-half the picture had changed considerably, since groups of five had increased to 24 per cent. Thus, the size of the play group increased with age during the preschool years. Parten also classified the behavior of the children into the following categories: (1) *unoccupied;* (2) *solitary* (independent play); (3) *on-*

looker; (4) *parallel activity* (playing alongside, but not with other children); (5) *associative activity* (common activity with borrowing, loaning and turns taken); and (6) *cooperative* (some common goal, different roles by various members that supplement one another).

The youngest children tended to engage either in solitary or in parallel play. The older children tended to engage in associative or cooperative play to a much greater extent than did the younger children. To bring together the results of the classification of their behavior, each category was given an arbitrary weight for cooperativeness with the highest category, *cooperative* play itself, considered the most cooperative and given the highest weight, and *unoccupied* considered the least cooperative and given the lowest weight. The social participation score derived from the weighting was correlated with age of the children and found to be 0.61. To put it in terms of the categories, as his age increased the preschool child engaged more in associative and cooperative play and less in idleness, solitary play, and serving as an onlooker. Parallel play was the only category which did not change materially over the years. It is evident that with increasing age between two and five years, social participation increased.

Another way of summarizing these findings about social participation, would be to put the results in the familiar framework of socialization theory. We already know that the two-year-old tends to be egocentric, and that during the preschool period, socialized responses increase. In social behavior, in the peer group, too, during the preschool period, there is a transition from egocentricity to increased socialization in the sense of increased cooperation.

Leadership. Closely related to social participation is leadership. One cannot lead others without participating in social settings; so it is not surprising that Parten (85) found a correlation of 0.97 between social participation and leadership. Using the same preschool subjects as before, she classified the child's role in the groups under these general headings: follower (F); neither leading nor following but following own inclinations (N); both directing some children and following some others (B); reciprocally directing with another child (R); and directing the group as a whole (D). A composite leadership score based on minus to plus scores extending from F to D was calculated for each child; it was then correlated with social participation scores with the finding mentioned.

Turning to the extent to which each kind of behavior was shown, the following of one's own independent inclinations was by far the more frequently indulged in by this group, but with wide individual variation. All but three of the children, at some time or another, were followers, although more than half only in a very small number of instances. Incidentally, even the greatest followers were sometimes directors, which suggests that the idea, sometimes advanced, that some individuals are born followers is fallacious. The reciprocal leaders tended to be older than children who did not follow this role. The children who were definite leaders were found to be of two types—the diplomat and the bully. The former were subtle and rendered suggestions; the latter employed sheer bossiness in their directive role.

Conflict. It has already been established that personality reactions to home situations, especially to parental attitudes, carry over into general tendencies toward social behavior. Aggression expressed in conflict is no exception. For example, in the Sears antecedent study (91) reported in detail in Chapter 10, it was found that for boys the more maternal punitiveness there was, the more aggressive the boys were in preschool. With girls, however, those with aggressive (punitive) mothers were less aggressive. Despite the sex differences in aggressive behavior, they show the effect of maternal behavior in expressing aggression in social settings.

The evidence presented in Chapter 10 demonstrated that aggressiveness increased within the preschool period as the children grew older. This has been verified in a study by Muste and Sharpe (81) which, because it did not relate these findings to parental influence, is reported here for the first time. Controlled settings were used by having paired children play with a selected array of toys. From their behavior in this setting, recordings of aggressive behavior were taken. A definite increase in aggression with age was found. Aggression is intimately related to conflict. A child faced with a conflict often tries to overcome the resistance of his peers by sheer forceful aggression. If he wants a toy, he tries to pull it away from the child who has it. In turn, that child holding the toy is apt to respond by counteraggression.

Increased social participation inevitably brings in its wake the chance of conflict between children. It will be remembered that Landreth (55) found that 75 per cent of the situations causing crying in the nursery school were conflicts with other children. Preschool children are still quite socially maladroit. They can blunder in and out of conflict with astonishing ease. We are again reminded of the tendency to "want what they want when they want it," noted as exemplifying the grip the pleasure principle has upon younger children. Preschool children continue to show the tendency noted earlier to find the other child an obstacle in doing what comes naturally and to manipulate him as he would inanimate objects. He is very much wrapped up in his own concerns. Jersild and Markey (53) found that about two-thirds of the conflicts of pre-school children were aggressive acts against another child's posses-sions, the space he occupied, or his play activities, whereas only one-third of the conflicts were brought on by aggression against the child himself. In other words, snatching toys, intruding on the space he was occupying, or blocking what the other child was doing were more common as causes of conflict than were direct attacks upon the other child. Sometimes, the child bringing on the conflict wanted the toy, or as it were, needed the space the other child was occupying and just came charging in. When the attack was directed upon the person of the other child, from the observer's viewpoint it appeared unprovoked in that there was no detectable behavior on the part of the child who was attacked that could be considered provocative of aggression.

They found these results through observations of nursery school children aged about two to four in free-play situations. On the average, a conflict occurred every five minutes of their observation time. In individual children the number of conflicts in which he engaged varied enormously. One child engaged in 141 conflicts, another in 17 conflicts during the same period of time. The number of conflicts also varied among the three nursery school settings in which information was collected; with one group the average number of conflicts was 34, whereas for a comparable period of observation the number in another group was 81 conflicts. Apparently, conflicts vary according to the setting.

A follow-up study by Jersild and Markey a year later showed that proneness to conflict is a fairly stable personality characteristic. Frequency of conflict was measured for some of the children in each of the various groups, and rank-order correlations ranging between 0.80 and 1.00 were found between the frequency of conflict behavior shown by children on two occasions a year apart. As compared to their behavior of a year before, a considerable increase in aggressive-ness was observed. While the average number of aggressions in nursery school per unit of observation had been six, a year later they now averaged 17.

The peer group serves to modify the aggressive behavior of children. Fite (29) observed children in free play on the playground and in staged play settings which were designed to draw the child out in respect to his attitudes toward aggression. She shows that children admonished not to fight by their parents will, when in a play group where there is a considerable amount of fighting, show a conflict, but eventually the need to stand up for one's rights forces the child to deviate from parental rules. The tendency for other children to regard aggressive behavior more leniently than did their parents tended to relax the standards of some children.

Sympathy. It is during the preschool years that children become capable of what we would call sympathetic behavior (79). A child of this age often will help other children in distress—try to help satisfy their physical and social needs, protect them, defend them, and help remove the cause of their distress. This is what is meant by sympathy. It comes about from a slow process of growth, since, in large measure, the ability to sympathize is dependent upon the child's ability to perceive what is happening. For example, one cannot sympathize with a child who is humiliated unless one knows what it is like to be humiliated and can recognize in him the signs that he is feeling humiliated. Murphy (79) found that two- and three-year-old children might recognize the sight of the flow of blood as an occasion for sympathy but not black and blue marks or swellings. Even when recognizing a distress situation, children of this age were more apt to stand about, with or without signs of anxiety, rather than doing anything actively. The ability to perceive subtle situations that will arouse sympathy increases as the child grows older. This results in a wider range of situations that become a signal that distress is present. It is not surprising that older preschool children show more sympathetic responses than do younger in the forms of activities of comfort, help, and defense.

Lois Murphy (79) studied the manifestations of sympathy in groups of preschool children in the settings of playgrounds which she supplemented by interviewing the parents as well as through a variety of experimental situations arranged so as to elicit sympathy.

Other factors than age seemed to influence the amount of sympathy, according to her findings. One especially prominent, positive relationship was the somewhat surprising one that sympathy and aggressiveness were related to one another. The more aggressive the child, the more often he tended to be sympathetic. Items from her rating forms show this association. They included association between a tendency to join in an attack on children and also to defend children attacked by others; an attempt to comfort other children and also to push or pull other children; and to help children out of painful situations and also to pummel children who fell accidentally. A definite relation for sympathetic and for aggressive behavior to be positively related to one another seems established. Jersild and Markey (53), in their study of conflict behavior referred to earlier, found the same relation between frequency of sympathy and of aggressiveness. Perhaps, sheer gregariousness helps to explain this apparently paradoxical relationship. The aggressive-sympathetic child was "in" on most social situations, including both those in which aggression might be elicited and in those in which sympathy might be forthcoming. The less aggressive and less sympathetic child, not being so psychologically close to the social settings, behaved as he did because of his detachment.

Intelligence, too, seems to be related to sympathetic behavior. In one group, Murphy found a correlation of about 0.50 between amount of sympathetic behavior and mental age. However, the relatively modest magnitude of correlation implies that there is still plenty of opportunity to feel that high intelligence does not necessarily insure sympathy. In maladjusted children we would not expect such correlations, as cases cited by Murphy herself illustrated; nor would this relationship necessarily hold as the child grows older. It may be that the less intelligent child she studied had not as yet attained the capacity for recognizing the situation as one in which sympathy would be appropriate as much as his more intelligent age peer. With increasing age, this relationship presumably would be sharply reduced or even disappear.

Murphy also utilized experimental situations in studying sympathetic behavior, such as leaving a child at the side of a playpen in which a two-year-old infant was confined. Toys for the infant, such as a doll and a ball, were *outside* the playpen. The child's reaction to the situation was studied. If at the end of 30 seconds he had done nothing to help the younger child, he was asked what he thought the infant wanted and otherwise encouraged to interact with the infant. Other situations designed to elicit sympathy were arranged as well. The children responded to them very differently—from complete inhibition to wholehearted sympathy. It was possible to find characteristic patterns concerning sympathy among the children. Of 18 children tested, 7 were consistently sympathetic in their behavior, 5 consistently unsympathetic, and 6 showed no consistency in their behavior.

Later Childhood

Many of the skills that make for socialization in our culture are learned in peer groups. How a child will react will depend not only upon that which he is exposed to in the group, but also upon his earlier established personality characteristics. His new experiences in the peer group do not mean that the effect of maternal attitudes and behavior is somehow erased or negated. To illustrate this point, only one study of maternal characteristics and the peer group age child will be used. Altman (1), in the course of a more extensive investigation, related the contentment-discontentment of mothers to their children's characteristics and found a positive relationship. They were mothers of boys and girls aged eight to ten. The measures for each of the mothers were based upon a rating by a psychiatrist on the happiness of the mother's own childhood and her satisfaction with her marriage and her husband. The ten mothers at each extreme on these rated dimensions were selected for further study. The Rorschach Ink Blot Examination was given the children and measures derived from it for intellectual freedom (originality, adaptability, and vigor); emotional freedom (spontaneity and stability); and anxiety control (freedom from conflict and tension, high frustration tolerance, and freedom from guilt). Statistically significant differences were found in the characteristics of the children of the mothers of the two extremes. The children of the "contented" mothers were found to show significantly greater intellectual and emotional freedom and better anxiety control. With this illustration we now return to our main theme—the peer group.

The shift from the family to the larger social setting which this chapter signalizes requires a shift in perspective concerning aggressive, independence, and sex tendencies. Heretofore, they have been examined as they originated in the family and as they were expressed in this and other social settings. These "other" social situations, such as the preschool, up to this point were treated merely as settings for the appearance of family-instigated tendencies. They were not considered as they modified or further elaborated these tendencies. This is part of our present concern. Instead of considering aggression, independence, and sex in and for themselves as separate topics, they are now seen as imbedded in these social settings. Aggression, for example, has already been reexamined in the setting of conflict at the preschool age level. In a later section of this chapter, sex is related to the latency period. At this point, independence will be considered.

During later childhood the twin problems of achieving some independence and of finding oneself as a person become prominent. These, too, are important problems at this period, even though it is customary to focus attention on adolescence as being the prime critical period. Reserving for later the question of the effect of the peer group on the individual's self-concept, we are now concerned with the child achieving independence. The seeking and finding of independence as an autonomous individual are continuous processes. It does not begin with later childhood, but before; it does not end with the close of this period, but continues through adolescence and into adulthood.

Independence as a tendency is expressed, so far as the peer group is concerned, as the continuing struggle to be more independent of the parents. In this connection one is reminded of the chart presented in the beginning of the chapter concerning the amount of time spent in the family and in community settings. A dramatic increase in time spent in the community occurred after preschool age. This is clear evidence that at least a certain form of independence from the home takes place. Most children not only leave home physically for more hours, they also leave emotionally to some extent.

In these years the child is seeking an independent existence. When younger, he identified only with his parents; he is now ready to be himself. He moves away from his parents into the world of his peers and the process of identification continues—but with figures outside the home. The young child does not question the wisdom and prowess of his parents. In his eyes they are all-knowing and all-powerful. Somewhere in later childhood cracks begin to appear in their armor of perfection. The child begins to question their knowledge and strength. They can be wrong and they can be weak. His own independent evaluation begins to emerge as an indispensable concomitant of emerging independence. Shifts in the direction of greater independence can be illustrated by changes in aspiration. The child of seven or eight can see himself, "when he grows up," only as like his father or mother; the child of ten thinks of himself as a cowboy, as a movie star, a pilot or athlete, or a similar glamorous person. (This finding by Havighurst, Robinson, and Dorr (47) is described in more detail in later discussion of the ideal self.)

If a child is to be successful with his peers, he must have some degree of independence. This may be illustrated in circumstances in which parental control is so strong that the child is forced to rebel. Not coming directly home after school is often an expression of too heavy an insistence on being precisely on time. Hounded about being a minute late can drive a child to being an hour late. Of course, rebellion of even greater proportion and a more pervasive form may occur. Other examples of unsuccessful children are those found by Levy (59) to be bound to their overprotective, dominant mothers. Although possessing many "virtues" such as docility, neatness, and politeness, they were promptly judged sissies by their peers.

The peer group is a means of socialization for the child. How does the peer group help a child meet his needs? In an analysis of this problem, Martin and Stendler (70) suggest a variety of ways in which the peer group influences the socialization of the child. Briefly, the peer group provides (1) rewards; (2) an identity for the child; and (3) support. A peer-age child sees in the behavior of other children that which he may model himself upon—a model for characteristics for which no adult can serve. He cannot model himself after his mother and father in seeking social acceptability— they are popular or unpopular in their own adult fashion through cocktails, bridge, or conversation on the latest novel (or through beer, pinochle, and the latest racing results). These forms of behavior are not yet within a child's ken. Other children must serve as models. To be accepted by the group is a reward. So he learns the way of the group in order to be accepted by that group. Once in the group he develops new needs—he acquires new secondary drives. No longer a means to an end—approval of the agents of socialization now becomes an end in itself. Thus, the peer group provides rewards. They also provide him with an identity of and for himself—not Mr. Brown's son Bob, but Bob. As Martin and Stendler indicate, he takes on successive identities from a first-grader, then to a Cub Scout, and so on up through the years. The group thus provides a series of identities. The group provides support through sheer numbers in presenting requests to do what others do or have what others have because "all the kids do (or have) it."

Although all of these positive, group-cohesive factors are present, one must also remember that groups and grouping carry within their very structure a measure of exclusiveness. One cannot have an airplane model club with a membership without excluding someone. Moreover, even in loosely knit groups, such as those that form on the playground, there still will be "outsiders" (83). These are the recessive children (listless, lacking in vitality, below normal in intelligence and careless); the socially uninterested; and the socially ineffective (the noisy, rebellious, boastful, and arrogant). Negative influences from the peer group will also be very evident in the discussion to follow.

With this introduction, we are now in a position to turn to three major facets of peer group relationships in later childhood—social acceptability, friendships, and cooperation and competition. Thereafter, the self and social perception as expressed in peer relationships will be examined.

Social acceptability. Consideration will now be given to what makes for the child's social acceptability with his peers. What is meant by social acceptability may be illustrated by anticipating the terminology used in the research studies of this topic. The investigators have referred to reputation, popularity, social success, social status, and prestige values in their specific studies. The common theme is what makes a person socially acceptable or not socially acceptable in his peer group.

One of the classes of tools that have been used to study social acceptability and other forms of group interactions has been called sociometric tests by their originator, Moreno (75). Sociometric tests have in common the fact that they may be used to elicit positive or negative or mutual responses about members of a group by the members of that group (62). They may be used to select or exclude companions for any group, actual or potential, of which the child might become a member. These positive or negative responses are shaped by a particular investigator to suit his needs. The test of social acceptability is concrete. Not mere liking in general, but the liking for someone in a particular setting or particular activity is found to be most conducive to precise results—a seat mate, a playmate, fellow TV watcher, a party guest, or what you will.

Closely related to sociometry, although developed independently by Hartshorne, May, and Maller (41), is the "Guess Who" technique, which is also used extensively in studies of social acceptability. A number of short word portraits of children are presented and the children are asked to guess which of their peer mates is being described. For example, "Guess who it is that is always bossing other

children?" Since the children's ratings may be pooled, high reliability may be achieved. Questions suitable to the intent of the
investigator can be framed with some ease and precision.

Constancy of social acceptability with increase in age during the
peer group ages has been established. Bonney (14) used the sociometric technique to differentiate socially acceptable from socially
unacceptable children in the second through the fifth grades in
three schools. The bases of choice of acceptability varied from
grade to grade, but in each there were from five to six bases of
choice, including with whom to have their pictures taken, partner
for a party, and to whom to give Christmas presents. The children
were also asked the names of their best friends. A composite score
for each child was derived. Bonney used a semilongitudinal approach, with most of the subjects tested in successive grades (although there was pupil population turnover). Consequently, correlation between general social acceptance at successive age levels
was possible, giving him a measure of social acceptance constancy.
Between the sociometric measure of the second and third grades
the correlation was 0.84; that between the third and fourth and
fourth and fifth grade was, respectively, 0.77 and 0.67. A high degree
of constancy in degree of social acceptability is exhibited from grade
to grade. To emphasize this point, the magnitude of the correlations
in social acceptability was approximately as large as that between
intelligence test scores for the same grades (0.75 to 0.86). In other
words, social acceptability is almost as constant as intelligence. This
constancy of social acceptability was checked by a study of children
who transferred from one school to another where, naturally, they
were unknown. Although the group was small, in every instance
their social acceptance scores at the end of the year in the new
school gave them very much the same degree of social acceptability
they had had in their previous schools. This constancy of social
acceptability has also been found by other investigators. For example, Criswell (22) found that both first and second choices in
elementary school children remained stable over a six-weeks period.
Nearly 70 per cent of the first choices did not change over this period.

In spite of constancy of social acceptability, the peer group members shift in their evaluation of desirable and undesirable personality
characteristics over the years of this age period. In other words,
personality characteristics making for social acceptability change
as the children grow older. This may be illustrated from data of
the longitudinal study reported by Macfarlane (66) using a "Guess

Who" technique. In the first grade "quiet" was given the highest mark by the children for what makes a real boy. By the third grade being "quiet" had almost dropped out of the pattern. If a given boy had maintained stability in the personality characteristic from the first grade to the third grade by remaining "quiet," he would thereby suffer change in reputational status as a "real boy." (Whether this bothered him or not is a different matter, dependent upon whether he wanted this form of prestige.) These findings were extended with a larger sample by Tuddenham (*104*) using the same "Guess Who" technique. Popularity in first grade girls was associated with "acting like a little lady," "being quiet," and "not being bossy or quarrelsome." In the fifth grade "acting like a little lady" had little to do with social acceptability. By this age characteristics such as good looks, being a good sport, friendliness, and tidiness were most highly correlated with social acceptability. The evidence seems clear that the children evaluate other children's social acceptability somewhat differently at different age levels in the light of standards and values characteristic of that age level.

At first, it may appear that there is a contradiction between the constancy of social acceptability found by Bonney, and the shifts in characteristics making for social acceptability found by Macfarlane and Tuddenham. This is not the case. Bonney dealt with *constancy of individual acceptability status;* Macfarlane and Tuddenham with *shifts in characteristics making for social acceptability.* So there is no contradiction between their results. Characteristics may shift in the socially acceptable child so that he maintains his acceptability but through different characteristics.

Social adaptability, whether deliberate or not, seems to be characteristic of the socially acceptable. He maintains his acceptability while changing his characteristics. This social adaptability is probably related to what has been called social compliance. Lippitt (*65*) found in a group of preschool children that social compliance was the most consistent positively related correlate of popularity of all the measures she used. Social compliance, more specifically, refers to the capacity of the child to make quick, unobtrusive adaptation to the situation prevailing in the group. The child who quickly adapts himself to the social demands of a given situation is the most popular and vice versa. Social compliance to a given situation and social adaptability with the passage of time have probably more than a superficial similarity.

Social acceptability varies at different socio-economic levels. Pope

(87) used children from two contrasting levels from different schools in different areas of a large city in studying this matter. One group was from the lower-lower class, the other from upper-middle and lower-upper class. Hereafter for convenience they will be referred to as the "lower" and "upper" groups, respectively. Both groups averaged 12 years in age, but it was impossible to avoid an IQ discrepancy of 104 in favor of the upper group as compared to 96 for the lower group. A variation of the "Guess Who" type of test yielded a reputational score for each child. The nature of the items may be inferred from the description of results which follow. Each of the 25 traits on which information was secured was intercorrelated for the upper and lower groups, separately for boys and girls. Cluster analysis (a modification of factor analysis) was then performed. Inspection revealed clusters of traits which were interrelated, yielding characteristic patterns of social behavior.

Among lower group boys three major patterns could be discerned. The members in the first pattern, in which only a few boys fell, were the leaders who had the homage of the other boys and the companionship of the girls. They were aggressive, belligerent, and domineering. The second pattern for lower group boys was the one involving most of the boys who were happy, sociable, able to enjoy a good joke, and considerably less aggressive than their leaders. The third pattern, the sissy, was the one the rest could not tolerate. This pattern included the studious and classroom conforming boys as well as what other groups would call "sissy."

Among boys of high socio-economic status, the group leader, although active and skilled in competitive games, was not expected to be aggressive; in fact, being bossy and given to fighting would tend to make him unpopular. Somewhat more numerous are instances of the pattern of the friendly, personable, good-looking boy who is accepted by both boys and girls. Instances of another pattern would be described as the classroom intellectual. He is not actively rejected; in fact, he enjoys a certain respect. The sissy, in the narrower sense, belongs to still another pattern, However, he is no more acceptable than he was among low socio-economic boys. Along with bossy, the unkempt, and the fighter, he is not accepted.

Among the girls of the lower socio-economic group, the type widely accepted is "the little lady" who is likeable, friendly, good, tidy, and a good student. She is, however, not likely to be a leader nor does she associate with boys. Another pattern which enjoys considerable prestige, but is less frequently encountered, is the somewhat rowdy, talkative, attention-getting, aggressive girl. She, rather than the little lady, associates with boys in the lower group.

High socio-economic girls instead of having two contrasting patterns of prestige, as did the lower group girls, has but one, that of the "little lady" pattern, but with certain differences. Although good-looking, friendly, and tidy, she is more vivacious than her low socio-economic counterpart and she is the one most likely to go out with boys. The tomboy has no place in the group since any form of aggressiveness or bossiness is rejected. From these results it is apparent that there are distinct differences in the value systems in the two peer cultures. In other words, the groups face different socialization pressures as shown by their differing criteria of what makes for acceptance. But in both, the peer group plays a direct role in personality formation.

For the moment, we are neglecting a systematic discussion of sex-linked characteristics as making for social acceptability. In later discussion of the latency period, it will be found that the characteristics conforming to cultural stereotypes—athletic skill, aggressiveness, and the like in boys, and docility, unassertiveness, and the like in girls—are definitely associated with social acceptability. Such generalizations as this, however, do not hold in all subcultures. For example, the tomboy of lower socio-economic status does not conform to this statement. Even here, however, there is an illustration of sex-related expectancy. Popularity with peers is related to conforming with expected patterns of sex-related characteristics.

Friendships. One factor, of course, that makes for friendship is propinquity—the sheer physical proximity or availability of someone to be a friend. Children may live near one another, or attend the same school, and thus be drawn together. This factor has little in the way of dynamic significance. Generally, it serves merely as a background factor—a necessary, but not a sufficient cause. This is demonstrated, once it is realized that in most instances an individual, child or adult, has a choice from among at least several more or less equally available potential friends. The factors which make for choice beyond mere availability need to be considered.

A study by Challman (18) of friendship in preschool children was dictated by the consideration that it was plausible to assume that similarity in some fashion or another is conducive to the formation of friendships. He selected for investigation likeness of sex, chronological age, mental age, intelligence quotient, height, and attractive-

ness of personality. He secured measures of each of these characteristics for boys and girls whose average age was about three-and-a-half.
They were observed in the nursery school setting, and the number
of times each child was with every other child was used as the
measure of the strength of friendship. The outstanding finding
was that even the youngest of these children discriminate in their
friendships very decidedly on the basis of sex. Only one boy and
one girl showed a more marked tendency to form friendships with
children of the opposite sex. All of the rest of the children tended
to form friendships within their own sex. This is also characteristic
of peer-age children. In the study of Tuddenham (104), referred
to earlier, his subjects chose children of their own sex almost without exception. As we shall later see in discussing latency phenomena,
sex segregation is characteristic of this age.

To return to the study of Challman, none of the other factors, with
the possible exception of chronological age, seemed to have any
influence on their friendships. Since the range of chronological age
was not particularly great as there were few cases at the extremes,
the study was not especially suitable for investigating the effect of
age.

This narrowness of age range was remedied in another nursery
school study, that by Green (35). Using the number of contacts as
her measure of friendship, she found that it increases with age.
From age two to three this is due to an increase in the number of
friends; from age three to five this is due to the depth of friendship
measured by their playing more often with specific children rather
than due to an increase in the total number of friends. These relationships in friendships may be interpreted in terms of behavior-
social learning theory. As Mussen and Conger state:

> This shift in friendship patterns may be viewed as a consequence of
> the child's learning in these new interpersonal situations. In his first
> experiences outside the home, the child may interact with many different
> children. Some of these early relationships do not bring rewards and
> may even bring punishment. With time, the child learns that relation-
> ships with certain children are more likely to be gratifying than others.
> Hence he forms closer attachments to these children (80, 276–277).[2]

In another phase of the same study (36) Green found by comparing solitary play and playing with one child, two children, and
three or more children, that the size of the group in which children

---

[2] From Mussen and Conger (80). Copyright 1956 by Harper and Brothers,
and published with permission.

play increased with age. She also investigated quarreling with the same subjects, finding that the ratio of quarreling to friendship contacts decreased regularly with age. Quarrels with friends correlated to the extent of a coefficient of 0.30. Boys were definitely more quarrelsome than girls. It will be remembered this is in agreement with the findings of Goodenough (33) on greater anger outbursts of boys. All her indices lend credence to the hypothesis that girls are more advanced in their social development expressed in their friendships than are boys—less quarrelsomeness, reaching their peaks of quarrelsomeness earlier, reaching their peaks in sheer number of friends earlier, and the ratio of their quarrels to their friendships.

Peer-aged children as they become older show greater stability in their choice of friends according to Horrocks, Buker, and Thompson (50, 51, 101). The data were simply collected. They asked about 350 suburban children from 5 through 10 years of age and 900 rural and 900 urban children from 11 to 18 years of age to write down the names of their three best friends. Two weeks later the same request was made of them. The investigators worked out an index of constancy of friendship, extending from identity of names and order on the two lists on the one hand to no similarity between the two lists on the other. They also presented data on whether or not the first choice of best friend on the two occasions remained the same. Both methods of analysis showed essentially similar results. As age increased, stability of friendships increased from years 5 through 18. For example, among urban children only about 40 per cent of the 11-year-old girls chose the same best friend two weeks later, but by age 15 the stability of choices over the same length of time had increased to over 60 per cent. Similar figures for the same ages in urban boys were 50 per cent and 60 per cent. These trends toward greater stability continued to the oldest age studied, that of the 18-year-old. The more fluctuating friendships of the younger child steadily gave way to relatively more permanent friendships of the mature person.

It will be remembered that Challman (18) found among preschool children that he could not establish very much relationship among similarities in the characteristics of friends. In the school-age child, personal characteristics do play a significant role in the formation of friendships. Furfey (31) found that 62 pairs of boy chums most resembled one another on social maturity, and somewhat resembled one another in chronological age, height, weight, and intelligence.

In general, nonintellectual factors were more crucial than intelligence in the maintenance of friendship ties. In the course of a more detailed study, Dymond and her associates (28) examined the differences in friendship qualities chosen by second and sixth graders. Drawing upon a list of descriptive phrases to characterize their friends, second graders stressed externals, such as a nice home, being good-looking, and having lots of spending money. The sixth graders, on the other hand, shifted to an emphasis on personality characteristics such as friendliness, cheerfulness, tidiness, and cleanliness. As they indicate, these changes in characteristics emphasized show an increase in socialization through the internalization of middle-class norms.

The causes of disruptions of friendships have also been investigated (10). After finding the three best friends of a group of 400 sixth-grade children, they checked on changes two weeks later. Sixty per cent changed in their choice of at least one of these friends. The major reasons for changing friends, in decreasing order of importance, were lack of recent contact, a quarrel, incompatibility, now considering them to be conceited or bossy, disloyal or underhanded, bullying or quarrelsome, or dishonest or untruthful. Sheer physical unavailability in lack of recent contact was thus a major factor. The second major factor, embracing all the rest of the reasons mentioned, is fluctuation in the child's social needs. In order for a friendship to endure, it must be mutually satisfying. Quarreling, incompatibility, and the like means that it is not, and the friendship is broken. If one or the other of the pair of friends gets nothing from it, or finds it frustrating, that friendship is headed toward dissolution.

Cooperation and competition. The nature and interrelation of cooperation and competition are enormously complicated and in many ways still not understood. Here we can refer to only a small percentage of available information. In our society, cooperation and competition are both considered as praiseworthy, and yet these tendencies may and do come in conflict. We play for the team, but we play for ourselves as well, both in childhood and adulthood.

The peer group provides opportunities for both cooperation and competition. Children may work together toward a common goal and, hence, cooperate, or they may vie with one another and, hence, compete. Often, of course, both cooperation and competition simultaneously are present. In a basketball game Johnny cooperates with his teammates in trying to beat his opponents, hence, he is cooperating with his own team and competing with the other one. But even among those with whom he cooperates, he is also competing in that he tries to be a better player than his teammates. In our classrooms the same confusing admixture occurs. Teachers ask that children cooperate and then place only a few in the best reading group, or hang only selected paintings on the wall. This is not meant as a criticism for behaving one way or the other—both cooperation and competition seem necessary to us. However, this does make it difficult to appraise their relative influence, since the same behavior may be motivated by either cooperation or competition.

Very young infants may hardly be said to compete. At the age of 6 to 8 months at the baby parties of Maudry and Nekula, infants did not, since their "fighting" over equipment was impersonal. Between 9 to 13 months, one may argue that since their conflicts became personal, there was competition over play equipment. The beginnings of cooperation seemed to occur later with the adjustment of one infant's behavior to that of the other, first occurring between 19 to 25 months. Their study, however, was not designed to measure cooperation and competition, specifically or definitely and, hence, must be considered as merely suggestive of the beginnings of these forms of social behavior.

Competition becomes more evident in the preschool period as studies by Leuba (58) and Greenberg (37) show. Leuba used a peg board situation with which preschool children played either singly or in pairs. The number of pegs placed properly in these two settings was compared. Two-year-olds were little affected by the presence of other children. Three- and four-year-olds, while competitive, were so distracted that they did more poorly when working in pairs than they did singly. Five-year-olds were not only competitive, but also definitely increased their output. In her study Greenberg encouraged a child to use building blocks competitively in building something bigger and (later) prettier than his companion. Using several criteria of rivalry, she found no competitive responses for children aged two to three, 43 per cent for children aged three to four, 69 per cent for children aged four to five, 75 per cent for children aged five to six and 86 per cent for children aged six to seven. At age two to three there was no competition, but in subsequent years there was a steady increase in amount of competition. Young children are not particularly competitive, but in our culture at least, children become progressively more competitive as age increases. Presumably, this reflects the child's assimilation of the competitive value of our society.

For competition to have an opportunity to appear, the task at which they are competing must be within the purview of the child concerned. Perhaps making something "bigger" or "prettier" was conceptually beyond the two-year-old child and consequently he did not compete. If it had been a task that they understood or were capable of doing, they, too, might have competed. Hence the finding that Maudry and Nekula's infants did compete, while Greenberg's two-year-olds did not, may be reconciled. A similar explanation may hold for Leuba's peg board study. At any rate, competition seems established in children in our culture at a relatively early age.

Aggression is not as closely related to competitive behavior as at first might be imagined. One might conceive of competition as simply a particular form of aggression. If this be the case, there should be a substantial correlation. However, it is possible that competitive behavior, or desire to excel, may develop independently of behavior with the aim of injury to another. McKee and Leader (67) investigated this comparison in 112 three- and four-year-old children, divided equally into groups on the basis of sex, age, and lower and higher socio-economic status. Each child was faced—first alone, and then later with a child matched in sex, age, and socio-economic status—with a table on which construction bricks were placed with which he was to play. Later analysis of the behavior was in terms of behavior in which the intent seemed to be to excel (competition) and behavior in which the intent seemed to be to injure (aggression). The relationship between competition and aggression was expressed in a correlation coefficient of only 0.22. In view of the small size of the correlation, competition and aggression can be conceived as independent patterns of behavior.

When the contrasting socio-economic groups were compared, the results verified the hypothesis held by McKee and Leader that competitive behavior was more intense among children from lower socio-economic groups. The explanation for this finding may lie in the fact that those deprived of status are likely to seek it more vigorously than those not so deprived. Or it is also possible that lower status youngsters have already learned the advantage of competing for material benefits which for them, in any event, are in limited supply. In the same study both boys and older children were more competitive than girls and younger children.

Unfortunately, there are few comparably precise studies of preschool children in cooperative situations. In a somewhat general and less precise way, all studies of social participation in which there was harmony are studies of cooperation.

There is no question, then, that cooperation is possible at the pre-school age. Wolfle and Wolfle (*108*) established that cooperative behavior was dependent upon communication skills. They did this by pairing children and pairing monkeys in an identical situation in which the pair could obtain a reward only if they cooperated. Child (or monkey) A must give his aid if child (or monkey) B is to obtain food from a cup. A, in this instance, must pull a string to bring the cup containing the food within range of B. The roles of A and B were reversed in the second phase of the study. The monkeys gave no cooperation to one another. The younger pre-school children cooperated only slightly. The older preschool children readily secured the cooperation of their companions.

There is some evidence that younger children are more coopera-tive (and friendly) than competitive (and hostile). Mengert (*72*) observed paired children in a playroom. Their overtly friendly responses outnumbered the overtly unfriendly ones by a ratio of over four to one. The greater amount of friendliness than aggres-siveness, a finding in earlier discussion from a variety of studies, points in the same direction. Sympathy, for example, frequently involves cooperation, so Murphy's results on sympathy in preschool children become relevant. Social participation itself may be pred-icated upon cooperation as was the case in Parten's studies reported earlier. To give a fresh illustration, Wright (*109*) found that when a newcomer is introduced into a group of children, they tend to be friendly toward him rather than hostile. The newcomer was given toys more frequently than they were given to already-established members of the group.

In older children, the study of Maller (*69*) is outstanding. He compared cooperation and competition in various groups of children, aged from 8 to 17, from different schools, and different socio-economic levels. The task was simple one-place addition. Various forms of cooperation and competition were arranged. For example, compe-tition was measured in an individual speed contest; from this result a list showing their ranks was to be posted. In addition, prizes for those scoring highest were offered. Cooperation was measured by staging a contest between classrooms.

Efficiency of work under competition was significantly and con-sistently higher than work under cooperation. When they were offered the choice between working for themselves or working for the group, the group was chosen in only 26 per cent of the choices. However, in one subsidiary experiment—a contest between boys and girls—the choice to work for the sex group among boys was higher than the choices to work for themselves. Nevertheless, in the over-all results, girls were more cooperative in that they chose more often than boys to work for the group (though still predominantly in favor of competition).

It would appear that competition for the self improved performance over that of cooperation for the group. Moreover, with but one such exception, competition was chosen by the children over cooperation. But as Doob (27) indicates, certain qualifications seem indicated. There is the fact that there were quite different rewards in the two situations. In competition both the prestige and prize were acquired. In cooperation there was no prize, and the given child could feel rewarded only if he belonged to a victorious group and he, himself, was strongly attached to the group. Classrooms of children are not necessarily conducive to *esprit de corps*. Moreover, competition was structured in a particular situation. Certain competitive-co-operative aspects of many other situations were absent. Interaction among the children was minimal. For example, competition often means that one tries to prevent competitors from reaching a goal, and cooperation requires constructive assistance of one another rather than merely contributing to a common goal. Any or all of these factors may contribute to different results concerning the relative influence of cooperation and competition. Hence, although Maller's study indicates competition was favored over cooperation, and this finding may even be typical of many situations, it does not prove that competition is always favored over cooperation.

The self and social perception. Each in his own way, a child reaches some sort of understanding of himself. As he moves through infancy and childhood, he acquires knowledge and attitudes about himself and others. The issues of self-perception and social perception continue in the setting of the peer group. Certainly, the peer-aged child has increased self-awareness, often expressed in self-consciousness. Attention to bodily grooming appears in boys as well as in girls. In the boy, earnest efforts to wet down the cowlick (or to cut the hair so close it no longer is there) may be said to epitomize these efforts.

Consideration of the self with peer group children will center on self-esteem (self-acceptance), the ego-ideal (ideal self), and an issue closely related to the self, empathy (ability to take the other person's role). Social perception has many ramifications. Chosen for exposition is the thorny question of race attitudes and awareness, particularly the social perception of the Negro. A return to consideration of the self-concept follows, in this instance that of the self-concept of the Negro.

SELF-ESTEEM, THE EGO-IDEAL, AND EMPATHY. The importance for self-esteem of the influence of the group is put forcefully by White:

> . . . it is fair to say that the crucial arena for self-esteem is the arena of one's age-mates. At home there is an age hierarchy. Even the siblings are bigger or smaller, so that differences of competence are expected. The home, moreover, continues to be the source of love and provision of basic wants, even when the child ventures forth to playground and school. At home he must be *love-worthy:* this may include being competent, but it is heavily weighted on the side of being good, obedient, and affectionate. On the playground the values are different: he must be *respect-worthy,* able to command respect because he shows competence and handles himself with ease. It is a sharp strain for many children when they pass from the atmosphere of a child-centered home into the competitive realities of even a friendly play group. They must now show what they have in the way of physical prowess, courage, manipulative skill, outgoing friendliness, all in direct comparison with other children of their age. The penalties for failure are humiliation, ridicule, rejection from the group (*105,* 144–145).[3]

Self-acceptance and social acceptability (popularity with one's peers) are positively related. Acceptance of one's peers is also positively related to popularity. These results were found in a study by Zelen (*111*) of sixth-grade children (almost all of whom had been together from the beginning grades) with a mean age of 10 years, 9 months. A sociometric measure, in which every group member rated every other member, gave the popularity or peer acceptance score in the form of the total score achieved. The total of the ratings which each of the children gave his peers is the measure of acceptance of others. Self-acceptance was a measure of the extent of expressed positive or negative feelings about oneself to the question, "Who are you—tell me about yourself." The correlations between peer acceptance and self-acceptance, and that between peer acceptance and acceptance of others, were positive, although relatively small. In other words, there is a small but stable

[3] Robert W. White, *The Abnormal Personality.* Copyright 1948, The Ronald Press Company,

relationship between the way a child perceives himself and the way his peers perceive him. If a child has positive accepting feelings about himself, he proves to be socially acceptable. Similarly, if he accepts others, they accept him and vice versa.

The development of the ideal self or ego-ideal was studied by a group of investigators (47) who asked several hundred children to write a brief essay on the topic, "The person I would like to be like." They were given instructions to describe a person whether he be real or imaginary or a combination of several people. Most of the subjects ranged in age from 8 to 18 and included both boys and girls. Several subgroups were used from widely scattered geographical regions and from varying levels of socio-economic status. The essays were first read by the investigators in order to arrive at categories of classification. Most of the essays fell into the categories of finding the ideal self in (1) parents; (2) glamorous adults (movie stars, athletes, and so on); (3) attractive and visible young adults (those within the range of observation of the child in question such as scout leaders, young uncles, and aunts, and so on); and (4) composite or imaginary characters (abstractions of a number of people).

The investigators studied age trends in these categorizations. The children from age 6 to about 8 tended more often to choose parents as ego-ideals. Children older than this move on to a choice either of a glamorous person or of a young adult. Sometimes, from about age 8 to 16 a glamorous person was consistently chosen. Other children chose the young adult at 8 or 10 and either continued choices falling in this category through adolescence, or else their choice shifted after this age to the more abstract ego-ideal or a composite imaginary person. Thus, a developmental trend concerning the ideal self was found. In the youngest years studied, it was still an identification with the parental figures, but who after about ten played a declining role; then moving on to a stage of romanticism or glamor, the ideal self finally culminating in late adolescence as a composite of desirable characteristics either symbolized by young adults known to them or by a purely imaginary figure. It should be noted that the choices of children, at first fanciful, become more realistic and more conforming to the norms of socialization.

The studies in the area of empathy essentially use the method of comparing a child's own estimate of another child's attitudes and then comparing his estimate with the actual attitudes as reported by this other child. Empathy, then, is this sensitivity to the attitudes of others.

Dymond and her associates (28) investigated the hypothesis that ability to empathize with others would increase with age. As a first step, cards, similar to those in the TAT but adapted to the children's ages, were given to small groups of second- and sixth-graders with mean ages, respectively, of about 7 and 11. After being told a simple story that accompanied each picture, each child was asked a standard series of questions about the thoughts and feelings of the characters in the story. Empathy was measured by the ease (lack of prodding or of the necessity for asking specific questions) with which the child could voice opinions about a pictured individual's thoughts and feelings, that is, what is he thinking and feeling. The mean score in "empathy" was significantly higher in the sixth as compared to the second grade. These results demonstrated that older children, as compared to younger, could express themselves more easily about others' thoughts and feelings. This potential for empathy, naturally, had no objective reference as to whether or not they were correct in their expressions. This was studied in the second phase of the study dealing with empathy, as such.

A second measure, the social insight test, was given. After judging sociometrically whom in the class he would like to sit with, invite home to a party, and so on, each child judged the extent to which he was liked or disliked by each other member of the class. Thus, there was a reverse sociometric test or social insight test following the sociometric one, since, by comparison of the two sets of data, one could get an empathy score. There was a measure, then, of how he thought he was liked and how he was actually liked. The empathy score was based on the degree of correspondence between the two measures. The children, who showed agreement on how much they thought they were liked to how much they were actually liked, showed high empathy. The children, who showed a discrepancy between how they thought they were liked and how they were actually liked, showed low empathy. There was a clear difference in favor of the greater empathy on the part of the sixth graders over the second graders. Within a grade, the sociometric and empathy scores correlated 0.26 for the second and 0.50 for the sixth grade. If every child more or less expects himself to be well-liked, only actually popular children can get a high score on empathy or insight. Hence the relation is about as high in the sixth grade as one might expect. The correlation is so low for the second graders it appears that they show relatively little relation between sociometric or popularity status and empathy or social insight. It will be remembered from the discussion in the section on friendships that Dymond and her associates (28) found that second graders were choosing friends on the basis of external qualities, such as money and a nice home. Certainly, these are not qualities which emphasize understanding or empathy, so it is hardly surprising that those who were most popular were not high in empathy at this age grade level. But, by the sixth grade and an average age of 11, children become more aware and better able to assess the feelings of others accurately, as shown by the increased correlation at that age.

In a somewhat similar study, Ausubel and his associates (9) used larger groups of subjects and separated the data for boys and girls for a more detailed analysis. They used a sociometric technique to determine the perceptions of one's own status and had him compare them with the perceptions held by others (the mean of the ratings given him by his classmates). The correlations were higher than those obtained by Dymond and were equally good for boys and girls. There was some increase with age as well.

Another facet of the self-social perception problem is the question of whether or not there is a relation between perceived similarity and the valuation given another person. Davitz (24) found that the highest sociometric choices tended to be perceived as more similar to the self than was the lowest sociometric choices, indeed, more similar to self than they actually were. He did this in a summer camp with a small group of boys and girls of an average age of about 10. They had been together 11 days when the study was conducted. Rankings gave sociometric choices, while social perception was measured by an activity inventory, with items consisting of two activities, such as dodge ball and ping pong; the subject was required to make choices between the pairs. Each child filled out this measure (1) for his own preferences; (2) for his highest sociometric choice; and (3) for his lowest sociometric choice. Perceived similarity was the degree of correspondence between his own responses and his prediction of the responses of the other child, both high or low sociometric choice as the case might be arrived at by counting the agreements between them. Actual similarity was the degree of correspondence between the child's own responses and those predicted for him. As mentioned before, Davitz found that the highest sociometric choices were perceived as those more like oneself than were the lowest choices. In fact, these highest choices were perceived as more similar to oneself than they actually were.

This may be interpreted as a tendency to wish to be similar to valued persons—in this case one's peers. One way this is expressed is in the usual pattern of identification of trying to make oneself like others. Here we have another way of being similar—trying to make the other person like oneself. In addition to identifying in the usual sense, one may identify others with oneself. This is what seems to have been happening in this study. It stands witness to the importance of the peer group.

RACE ATTITUDES AND AWARENESS. The question of self and social perception is an enormously complicated affair with interrelationships extending into most aspects of the life and experience of the child. Radke and her associates state the issue vividly:

> When the child arrives at school, he is not just "Bill," the individual personality. His concept of himself and his place among his peers and teachers are influenced by a great many variables such as his family's socio-economic status, his father's occupation, the street on which he lives, the language of his parents, his national background, his race and religion. In many ways and in repeated situations, differences among people, such as these, which are group-derived differences, are reinforced. "Bill" knows that how his family lives is different from the families down the street; and that his parents want to move because there are too many colored or foreign or Catholics in the neighborhood. He learns that his family goes to one place of religious worship, his playmates to another, a second playmate to none at all. His mother's advice and admonitions help him to sense the meaning of group differences; one day as he is playing on the corner lot, his mother calls him in and warns him never again to play with those children with some group designation because they are "bad," "tough," "dirty" and so on. His response is uncertain when some boys call his brother a derogatory group name, but he quickly senses all the anger, fear, or shame of it from the way his brother reacts to the situation (89, 331).[4]

Only one of the problems of social perception of the white child (and the self-perception of the Negro child) will be treated in discussing race attitudes and race awareness. This, however, is but an aspect of a larger social context.

The awareness of and prejudice toward the Negro will be used for illustrative purposes. Ordinarily, this problem is sketched in terms of an ethnic attitude, by which is meant a point of view toward some or all members of an ethnic (minority) group (38).

---

[4] From Radke, Trager, and Davis (89). Copyright 1949 by The Journal Press, and published with permission.

Prejudice in this sense is an unfavorable ethnic attitude, that is, one in which negative reaction tendencies predominate. In these attitudes there are cognitive components—beliefs, perceptions, and expectations the individual holds toward the ethnic group, and affective components—the feelings toward minority group members. This distinction between perceptions and feelings is important in unraveling the development of attitudes toward the Negro. One may have perceptions of differences, that is, be aware of race differences but feelings may be absent, confused, negative or positive.

Certain major studies will be discussed in some detail in order to give a normative perspective of the development of racial attitudes with age. Thereafter, these and other more briefly described studies will be used to examine the determinants of racial attitudes.

Race awareness in the sense of awareness of racial characteristics appears early. Goodman (34) studied this problem among preschool-aged children, who lived in, or near, a mixed Negro-white area in a large northern city. She used tests, interviews, and observation of both parents and children, while she herself lived in the area and had children enrolled in one of the nursery schools that she used for information. As she defined it, high awareness in both Negro and white children is characterized by (1) clear perception of color and other ethnic attributes; (2) use of numerous and accurately expressed race terms; and (3) the possession of strong values about these matters. Low awareness, on the other hand, meant unclear awareness, inaccurate and infrequent use of race terms, and no strong values held about them. Naturally, there were degrees of awareness between these two extremes, but for some presentations she divided the group into those showing high and those showing low awareness. She found that some awareness of ethnic differences appeared even among children aged four. As might have been expected, she found a relationship between awareness and age, with greater awareness among the older children and lower awareness among the younger children. High awareness did not appear before the age of four years-three months, but low awareness had entirely disappeared in her sample before five years of age. In addition, in the Negro children conflicts over racial matters and rejection of Negro attributes were strong. Both Negro and white children, even those with low awareness, showed some rejection of Negro attributes. In her sample among the white children, 15 per cent showed low awareness, 61 per cent showed medium awareness, and 24 per cent showed high awareness. Among the Negro children, the percentages were, respectively, 15, 45, and 40 per cent. Three-quarters of the Negro children with whom it could be established projectively and otherwise showed preferences for being white. This was shown in fairly consistent preference for white dolls, white characters in stories, and (presumably) for real individuals.

Only a minority of the children showed signs of racial hostility. For example, 84 per cent of the Negro children expressed some positive friendliness toward white children. Only 9 per cent expressed antagonism, although many more were disturbed by the problem of color. Among white children the corresponding percentages were, respectively, 56 and 33.

In a now classic investigation, Horowitz (48) studied ethnic preferences of white children (1) through the ranking of the order of pictures preferred of Negro and white children; (2) by their selecting from the pictures Negro and white companions for eating together, swimming together and so on; and (3) by asking the children whether or not they wanted to join in pictured activities, such as baseball, a school scene, or an ice cream parlor scene. There were two series of pictures; in one the pictures showed four white boys and in the other series a Negro boy was substituted for one of the group. For the last test, he found a gradual increase from ages 5 to 12 in the number of situations in which the children said they would participate if they were all white but would not if a Negro child were included. Somewhat similar results were found in selecting white or Negro companions. But the first or ranking test, which is a relatively pure test of affective orientation toward the Negro, unaffected by the behavioral situation as were the other tests, showed no change of relationship with age. Instead, generalized preference for whites was well-established by age five and continued without noticeable alteration with increased age.

Radke and her associates (89) studied social perceptions and attitudes in white and Negro children aged five to eight from kindergarten to the first and second grades. The 250 lower-middle class children drawn from six schools in a metropolitan area were selected so as to represent various social and religious groups. A series of pictures, the Social Episodes Tests, were given these children. The pictures consisted of scenes on the playground, in school, and on the street. Pictures were so drawn that differences in race (or religion) was suggested by each picture. A typical one involved a play scene in which several children were playing, with one child prominently in the foreground who was so drawn that he could be interpreted by the child either as being in the group or isolated from it. Two forms of the picture were used: one, a white boy in the foreground with the rest of the children Negro and the other, vice versa. The other pictures used were similar in intent. The racial (or religious) identification was defined by the tester if the child did not state it in his initial interpretation, and the child was then asked to tell a story about the picture. Even the youngest children were aware of Negro and white differences. When aggression was involved in the stories, there were two major ways it was handled by the white children. When it took the form of exclusion and rejection, it was said to be expressed by whites; when it took the form of physical aggression, it was attributed to Negroes. In general, Radke and her associates found that racial attitudes are learned early in childhood. There was a progressive crystallization of attitudes with increase in age, that is, they became more fixed and more extensive as the children studied were older in age.

In general, these results support the conclusion that by four years of age, skin color is perceived as having both ethnic and social significance. Socialization is shown in this process by the increasing conformity to social and cultural norms. Criswell (21) found, with increasing age, increasing preference of whites to associate with whites and Negroes with Negroes. By the fifth and sixth grades there was relatively little crossing over the ethnic line in selection of preferred associates. Among younger children there was by no means as marked a barrier. That these changes are due to sensitivity to cultural expectations is a plausible inference. The other studies reviewed earlier also indicate the importance of socialization. Goodman found both her Negro and white subjects sensed social differentiation and separation. The dawning desire of white children to exclude Negroes from their activities, as shown by Horowitz, is also pertinent. We shall now examine some of the determinants of race awareness.

Among white children the reaction is partly dependent upon social and other contacts. Although we are considering peer group phenomena, parents are not without their influence. Goodman (34) found that much race awareness and many of the specific characteristics her subjects attributed to the other group arose from parental teaching. Horowitz and Horowitz (49) found that in grade school children from the South, the parents were the primary source from which racial attitudes were learned. In fact, until the years of adolescence, the children were consciously aware that this was the case. Thereafter, they lost awareness of the origins of their attitudes and began to offer rationalizations to support their attitudes. Radke and her associates (89) also verified that the child accepted adult attitudes toward Negroes, shown in their reference to the parents in the course of their reactions to the pictures. Radke-Yarrow and her associates (90) interviewed parents and found that they controlled their children's social relationships in the home, neighborhood, and at school by placing restrictions on or encouraging friendships. Thus, we have an instance of the influence of reinforcement of certain responses upon learning; in this instance, the learning of attitudes toward the Negro.

Socio-economic circumstances are also evident as a determinant. For example, Landreth and Johnson (56) found that white children of upper socio-economic status, although aware of skin differences, handled the problem more cognitively, but that white children of lower socio-economic status saw it in affective terms. From about five onward, there are age changes in regard to association with Negroes on the part of white children. They are more and more inclined to reject them as persons with whom to come in contact. The social desirability of being white was recognized by white and Negro alike.

Although lack of contact may result in different attitudes from the usually prevailing ones, as in the Landreth study, this is not necessarily the case. In a particular school where there were few or no Negro children, among those studied by Radke (89), there was just as much prejudice expressed as in a school where there were many more Negro children. Radke and Sutherland (88) found a well-developed stereotyped attitude towards Negroes in a group of midwestern children who had little or no contact with them. Hartley (39) even found that children would express attitudes toward groups that were entirely fictitious. Horowitz (48) in his investigation found that there was very little difference between Northern and Southern white children in prejudice, and that living as neighbors or going to a common school did not materially affect attitudes. Contact in which the general interaction is favorable and pleasant does not necessarily change attitudes. Radke (89) concluded that white children do not change their stereotyped attitude on the basis of pleasant association with Negroes. Instead, they consider their experiences exceptions to the rule! White children's attitudes, more often than not, seem independent of the degree of contact they have had with Negroes. As Horowitz concludes, "It seems that attitudes toward Negroes are now chiefly determined not by contact with Negroes but by contact with the prevalent attitudes toward Negroes" (48, 34–35).[5]

THE SELF-CONCEPT OF THE NEGRO. Consequences of these social pressures upon the self-concept of the Negro need examination. It is apparent that the peer group has been shown to have an effect upon the self-concept. We have some suggestive results in studies already referred to. Goodman found that the Negro children she worked with, when required to make racial self-identifications, reacted uneasily, tensely, and evasively, whereas there were no similar tendencies among the white children. Many of Radke's (89) children, whites as well as Negroes, indicated a sense of group membership in regard to ethnic belonging. He placed himself in his own race in responding to the pictures. Although some white children found security in this group membership, saying they were glad they were white, others, particularly Negroes, felt insecure and anticipated rejection from white children. Psychological insecurity characterizes the self-identification of many Negroes.

A definitive study in this area was performed by Clark and Clark (20). They studied attitudes of Negro children, using the technique of doll selection. Dolls, identical except for skin and hair color, were presented to over 250 Negro children, aged three to seven, who were asked successively to give that doll to the investigator which (1) they would like to play with best; (2) is "nice"; (3) "looks bad"; (4) has "nice color"; (5) is a "white child"; (6) is a "colored child"; (7) is a "Negro child"; and (8) is "like you." Requests one through four were designed to reveal ethnic preferences; requests five through seven to demonstrate knowledge of ethnic differences; and request eight to show self-identification. Results on ethnic differences, self-identification, and ethnic preferences will be discussed in that order. To the requests for the white doll and for the colored one, knowledge of ethnic differences was shown by the very high percentage of choice for the correct doll. The "Negro" concept, a more abstract one, was not as well-established since only 72 per cent chose the brown doll on this request. In reference to identification, 66 per cent chose the brown doll and 33 per cent identified themselves with the white doll. It would appear that knowledge of ethnic differences does not necessarily mean a racially

[5] From Horowitz (48). Copyright 1936 by the American Psychological Association, and published with permission.

oriented self-identification. Turning to racial preferences, 67 per cent chose the white doll to play with. The relation of preference to age was curvilinear. A white doll to play with was preferred by 55 per cent of the three-year-olds, 76 per cent of the four-year-olds, 74 per cent of the five-year-olds, 71 per cent of the six-year-olds and 60 per cent of the seven-year-olds.

Other results they found are also of interest. Light-skinned Negro children chose a white child as more like themselves more often than did Negro children with darker skins. The light-skinned Negroes had greater difficulty in identifying themselves on the basis of their color than did the darker children. Self-identification was measured by their responses to the request to give the experimenter "the doll that looks like you." The youngest children were not certain of their identification. With increasing age there was a marked rise in the percentage of the children who identified themselves with the colored doll, reaching 87 per cent in the seven-year-olds.

The identifications made by Negro children are a matter of socialization. Identification to the Negro means in part an acceptance of himself as a member of an ethnic group. The Clark study (20) brought out vividly the difficulty their subjects had in identifying with the "colored" or "Negro" doll. Awareness of ethnic differences does not mean he has made a personal identification. Clark and Clark found then that knowledge of ethnic differences precede socially accurate self-identification, but that, with increase in age, both were accurately perceived. In these studies we have been examining the beginnings of a child's awareness of self through his recognition of differences between his skin color and the skin color of others.

In the Negro, self-acceptance goes along with social acceptance. Trent (103) found that self-accepting Negro children tended to express more positive attitudes both toward other Negroes and toward whites than did Negro children who were less self-accepting. A sentence completion test was utilized to estimate the degree of self-acceptance. Some items had to do with what they were afraid of, what they worried about, and so on. Judges classified the sentence completion protocols into these categories: most self-accepting, least self-accepting, and ambivalent. An attitude measure was developed for measuring attitudes towards whites and Negroes—the perceptions the Negro had of whites and other Negroes as threats, as inferiors, his feeling of trust, contempt, and the way he felt; and the actions taken such as rejection, aggression, exclusion, and so on. He found that Negro children who were most self-accepting had significantly more positive attitudes toward both whites and Negroes than did Negro children who were least self-accepting. In other words, to put forth the point of view of the least self-accepting, if the child did not accept himself as a person of worth, he tended to perceive groups, including his own, in a derogatory or hostile fashion. Many of the Negro children who showed low self-acceptance said they wished they were whites; in repudiating themselves they repudiated their group. Again it is found that attitudes toward self and toward others are intertwined. Prejudice is seen to be not only a social problem but a symptom of individual maladjustment.

There is, apparently, a particular pattern of feelings of inferiority, low self-esteem, and ambivalent attitudes towards one's own group that characterizes an unknown but a not insignificant proportion of Negroes (107). It is hardly necessary to add that how it is expressed and the extent to which it is held vary widely in degree among Negro individuals. Probably, security within the family and differences of social and economic level contribute to the particular form adjustment may take. For the different forms of adjustment patterns in the self-concept of Negro children, the effect of the peer group is at least partially responsible.

The school age

In the discussion to follow, although the teacher as a person and the setting of the school and their effect upon the school-age child will be the center of focus, a somewhat broader personnel and framework will be utilized. The influence of all adults, other than parents, will be considered. Moreover, the group settings, with which we shall be concerned, will include all such settings other than the home. Consequently, adults significant to the life of the child (such as recreation leaders), and adult-led settings (such as clubs) are included.

Socialization and the Teacher

There is no question of the importance of the influence of the peer group upon the child. Social behavior in this sense is oriented to the child and his peers. But there is the equally uncontrovertible fact that social behavior takes place under the watchful eye of adults (in this case, other than parents), who constantly impose upon the child their own standards of socialization.

Wright (*110*), in the study cited for information about the amount of time spent by children in community settings, also investigated who were the leaders in the various community settings. Almost all leaders were adults—in only eight per cent of all community settings had children assumed leadership. In effect, this means that adults were almost always on hand to look after the children. To put it concretely, every cub scout den had its den mother. To be sure, in other communities, especially in the large cities and in lower socio-economic groups, children are much more "on the loose." Too little supervision can naturally have a pernicious effect, but also it is possible that these findings of Wright imply that too much supervision is being given the children he studied.

At any rate, the school-age group is certainly vocal about wanting freedom from adult supervision. In this connection, the writer is reminded of a certain local model club of ten-year-olds whose principle contention about its charm is that "the mothers have nothing to do with it."

These adults, teachers, recreation leaders, ministers, rabbis, priests, and the like are intent upon bringing about in the child behavior that they consider proper. In general, they wish to bring about an increase in cooperation, a diminution of conflict, and other values of our society. The school is made up of teachers and pupils. This trite, bald statement is made in order to make clear that the school, as an institution, is relevant to the present discussion. The school, expressed through teacher practices, reflects educational philosophy and practices.

It is not within our province to examine the current and past conceptions of the school's task, but it must be mentioned that it has enormously broadened within the years of this century (*107*). At the turn of the century, the schools were dedicated to imparting certain knowledge and skills. Today, the doctrine of the "whole" child brings within its wake concern over personal, social, economic, political, and health development, and the imparting of knowledge and skills is a "minimal program."

Havighurst puts this issue in terms of developmental tasks:

> In some societies the school goes far beyond this minimal program. The middle-class part of American society uses the school for a wider variety of purposes than any other society. Since American boys and girls are thrown together in the school by age-groups, the school becomes

a place where they may learn the tasks of social development, and American educators consider the teaching of these tasks an important part of the school's responsibility. Also the American school is expected to help out other training institutions of society—the family, church, industry, youth-serving organizations—in the teaching of such diverse tasks as learning physical skills, selecting and preparing for an occupation, preparation for marriage, and learning a scale of values.

There is no developmental task of children or adolescents which the school can completely ignore, for the reason that the tasks are so closely interrelated that difficulty in one task, which may show in the school, is often tied up with difficulty in another task for which the school has little direct responsibility. For instance, failure in academic work may be due to failure in some other developmental task (44, 25–26).[6]

This becomes relevant when it is indicated that the teachers not only share this view but also are actively engaged in carrying it out in the classroom. The various ramifications of this topic could, and does, fill volumes. All that can be done here is to indicate how the teacher serves as an agent of socialization and to sample certain relevant research results which bear upon this particular influence of the teacher.

The teacher chooses certain activities in preference to others, she sets up certain standards and not others; thus, she is structuring the group. She, of course, makes her choices on the basis of her conception of what children are like, how they should behave, and what they should learn. Moreover, she makes it on the basis of her own system of values—most often that of the middle-class (43).

The teachers proceed to socialize the child using much the same methods as does the mother, as described in Chapter 4. She sets up standards of conduct to which the child is expected to conform. In addition to teaching subject matter, she performs a variety of socializing practices. For example, she helps individual children in the school group by a variety of consciously recognized devices—of creating situations in which it would be possible to see a previously objectionable child in a new role, getting a child previously ignored to contribute a talent which the other children have not recognized, helping a child to accept her as a person by accepting him as a person of worth, hoping this will lead to peer acceptance.

The teacher uses rewards and punishments in her socialization efforts (17). Not only are they used at the formal level epitomized by the "gold star" or "staying after school," but also in a variety of

[6] From Havighurst (44). Copyright 1953 by Longmans, Green and Co., and published with permission.

more subtle and much broader ways (70). In the setting of behavior-social learning theory any behavior which serves as reinforcement may work toward socialization. A nod, a frown, a smile are
means of reinforcing certain forms of behavior while attempting to
extinguish others. Martin and Stendler offer the following illustration concerning Miss A, a third grade teacher:

> Miss A's class is writing a letter to Tony who is ill at home. Miss A
> walks up and down the aisles supervising the children's work. She stops
> at Pete's desk and picks up his paper.
> "Boys and girls," she says to get the attention of the group. "May I
> have your attention? That means you too, Matilda. This is Pete's
> paper. I want you to notice how carefully Pete has followed my direc-
> tions. See? He has left margins at both sides and has written the head-
> ing exactly right. See how neat and clean his paper is, too?"
> Miss A returns Pete's paper with a beam of approval and goes on. She
> stops at Raymond's desk. Raymond does not fare so well. "Boys and
> girls." Again the heads go up. "Look at Raymond's paper. Raymond
> needs some help. See the smudges and spots on his paper? What can
> we tell Raymond to help him improve?"
> "He should wash his hands before he starts and not erase," say the
> children.
> The teacher returns the paper to Raymond with a look of disapproval.
> "It will have to be done over, Raymond, and that's wasting paper, you
> know."
> Some of the children finish their letters and must wait for all to finish.
> Several sit and do nothing. Miss A comments to the class.
> "I like the way some people are finding jobs to do when they finish.
> I saw two children studying spelling and one boy doing his workbook.
> That's using time wisely, isn't it, boys and girls? You'll have five more
> minutes to finish and I expect all of you to be done, if you haven't been
> dawdling" (70, 415).[7]

The material the teacher selects in her teaching also influences the
socialization process—the examples she uses with approval or disapproval, the events she talks about, and the textbooks she uses.
Textbooks supply material for the development of academic skills
and certainly none bear the title *Socialization: Grade 3*. Nevertheless, they also influence socialization.

Child, Potter, and Levine (19) analyzed the contents of a considerable number of third-grade readers according to motivational
categories applied to the characters involved in the stories. The
theoretical background was that of behavior-social learning theory,
in that reinforcements and punishments expressed in the stories were

[7] From Martin and Stendler (70). Copyright 1953 by Harcourt, Brace and
Company, and published with permission.

analyzed on the assumption that rewarded behavior would tend to increase the likelihood of similar future behavior, whereas punishment would tend to decrease similar future behavior. There was unequivocal evidence that certain motives were encouraged and others discouraged. Seeking help, information, or friendship were rewarded, but being aggressive, independent, or avoiding blame were punished. In general, the investigators concluded that the stories were of a sort which would encourage adjustment to our society. They went on to indicate, however, that they tended to be unreasonably optimistic (good behavior is always rewarded and children are rarely asked to adjust to failure of any sort) and failed to encourage independent behavior. However, this may reflect our own confused value-system and we cannot blame the textbooks. They can do no more than reflect society, not lead it.

Individual differences in personality among teachers are almost as great as those to be found among their pupils. The only reason for even as much restriction as the previous remark implies is that their predominately middle-class background, specific choice of teaching as a profession, some degree of similarity of education, the predominance of women in the profession, and related factors presumably make for at least somewhat less variability than would be found in their pupils. Nevertheless, there is still a tremendously wide range of personality variation.

A topic of particular interest in this connection is the issue of teachers who show personality maladjustments. A considerable body of opinion has developed which would allege that if a teacher's personal adjustment is poor, her pupils also will show signs of maladjustment. Gladstone (32) made an analysis of the available data and reaches the conclusion that there is no necessary relationship between maladjustment in the teacher and maladjustment in her pupils. It would seem that both adjusted and maladjusted teachers can bring about pernicious effects upon their pupils. More important than any fuzzy concept such as general adjustment appears to be her empathy with, and acceptance of, children. These qualities are not confined to "adjusted" teachers only. Indeed, some teachers with emotional difficulties may be especially sensitive to particular kinds of problems in their students. Others, of course, release their pent-up aggression upon their hapless pupils. Not the presence or absence of maladjustment, *per se*, but the form the maladjustment takes should be the criterion of fitness to teach.

Several studies have been concerned with the question of teachers' attitudes toward the behavior problems they encounter. In one such study Thompson (99) asked 500 teachers and 42 psychologists, along with other groups, to rank the seriousness of various forms of behavior problems. Table 25 presents the relevant results. A rank of "1" means the most serious in their opinion, a rank of "2" the next most serious, and so on. The ratings of parents and pupils resembled

TABLE 25

ATTITUDES OF TEACHERS AND CHILD PSYCHOLOGISTS TOWARD BEHAVIOR PROBLEMS *

	Average Rank Order of Seriousness of Behavior, as Rated by		
Behavior Problems	2500 Children, Parents, and Teachers	500 Teachers	42 Psychologists
Stealing	1	2	11
Cheating	2	3	16
Untruthfulness	3	1	14
Disobedience	4	6	21
Cruelty	5	16	5
Destroying school property	6	11	18
Bullying	7	14	10
Impertinence	8	7	19
Resentfulness	9	5	9
Domineering	10	10	12
Obscene notes	11	18	20
Truancy	12	23	17
Defiance	13	12	13
Masturbation	14	20	22
Overcriticalness	15	17	15
Unsocialness	16	4	2
Suspiciousness	17	21	4
Heterosexual activity	18	22	23
Depression	19	13	1
Sensitiveness	20	9	6
Shyness	21	8	7
Fearfulness	22	19	3
Dreaminess	23	15	8
Puppy love	24	24	24

* Adapted from Thompson (99). Copyright 1940 by the American Psychological Association, and published with permission.

much more those of the teachers than they did those of the psychologists. The teachers rank the following as the most serious problems— untruthfulness, stealing, cheating, unsocialness, impertinence, and disobedience. Psychologists, on the other hand, while agreeing about unsocialness, stress the seriousness of depression, fearfulness, suspiciousness, cruelty, and sensitiveness, while ranking almost all of those stressed by the teacher as of no great importance. It is evident that teachers were defining seriousness in terms of a moralistic viewpoint, with stress on aggressiveness against persons and property. Many of the problems the teachers placed as most serious were, in one way or another, challenges to her authority in the classroom. Evidently, seriousness was equated with seriousness as a threat to her smooth-running functioning of the classroom. The child psychologists had a different frame of reference, being much more concerned with behavior they knew had an ominous implication for the child's future emotional and personal development. The withdrawing type of symptom, unsocialness, as well as depression, suspicion, fearfulness, and sensitiveness have been demonstrated to be most difficult to overcome in treatment and sometimes to be the precursors of a more serious form of maladjustment. There was, however, one point of agreement—that concerning unsocialness. In a very similar study by Wickman (106) more than 12 years before that of Thompson, there was not even this much resemblance between the opinion of teachers and mental hygiene specialists. It may be that to a slight degree teachers are showing greater appreciation of mental hygiene concepts.

Nevertheless, it is somewhat disturbing to see how little appreciation of the seriousness of certain forms of behavior problems in children this sample of teachers showed. Perhaps, some comfort may be derived from the fact that this sample, though newer than Wickman's, is at the time of this writing 18 years old! Before these results are interpreted as too critical of the teachers' attitudes, it is worth while to indicate that if the teacher is to do her job of communicating skills and values, this can be done only in an orderly environment. The aggressive child disrupts the class, the withdrawing child at least does not do this.

Pupil's Evaluations of Teachers and of School

Since teachers are the visible symbols of school, it is not too far-fetched to include, in the presentation to follow, information we have about attitudes of children toward school in general and teachers in particular. There is no question that entrance into school is a stirring experience, whether favorably received or not. Let me quote Murphy and his associates on this point:

> Entrance into the conventional first grade marks a sharp break in the actual structure of the child's experience. For the first time in the case of many children, they are expected to conform to a group pattern imposed by an adult who is in charge of too many children to be constantly aware of each child as an individual. Flash cards are flashed at the group all at once. Stories are told and everybody must listen whether he will or no. Drawing paper and crayons are meted out whether you happen to feel like drawing at that moment or not. One child who found this shift quite beyond endurance remarked after his first day in school, "It's awful; all you do is mind all day long." And another day he added, "It really is awful. All you do is sit and sit and sit" (78, 652).[8]

This new pattern of conformity expected of the child is often softened by a somewhat less rigorous atmosphere in the modern school, but the teacher, no matter how progressive, cannot be aware of all the children at once. Group, not individual, methods must be used. Many children find entrance to school to be a pleasurable experience while others do not. Children come to school with different expectancies. Some view it suspiciously, are reluctant, and prepared to dislike it and all that it stands for.

A child's feelings about himself are at least partially related to his parents' attitudes. This was demonstrated in earlier chapters and does not need to be belabored again. The child, accepted by his parents and motivated to learn what they have to teach, will generalize this situation to the teacher in school (8). The child may see the teacher as a mother substitute and, if he receives the same acceptance from her that he does at home, will readily accept her teachings. He will be confident and eager to learn. If he is not so motivated, learning in school becomes less attractive and less necessary.

One of the sources of difference in attitudes is social class. The resultant attitudes are a function of the teacher, the pupil, and his parents. As a broad generalization later to be qualified, upper- and middle-class children are favorably disposed, while lower-class children in varying degrees are not favorably disposed toward school. In reviewing a series of studies on the subject of social class (43), it was found that the social environment is essentially middle-class

---

[8] From Murphy, Murphy, and Newcomb (78). Copyright 1937 by Harper and Brothers, and published with permission.

in its values. It follows that holding these values means that the teachers reinforce the attitudes and habits taught in middle-class homes.

Middle- and upper-class parents often display a marked interest and favorable attitude toward scholastic success. They may reward scholastic success by tangible steps, such as presents and trips. The child himself sees the effect of education upon the success of friends of the family and relatives and neighbors who have gone into activities for which education has prepared them. So the prospect of future rewards reinforces pressures from the family. Lower-lower class parents view education with suspicion and distrust, very often actively rejecting its values. The lower-class peer group reinforces these negative attitudes toward education. As Davis (23) indicates, the child from the slum is taught by his gang to view education as a trap, not to be taken in by the teacher and the disgraceful nature of doing homework. If by some mistake he were to get good grades, this must be concealed at all costs. Lower-class children find contradictions between what they have been taught at home and what they are taught in school. These weaken tendencies of liking school and the teacher in most pupils in this group, while strengthening it in others. Some may turn to school for what the family cannot teach them, but a greater number reject school. In upper-lower class groups parental interest is somewhat greater although not to the extent that it is in the upper- or middle-class groups (45, 46). They see it as a means of vocational preparation perhaps, but do not believe in education *per se*.

In a sample of middle-class children, Stendler and Young (95) found that starting school gave them feelings of being "grown-up" and important. After three months they still liked school very much. After three months in school, the mothers on interview were asked whether their children liked school more, the same, or less than when they started. They found 47 per cent liked it more, 48 the same, and only 5 per cent liked it less.

Stendler (94) found through interview of first grade mothers that almost 100 per cent of upper and upper-middle class parents sent their children to preschool, while only 14 per cent of lower-lower class parents did so. She showed that economic circumstances alone cannot be the cause of the difference. Similarly, parental expectations for schooling go down as one descends the social ladder. More upper- and upper-middle class mothers prepared their children for first grade by teaching at home the alphabet and the beginnings of reading and writing than did the other groups. Higher standards were expected in the higher groups. That these attitudes communicate themselves to the children there can be no doubt. Milner (74) administered measures of reading readiness, and found that children from middle-class families were better prepared for reading than were children from lower-class families. These differences, it is obvious, temper the attitudes of children toward school and teachers differentially.

There are, of course, other sources of differences of evaluation of school and teachers. Sources of differences extending over the gamut of psychological characteristics by which we distinguish one child from another all may affect attitudes toward school. Social factors will be important. For example, the nature of the child's reception by the peer group in school will undoubtedly influence his attitudes. Similarly, his self-concept, as already determined by experiences prior to school, will bring him to school receptive either to a favorable or an unfavorable attitude. It will be remembered from the account in Chapter 10 that Merrill-Bishop found that when children were placed with a "neutral" stranger, if their mothers were restrictive and, hence, produced aggression in their children, they behaved aggressively toward the strange woman. This was in contrast to the nonaggressive children who continued their nonaggressive behavior. Their behavior toward the mother consistently generalized to other adults. Presumably, this includes behavior toward the teacher.

Attitudes at home in their interplay with school behavior are maintained as the school years go on. Hartshorne, May, and Shuttleworth (42), in the course of an extensive study of moral character, had occasion to administer a series of tests of honesty to pupils in grades five through eight. They used two summary measures that are relevant here—(1) a combined honesty measure; and (2) an integration score which had to do with the stability of these measures, that is, the degree to which one was stable or consistent in honesty from test situation to test situation in the classroom. These measures were obtained in two school populations. Population Y is located in a small town with a fairly stable population; population Z is the underprivileged, slum section of a large city. Population Y is the more favored in intelligence, emotional stability, and cultural and economic background. In the pupils drawn from that population, the correlations of age with honesty and with integration although low were significant. In other words, the pupils tended to become both more honest and more integrated in classroom behavior as they grew older. Children in population Z showed the opposite tendency with correlations with increasing age being negative. As they grew older these children became more dishonest and more inconsistent. In the first group, presumably pressure from home and neighborhood and school worked together; in the second group, they probably were at odds with one another.

Relevant to the school age are many other important issues. Two are chosen for exposition. These are the qualities of teachers which pupils like and their views of the teachers' dispensing of approval and disapproval.

In the course of a more extensive investigation, Jersild (52) asked children in grades one through twelve what the characteristics were of the teacher they liked best. They reported that these teachers showed certain (1) human qualities, such as being kind, sympathetic, and considerate; (2) disciplinary qualities, such as being fair, consistent, and not scolding; and (3) performance as a teacher, through being helpful and interesting. Attractive physical appearance, grooming and voice, unimportant for the youngest group, was mentioned as a quality by children from the fourth grade onward. The youngest group in the first three grades stressed participation in activities, such as joining in games. Adults were asked to recall their teachers they had liked best, and substantially the same pattern was found, except for more stress on the human qualities. It would appear that most of the children and adults were probably of middle-class status.

From the pupil's point of view, teachers distribute approval and disapproval in a consistent, but unfair manner. A "Guess Who" technique was used by deGroat and Thompson (25) to find those pupils to whom the teacher gave approval and disapproval. The nominations were consistent in showing that a few children received most of the teacher's approval, and another small group the burden of his disapproval. Moreover, a recheck, five weeks later, showed a correlation of 0.80 in the two inquiries into teacher approval-disapproval. The pupils receiving the greatest teacher approval were the most intelligent, showed the highest academic achievement, and had the best personality adjustment as measured by a personality questionnaire. Whether the approval or disapproval the teacher gives, as described in the previous section, is actually assimilated, Martin and Stendler (70) indicate is dependent upon the relationship between the teacher and the pupil. If there is acceptance of the teacher by the pupil, if the learning situation is a rewarding one, then he learns from her. If it is not a rewarding one, he does not. It is not only what the teacher teaches that is important, but also what the pupil finds rewarding enough to learn. Learning, in this instance, takes place in an interaction between teacher and pupil.

Pupil-Teacher Interaction

The already familiar study of conflict in preschool children by Jersild and Markey (53) will be used to introduce the question of pupil-teacher interaction. The role of the teacher in the conflicts of the children was studied. They found that teachers injected themselves into about one-third of the children's conflicts. In many instances, the teacher did so before the children had ceased their struggles. Less frequently, but still fairly often, she stepped in *after* the children had ceased their conflict, either to renew the issue in an effort to bring about a compromise solution or to reverse the decision the children had reached. Often this took the form of giving the advantage to the child who had lost, thus depriving the victor of what he had gained. In about 70 per cent of the occasions in which she stepped in, the teacher decided definitely in favor of one child or the other. Almost always, the decision was against the child who had been the aggressor. It is significant to add that he often interferred in situations so mild that they could not be construed as either dangerous or one-sided for the children concerned. It is quite possible that, in these instances, the children would have been better off if left to their own devices.

Another finding was the tendency of the teacher, irrespective of the severity of the problem, to use the same bland methods. Since mild and severe problems were handled alike, it made it difficult for the child to distinguish between what was a grave trespass upon the person or rights of others and something which was relatively innocuous in nature. Consequently, the practice of differential severity on the part of the teachers is urged by Jersild and Markey.

In some school groups there has been found to be a substantial relation between the extent of fighting and quarreling with one's peers and aggressive, resistant acts directed by the children toward the teacher. This was also a finding of Jersild and Markey (53). However, they found this relation to vary from group to group. In their three groups the correlations between frequency of conflicts with other children and frequency of conflicts with teachers were 0.47, 0.08, and 0.73. Over-all, for the three groups combined, the correlation was 0.28. In the second group in which the correlation was lowest, there were certain distinguishing characteristics. In this group the children were the oldest, they had the least conflicts among themselves, and teachers interfered the most when conflicts between children occurred. These findings, although not definitive, would tend to indicate that these factors may be important in influencing the nature of pupil-teacher interaction. We do know that the attitude of the teacher affects this interaction. The particular situation effects the patterns of aggression and related behavior.

This question of the effect of the particular situation upon the patterns of aggression was investigated by Thompson (*100*). He equated two groups of four-year-old children for IQ, socio-economic status, and ratings by teachers on general personality characteristics. With one, a nursery school group, the teachers, although understanding and interested, were somewhat aloof and allowed the children to plan their own activities to a considerable extent. In the other group, the teachers were much more cooperative, maintained a great deal of personal contact, and to a much greater degree helped to guide their activities. The teachers shared equal time in both groups and the equipment used was identical, thus controlling the effect of these factors. After eight months of this experience, the children in the more highly guided group were found to be more ascendant, more constructive when faced with possible failure, and higher in social participation and in leadership. They were also less destructive. Teacher guidance, when it has certain goals, can bring about these goals by the kind of behavior adopted. Positive gains in social maturity seem indicated when the teachers adopt certain attitudes.

Also illustrative of the effect of teacher attitudes in their interaction with their pupils is an experiment by Trager and Yarrow (*102*) in which substantial changes in attitude and behavior were found in one group of first and second grade children which did not appear in another. With 14 sessions in each, two contrasting procedures were followed. In one group the adult leader accepted status differences and worked toward creating an atmosphere of intergroup understanding. Comparable groups of control children had comparable sessions without the intercultural content. Changes were measured through projective devices both before and after the sessions and through systematic observations during the sessions. They indicated changes in the children's responses in the direction of the atmospheres established by the leaders.

In the investigation of teacher behavior, a guiding theme of a considerable number of investigators (2, 3, 4, 5, 6, 7, 61, 63, 64) has been that teachers' behavior in working with children may be related to a contrast between a dominating or authoritarian attitude on the one hand, and a socially integrated or democratic one on the other. These investigators related these contrasting attitudes to the behavior shown by the children, stressing the greater growth value, greater productivity, cooperation, and engagement in integrative-democratic procedures.

A series of studies was conducted by Anderson and his associates (2, 3, 4, 5, 6, 7). Dominative behavior was said to be shown by teachers who used force, commands, threats, bribes, shaming, and insistence upon conformity in dealing with their pupils. They resist differences or change, thus being rigid or inflexible (3). In integrative behavior, in contrast, they are alleged to be yielding to other persons, finding with them common purposes and, consequently, to be spontaneous and flexible. Anderson and his colleagues proceeded to study the relationship of teachers' dominative or socially integrated behavior to their pupils' behavior. They hypothesized that (1) integrative behavior in one person tends to increase similar behavior in others; and (2) dominative behavior, likewise, tends to bring about dominative behavior in others (4). Although these hypotheses were also investigated in the interrelationship of child with child, for example, (2), present concern is with teacher-pupil relationships.

In collaboration with Anderson, Brewer (6), using an observational technique, made records of dominative and integrative behavior in two second grade rooms in the same elementary school. Assignment to one room or the other had been by lot, minimizing the possibility of systematic differences between the children in the two rooms. The teacher in one room was found to be consistently more integrative; the other was found to be consistently more dominative. The comparison of the behavior of the children under these contrasting teachers forms the basis of reporting the results of their study. The children with the more integrative teacher showed considerably more spontaneity in offering suggestions, in expressing appreciation, in making social contributions, and in telling of their own experiences, upon invitation by the teacher. The children under the more dominative teacher not only showed less of the behavior just described, but they also were more distractible and wasteful of time and nonconforming to teacher domination. The investigators considered that their hypotheses were verified—integrative behavior and dominative behavior in the teachers induced corresponding behavior in their pupils. However, differences between the teachers were not significant for *spontaneous* offering of suggestions and in telling of their experiences. Since the "integrative" teacher was selected as being responsive, the fact that they proved she was responsive is hardly surprising.

Reed (7), in following up Brewer's two teachers with new classes a year later, found that they and their new pupils repeated their contrasting performances of the year before. Meanwhile, the pupils Brewer had studied had moved on to new teachers in the third grade. With their new teachers the children's behavior showed practically a zero correlation with their behavior a year before, attesting to the great (and fortunate) flexibility of children. Their behavior in the classroom seemed highly dependent on the behavior of their teachers. If presented with integrative behavior by their teacher, children respond with similar behavior; if they meet dominative behavior from their teachers, they become distractible and resistant. These results are interpretable in terms of behavior-social learning theory. As Mussen and Conger indicate:

> These findings seem quite consistent with what we would expect on the basis of a reinforcement theory of learning. The integrative teacher, like the dominative one, has the responsibility for teaching the child to behave in a socially acceptable and constructive fashion. But the integrative teacher does so in ways which make socially constructive responses rewarding. As a consequence, the child is motivated to learn these responses because they also satisfy his own needs. Furthermore, the integrative teacher has a broader conception of what constitutes socially acceptable behavior than the dominative one. Thus she views fewer of the child's spontaneous responses as requiring elimination or modification than does the dominative, authoritarian type of teacher (80, 396).[9]

Procedures and findings closely related to those just cited have been obtained by Lewin, Lippitt, and White (61, 63, 64). Kurt Lewin, himself a refugee from Nazi Germany, was interested in the question of the relative psychological effects of authoritarianism and democracy. He and his collaborators first conceived of their prob-

[9] From Mussen and Conger (80). Copyright 1956 by Harper and Brothers, and published with permission.

lem in terms of a contrast between authoritarian and democratic conditions in a fashion quite similar to the dominative and integrative conditions of Anderson. Later, they made the significant advance of reaching the conclusion that they were dealing not with a bipolar, but with a tripolar relationship in the behavior of groups under different kinds of leadership. In addition to authoritarian and democratic leaders, they discovered another pattern of leadership, that of the laissez-faire leader. He may be described essentially as a benevolent bystander, somewhat akin to the aloof teacher in the study of Thompson (100). The laissez-faire group leader has more than an accidental similarity to the teacher in extremely "progressive" school settings since, as it will be found, the "democratic" teacher does not give up her adult responsibility and authority, the relinquishment of which is the most conspicuous characteristic of the laissez-faire leader or teacher.

The study to receive detailed consideration was performed by Lewin, Lippitt, and White (61, 64). Four comparable groups of ten-year-old boys were studied, each of which passed successively through three club periods in such a fashion that, for all four groups combined, there were five democratic periods, five autocratic periods, and two laissez-faire periods. Personality differences were controlled by having each group pass through democratic and then autocratic leadership, or vice versa. Transition periods from one kind of atmosphere to another and from one leader to another were provided. Leadership factors were controlled by having each of the four group leaders playing both the autocratic and the democratic role at least once. Careful observational check showed that they were successful in modifying their behavior to fit their particular role of the moment. The physical setting for the club meetings was the same throughout. Prior to the formation of the groups, the boys in the setting of the larger group from which they were drawn were studied by sociometric techniques to find rejections, friendships, and leadership. Teacher ratings and observations were also made. The groups were then equated on these findings. Activities, such as mask making, mural painting, and model airplane construction, were selected to be carried on during the sessions by arranging the democratic clubs to meet, first to decide what to do through a discussion with the leader and then having the authoritarian leaders dictate these same activities to their clubs; at the same time supplying to the laissez-faire leaders the entire range of materials the others had used from which the boys were expected to make their own choice as to what they wished to use. These three different ways of selecting the materials aptly catches the differences among the three atmospheres they were creating in the groups. The roles and methods of the leaders in creating these group atmospheres, agreed upon in advance, are those given in Table 26.

The effect of these atmospheres upon the behavior of the boys was obtained from observation of the club sessions and individual interviews with the children, their parents and teachers, and administration of Rorschach tests. We are now in a position to consider their findings.

Group morale was decidedly higher in the democratic groups than in either the autocratic or laissez-faire groups (64). By morale, they meant spontaneous group cohesion—the working together toward common goals with sense of "we," rather than "I," and with a friendliness, rather than hostility toward other group members. Spontaneous, in this context, meant that this cohesiveness rose from the attitudes of the boys themselves, rather than cohesiveness being induced by the leader. Several types of quantitative findings demonstrate this. The democratic groups used "we" as compared to "I" in their speech more than did the autocratic-submissive group, made more friendly remarks to one another than did any of the other groups, and expressed less discontent either to the leader or to one another. When compared to the laissez-faire group, more spontaneity was shown in their continuing activity in the task at hand when the leader deliberately left the room and in the length of time devoted to the activity.

Two reactions to autocracy were found, not just one. There was an aggressive, self-centered irritability in some groups and a submissive, dependent apathetic reaction in others. In either reaction to autocracy the boys showed less spontaneous group cohesiveness.

There were three major reasons for group disruption in autocracy. Especially important in the aggressive reaction to autocracy (as distinguished from the submissive reaction) was what they called "restricted space of free movement." This restriction pertained to the orders, the strictness which "fenced in" these children, so that they complained the leaders were too strict and did not permit them to do what they wanted to do. In the submissive autocratic reaction, the boys gave up and, hence, ceased to be frustrated by this restriction in itself. But this came about only by surrendering independence and autonomy. In this connection, one is reminded of one of the major reactions in adults to the effects of a concentration camp.

TABLE 26

THE ROLES AND METHODS ADAPTED TO CREATE GROUP ATMOSPHERES *

Authoritarian	Democratic	Laissez faire
1. All determination of policy by the leader	1. All policies a matter of group discussion, encouraged and assisted by the leader.	1. Complete freedom for group or individual decision, without any leader participation.
2. Techniques and activity steps dictated by the authority, one at a time, so that future steps were always uncertain to a large degree.	2. Activity perspective gained during first discussion period. General steps to group goal sketched, and where technical advice was needed the leader suggested two or three alternative procedures from which choice could be made.	2. Various materials supplied by the leader, who made it clear that he would supply information when asked. He took no other part in work discussions.
3. The leader usually dictated the particular work task and work companions of each member.	3. The members were free to work with whomever they chose, and the division of tasks was left up to the group.	3. Complete nonparticipation by leader.
4. The dominator was "personal" in his praise and criticism of the work of each member, but remained aloof from active group participation except when demonstrating. He was friendly or impersonal rather than openly hostile.	4. The leader was "objective" or "factminded" in his praise and criticism, and tried to be a regular group member in spirit without doing too much of the work.	4. Very infrequent comments on member activities unless questioned, and no attempt to participate or interfere with the course of events.

* From Lewin, Lippitt, and White (*61*). Copyright 1939 by The Journal Press, and published with permission.

The lack of aggression in the autocratically led, apathetic group was not due to a lack of frustration, as shown by the sharp rise of aggression when the autocratic leader left the room, the outbursts of aggression on the days in which there was a transition to a freer atmosphere, other indices of generalized apathy, such as lack of smiling and joking, and the fact that more children disliked their autocratic leader much more than their later or earlier democratic or laissez-faire leader.

The second major finding was the way the autocratic groups, especially the submissive ones, gave up free and easy sociability among themselves. For example, child-to-child conversation was lower in general, and discussion of "nonclub" centered activities even smaller in comparison to these activities in the democratic groups. The investigators interpreted these findings on sociability as a transfer from one aspect of the club, its leadership, to the group itself and the work in which it was engaged. Thus, there was what they called a spread of dissatisfaction. The third factor they found was a sharp division into two portions of the boy's psychological field—the portion belonging to the leader and the portion belonging to the boy himself and to the boys collectively. What was perceived in one field was sharply separated from what was perceived in the other. Specifically, the boys saw it "as what *he* (the leader) wants me to do, and what *I* want to do." In contrast, in the democratic group, the boys identified with the leaders and what "*we* want to do" was the result. This finding was verbalized in the democratic groups as the leader working right along "with them."

In the laissez-faire groups, group disruption centered on one of the same factors which was evident in the autocratic group. Restricted space of free movement again appeared, but this time in the forms of restriction by ignorance of what to do and by the absence of accomplishment on the part of the boys. The boys wanted to be workmanlike and to work together, but they could not since they lacked leadership. Although there was a lot of "group-minded" conversation directed to the tasks at hand in the laissez-faire groups, it was fruitless in that they could not carry through to completion because of lack of guidance. They verbalized the leader's behavior as "too easy-going." The second factor in the laissez-faire groups was referred to as a need for "clearness of structure" which most of the boys seemed to need. The uncertainty, the chaos, and the confusion in their club meetings made them uneasy—"he let us figure out things too much." The third factor in the laissez-faire groups was the already familiar vicious circle of frustration leading to aggression, which in turn leads to further frustration, and then further aggression, in endless fashion.

Group goals, in terms of accomplishment, were influenced by the various atmospheres. The masks made in the democratic atmosphere were said to be of higher quality than those produced in the other atmospheres. Work was initiated or continued in the democratic group even when the leader was "late" or left the room. An authoritarian leader arriving late would find no work started, and when he left the room, work dropped considerably.

As Mussen and Conger (80) indicate, a caution must be offered that these results cannot be generalized to all children. These studies, it must be remembered, were performed with boys who, for the most part, were from democratic homes. Cues from the democratic atmosphere were familiar and accepted by them. Therefore, the authoritarian atmosphere would be more frustrating. However, if they had been children from authoritarian homes, it is quite possible they might have found that this atmosphere was easier for them to cope with. In fact, the one boy who preferred authoritarian leadership was the son of an Army officer who liked that leader because "he was strictest." Consequently, we cannot generalize these results to all groups or individuals or under all conditions. Even more important, as Sechrest (92) indicates, these studies have not demonstrated that there is more than a situational effect. Both groups of investigators showed that the children could shift rapidly in behavior when moved from one atmosphere to another. Neither group showed that the changes they found were permanent, or that they generalized to other situations. Without such effects being demonstrated their results may or may not be of much consequence. If verified and extended their findings would have obvious implications for our school settings, showing the dangers both of "old-fashioned" authoritarianism in a setting of no whispering and sitting-up straight and of the anarchy of laissez faire where the teacher is only a benevolent spectator in an effort to be "progressive" in education. This laissez-faire role is but a caricature of progressive education, similar in spirit to those cartoons which picture the child as a little destructive monster with the adult in the cartoon standing helplessly by (generally with a book labeled *Child Psychology* clutched in hand.) A truly democratic leader or teacher gives assistance and direction, while allowing freedom of action only within the limits of the child's capabilities to handle this freedom.

The latency period

Discussion of sex tendencies in later childhood has been deferred until this point because of its obvious relevance to the current topic of the latency period. In a setting of peer relationships and related problems, these tendencies will now be considered. A neo-Freudian interpretation of latency will follow.

Sex Tendencies and Peer Relationships

At the preschool level, the differences in behavior of boys and girls were noted. Development during the years of later childhood continues and sharpens these differences. An increase in greater social centering of these tendencies is prominent. Their social cast now becomes much more pronounced. Sex cleavage existed even before the latency period, as discussion in an earlier chapter indicated. But essentially these differences in social behavior were somewhat casual and "unplanned." Boys and girls went their separate ways, but gave it no particular thought. Sometime after the middle of the present period, this cleavage becomes conscious and ritualized. They deliberately shun one another, rather than having it happen more or less "naturally." Virtually all boys, for example, go through a period in which they vehemently reject all females (with the honorable exception of the mother), perhaps going so far as to swear celibacy till death. Girls, although finding the boys that they know "horrid," still manage to keep a romantic vision of a Prince Charming, along with an interest in love stories and movies which their brothers indignantly dismiss as trash.

There are characteristic patterns of social relationships between and among boys and girls during the latency period. This was clearly brought forth by Campbell (16) in her account of an observational study made in the setting of recreational clubs, whose memberships were made up of the "alumni" of a large, well-known nursery school. The groups they formed, the relationships between boy and girl groups that they established, the kinds of relationships (or lack of it) between individual boys and girls all were largely a matter of choice on the part of the children. Her summaries for boys and girls, respectively, follow:

A. Social-Sex Development of the Boy

1. Youngest Stage (Ages 5–8)

A boy at this stage will play with a group otherwise made up entirely of girls, because he is not yet conscious of sex differences, nor is he embarrassed to be found in such a group. He does not object to having adults of either sex show physical affection for him. He is not yet modest as to posture, gesture, clothing, etc. He does not differentiate games according to sex. He shows no protective habits toward women and girls. When in a game not involving physical skill, he is not inclined to choose his own sex over the other. He fights physically with girls. He is not yet self-conscious or embarrassed by physical contact with girls. He is careless of his personal appearance. Work is work to him, and he does not regard any one kind of work as suitable to boys and another as suitable to girls. The concept of "sissy" is still to be discovered. He is not concerned with girls as attractive creatures. On the whole, he prefers women to girls; at least, women who play with him. He is in a creative period in handicrafts and keeps very busy, and is not tempted to leave his work to play with girls, as he will be later.

2. Middle Period (Ages 9–14)

At this stage the boy is found playing pursuit games with girls, such as informal tag games indoors. So much attention he will pay to girls, but in general he shows no interest in what they are doing and even in games not involving physical skill he prefers boys on his "side." When allowed to choose, he always sits next to boys rather than girls. He will not join in a game in which he is the only boy, but must have other boys with him when he plays with girls. Toward the end of the period he becomes sufficiently conscious of sex so that he does not wish to touch girls or show them any attention except under socially approved conditions, such as in games or dancing. If he finds himself in a group of girls, he leaves quickly. Still later in this period he begins a teasing derogatory kind of talk about his friends who have girls, with the intention of "fussing" the boy in question. He is extremely self-conscious and modest about the physical aspects of sex and would not for the world undress or go to the toilet before girls or even women, except where the relationship is parental. . . .

B. Social-Sex Development of the Girl

1. Youngest Stage (Ages 5–8)

The girl of these ages is perfectly willing to play in groups composed entirely of boys. In choosing sides in games not involving physical skill she has no particular preference for one sex over the other. She is not yet modest about physical matters, will sit in any posture without embarrassment, show her underclothes, and go to the toilet where boys are. She is not embarrassed in a group of boys, as she will be later. She pays no attention if a boy touches her. She likes to have either men or women show physical affection for her. She is careless about her personal appearance, even when with boys. It has never occurred to her that tasks should be allotted on sex lines.

2. Middle Period (Ages 8½–12½)

In this period the girl shows no interest in what boys are doing merely because they are boys. She will not stay long in a group of boys if she is the only girl. In choosing sides she is likely to choose girls unless it is a game involving physical skill, when she may choose a boy in the interests of victory. She prefers men to boys. She sits next to girls if given a choice. She will not participate in an activity unless other girls are included. She will invite men to sit next to her, but never boys. She begins to be sufficiently conscious of sex so that she will not deliberately touch boys except under conventional circumstances, as in games or dancing. She classifies games according to sex—boys play this, girls play that.

Later she enters the "whispering period" with her girl contemporaries. She is shyer with a group of boys than with a single boy. If she dances, she prefers to dance with other girls. She would not admit that a certain boy is attractive to her, though she begins to take a covert interest. By this time she is modest about exposing her body and underclothing before boys—probably more so than she will ever be again. She is sufficiently conscious of the sex attraction of clothes to admire the clothing of women and her girl friends. She begins frankly to enjoy dancing (*16*, 523–526).[10]

Her results give a vivid picture of the patterns of social relationships in the latency-aged child. However, a caution must be offered that patterns of social interaction among boys and girls may vary greatly with socio-economic status and other variables. It is very evident that the groups Campbell described are those composed of middle-class children. Patterns in other classes probably differ in some measure.

Her results also bring out vividly that when we are talking about latency period phenomena of a sexual nature, we are emphasizing the latter half from about age nine onward. This will be the case with the evidence and opinions which follow.

Extent and nature of sex behavior. Some socially approved forms of behavior indicate interests in sex. Much of teasing and tussling going on among boys and girls is a crude form of amorous play. Under the ritualized content of games, such as Post Office, there is

[10] From Campbell (*16*). Copyright 1939 by The Journal Press, and published with permission.

a sexual undercurrent. By and large, however, their sexual behavior is not of a self-evident or obvious sort.

The child's interest in sex may not be as submerged as parents and other adults think. Awareness of their disapproval may result in his keeping his thoughts and actions to himself. There is a considerable amount of socially hidden sex behavior occurring in children of these ages as Kinsey and his associates (54) show in their studies of sex behavior. This behavior may take the form of tentative heterosexual exploration, but such behavior may include deviations from heterosexual behavior. Kinsey *et al.* show that among boys from ages five to ten the incidence of all sexual play increased from 10 per cent to over 35 per cent, with both heterosexual and homosexual incidents in evidence. For many of the children, activities of this sort were limited to a single experience. Some had much more extensive experience, since a third of the males continued sexual play of heterosexual or homosexual sort for five years or more. They conclude that this play did not extend further than it did because of cultural restraints.

Cultural pressures and sex differences. Quite apart from social relationships between the sexes and actual sex practices, the process of socialization concerning sexual matters shows itself through some of the social pressures which exist.

Cultural pressures from adults for differentiated behavior of boys and girls continue during these years. In a cross-cultural study akin to those by Whiting and Child described in Chapter 1, Barry, Bacon, and Child (13) made a search of reports of primitive societies for evidence of differential treatment of the sexes. In terms of indulgence in infancy, the judges agreed in finding no evidence of sex differences. But in childhood there was considerable evidence that among these societies there was a widespread pattern of pressure on girls for greater nurturance (helpfulness), obedience, and responsibility; and greater pressure on boys for self-reliance and achievement strivings (high standards of excellence in performance).

The formation of more and deeper friendships with children of the same sex, reported in discussing this topic earlier, is an indication of the sharpening sense of sex awareness. These mutual attractions between members of the same sex may be interpreted in terms of behavior-social learning theory. Reinforcement by adults, parents, teachers, and others is given in our society for association with, and imitating the behavior of, individuals of the child's own sex.

Differences in school achievement in which girls excel boys (97) may be related to cultural expectations. Girls are expected to be more interested in writing, reading, and arithmetic, whereas boys are expected to be more aggressive toward teachers and not interested in school subjects. Of course, there are large and varied exceptions, but no one can deny that scholarship is occasionally confused in the peer group with being a "sissy," as witness the lower-class group studied by Pope (87).

Even textbooks may be used for sex-socialization purposes. The texts analyzed by Child and his associates (19) referred to in connection with the school-aged child, portrayed females as sociable, kind, timid, easily frightened, unambitious, and uncreative. Heroes are invariably boys or men; females have unimportant roles. Girls satisfy their needs by passive dependence or by rivalry with overtones of rather emotional immaturity; nor is there a realistic appraisal of natural relationships between the sexes. Presumably what is read by children is still another source of differential socialization of the sexes—with most of the advantages going to the male.

Children's opinions about sex differences. An ingenious study by Smith (93) demonstrates that opinions about sex differences held by boys and girls show a progressive change with age. He found that both boys and girls have a progressively better opinion of boys and a progressively poorer opinion of girls, as age increased from 8 to 15 years. He asked 100 boys and 100 girls at each of these ages to vote whether boys or girls possess to a greater degree each of 19 desirable and 14 undesirable traits. The questions were in the form "Who are . . . kinder to animals (bossy, selfish, honest, generous, good sports) . . . boys or girls?" In graphic form the curve, with increase in age for the boys, shows that the proportion favoring their own sex for more possession of desirable traits and less possession of undesirable traits combined is steadily upward; for girls the curve is steadily downward. Each sex thought better of its own than of the other sex, but by age 14 girls think almost as well of boys as they do of themselves. There are, of course, exceptions, such as being bright in school or kind to animals, in which both boys and girls are overwhelmingly of the opinion that girls excel. Nevertheless, the results show that, for the traits included, boys and girls both have a progressively higher opinion of boys and a progressively lower opinion of girls.

Tuddenham (104) using the "Guess Who" technique in the first, third, and fifth grades shows that social acceptability as seen by the boys and girls he studied conforms to the expected picture of sex differences. He says of his results:

> The picture of the typical boy and girl as conceived by children even in the primary grades seems to be almost a photostat of the common identification by adults in our society of aggressiveness, restlessness, and daring with masculinity, and of amiability, docility, and timidity with femininity (104, 19).[11]

Sex differences in recreational interests. During the school years, sexual behavior has the characteristic social orientation of these years. However, our culture restricts severely manifestations of behavior of a directly and narrowly sexual nature. Consequently, some of the manifestations of sex to be discussed are the emerging sex differences in psychological areas other than the narrowly sexual. These will be illustrated by discussion of sex differences in recreational interests.

In a masterly survey of sex differences in general, Terman and Tyler (97) included discussion of differences among boys and girls in recreational interests. Although such interests as these are subject to superficial changes based on momentary fads, the findings, most of which were collected some years ago, are still of concern. Terman and his associates had developed a masculinity index based on the pursuit of various activities by boys and by girls of elementary school age. The masculine activities, more or less in order of descending masculinity, were using tools, shooting, playing with kites and marbles, wrestling, boxing, football, baseball, fishing, garden work, basketball, swimming, rowing, hunting, racing, coasting, hiking, riding, playing checkers, chess, and billiards. A line of neutrality occurred at this point and included such activities as Red Rover, follow the leader, croquet, volley ball, dominoes, snap, and cards. As for the characteristically feminine activities from least to most feminine they were Jackstraws, post office, fox and hounds, tennis, authors, tag, hide and seek, solving puzzles, jackstones, skating, drop the handkerchief, ring around the rosy, London Bridge, farmer in the dell, cat and mouse, jumping rope, guessing games, charades, dancing, sewing, playing store, knitting, playing school, cooking, playing house, hopscotch, dressing-up, and dolls. The most im-

---

[11] From Tuddenham (*104*). Copyright 1952 by the American Psychological Association, and published with permission.

mediately obvious feature of this list is the predominance of strenuous activities at the masculine end of the listing.

Lehman and Witty (57) found similar results and, in addition, found that boys more often engage in competitive and more highly organized games than did girls. Games become more and more clearly sex-linked as age increased until the ages of about eight-and-a-half to ten-and-a-half, the period during which the social separation among boys and girls is at its greatest.

Sex differences are also reflected in the reading, movie and radio listening interests (97). Although not particularly different in percentages of books read of an informational or classical sort or in fairy tales and legends, boys predominantly read stories of adventure, while girls read stories of home or school life or what was described as "emotional" fiction. Boys almost never read girls' books but boys' books were sometimes read by girls. As might be guessed, girls read more than boys. Similar tastes to those just described were shown in radio listening and in movies.

A Neo-Freudian Interpretation of Latency

According to psychoanalytic theory, the latency period follows the highly sexually charged phallic stage. The Oedipus situation was supposed to have resulted in repression of sexual interests. Latency is supposed to be a period of relative quiescence with a reduction of sexual interests, and, consequently, of considerably less dynamic interest than the psychosexual stages, so far as the effects of events occurring during this period are concerned. They are of less significance for the formation of personality than are the earlier stages or the later stage of adolescence. Consequently, there has been a relative neglect of these years by orthodox psychoanalytic workers. Relatively few articles have appeared concerned with latency or its effects. The neglect can be made specific by citing the fact that Munroe (76), in an authoritative account of psychoanalytic schools of thought, devotes less than two pages to the latency period out of the 330 which she devoted to Freud. According to the index, no other direct reference to latency is made anywhere in the volume.

Whether the repressions of the Oedipus situation are responsible for events in the latency period is a disputed question. In Chapter 10 evidence was offered which tended to cast doubt on the omnipresence of the Oedipus situation. In keeping with that earlier discussion, emphasis would then be placed upon social pressures preventing too open manifestations of sexual interests during the school years. Certainly, sex interests and sex play are not given up during the latency period.

The psychoanalytic description of the latency period is not too inaccurate a description of the public sex behavior of latency-aged children in our culture. But as we have seen from previous discussion, everything is not quite as serene and asexual as it appears. An active sex life may be still very much present.

The latency period is not a universal phenomenon. Malinowski (68), in his study of the Trobriand Islanders referred to in Chapter 10, has given us an instance of a society in which genital sexuality continues during the so-called latency period. There were no moral sanctions and no adult authority against sexual behavior. Sexual behavior gradually became more direct and "adult" as the child grew older with no break in the continuity. Consequently, it was individual temperament which decided a child's behavior in this sphere. There was no evidence of latency. Other primitive societies show similar attitudes. In the Mohave, Devereux (26) attributes the absence of latency to the tolerant attitudes of adults toward sexuality in the child.

Cultural determinants of the presence or absence of the latency period seem evident. In our culture, emphasis is upon a suppression of the specifically sexual aspects of masculine and feminine behavior during the age span with which we are concerned. As Devereux (26) indicates, it is the presence, not the absence, of the latency period which needs explanation. Its appearance seems to be due to socialization pressure present in major segments of our society.

Sullivan (96) emphasizes cooperation and competition as part of normal development in what he calls the juvenile period. This comes about because the child has now reached the age where he can view his peers with some objectivity and thus is able to develop these tools of social living. It is an age when children try out their abilities and gain or fail to acquire self-confidence and self-reliance.

With Thompson (98) the writer is in agreement that, in addition to disapproval of sexual interests, there is a widening of the social horizon during this age period. The child's school and play interests absorb him in the world of his contemporaries. With this widening, sexual interests may assume less importance simply because his scope of interest has widened.

Perhaps, Freud himself was coming to a more culturally oriented interpretation in his later years. In an autobiographical study (30) originally published in 1935, he comments that, although latency is a maturational phenomenon, it can lead to a complete interruption of sexual behavior only in a culture which has suppression as a part of its way of life. It can perhaps be argued that no culture can succeed in carrying through this suppression completely. At any rate, Hartmann, Kris, and Loewenstein (40), after quoting Freud on the matter above, proceed to discuss a variety of psychoanalytic topics in cultural perspective. It is significant that they at least consider themselves as working within an orthodox psychoanalytic framework.

Latency, insofar as it occurs, would appear to be learned, as the evidence adduced earlier suggests. This conclusion is reinforced by evidence from endocrinology. No shift in endocrine balance has been observed during these years (82). Instead, the concentration of hormonal substances (androgens and estrogens) shows a progressive rise throughout childhood to a peak at puberty. There is no qualitative change from the phallic age to the latency period to adolescence—only this progressive rise.

We have attempted throughout this chapter to show what is happening to children during these years. In general, the years appear important for the formation of social relationships. In their formation, events of infancy and early childhood have contributed their share, but events happening during latency itself, too, have their effect. Orthodox psychoanalytic formulation for these years in the concept of the latency period seems to minimize unduly this extremely important age period.

General evaluation of orthodox psychoanalytic formulations

It is now appropriate to present a general evaluation of psychoanalytic formulations of personality development. It is appropriate at this point because of the limitation of the age span considered in this book. Adolescence and adulthood are ages beyond its scope. Hence, a summing-up is now offered.

Psychoanalytic hypotheses are in crying need of systematic research verification. Lack of research personnel and skills and attitudes, the demand for treatment, and the position that clinical find-ings do not require research verification help to account for this paucity of research. Research is deterred because of the general nonoperational terms in which findings are stated and the amorphous-ness of the theory which makes coming to grips with it very difficult. The sheer complexity and subtlety of this theory are both a challenge and a deterrent. Often research done on some small segment can be cogently criticized by the psychoanalysts either as not paying sufficient attention to, or as not showing adequate understanding of, other related aspects of psychoanalytic theory. Often, research critical of the position can be dismissed as irrelevant or immaterial by those sufficiently acquainted with psychoanalysis as a theory and as a clinical approach. The fact remains that frequently psycho-analytic propositions are stated in a manner incapable of proof or disproof.

Often what is demonstrated by controlled research which is con-cerned with psychoanalytic hypotheses is not crucial to psycho-analytic theory. Miles puts this matter cogently.

It may be said, for example: "According to psychoanalytic theory, the girl at this stage loves her father more than she loves her mother, and therefore this thing will happen in my sample of her behavior." It does happen. But does not the theory, in its controversial aspects, the really interesting ones, say: "The girl loves her father more than she does her mother *because* she has sexual desires toward her father *because* she blames her mother for her lack of a penis?" The greater love of the girl for her father, while it may have been pointed out as a fact by the origi-nator of the theory, is not the theory itself. The theory **is not only that it is so, but why it is so.** In fact, is not the reason the real theory? That it is so, that she loves her father more than she does her mother, might be in accord with other theories that would have different reasons to offer. On at least one occasion, the psychoanalytic theory stated that the girl may love her father more than her mother for the simple reason that masculinity is preferred by femininity naturally, or, that the male appeals most strongly to the female, at any age, or at any rate as soon as the developing organism can be said to be female psychologically, or in so far as the female organism has femininity. This would mean that sexual preference and ambivalence could be a simple matter of the dominant and subordinate sexuality of the organism. . . .

Evidence may be found that boys, especially at certain ages, fear loss of the penis, or that girls resent fancied loss of the penis. This evidence is then taken as "support for the psychoanalytic concept of the castration complex." But is not the essence of that concept not merely that there is such a fear, but rather the part that such a fear plays in the formation of character, relative to other fears? Probably no one would deny that to most men loss of the penis would actually be the greatest loss, and therefore, a fearful thing to contemplate, and a danger to be habitually alerted to. But "the psychoanalytic theory" referred to assumes, does it not, in the first place that this fear is the only one worth considering in the boy? It is true that Anna Freud rebuked Henry Murray . . . for saying that, but other fears seem in practice to get short shrift. It is *the* reason for the boy's identification with the father, for example. And the theory assumes in the second place, does it not, that the boy fears this loss because of his sexual desires toward the mother? It is necessary to ask what the evidence has shown about these components of the concept.

It is difficult to see what will be gained for genetic theory by repeatedly showing facts about the relationship of traits of character to complexes about infantile oral, anal, and phallic experiences, without relating them to controversies about the origin of the traits, and about the meaning of the complexes. Contentions about the origin of either, and about the part that either plays in the formation of character appear to be the essence of the theories. To show that stubbornness, retentiveness, miserliness and the like are associated with anal complexes is not to present evidence that those traits, viewed as strategic or defensive relationships to the world, are the result of thwarting or overindulgence of the partial sexual instinct about which there is a complex, and solely of that. It has been shown only that those causes or conditions which engender retentiveness, or stubbornness, are also likely to engender anal complexes, since the trait and the complex are found together with greater frequency than would be expected by chance. A single exception would refute the theory that an anal complex is a necessary or the only sufficient condition for the development of the trait in question. Even if no such exception were found as, say, a pathological miser with no anal complex, that would be evidence that the anal complex was necessary, not that it was sufficient (73, 245–246).[12]

Freud's influence upon child psychology involves a paradox. More than any other man his work has made us recognize the importance of the influence of family members upon the child's development. And, yet, in his own theoretical framework, its influence is given a subordinate, almost incidental place. A serious neglect chargeable against orthodox psychoanalysis is its neglect of the influence of learning on development. This is expressed not only in neglect in learning in its narrow sense, but also learning as expressed in socialization and culture. The constitutional factor has been emphasized over environmental ones. Even the external events considered, such as castration anxiety, are supposed to produce relatively fixed and inevitable results.

What has Freud contributed to our knowledge?   The writer knows of no more sweeping and acute summing-up than that offered by Gardner Murphy in discussing the current impact of Freud upon psychology.   What he has to say he says for child psychology as well.

. . . first, the specification of drive; second, the conception that life tendencies are deeper, more primordial then the phenomenon of consciousness, which is at best an elaboration or screening technique which can in no way obliterate or weaken the basic drive modulations; third, as James Harvey Robinson said, the discovery that, "as children, we are at our most impressionable age"; fourth, the conception that the ego is a derivative rather than a primary expression of life; and fifth, most general of all propositions, that all psychological activity is motivated, driven, guided, directed by life tensions seeking resolution.   It is in this latter sense that psychoanalysis is a consistently dynamic psychology.   It begins with force and ends with the dissipation of force through a tension-reducing process always to be followed by fresh tension accumulations and further discharges.   Every idle fancy, every quick calculation, every odd remark, every whim and every great decision alike, spring basically from the tensions of the tissues within us (77, 664).[13]

To be sure, he goes on to say that child psychology has so far only been influenced by psychoanalysis in a relatively limited way. What has been presented in this book is an attempt to show the relevance of psychoanalysis to child psychology.

Whatever the eventual outcome of psychoanalytic formulations of personality development, they have had and will continue to have a profound effect upon thinking and studying and working with children.   To what extent they will be assimilated into child psychology as a science is a solution of the future, not of the present. But that it will be assimilated in the course of its modification is certain.

Summary

In the years of later childhood, the child spends relatively more time outside of the home than he did in his earlier years.   It is no wonder, then, that these years are referred to as the peer group age

[13] From Murphy (77).   Copyright 1956 by the American Psychological Association, and published with permission.

and the school age. Their further designation as the latency period is in keeping with psychoanalytic contention.

Prior to the peer group age, as an infant and as a preschool child, the child's contacts with peers were primitive and crude. Nevertheless, even during infancy, he moved from passivity to a sufficiently high level of social contact in which there was necessity for reciprocal adjustment to other infants. During early childhood social participation increased in versatility and complexity: some children emerged as leaders, the variety and nature of conflict among children increased, and they became capable of sympathetic behavior.

The peer group serves as a means whereby the older child finds some independence from parental restrictions as well as finding himself in relation to the social group. Social acceptability, friendships, and cooperation and competition are used for illustrative purposes. During the peer group age, as age increases constancy of social acceptability goes hand in hand with shifts in characteristics making for this social acceptability. What makes for social acceptability is found to vary at different socio-economic levels. Peer group age friendships are found to rest upon propinquity and similarities in nonintellectual factors rather more than in intellectual ones. Greater stability of friendships with increasing age is found. Reflecting society's stand, cooperation and competition are found to exist side-by-side in children. Both cooperation and competition were clearly manifest in the preschool years and may well have had their beginnings in infancy. Competition is more intense in lower socio-economic groups than it is in other groups. Whether competition or cooperation is stronger in children in general is, in a sense, a pointless question. Relative strength of competition or cooperation when either or both are possible depends upon the situation and the child.

The influence of the peer group is shown by the fact that there is a stable (although not pronounced) relationship between the way a child perceives himself and, in turn, the way his peers perceive him. Self-acceptance and the acceptance on his part of his peers are both positively related to popularity. The ideal self of younger peer group age children is relatively fanciful, but, as they grow older, their conceptions of the ideal self become more realistic. This change in views on the ideal self demonstrates vividly the influence of socialization pressures.

Race attitudes and awareness are used to illustrate social perception of the peer age child. It was found that race awareness appeared early and increased with age. The relation of race awareness to the behavior of the peer age group was demonstrated.

The school age child has the teacher as the prime agent of socialization. However, other adults in the community who are leaders of groups in which he participates also impose standards on the child. The teacher brings pressures to bear upon the child through her reflection of the school's philosophy and through her reflection of her own background. To further these socialization aims she helps children, uses rewards and punishment, and selects material for teaching purposes.

Pupils react variously to these pressures from teachers and other adults. Nevertheless, social class differences are found—upper- and middle-class children are more favorably disposed toward school and lower-class children are less favorably disposed. Other factors are also shown to influence the evaluation the child makes of school and of his teachers.

Pupil-teacher interaction was found to take many forms. In the instance of conflicts among pupils, teachers were found to inject themselves, sometimes arbitrarily and not always without what may be unhealthful results. Dominating (authoritarian), socially integrated (democratic), and laissez-faire attitudes on the part of the teachers and other group leaders were found to have dramatically different effects upon the characteristic behavior of the children in these group atmospheres. The same children, shifted from one group atmosphere to another, showed changes of behavior congruent with the particular atmosphere.

Turning to the older child conceptualized as going through the latency period, sex tendencies were found to be now more related to the ones shown by the peers of the child than was the case when he was younger. Characteristic patterns of social relationships of boys and girls at various ages were sketched in order to show changes with age in relation to their social groups. Sex behavior and interest are not as submerged during the so-called latency period as conventional opinion would have it. The cultural pressures which help to create and perpetuate differences between boys and girls are considered. Even children's opinions about sex differences show the effect of these pressures. Discussion of sex differences in recreational interests, showing progressive changes with age, closes the section.

The psychoanalytic description of the latency period, it is agreed, is not too inaccurate a description of the public sex behavior of children of this age. However, the period is neither as serene nor as asexual as might be expected. Differential cultural pressures make for differences among children in different groups. Latency, it would appear, is more culturally determined than the orthodox psychoanalytic interpretation would have it. Sheer learning is found to be very important in establishing the characteristics of children of this age.

A general evaluation of orthodox psychoanalytic formulations closes the chapter. Many of the phenomena of childhood have been illumined by psychoanalytic hypotheses. Many of the forms of behavior and experience in childhood are compatible with their views without, however, excluding the possibility of other interpretations. Very little in the way of crucial research has appeared which would prove unequivocally that their views are valid and opposing views are invalid. The relative neglect of the influence of learning is the most serious charge that can be made against orthodox psychoanalytic contentions. The assimilation of their positive contributions into the main stream of child psychology has begun, and will continue.

For Further Reading

Much more than others L. Joseph Stone and Joseph Church in their book, *Childhood and Adolescence* (New York: Random House, 1957), have captured a child's-eye view of these years. Based on their intimate acquaintance with children rather more than on accounts of research findings, the book gives a realistic, but empathetic view of the struggle of growing-up.

References

1. Altman, Charlotte. Relationships between maternal attitudes and child personality structure. *Amer. J. Orthopsychiat.*, 1958, 28, 160–169.
2. Anderson, H. H. Domination and integration in the social behavior of young children in an experimental play situation. *Genet. Psychol. Monogr.*, 1937, 19, 341–408.
3. Anderson, H. H. Domination and social integration in the behavior of kindergarten children and teachers. *Genet. Psychol. Monogr.*, 1939, 21, 287–385.
4. Anderson, H. H., and Anderson, Gladys L. Social development. In L. Carmichael (Ed.), *Manual of child psychology* (2nd ed.). New York: Wiley, 1954.

5. Anderson, H. H., and Brewer, H. M.   Dominative and socially integrative behavior of kindergarten teachers.   *Appl. Psychol. Monogr.*, 1945, No. 6.

6. Anderson, H. H., and Brewer, J. E.   Effects of teachers' dominative and integrative contacts on children's classroom behavior.   *Appl. Psychol. Monogr.*, 1946, No. 8.

7. Anderson, H. H., Brewer, J. E., and Reed, Mary F.   Studies of teachers' classroom personalities: III. Follow-up studies of the effects of dominative and integrative contacts on children's behavior.   *Appl. Psychol. Monogr.*, 1946, No. 11.

8. Ausubel, D. P.   Ego development and the learning process.   *Child Develpm.*, 1949, 20, 173–190.

9. Ausubel, D. P., Schiff, H. M., and Gasser, E. B.   A preliminary study of developmental trends in sociempathy: accuracy of perception of own and others' sociometric status.   *Child Develpm.*, 1952, 23, 111–128.

10. Austin, M. C., and Thompson, G. G.   Children's friendships: a study of the bases on which children select and reject their best friends.   *J. educ. Psychol.*, 1948, 39, 101–116.

11. Baldwin, A. L.   The effect of home environment on nursery school behavior.   *Child Develpm.*, 1949, 20, 49–62.

12. Baldwin, A. L., Kalhorn, Joan, and Breese, Fay H.   Patterns of parent behavior.   *Psychol. Monogr.*, 1945, 58, No. 268.

13. Barry III, H., Bacon, Margaret K., and Child, I. L.   A cross-cultural survey of some sex differences in socialization.   *J. abnorm. soc. Psychol.*, 1957, 55, 327–332.

14. Bonney, M. E.   The constancy of sociometric scores and their relationship to teacher judgments of social success, to personality self-ratings.   *Sociometry*, 1943, 6, 409–424.

15. Buhler, Charlotte.   The social behavior of children.   In C. Murchison (Ed.), *Handbook of child psychology* (2nd ed. Rev.).   Worcester: Clark University Press, 1931, 374–416.

16. Campbell, Elise H.   The social-sex development of children.   *Genet. Psychol. Monogr.*, 1939, 21, 461–552.

17. Campbell, Nellie M.   The elementary school teacher's treatment of classroom behavior problems.   *Teach. Coll. Contr. Educ.*, 1935, No. 668.

18. Challman, R. C.   Factors influencing friendships among preschool children.   *Child Develpm.*, 1932, 3, 146–158.

19. Child, I. L., Potter, E. H., and Levine, Estelle M.   Children's textbooks and personality development; an exploration in the social psychology of education.   *Psychol. Monogr.*, 1946, 60, No. 279.

20. Clark, K. B., and Clark, Mamie P.   Racial identification and preference in Negro children.   In T. M. Newcomb and E. L. Hartley (Eds.), *Readings in social psychology*.   New York: Holt, 1947, 169–178.

21. Criswell, Joan H.   A sociometric study of race cleavage in the classroom.   *Arch. Psychol., N. Y.*, 1939, No. 235.

22. Criswell, Joan H.   Social structure revealed in a sociometric retest.   *Sociometry*, 1939, 2, 69–73.

23. Davis, W. A.   *Social class influences upon learning*.   Cambridge, Mass.: Harvard University Press, 1948.

24. Davitz, J. R.   Social perception and sociometric choice of children.   *J. abnorm. soc. Psychol.,* 1955, 50, 173–176.
25. deGroat, A. F., and Thompson, G. G.   A study of the distribution of teacher approach and disapproval among sixth grade children.   *J. exp. Educ.,* 1949, 18, 57–75.
26. Devereux, G.   The primal scene and juvenile heterosexuality in Mohave society.   In G. B. Wilbur and W. Muensterberger (Eds.), *Psychoanalysis and culture.*   New York: International Universities Press, 1951, 90–107.
27. Doob, L. W.   *Social psychology.*   New York: Holt, 1952.
28. Dymond, Rosalind F., Hughes, Anne S., and Raabe, Virginia L.   Measurable changes in empathy with age.   *J. consult. Psychol.,* 1952, 16, 202–206.
29. Fite, Mary D.   Aggressive behavior in young children and children's attitudes toward aggression.   *Genet. Psychol. Monogr.,* 1940, 22, 151–319.
30. Freud, S.   *An autobiographical study.*   London: Hogarth, 1936.
31. Furfey, P. H.   Some factors influencing the selection of boys' "chums."   *J. appl. Psychol.,* 1927, 11, 47–51.
32. Gladstone, R. D.   Do maladjusted teachers cause maladjustment?   A re-review.   *J. except. Child.,* 1948, 15, 65–70.
33. Goodenough, Florence L.   Anger in young children.   *Univ. Minn. Inst. Child Welf. Monogr. Ser.,* 1931, No. 9.
34. Goodman, Mary E.   *Race awareness in young children.*   Cambridge, Mass.: Addison-Wesley, 1952.
35. Green, Elise H.   Friendships and quarrels among preschool children.   *Child Develpm.,* 1933, 4, 237–252.
36. Green, Elise H.   Group play and quarreling among preschool children.   *Child Develpm.,* 1933, 4, 302–307.
37. Greenberg, Pearl J.   Competition in children: an experimental study.   *Amer. J. Psychol.,* 1932, 44, 221–248.
38. Harding, J. et al.   Prejudice and ethnic relations.   In G. Lindzey (Ed.), *Handbook of social psychology.*   Cambridge, Mass.: Addison-Wesley, 1954.
39. Hartley, E. L.   *Problems in prejudice.*   New York: King's Crown Press, 1946.
40. Hartmann, H., Kris, E., and Loewenstein, R. M.   Some psychoanalytic comments on "culture and personality."   In G. B. Wilbur and W. Muensterberger (Eds.), *Psychoanalyses and culture.*   New York: International Universities Press, 1951, 3–31.
41. Hartshorne, H., May, M. A., and Maller, J. B.   *Studies in the nature of character: II. Studies in service and self-control.*   New York: Macmillan, 1929.
42. Hartshorne, H., May, M. A., and Shuttleworth, F. K.   *Studies in the organization of character.*   New York: Macmillan, 1930.
43. Havighurst, R. J.   Child development in relation to community social structure.   *Child Develpm.,* 1946, 17, 85–90.
44. Havighurst, R. J.   *Human development and education.*   New York: Longmans, Green, 1953.
45. Havighurst, R. J., and Breese, Fay H.   Relation between ability and social status in a midwestern community: III. Primary mental abilities.   *J. educ. Psychol.,* 1947, 38, 241–247.

46. Havighurst, R. J., and Janke, L. L.   Relation between ability and social status in a midwestern community: I. Ten-year-old children.   *J. educ. Psychol.*, 1944, 35, 357–368.

47. Havighurst, R. J., Robinson, Myra Z., and Dorr, Mildred J.   The development of the ideal self in childhood and adolescence.   *J. educ. Res.*, 1946, 40, 241–257.

48. Horowitz, E. L.   The development of attitude toward the Negro.   *Arch. Psychol., N. Y.*, 1936, No. 194.

49. Horowitz, E. L., and Horowitz, Ruth E.   Development of social attitudes in children.   *Sociometry*, 1938, 1, 301–338.

50. Horrocks, J. E., and Buker, Mae E.   A study of the friendship fluctuations of preadolescents.   *J. genet. Psychol.*, 1951, 78, 131–144.

51. Horrocks, J. E., and Thompson, G. G.   A study of the friendship fluctuations of rural boys and girls.   *J. genet. Psychol.*, 1946, 69, 189–198.

52. Jersild, A. T.   Characteristics of teachers who are "liked best" and "disliked most."   *J. exp. Educ.*, 1940, 9, 139–151.

53. Jersild, A. T., and Markey, Frances V.   Conflicts between preschool children.   *Child Develpm. Monogr.*, 1935, No. 21.

54. Kinsey, A. C., Pomeroy, W. B., and Martin, C. E.   *Sexual behavior in the human male.*   Philadelphia: Saunders, 1948.

55. Landreth, Catherine.   Factors associated with crying in young children in the nursery school and in the home.   *Child Develpm.*, 1941, 12, 81–97.

56. Landreth, Catherine, and Johnson, Barbara C.   Young children's responses to a picture and inset test assigned to reveal reactions to persons of different skin color.   *Child Develpm.*, 1953, 24, 63–80.

57. Lehman, H. C., and Witty, P. A.   *The psychology of play activities.*   New York: A. S. Barnes, 1927.

58. Leuba, C.   An experimental study of rivalry in young children.   *J. comp. Psychol.*, 1933, 16, 367–378.

59. Levy, D. M.   *Maternal overprotection.*   New York: Columbia University Press, 1943.

60. Lewin, K.   Experiments in social space.   *Harvard Educ. Rev.*, 1939, 9, No. 1, 21–32.

61. Lewin, K., Lippitt, R., and White, R. K.   Patterns of aggressive behavior in experimentally created "social climates."   *J. soc. Psychol.*, 1939, 10, 271–299.

62. Lindzey, G., and Borgatta, E. F.   Sociometric measurement.   In G. Lindzey (Ed.), *Handbook of social psychology.*   Cambridge, Mass.: Addison-Wesley, 1954, 405–448.

63. Lippitt, R.   An experimental study of the effect of democratic and authoritarian group atmospheres.   *Univ. Iowa Stud. Child Welf.*, 1940, 16, No. 3.

64. Lippitt, R., and White, R. K.   The "social climate" of children's groups. In R. G. Barker, J. S. Kounin and H. F. Wright (Eds.), *Child behavior and development.*   New York: McGraw-Hill, 1943, 485–508.

65. Lippitt, Rosemary.   Popularity among preschool children.   *Child Develpm.*, 1941, 12, 305–332.

66. Macfarlane, Jean W.   Study of personality development.   In R. G. Barker, J. S. Kounin and H. F. Wright (Eds.), *Child behavior and development.* New York: McGraw-Hill, 1943, 307–328.

67. McKee, J., and Leader, Florence B. The relationship of socio-economic status and aggression to the competitive behavior of preschool children. *Child Develpm.*, 1955, 26, 135–142.
68. Malinowski, B. Prenuptial intercourse between the sexes in the Trobriand Islands, N. W. Melanesia. *Psychoanal. Rev.*, 1927, 14, 26–36.
69. Maller, J. B. Cooperation and competition: an experimental study of motivation. *Teach. Coll. Cont. Educ.*, 1929, No. 384.
70. Martin, W. E., and Stendler, Celia B. *Child development: the process of growing up in society.* New York: Harcourt, Brace, 1953.
71. Maudry, Maria, and Nekula, Maria. Social relations between children of the same age during the first two years of life. *J. genet. Psychol.*, 1939, 54, 193–215.
72. Mengert, Ida G. A preliminary study of the reactions of two-year-old children to each other when paired in a semi-controlled situation. *J. genet. Psychol.*, 1931, 39, 393–398.
73. Miles, D. The impact for clinical psychology of the use of tests derived from theories about infantile sexuality and adult character. *Genet. Psychol. Monogr.*, 1954, 50, 227–288.
74. Milner, Esther. A study of the relationship between reading readiness in grade one school children and patterns of parent-child interaction. *Child Develpm.*, 1951, 22, 95–112.
75. Moreno, J. L. *Who shall survive? A new approach to the problem of human interrelations.* Washington, D. C.: Nervous and Mental Diseases Publishing Co., 1934.
76. Munroe, Ruth L. *Schools of psychoanalytic thought: an exposition, critique, an attempt at integration.* New York: Dryden, 1955.
77. Murphy, G. The current impact of Freud upon psychology. *Amer. Psychologist*, 1956, 12, 663–672.
78. Murphy, G., Murphy, Lois B., and Newcomb, T. M. *Experimental social psychology: an interpretation of research upon the socialization of the individual* (Rev. ed.). New York: Harper, 1937.
79. Murphy, Lois B. *Social behavior and child personality.* New York: Columbia University Press, 1937.
80. Mussen, P. H., and Conger, J. J. *Child development and personality.* New York: Harper, 1956.
81. Muste, Myra J., and Sharpe, Doris F. Some influential factors in determination of aggressive behavior in preschool children. *Child Develpm.*, 1947, 18, 11–28.
82. Neustadt, R., and Myerson, A. Quantitative sex hormone studies in homosexuality, childhood and various neuropsychiatric disturbances. *Amer. J. Psychiat.*, 1940, 97, 542–551.
83. Northway, M. L. Outsiders: a study of the personality patterns of children least acceptable to their age mates. *Sociometry*, 1944, 7, 10–25.
84. Parten, Mildred B. Social participation among preschool children. *J. abnorm. soc. Psychol.*, 1932–33, 27, 243–269.
85. Parten, Mildred B. Leadership among preschool children. *J. abnorm. soc. Psychol.*, 1932–33, 27, 430–440.
86. Parten, Mildred B. Social play among preschool children. *J. abnorm. soc. Psychol.*, 1933, 28, 136–147.

87. Pope, B. Socio-economic contrasts in children's peer culture prestige values. *Genet. Psychol. Monogr.*, 1953, 48, 157–220.
88. Radke, Marian, and Sutherland, Jean. Children's concepts and attitudes about minority and majority American groups. *J. educ. Psychol.*, 1949, 40, 449–468.
89. Radke, Marian, Trager, Helen G., and Davis, H. Social perceptions and attitudes of children. *Genet. Psychol. Monogr.*, 1949, 40, 327–447.
90. Radke-Yarrow, Marian, Trager, Helen G., and Miller, Jean. The role of parents in the development of children's ethnic attitudes. *Child Develpm.*, 1952, 23, 13–53.
91. Sears, R. R., Whiting, J. W. M., Nowlis, V., and Sears, Pauline S. Some child-rearing antecedents of aggression and dependency in young children. *Genet. Psychol. Monogr.*, 1953, 47, 135–236.
92. Sechrest, L. Unpublished manuscript.
93. Smith, S. Age and sex differences in children's opinion concerning sex differences. *J. genet. Psychol.*, 1939, 54, 17–25.
94. Stendler, Celia B. Social class differences in parental attitude toward school at Grade I level. *Child Develpm.*, 1951, 22, 37–46.
95. Stendler, Celia B., and Young, N. The impact of beginning first grade upon socialization as reported by mothers. *Child Develpm.*, 1950, 21, 241–260.
96. Sullivan, H. S. *Conceptions of modern psychiatry*. Washington: William Alanson White Psychiatric Foundation, 1947.
97. Terman, L. M., and Tyler, Leona E. Psychological sex differences. In L. Carmichael (Ed.), *Manual of child psychology* (2nd ed.). New York: Wiley, 1954, 1064–1114.
98. Thompson, Clara. *Psychoanalysis: evolution and development*. New York: Hermitage, 1950.
99. Thompson, C. E. The attitudes of various groups toward behavior problems of children. *J. abnorm. soc. Psychol.*, 1940, 35, 120–125.
100. Thompson, G. G. The social and emotional development of preschool children under two types of educational program. *Psychol. Monogr.*, 1944, 56, No. 258.
101. Thompson, G. G., and Horrocks, J. E. A study of the friendship fluctuations of urban boys and girls. *J. genet. Psychol.*, 1947, 70, 53–63.
102. Trager, Helen G., and Yarrow, Marian R. *They learn what they live: prejudice in young children*. New York: Harper, 1952.
103. Trent, R. D. The relation between expressed self-acceptance and expressed attitudes toward Negroes and whites among Negro children. *J. genet. Psychol.*, 1957, 91, 25–31.
104. Tuddenham, R. D. Studies in reputation: I. Sex and grade differences in school children's evaluation of their peers. II. The diagnosis of social adjustment. *Psychol. Monogr.*, 1952, No. 333.
105. White, R. W. *The abnormal personality: a textbook*. New York: Ronald, 1948.
106. Wickman, E. K. *Children's behavior and teacher's attitudes*. New York: Commonwealth Fund, 1928.
107. Witmer, Helen L., and Kotinsky, Ruth (Eds.). *Personality in the making; the fact-finding report of the Midcentury White House conference on children and youth*. New York: Harper, 1952.

108. Wolfle, D. L., and Wolfle, Helen M. The development of cooperative behavior in monkeys and young children. *J. genet. Psychol.*, 1939, 55, 137–175.
109. Wright, Beatrice A. Altruism in children and the perceived conduct of others. *J. abnorm. soc. Psychol.*, 1942, 37, 218–233.
110. Wright, A. F. Psychological development in Midwest. *Child Develpm.*, 1956, 27, 265–286.
111. Zelen, S. L. The relationship of peer acceptance, acceptance of others and self acceptance. *Proc. Iowa Acad. Sci.*, 1954, 61, 446–449.

part

Psychological Disturbances in Childhood

chapter 13

Psychological Disturbances
in Childhood

IT MAY HAVE BEEN NOTED THAT THE PRESENTATION OF the chapters devoted to early childhood did not include discussion of psychological disturbances. It is difficult to separate psychological disturbances in early childhood from those of later childhood. Rather than force an artificial division it was decided to consider psychological disturbances in children between the ages of two or three and twelve as one unit.

Personality disorders in childhood may be examined in several classificatory perspectives. In Chapter 8, in discussing disorders of infancy, a classification in terms of psychoanalytic psychosexual stages was one of those followed. Present discussion might continue that presentation by centering on personality disturbances in terms of the phallic stage and of the latency period. It was decided, however, to use a classificatory system based on distinction among personality disorders which still permitted psychoanalytic findings to be used.

With increasing age beyond infancy other major categories of disorders individuate from the total mass. Greater clarity and the advantage of more common clinical usage may be obtained if these generally accepted and understood categories are followed. Various other patterns of specific disorders thus emerge during childhood

605

in a sufficiently recognizable form to warrant their use as a classificatory system. In childhood it is customary to distinguish among primary behavior disorders, psychotic reactions, and psychosomatic conditions. The primary behavior disorders include neurotic traits, habit disturbances, and conduct disturbances. Psychotic reactions, the second major category to be used, are generally conceived to be of a more severe and inclusive nature than are primary behavior disorders. Schizophrenia, the major psychosis of childhood, receives special consideration in a section to follow. Psychosomatic reactions, unlike the more global and all-pervasive reactions of infancy, in childhood take on the form of relatively specific, more distinct entities. One characteristic class of psychosomatic conditions, the allergies, receives major consideration. In the child, the distinction between psychological and physical has continued to develop to such an extent that it is both convenient and customary to speak of some physical disorders as sharply distinguished from psychological ones. Crippling, a debilitating disease, or blindness are neither brought about by psychological forces nor treated directly by psychological means. Nevertheless, there is a psychological reaction to these physical conditions. Hence, there must be consideration of personality reactions to physical handicap.[1] Although reference to treatment of psychological disturbances in childhood is made more or less incidentally throughout these sections, it was considered appropriate to present psychological forms of treatment of personality disorders in a more systematic fashion. This discussion of psychological treatment closes the present chapter.

Primary behavior disorders

The so-called primary behavior disorders of childhood receive this designation because the behavior difficulties exhibited are primary, not secondary, manifestations to disorders in other classificatory groups. The same disturbances, for example, habit difficulties or anxiety states, may appear in the setting of another disturbance such as in a psychosis, but in such instances they are secondary to the psychotic states. In the difficulties now being considered, habit

---

[1] Structural or physiological alterations of the brain also produce psychological disturbances and could logically be included as an additional classificatory category. Space limitations preclude discussion.

difficulties and anxiety states stand on their own and are the disorders.

It is customary to classify the primary behavior disorders into (1) habit disturbances; (2) conduct disturbances; and (3) neurotic traits (33). Nevertheless, behavior characteristics of all three almost always appear in a particular child's functioning. A child's classification in a given category essentially depends upon the predominance of disturbances from one of these categories, not the absence of indications of the others. Despite this, for the sake of clearness of exposition, each category will be discussed as if it were relatively independent of the other two.

Habit Disturbances

Habit disturbances are behavior problems in which there has been a disturbance in the performance of major biological functions. Some manifestations of habit disturbances are already familiar from earlier considerations of disorders of infancy. Thus, infantile disturbances of feeding, elimination, and sleep have been considered. In growing into childhood either there is a continuous prolongation of infantile pleasure habits (fixation) or a reactivation (regression) of these habits after a period in which they are not practiced. These disturbances may continue essentially unchanged from infancy or they may take on new forms. Some of the habit disturbances of mouth or feeding function include thumb sucking, nailbiting, eating too much or too little, and vomiting. Disturbances in elimination include bedwetting and soiling, constipation, and diarrhea. Sleep disturbances involve, among others, inability to fall asleep and night terrors. Faulty speech development is considered to be a habit disturbance. Sexual disturbances, such as excessive masturbation, also are classified as habit disturbances.

Habit disturbances appear to be most closely related to anxiety and tension. A case described by Kanner brings out the relation of a habit disturbance, which in this instance was nailbiting, and tension and anxiety. The case follows:

Pauline B., 10 years old, had been under an enormous burden of too much home responsibility, housework, too difficult school requirements with insufficient endowment and not enough time, and fear imposed by an ignorant, superstitious mother. When relieved of some of her responsibilities, she stopped biting her nails, and there was also decided improvement in her other personality difficulties. Her pride in her appearance was easily stimulated and she wanted to let her nails grow.

Some time afterwards, a sick sister who had been in a convalescent home and her younger brother who had been away returned home and the whole burden for caring for them again fell on Pauline's shoulders, and she promptly resumed her nail biting. This happened especially when she had the task of watching her brother: "When Sonny gets away from me, I am nervous and bite my nails" (26, 536).[2]

In addition to the ebb and flow of nailbiting in relation to the ebb and flow of tension there is another important factor worth noting in this case. Pauline's habit disturbance occurred in a setting of interpersonal relations. Her difficulties centered around shifting interpersonal relations. Overwhelmed with work by school and mother she developed tension expressed in nailbiting. Relieved of some of this she stopped, but then a sick sister and the return of a brother brought back the burden and a return of the difficulty. A conflict with the environment is evident.

Although not entirely evident from the case note, it is also characteristic of many habit disturbances that they are ways of withdrawing from contact with the environment. There is a seeking of relief of tension by autoerotic activities such as nailbiting, thumb sucking, masturbation, and overeating. They serve the function of soothing the child's anxiety. To be sure there are some habit disturbances where it is less evident that this dynamic factor is at work. In vomiting, for example, an aggressive component is manifest. But, by and large, habit disturbances are to some extent soothing to the child. Maladaptive though they may be, they are attempts at a solution of his problem arising out of a conflict with his environment.

Many of these habit disturbances, especially noticeable in the preschool child, tend to decrease as the child grows older and enters school. The Macfarlane study (30) of normal children shows that habit disturbances practically disappeared as her subjects grew older. Many, if not most, children as they become more socialized no longer needed the sources of solace which habit disturbances provided. Macfarlane and her associates (30), whose work was just mentioned, were concerned with the behavior problems exhibited by a group of such children. The children, part of a long continued psychological study at the Institute of Child Welfare at the University of California, had been chosen by chance drawing from a birth certificate registry. They were *not* chosen on the basis of problems they presented. Consequently, they were representative of typical

[2] From Kanner (26). Copyright 1950 by Charles C Thomas, and published with permission.

children in their community. Both before sample shrinkage over the years and in an accentuated fashion later, the sample represented a higher socio-economic-educational level than the average of the population in general. Otherwise, they are representative of children of their age levels.

The children's first visit to the Institute was made at the age of 21 months. The mothers were questioned at that time about the problems the children showed. What constituted a problem had been agreed upon in advance by the investigators and the same sensible, but arbitrary, standards were followed consistently throughout the years of the study.

Table 27 gives the percentage of boys and girls separately who showed some of the more important problems they investigated. Data for the other problems and for other yearly intervals are contained in their detailed report (30). Inspection shows that these problems include many just discussed as habit disturbances, whereas others are conduct disturbances and even neurotic traits.

From the point of view of the reader, probably the most striking finding is the persistence, variety, and magnitude of problems these "normal" children exhibited. Practically every one of the problems reported in the table was present in a few children even at age 14. Many problems, such as excessive modesty, nailbiting, oversensitiveness, somberness, irritability, temper tantrums, and jealousy were exhibited by over 20 per cent of either the boys or girls or both.

The longitudinal changes of the findings in the table may be summarized by the following. (1) Some problems decreased with age. Early and rapid decline was shown in connection with elimination control. Somewhat later in starting to decline were speech problems, fears, and thumb sucking. Still later, overactivity, destructiveness, and temper tantrums started to decline. (2) Only one problem increased with age—nailbiting—which did not reach its peak in girls until the end of pubescence. It was still high with boys at age 14 but would have declined if the data they presented had extended beyond this age. (3) Problems reaching a peak and then definitely subsiding before age 14 were insufficient appetite and lying. (4) Other problems showed two elevations of frequency. One group showed these elevations at the preschool age and again in late pubescence—restless sleep, disturbing dreams, physical timidity, irritability, and attention demanding. For other problems the first peak was at the age of entering school and again at the beginning of adolescence—overdependence, somberness, and jealousy.

TABLE 27

PERCENTAGE OF PROBLEM INCIDENCE OF NORMAL CHILDREN *

Problem	Sex	Age in Years						
		1¾	4	6	8	10	12	14
Sleep								
Disturbing dreams	B	16	24	24	22	33	9	6
	G	13	22	35	23	47	26	4
Restlessness in sleep	B	38	2	12	9	22	13	11
	G	27	2	2	12	15	17	0
Elimination								
Nocturnal enuresis	B	75	13	9	12	11	9	11
	G	73	20	10	14	6	7	0
Eating								
Insufficient appetite	B	7	31	29	16	7	9	0
	G	10	29	37	21	9	14	0
Food finickiness	B	30	31	29	12	4	17	6
	G	37	31	51	16	9	24	4
Sex								
Excessive modesty	B	0	16	12	22	15	17	22
	G	5	24	16	5	26	21	17
Masturbation	B	9	16	6	6	4	4	0
	G	8	8	2	2	0	0	0
Motor Habits								
Nailbiting	B	5	9	12	16	18	22	33
	G	3	14	20	23	32	31	22
Thumb sucking	B	21	7	6	3	0	0	0
	G	33	27	16	12	6	2	0
Excessive activity	B	29	44	32	38	26	26	11
	G	17	35	29	16	15	2	0
Speech problems	B	30	16	12	6	11	9	0
	G	17	10	8	12	3	5	4
Social Standards								
Lying	B	0	33	53	41	15	9	6
	G	0	49	49	19	12	0	0
Destructiveness	B	14	20	24	22	11	4	0
	G	2	12	8	5	6	2	0
Personality Characteristics								
Excessive emotional	B	21	27	18	3	15	13	11
dependence	G	8	14	20	7	21	17	9
Excessive demanding of	B	20	27	9	22	26	13	0
attention	G	27	18	18	14	12	5	0

TABLE 27 (*Continued*)

Problem	Sex	1¾	4	6	8	10	12	14
Oversensitiveness	B	9	42	32	50	59	39	17
	G	18	51	53	49	38	48	52
Physical timidity	B	23	16	18	16	30	4	0
	G	25	24	31	30	24	21	13
Specific fears	B	30	47	38	34	22	17	6
	G	33	45	41	35	26	21	17
Somberness	B	0	16	26	16	18	26	6
	G	0	14	33	19	21	29	22
Irritability	B	16	18	9	9	15	13	11
	G	3	24	16	7	12	10	4
Temper tantrums	B	59	53	59	53	44	39	22
	G	43	47	51	28	32	29	9
Jealousy	B	30	29	24	44	41	44	22
	G	20	22	26	28	35	31	22

* Adapted from Macfarlane *et al.* (*30*). Copyright 1954 by the University of California Press, and published with permission.

(5) One problem showed no definite progression with age—oversensitiveness. With girls it stayed high throughout the ages studied; with boys it remained high until age 11, at which time it dropped dramatically.

Although the children of the Macfarlane study (*30*) were randomly selected from birth records, any random sample would include some children who would become disturbed as they grew older. Hence, some of the children in this group were disturbed individuals. But there is considerable evidence that this cannot be the case with the great majority of the children in this group.

Sometimes it is thought that for the child to be normal he must have no problems. According to this view, by definition, a normal child has no problems. It has just been shown that this is emphatically not the case. Normal children show problems differing only in relative mildness, infrequency, and lack of patterning from children who are considered nonnormal or disturbed.

Conduct Disturbances

The term, conduct disturbances, commonly brings to mind aggressive, destructive, delinquent behavior. Developmentally, conduct disturbances become manifest at a later age than habit disturbances. Later childhood and adolescence are the ages where conduct disturbances assume prominence. After all, conduct disturbances require a level of psychomotor maturity requisite for attacking the environment and which is lacking until this age. Speaking in general and, therefore, in crude terms, the child showing a conduct disturbance is attempting to meet his needs through coercing his environment. There may be a background of parental hostility. If present, it is argued that there is no reason for the child to submit to restraint in learning to live with others. In the words of Ackerman, "it does not . . . pay the child to inhibit his infantile impulses" (*1*, 214).[3] The child defends himself against parental deprivation or rejection by direct aggression. In common with habit disturbances, the conduct disturbances indicate that the child is experiencing a conflict with the environment both within the home and outside of it.

Neurotic Traits

In contrast to habit and conduct disturbances, with their focus on conflict of the child with his environment, neurotic traits are at least partially internalized and show a conflict with the self. Jealousy, inhibition of aggression, and phobias are three characteristic neurotic traits. Jealousy of a sibling is especially prominent. Inhibition of aggression makes the child appear self-effacing and timid, not ready to stick up for his rights. Phobias take manifold forms: fear of animals, of the dark, of strangers, or of certain places are illustrative.

It can often be elicited by careful clinical investigation that there is conflict present when these traits occur. In jealousy the person is torn between knowing he should love the person in question and yet not loving him. In inhibition of aggression the child wants to strike out at someone but cannot do so. In phobias the individual has hostility toward someone, most often his parents, which he cannot express directly and, since he anticipates retaliation, he develops

[3] From Ackerman (*1*). Copyright 1953 by Grune and Stratton, and published with permission.

a fear of a symbol of that parent. Still infantile, though now a child in years, his urges are only partly restrained, and yet the superego is in the process of formation. Fear of parental hostility is displaced elsewhere on thunder, the dark, or the bogeyman. Some external object is the symbol of the developing superego which is not yet fully internalized. Psychoanalytically speaking, all children have phobias. They are characteristic phenomena of the phallic stage. They disappear when the emotional conflict is solved. English and Pearson report a child who solved his particular emotional conflict most dramatically:

> He got out of bed in the middle of the night, shot the bear that troubled him and was no longer troubled by a phobia of bears. In reality he had apparently acquired enough courage to admit and play out his hatred of his father. These phobias are not prognostically serious but are what Freud calls "the normal neurosis of childhood" (*19*, 131–132).[4]

From a developmental point of view, neurotic traits are not yet organized into a pattern of personality. Some authorities would not only accept the category of neurotic traits as one aspect of primary behavior disorders, but also go beyond and consider the psychoneuroses as another independent major category of personality disturbances in childhood. The psychoneuroses are distinguished from the neurotic traits of a primary behavior disorder since there is a structured pattern of pathology expressed in such labels as anxiety hysteria, conversion hysteria, obsessive-compulsive neuroses, and hypochondriac neuroses. Because the presence of a psychoneurosis is taken to imply a high level of organization of personality, it is generally agreed that its appearance is not as common or as characteristic in children as it is in adults. It would take us too deeply into pathology for us to consider here these psychoneurotic constellations in any detail.

Two difficulties characteristic of the latency stage (*19*) will be used to discuss further neurotic traits and neuroses. These are anxiety states and obsessive-compulsive reactions.

Anxiety, as we have seen earlier, is not easily defined. By its very nature it is a somewhat amorphous state. The feeling of fear is there, but fear often without an object. There is no real cause for fear, but it is present nevertheless. There is a sense of something going to happen. It is in the "air," ranging from a state of uneasiness to the screaming terror of a nightmare. It is the lost child or the adult experiencing "a world he never made" and shrinking from that world. It is also the physiological indicators, the manifest anxiety as it is called, the trembling, the sinking feeling in the pit of the stomach, restlessness, sweating, and fitful sleep.

A clue to the nature of anxiety may be obtained from the examples that English and Pearson (19) give of a child lost in the department store, the child sent away from London during the blitz, or a girl whose father is going away—all of whom show anxiety. They are not in any danger. What is the common element for these children? English and Pearson point out that for each of these children it is the separation from the person he loves and on whom he is dependent. He becomes afraid that, if separated, his needs will be unsatisfied. They go on to indicate that the child usually blames himself for the separation, regardless of the real cause. He is convinced that his feelings of loneliness upon separation are because of his doing something forbidden. The feeling of punishment generalizes so that desires for gratification, any gratification, are regarded as something forbidden expressed in consciousness as a feeling of anxiety. As English and Pearson remind us, "It's the burnt child who fears the fire." Even if the parents are loving and reasonable with the child, anxiety will occur if they are overstrict and place too high demands upon him. Anxiety results from a conflict over his need to gratify his childish impulses and the fear that, if he does, his parents will no longer love him. Anxiety is also increased by prolonged absence of a parent.

Control of impulses by the ego becomes weakened by fatigue and during sleep. Hence, anxiety attacks at night are not uncommon. In discussing this, English and Pearson consider that in our culture, with its restrictions on infantile sexuality, anxiety arises most commonly in connection with some interference with masturbation. The child tries to stop and often succeeds in doing so during the day, but the impulse gets out of control at bedtime or while he is asleep. He struggles against it while awake and, when asleep, wakens from a frightening dream. Why is it a frightening dream? It is, according to them, because the dream in symbolic form is a repetition of the threat to him which masturbation has become. The dream does not gratify his wish to masturbate, but does gratify his punitive superego and serves to stop the masturbation.

All children show some anxiety. All children meet many new

situations and new feelings which bring them pain and fear of loss. This process is a part of growing up. But if faced with excessive emotional strain (often preventable), they take a traumatic turn, as a neurotic trait or even as a full-blown psychoneurosis.

Obsessive-compulsivelike reactions are common in children of latency age. Walking (or not walking) on cracks, touching certain fence posts or telephone poles become important and absorbing. But more than that, a certain anxiety is present if a miss is made. The child may go back perhaps, as he puts it, "to avoid bad luck." Other rituals are not uncommon. Binding by some vow or another is not uncommon. Once made, they may be difficult to escape from. English and Pearson speak of experiences from their practice:

> Another girl vowed never again to tell her father anything about herself. As she grew up she found it impossible to be confidential with any man in authority, even though this attitude was detrimental to her. A boy vowed that when he grew up he would kill his father. When he did grow up he found it impossible to have a satisfactory relationship with his bosses. He either attempted to do them some injury or else he behaved toward them as if no act of theirs could ever anger him (19, 266).[4]

The child may show the same phenomena through a form of thinking about the same thing over and over, or a snatch of tune may "run through the head"—obsessive thoughts as differentiated from compulsive actions.

In explaining these phenomena in psychoanalytic terms, English and Pearson assert that sometimes the act is a symbolic expression of an inner impulse which would meet some social disapproval if openly expressed. They illustrate this with the rhyme which sometimes accompanies walking without stepping on a crack.

> "Don't step on a crack, or you'll break your mother's back." We are not certain whether this game is based on the same inner impulse—that is, hostility toward the mother—among all children who play it. To step on the crack is to injure the mother. The child uses the idea of stepping on a crack as a symbol of an inner wish and then avoids the expression of the wish by refusing to step on the crack. The impulse is displaced onto an action toward an indifferent object and then the child can avoid the action (19, 265).[4]

They close their discussion of obsessive-compulsive reaction with the encouraging (and to the reader by now familiar) note that in the child these reactions serve as a step along the road to socialization. With the skills open to his ego, he is not yet ready to control them in more realistic ways. This weakness of the ego allows the obsessive-compulsive reactions to occur in his seeking to avoid painful feelings of guilt. With greater maturity, the child will no longer need these reactions to cope with similar situations.

Relations among the Primary Behavior Disorders

The primary behavior disorders are mutually interrelated. This is true in the sense of overlap among symptoms previously mentioned, but more importantly, they show an interrelation because they are fundamentally related reactions to stress. Moreover, they form the substratum for the development of more structured disorders such as the psychoneuroses and psychoses. Ackerman puts it so cogently that a quotation is in order. He writes:

> All primary behavior disorders are conceived as a reaction to an unfavorable environment. A child attempting to cope with hostile, depriving parents can react in one of several ways:
> 1) The child can attack his personal environment and attempt, thereby, to coerce gratification of basic needs. In this category fall the aggressive conduct disorders and the psychopathic forms of maladaptation.
> 2) The child can narrow or withdraw from contact with his environment. In this category fall the recessive personality developments and the habit disorders. The effort to soothe inner tensions and frustrations through such autoerotic activities as thumb sucking, masturbation and scratching implies the existence of some emotional barrier to close contact between child and parent.
> 3) Finally, the child may react to conflict with his environment with excessive anxiety, internalization of the conflict and with the production of one or another structured form of psychopathology:
>   a) excessive anxiety, with localization and encapsulation of specific unconscious conflict, as in the production of specific psychoneurosis;
>   b) excessive anxiety, defective emotional control, decompensation of defenses against anxiety, paralysis or disorganization of adaptive functions with resulting psychosomatic dysfunction;
>   c) excessive anxiety, disorganization of adaptive behavior, arrest of development and/or regression and reintegration at a primitive psychic level, as in psychosis (1, 211–214).[3]

This formulation centers upon the manner in which a child reacts to an unfavorable environment. His attempt to cope with it, which incidentally leads to his symptoms, takes various paths. He may show behavior characteristic of one of the primary behavior disorders. Through attacking techniques the conduct disorders appear. By narrowing or withdrawing, the habit disorders come about. By showing anxiety and internalization in his conflicts, neurotic traits manifest themselves. Through the process of greater structuring and depth to this latter form of dealing with the situation, there emerges the structured forms of psychopathology—the psychoneuroses, the psychosomatic disorders, and the psychoses. The latter two, psychosomatic disorders and the psychoses, are discussed next.

Psychosomatic disorders

Psychosomatic disorders have been conceptualized in a variety of ways. A hard core of general agreement appears to exist, despite the diversity of ways of expressing the relationships in this group of disorders. The formulation given by Kubie (29) has much to recommend it and will be followed here. He speaks of two fundamental aspects—susceptibility and somatization. In a psychosomatic disorder individuals differ in *susceptibility* to different disorders. These differences among individuals rest in the structure, or morphology; the function, or physiology; and the behavior and experience, or psychology of the organism and person. Thus, individuals differ in the threshold of tolerance or degree of susceptibility to certain disorders (in this instance, the psychosomatic disorders). *Somatization,* as he uses it, is a term "for any process by which tensions are generated at the level of psychological experience [and] are given some form of bodily representation and a partial discharge through anatomical and physiological disturbances" (29, 47).[5] Rising psychological tensions overflow into anatomical and physiological channels. Thus, there is a psychosomatic disorder showing both anatomical, physiological, and psychological components.

A variety of psychosomatic reactions appear in childhood. Maslow and Mittelmann (33), in their text, for example, describe gastrointestinal pain, fever and headache, allergic conditions, and ulcerative colitis as prominent psychosomatic disorders of childhood. The allergies will serve to illustrate children's psychosomatic disorders.

The Allergies

The allergies are spoken of in the plural because they include a variety of conditions, including bronchial asthma, eczema, and hives.

[5] From Kubie (29). Copyright 1944 by The New York Academy of Medicine, and published with permission.

Often the allergies occur in combination in the same patient. They are most frequently based on reactions to certain substances, mostly of a predominant protein base, which enter the body as food or inhaled as pollens or feathers. To most people these substances are harmless; to the allergic they bring on certain symptoms. Physical treatment consists of attempting to find the substance to which the child is sensitive, application of local medications to the affected parts, and the administration of drugs, particularly the antihistamines. The symptoms depend upon the mode of contact. When the allergy centers in the chest, the child wheezes and is said to have asthma; when the allergy centers in the skin, it erupts and itches, and he is said to have eczema or hives.[6]

There are differences of opinion concerning the extent of psychogenesis in the various allergic disorders. Asthma, for example, traced down to the substance bringing on the attack, can be cured by inoculation. There is no ground for assuming that all asthmas have a psychological component. Our concern, however, is with those instances in which psychological factors are present.

Hostility in the allergic. A prominent psychological factor in allergic children is the apparent relation their symptoms have to the way they express hostility. Miller and Baruch (*34*) brought out some differences between the way allergic and nonallergic children express hostility. As a working team of allergist and psychologist, they drew upon their practice, using as subjects every allergic child seen over a three-year period. The nonallergic children were those referred during the same period for diverse problems excluding mental deficiency, epilepsy, brain damage, or psychosis. The children in both groups were studied through play and interview sessions with the child, through interviews with the mother, and, often, with the father. The allergic group consisted of 51 boys and 39 girls; the nonallergic group of 24 boys and 29 girls. The mean ages of the groups were respectively 8 years, 8 months and 8 years, 2 months.

They found that blocking of outgoing hostility was more common in the allergic than in the nonallergic children. That is, the children with allergies significantly more often than nonallergic children brought out their hostility with hesitance, or displayed no overt hostility at all. For example, in play interviews when it was structured that, "Now the boy (or girl) does something naughty," the allergic children tended to hesitate, but the nonallergic children

---

[6] These last two conditions for our purposes do not need to be distinguished.

entered readily and immediately into the spirit of the situation. They had the doll go to the movies instead of school, "sock" the mother, "sock" the father and get a new mother, or dump the mother's dresses into the water. To quote Miller and Baruch:

> In contrast, among the allergics, Phyllis (14) says, "I have no troubles. They don't ever bother me!" And from Caroline (12), "I've got no problems. I don't mind how they act. I don't care at all, I never feel mean." Jacqueline (14) explains, "I just sit and stare into space, just blank most of the time, so I won't think of anything."
>
> Jimmy (9/7) in his play session admits that he wants to make the mother cry and then shows his block saying, "But I never can manage to get at it, so I stop wanting to. The trouble is as soon as I want to I feel like crying so it doesn't ever work out."
>
> Sam (7/7) similarly shows his desire and his block, "He'd like to knock the chair down and make the mother fall over. But he can't. He only cries." Hans (9) sits completely blocked and can do nothing. "I can't think," he says, "I feel awful. I wish I could think up something to do to them but I can't" (34, 513).[7]

In the allergic group 83 of the 90 children (92 per cent) were blocked while only 9 of the 53 (17 per cent) of the nonallergics were blocked in expressing their hostility. The allergic child apparently does not express his hostile feelings as freely as the nonallergic child.

It was also characteristic of the allergic group that they directed their hostility inwardly upon themselves.

> Larry (8/9) illustrated this type of hostility against self both in his play and his daily behavior. He was an obese boy with asthma and hay fever, uncertain in his speech and movement, almost viciously rejected by his mother, who also overprotected him. In his play he makes the doll representing himself not eat, "even though," as he says, "it is the best dinner." He makes various uncomfortable things happen to the child. For instance, he has to bathe in freezing water. He says, "Poor little boy, he doesn't have his own bed, he has to sleep on the floor." As to his behavior, the schoolteacher reported that he repeatedly tattled on himself, even to making false accusations as if seeking punishment. He threatened suicide frequently (34, 512).[7]

In the allergic group both in their daily behavior and in the play situation the children showed statistically significantly greater hostility against the self.

Maternal rejection. These factors of blocking and inwardly directed hostility were attributed by Miller and Baruch to the much

---

[7] From Miller and Baruch (34). Copyright 1950 by The American Orthopsychiatric Association, and published with permission.

greater incidence of maternal rejection in the allergic group (98 per cent) as contrasted with the nonallergic group (24 per cent). They write:

> In a way, the allergic child is like a cornered animal. He feels and hates the impact of his mother's rejection as all children do. But he fears to bring out hostility directly to his parents. He tries to bring it out by indirection, but again is apparently too guilty and blocks. He turns to displacing it but even so cannot seem to vent it sufficiently. In short, he cannot get release from the tension of his hostile feelings by expressing them in outgoing fashion. He seeks to punish himself. Still he does not gain absolution or peace, so he goes on trying to shut off the expression of his hostile feelings and to deny them. The inner conflict, however, apparently remains and so he must draw from other resources within him to solve his dilemma. Here is probably where his allergic constitution comes in. It becomes useful to him. He can muster it to his aid.
>
> With remarkable acuity, some of the allergic children seem to see this. Says Jeff (6/5), "When they punish and whip me I want to slam the door and break things and run away and get out. But I can't. I can't do nothin' to my little brother, he's sleeping. I can't do nothin' to my mother and father, I just can't. I just want to get out. But I can't. I get sick. Then mother brings me stuff and daddy does too, to make me better." Or, as Alice (7/9) expressed it, "Most days I'm good and my mother loves me. But when I'm sick I make my mother good and mad. She thinks I'm a regular nuisance 'cause she can't go out with her friends." Or as Eddie (4/9) says gleefully, "When I'm sick my daddy has to walk around at night for me and he says 'God damn'" (34, 517).[7]

This way of handling the expression of hostility is, of course, not the only characteristic of allergic children, but it serves as one of the major factors which has enlarged our understanding of allergic children through research.

Emotional trauma. Certain events apparently precipitate the appearance of allergic symptoms. Physical illness, such as pneumonia or operations, naturally conducive to emotional upset, has been frequently noted as preceding allergic symptoms. Emotional traumata without physical aspects also have been observed. It is characteristic of psychosomatic disorders that the process emerges when the child meets an emotionally upsetting experience. In a minority no such events can be elicited, but a considerable majority do seem to show this relationship between an upsetting experience and the appearance of the allergies.

In another study Miller and Baruch (35) investigated, medically and psychologically, 90 allergic children with an average age of 8 years, 8 months. The investigators were able to trace down in about 70 of these children traumatic episodes preceding the first allergic symptoms. More than half of these episodes had to do with either the loss or threatened loss of a parent or a marital conflict in the home. Other traumatic events found in these children's histories were the birth of a sibling, oversevere habit training, threats about masturbation, physical violence, and surgical operations. The common denominator throughout was separation from the parent or some threat in this direction. This can easily be seen in the first group where this, in itself, was the emotional trauma. Marital conflict also breeds the fear of the loss of the parent. Similarly, the birth of a sibling in addition to the realistic loss of part of the parent's time can be seen by the child as the loss of part of the parent's love as well. In the case of oversevere habit training it is as if the child were told, "You are not good enough" and thus the possibility of being disowned occurs. Even surgery means removal into a frightening experience alone. Thus, the child received what appears to him to be confirmation of his fear that his mother does not love him as much as he would like. When this is coupled with the finding previously reported, of her often being a rejecting mother, these "threats" have a powerful effect upon the child in the insecurity it breeds. Ordinarily, a child when insecure becomes resentful, but the allergic child feels unable to show resentment as does the ordinary child. He expresses his resentment through his allergies even though most often he is unaware that he does so.

For some of the children no history of traumatic episodes could be found. Moreover, as the investigators themselves state, these incidents are not unique to children developing allergic symptoms. They occur in some children without being followed by any apparent difficulties, allergic or otherwise. The addition of a control group of children would have allowed a more careful exploration of the extent of these traumata in a nonallergic normal sample. Nevertheless, the results are impressive and suggest that emotional trauma of threatened loss of a parent often precedes allergic symptoms.

That severe illness followed these traumatic episodes (which other children weather successfully) can only be explained, they go on to say, by the assumption that the allergic children had a susceptibility for difficulties of this sort, thus indicating in them the presence of reagin, which is the abnormal antibody of the allergies. Thus, allergies illustrate the twin factors of susceptibility and somatization.

The psychoses

Psychotic children are exceedingly rare relative to the total number of disturbed children. In 1942, Bender (8) could indicate that some experts did not accept the diagnosis of childhood schizophrenia because they had never seen a case. Opinion has now shifted to the extent that if an expert disputes the existence of a psychotic reaction in children, he does so on some relatively technical ground while admitting the existence of a "psychoticlike" reaction.

English and Pearson (19) indicate that, if the phobia be the "normal" neurosis of the phallic stage, then the temper tantrum is the "normal" psychosis of the same age. Consider a typical temper tantrum. The child has had a busy, exciting day, and he is overtired. A favorite TV program is anticipated. But mother, knowing his tiredness, suggests bed. He protests. She insists. He becomes excited and demands to stay up. She continues to insist on his going to bed. At some point in this interchange, he begins to cry and scream. He begins to jump up and down, hit and kick at the wall. He may even bang his own head against the wall. He pays no attention to entreaties, cajoleries, or commands. If severely spanked, he may stop; otherwise, he continues for some time, with the screaming subsiding to low sobbing. After a while, he seems all right again.

It is characteristic that during this behavior the child is oblivious to his surroundings. He strikes out blindly and hears nothing unless very forcefully handled. He reacts out of all proportion to the situation. In these characteristics he is reacting psychotically. He is still unable to control his desires, so, when frustrated, he takes it out on his environment or on himself.

Temper tantrums are evaluated for their seriousness by how severe, prolonged, and frequent they are. If extreme, they are pathological and require treatment because they are indicative that the child's personality development is not proceeding properly. On the other hand, their presence in milder form is indicative merely of the stage of development.

Earlier, primary behavior disorders in childhood were considered. Psychotic reaction patterns differ from primary behavior disorders in several respects. There is general agreement that a psychosis is a more severe disturbance and that the disturbance often extends over more of the behavior repertoire of the child. In short, personality disorganization is extensive. It is also accepted that childhood psychoses fall at a more advanced point along a continuum of severity and disorganization than do the primary behavior disorders. It is still an unsettled question whether the primary behavior disorder and psychoses have different etiological bases and obey different laws of pathology. In other words, it is still not certain whether or not they differ qualitatively as well as quantitatively. The basic similarity, or lack of it, between psychotic behavior in children and psychotic behavior in adults is not yet clear. Certainly, childhood psychoses are less structured or patterned than are psychoses in the adult. Psychoses manifest themselves more often during the latency period rather than during the phallic stage.

Characteristics of Psychotic Reactions

Escalona (20) offers certain descriptive criteria for the identification of psychosis in childhood. She points out that interchangeable terms are "childhood psychosis," "grossly atypical development," and "severe disintegration of personality." Previous discussion in this book has given meaning to the latter two terms. These two terms, summarizations of the question at hand, help one to grasp what is meant by childhood psychosis. Surveying over a period of years all children diagnosed as psychotic in a children's unit of a psychiatric institute, she found certain outstanding characteristics:

(1) The development had been atypical and irregular since earliest infancy. Not all deviant development was a question of retardation; sometimes there was acceleration in some areas, but with a concomitant retardation in another area, for example, walking early or advanced neuromuscular development but retardation in speech in the same child. Sometimes there were developmental gains which were later lost, for example, learning to speak quite early but lapsing into mutism later. General intellectual functioning tended to be uneven with some accomplishments considerably above and some considerably below the norms for the age of the child.

(2) Disturbances in the earliest and most basic interpersonal relationships were present. The familiar indices of infantile maladjustment were present—feeding difficulties, weaning and toilet training difficulties, and sleep disturbances. In this connection, the mothers reported that they felt there was something "different" about their

children, that they could not get close to them or know what to expect from them.[8]

(3) On seeing the child there was found to be present a generalized and far-reaching inadequacy. Frequently encountered were:

(a) Speech disorders including mutism, or a peculiar deviantly structured speech.

(b) Deviant thought processes such as autistic logic.

(c) Bizarre preoccupations and unusual interests occupying much of the time of the child, such as intense interest in machinery, skin, frogs, circuses, marine life and the like.

(d) Low frustration tolerance to the extent of a kind of hypersensitivity. On experiencing frustration no matter how slight, the child may respond excessively by rage or withdrawal.

(e) Excessive fantasy of an unrealistic kind; often to the point of their inability to distinguish fantasy from reality.

(f) Learning ability, either intact but failing to function because of inability in the social sphere, or gross learning disability.

The publications of others to which she refers as bringing out further the nature of the psychotic reactions of childhood are specifically concerned with schizophrenia and schizophreniclike reactions. Schizophrenia, now to be considered, is the major psychosis of childhood. The psychotic characteristics given by Escalona will form the basis for the discussion of the characteristics of schizophrenic children.

Schizophrenia

Consideration of the psychological processes appearing in the schizophrenic child will be introduced by a consideration of some characteristic psychological test results showing the way these children conceptualize themselves and their world. In the Children's

---

[8] Escalona points out that it is possible that a source of error in thinking about casual relationships sometimes occurs about this point. It is commonly accepted that behavior deviations of this kind are often the result of parental attitude. It may be, however, that maternal rejection in these psychotic children is produced by child "rejection" which first leads the mother to try everything including going to extremes of both strictness and indulgence. After years of unsuccessful attempts, such feelings of rejection will develop on the part of the mother, and the clinician now seeing them may confuse cause with effect. It may be that the mother would not have tried these methods which culminated in her rejection of the child if the child had not been difficult in the first place,

Ward of the Psychiatric Division of Bellevue Hospital, Des Lauriers and Halpern (*18*) administered a battery of tests to 100 schizophrenic children before they received treatment. They ranged in age from four to eleven years. They report what they consider to be characteristic findings.

A disturbance of functioning was found in these children in all areas which they tested. In a specific child it might appear in one or several areas, with a different pattern appearing in the next child. There were, nevertheless, certain fairly prominent characteristics.

On an intelligence test made up of a series of tests composed of different items, such as the Stanford-Binet, there would be a run of successes and then an unexpected and unpredictable failure followed by later successes. These failures are not related to the difficulty of the task as they are in the normal child whose failures on items of the same test increase in proportion to the difficulty of the task. Their failures occurred in an unpredictable jumble. Sometimes their errors were not merely incorrect, they also appeared illogical in relation to the initial connection. Consider the answer of a child who was asked to tell what was foolish about the statement: "A man called at the post office and asked if there was a letter waiting for him. 'What is your name?' asked the postman. 'Why,' said the man, 'you will find my name on the envelope.' The child responded, 'He shouldn't have called. There was a strike. The people have to work hard.' After considerable interrogation it became clear that the child had responded to the word 'called,' had associated this with telephoning, and from that had gone on to the threatened phone strike" (*18*, 59).[9]

Sometimes the child may give an answer which appears satisfactory until the reasoning behind it is elicited. For example, "Asked what he would do if he found on the streets a three-year-old baby who was lost, one schizophrenic child replied, 'Take it to the cops.' This was the expected answer. However, when asked why he would do this, he said, 'Blue, they all wear blue.' Further questioning elicited the fact that his father was a sailor, that he felt lost, and associated the blue uniform of the police with the blue sailor uniforms" (*18*, 59).[9] In Escalona's terms, deviant thought processes of an autistic kind were present.

On being asked to draw a human figure, the schizophrenic child reveals both the confusion which he manifests concerning himself as

[9] From Des Lauriers and Halpern (*18*). Copyright 1947 by The American Orthopsychiatric Association, and published with permission.

a person and the confused distinction between himself and his environment. Inner disorganization or confusion is shown by disturbed spatial relationships in his drawings—arms coming from the head, hands protruding from the trunk without arms, or even heads "coming out" all over the body. He elongates parts, omits others, overemphasizes others down to the tiniest detail. The child's confusion of himself in relation to his environment is shown by an inability to delimit clearly the boundaries of the body he draws—even to the extent of having the body drawn transparent with all manner of objects seen as if beneath the flesh. This problem of inability to establish ego-boundaries, or dys-identity, as it is called, is, according to Rabinovitch's summary of the literature (36), the core of the problem of schizophrenia. Certainly, there is no question that it is an important factor in the schizophrenic process.

The Thematic Apperception Test brought out certain of the ways in which the schizophrenic child deals with his problems. To quote:

> What may be called his denial of reality as well as his struggle to gain some true contact with the world around him often appears dramatically in his stories. Even more significant than the actual content of the stories, however, is the way the child proceeds to build these up. Thus the test picture may actually serve little or not at all in determining the story that is produced. The child may start making up a fantastic tale in which he covers problems ranging from high heaven (astronomical or angelical stories) to the depths below (death, devils, ocean bottoms), but these will have no relation to the presented picture. It is as though he dare not accept any part of the situation which faces him, but denies it by ignoring it. Such behavior illustrates the method he employs for escaping reality and also reveals some of his own problems and preoccupations. Another child may choose only one incidental element of a picture on which to build up his fantasy. Thus, seeing two adults embracing with their eyes closed, the child makes up a tale where "eyes closed" is the main theme and says, "Those people are unconscious. Those people bumped their heads and are dizzy. They fell off a trolley car, one after the other and hit their heads. In other words they are sleepwalkers."
>
> Self-reference and autistic thinking also appear frequently in the productions of these children. They are likely to exclaim, "This is me," or "Oh, that happened to me," or "That lady is staring at me, I'm bad," etc. These comments are usually made when the card is first presented and the story which follows is generally not related to any event in the child's life, but seems to be an attempt at repressing the anxiety which is aroused in association with these remarks (18, 64–65).[10]

[10] From Des Lauriers and Halpern (18). Copyright 1947 by The American Orthopsychiatric Association, and published with permission.

To use the terms of Escalona's analysis, autistic logic, bizarre pre-occupations, excessive fantasy, and inability to distinguish fantasy from reality are all shown.

Illustrations may be drawn from the work of other investigators. Consider the capsule description of Adriene, a white girl who was three-and-a-half-years old when admitted to Bellevue Hospital.

> At the time when the psychotherapeutic treatment started the patient was strongly withdrawn, autistic, unable to form a rapport, and extremely retarded in her behavior and development. She hardly spoke, was not toilet trained, her way of walking showed lack of coordination, and she refused any contact, physically or otherwise (25, 147).[11]

Withdrawal, lack of uniformity of development, disturbance of interpersonal relationships, and impaired communication are all illustrated within the compass of this brief note.

> Or consider this letter ten-year-old Francine wrote to her doctor: "For the doctor, I am sure I will escape though and go to the real world. It is better there. He isn't a guardian angel and neither is this a guardian angel hospital meant for all who come here. I, Francine, that is what they call me, was very unhappy there. It was a terrible world. I thought it was a real one but it seems it isn't. I may some day go to the real one" (9, 44).[12]

Withdrawal into fantasy with confusion of reality and deviantly structured speech are both illustrated.

It is possible to get the impression that schizophrenic children all follow the general pattern just outlined. This is not the case. Other schizophrenic children show other, even opposite, trends in behavior from these chosen as characteristic. Bender (10) indicates, for example, that some schizophrenic children have high language skills instead of ineptness, and relate too well with individuals to the point of overidentification instead of being withdrawn from human contact. Hence, she emphasizes the concept of plasticity, with schizophrenic children showing a high degree of plasticity in every area of function. This helps to account for the wide variety of clinical pictures found. Nevertheless, support for the generality of the earlier description to fit at least a substantial proportion of cases of childhood schizophrenia can be found. Certainly the lack of uniformity of development as a diagnostic feature is underscored.

[11] From Gurevitz (25). Copyright 1952 by the *Quarterly Journal of Child Behavior,* and published with permission.

[12] From Bender (9). Copyright 1947 by The American Orthopsychiatric Association, and published with permission.

The causes of schizophrenia. Both in children and in adults precise specification of the causes of schizophrenia is impossible. Bellak (6), who made an extensive survey of theories of, and research into, the causes of schizophrenia, concluded that no one position was definitive. At the present time one must be content with knowledge of some of the more prominent and plausible etiological factors.

It is possible to start with the generally accepted position that schizophrenia is the result of an interaction of constitutional and psychological factors. Beyond this point the experts part company. Some minimize constitutional factors, stressing psychological; others, the reverse. Sometimes, for example, schizophrenia is viewed as a very specific type of organic brain deficit (for example, 5).

The general unevenness of development, previously discussed, may well be due to a constitutional factor. So far as psychological factors of etiological importance, there is general agreement that they center in disturbances of early parent-child relationships. This may take the form of extreme emotional unavailability or overprotection on the part of the mother, physical separation, and the like. Reichard and Tillman (37) have summarized the clinical reports of several investigators and added cases of their own. They categorize the mothers as overtly rejecting, covertly rejecting (overprotective), or ambiguous. Only 15 per cent of the fathers are described as domineering, sadistic, or rejecting.

Several investigations have been conducted on the problem of parental attitudes of schizophrenics (21, 22, 31, 32). Information has been gathered either through examination of early records of children who later became schizophrenic or through questionnaires completed by mothers after the appearance of the disorder in their children.

Frazee (21), using clinic data, compared with a control group 23 male children who later become schizophrenic. She found that a high percentage of the schizophrenic children had overprotective, infantalizing mothers. Indifference and lack of consistency also characterized these mothers. Overt rejection was present in six mothers of schizophrenic children while not appearing in a single control mother. The prominence of the ineffectual, passive father, so often mentioned in the literature, was not borne out by her findings.

McKeown (31) used essentially the same procedure. He categorized the mothers of schizophrenic children and nonschizophrenic children as demanding-antagonistic (dictating high standards), superficial (slightly concerned or indifferent, preoccupied), encouraging (assisting, helping, attempting to understand), and protective-indulgent (reluctant to employ any discipline, encouraging dependence, defending child's inadequacies). The case records showed that the mothers of schizophrenic children tended to be demanding-antagonistic and protective-indulgent, while the mothers of the normal children predominantly tended to be encouraging.

Two studies employed the technique of a questionnaire study of maternal attitudes as applied to the mothers of young male schizophrenics and to the mothers of nonschizophrenics (22, 32). Both studies agreed in showing that mothers of schizophrenics exhibited generally poorer parental attitudes than did the mothers of the controls. The finding assumes even greater significance when one thinks of the probable stronger desire of the mothers of schizophrenic children to make a good showing on such questionnaires. In one study (22), examination of items which significantly differentiated the schizophrenic from the control group showed a fairly definite pattern. Characterizing the mothers of schizophrenics were attitudes of self-sacrificing martyrdom, subtle domination, and overprotectiveness. In the other study (32), the mothers were characterized as restrictive and also exhibiting excessive devotion along with cool detachment.

Evidently there is a pathological familial influence present in the development of schizophrenia. But this finding does not throw light on the relative influence of constitutional and psychological factors. Those adhering to a theory of hereditary or constitutional weakness can maintain that this manifests itself in a child who is weak. Overprotectiveness, for example, then becomes a reaction to a basic weakness and is not in itself the cause of the difficulty. At the present stage of our knowledge it probably reflects current thinking to admit the influence of both constitutional and psychological factors. Sometimes one or the other is stressed. Both are probably operative. Overprotectiveness, then, to select one example, is sometimes the cause, sometimes the result of the disorder, or even more aptly it is both the cause *and* the result of the schizophrenic process.

Other Psychotic Reaction Patterns

There are other forms of psychotic reaction patterns in childhood. Manic depressive psychosis with its characteristic swing of elation and depression is rarely found (27). Relatively more common (although affecting only a very, very small proportion of children) are the psychoses associated with organic brain diseases. These brain diseases may be brought about by trauma such as a blow, by a neoplasm or growth such as a tumor, by an inflammation, or an injection. Whooping cough, encephalitis, or any acute infectious disease may, in some instances, leave in its wake a behavioral disturbance of a psychotic nature. In one evaluation (24) of the behavior complications of encephalitis, it was found children so affected could be placed into three groups: (1) simple behavior disturbances; (2) psychopathic behavior; and (3) psychotic behavior. In their series of 78 cases, 26 showed simple behavioral difficulties, 36 showed psychopathic kinds of behavior, and 16 were psychotic. The psychotic children were careless of personal appearance and slovenly in habits. Often moodiness, crying spells, outbursts of screaming and laughter, and irrelevant talk were present. It was impossible to establish a warm friendly relationship with these children. These clinicians noted that some of the children had previously been diagnosed as schizophrenic. This again reminds us of the confused etiological picture that is so characteristic of childhood psychoses.

The reactions to physical handicap

Any accident or illness which produces a definite change in body structure or causes a pervasive limitation in freedom of general action inevitably must have an effect upon personality functioning. The amputee, the poliomyelitic, the blind, the deaf, and others bear upon their person the indication of their crippling disorder. The cardiac, the diabetic, and the tubercular, although their condition is not as open to the casual glance, are sometimes equally crippled.

Within a given crippling condition, such as blindness, uniformity of reaction cannot be expected (17). No matter how similar the disorder in two children, each is still an individual and each brings to bear upon this new crisis, this private and unique critical period, all of their previously acquired patterns of adjustment. Nevertheless, there are certain general factors, child-centered and parental, which can be discerned. Factors in the child will be considered first.

Age and all that goes with it in the behavior repertoire characteristic of that age are of varying significance in deciding the reactions to physical handicap. Some authorities would argue the older the child is at the time he receives his handicap, the less the likelihood of emotional trauma.   This rests on the assumption of the vulnerability of the young child.   But diametrically opposed is the position that the younger the person at the time he receives his handicap, the less the likelihood that he will manifest emotional difficulties.   The argument rests upon the presumed pliability of the young child.   These opposing opinions are not necessarily contradictory.   One or the other may operate in such a fashion as to be of critical significance for a given child.

Age in other children may be of only incidental etiological significance.   In this connection Caldwell states:

> Perhaps the influence of age is more related to other factors that vary with age than it is to age per se.   For example, the values held by a child (or an adult) at the time of acquisition of the handicap will likely have considerable importance in determining his attitude toward the disability.   For the young child of 4 or 5 years motor activity is extremely important.   He is in the process of rapidly acquiring many new skills which involve expressive movements of the entire body, particularly the arms and legs.   In his own private reaction to the residual effects of poliomyelitis, the necessary restrictions of motor activity might be the only deprivation he would feel.   During adolescence, a time when physical appearance is assuming greater importance, the limitations in motor activity might assume a subordinate role while the cosmetic injury would be regarded as the most traumatic aspect of the illness.   In subsequent years, this feeling might disappear from the top of the hierarchy of deficit, with vocational limitation usurping the leading role.   The concept of a "cripple" is by no means a unitary one—one is crippled only in terms of specific activities and skills, and this pattern will vary from one individual to another and within the same individual from time to time (17, 220).[13]

Reaction to crippling on the part of the child is dependent not only upon his personality structure but the relevance or irrelevance of the particular form of handicap to the critical periods in which he is immersed at the time or shortly thereafter.

As has been amply demonstrated elsewhere in this book, children have an active fantasy life.   One fantasy theme appears regularly in many children.   Parents are regarded as omnipotent—both in giving and in depriving they are all powerful.   Physically handicapped children also have this fantasy—but they are crippled.   Small wonder they are likely to blame their parents for their crippling.   Feelings of hostility toward their parents who "punished" them in this way

[13] From Caldwell (17).   Copyright 1952 by the Missouri State Medical Association, and published with permission.

are, under the circumstances, inevitable. Aggressive and antisocial acts may be carried out which, in turn, bring disapproval and disappointment on the part of the parents. A vicious circle then is set in motion. Another kind of reaction to the same situation would be the repression of these hostile impulses, thus laying the foundations for anxiety and feelings of guilt.

Crippling may also be interpreted by the child as punishment for some unacceptable act. A poignant finding by Beverly (15) is relevant. He reports that 90 per cent of cardiac and diabetic children interviewed in a large hospital responded to the question, "Why do children get sick?" with answers which had the meaning, "Because they are bad."

The attitudes of the parent weigh heavily in determining the reactions of the child. Bender (7) goes so far as to say that a child will be able to tolerate a disfigurement to the extent to which his *mother* is able to accept it. The presence of a crippled child lends itself to the appearance of all the manifold facets of rejection including its compensatory form of overprotection. Irritation toward, resentment of, and shame for the crippled child, with the inevitable limitations it brings down upon the parent, are perhaps understandable. Simultaneously, genuine sympathy for the child is also felt by the parent. With both of these attitudes operating it is not unusual for inconsistent behavior to be shown—one moment babying, the next punishing the child. Whatever is done, the greatest hope for psychological health in the crippled child lies with the parent.

Treatment

The nature of personality disorders in childhood was examined in previous sections, but treatment was considered only incidentally. Similarly, there has been incidental reference to psychotherapy in other chapters, but explicit examination of the treatment of psychological disturbances in children has not been made. This is done in the present section.

Diagnostic appraisal and treatment were described in Chapter 2 as the intertwined aspects of the clinical method. The position of treatment in the foreground of present interest should not obscure the fact that it is preceded by diagnosis. Work on classificatory diagnoses of many clinicians over the years was what made it possible to present the classification of personality disorder on which the earlier portions of the chapter were based. Nosology or classification per se was the basis of what Rabinovitch (36) has called the current antidiagnostic feeling in clinical work. Some clinicians have raised objection to carrying on the task of classification, claiming it to be sterile so far as giving leads in treatment is concerned. In a more dynamic and subtle sense, diagnosis, as Rabinovitch goes on to point out, *must* precede treatment. In this sense we are only incidentally concerned with labeling. The emphasis is much more on getting some conception of the personality of the individual child patient and of the conditions which contributed to its development in this particular child. Diagnostic insights thereby gained are applied in treatment and make diagnosis essential (36).

Treatment may be conceptualized as having two interrelated forms. One of these forms, organic treatment, that is, treatment by drugs, operations, diet, exercise, and the like, is inappropriate for discussion. Instead, the second form, treatment by psychological means, will receive attention. Psychological treatment, in turn, has two aspects—direct methods (psychotherapy) and indirect methods of treatment.

Direct Methods of Treatment

Psychotherapy is the term used to designate direct methods of psychological treatment.[14] In psychotherapy there is a one-to-one interpersonal relationship between a specific child and a specific therapist. The therapist has in the words of Allen, "nothing to offer except himself" (2, 698).[15] As this writer elsewhere put it:

> All forms of psychotherapy demand a personal interrelationship of therapist and patient. In a sense this is a truism so obvious that it may be regarded as hardly worth mentioning. It might be said that you can hardly have psychotherapy without both there, any more than you can dispense with some means of communication between them. It is not in this sense of being required merely to permit such sessions—a necessary but not a sufficient cause—that the clinician-patient relationship is given a position of prominence here. The relationship is regarded by many therapists as effective in psychotherapy of and for itself. . . . This relationship, if properly established, assures the emotional participation of the patient, an essential to the assimilation of the material that emerges. The patient must feel secure in this relationship and must

[14] Sometimes in a more general sense, the term, psychotherapy, is used to designate both direct and indirect methods of treatment.

[15] From Allen (2). Copyright 1940 by The American Orthopsychiatric Association, and published with permission.

feel that he is accepted whether he is expressing positive, ambivalent, or negative feelings (40, 554).[16]

This relationship between patient and therapist is considered one of the basic factors in all forms of direct psychotherapy, but other factors are operative as well. For example, release of emotional tension and insight into the sources and nature of the difficulties are considered important factors. Nevertheless, there is common agreement that some form of relationship between therapist and patient allows these other factors to operate (40).

Psychotherapeutic approaches with children take many forms. Psychoanalytic therapy has already been described. In addition, there is considerable use of "relationship" therapy (3) and "nondirective" therapy (38) as well as other approaches. Their detailed consideration is manifestly impossible. Instead, the nature of psychotherapy with children will be illustrated by consideration of the use of the play technique in the general dynamic, neo-Freudian tradition prevalent in the child guidance clinics of today.

Psychotherapy and play technique. Play is the natural medium of expression of the younger child. It is an apt illustration of the theme, "doing what comes naturally." It is a younger child's way of "telling" and "living" for which adults use words. Before considering play as a means of psychotherapy it should be noted that in the telling through play a diagnostic function is thereby served. Through play we are better able to understand the significance of the child's behavior and what are the cross-currents in the personality that make the child experience and behave in his own individual way. In other words, observation of and participation in play helps the therapist to gain some insight into the child's motives, his characteristic ways of behaving, and the causes of his behavior.

Play technique is also a medium of psychotherapy. In itself, play is not curative any more than words in adult psychotherapy. Play and words, each in its own way, are the *media* of psychotherapy. Often they are combined. A difficulty in verbal communication is not always present in working with children. Older, brighter children can verbally communicate very well. In this instance a play *setting* for verbal communication is maintained. A formal conversational situation is suitable for adult psychotherapy, whereas an informal situation in which the child may play or draw as he talks

---

[16] From Watson (40). Copyright 1951 by Harper and Brothers, and published with permission.

is comfortable and natural for the child. Thus, both play and verbal communication may be used rather than their standing in sharp contrast.

The two closely related, in fact inseparable, functions of diagnosis and psychotherapy might be illustrated by drawing from an account of a psychiatric social worker, Fanny Amster, some of the uses of play therapy. She writes:

Play can be used to help a child verbalize certain conscious material and the associated feelings. This use is helpful when a child blocks in discussing certain material and an impasse in treatment is created.

> Stanley, 10, doggedly refuses to discuss his encopresis and his mother's attitude toward him. As he is interested in building with blocks, I suggest he build a house. He builds one but omits the bathroom. We discuss what such an omission might mean to the imaginary family who lives in the house. We discuss this in terms of the inconvenience to the family. The boy comments that he dislikes the simple bathroom in his home. Later, he relates that he soils himself; that his mother punishes him by whipping and by rubbing his faeces on his face; that he gets even because she has to wash his trousers. We discuss the pleasurable aspects of his soiling and whether through his "getting even" he can achieve the escape he wants from his mother's domination.

In this situation, the therapist uses material in which the boy is interested at this point in treatment; initiates a general play situation and permits the boy to fill in the details, discusses his omission of a reality, makes interpretative remarks geared to the content of the play and, later, when the boy makes his own associations, the therapist makes interpretations which point up the symptomatic nature of his soiling and which fits this into his general problem. The boy is helped to verbalize material which represents failure, punishment and retaliation; secures release of his feelings, surrenders some of his negativism, gradually accepts the reality of bathrooms, verbalizes his role in his relationship to his mother, and is helped to doubt the effectiveness of his method. Some of his discomfort is alleviated and an impasse in treatment is worked out.

> Leon, 7, who was referred for refusal to attend school, denies any concern as to what his mother and I discuss, yet he always stands outside my door when I am interviewing his mother. In an interview with him I initiate a play situation with three dolls which are designated as a boy, his mother, and myself. Leon quickly uses chains of paper clips to outline the floor plan of my office and the small outside foyer, and uses strips of paper for the office furniture. As he moves the dolls around, he talks freely: "I am standing outside. I can't hear. I smack you down 'cause I can't hear what you tell my mother. I can't smack her down—she's my mother."

He acts out and verbalizes what happens from the time he and his mother arrive for their appointments: "We come in. We ask for you. You tell me, 'come in.' You ask questions. Then you say, 'time is up. I want to see your mother.' I say 'Oh, yeh?' I knock you down. I go home with my mother. Now it is next week. We come here. . . ." Leon demonstrates and verbalizes this scene three times and the intensity of his feelings diminishes. He then starts the same scene but shows that he permits the mother to come into my office and he accompanies her. He shows that I tell him to go outside and says: "I go out. I try to open the door but you won't let me in. I listen. I can't hear." He quickly draws two figures, designates them as he and I, and says I am shooting and killing him. I recognize his fearfulness, his concern about what will happen to him, and his feeling that I am mean because I limit his desire to control. Leon now draws me a valentine, then decides it is too good for me and he will keep it.

In this situation, the therapist initiates a general play situation and permits the boy to fill in the details, allows him to continue the play activity until the intensity of his feelings diminishes and, after the boy has expressed his hostility and fearfulness, the therapist verbalizes his feelings and his wishes. Leon secures release of his feelings of exclusion and fearfulness, feels omnipotent and retaliatory in his play, reduces the intensity of his feelings through the repetitive play, recognizes the unreality of the power he desires, verbalizes guardedly his hostility toward his mother while he uses the therapist as a substitute foil for her, and expresses mixed feelings for the therapist. Some of his discomfort in the therapeutic relationship has been alleviated and the barrier in treatment has been removed. . . .

Play can be used to help a child act out unconscious material and to release the accompanying tension. This cathartic use of play deals with symbolic material which has dangerous significance to the child. The therapist must be aware of how much release in play the particular child can tolerate without panic and must be aware of the kind of participation and interpretation in which to engage.

Morton, 7, is referred for a sudden onset of sleeplessness. He anxiously relates that Max is the name of a neighborhood bully who beat him severely. He slowly writes out: "Max is a triple based (bastard)," and walks restlessly about the room as he shows me how well he can bounce a ball. He quickly accepts my suggestion that we make up a story about a little boy and a big boy. I draw the stick figures while Morton tells the story. He relates that the little boy meets the big boy who beats the little boy until the little boy loses his nose and legs. The little boy is disappointed because his mother does not kiss him. A doctor makes the little boy well. The second scene shows the little boy challenging the big boy to a fight. . . . In the fight the little boy knocks off the bully's nose, legs and arms. The last scene shows the big boy covered with bandages, confined to his bed and weeping. A doctor is preparing painful remedies and the little boy who is standing outside the bedroom window is laughing heartily.

In subsequent interviews, Morton acts out through stories and jokes, various dangers which overtake small boys and how these boys emerge victorious. After this play activity Morton spontaneously relates that he and Max are friends and share activities. His mother reports that Morton is now able to sleep.

This boy contributed through play activity additional diagnostic understanding. He revealed his feeling of weakness, desire for consolation from his mother, concern about injury, and his need to feel strong (4, 65–67).[17]

In the last sentence of the quotation it will be noted that Morton by his play has not only released tension but also supplied additional diagnostic information. This inseparability of diagnostic and therapeutic facets of play therapy is again illustrated.

When examined subjectively by its proponents play therapy is reported as working very well with many sorts of disturbed children. Nevertheless, crucial research evidence concerning its validity is still lacking. It would appear that the use of the controlled research is called for. The personal adjustment of two randomly assigned but equated groups tested before therapy could then be compared by a post-therapy evaluation after one group received play therapy while the other did not.

Concerning play techniques, the greatest need at the present is further work in systematizing the situational variables concerned. Illustrative are systematic experimental variation of such factors as kind and degree of realism of materials, extent of experimenter-child interaction, and duration, to mention some of the variables referred to by Sears (39). It is to Robert Sears and his associates that we owe much of our present knowledge concerning the effect of these factors, but the work is only at its beginning. As Sears puts it, "They are simply the necessary brush-clearing and hump-leveling required before we go on to erect a structure of facts and theories that will relate to *experiential* determinants of doll play behavior" (39, 196).[18] The interpretations that psychotherapists make from play therapy seem real, vivid, and plausible in some circumstances. On other

[17] From Amster (4). Copyright 1943 by The American Orthopsychiatric Association, and published with permission.

[18] From Sears (39). Copyright 1947 by the Society for Research in Child Development, and published with permission.

occasions, they do not and skepticism and repudiation seem called for. But is one right in his acceptances and in his rejections? Only research, such as just referred to, will demonstrate the nature and extent of the trustworthiness to be placed in findings from play therapy.

Indirect Methods of Treatment

Indirect methods of treatment are also used with children. Broadly speaking, indirect methods of treatment involve the use of procedures and materials ordinarily not considered therapeutic but which have been adapted to therapeutic ends. Going to summer camp is hardly a form of therapy in and of itself. Placement in an institution may be intended as punishment of the individual, a way of protecting society, and as a matter of sheer convenience. Yet, both camp and institutionalization may be used for therapeutic ends and consequently become indirect methods of treatment. Often indirect methods are supplementary in the sense that psychotherapy involving a direct relationship of therapist and child is carried on simultaneously with them.

Two major forms of indirect treatment used with children may be distinguished: (1) *environmental manipulation,* the outright removal of the child from the present unsuitable environment and placement elsewhere; and (2) *environmental modification,* the change of some aspects of the present environmental forces which are working on the child without removing him from this environment completely. The first form is exemplified by institutionalizing, the second by attempting to change pernicious parental attitudes toward the child while he continues to live at home.

Both environmental manipulation and environmental modification are intended to remove stimuli which may be contributing to the disturbance of the child. If the manipulation or the modification is successful, the stimulus configuration facing the child is different, permitting the extinguishing of old inadequate patterns of behavior and the formation of newer, more adaptive ones. If the environment is judged one in which the chances of modifying are so remote that he could never achieve healthful adjustment, then outright removal or manipulation is indicated. On the other hand, if it would appear that modifying certain factors through working with the disturbing influences (individuals), eliminating the disturbing element, or adding new experiences will create a changed field, then environmental modification is indicated.

The choice of particular indirect therapeutic approaches depends upon the diagnostic appraisal which is formulated in a specific case. This depends upon many factors specific to the needs of each child. Some of the more general forms and values of environmental manipulation and modification will now be characterized.

Environmental manipulation. The two major forms of agencies used in environmental manipulation are foster homes and institutions. In broadest and simplest terms the choice between a foster home and an institution is in part decided on the basis of whether the needs of the child are likely to be best met through the individual, personal, and intense relation which a foster home is more likely to provide, or through a group, impersonal, diluted relationship which the typical institution provides. A factor related to this decision is the age of the child. A younger child (up to about 10) is generally considered to be better suited for foster-home placement and an older one (10 or older) for institutional placement. Still another factor to be taken into consideration is the severity of the condition affecting the child. If he is seriously disturbed, is psychotic, low grade mentally retarded, is an advanced delinquent or has symptoms difficult to tolerate in a home setting, then an institution probably is indicated, no matter what the age of the child may be. If he shows milder behavior difficulties, neurotic conditions or symptoms arising from needs for interpersonal relationships, then foster home placement is more likely to be indicated.

Closed institutions, particularly those for delinquents are often based on the idea of protective custody—protecting the child from himself and from harming others (11). Unfortunately, this idea of protective custody, which can be defended on theoretical grounds, sometimes becomes confused with restraint as a form of punishment. As a result, many so-called curative institutions take on the character of jails in the narrow sense and thus fail in their therapeutic function. But this custodial or punishment motif is not inherent in an institutional setting.

The very environment of an institution where children live may create a therapeutic milieu. Instead of being merely a convenient place to house children, the institution may be used to create a therapeutic atmosphere appropriate to the children. Naturally, the nature of this atmosphere in a particular institution varies with the difficulties of the children they house. This therapeutic character of the institutions concerned with emotional difficulties is caught by their new designation, "residential treatment centers" (28).

It is recognized that some children cannot be treated with any success while they remain at home with their parents. Some of the general therapeutic values of institutions are their freedom from emotionally unhealthy distractions, their neutral environment, their regularity of regimen, and even their freedom from contact with realities. All of these values are sometimes contraindicated in the case of a particular child. An institution may then systematically vary in any or all of these.

It will be remembered that one of the advantages of the typical institution is its freedom from too close interpersonal contact. It was indicated that foster homes which supply this are not suitable for seriously disturbed children. But what of the seriously disturbed child who does need deep and steady interpersonal contacts and yet cannot form them? Because of the seriousness of the disturbance, institutionalization is indicated, but the typical institution does not supply the opportunity for the interpersonal contact he needs. In an attempt to meet this need, Bettelheim and Sylvester introduced the principle of the therapeutic milieu as a basis for organization in an institution with which they were connected. They describe it as follows:

> In a therapeutic milieu . . . the child's development toward increasing mastery must be facilitated. Training in skills and achievements, specialized programs and activities are of peripheral importance only. They are therapeutically justified solely if they originate from the central issue of the therapeutic milieu. A therapeutic milieu is characterized by its inner cohesiveness which alone permits the child to develop a consistent frame of reference. This cohesiveness is experienced by the child as he becomes part of a well defined hierarchy of meaningful interpersonal relationships. Emphasis on spontaneity and flexibility—not to be misconstrued as license or chaos—makes questions of schedule or routine subservient to the relevance of highly individualized and spontaneous interpersonal relationships. Such conditions permit the emergence and development of the psychological instances, the internalization of controls, and the eventual integration of the child's personality (13, 192).[19]

This milieu is particularly appropriate for either children whose ability to maintain interpersonal relations with a parent figure has

[19] From Bettelheim and Sylvester (13). Copyright 1948 by The American Orthopsychiatric Association, and published with permission.

been destroyed or children who lack the tools to build this or any other personal relationship. Illustrative of this first group would be the boy they describe whose presenting symptoms were truancy and an inhibition of learning. It was found that he had interpreted his mother's divorcing two husbands in rapid succession as being brought about by him. "His need for gratification and reassurance made him hunger for closeness to adults and made him approach them, while his fear of destroying them made him flee from them in panic. In this sense, his truancy was an attempt to escape from his own destructiveness, and he had further to avoid all learning because of his doubts about his own personal identity and that of his delusionally destroyed victims" (14, 56–57).[20]

The second group, those lacking ability to form personal relationships, typically would include many children who had grown up in orphanages. Baldly put, the child needs love, but as Bettelheim reminds us in the very title of one of his books, *Love is Not Enough.* Sometimes, incorrectly, he is offered this love immediately and in an overwhelming fashion; forcing the "rights of infants" on him as it were, whether he wants it or not! Often he is not ready. Instead, in the therapeutic milieu of Bettelheim he is offered casual acquaintance and his other needs are taken care of until he is ready to choose a deeper relationship, at his own time and in his own way and from whom he wishes. A one-to-one relationship with this person, once developed while still in the midst of a milieu therapy, expresses, as much as can be done in one sentence, the essence of this approach.

There is a close, uninterrupted relationship between the child and the residential worker who is genuinely fond of the child and capable of understanding and helping to meet his emotional needs. Emphatically this does not mean that there will be no individual relationship of the sort characteristic of direct individual therapy. This, too, will be present. The contact with the residence worker in the setting of the therapeutic milieu is an integral but indirect part of the total program of treatment.

Environmental modification. In many instances a child's personality disturbance may be treated while he remains at home. This does not mean that there are no pernicious influences in the home atmosphere which adversely affect the child's development and adjustment. Any one of three forms of environmental modification may

[20] From Bettelheim and Sylvester (14). Copyright 1949 by the Smith Ely Jelliffe Trust, and published with permission.

be brought to bear—elimination, addition, and attitude change. On a few rare occasions it takes the drastic form of arranging for the removal of some peripheral member of the family such as a boarder or an aunt who is serving as a disturbing element. Thus, *elimination* is introduced. Also useful is the introduction into the life of the child of some new environmental experience. Individualization of school experiences, or placement in special classes to help match educational demands to the needs and capacities of the particular child also are forms of environmental modification used for therapeutic as well as educational ends. Summer camps, settlement houses, and Boy Scout troops are also illustrations of *additions* as forms of environmental modifications. But often most significant of all is attempts at *change of attitudes* of the members of the family which may be interfering with the adjustment of the child. This form of modification will be explored in more detail.

When a child is brought to a psychiatrist or psychologist, naturally a parent accompanies him. The adult is given an opportunity to state his version of what it is about the child that necessitates his being brought for help. The clinician listens sympathetically not only for the sake of the information elicited, but also because this talking helps relieve the parent of excessive self-criticism and needless accusations. Even more important, experience has taught him that a parent's problems often contribute to those of the child. His patient is the child, not the parent. But since the parent has created or exacerbated the problem the child faces, he must, to that extent, pay attention to and work with the parent's difficulties. For example, in seeing the mother, a therapist may emphasize modification of the mother's attitude toward the child by facilitating insight into her influence on the child's behavior. One session from a case quoted by Green is appropriate.

The mother of an eight year old girl was in the clinic for her first interview. She talked a great deal of Linda's bed-wetting and thumb-sucking. The mother said she feared Linda had not had as much affection as she needed (many illnesses and hospitalizations); also, that she herself had had no affection and frankly expressed hostile feelings to her own mother. She resented her mother's influence with Linda, and against herself. She felt somehow that Linda's bed-wetting might be tied in with this conflict. Among other points of activity, the case worker helped this mother to describe and discuss the behavior that worried her. With much feeling for the mother, the worker's activity focused clearly on the mother's involvement in her relationship problems with her daughter. In all her inquiries and responses, the worker remembered that this mother had come to the clinic because of her *re-sponsibility* as a parent. Toward the end of the interview, the mother was able to say she thought Linda's behavior was retaliative: "When I lose my temper, she sucks her thumb; and when she sucks her thumb a lot, she wets the bed."

This insight on the mother's part is very likely the result of the worker's acceptance of, and focus upon, the mother's coming to the clinic in the role of parent. A different case worker might have focused on the mother's resentment toward her own mother. Focus on this area as the problem would have been accepting her role of daughter rather than mother, and would have tended to dissipate the impetus and strength upon which this mother came to the clinic (23, 444).[21]

The emphasis here was on the mother as a *parent* of the child. If she had been the primary patient it might well have been that her role as daughter would have been emphasized. The mother's own difficulties insofar as they did touch upon her relations with the disturbance of the child were minimized. In this sense, then, with the child in focus as the patient, treatment of the mother is an indirect form of treatment of the child.

Sometimes, interpretation of the child's behavior is necessary so that the parent can accept the child as he is. It is well known to clinicians that during treatment an *increase* in disturbing symptoms may appear. In a timid fearful child his first few attempts at self-assurance may be met by his parents with consternation and even loss of faith in treatment. Consider the following excerpt from a case history of just such a boy.

After a few interviews with the therapist, the little boy began to be somewhat less fearful, but also he became less docile and obedient. "He refused his spinach one day last week," said his mother. "He never did that before. I never even knew that he disliked spinach." She went on to question whether she could continue to bring the boy to the clinic, giving as a reason that the trip was too long and expensive. The social worker did not leave the question of the mother's continuing to bring the boy to the clinic on the basis of the trip, but inquired whether the mother might be worried over the changes in the boy and his being a little less obedient. The mother replied that he never had been disobedient before she brought him to the clinic, but then she was able to go on to talk of how she always had demanded docility and obedience of the boy. She ended this description with the query as to whether this way of bringing up the boy might have some connection with his having become such a fearful child. The social worker agreed that this was a real possibility and the mother decided that she

[21] From Green (23). Copyright 1948 by The American Orthopsychiatric Association, and published with permission.

would continue to bring the boy for treatment because she preferred him to be less fearful even at the expense of his being a little less submissive to authority (*16*, 121–122).[22]

Interpretation of the boy's behavior to the mother was obviously necessary both to see to it that he remained in treatment and to allow the mother to understand the child somewhat better. She would to that extent create a more healthful environment for him. In general, it has been found that interpretation to parents is often necessary in helping to deal with any kind of disturbed child.

The Parent and Treatment

It is evident there is great parental responsibility for the appearance of psychological disturbances in childhood. A vast literature of writings designed for general consumption, concerned with the pernicious effects of wrong parental practices has been available for some years. Along with undoubted benefit to parents and to children from these writings has come unwittingly a danger—that of a paralyzing anxiety on the part of the parent about doing the right thing. Slavish following of the new dogma of child care can itself produce its own difficulties.

It is even not enough to do the right thing at the right time. As Bettelheim (*12*) reminds us, it must be carried out with the appropriate feelings. Illustrative of this point is the mother who does not scold her child who wets the bed, "knowing she shouldn't," but kicks up a fuss at washing the sheets. This "permissive" mother may be creating greater guilt feelings than if the child had been given an outright scolding. Or a mother may not toilet train her child too early, thus sticking to the rules as she understands them, but instead bring pressure for him to develop an ever larger vocabulary before the child is ready.

It would be inappropriate in this book to devote direct attention to the matter of the do's and don't's of child care. In connection with treatment only one specific bit of advice will be offered. Willingness on the part of the parents to seek counsel when problems arise which are beyond their understanding is one of the hopes for optimal development. There are in practically every community sources which can put one in touch with the appropriate specialist be he psychiatrist, clinical psychologist, social worker, or remedial expert. Welfare

[22] From Blanchard (*16*). Copyright 1940 by the American Psychological Association, and published with permission.

agencies, school systems, medical school departments of psychiatry, and college departments of psychology are often in a position to know the resources available. It is a sign of maturity to know when to seek help and be able to take the step of seeking it.

Summary

Habit disturbances, conduct disturbances, and neurotic traits, which make up the primary behavior disorders of childhood, are first considered. Habit disturbances are those in which there has been psychological interference with a major biological function. They often center in feeding, elimination, sleep, speech, or sex func-tions, and are shown to be related to tension in the child and to the interpersonal difficulties he may encounter. "Normal" children show many of the same problems, but with them they are milder, less frequent and not as much organized into multifaceted patterns of disturbance. Conduct disturbances generally emerge at a somewhat later age and include aggressive, destructive, and delinquent behavior. As in habit disturbance, a conflict with the environment is prominent. Neurotic traits, in contrast, are at least partially internalized. Jealousy, inhibition of aggression, and phobias are characteristic neurotic traits. From a developmental point of view they are not yet organized into patterns of personality. Hence they are referred to as neurotic traits rather than as neuroses, although conflict is both with oneself and with the environment. The neuroses, as such, also appear in children. All forms of primary behavior disorders are interrelated in that they are reactions to an unfavorable environment.

Psychosomatic disorders are discussed in terms of susceptibility and somatization with particular reference to the allergies. Interpretation was in terms of the blocking of outward-directed hostility of the allergic children and its direction upon themselves. Maternal rejection appears to be a prominent causative factor in allergic children, with emotional trauma being a precipitating factor.

The psychoses may or may not occur in children, but at least psychoticlike reactions do occur. Atypical development and disturbances in the earliest and most basic interpersonal relationships are present in these children. Schizophrenia, a condition which defies

short summarization, is considered as a characteristic psychotic disorder of children.

Reactions to physical handicap are found to bring forth a variety
of psychological reactions. Hostility and guilt appear prominently
in physically handicapped children. The attitudes of the parents
toward the child's handicap are important in deciding the child's
reaction to his handicap.

Psychological treatment of psychological disturbances in childhood
has two aspects, direct methods (psychotherapy) and indirect method
of treatment. Psychotherapy is essentially a form of interpersonal
relationship between therapist and child. It is illustrated through the
medium of play therapy. Indirect methods of treatment may be
divided into environmental manipulation and environmental modification. A discussion of the importance of the parent in the treatment
of the child closes the section.

For Further Reading

The chapter on disorders in childhood in *Principles of Abnormal Psychology,
Revised Edition* (New York: Harper, 1951), by Abraham Maslow and Bela Mittel-
mann is recommended for a short account. The case approach used in the book,
Emotional Disorders of Children (New York: Norton, 1949), by Gerald H. S.
Pearson is recommended for its clarity and system. For a vivid and poignant story
of an allergic child, *One Little Boy* (New York: Julian Press, 1952), by Dorothy
W. Baruch is recommended.

In the book edited by Helen L. Witmer, *Psychiatric Interviews with Children*
(New York: Commonwealth Fund, 1946), will be found a series of case presentations of disturbed children with emphasis on a step-by-step account of their treatment. Although no account of the psychoanalytic treatment of a child can be
simply and yet fully presented, a relatively clear and yet subtle picture may be
obtained from a case presented by Margaret W. Gerard in the *American Journal
of Orthopsychiatry*, 1938, 8, 1–18, 409–435. The day-to-day life of a residential
treatment center is vividly presented in the book of Bruno Bettelheim, *Love is
Not Enough* (Glencoe, Ill.: Free Press, 1950). In another book by the same
writer, *Truants from Life* (Glencoe, Ill.: Free Press, 1955), detailed case histories
of disturbed children are given.

References

1. Ackerman, N. W. Psychiatric disorders in children—diagnosis and etiology in
   our time. In P. H. Hoch and J. Zubin (Eds.), *Current problems in psychiatric diagnosis.* New York: Grune and Stratton, 1953, 205–230.

2. Allen, F. H. In G. Watson (Chm.), Areas of agreement in psychotherapy. *Amer. J. Orthopsychiat.*, 1940, 10, 698–709.
3. Allen, F. H. *Psychotherapy with children.* New York: Norton, 1942.
4. Amster, Fanny. Differential uses of play in treatment of young children. *Amer. J. Orthopsychiat.*, 1943, 13, 62–68.
5. Anderson, Camilla M. Organic factors predisposing to schizophrenia. *Nerv. Child*, 1954, 10, 36–42.
6. Bellak, L. *Dementia praecox.* New York: Grune and Stratton, 1948.
7. Bender, Lauretta. Neuropsychiatric contributions to the mental hygiene problems of the exceptional child. *Ment. Hyg., N. Y.*, 1942, 26, 617–630.
8. Bender, Lauretta. Childhood schizophrenia. *Nerv. Child,* 1942, 1, 138–140.
9. Bender, Lauretta. Childhood schizophrenia; clinical study of one hundred schizophrenic children. *Amer. J. Orthopsychiat.*, 1947, 17, 40–56.
10. Bender, Lauretta. Childhood schizophrenia. *Psychiat. Quart.*, 1953, 27, 663–681.
11. Bettelheim, B. Closed institutions for children? *Bull. Menninger Clin.*, 1948, 12, 135–142.
12. Bettelheim, B. *Love is not enough.* Glencoe, Ill.: Free Press, 1950.
13. Bettelheim, B., and Sylvester, Emmy. A therapeutic milieu. *Amer. J. Orthopsychiat.*, 1948, 18, 191–206.
14. Bettelheim, B., and Sylvester, Emmy. Milieu therapy; indications and illustrations. *Psychoanal. Rev.*, 1949, 36, 54–68.
15. Beverly, B. I. The effect of illness upon emotional development. *Pediatrics,* 1936, 8, 533–544.
16. Blanchard, Phyllis. Interpreting psychological data to parents. *J. consult. Psychol.*, 1940, 4, 120–123.
17. Caldwell, Bettye M. Factors influencing psychologic reactions to crippling disorders. *J. Mo. State Med. Ass.*, 1952, 49, 219–222.
18. Des Lauriers, A., and Halpern, Florence. Psychological tests in childhood schizophrenia. *Amer. J. Orthopsychiat.*, 1947, 17, 57–67.
19. English, O. S., and Pearson, G. H. J. *Emotional problems of living* (Rev. ed.). New York: Norton, 1955.
20. Escalona, Sibylle. Some considerations regarding psychotherapy with psychotic children. *Bull. Menninger Clin.*, 1948, 12, 126–134.
21. Frazee, Helen E. Children who later became schizophrenic. *Smith Coll. Stud. soc. Wk.*, 1953, 23, 125–149.
22. Freeman, R. V., and Grayson, H. M. Maternal attitudes in schizophrenia. *J. abnorm. soc. Psychol.*, 1955, 50, 45–52.
23. Green, Rose. Trends in orthopsychiatric therapy: VIII. Treatment of parent-child relationships. *Amer. J. Orthopsychiat.*, 1948, 18, 442–446.
24. Greenebaum, J. V., and Lurie, L. A. Encephalitis as a causative factor in behavior disorders of children. *J. Amer. Med. Ass.*, 1948, 136, 923.
25. Gurevitz, S. Treatment of a schizophrenic child through activation of neurotic symptoms. *Quart. J. Child Behav.*, 1952, 4, 139–155.
26. Kanner, L. *Child psychiatry* (2nd ed.). Springfield, Ill.: Thomas, 1950.
27. Kasanin, J., and Kaufman, M. R. A study of the functional psychoses in childhood. *Amer. J. Psychiat.*, 1929, 86, 307–384.
28. Krugman, M. The education of emotionally disturbed children: 1. introduction. *Amer. J. Orthopsychiat.*, 1953, 23, 667–669.

29. Kubie, L. S. The basis of a classification of disorders from the psychosomatic standpoint. *Bull. N. Y. Acad. Med.*, 1944, 20, 46–65.
30. Macfarlane, Jean W., Allen, Lucile, and Honzik, Marjorie. *A developmental study of the behavior problems of normal children between 21 months and 14 years.* Berkeley, Calif.: University of California Press, 1955.
31. McKeown, J. E. The behavior of parents of schizophrenic, neurotic, and normal children. *Amer. J. Sociol.*, 1950, 56, 175–179.
32. Mark, J. C. The attitudes of the mothers of male schizophrenics toward child behavior. *J. abnorm. soc. Psychol.*, 1953, 48, 185–189.
33. Maslow, A. H., and Mittelmann, B. *Principles of abnormal psychology: the dynamics of psychic illness* (Rev. ed.). New York: Harper, 1951.
34. Miller, H., and Baruch, Dorothy W. A study of hostility in allergic children. *Amer. J. Orthopsychiat.*, 1950, 20, 506–519.
35. Miller, H., and Baruch, Dorothy W. Emotional traumata preceding the onset of allergic symptoms in a group of children. *Ann. Allergy*, 1950, 8, 3–11.
36. Rabinovitch, R. D. An evaluation of present trends in psychotherapy with children. *J. Psychiat. soc. Wk.*, 1954, 24, 11–19.
37. Reichard, Suzanne, and Tillman, C. Patterns of parent-child relationships in schizophrenia. *Psychiatry*, 1950, 13, 247–257.
38. Rogers, C. R. *Counseling and psychotherapy.* Boston: Houghton Mifflin, 1942.
39. Sears, R. R. Influence of methodological factors on doll play performance. *Child Develpm.*, 1947, 18, 190–197.
40. Watson, R. I. *The clinical method in psychology.* New York: Harper, 1951.

Index of Names

649

Index of Subjects

DATE DUE